The Fintech Matrix

Connecting Innovation, Regulation, and Technology

RIVER PUBLISHERS SERIES IN COMPUTING AND INFORMATION SCIENCE AND TECHNOLOGY

Series Editors

K.C. CHEN
National Taiwan University, Taipei, Taiwan
University of South Florida, USA

SANDEEP SHUKLA
Virginia Tech, USA
Indian Institute of Technology Kanpur, India

The "River Publishers Series in Computing and Information Science and Technology" covers research which ushers the 21st Century into an Internet and multimedia era. Networking suggests transportation of such multimedia contents among nodes in communication and/or computer networks, to facilitate the ultimate Internet.

Theory, technologies, protocols and standards, applications/services, practice and implementation of wired/wireless networking are all within the scope of this series. Based on network and communication science, we further extend the scope for 21st Century life through the knowledge in machine learning, embedded systems, cognitive science, pattern recognition, quantum/biological/molecular computation and information processing, user behaviors and interface, and applications across healthcare and society.

Books published in the series include research monographs, edited volumes, handbooks and textbooks. The books provide professionals, researchers, educators, and advanced students in the field with an invaluable insight into the latest research and developments.

Topics included in the series are as follows:-

- Artificial intelligence
- Cognitive Science and Brian Science
- Communication/Computer Networking Technologies and Applications
- Computation and Information Processing
- Computer Architectures
- Computer networks
- Computer Science
- Embedded Systems
- Evolutionary computation
- Information Modelling
- Information Theory
- Machine Intelligence
- Neural computing and machine learning
- Parallel and Distributed Systems
- Programming Languages
- Reconfigurable Computing
- Research Informatics
- Soft computing techniques
- Software Development
- Software Engineering
- Software Maintenance

For a list of other books in this series, visit www.riverpublishers.com

The Fintech Matrix

Connecting Innovation, Regulation, and Technology

Neha Garg
Bhagwan Parshuram Institute of Technology,
affiliated to GGSIP University, New Delhi, India

Anoop Pandey
Hemvati Nandan Bahuguna Garhwal University,
Uttarakhand, India

Nupur Tyagi
Bhagwan Parshuram Institute of Technology,
affiliated to GGSIP University, New Delhi, India

River Publishers

Routledge
Taylor & Francis Group
NEW YORK AND LONDON

Published 2026 by River Publishers
River Publishers
Broagervej 10, 9260 Gistrup, Denmark
www.riverpublishers.com

Distributed exclusively by Routledge
605 Third Avenue, New York, NY 10017, USA
4 Park Square, Milton Park, Abingdon, Oxon OX14 4RN

The Fintech Matrix: Connecting Innovation, Regulation, and Technology / Neha Garg, Anoop Pandey and Nupur Tyagi.

Routledge is an imprint of the Taylor & Francis Group, an informa business

ISBN 978-87-438-1122-0 (hardback)
ISBN 978-87-438-1128-2 (paperback)
ISBN 978-87-438-1125-1 (online)
ISBN 978-87-438-1127-5 (e-pub)
ISBN 978-8-743-81124-4 (ebook master)
DOI: 10.1201/9788743811244

Dedication

This book is dedicated to my mother, Late Tanuja Gupta, father, Shiv Kumar Gupta, super-supportive husband, Amit, and two lovable kids, Araina and Aarav.

Neha Garg

This book is dedicated to my mother, Maya Devi, father, D.S.Pandey, wife, Meenu, and two sons, Aaryan and Atharv.

Anoop Pandey

This book is dedicated to my mother, Pavitra Tyagi, father, Ashok Tyagi, my husband, Raghav Tyagi, and my beloved daughter, Radhika.

Nupur Tyagi

Contents

Preface

We are living through a financial renaissance. The convergence of finance and technology, known globally as FinTech, has not merely introduced new tools and systems but has fundamentally redefined how the world perceives, accesses, and interacts with financial services. This book is both a response to and a reflection of this monumental transformation. It aims to provide a structured, multidisciplinary, and internationally oriented exploration of the FinTech ecosystem, designed to serve as a foundational text for scholars, students, practitioners, academicians, and policymakers alike.

The digital revolution has left no sector untouched, but in finance, its impact has been particularly profound. Technologies such as blockchain, artificial intelligence, machine learning, cloud computing, big data analytics, and digital identity systems are not just enabling greater financial inclusion; they are also reshaping the architecture of global finance itself. This transformation is not limited to any single region or economy; it is a global phenomenon. From digital wallets in Kenya to real-time payment platforms in India, from regulatory sandboxes in the United Kingdom to central bank digital currencies being piloted in China, the FinTech wave is sweeping across continents, cultures, and economic models.

The purpose of this book is to provide a comprehensive and globally contextualized perspective on the evolution, mechanisms, challenges, and future of FinTech. Each chapter delves deeply into specific themes – ranging from digital banking, blockchain, and robo-advisory systems to cybersecurity, regulatory frameworks, and financial ethics. This diversity of content reflects the complexity of FinTech, which exists at the intersection of finance, technology, law, sociology, and data science. This work is also an academic commitment. As educators and researchers, the authors have observed a growing demand among students and professionals for clear, structured knowledge that bridges theory with real-world application. This book endeavors to meet that demand by incorporating both foundational concepts and contemporary case studies that span the globe. Through critical analysis and comparative perspectives, it seeks not only to inform but also to inspire critical thinking and innovation. AI

Moreover, in a time when financial literacy, digital inclusion, and data ethics are becoming essential pillars of economic development, this book serves as a timely contribution. It encourages dialogue around key questions: How do we democratize financial access without compromising security? What role should governments and central banks play in this evolving ecosystem? How can startups, traditional banks, and tech giants co-exist and collaborate? And most importantly, how can we ensure that technological advancement in finance remains inclusive, ethical, and sustainable?

We are deeply grateful to our colleagues, mentors, students, and the broader academic and professional communities who have contributed ideas, feedback, and encouragement throughout the development of this book. We also extend our appreciation to global innovators, regulators, and entrepreneurs whose work continues to push the boundaries of what is possible in the financial world. I hope that this book will serve as a valuable reference not only for those seeking to understand FinTech but also for those who aim to shape its future. Whether you are a student aspiring to enter the financial technology space, an academician teaching technological transformation in the financial landscape, a policymaker designing inclusive frameworks, a technologist building next-generation tools, or an investor evaluating emerging trends – this book is written keeping you in mind.

In keeping with the spirit of innovation that defines FinTech, this book has been thoughtfully crafted with the support of advanced AI tools and techniques; an embodiment of the very technology it seeks to explore. Let us embark together on this exploration of FinTech - a journey that is as dynamic as it is essential to the future of our interconnected global economy.

Acknowledgment

At the very outset, we offer our humble gratitude to Lord Ganesha, whose divine blessings and inspiration have guided us in undertaking this work on the transformative power of emerging technologies shaping the global financial ecosystem.

This book is the result of a collective journey, and we are deeply indebted to all who have played a part in its realization. We extend our heartfelt thanks to our families, whose unwavering love, patience, and support have been our steadfast foundation throughout this endeavor. Your belief in us has been our greatest source of strength.

We express sincere appreciation to our academic mentors and professional colleagues, whose invaluable insights, thoughtful critiques, and continuous encouragement helped shape the structure and depth of this book. Their expertise in financial innovation and your commitment to knowledge have left an indelible mark on our thinking. Our gratitude also goes to the FinTech professionals, industry experts, and regulatory leaders, whose real-world experiences and perspectives brought practical relevance to the pages of this work. Their pioneering efforts continue to inspire the vision of an inclusive and digitally empowered financial future.

To our students and fellow researchers, we owe special thanks. Their curiosity, challenging questions, and enthusiasm for learning have constantly pushed us to explore deeper and think broader. Special thanks to Bhagwan Parshuram Institute of Technology, Bank of Maharashtra and Hemvati Nandan Bahuguna Garhwal University. May this book return the favor by serving as a useful guide in your intellectual pursuits. We are also thankful to the editorial and publishing teams, whose dedication, professionalism, and attention to detail helped transform this manuscript into its final form.

Lastly, it is worth noting that in harmony with the book's theme, AI tools and techniques were thoughtfully employed throughout its development. In embracing these very technologies, we hope to reflect the essence of FinTech - where innovation meets application, and tradition meets transformation. To everyone who contributed directly or indirectly, we offer our deepest gratitude. This book is as much yours as it is ours.

About The Book

In a rapidly evolving world, the financial landscape is undergoing a profound transformation. FinTech offers a comprehensive exploration of this transformation, providing readers with an in-depth understanding of FinTech – the fusion of finance and technology. This book takes a deep dive into the forces driving the revolution in financial systems and services, from digital payments and blockchain to artificial intelligence and regulatory technologies.

Structured in seven detailed parts, this book serves as both an essential academic resource and a practical guide for professionals looking to navigate the complex and dynamic world of FinTech. The chapters cover foundational financial concepts, the evolution of financial innovation, the diverse ecosystem of FinTech, digital services, and the application of emerging technologies. With a focus on real-world case studies, business models, regulatory challenges, and future trends, the book provides readers with a well-rounded perspective on the future of finance.

Key themes explored in the book include:

- The foundational structures of financial systems and the historical evolution of finance
- The global FinTech ecosystem, key players, and funding channels
- How FinTech is transforming banking, lending, insurance, and other financial sectors
- The role of blockchain, cryptocurrencies, and digital assets in reshaping financial markets
- Innovations in data analytics, AI, and emerging technologies such as IoT, AR/VR, and cybersecurity in financial services

- The regulatory landscape and the impact of regulatory technologies (RegTech) and supervisory technologies (SupTech)
- Ethical considerations in the digital financial world and the path forward for FinTech

List of Figures

List of Tables

List of Abbreviations

3D	Three dimensional
AD	Authorized dealer
ADA	Cardano
ADAA	Abu Dhabi Accountability Authority
AI	Artificial Intelligence
AMC	Asset Management Company
AML	Anti-money laundering
API	Application programming interface
APT	Advanced persistent threat
AR	Augmented reality
ART	Asset-referenced token
ASEAN	Association of Southeast Asian Nations
ATM	Automated teller machine
AWS	Amazon web services
B2B	Business-to-business
BC	Business correspondent / blockchain
BCBS	Basel committee on banking supervision
BCE	Banque Centrale Européenne (European Central Bank)
BEC	Business email compromise
BHIM	Bharat interface for money
BIG TECH	Big Technology Companies (e.g., Google, Amazon, Facebook, Apple)
BIS	Bank for International settlements
BNB	Binance coin
BNPL	Buy now pay later
BSE	Bombay stock exchange
BTC	Bitcoin
CAGR	Compound annual growth rate
CBDC	Central Bank Digital Currency
CCPA	Central consumer protection authority
CDSL	Central depository services limited

CFTC	Commodity futures trading commission
CRM	Customer relationship management
CRR	Cash reserve ratio
CTF	Counter terrorism financing
CTORO	Possibly a typo – might refer to etoro (social trading platform)
DAO	Decentralized autonomous organization
DBS	Development Bank Of Singapore
DCP	Data control platform
DDOS	Distributed denial of service
DEFI	Decentralized finance
DEX	Decentralized exchange
DLT	Distributed Ledger Technology
DOGE	Dogecoin
DOT	Polkadot
DPDP	Digital personal data protection (India bill)
E-CNY	Electronic chinese yuan (CBDC of China)
E-COMMERCE	Electronic commerce
ED	Enforcement directorate (India)
ED TECH	Education technology
EIDAS	Electronic identification, authentication and trust services (EU)
E-KYC	Electronic know your customer
EMH	Efficient market hypothesis
EMI	Equated monthly installment
EMT	E-money token
ENAIRA	Electronic naira (CBDC of Nigeria)
EPFO	Employees' Provident Fund Organisation
ESC	Electronic stability control / Escrow (context-dependent)
ETC	Ethereum classic
ETH	Ethereum
EU	European Union
EXMI	Exchange member identifier (used in stock exchange systems)
FATF	Financial action task force
FCA	Financial conduct authority (UK)
FINCEN	Financial crimes enforcement network (US)
FINRA	Financial industry regulatory authority
FINTECH	Financial technology

FSB	Financial stability board
FSCS	Financial services compensation scheme (UK)
FSD	Financial sector development
GDPR	General data protection regulation
GPI	Global payments innovation
GPS	Global positioning system
GST	Goods and services tax
HDFC	Housing Development Finance Corporation
HFT	High-frequency trading
HSBC	Hongkong and Shanghai Banking Corporation
ICICI	Industrial Credit and Investment Corporation of India
ICO	Initial coin offering
IDO	Initial dex offering
IDS	Intrusion detection system
IDV	Identity verification
IEO	Initial exchange offering
IFI	International Financial Institution
IMF	International monetary fund
INSUR TECH	Insurance technology
IOSCO	International Organization of Securities Commissions
IOT	Internet of things
IPA	International payments association
IPO	Initial public offering
IPS	Intrusion prevention system
KPMG	Kpmg consulting
KYB	Know your business
KYC	Know your customer
LTC	Litecoin
LVPS	Large value payment system
M & A	Mergers and acquisitions
MAS	Monetary Authority of Singapore
MF	Mutual fund
MFA	Multi-factor authentication
MiCA	Markets in crypto-assets regulation (EU)
MICLV	Minimum initial capital and liquidity value
MIFID	Markets in financial instruments directive
MII	Market infrastructure institution
MIT ID	MIT Identification (Massachusetts Institute of Technology id)
MITM	Man in the middle (attack)

MKA	Mutual knowledge agreement (less common)
ML	Machine learning
M-PESA	Mobile money transfer service (by safaricom)
MPT	Modern portfolio theory
MVP	Minimum viable product
NABARD	National bank for agriculture and rural development
NASDAQ	National association of securities dealers automated quotations
NEFT	National electronic funds transfer
NEM ID	National eID (Denmark)
NFC	Near field communication
NFT	Non-fungible token
NLP	Natural language processing
NPA	Non-performing asset
NPCI	National payments corporation of India
NPS	National pension system
NSDL	National securities depository limited
NSE	National stock exchange
OBIE	Open banking implementation entity (UK)
OCC	Office of the comptroller of the currency (US)
OCR	Optical character recognition
OECD	Organisation for Economic Co-operation and Development
OTC	Over the counter
OTP	One-time password
PEM	Privacy-enhanced mail / portable encoding mechanism (contextual)
PFM	Personal financial management
PFOF	Payment for order flow
PIM	Personal investment management
PLP	Peer lending platform
POS	Point of sale
PoS	Proof of stake
PoW	Proof of work
PPP	Public-private partnership
PSD	Payment services directive
PWC	Pricewaterhousecoopers
QR	Quick response (code)
RAAS	Robotics as a service
RBI	Reserve Bank of India

REG TECH	Regulatory technology
RPA	Robotic process automation
RTGS	Real-time gross settlement
SBI	State bank of india
SBIR	Small business innovation research
SDC	Secure digital card / smart data capture (context-specific)
SEC	Securities and exchange commission
SIDBI	Small Industries Development Bank of India
SIEM	Security Information and Event Management
SLR	Statutory liquidity ratio
SME	Small and medium enterprises
SOFI	Social Finance Inc.
SOL	Solana
STO	Security token offering
SWIFT	Society for Worldwide Interbank Financial Telecommunication
T-BILL	Treasury bill
TDS	Tax deducted at source
UBI	Universal basic income
UBO	Ultimate beneficial owner
UK	United Kingdom
UPI	Unified payments interface
USA	United States of America
USD	United States Dollar
USDC	USD coin
USDT	Tether (USD-pegged stablecoin)
USSD	Unstructured Supplementary Service Data
UX	User experience
VAR	Value at risk
VR	Virtual reality
XAI	Explainable Artificial Intelligence
XMR	Monero
XRP	Ripple
YNAB	You need a budget

UNIT 1

Foundations of Financial Systems and Innovation

1

Understanding Financial Systems

Abstract

This chapter provides a comprehensive foundation for understanding the architecture, functions, and critical importance of financial systems in driving economic development. At its core, the financial system serves as the backbone of any economy, facilitating the efficient allocation of resources, promoting investment, and supporting sustainable growth through the mobilization of savings and distribution of credit. The chapter begins by explaining the structure of the financial system, detailing the interrelated components that include financial institutions, markets, instruments, services, and regulatory bodies. It introduces key institutional players such as banks, insurance companies, and non-banking financial companies (NBFCs), which act as intermediaries to channel funds from savers to borrowers, enabling capital formation and economic diversification.

A thorough exploration of financial markets – both money and capital markets – is presented, underscoring their role as dynamic platforms for investment, risk management, and liquidity enhancement. The chapter also clarifies the purpose and functioning of various financial instruments like equity shares, debt securities, and derivatives, which represent contracts and claims that facilitate financial transactions and risk transfers. Critical financial infrastructure, including payment and settlement systems, is examined to highlight the mechanisms that ensure seamless, secure, and timely transfer of funds. The discussion includes real-time gross settlement (RTGS) and deferred net settlement (DNS) systems, vital for the smooth operation of financial transactions in modern economies.

Regulatory oversight is another focal point, with detailed insights into the roles of major Indian regulatory authorities such as the Reserve Bank of India (RBI), Securities and Exchange Board of India (SEBI), and Insurance Regulatory and Development Authority of India (IRDAI). Their mandates to

DOI: 10.1201/9788743811244-2

ensure market integrity, investor protection, and systemic stability are analyzed within the broader regulatory ecosystem. The pivotal role of central banks is also emphasized, especially their responsibilities in issuing currency, managing inflation, formulating monetary policy, and supervising banking institutions. Additionally, the chapter touches on the legal and technological frameworks that constitute the financial infrastructure necessary to support digital innovation, cybersecurity, and regulatory compliance.

Lastly, the chapter outlines key financial services, including credit provision, insurance, asset management, and investment advisory, essential for individuals and institutions alike in managing wealth, mitigating risks, and achieving financial goals. Through this multidimensional exploration, the chapter equips readers with a solid conceptual and practical understanding of how financial systems operate, their interdependencies, and their critical impact on economic stability, growth, and individual well-being.

Introduction

This chapter provides a foundational understanding of the components that make up the financial system, which is essential for the smooth functioning of any economy. It begins by discussing financial institutions, such as banks, insurance companies, and investment firms, which serve as intermediaries that mobilize savings and allocate credit. These institutions play a key role in channeling funds from savers to borrowers and ensuring the efficient functioning of the financial ecosystem. The chapter then explores financial markets, including money markets and capital markets, which facilitate the buying and selling of financial instruments. These markets offer platforms for raising capital, managing risks, and ensuring liquidity in the economy. Financial instruments such as stocks, bonds, and derivatives are introduced as tools that represent financial claims and obligations, helping investors and institutions manage wealth and risk. Another crucial component is the payment and settlement systems, which ensure the secure and timely transfer of funds between financial parties. These systems support both retail and wholesale transactions and are vital for maintaining trust and efficiency in financial operations. The chapter also elaborates on regulatory authorities, which oversee financial activities and enforce compliance to maintain market integrity and protect consumers.

The central banks are presented as the core monetary authorities responsible for issuing currency, managing monetary policy, and ensuring financial stability. The discussion further extends to financial infrastructure, including technology, legal frameworks, and communication networks that support financial transactions and services. Finally, the chapter concludes with financial services, which encompass a wide array of offerings such as loans, insurance, wealth management, and advisory services that meet the diverse needs of individuals and businesses. Together, these components form a robust financial system that supports economic development, promotes savings and investments, and enables smooth financial intermediation in the economy.

1.1 Financial Institutions

Financial institutions are the backbone of any financial system. They act as intermediaries between savers and borrowers and facilitate the flow of money within the economy. These institutions include commercial banks, investment banks, insurance companies, mutual funds, pension funds, credit unions, and non-banking financial companies (NBFCs). Financial institutions act as the backbone of the financial system by mobilizing savings and allocating capital efficiently, while simultaneously innovating to manage risk and enhance stability [1], [2]. Each type of institution has a unique role in enhancing capital formation, promoting economic stability, and fostering inclusive growth.

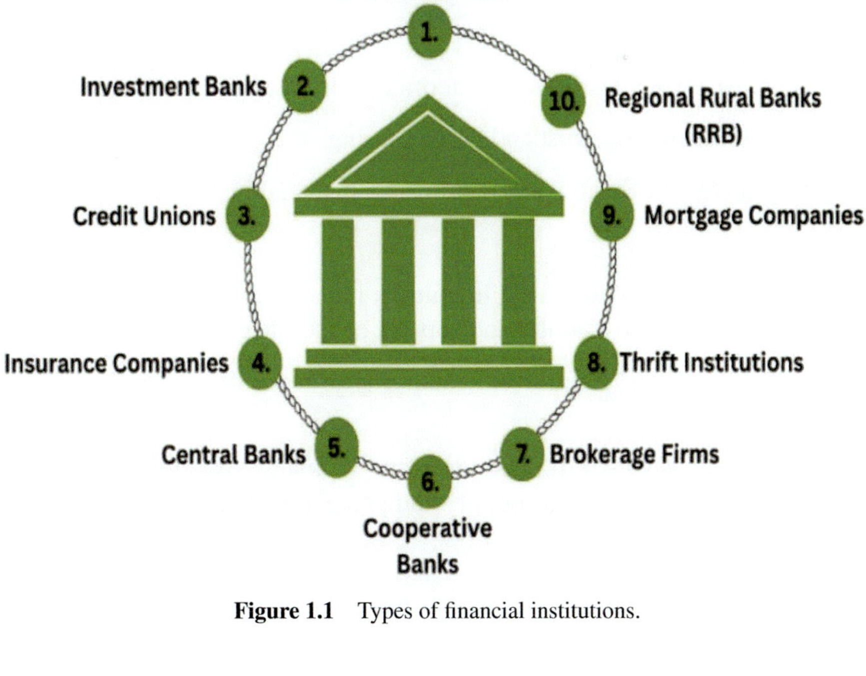

Figure 1.1 Types of financial institutions.

1.1.1 Types of financial institutions

Commercial banks

- Accept deposits and offer savings and checking accounts.
- Provide loans to individuals, businesses, and governments.
- Offer services like ATM facilities, internet banking, debit/credit cards.
- Example: SBI, ICICI Bank, HDFC Bank.

Investment banks

- Help companies raise capital through equity and debt markets.
- Advise on mergers and acquisitions, corporate restructuring, and IPOs.
- Engage in trading and securities underwriting.
- Example: Goldman Sachs, Morgan Stanley.

Insurance companies

- Provide risk protection through life, health, property, and liability insurance.
- Collect premiums and invest funds to generate returns.
- Example: LIC, HDFC Life, ICICI Lombard.

Credit unions

- Member-owned institutions that offer savings, credit, and small loans.
- Operate on mutual trust and profit-sharing.
- Play a key role in rural and semi-urban financial inclusion.

Central bank

- Monetary policy authority: It controls money supply and interest rates to maintain price stability and support economic growth.
- Currency issuer: It is the sole authority to issue the national currency of a country.
- Regulator of banks: It supervises and regulates commercial banks to ensure financial system stability and prevent banking crises.

Cooperative banks

These banks are similar to credit unions but are usually larger and may serve a broader community. Key features:

- Owned by their members.
- Offer banking and credit services, especially in rural areas.
- Promote financial inclusion and cooperative values.

Brokerage firms

Brokerage firms act as intermediaries between buyers and sellers in financial markets. They:

- Enable clients to buy/sell stocks, bonds, mutual funds, etc.
- Offer portfolio management, investment advice, and research.
- Some large brokerage firms also offer banking services.

Thrift institutions

Also known as **savings and loan associations** or **savings banks**, they focus on:

- Encouraging personal savings.
- Providing home loans and mortgages.
- They help promote home ownership and serve low- to middle-income individuals.

Mortgage companies

Specialized financial institutions that:

- Focus primarily on providing home loans and refinancing services.
- May operate independently or be part of a larger financial group.
- They play a vital role in the real estate and housing finance sector.

Regional rural banks (RRBs)

RRBs are government-backed banks in countries like India that:

- Serve rural and semi-urban areas.
- Provide credit and other financial services to small farmers, artisans, and rural businesses.
- They help bridge the urban-rural financial divide and support agricultural development.

Functions of financial institutions:

- **Mobilizing savings**: Convert idle money into productive capital.
- **Providing credit**: Offer loans for personal, industrial, and infrastructural use.

- **Risk management**: Through insurance and diversification.
- **Investment services**: Facilitate access to capital markets and investment products.
- **Foreign exchange services**: Enable global trade and currency exchange.
- **Payment systems**: Offer payment and settlement services via cheques, cards, UPI, NEFT, etc.

Importance of financial institutions:

- **Promote economic growth**: By financing industries, startups, and infrastructure.
- **Ensure financial inclusion**: Provide banking and financial services to underserved sections.
- **Maintain financial stability**: Act as shock absorbers during economic downturns.
- **Support government policies**: Implement schemes like PMJDY, Mudra Loans, etc.

Challenges faced:

- Non-performing assets (NPAs) in banking.
- Cybersecurity threats in digital finance.
- Regulatory compliance and capital adequacy norms.
- Balancing profitability with social responsibility.

Financial institutions are the pillars of a modern economy. They ensure that financial resources are efficiently allocated, risks are managed, and monetary transactions are smoothly conducted. With the rise of digital finance and FinTech, traditional institutions are evolving to become more accessible, efficient, and innovative. Their continued development and regulation are essential for fostering sustainable and inclusive economic growth.

Commercial banks are perhaps the most recognizable type of financial institution. They accept deposits from the public and provide loans to individuals, businesses, and governments. By doing so, they help in mobilizing idle savings and directing them toward productive uses. Investment banks, on the other hand, specialize in helping corporations raise capital through the issuance of stocks and bonds. They also provide advisory services for mergers, acquisitions, and other corporate restructuring. Insurance companies manage risk by pooling premiums from policyholders and providing compensation in the event of insured losses. Pension funds collect and invest retirement savings of employees to ensure post-retirement financial security. Mutual funds aggregate money from numerous investors and invest it in diversified portfolios of stocks and bonds, offering small investors access to professionally managed investment options. The integration of digital technologies with traditional financial infrastructures has enhanced risk management, credit assessment, and transaction security, underscoring a shift from paper-based to electronic systems [3]; [4].

NBFCs also play a crucial role, especially in emerging markets like India. They often cater to underserved segments such as small businesses, low-income individuals, or rural populations who might not have access to formal banking services. Credit unions, typically cooperatives owned by their members, also serve specific communities or employee groups with a focus on affordable credit and savings products. The importance of financial institutions lies in their ability to reduce information asymmetry, mitigate transaction costs, and provide liquidity. They evaluate the creditworthiness of borrowers, thereby minimizing risks for depositors and investors. Moreover, they offer a range of financial products like savings accounts, term deposits, loans, insurance policies, and investment products to cater to diverse financial needs. In addition, financial institutions help implement the monetary policy of a country. For instance, central banks often rely on commercial banks to transmit changes in interest rates or reserve requirements into the broader economy. Through lending and deposit-taking activities, financial institutions also influence money supply and credit availability. With advancements in digital technology, many traditional financial institutions are now undergoing transformation. Online banking, digital lending platforms, robo-advisors, and insurtech solutions have expanded the reach and efficiency of financial institutions. This evolution is enabling broader financial inclusion, especially in remote and rural areas.

In summary, financial institutions are vital for economic development. They channel funds from savers to borrowers, reduce financial risks, support investment, enhance capital allocation, and provide a wide array of financial services that support both individuals and enterprises. Their efficiency and integrity are crucial to the health of the financial system and the economy as a whole. The structure and growth of banks, non-banking financial companies, and other intermediaries highlight how institutional diversity supports credit delivery, risk transformation, and market liquidity[5].

1.2 Financial Markets

Financial markets are platforms or systems where financial instruments such as stocks, bonds, commodities, and currencies are bought and sold. They are critical components of the financial system as they facilitate the efficient allocation of resources, promote liquidity, enable price discovery, and allow risk sharing. These markets play a pivotal role in linking investors (who have surplus funds) with borrowers or institutions in need of funds.

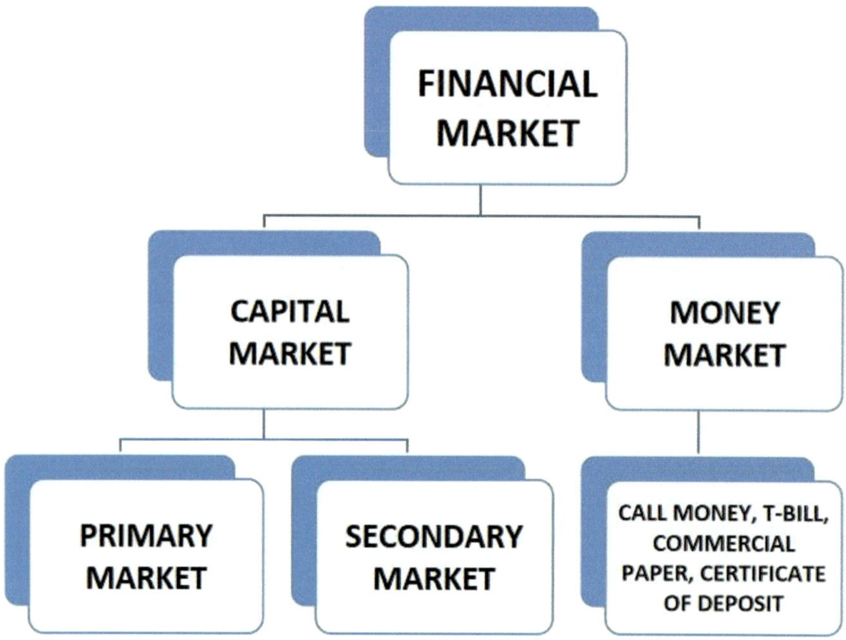

Figure 1.2 Types of financial markets.

Financial markets are broadly categorized into two types: **money markets** and **capital markets**. **Financial markets,** including money markets, capital markets, facilitate price discovery, liquidity, and resource allocation, linking domestic economies to global capital flows [4], [5].

Money markets deal with short-term debt instruments, typically those with maturities of one year or less. Common instruments include treasury bills, certificates of deposit, commercial paper, call money, and repurchase agreements. These markets are used by governments, financial institutions, and corporations to manage their short-term liquidity needs. They are known for their high liquidity and low risk.

Capital markets, on the other hand, facilitate the trading of long-term financial instruments such as stocks (equity) and bonds (debt). The capital market includes:

1.2.1 Primary market

The **primary market** is where **new securities are issued for the first time**. This is also called the **new issue market**. Companies raise capital by selling their shares or bonds directly to investors. The proceeds go directly to the issuing company, helping them finance new projects, repay debt, or expand operations.

Initial public offering (IPO)

An **IPO** is the first time a company offers its shares to the public. Through an IPO, a private company becomes a publicly traded company by listing on a stock exchange. Investors purchase these shares directly from the company at a fixed or market-determined price. Example: When Zomato Ltd. launched its IPO in India, it raised capital from the public for the first time. Purpose: Raise large capital, increase visibility, and establish a market value.

Right issue

A **Right issue** is when a company offers additional shares to its existing shareholders, usually at a discounted price, in proportion to their current holdings. This allows companies to raise additional funds without diluting ownership too much. Example: If a shareholder owns 100 shares and the company announces a 1:5 right issue, they can buy 20 additional shares at a discounted price. Purpose: Meet urgent financial needs, reduce debt, or fund expansion.

Key features of the primary market:

- Only new securities are issued.
- Funds go directly to the issuing company.
- No trading between investors – only between the company and investor.
- Requires underwriters and regulatory approval (e.g., SEBI in India).

1.2.2 Secondary market

The **secondary market** is where **existing securities are traded among investors**. It provides liquidity to investors and allows them to buy and sell securities post-IPO. The issuing company is not involved in these transactions, and the prices fluctuate based on market demand and supply.

Stock market

The **stock market** is a formal, regulated platform (like the NSE or BSE in India) where securities are bought and sold. It is transparent, offers real-time price discovery, and is supervised by regulatory bodies to protect investors. Example: Buying TCS shares on the National Stock Exchange. Investors profit or lose based on market price movements.

Over the counter (OTC)

OTC markets are decentralized markets where trading occurs directly between parties, often without a formal exchange. These are used for securities that are not listed on stock exchanges, such as derivatives, debt instruments, or small company shares. Example: Trading of corporate bonds or customized derivatives contracts. These are less liquid and carry higher risk but may offer higher returns.

Key features of the secondary market:

- Enables trading of existing securities.
- Provides liquidity and continuous pricing.
- Involves brokers, stock exchanges, and clearing houses.
- Prices are market-driven based on investor sentiment, news, and performance.

Table 1.1 Primary market and secondary market.

Aspect	Primary market	Secondary market
Purpose	To raise fresh capital	To facilitate the trading of existing securities
Participants	Issuer and investors	Investors trading among themselves
Pricing	Fixed or market-driven at issue	Fluctuates with demand and supply
Role of company	Company is directly involved	Company is not involved in trades
Examples	IPO, right issue	Stock exchange, OTC market

Another crucial classification is between **organized markets** and **over-the-counter (OTC)** markets. Organized markets, such as stock exchanges, are regulated and provide a transparent trading environment. OTC markets are decentralized and involve direct trades between two parties without a formal exchange, often used for derivatives and debt instruments.

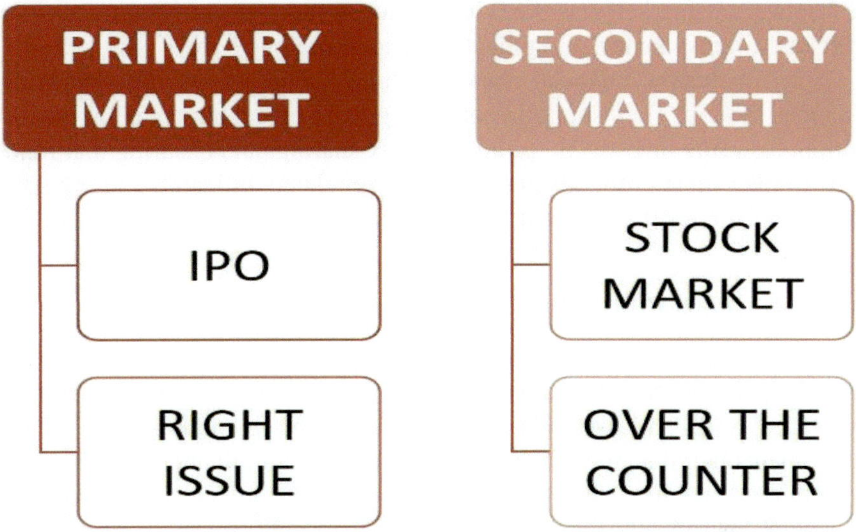

Figure 1.3 Primary and secondary market.

Foreign exchange (forex) markets form a global marketplace for trading currencies. These markets are essential for international trade and investment. They help determine currency values and allow businesses to hedge against currency risks. FinTech innovations such as algorithmic trading, AI-driven analytics, and real-time digital platforms have significantly transformed the forex market by enhancing speed, transparency, and trading efficiency [6].

Commodity markets allow the trading of physical goods like gold, oil, wheat, and other raw materials. These markets are essential for producers and consumers to manage price risk through futures and options contracts.

Financial markets are vital for price discovery, which refers to the process through which asset prices are determined based on supply and demand. They also enhance liquidity, ensuring that assets can be quickly bought or sold with minimal price fluctuation. Through diversification and various instruments like derivatives, markets also enable risk management and hedging. Moreover, financial markets play a key role in economic development. They help businesses raise long-term capital, support public sector infrastructure financing through bonds, and allow households to invest in wealth-creating opportunities. They also support monetary policy transmission by reflecting interest rate changes in asset prices and yields. In recent years, technological advancements have transformed financial markets. Algorithmic trading, blockchain, digital asset exchanges, and decentralized finance (DeFi) are reshaping how markets operate. These innovations are improving transaction efficiency, transparency, and global participation.

In conclusion, financial markets are indispensable mechanisms in the financial system. They support economic growth by enabling capital mobilization, fostering investment, promoting risk sharing, and ensuring that funds flow to their most productive uses. A well-regulated, efficient, and transparent financial market is fundamental to a healthy financial ecosystem.

1.3 Financial Instruments

Financial instruments are contracts or documents that represent a legal agreement involving monetary value. They can be created, traded, modified, or settled, and serve as the building blocks of the financial system. These instruments facilitate the transfer of capital and risk in financial markets and institutions, enabling savings to be channeled into productive investments. Financial instruments ranging from equity and debt securities to complex derivatives represent the contractual vehicles through which funds flow between surplus and deficit units in the economy [7]; [8]. Financial instruments are broadly categorized into **equity instruments**, **debt instruments**, **derivatives**, and **hybrid instruments**.

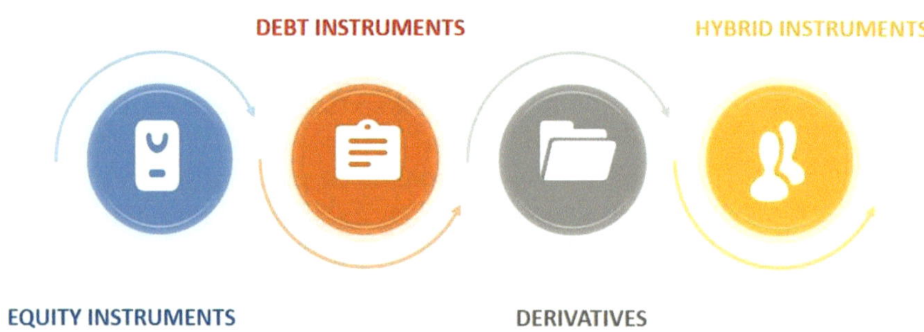

Figure 1.4 Types of financial instruments.

1.3.1 Equity instruments

These represent ownership in a company. The most common equity instrument is **common stock** or shares, which entitle the holder to a portion of the company's profits (in the form of dividends) and a claim on assets in case of liquidation. Shareholders also gain voting rights in corporate governance. Equity instruments are typically riskier than debt, but they offer higher potential returns.

1.3.2 Debt instruments

These represent a loan made by an investor to a borrower, typically with a fixed return in the form of interest. These instruments specify repayment terms, interest rates, and maturity dates. Debt instruments are crucial for raising capital while maintaining ownership control. Common debt instruments include:

- **Bonds** (government or corporate)
- **Debentures**
- **Commercial papers**
- **Treasury bills**

Derivatives

Derivatives derive their value from an underlying asset, index, or interest rate. They are primarily used for **hedging** risk or **speculation**. Common derivatives include:

- **Futures**: Standardized contracts to buy/sell an asset at a future date.
- **Options**: Give the right (but not obligation) to buy/sell.
- **Swaps**: Agreements to exchange cash flows or financial instruments.

  Derivatives play a vital role in managing risks related to interest rates, currency exchange rates, and commodity prices.

Hybrid instruments

These instruments combine features of both debt and equity. Examples include:

- **Convertible bonds** (can be converted into equity)
- **Preference shares** (offer fixed dividends with limited voting rights)

  Hybrid instruments are popular in corporate finance for balancing risk and capital structure.

Characteristics of financial instruments:

- **Liquidity**: The ease with which an instrument can be bought or sold in the market without affecting its price.
- **Risk and return**: Each instrument carries a specific risk profile and expected return.

- **Maturity**: The lifespan of the instrument, especially important for debt securities.
- **Legal enforceability**: The contracts are legally binding and enforceable under financial laws.

Financial instruments serve numerous functions:

- **Facilitating investment**: They allow individuals and institutions to invest savings.
- **Enabling financing**: Help companies, governments, and institutions raise funds.
- **Risk transfer**: Derivatives and insurance contracts shift risk from one party to another.
- **Monetary policy transmission**: Interest-bearing instruments like bonds help central banks manage inflation and liquidity.

With the rise of FinTech and digital innovation, new-age financial instruments have emerged, including tokenized assets, crypto derivatives, and digital securities. These offer faster settlement, fractional ownership, and global accessibility.

In summary, financial instruments are the essential tools through which financial transactions occur. They underpin capital formation, enable efficient risk sharing, and support economic activities across all sectors. A well-developed system of instruments expands financial inclusion and strengthens the overall resilience and functionality of the financial system.

1.4 Payment and Settlement Systems

Payment and settlement systems are fundamental infrastructures within the financial system that facilitate the transfer of money between individuals, businesses, financial institutions, and governments. These systems ensure that monetary transactions ranging from small retail payments to large interbank transfers are completed securely, efficiently, and reliably. At the core, a **payment system** is a mechanism that allows parties to exchange funds for goods, services, or financial assets. Global experiences show that innovative payment platforms such as India's UPI and cross-border instant transfer systems reduce transaction costs and broaden financial inclusion [9];[10]; [11]. A **settlement system**, on the other hand, finalizes these transactions by transferring the ownership of funds or securities, thereby completing the transaction cycle. The design of **payment and settlement systems** underpins financial stability by reducing counterparty risk, increasing operational efficiency, and ensuring trust in large-value and retail transactions [12], [13].

1.4.1 Types of payment systems

Retail payment systems

These systems handle low-value, high-volume transactions made by individuals and businesses. They include:

- **Debit and credit card networks**
- **Mobile wallets** (e.g., Google Pay, PhonePe, Paytm)
- **Internet banking**
- **UPI (Unified Payments Interface)** in India

  Retail payments are crucial for day-to-day economic activities and promote financial inclusion by providing accessible and digital alternatives to cash.

Large-value payment systems (LVPS)

These are used for high-value, time-critical interbank transfers. Examples include:

- **Real-Time Gross Settlement (RTGS)**: Settles payments individually and instantly.
- **National Electronic Funds Transfer (NEFT)** in India: Operates in batches. These systems ensure the safe and timely transfer of large funds between financial institutions, corporations, and government bodies.

Cross-border payment systems

Facilitate international money transfers through systems like:

- **SWIFT** (Society for Worldwide Interbank Financial Telecommunication)
- **TARGET2** in Europe
- **RippleNet** using blockchain

  Cross-border payments are complex due to currency conversion, regulations, and time zones, making robust systems essential for global commerce.

Settlement systems

Settlement systems ensure that once a payment instruction is given, the transfer of value (cash, securities, or derivatives) actually occurs. These can be:

- **Gross settlement** (e.g., RTGS): Each transaction is settled individually.
- **Net settlement**: Transactions are accumulated and settled in bulk after netting debit and credit positions, reducing the need for liquidity.

The **clearing process** (matching, confirming, and netting obligations) often precedes the settlement. Organizations like **clearing houses** and **central counterparties (CCPs)** manage this process to reduce counterparty risk.

1.4.2 Importance of payment and settlement systems

- **Stability and trust**: A secure and efficient payment infrastructure reduces systemic risk and fosters trust in the financial system.
- **Liquidity management**: Helps banks and businesses manage their cash positions in real time.
- **Economic efficiency**: Fast and reliable payments promote consumption, investment, and economic participation.
- **Financial inclusion**: Digital systems bring banking and payments to rural, remote, or underserved populations.

Figure 1.5 Payment and settlement services.

In conclusion, payment and settlement systems are vital arteries of the financial system, enabling smooth, secure, and instantaneous financial transactions across different layers of the economy. Their efficiency determines the speed and reliability of financial operations, making them foundational to economic stability and growth. In India, the Reserve Bank of India (RBI) and the National Payments Corporation of India (NPCI) have spearheaded real-time payment innovations such as UPI, creating a safe, secure, and efficient digital ecosystem [14]. RBI's Digital Payments Index recorded a 10.7% rise in FY25, reflecting robust supply-side infrastructure and accelerating adoption of cashless modes of settlement.

1.5 Regulatory Authorities

Regulatory authorities are the guardians of the financial system, entrusted with overseeing, monitoring, and regulating various financial institutions, markets, instruments, and practices to ensure stability, transparency, and fairness. These bodies play a critical role in maintaining investor confidence, preventing systemic crises, protecting consumers, and promoting orderly financial development. At the national level, regulatory authorities are often established by governments or central banks to enforce financial laws, set standards, issue licenses, and supervise market participants. The primary objective is to mitigate risks such as fraud, default, money laundering, and unethical financial practices that could undermine economic integrity.

1.5.1 Key roles and functions

- **Licensing and supervision**
  Regulators are responsible for granting operating licenses to banks, insurance companies, stock exchanges, mutual funds, and other financial intermediaries. After licensing, they monitor operations to ensure compliance with laws and guidelines.

- **Setting prudential norms**
  They establish capital adequacy norms, liquidity ratios, exposure limits, and asset classification norms to ensure that financial institutions remain solvent and capable of absorbing shocks.

- **Market regulation**
  Regulators enforce fair trading practices, monitor market manipulation, and promote investor protection through surveillance of securities markets and financial disclosures.

- **Consumer protection**
  They ensure that consumers are not misled by unfair practices, hidden fees, or predatory lending. Grievance redressal mechanisms and ombudsman services are part of this framework.

- **Systemic risk management**
  Regulators monitor systemic risks that could trigger a financial crisis. They engage in stress testing, monitor macroeconomic indicators, and act proactively to stabilize markets during times of volatility.
- **Promoting financial inclusion**
  Modern regulatory frameworks also promote inclusive finance by encouraging innovations such as mobile banking, microfinance, and digital KYC processes.

1.5.2 International regulatory bodies

Global financial interconnectedness has led to the emergence of coordinated global regulatory bodies such as the BCBS, IOSCO, and FSB, which establish international standards for banking, securities, and financial stability (Claessens, 2021) [15]

- **The Basel Committee on Banking Supervision (BCBS)**: Sets global banking standards (e.g., Basel III norms).
- **International Organization of Securities Commissions (IOSCO)**: Sets global standards for securities regulation.
- **Financial Stability Board (FSB)**: Promotes international financial stability and coordination.

Regulatory authorities are vital pillars of a sound financial ecosystem. By enforcing compliance, managing risk, and promoting transparency, they uphold the integrity and efficiency of the financial system. Strong and adaptive regulatory institutions ensure that markets operate smoothly, instill public confidence, and support sustainable economic growth. Strengthened regulatory oversight by central banks and international bodies has improved the resilience of financial institutions and markets, mitigating systemic vulnerabilities and contagion risks [16]; [17].

1.6 Central Banks

Central banks are apex monetary authorities that lie at the heart of every financial system. They are independent institutions tasked with formulating and implementing a nation's monetary policy, managing currency issuance, ensuring price stability, and supervising the banking sector. By influencing the availability and cost of money and credit, central banks play a pivotal role in steering economic growth, employment levels, and inflation.

1.6.1 Core functions of central banks

- **Monetary policy implementation**
  One of the primary roles of a central bank is to control inflation and support economic growth through monetary policy. This is done by adjusting key interest rates (e.g., repo rate) and managing liquidity in the economy. An expansionary policy lowers interest rates to stimulate borrowing and spending, while a contractionary policy raises rates to curb inflation.
- **Issuance of currency**
  Central banks have the exclusive authority to issue a nation's legal tender. They ensure that the currency in circulation matches the economic activity and is protected against counterfeiting. This function preserves the public's trust in the monetary system.
- **Lender of last resort**
  During times of financial distress or liquidity crunch, central banks provide emergency funding to commercial banks and financial institutions to prevent systemic collapse. This function stabilizes the financial system and maintains confidence.
- **Regulation and supervision of banks**
  Central banks set prudential norms for commercial banks and NBFCs to ensure financial stability. This includes regulating capital requirements, reserve ratios (like CRR and SLR), provisioning norms, and risk management practices.
- **Foreign exchange management**
  Central banks manage the country's foreign exchange reserves and intervene in the forex market to stabilize currency fluctuations. In economies with a fixed or managed exchange rate, this role is particularly critical.
- **Government's banker and debt manager**
  The central bank acts as a banker to the government by managing its accounts, issuing public debt instruments like bonds and treasury bills, and helping in fiscal deficit financing.

Central banking in India: Reserve Bank of India (RBI)

The **Reserve Bank of India (RBI)** is India's central bank, established in 1935. It operates under the RBI Act of 1934 and serves as the country's monetary authority, regulator of the financial system, and currency issuer. Key functions include:

- Managing inflation through repo and reverse repo rates
- Regulating banks and NBFCs
- Supervising payment systems like RTGS and NEFT
- Managing India's foreign exchange reserves
- Promoting financial inclusion (e.g., Priority Sector Lending, PMJDY)

Central banks are the architects of monetary stability and financial soundness. Their ability to manage money supply, interest rates, and banking supervision ensures the orderly functioning of the entire economy. A credible and transparent central bank strengthens investor confidence, protects the value of money, and enhances the resilience of the financial system.

1.7 Financial Infrastructure

Financial infrastructure refers to the foundational systems, institutions, technologies, and frameworks that support the functioning, safety, efficiency, and accessibility of financial services and markets. Financial market infrastructures include clearinghouses, securities settlement systems, and real-time gross settlement networks, and also act as the "plumbing" of the financial system, enabling high-volume transactions with minimal risk [18]. It serves as the backbone that enables seamless financial transactions, regulatory compliance, market operations, data management, and risk control. Comparative evidence shows that strong financial market infrastructures, including central counterparties, payment systems, and securities settlement systems, are indispensable for maintaining global financial stability [19]; [20]. A robust financial infrastructure ensures that the financial system operates smoothly, fosters trust, and drives economic development.

1.7.1 Core components of financial infrastructure

- **Payment and settlement systems**
  At the center of financial infrastructure are reliable and secure payment and settlement systems, which facilitate the transfer of funds between institutions, individuals, and countries. Systems like (RTGS), NEFT, and UPI in India are part of this infrastructure, enabling real-time, large-scale, or batch processing of payments.

- **Clearing houses and central counterparties (CCPs)**
  These institutions ensure that trades – especially in securities, derivatives, and foreign exchange – are settled efficiently. Clearing houses calculate obligations, manage risks, and guarantee settlement even if one party defaults. CCPs reduce counterparty risk by acting as intermediaries between buyers and sellers.

- **Depositories and custodians**
  Financial infrastructure includes entities like **Central Depository Services Ltd. (CDSL)** and **National Securities Depository Ltd. (NSDL)** in India, which maintain and transfer ownership of securities electronically. Custodians safeguard clients' financial assets and ensure secure and accurate processing of financial transactions.

- **Credit information systems**
  Credit bureaus such as **CIBIL**, **Equifax**, and **Experian** collect and maintain credit histories of individuals and businesses. These systems provide critical inputs for lenders to assess creditworthiness and manage credit risk effectively.

- **KYC and identity verification mechanisms**
  Infrastructure such as **Aadhaar-enabled e-KYC** systems allows financial institutions to onboard customers while ensuring compliance with anti-money laundering (AML) and counter-terrorism financing (CTF) regulations. Digital identity systems make onboarding faster and more secure.

- **Regulatory and supervisory technology (RegTech and SupTech)**
  These are tools used by regulators and institutions to monitor compliance, detect financial crime, analyze data, and implement regulations efficiently. RegTech solutions enhance transparency and reduce the cost of regulatory compliance.

- **Cybersecurity frameworks**
  Given the increasing digitization of financial services, a secure infrastructure to protect systems from cyber threats is a vital component. Firewalls, encryption, multi-factor authentication, and data protection laws form part of this defense layer.

- **Market infrastructure institutions (MIIs)**
  In India, MIIs include stock exchanges (like NSE and BSE), depositories, and clearing corporations. These institutions ensure efficient capital market functioning through transparency, automation, and operational integrity.

1.7.2 Importance of financial infrastructure

- **Enhances stability**: Prevents systemic crises by ensuring the secure and timely execution of financial transactions.
- **Improves efficiency**: Reduces transaction costs, settlement times, and risks.
- **Fosters trust**: Transparent systems inspire confidence among investors, lenders, and the public.
- **Enables innovation**: Supports FinTech developments like digital lending, robo-advisory, and blockchain-based transactions.
- **Promotes financial inclusion**: Mobile banking, e-KYC, and micro-ATMs extend services to rural and unbanked populations.

Financial infrastructure is the invisible framework that powers the visible operations of the financial system. It underpins every financial interaction – whether it is a retail payment, a bond issuance, or an equity trade. Cross-border capital movements and geopolitical tensions are prompting a shift toward alternative financial networks and regional market infrastructures ([21]; [22]). A strong and inclusive financial infrastructure is essential for economic resilience, innovation, and inclusive growth.

1.8 Financial Services

Financial services refer to the wide range of services provided by the finance industry to individuals, businesses, and governments to facilitate various financial activities, including borrowing, lending, investing, insuring, saving, and transferring money. These services are the visible outputs of the financial system that directly impact people's financial well-being and economic activity. Financial services are delivered by various financial institutions such as commercial banks, insurance companies, investment firms, mutual funds, pension funds, FinTech companies, and non-banking financial corporations (NBFCs). They form the interface between the financial infrastructure and end users, translating financial products and instruments into actionable offerings. Innovations in securitization, digital assets, and hybrid securities are reshaping the risk-return profiles available to investors, reflecting a dynamic interplay of market demand, regulation, and technology [23].

1.8.1 Categories of financial services

Banking services: This includes retail and commercial banking activities, like:

- Savings and checking accounts
- Fixed and recurring deposits
- Personal, housing, auto, and business loans
- Credit and debit card issuance
- Internet and mobile banking
- Banks also offer services like safe deposit lockers, fund transfers, and wealth management.

Investment services: These involve helping individuals and organizations grow their wealth through:

- Mutual funds
- Portfolio management
- Stockbroking and trading
- Asset management
- Financial advisory services
  Investment services match risk profiles with suitable financial instruments to achieve long-term financial goals.

Insurance services

Insurance companies offer products that protect against financial loss from unforeseen events. Common offerings include:

- Life insurance
- Health insurance
- Vehicle and property insurance
- Business and liability insurance
  These services provide financial security, manage risk, and support recovery in times of loss.

Payment services

These services facilitate money movement, such as:

- Electronic fund transfers (EFTs)

- Unified Payments Interface (UPI)
- Mobile wallets (Paytm, Google Pay)
- Point-of-sale (POS) services
- International remittance

The evolution of digital payment services has revolutionized financial access and speed.

Capital market services

These are services that help companies raise capital and investors earn returns, including:

- IPO facilitation
- Bond issuance
- Underwriting
- Market making
- Clearing and settlement

These services are essential for capital formation and liquidity in the economy.

Wealth management and financial planning

These services are personalized offerings for high-net-worth individuals and families to manage and grow wealth efficiently, including:

- Tax planning
- Estate planning
- Retirement planning
- Trust and fiduciary services

FinTech services

Technology-driven financial services have emerged rapidly in recent years, such as:

- Peer-to-peer lending platforms
- Robo-advisors
- Buy Now Pay Later (BNPL)
- InsurTech platforms
- Digital-only banks (neo-banks)

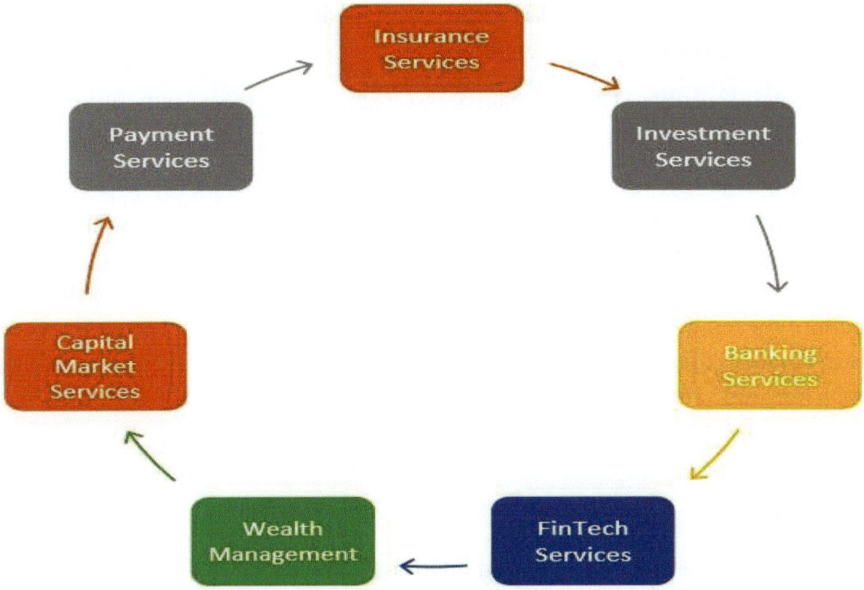

Figure 1.6 Types of financial services.

1.8.2 Importance of financial services

- **Resource mobilization**: Converts savings into productive investments.
- **Economic growth**: Facilitates business expansion, infrastructure projects, and consumption.
- **Risk management**: Enables individuals and businesses to hedge against uncertainties.
- **Liquidity**: Ensures that funds are available where needed through credit and capital markets.
- **Financial inclusion**: Extends financial access to marginalized populations using technology and tailored services.

1.8.3 Emerging trends and challenges:

- **Digitization**: AI, blockchain, and big data analytics are reshaping service delivery.
- **Cybersecurity**: As services go digital, ensuring data privacy and fraud prevention is paramount.

- **Customer experience**: Hyper-personalization, 24/7 support, and seamless interfaces are now expected.
- **Sustainability**: Green finance and ESG investing are redefining financial service priorities.

Financial services represent the dynamic and customer-facing aspect of the financial system. They not only support day-to-day economic functions but also empower individuals to achieve financial security and prosperity. An inclusive, innovative, and regulated financial services sector is critical to building a resilient and equitable economy. The interplay between financial instruments, markets, and payment systems determines overall monetary transmission and liquidity conditions, affecting both domestic growth and cross-border capital flows [23].

Summary

This chapter outlines the fundamental components of the financial system and their individual roles within the broader economic structure: **Financial institutions** act as intermediaries that mobilize savings and extend credit, playing a central role in economic development. **Financial markets** provide platforms for trading securities, enabling efficient capital allocation and liquidity. **Financial instruments** serve as the tools or contracts for investment, lending, or risk management. **Payment and settlement systems** ensure the secure and timely transfer of funds and securities in both domestic and international transactions. **Regulatory authorities** supervise and control various financial entities, protecting stakeholders and ensuring market integrity. **Central banks** govern monetary policy, maintain financial stability, and serve as the apex financial institutions in any economy. **Financial infrastructure** encompasses the technological and operational frameworks, such as clearinghouses, exchanges, and information systems. **Financial services** include banking, insurance, asset management, and other customer-facing functions that support financial transactions. Together, these components form a dynamic and interdependent structure that drives financial innovation, ensures regulatory compliance, and supports national and global economic systems.

Case Study: "India's Demonetization and the Rise of Digital Payments"

Overview: In a landmark economic move on November 8, 2016, the Government of India announced the demonetization of all ₹500 and ₹1,000 banknotes – effectively invalidating 86% of the currency in circulation at the time. This unexpected and unprecedented decision, initiated by Prime Minister Narendra Modi, was aimed at combating issues such as black money, fake currency, and terror financing. However, beyond these immediate goals, the policy also had a transformative agenda: to catalyze India's transition toward a digital and less-cash economy. The sudden cash crunch created by demonetization forced individuals and businesses to explore alternative payment mechanisms. With limited access to physical currency, digital payment platforms experienced exponential growth. Services such as Paytm, PhonePe, FreeCharge, and MobiKwik saw a sharp rise in new users and daily transaction volumes. Simultaneously, the government's push through initiatives like Digital India, BHIM app, and Unified Payments Interface (UPI) accelerated the adoption of electronic payment modes. UPI, in particular, became a game-changer, allowing seamless real-time transactions directly between bank accounts using mobile devices.

Prior to demonetization, India's economy was predominantly cash-driven, especially in rural and unorganized sectors. Many small businesses operated outside the formal banking system. But post-2016, there was a noticeable behavioral shift toward digital financial inclusion. More people opened bank accounts, embraced mobile wallets, and began using QR codes for transactions. The introduction of Aadhaar-linked payments, combined with Jan Dhan Yojana bank accounts, facilitated greater access to digital finance among previously unbanked populations. Despite the progress, the transition was not without challenges. Rural and semi-urban areas faced barriers such as low internet penetration, digital illiteracy, and concerns over cybersecurity. Many small merchants and daily wage earners found it difficult to adopt digital tools overnight. Moreover, consumer trust and data privacy became critical issues as digital transactions grew. Nevertheless, the policy succeeded in breaking the inertia around digital payments. By 2020, India had become one of the world's fastest-growing digital payment markets, with a vibrant fintech ecosystem and increasing government and private investments in payment infrastructure. The long-term impact of demonetization laid the foundation for the ongoing decline in paper currency dependency and the rise of digital currencies and services, including discussions around the Central Bank Digital Currency (CBDC), or the Digital Rupee. In retrospect, demonetization served as both a disruptive challenge and a powerful catalyst for digital financial transformation in India. It demonstrated how policy-driven interventions, when coupled with technology and public readiness, can reshape the foundations of a nation's financial behavior.

Key aspects of the case:

1. In November 2016, the government of India announced the demonetization of ₹500 and ₹1,000 notes – removing nearly 86% of the country's paper currency in circulation overnight. This drastic move was aimed at curbing black money, counterfeit currency, and promoting a shift toward a digital economy.
2. While it caused short-term disruptions, it significantly accelerated the adoption of digital payment systems, including mobile wallets, UPI (Unified Payments Interface), and online banking.
3. India had a largely cash-based economy. Demonetization was a push toward transparency and formalization. It was an opportunity to transition users toward digital financial platforms.
4. Government initiatives like Digital India and Jan Dhan Yojana played supportive roles. A rise in smartphone and internet penetration supported digital currency use. Banks, fintechs, and the government invested in building cashless payment ecosystems.

Rural populations struggled due to a lack of digital literacy and internet access. Cybersecurity threats and digital fraud have become a growing concern. A sustained rise in digital transactions even after cash availability is normalized. India emerged as one of the global leaders in digital payment innovation. Paper currency usage declined proportionally, though not completely eliminated. Use of mobile wallets (e.g., Paytm, PhonePe) surged dramatically. UPI transactions grew from less than a million per month in 2016 to over 10 billion per month by 2024.

Case Discussion Questions

1. What were the primary economic and social motivations behind India's demonetization?
2. How did the policy impact consumer behavior regarding paper vs. digital currency?
3. What infrastructure and policy changes were critical in enabling the rise of digital payments?
4. What lessons can other countries learn from India's push toward a cashless economy?
5. What challenges remain in achieving full digital currency adoption in developing economies?

Keywords

- **Financial system:** A network of institutions, markets, instruments, and regulations that facilitates the flow of funds between savers and borrowers. It supports savings, investment, and economic growth.
- **Financial services**: Services provided by the finance industry, including banking, insurance, investment, and asset management, which help individuals and businesses manage money.
- **Core financial functions:** The main roles of a financial system – such as mobilizing savings, allocating resources, managing risk, and facilitating payments and settlement
- **Financial institutions:** Organizations like banks, insurance companies, pension funds, and mutual funds that provide financial services to customers.
- **Money:** A medium of exchange, a unit of account, and a store of value used to facilitate economic transactions.
- **Monetary system**: The set of institutions and rules that govern the supply and value of money in an economy, including central banks and monetary policy mechanisms.
- **Economic impact:** he influence of financial systems or policies on a country's economic indicators, such as growth, inflation, employment, and investment.

- **Intermediaries:** Institutions like banks or brokers that act as a bridge between savers and borrowers by channeling funds and reducing transaction costs.
- **Clearing:** A process that confirms and matches the details of financial transactions (such as buying/selling stocks) before they are settled.
- **Settlement system**: The final stage of a financial transaction where the transfer of money and/or securities is completed between parties.
- **Capital allocation:** The process of distributing financial resources to different sectors or projects based on expected returns and risk.
- **Risk management:** The process of identifying, assessing, and minimizing financial risks through insurance, diversification, or hedging.
- Price discovery: The process through which markets determine the price of a financial asset based on supply and demand factors.

Discussion Questions

1. What are the primary functions of a financial system, and how do they contribute to economic development?
2. How do different financial institutions (e.g., banks, insurance companies, NBFCs) differ in their roles within the financial system?
3. Explain the relationship between the monetary system and macroeconomic variables such as inflation and interest rates.
4. Why are financial intermediaries important for ensuring liquidity and stability in the economy?
5. What is the significance of clearing and settlement systems in maintaining trust and efficiency in financial markets?
6. In what ways does the financial infrastructure support secure and timely financial transactions in a digital economy?
7. Discuss how financial markets help in price discovery and what role they play in investment decisions.
8. How do modern financial systems differ from traditional systems in terms of technology and accessibility?

References

[1] Bhole, L. M., & Mahakud, J. (2017). *Financial Institutions and Markets: Structure, Growth and Innovations* (5th ed.). McGraw Hill Education.

[2] Saunders, A., & Cornett, M. M. (2018). *Financial Institutions Management: A Risk Management Approach* (9th ed.). McGraw-Hill.

[3] Merton, R. C. (1995). A functional perspective of financial intermediation. *Financial Management, 24*(2), 23–41.

[4] World Economic Forum. (2025). *Navigating global financial system fragmentation.* WEF Reports.

[5] Mishkin, F. S. (2018). *The Economics of Money, Banking, and Financial Markets* (12th ed.). Pearson.

[6] Zetzsche, D. A., & Arner, D. W. (2023). *FinTech and the evolution of digital financial markets.* Journal of Financial Regulation, 9(2), 145–167

[7] Fabozzi, F. J., Modigliani, F., & Jones, F. J. (2013). *Foundations of Financial Markets and Institutions* (4th ed.). Pearson.

[8] Cecchetti, S. G., & Schoenholtz, K. L. (2021). *Money, Banking, and Financial Markets* (6th ed.). McGraw-Hill.

[9] IMF. (2022). *How India's central bank helped spur a digital payments boom.*

[10] IdRBT. (2020s). Reserve Bank of India's initiatives and infrastructure enhancements for safe, secure, efficient payment systems. *Banking Technology Journal.*

[11] National Payments Corporation of India Report. (2025).

[12] Kamesam, V. (2003). Payment and settlement systems. *BIS Review.*

[13] Norman, B. (2011). *The Risk Controllers: Central Counterparty Clearing in Globalised Financial Markets.* Wiley.

[14] Reserve Bank of India. (2025). Digital Payments Index rises 10.7% in FY25, showing steady growth in supply-side infrastructure. *News Report.*

[15] Claessens, S. (2021). Global financial regulation: Institutions, standards, and challenges. *Journal of International Money and Finance*, 115, 102398.

[16] International Monetary Fund. (2023). *Global Financial Stability Report.* https://www.imf.org

[17] Saunders, A., & Cornett, M. M. (2020). *Financial Institutions Management: A Risk Management Approach* (9th ed.). McGraw Hill.

[18] Badruddin, A. (2015). Financial market infrastructures: A study on payment and settlement system in India banking sector. *International*

Journal of Engineering Technology, Management and Applied Sciences, 3(2), 179–190.
[19] World Bank. (2019). *Payment Systems Worldwide: A Snapshot.* Washington, DC: World Bank Publications.
[20] International Monetary Fund. (2023). *Global Financial Stability Report.* https://www.imf.org
[21] Ballis, A. (2025). Geopolitical tensions and financial networks: Strategic shifts toward alternatives.
[22] Jenkins, P. J. (2025, July 28). What India's economy can teach the UK. *Financial Times.*
[23] Blanchard, O., & Johnson, D. R. (2017). *Macroeconomics* (7th ed.). Pearson. IMF.

2

The Roots of Financial Innovation

Abstract

This chapter provides a foundational exploration of the historical and conceptual journey of financial innovation, tracing its evolution from primitive exchange systems to the sophisticated digital platforms of today. By examining the deep-rooted origins of financial tools and practices, it sets the stage for understanding the current digital revolution within a broader socio-economic and technological context. The discussion begins with an overview of finance in its earliest forms, such as barter trade, commodity money, and the emergence of rudimentary credit systems, laying the groundwork for understanding how early societies facilitated value exchange and resource allocation. It then moves through milestone events such as the invention of coinage, the rise of banking in medieval Europe, the establishment of stock markets, the creation of central banking systems, and the development of paper currency – all of which significantly influenced the architecture of modern financial systems.

A key focus of the chapter is on the technological, economic, and social drivers that have historically propelled financial innovation. From the printing press enabling mass issuance of financial instruments to the internet ushering in online banking and mobile wallets, innovation has consistently been shaped by a dynamic interplay between necessity, opportunity, and technological progress. The chapter further explores the shift from traditional, paper-based financial systems to digitized solutions, highlighting how digital platforms have enabled faster transactions, greater transparency, improved financial inclusion, and increased access to capital. This transformation is not only operational but also cultural, reshaping consumer expectations and redefining regulatory boundaries.

DOI: 10.1201/9788743811244-3

While the benefits of digital financial systems are considerable – including cost- efficiency, real-time analytics, and broader outreach – the chapter does not overlook the challenges that accompany this transformation. These include cybersecurity threats, data privacy concerns, regulatory gaps, and digital divides that hinder equitable access. Concluding with a forward-looking perspective, the chapter emphasizes the importance of ongoing innovation that is inclusive, ethical, and resilient. It calls for cross-sector collaboration and anticipatory regulatory frameworks to ensure that the future of finance remains both progressive and stable. By grounding modern financial developments in historical insight, this chapter equips readers with a deeper appreciation of how finance has continually adapted to meet the needs of society – an evolution that continues to this day through digital disruption and beyond.

Introduction

The foundations of modern finance are deeply rooted in centuries of economic evolution, institutional development, and technological ingenuity. Understanding the historical trajectory of financial systems offers vital insight into how innovations emerge in response to changing societal needs and economic complexities. This chapter traces the chronological evolution of finance, from the rudimentary practices of barter and coinage to the sophisticated mechanisms of global digital banking. It highlights the pivotal milestones that have reshaped financial landscapes – such as the invention of paper currency, the rise of central banking, and the emergence of capital markets – while identifying the key forces driving continuous innovation, including globalization, regulation, and technology. Special emphasis is placed on the transformative shift from paper-based processes to digital platforms, marking a critical inflection point in the financial sector's journey. By revisiting the roots of financial innovation, this chapter sets the stage for understanding the disruptive trends shaping today's FinTech-driven world.

2.1 The Historical Evolution of Finance

2.1.1 Origins of finance in ancient civilizations

Finance, in its earliest form, emerged as a response to the limitations of barter systems. Ancient civilizations developed rudimentary financial practices to facilitate trade, manage resources, and record transactions. Early financial systems emerged in Mesopotamia through commodity money and debt arrangements [1].

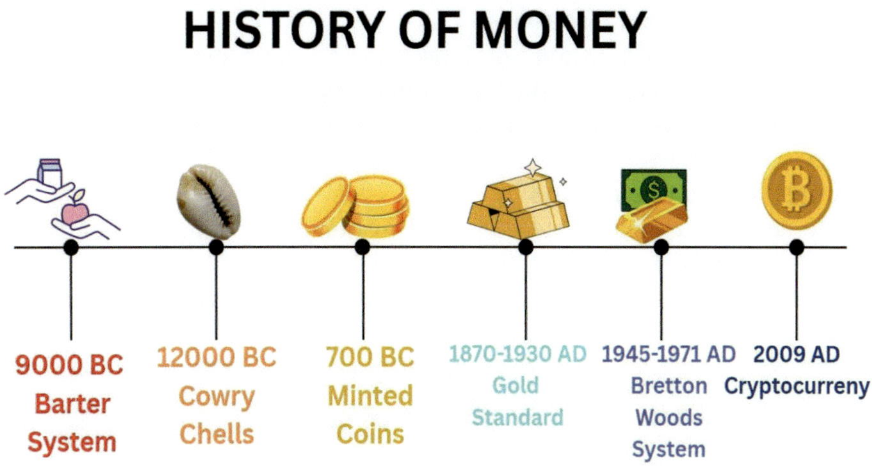

Figure 2.1 History of money.

Barter systems and the need for money

In prehistoric societies, goods and services were exchanged directly. However, the inefficiencies of barter – such as the double coincidence of wants – necessitated the creation of a more versatile medium of exchange. This led to the adoption of commodity money, including items like cattle, grain, and shells.

The advent of coinage

The first standardized coins appeared in Lydia (modern-day Turkey) around 600 BCE, made from electrum, a natural alloy of gold and silver. Coinage provided a reliable and divisible medium of exchange, facilitating trade across regions. Ancient civilizations like Greece and Rome established the foundations of coin-based economies [2].

Financial practices in ancient Mesopotamia and Egypt

In Mesopotamia, temples and palaces acted as financial centers, recording transactions on clay tablets. They provided loans, collected taxes, and managed large-scale agricultural projects. Similarly, ancient Egypt utilized grain banks, where grain deposits could be used as a form of currency. The transition from metal to paper currency marked a turning point in global trade systems [3].

2.1.2 Financial innovations in classical antiquity

The classical civilizations of Greece and Rome introduced significant financial innovations that laid the groundwork for modern finance.

Banking in ancient Greece

Greek bankers, known as trapezitai, operated private banks offering deposit and loan services. They facilitated currency exchange and provided credit to merchants, playing a crucial role in the commercial activities of the time.

Roman financial systems

Rome developed sophisticated financial instruments, including promissory notes and complex contracts. The Roman legal system codified financial transactions, providing a legal framework that influenced future financial practices.

2.1.3 Medieval finance and the rise of banking

The medieval period witnessed the resurgence of trade and the evolution of financial institutions to support expanding economies. The Renaissance banking era, led by families such as the Medicis, transformed credit and capital mobility [4].

The role of moneylenders and merchant guilds

With the decline of centralized Roman authority, local moneylenders and merchant guilds filled the financial void. They provided credit and facilitated trade fairs, which became hubs of commercial activity.

Emergence of banking families

Prominent families, such as the Medici in Florence, established banking houses that offered a range of services, including currency exchange, loans, and investment opportunities. These banks played a pivotal role in financing trade and political endeavors.

Development of bills of exchange

To mitigate the risks of transporting large sums of money, merchants developed bills of exchange. These financial instruments allowed for the transfer of funds across regions without the physical movement of currency, enhancing the safety and efficiency of trade.

2.1.4 Financial expansion during the Renaissance

The Renaissance era brought about a renewed interest in commerce and finance, leading to the establishment of more structured financial institutions. The Industrial Revolution accelerated joint-stock companies and organized stock markets, shaping modern finance [5]. Financial innovation in Islamic economics reflected evolving trade ethics and contracts across centuries [6]. The rise of digital finance, open banking, and FinTech symbolizes the ongoing 150-year revolution in financial technology [7].

Birth of stock exchanges

The Amsterdam Stock Exchange, established in 1602, is considered the world's first official stock exchange. It facilitated the trading of shares in the Dutch East India Company, allowing investors to participate in the profits of overseas ventures.

Joint-stock companies and risk sharing

Joint-stock companies emerged as a means to pool capital for large-scale enterprises, such as exploration and colonization. Investors shared in the profits and losses, distributing risk and encouraging investment in ambitious projects.

Evolution of banking practices

Banks began to offer more sophisticated services, including checking accounts and letters of credit. These innovations enhanced the liquidity of capital and supported the growing needs of commerce.

2.1.5 Financial systems in the industrial age

The Industrial Revolution transformed economies, necessitating the development of advanced financial systems to support industrial growth. Central banking and institutional credit systems enhanced monetary stability in the 19th century (Berk, 2012) [8].

Expansion of credit and capital markets

Industrialization required substantial capital investment. Banks and financial markets expanded to meet this demand, offering loans and facilitating the issuance of stocks and bonds to fund industrial enterprises.

Central banking and monetary policy

Central banks, such as the Bank of England, began to play a more prominent role in managing national currencies and monetary policy. They acted as lenders of last resort and worked to stabilize financial systems.

Emergence of modern insurance

The growth of commerce and industry led to increased risks, prompting the development of insurance companies. These institutions provided financial protection against losses, contributing to economic stability.

2.1.6 The globalization of finance in the 20th century

The 20th century saw the globalization of financial markets and the integration of economies.

The gold standard and its collapse

The gold standard, which pegged currencies to gold, provided stability but limited monetary policy flexibility. Its collapse during the Great Depression led to the adoption of fiat currencies and more active monetary management.

Bretton Woods system and international institutions

Post-World War II, the Bretton Woods Agreement established a new international monetary system, leading to the creation of the International Monetary Fund (IMF) and the World Bank. These institutions aimed to promote global economic stability and development.

Rise of financial deregulation

In the latter half of the century, many countries moved toward financial deregulation, liberalizing markets and encouraging innovation. This period saw the proliferation of complex financial instruments and increased capital flows across borders.

2.1.7 Contemporary finance in the digital era

The digital transformation of the financial sector has been one of the most profound shifts in the history of modern economics. This chapter explores the key developments that define finance in the digital age, focusing on technological innovation, the emergence of decentralized finance, and the pressing regulatory and security challenges that accompany this evolution.

Electronic trading and FinTech innovations

Electronic trading platforms

Electronic trading has replaced the traditional floor-based systems in stock exchanges with algorithmic and online trading mechanisms. Platforms like NASDAQ and BSE now handle billions of dollars in transactions daily using high-frequency trading (HFT) and automated order-matching systems. This transition has increased market liquidity, improved pricing transparency, and significantly lowered transaction costs for investors.

Fintech disruption

Fintech (financial technology) companies have emerged as agile competitors to traditional banks, leveraging data analytics, artificial intelligence, and mobile technology to provide services that are faster, cheaper, and more personalized.

- **Mobile banking**: Through apps, consumers can transfer money, pay bills, and even invest without visiting a physical bank.
- **Peer-to-Peer (P2P) lending**: Platforms like LendingClub and Prosper enable borrowers to access funds directly from investors, bypassing traditional bank intermediaries.
- **Robo-advisors**: Services such as Betterment and Wealthfront offer automated, algorithm-driven investment advice, making wealth management more accessible and cost-effective.

These FinTech innovations have democratized access to financial services, particularly benefiting underserved populations and small businesses.

Cryptocurrencies and blockchain technology

Cryptocurrencies

The rise of cryptocurrencies such as Bitcoin (BTC), Ethereum (ETH), and Ripple (XRP) has challenged the traditional financial paradigm by introducing digital currencies that operate independently of central banks. These assets offer the benefits of fast, low-cost, borderless transactions and are increasingly viewed as stores of value or speculative investment instruments.

Figure 2.2 Types of cryptocurrencies.

Blockchain technology

At the core of most cryptocurrencies lies blockchain, a distributed ledger technology (DLT) that records transactions across a decentralized network of computers. Blockchain ensures transparency, immutability, and security, enabling:

- **Smart contracts**: Self-executing agreements encoded on the blockchain, eliminating intermediaries.
- **Decentralized Finance (DeFi)**: Platforms that allow users to borrow, lend, and trade assets without traditional financial institutions.
- **Tokenization of assets**: Real-world assets like real estate, art, or stocks can be represented as digital tokens, allowing fractional ownership and improving liquidity.

These technologies signal a shift from centralized control to user-governed systems, disrupting conventional banking, payment processing, and asset management structures.

Regulatory challenges and cybersecurity Regulatory landscape

The rapid pace of financial innovation has outstripped the development of regulatory frameworks, creating a lag that presents risks to consumer protection and market stability.

- **Cross-border compliance**: Cryptocurrencies and global FinTech platforms often operate in regulatory gray zones, complicating enforcement and tax compliance.
- **Consumer protection**: With many digital platforms operating outside traditional banking safeguards, ensuring transparency and accountability is a growing concern.
- **Anti-money laundering (AML) and know your customer (KYC)**: Regulators face challenges in enforcing AML and KYC norms in decentralized or pseudonymous networks.

Governments and financial authorities worldwide are racing to develop adaptive, technology-neutral regulations that balance innovation with risk management.

Cybersecurity concerns

As financial operations increasingly migrate online, the sector has become a prime target for cybercriminals. Threats include:

- **Phishing attacks and ransomware**: Targeting financial institutions and customers alike.

- **Data breaches**: Breaches expose sensitive personal and financial data, leading to identity theft and financial loss.
- **Systemic risk**: A large-scale cyberattack on interconnected financial networks could have devastating consequences for the global economy.

To combat these risks, institutions are investing heavily in advanced cybersecurity frameworks, employing AI for real-time threat detection, and adopting zero-trust architectures.

The history of finance is a testament to human ingenuity in developing systems to manage resources, facilitate trade, and support economic growth. From ancient barter systems to sophisticated digital platforms, finance has continually evolved to meet the changing needs of societies. Understanding this evolution provides valuable insights into current financial practices and future developments.

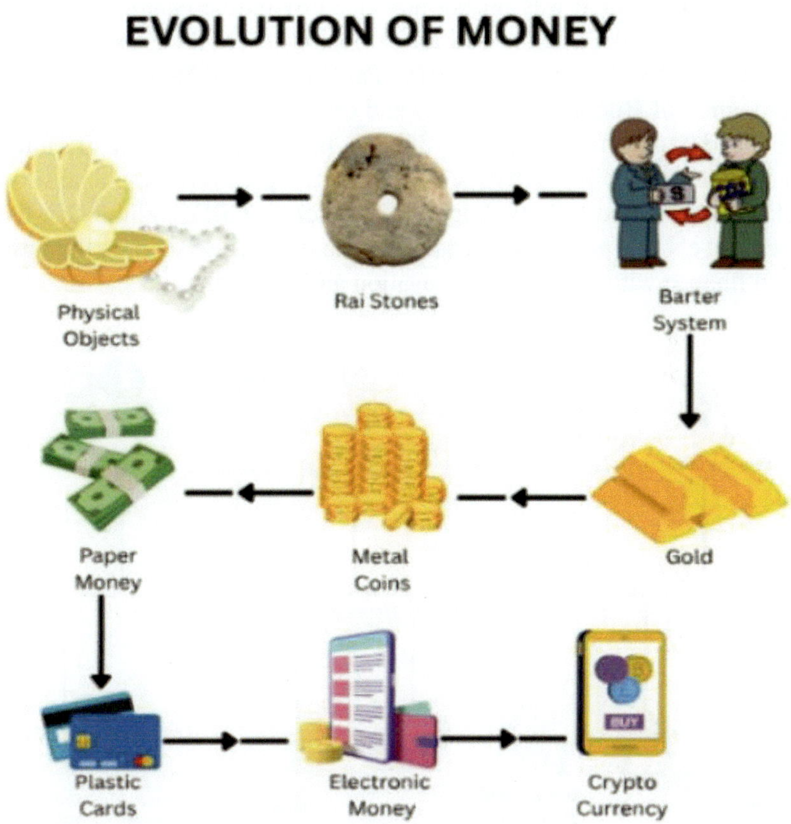

Figure 2.3 Evolution of money.

2.2 Milestones in Financial Innovation

The history of financial innovation reflects humanity's continuous quest for efficiency and trust in transactions. The invention of money between 3000 BCE and 600 BCE marked a major shift from the cumbersome barter system to the use of coins as a standardized medium of exchange. During the 12th to 15th centuries, proto-banking practices emerged in Italy, laying the groundwork for modern banking. This evolved into the establishment of central banks in the 17th and 18th centuries, notably with the founding of the Bank of England in 1694, to stabilize national economies. The emergence of stock markets, starting with the Amsterdam Stock Exchange in 1602, revolutionized capital formation. In the following centuries, paper currency and cheques became widespread. The 1950s saw the introduction of credit cards like the Diners Club and BankAmericard, transforming consumer finance. The launch of the first ATM by Barclays in 1967 initiated the era of electronic banking, which was further advanced by online banking platforms in the 1990s. The 2010s witnessed an explosion in FinTech and mobile payments, driven by platforms such as PayPal, Alipay, and Paytm. Following the 2009 launch of Bitcoin, blockchain and cryptocurrencies have significantly challenged traditional financial paradigms. In the 2020s, the integration of AI and big data is enabling hyper-personalized and predictive financial services. Additionally, Central Bank Digital Currencies (CBDCs) like the Digital Rupee and eNaira, along with regulatory sandboxes, are shaping the future of digital finance with a focus on innovation and oversight.

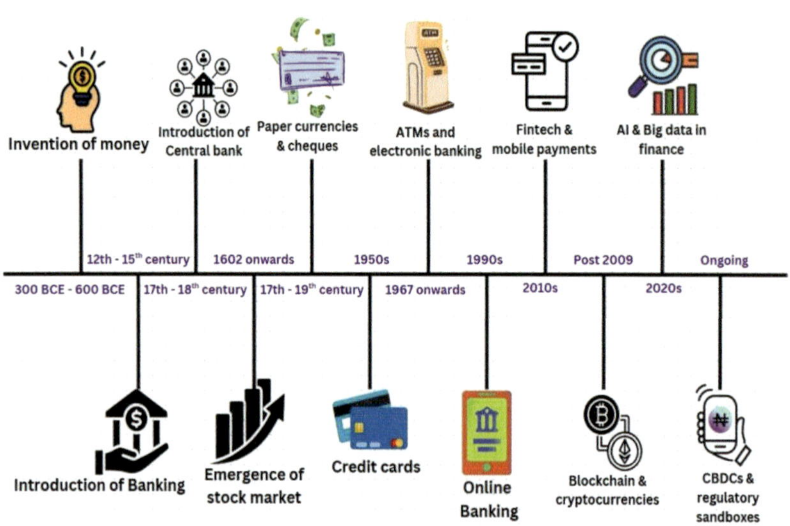

Figure 2.4 Milestone in financial innovation.

Table 2.1 Milestones in financial innovation.

Milestone	Context	Impact	Innovation value
Invention of money (circa 3000 BCE – 600 BCE) Shift from barter to coinage	Ancient civilizations like Mesopotamia, Egypt, Greece, and Rome replaced barter systems with metal coins.	Standardized value, enabled trade scalability	Introduced universal value representation for complex economies
Introduction of banking (12th–15th century) Proto-banking in Italy	Merchants in Florence, Venice, and Genoa developed bills of exchange and deposit systems.	Safe wealth storage, international trade facilitation	Foundation for modern banking: deposits, loans, exchanges
Creation of central banks (17th–18th century) Bank of England (1694)	Central banks established to manage debt and currency issuance.	Centralized monetary control	Enabled government monetary management and policy
Emergence of stock markets (1602 onwards) Amsterdam Stock Exchange	Dutch East India Company issued public shares.	Joint-stock structure encouraged investment	Origin of equity financing and securities trading
Paper currency and cheques (17th–19th century)	Banknotes and cheques replaced metal coins, backed by gold reserves.	Enhanced liquidity and convenience	Safer, portable transactions with greater economic mobility
Introduction of credit cards (1950s) Diners Club, BankAmericard	Enabled deferred payments and became globally adopted.	Stimulated consumer spending and instant credit access	Birth of consumer credit industry

(Continued)

Table 2.1 *Continued*

Milestone	Context	Impact	Innovation value
ATMs and electronic banking (1967 onwards) First ATM by Barclays	Allowed 24/7 cash access without tellers.	Customer convenience, reduced branch dependency	Start of banking automation and self-service model
Online banking (1990s) Internet-based platforms	Offered round-the- clock access to financial services.	Lowered costs, increased accessibility	Digitized financial operations and user empowerment
Fintech and mobile payments (2010s) PayPal, Alipay, Paytm, etc.	Mobile apps enabled real-time transactions and planning.	Disrupted legacy banking, improved inclusion	User-centric, fast, borderless finance solutions
Blockchain and cryptocurrencies (Post-2009) Bitcoin, Ethereum	Peer-to-peer transactions without intermediaries.	Challenged traditional finance systems	Decentralized, transparent, secure finance paradigm
AI and Big Data in finance (2020s)	Used in risk management, trading, and customer service.	Boosted efficiency and personalization	Intelligent, adaptive financial decision systems
CBDCs and regulatory sandboxes (Ongoing) Digital Rupee, eNaira	Digital fiat currencies piloted by governments.	Improved monetary control and reduced fraud	Combines fiat security with digital efficiency

2.3 Drivers of Innovation in the Financial System

The financial system, historically known for its rigid structures and traditional methodologies, has experienced a transformative shift in recent decades. This transformation is primarily attributed to a diverse array of innovation drivers that compel financial institutions and market participants to evolve continuously. These drivers, encompassing technological advancements, regulatory developments, shifting consumer expectations, economic pressures, and socio-demographic changes, have fundamentally redefined the architecture of financial systems worldwide. Technological progress and globalization continue to reshape financial intermediation and product design [9]. Expanding digital infrastructure and customer-centric models have made banks increasingly invisible in the digital economy [10].

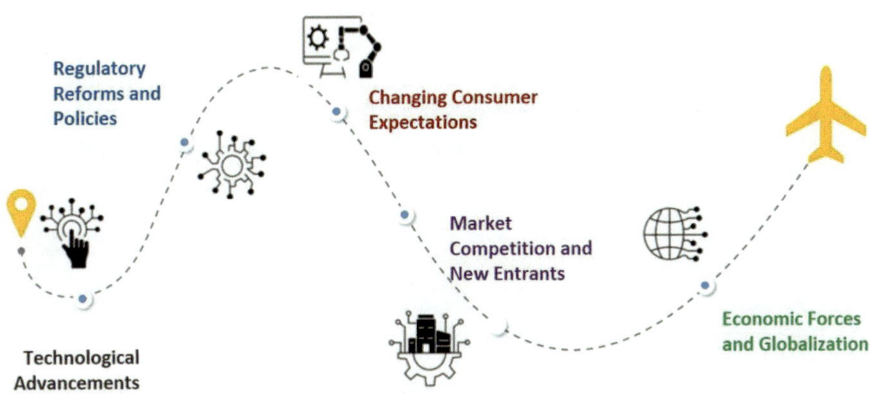

Figure 2.5 Drivers of innovation – financial system.

2.3.1 Technological advancements

One of the most influential drivers of financial innovation is the rapid progress in technology. The proliferation of digital tools and platforms has enabled financial service providers to deliver more efficient, accessible, and customized services.

- **Digital transformation:** The integration of digital technologies such as artificial intelligence (AI), machine learning (ML), and blockchain has allowed banks and financial institutions to automate processes, reduce human error, and offer real-time services. Robo-advisors, for instance, utilize AI algorithms to provide investment advice tailored to individual preferences, reducing dependency on traditional financial advisors.

- **Mobile and internet penetration:** The widespread adoption of smartphones and increased internet connectivity have facilitated the emergence of mobile banking and digital wallets. Services like M-Pesa in Kenya and Paytm in India exemplify how technology can bridge the gap between financial institutions and underserved populations.
- **Big Data and predictive analytics:** Financial institutions now rely heavily on data analytics to derive insights about customer behavior, creditworthiness, and market trends. Predictive models allow for more informed decision-making, risk mitigation, and enhanced customer engagement.

2.3.2 Regulatory reforms and policies

Regulatory frameworks have evolved to encourage financial innovation while ensuring consumer protection and market integrity. Regulatory frameworks and governance mechanisms are essential for responsible financial innovation [11]. Strategic responses to geopolitical tensions have driven nations to seek alternative financial networks [12].

- **Financial deregulation:** The removal of restrictive financial regulations, particularly in emerging markets, has opened the doors for private and foreign banks. This liberalization has fostered competition and incentivized the development of novel financial products.
- **Regulatory sandboxes:** To support innovation without compromising systemic stability, many countries have introduced regulatory sandboxes. These environments allow FinTech firms to test new products under regulatory oversight, thus balancing innovation with compliance.
- **Financial inclusion policies:** Governments and international organizations have emphasized the importance of financial inclusion. Policy initiatives aimed at reducing the unbanked population have encouraged banks to innovate in areas such as microfinance, digital KYC, and agent banking.

2.3.3 Changing consumer expectations

Modern consumers are more informed, digitally savvy, and demanding. Their expectations for convenience, speed, and personalization drive financial institutions to innovate continuously.

- **On-demand services:** Consumers expect 24/7 access to financial services, real- time transaction capabilities, and seamless digital interfaces. This has led to the proliferation of digital-only banks, also known as neobanks.
- **Customized financial products:** The demand for personalized financial services has increased. AI and ML technologies help institutions offer tailored credit lines, insurance packages, and investment portfolios.

2.3.4 Market competition and new entrants

The entry of agile FinTech startups and big tech companies into the financial services space has intensified competition.

- **Fintech disruption:** Startups like Revolut, Stripe, and Robinhood have redefined customer experience with cost-effective, user-friendly platforms. These companies have challenged traditional banks, compelling them to innovate or collaborate.
- **Platformization of finance:** Tech giants like Google, Apple, and Amazon are integrating financial services into their ecosystems. Their scale and technological prowess force conventional banks to adapt rapidly to retain customer loyalty.

2.3.5 Economic forces and globalization

Economic globalization and financial integration have created both opportunities and pressures for innovation.

- **Cross-border transactions:** With increased global trade and migration, there is a growing demand for low-cost, fast, and reliable cross-border payment solutions. Innovations like Ripple and SWIFT GPI address this need effectively.
- **Cost optimization:** Banks face immense pressure to cut costs while maintaining service quality. Technologies such as robotic process automation (RPA) and cloud computing allow institutions to streamline operations and achieve operational efficiency.

As financial systems become more digitized, the importance of risk management and cybersecurity grows. The rise in cyber threats has led to the development of advanced security measures, including biometric authentication, blockchain-based transaction ledgers, and multi-factor authentication systems. To comply with increasingly complex regulations, financial institutions are adopting RegTech solutions that automate compliance monitoring, reporting, and risk assessment. The innovation in the financial system is not driven by a single factor but by an intricate interplay of technological evolution, regulatory facilitation, customer-centric approaches, and broader economic and social transformations. These drivers not only redefine how financial services are delivered but also shape the very foundations of financial systems. As we move further into the digital age, the impetus for innovation will continue to grow, compelling financial institutions to remain agile, proactive, and responsive to the changing landscape.

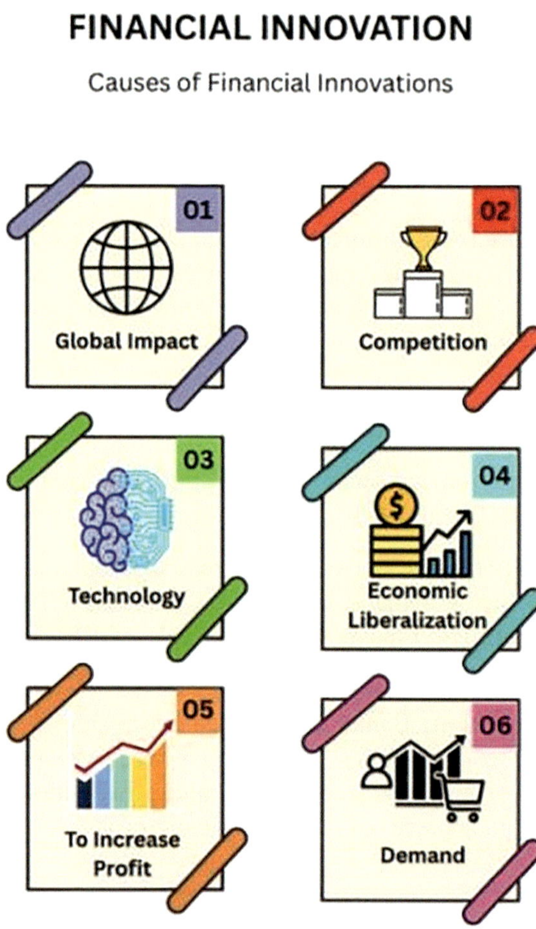

Figure 2.6 Causes of financial innovation.

2.4 From Paper to Digital: A Paradigm Shift in Financial Systems

The global financial system has undergone a monumental transformation over the past few decades, shifting from traditional paper-based operations to a highly digitized, technology-driven ecosystem. This paradigm shift – often referred to as the "digital transformation of finance" – has fundamentally redefined how money is created, managed, transacted, and regulated. It is not merely a technological change but a structural overhaul with significant implications for financial inclusion, efficiency, transparency, and innovation. The evolution from physical to electronic currency has enabled seamless, global transactions [13]. The rapid adoption of digital finance fosters inclusion but also raises concerns over debt expansion [14]. Blockchain-based systems underpin the growth of decentralized finance, enhancing transparency and autonomy [15]. Cryptocurrency represents a major milestone in redefining monetary sovereignty and trust [16]. Cybersecurity has emerged as a central concern as digital ecosystems expand globally [17]. The continuous ascent of money from tangible to digital forms reflects humanity's evolving relationship with value and technology.

2.4.1 The age of paper-based finance

Historically, financial transactions were conducted through manual processes and physical documentation. Paper currency, cheques, passbooks, and ledgers formed the backbone of financial record-keeping and operations. Banking services required physical presence, with long queues, limited service hours, and high transaction costs. Institutions operated in siloed environments with minimal real-time data exchange. During the 19th and early 20th centuries, financial systems were mostly localized, and the use of instruments such as promissory notes, bills of exchange, and paper-based stock certificates was common. Clearing houses were introduced to settle interbank payments, but even these relied heavily on paper trails and manual reconciliation.

2.4.2 Emergence of electronic finance

The first wave of change came with the advent of computing technologies in the mid-20th century. Banks began to adopt mainframe computers to automate back-office operations. The introduction of the Society for Worldwide Interbank Financial Telecommunication (SWIFT) in the 1970s revolutionized cross-border transactions by replacing telex-based systems with encrypted electronic messaging. The 1980s and 1990s saw the proliferation of Automated Teller Machines (ATMs), credit and debit cards, and electronic point-of-sale (POS) systems. These innovations reduced reliance on cash and facilitated more convenient consumer interactions with financial institutions. Nevertheless, the infrastructure was still heavily centralized and primarily benefited urban populations with access to banking infrastructure.

2.4.3 The rise of the internet and online banking

The internet era ushered in a transformative phase in the late 1990s and early 2000s. Commercial banks launched online banking portals, enabling customers to perform a range of transactions remotely – view balances, transfer funds, and pay bills. The digitization of customer interfaces reduced the need for branch visits, improved service efficiency, and laid the groundwork for a customer-centric financial model. E- commerce platforms, digital marketplaces, and online payment gateways like PayPal further accelerated the shift toward digital finance. As financial data began to be stored in centralized databases and cloud platforms, the scope for real-time analytics, fraud detection, and automated decision-making expanded significantly.

2.4.4 FinTech revolution and mobile finance

The 2010s witnessed the meteoric rise of FinTech – technology-driven financial services. Startups and non-banking entities began offering tailored financial products, leveraging technologies such as artificial intelligence (AI), big data, blockchain, and cloud computing. Fintech democratized access to financial services by offering solutions such as **mobile wallets** (e.g., Paytm, Apple Pay, Google Pay), **peer-to-peer lending platforms, robo-advisors** for automated investment management, **Insurtech** for digital insurance solutions, and **Regtech** for regulatory compliance automation. Simultaneously, the global adoption of smartphones brought banking to the fingertips of users. In developing countries, mobile banking helped bridge the financial inclusion gap by providing access to underserved populations without the need for physical branches.

2.4.5 Cryptocurrencies and the decentralized finance movement

Another major leap in the digital finance journey was the creation of Bitcoin in 2009, which introduced the concept of decentralized, trustless transactions using blockchain technology. Unlike traditional currencies, cryptocurrencies are not issued by central banks but rely on distributed ledger technologies (DLT) to record and validate transactions. This gave rise to **Decentralized Finance (DeFi)** – a movement aiming to create open, permissionless, and transparent financial systems. Through smart contracts, DeFi platforms offer services such as lending, borrowing, asset trading, and insurance, without the need for intermediaries. Although highly volatile and still evolving, cryptocurrencies and DeFi have challenged conventional notions of monetary policy, trust, and financial control. They represent a radical departure from paper and centralized record-keeping systems.

The digitalization of finance has necessitated corresponding changes in regulation. Central banks and regulatory bodies have adopted digital tools for monitoring, supervision, and enforcement. Innovations like e-KYC (electronic Know Your Customer), digital signatures, and Aadhaar-linked services in India have streamlined identity verification and reduced financial fraud. However, the shift to digital has also introduced complex cybersecurity threats. Financial institutions are now prime targets for data breaches, ransomware attacks, and phishing schemes. The need for robust cybersecurity frameworks, data encryption, and international cooperation has become more critical than ever.

2.4.6 Benefits of the digital paradigm

The transition from paper to digital finance has yielded multiple benefits:

Enhanced efficiency: Automation has reduced transaction processing times and errors.

Financial inclusion: Digital platforms have reached populations previously excluded from the formal financial system.

Transparency and traceability: Digital records enhance auditability and reduce corruption.

Personalization: AI and data analytics allow tailored financial products for consumers.

Real-time access: Transactions and data can now be accessed instantly, improving user satisfaction.

Despite these advantages, the digital transformation of finance also poses several challenges:

Digital divide: Rural and low-income populations may lack access to digital infrastructure.

Privacy concerns: Handling large volumes of sensitive data raises questions about privacy and surveillance.

Regulatory lag: Innovations often outpace the ability of regulators to adapt quickly.

Job displacement: Automation threatens traditional banking roles.

Going forward, the focus must be on building inclusive, secure, and ethical digital finance ecosystems. Public-private partnerships, digital literacy campaigns, and investment in infrastructure are crucial to ensuring that the digital revolution benefits all segments of society.

Figure 2.7 Paper currency vs electronic currency.

Table 2.2 Comparison table between paper currency and electronic currency.

Aspect	Paper currency	Electronic currency
Definition	Physical money, such as banknotes and coins	Digital representation of money used in electronic transactions
Form	Tangible, physical medium	Intangible, stored electronic platforms digitally on
Storage	Wallets, safes, cash registers	Digital wallets, bank accounts, apps, cloud platforms
Transfer method	Hand-to-hand exchange	Online transfers, mobile payments, digital wallets
Transaction speed	Slower, requires physical presence	Instant or near-instant across the globe

Aspect	Paper currency	Electronic currency
Security	Prone to theft, loss, and counterfeiting	Vulnerable to cyber threats but secured through encryption & MFA
Cost of handling	High (printing, transport, storage, security)	Lower (no physical handling or printing required)
Accessibility	Accessible without internet or devices	Requires electronic devices and internet connectivity
Traceability	Difficult to trace transactions	Easily traceable and recordable
Environmental Impact	Uses paper, ink, and physical resources	Reduced physical waste, but relies on energy-consuming data centers
Usage in informal sector	Common in cash-dominated economies	Less prevalent, although increasing with digital literacy
Government control	Fully issued and controlled by central banks	Includes both central bank digital currencies (CBDCs) and private e-money

The journey from paper to digital finance marks one of the most significant paradigm shifts in economic history. What began as an incremental adoption of computing tools has now evolved into an intelligent, data-driven, and interconnected financial ecosystem. This transformation is not just about technology – it represents a re-imagining of the very principles that govern the flow of money, credit, and economic value. As digital finance continues to evolve, its success will hinge on striking a balance between innovation, regulation, and inclusivity.

Summary

Chapter 2 delves into the foundational history and evolution of financial innovation, tracing the journey from early financial systems to today's digital age. It begins with an overview of the historical evolution of finance (Section 2.1), highlighting how societies developed tools and institutions to facilitate trade, credit, and capital allocation over centuries. The chapter then identifies key milestones in financial innovation (Section 2.2), such as the introduction of paper money, the creation of stock exchanges, and the rise of electronic payment systems, which have fundamentally transformed how financial transactions are conducted. In Section 2.3, the focus shifts to the drivers of innovation in financial systems. These include technological advancements, regulatory changes, economic needs, and shifts in consumer behavior that collectively push the boundaries of financial products and services. Finally, Section 2.4 explores the critical paradigm shift from paper to digital finance, underscoring how digitization has revolutionized financial services by enabling faster, more secure, and accessible transactions, thus reshaping the entire financial ecosystem. Overall, this chapter provides a comprehensive understanding of the origins and forces behind financial innovation, setting the stage for grasping contemporary transformations in finance.

Case Study: SWIFT GPI and RTGS Modernization – A FinTech-Enabled Transformation In Cross-Border Payments

One of the most significant global transformations in the RTGS landscape is the modernization of cross-border payment systems through SWIFT GPI (Global Payments Innovation), in collaboration with FinTech partners and central banks. Traditionally, RTGS systems operated domestically within a country's central banking framework, enabling high-value transactions between banks. However, cross-border transactions remained slow, opaque, and costly due to fragmented correspondent banking networks. To solve these challenges, SWIFT, a global financial messaging network, launched SWIFT GPI, integrating advanced FinTech solutions with traditional RTGS systems to enable real-time tracking, fee transparency, and same-day settlement of international payments.

A notable example of this transformation is the partnership between SWIFT, FinTech providers, and the Bank of England, which launched the RTGS Renewal Programme. This initiative modernized the UK's RTGS system by enabling API-based access, real-time transaction data sharing, and interoperability with FinTech platforms and blockchain networks. As part of this collaboration, SWIFT gpi was integrated with central banks and commercial banks using cloud-based FinTech solutions for message routing, data analysis, and fraud detection. The modernization allowed banks and corporate clients to make cross-border payments with full traceability, faster processing, and better liquidity management.

For instance, global banks like HSBC and BNP Paribas, along with FinTech firms such as Form3 and Volante Technologies, adopted

SWIFT gpi to build platforms that offer real-time settlement status updates, fee disclosures, and instant reconciliations. These systems leverage APIs, artificial intelligence, and cloud computing to extend traditional RTGS functions beyond domestic use, optimizing international treasury operations for multinational corporations. With these FinTech-driven enhancements, settlement cycles that previously took 2–3 days were reduced to a few minutes, enhancing efficiency, transparency, and customer experience.

This FinTech-powered evolution of RTGS systems has had a profound global impact, particularly in regions like the EU, UK, Singapore, and Australia, where central banks have encouraged open banking and real-time settlements. The Bank of England's new RTGS platform, for example, allows non-bank payment firms to access RTGS services directly through APIs – a major breakthrough for FinTechs previously dependent on commercial banks for real-time settlement access. Additionally, Singapore's MAS (Monetary Authority of Singapore) has partnered with FinTechs to explore RTGS integration with cross-border digital currencies (CBDCs), further accelerating innovation.

In conclusion, this global case study demonstrates how traditional RTGS systems are being revolutionized through FinTech integration, particularly in the realm of cross-border payments. By combining SWIFT's global infrastructure with modern technologies and real-time capabilities, FinTechs and central banks are jointly enabling faster, safer, and more transparent financial transactions. This reflects a broader shift toward next-generation financial systems that prioritize speed, interoperability, and digital inclusion across international markets.

Case Discussion Questions

1. How does the integration of FinTech solutions like APIs and AI into traditional RTGS systems challenge the role of commercial banks in cross-border transactions?
2. In what ways could the modernization of RTGS systems through FinTech partnerships impact financial inclusion and access to global financial markets for developing economies?
3. What risks and governance challenges arise when FinTech companies gain direct or indirect access to central bank systems like RTGS, and how should policymakers address them?

Keywords

- **Deregulation:** The removal or reduction of government rules and controls in a particular industry.
- **Disruption:** A big change in the way things are usually done, especially when a new idea or technology replaces an old one.
- **Moneylender:** A person or small business that lends money to others, usually at a high interest rate, and often outside formal banks.
- **Bill of exchange:** A written order used in business that tells someone to pay a certain amount of money to another person on a future date.
- **Barter system**: A way of trading goods and services directly without using money.
- **Demonetization**: When a government removes the value of a certain type of money, making it no longer usable.

Discussion Questions

1. What were the key developments in ancient trade and currency systems that influenced contemporary financial practices?
2. In what ways did the Industrial Revolution drive changes in financial systems and institutions?
3. Consider the development of banking infrastructure, credit systems, and financial markets during this era.
4. What are some key milestones in financial innovation that have had a lasting impact on global markets?
5. Discuss innovations such as the creation of credit cards, electronic payments, and online banking platforms.
6. What role did technological advancements, such as computers and the internet, play in driving financial innovation?
7. Discuss the rise of algorithmic trading, digital currencies, and the advent of FinTech in recent decades.
8. What are the primary factors that drive innovation in the financial sector?
9. Discuss the roles of technological advancement, regulatory changes, customer demand, and market competition in driving financial innovation.

10. How does globalization influence financial innovation?
11. Evaluate whether regulators are supportive of innovation or more focused on controlling potential risks to financial stability.
12. What is the role of competition in spurring financial innovation?
13. How have new entrants, such as FinTech companies, challenged traditional financial institutions, and how have these challenges led to innovation?
14. How has the shift from paper-based to digital financial systems transformed the way consumers interact with their finances?
15. Explore both the opportunities and risks posed by the digitalization of finance, such as cybersecurity threats and financial inclusion.

References

[1] Arthur, F., & Geanakoplos, J. (2016). *Commodity money and early financial arrangements in Mesopotamia.* In *Evolution of Financial Innovation and Innovative Financial Instruments.*

[2] Davies, G. (2002). *A History of Money: From Ancient Times to the Present Day.* University of Wales Press.

[3] Eich, S. (2022). *The Currency of Politics: The Political Theory of Money from Aristotle to Keynes.* Princeton University Press.

[4] Ferguson, N. (2008). *The Ascent of Money: A Financial History of the World.* Penguin Press.

[5] Chew, D. H. (2025). *The Making of Modern Corporate Finance.* Financial Times Publishing.

[6] Arthur, S. (2017). *A Historical Analysis of Financial Innovation in Islamic Economics and Finance from Inception to the Sixteenth Century.* In *Financial Innovation and Engineering in Islamic Finance.* Springer. https://doi.org/10.1007/978-3-319-52947-9_4

[7] Hernández de Cos, P. (2019). *Financial technology: The 150-year revolution.* Basel Committee on Banking Supervision, Frankfurt, Germany.

[8] Berk, J. M. (2012). *Central banking and financial innovation: A survey of the modern literature. PSL Quarterly Review, 55*(222). https://doi.org/10.13133/2037-3643/9912

[9] Nejad, M. G. (2022). *Research on financial innovations: An interdisciplinary review. International Journal of Bank Marketing, 40*(3), 578–612. https://doi.org/10.1108/IJBM-07-2021-0305

[10] Stefanelli, V., Manta, F., & Toma, P. (2022). *Digital financial services and open banking innovation: Are banks becoming invisible?*

[11] Llewellyn, D., White, L., & Tufano, P. (2017). *Financial innovation and its governance: Cases of two major innovations in the financial sector. Financial Innovation, 3*, Article 60. https://doi.org/10.1186/s40854-017-0060-2

[12] Ballis, A. (2025). *Geopolitical tensions and financial networks: Strategic shifts toward alternatives.*

[13] McWilliams, D. (2023). *Money: A Story of Humanity.* Gill Books.

[14] Yue, P., Korkmaz, A. G., Yin, Z., & Zhou, H. (2022). *The rise of digital finance: Financial inclusion or debt trap.*

[15] Durigan Junior, C. A., Kissimoto, K. O., & Laurindo, F. J. B. (2024). *IT enabling factors in a new industry design: Open banking and digital economy.*

[16] Hyman, L. (2011). *Debtor Nation: The History of America in Red Ink.* Princeton University Press.

[17] Arthur, C. P. (2002). *Technological Revolutions and Financial Capital: The Dynamics of Bubbles and Golden Ages.* Edward Elgar Publishing.

3

Digital Transformation in Finance

Abstract

This chapter delves into the profound impact of digital transformation on the financial services industry, offering a strategic and forward-looking perspective on how technology is redefining the structure, operations, and customer experience within traditional financial institutions. As digital innovation becomes central to competitiveness and resilience, financial entities worldwide are undergoing foundational shifts in strategy, service delivery, and infrastructure.

The chapter begins by examining the strategic approaches adopted by financial organizations to embrace digital finance, including digital-first models, customer-centric service design, and agile operational frameworks. It evaluates how institutions are integrating digital technologies into their core processes to improve efficiency, reduce costs, and enhance real-time decision-making. A key focus is on how digital transformation is reshaping legacy financial institutions, compelling banks, insurance companies, and other financial entities to rethink their business models. The integration of mobile banking, cloud computing, robotic process automation (RPA), and digital onboarding has led to greater operational agility and improved customer engagement, while simultaneously introducing new risks and compliance challenges.

Additionally, the chapter explores emerging technological trends that are fueling the next wave of innovation in finance. These include blockchain for secure, decentralized transactions; artificial intelligence (AI) for personalized financial services and fraud detection; big data analytics for predictive modeling; and application programming interfaces (APIs) that enable open banking ecosystems. Together, these technologies are creating a more inclusive, transparent, and intelligent financial system. The chapter concludes by emphasizing that successful digital transformation is not merely

DOI: 10.1201/9788743811244-4

a technological shift but a cultural and organizational one. It requires strategic alignment, investment in digital talent, robust cybersecurity frameworks, and a commitment to regulatory compliance. Through real-world examples and forward-thinking analysis, this chapter provides readers with a nuanced understanding of the digital revolution transforming finance and its implications for institutions, regulators, and customers alike.

Introduction

The rapid proliferation of digital technologies has revolutionized the financial services industry, necessitating a fundamental shift in how businesses strategize, operate, and deliver value to customers. Digital finance is not merely a technological transformation; it is a strategic reorientation that affects organizational models, customer engagement, product offerings, and competitive positioning. In this chapter, we delve into the core components of business strategy for digital finance, exploring how financial institutions can harness digital innovation to achieve sustainable growth, resilience, and market leadership.

3.1 Business Strategy for Digital Finance

In today's rapidly evolving financial ecosystem, the integration of digital technologies has moved from being a competitive advantage to a strategic necessity. Digital finance encompasses a wide range of financial services delivered through digital platforms, including digital banking, mobile wallets, automated investment platforms, cryptocurrency solutions, and more. As the demand for real-time, personalized, and seamless financial services grows, institutions must adopt well-crafted business strategies to navigate the digital landscape successfully. A strong business strategy for digital finance is not merely about adopting technology but aligning digital initiatives with organizational goals, customer needs, regulatory requirements, and market opportunities. The emergence of digital finance strategies in emerging markets reflects an adaptive response to evolving consumer behaviors [1]. Post-crisis FinTech development has transformed business models toward resilience, inclusion, and agility [2]. Corporate finance today must integrate FinTech tools to enhance efficiency and competitiveness in digital environments [3].

At the core of any digital finance strategy lies **customer-centricity**. Modern consumers expect instant access, ease of use, security, and personalization. Therefore, a winning strategy must prioritize understanding customer behavior and preferences through data analytics, surveys, and engagement tools. Institutions need to design digital experiences that are intuitive, mobile-first, and available across multiple touchpoints. This involves streamlining user interfaces, offering self-service options, and delivering financial products tailored to different customer segments using AI and machine learning. By placing the customer at the center of the strategy, financial service providers can foster trust, satisfaction, and long-term loyalty.

Another key pillar of a digital finance strategy is **operational agility and innovation**. Legacy systems and rigid workflows can inhibit digital progress. Financial institutions must embrace cloud computing, agile development practices, and scalable digital platforms that support rapid innovation. Adopting a modular architecture using APIs (Application Programming Interfaces) allows institutions to integrate third-party FinTech solutions, enhance product offerings, and reduce time-to-market for new services. Strategic partnerships with FinTech startups, technology providers, and even non-financial entities enable access to new capabilities, customer bases, and business models. Innovation labs, incubators, and dedicated digital transformation teams are essential for fostering a culture of experimentation and agility.

Data strategy is another critical aspect of digital finance. The ability to collect, analyze, and act on real-time data gives institutions a powerful edge. Financial firms must invest in robust data infrastructure, business intelligence tools, and advanced analytics to drive decision-making across functions – whether it is credit underwriting, fraud detection, customer segmentation, or product development. However, this also requires a strong focus on data governance, privacy, and ethical use. Regulatory compliance, especially with laws like GDPR, is integral to building a responsible data-driven strategy.

A robust **risk management and cybersecurity strategy** must accompany digital finance initiatives. As more transactions move online, threats such as data breaches, identity theft, and cyberattacks become more frequent and sophisticated. Institutions must integrate cybersecurity into the core of their digital strategy, using tools like biometric authentication, encryption, intrusion detection systems, and real-time monitoring. Simultaneously, risk models need to evolve to account for emerging threats and digital behaviors. Regulatory compliance and digital identity management should be seamlessly embedded in digital products to ensure trust and accountability.

Moreover, the strategy should also encompass **financial inclusion** and **sustainability**. Digital finance offers a unique opportunity to reach unbanked and underbanked populations through mobile technology, digital wallets, and low-cost financial products. By extending services to rural and remote regions and designing inclusive financial products, institutions can tap into new markets while contributing to social and economic development. Integrating environmental, social, and governance (ESG) considerations into digital finance strategies also aligns businesses with global sustainability goals and enhances brand reputation.

Lastly, **leadership** and **change management** are vital components of a successful digital finance strategy. Digital transformation requires cultural shifts, upskilling of employees, redefined roles, and clear communication from leadership. A long-term vision with measurable goals, key performance indicators (KPIs), and cross-functional collaboration is essential to sustain digital progress. Continuous learning, employee empowerment, and stakeholder engagement are crucial to navigating the dynamic nature of digital finance.

In conclusion, a sound business strategy for digital finance is holistic, dynamic, and customer-driven. It integrates advanced technologies, data intelligence, agile operations, cybersecurity, financial inclusion, and strong leadership to deliver value in a digital-first financial landscape. Institutions that craft and execute such a strategy are well-positioned to innovate, grow, and lead in the future of finance. The global FinTech landscape continues to expand, reshaping financial intermediation and innovation frameworks [4].

3.1.1 Strategic imperatives for digital finance customer-centricity

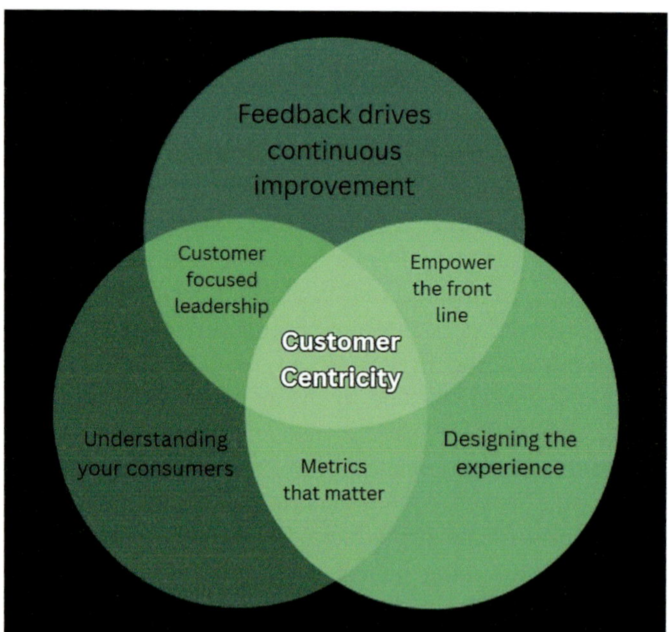

Figure 3.1 Customer centricity.

Modern digital finance strategies prioritize customer experience above all. Financial institutions must show a transition from product-centric models to customer-centric frameworks that prioritize personalization, ease of access, and real-time support. **Strategy**: Use AI and data analytics to offer hyper-personalized services based on behavioral data and predictive modeling.

Innovation and agility

Innovation is no longer optional; it is a strategic imperative. Agile business models that encourage experimentation, iterative development, and rapid go-to-market strategies are critical. **Strategy**: Establish digital innovation labs and foster a culture that supports rapid prototyping and failure tolerance.

Digital ecosystems and partnerships

The rise of platforms and open banking has ushered in a new era of collaboration. Instead of building everything in-house, financial institutions can leverage FinTech partnerships and open APIs to co-create value. **Strategy**: Develop an API strategy and seek synergistic alliances with FinTech startups, tech giants, and even non-financial players.

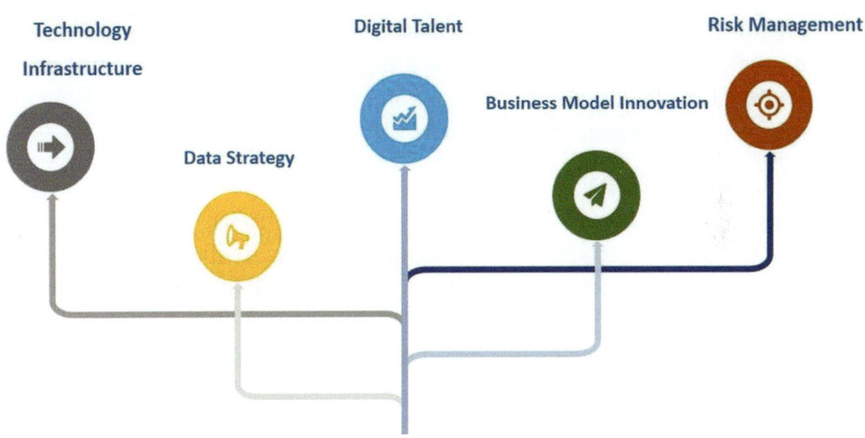

Figure 3.2 Components of digital finance strategy.

3.1.2 Core components of digital finance strategy

- **Technology infrastructure**
  The foundation of digital finance lies in a robust and scalable technology stack. Cloud computing, microservices architecture, and cybersecurity are non-negotiable components. **Strategy**: Migrate legacy systems to

the cloud to enhance flexibility and reduce operational costs. Invest in zero-trust security models.

- **Data strategy**
  Data is the currency of the digital economy. A comprehensive data strategy encompasses data governance, quality, integration, and analytics capabilities. **Strategy:** Implement enterprise-wide data lakes and AI-powered analytics platforms to derive actionable insights and enable real-time decision-making.

- **Digital talent**
  Digital transformation demands a workforce with new skills and a mindset aligned with innovation. Talent strategy must focus on reskilling, upskilling, and cultivating digital fluency. **Strategy**: Foster a digital-first culture through leadership training, agile methodologies, and a cross-functional team structure.

- **Business model innovation**
  Traditional banking models based on branch networks and manual processes are being replaced by innovative models such as platform-based banking – offering banking-as-a-service (BaaS) through APIs, subscription models – charging flat fees for premium digital services, and marketplace banking – acting as a digital marketplace for third-party financial products. **Strategy**: Redefine the value proposition by focusing on convenience, personalization, and inclusivity.

- **Risk management**
  The digital finance landscape brings new risks, including cyber threats, data breaches, and algorithmic biases. At the same time, regulatory frameworks are evolving to accommodate digital innovation. **Strategy**: Develop an integrated risk and compliance framework that uses RegTech (regulatory technology) to automate compliance, detect anomalies, and ensure auditability.

To track the success of a digital finance strategy, institutions must adopt new performance indicators: Digital adoption rate, customer lifetime value (CLV), digital channel engagement, innovation pipeline yield, and operational cost reduction through automation. **Strategy**: Use a balanced scorecard that integrates digital KPIs with traditional financial metrics. Looking ahead, digital finance strategies must embrace emerging trends:

- **AI-driven finance**: Expand use of generative AI for financial advice and operational efficiency.
- **Embedded finance**: Integrate financial services into non-financial platforms such as e-commerce or ride-sharing apps.
- **Decentralized finance (DeFi)**: Explore opportunities in blockchain-powered, non-intermediated finance.
- **Sustainable finance**: Incorporate ESG (Environmental, Social, Governance) metrics into digital finance offerings.

A robust business strategy for digital finance is no longer a differentiator – it is a prerequisite for survival and growth in an increasingly digital world. Financial institutions must reimagine their value chains, embrace data and technology, and build agile, customer-first cultures. As the digital finance ecosystem continues to evolve, success will hinge on strategic foresight, execution excellence, and continuous innovation. Leading fund managers are shifting towards digital-first approaches to improve operational scalability [5]. Organizations must adopt structured digital roadmaps to remain adaptive and continuously innovative in financial ecosystems [6]. Strategic digital transformation in banking involves building collaborative ecosystems with FinTech partners [7].

3.2 Impact of Digitalisation on Traditional Financial Institutions

The financial sector has witnessed an unprecedented wave of transformation driven by digitalisation. This digital shift – marked by technologies such as mobile banking, artificial intelligence (AI), blockchain, and big data – has disrupted traditional financial institutions (TFIs) and redefined how financial services are delivered, accessed, and consumed. While digitalisation presents significant opportunities for efficiency and innovation, it also poses formidable challenges to legacy institutions. This chapter explores the multidimensional impact of digitalisation on traditional financial institutions, analyzing both strategic threats and transformational pathways. FinTech innovation has disrupted traditional banking by redefining customer experience and service delivery [8]. The rapid rise of RegTech enables banks to navigate complex compliance environments more efficiently [9]. Artificial intelligence is revolutionizing decision-making in both personal and corporate finance operations [10].

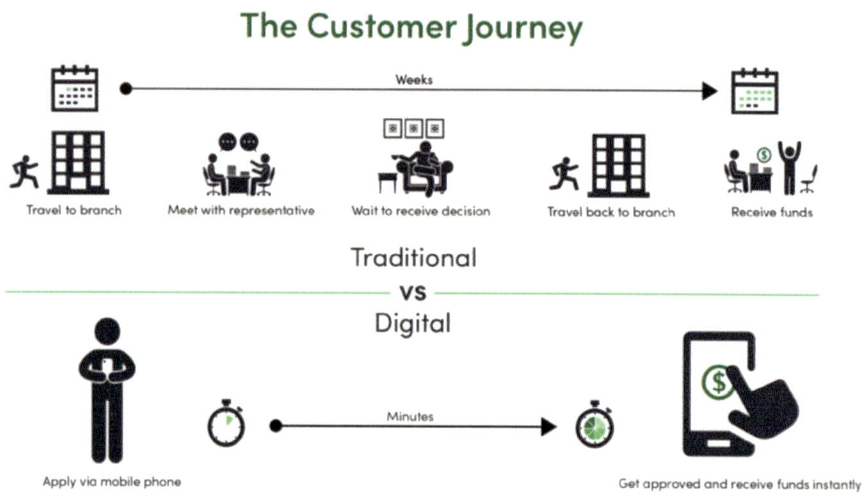

Figure 3.3 The customer journey.
Source: https://www.smartinsights.com/digital-marketing-strategy/financial-services-marketing/

3.2.1 Rise of the digital customer

The rise of the digital customer has transformed expectations across the financial services sector. Today's customers demand convenience, speed, personalization, and seamless service across channels – comparing their banking experiences to those offered by tech giants like Amazon and Google. This has forced traditional financial institutions (TFIs) to rethink their engagement strategies or risk falling behind. In response, many have introduced mobile apps, chatbots, and online portals to improve user experience. Alongside this, there has been a notable shift toward self-service banking. As digital literacy improves, customers prefer managing tasks such as fund transfers, account updates, and even loan applications on their own. This shift has led to a decrease in branch visits, prompting banks to either scale down or repurpose physical locations into digital hubs.

3.2.2 Operational transformation through automation and data

Operationally, digitalisation has brought significant transformation. One key aspect is the automation of back-office processes using robotic process automation (RPA) and artificial intelligence (AI). This has greatly improved operational efficiency and reduced costs. However, integrating such advanced technologies into older legacy systems remains a complex and expensive challenge. Another operational advancement is data-driven decision-making. With access to large volumes of real-time data, financial institutions are now better equipped to make accurate decisions in areas such as risk assessment, fraud detection, and credit scoring. Consequently, banks are investing more in building strong data analytics capabilities and hiring skilled professionals.

3.2.3 FinTech disruption and competitive pressure

The competitive landscape of financial services has also been reshaped by FinTech disruption. Agile FinTech startups are attracting customers by offering more affordable, faster, and user-friendly financial solutions. Their rise is particularly evident in segments like digital payments, lending, and investment management, which were traditionally dominated by banks. In response, many TFIs are setting up their own digital arms, acquiring FinTech startups, or collaborating through open banking platforms. Additionally, the growth of the platform economy and embedded finance has allowed BigTech companies like Apple, Google, and Amazon to integrate financial services into their ecosystems. This trend threatens to disintermediate banks and reduce them to behind-the-scenes service providers unless they quickly adapt to these platform-based models.

3.2.4 Regulatory and cybersecurity challenges

The digital shift has brought with it serious regulatory and security challenges. As the number of online financial transactions grows, so do the threats from cyberattacks, fraud, and data breaches. This has created a need for banks to make substantial investments in cybersecurity infrastructure and monitoring systems. At the same time, regulatory compliance has become more complex in the digital age. Regulators are updating frameworks to cover areas such as digital KYC (Know Your Customer), data protection, and cross-border transactions. To keep pace, TFIs are increasingly turning to RegTech solutions that automate compliance and regulatory reporting processes.

3.2.5 Cultural shifts and talent gaps

Beyond technology and competition, cultural and structural factors are also barriers to transformation. Many traditional banks are weighed down by legacy mindsets and rigid hierarchies that resist change. This slows innovation and reduces their ability to respond quickly to market trends. To overcome this, leadership must promote a digital-first culture by encouraging innovation through internal incubators and digital champions. Moreover, as digital finance grows, so does the demand for skills in fields like AI, cybersecurity, data science, and UX/UI design. Many existing employees lack these skills, creating talent shortages. TFIs are addressing this gap through training programs, digital academies, and by recruiting from the technology sector.

3.2.6 Reimagining business models in a digital era

Finally, the need to reimagine banking business models has become urgent. The traditional product-centric model – where banks focused on pushing their own services – is giving way to platform-based models that allow third-party services to be integrated through APIs and cloud platforms. This transformation is redefining how banks create value and generate revenue. One of the biggest shifts is the adoption of open banking. By allowing third-party developers access to customer data (with consent), open banking enables the creation of innovative apps and services. While this increases competition and the risk of customer churn, banks that proactively adopt open APIs can stay relevant and retain customer trust in a rapidly evolving digital landscape.

To remain relevant, traditional financial institutions must:

1. **Accelerate digital transformation**: Prioritize digital channels and cloud-native architectures.
2. **Build strategic alliances**: Partner with FinTechs and technology providers.
3. **Adopt agile governance**: Replace hierarchical structures with agile frameworks.
4. **Invest in digital talent**: Foster continuous learning and digital leadership.

3.2.7 Benefits of digital transformation in financial services

Digital transformation is revolutionizing industries across the globe, and the financial services sector is at the forefront of this shift. By leveraging cutting-edge technologies such as artificial intelligence (AI), machine learning (ML), blockchain, big data analytics, cloud computing, and robotic process automation (RPA), financial institutions are redefining their operations, customer engagement strategies, and service delivery mechanisms. Digital transformation in financial services refers to the strategic adoption of digital technologies to improve operational efficiency, enhance customer experiences, ensure regulatory compliance, and drive innovation. Banking-as-a-Service models allow traditional banks to unbundle products and collaborate with digital providers [11]. Digital transformation challenges legacy institutions to rethink their operational infrastructure and data use [12]. FinTech disruption has compelled financial incumbents to restructure their strategies to remain relevant [13]. Open banking innovations are making conventional banks increasingly invisible in customer-facing operations [14].

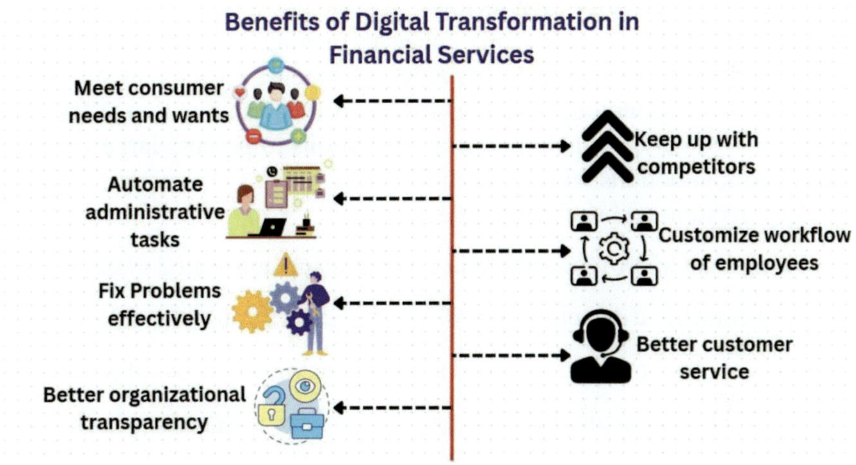

Figure 3.4 Benefits of digital transformation in financial services.

This chapter explores the multifaceted benefits of digital transformation in financial services and explains how it enables institutions to remain competitive, resilient, and customer-centric in an increasingly digital world.

Enhanced customer experience

One of the most significant benefits of digital transformation in financial services is the dramatic improvement in customer experience. With the rise of digital banking platforms, mobile applications, and AI-powered chatbots, customers can now access financial services anytime, anywhere, and on any device.

Financial institutions can offer:

- Personalized product recommendations based on customer behavior and financial history.
- 24/7 support through chatbots and virtual assistants.
- Real-time transaction notifications and account updates.
- Seamless onboarding and Know Your Customer (KYC) processes via digital documentation.

By embracing digital tools, banks and financial service providers are able to move from transactional engagement to relationship-based engagement, fostering long-term customer loyalty.

Increased operational efficiency

Digital transformation significantly enhances operational efficiency by automating routine and repetitive tasks, reducing manual errors, and streamlining workflows. Technologies such as robotic process automation (RPA) and intelligent automation enable financial institutions to process large volumes of data and transactions with speed and accuracy.

Key operational benefits include:

1. Faster loan approvals and credit scoring using automated systems.
2. Real-time fraud detection and risk management through AI and analytics.
3. Efficient data management and reporting using cloud-based platforms.
4. Paperless documentation and digital signatures to speed up workflows.

This improved efficiency reduces turnaround time, cuts costs, and allows institutions to focus on strategic initiatives.

Data-driven decision making

Modern financial services generate vast amounts of data on customer transactions, behavior, and preferences. Digital transformation empowers institutions to harness the power of big data analytics to derive actionable insights, identify patterns, and make informed decisions.

Applications of data-driven decision-making include:

1. Credit risk assessment and underwriting.
2. Investment portfolio optimization.

3. Personalized marketing campaigns.
4. Predictive modeling for customer churn and product uptake.

By using advanced analytics and AI, financial firms can shift from reactive to proactive strategies, thus improving business performance and customer satisfaction.

Cost reduction and resource optimization

Digital transformation leads to significant cost savings by reducing reliance on physical infrastructure, manual labor, and legacy systems. Cloud computing allows financial organizations to shift from capital expenditure (CapEx) to operating expenditure (OpEx), paying only for what they use.

Examples of cost optimization include:

1. Lower costs in customer servicing through AI-based chatbots.
2. Reduced branch overheads due to digital banking platforms.
3. Minimal maintenance of outdated IT systems by adopting cloud-native solutions.
4. Automation of compliance and reporting, saving labor hours and reducing human errors.

These savings not only improve the bottom line but also free up resources for innovation and expansion.

Improved agility and innovation

In a rapidly evolving financial ecosystem, agility is critical. Digital transformation fosters a culture of continuous innovation and adaptability, enabling financial institutions to launch new products and services faster, respond to changing customer needs, and pivot operations when necessary.

FinTech collaborations and open banking application programming interfaces (APIs) have made it possible for traditional banks to integrate third-party services, create new revenue streams, and deliver holistic financial solutions. Agile methodologies and DevOps practices further accelerate product development cycles and promote innovation.

Strengthened regulatory compliance and risk management

Compliance with regulatory frameworks is a major concern for financial institutions. Digital tools simplify the process of adhering to complex and dynamic regulations such as Anti-Money Laundering (AML), General Data Protection Regulation (GDPR), and Know Your Customer (KYC) norms.

Key compliance advantages include:

1. Real-time tracking and monitoring of transactions to detect suspicious activity.
2. Automated reporting tools to meet audit and regulatory requirements.
3. Secure data storage and access control using blockchain and encryption technologies.
4. Improved transparency and traceability across the financial supply chain.

Digital compliance solutions not only mitigate risks but also build trust with stakeholders and regulators.

Enhanced cybersecurity and fraud prevention

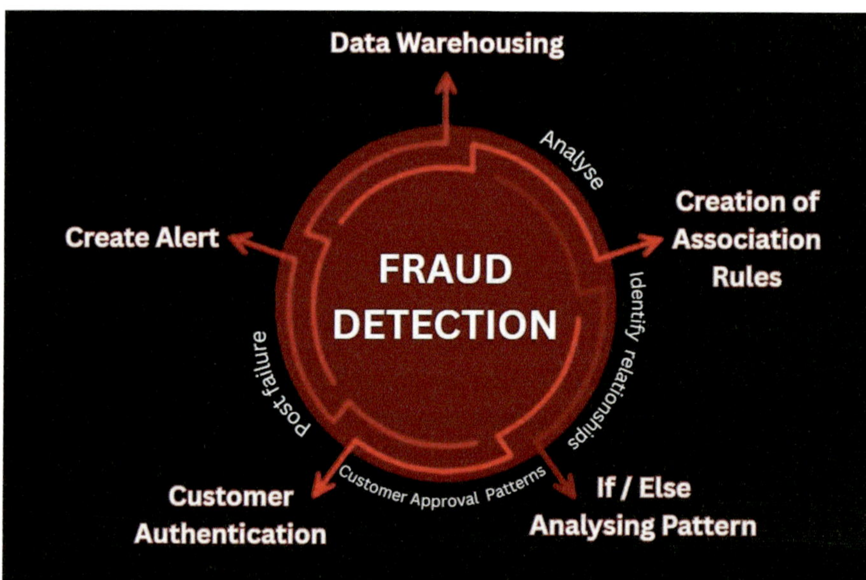

Figure 3.5 Fraud detection.

As cyber threats evolve, digital transformation equips financial institutions with advanced cybersecurity frameworks to protect customer data and financial assets. Machine learning algorithms, biometric authentication, and behavioral analytics play a vital role in identifying anomalies and preventing fraud.

Security benefits include:

1. Real-time threat detection systems.
2. Multi-factor authentication (MFA) for secure access.
3. End-to-end encryption for data privacy.
4. Blockchain for tamper-proof record keeping.

With growing concerns over data breaches and identity theft, investing in digital security infrastructure has become a top priority for financial service providers.

Greater financial inclusion

Digital transformation has widened the reach of financial services to underserved and remote populations. Mobile banking apps, digital wallets, and micro-lending platforms have made it possible for individuals without access to traditional banking to participate in the formal financial system.

Benefits for financial inclusion include:

1. Low-cost banking through mobile platforms.
2. Access to microloans and insurance via FinTech solutions.
3. Digital identity verification enabling easier onboarding.
4. Support for rural banking and small enterprises.

By bridging the gap between the banked and the unbanked, digital transformation contributes to inclusive economic growth.

Scalability and future-readiness

Digital infrastructure provides financial institutions with the scalability needed to handle growth and market fluctuations. Cloud-based solutions and platform-driven architectures allow institutions to expand their customer base and services without massive investments in physical infrastructure.

Digital transformation ensures future-readiness by:

1. Supporting remote operations and hybrid work environments.
2. Enabling real-time collaboration and decision-making.
3. Offering API-based integrations for flexibility and scalability.
4. Keeping pace with emerging trends like Central Bank Digital Currencies (CBDCs), embedded finance, and AI-powered wealth management.

Institutions that invest in scalable digital frameworks position themselves as future leaders in the financial landscape.

Digital transformation in financial services is not just a technological upgrade; it is a fundamental shift in how institutions operate, engage with customers, manage risk, and pursue growth. From improving customer experience to strengthening compliance, reducing costs, and driving innovation, the benefits are comprehensive and far-reaching. In an era where customer expectations are rising and market dynamics are constantly evolving, digital transformation is no longer optional; it is essential. Financial institutions that embrace digital change with a strategic mindset will not only survive but thrive in the digital economy.

3.3 Technological Trends Driving Transformation in the Financial Sector

The financial sector is undergoing a profound transformation, largely driven by rapid advancements in digital technologies that are reshaping traditional business models, customer expectations, and regulatory landscapes. Among the most influential trends is the rise of artificial intelligence (AI) and machine learning, which enable financial institutions to automate processes, personalize services, detect fraud, and make data-driven decisions with unprecedented accuracy. Equally transformative is the adoption of blockchain and distributed ledger technologies, which enhance transparency, security, and efficiency in areas such as payments, settlements, and identity verification. The integration of cloud computing has allowed for scalable, cost-effective infrastructure that supports real-time processing and innovation. Meanwhile, robotic process automation (RPA) is streamlining back-office operations and reducing manual errors, thereby increasing operational efficiency. The expansion of mobile and digital banking, powered by intuitive user interfaces and seamless connectivity, is redefining customer engagement by offering 24/7 access to services. Furthermore, the emergence of open banking and APIs is fostering collaboration between traditional banks and FinTechs, enabling the creation of integrated, customer-centric financial ecosystems. Cybersecurity technologies are also evolving rapidly to protect digital assets and ensure data privacy in an increasingly interconnected world. Blockchain and FinTech integration are reshaping global financial markets and service models [15]. Technological revolutions consistently realign capital and innovation cycles in finance [16]. Data analytics and automation are now key drivers of competitive differentiation in financial services [17]. Emerging technologies like AI, blockchain, and quantum computing are transforming CFO decision-making [18]. Together, these technological trends are not only revolutionizing the delivery and management of financial services but also fostering innovation, inclusivity, and resilience across the global financial system.

3.3.1 Artificial intelligence (AI) and machine learning (ML)

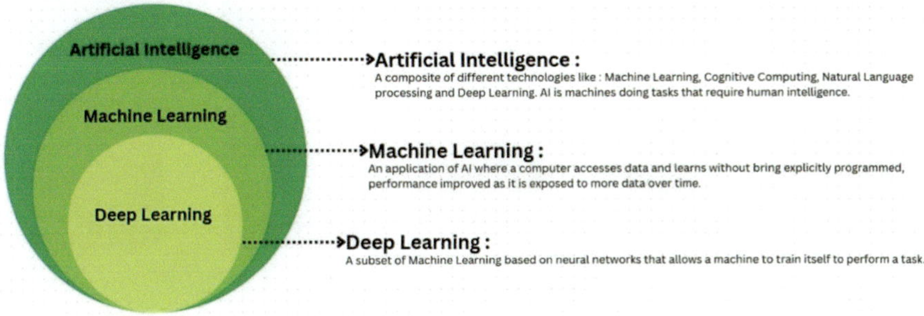

Figure 3.6 Difference between AI and ML.

Artificial intelligence (AI) and machine learning (ML) are at the forefront of digital transformation in finance. These technologies enable institutions to analyze vast amounts of structured and unstructured data for informed decision-making. From personalized product recommendations to automated credit scoring, AI and ML are improving both customer experience and internal efficiency. Example: JPMorgan Chase uses its COIN platform to analyze legal documents in seconds, saving thousands of human hours annually. It helps in enhancing operational efficiency, fraud detection, risk assessment, and customer satisfaction. AI-powered predictive analytics can forecast market trends, customer behavior, and financial risks. This capability is critical for portfolio optimization, dynamic pricing, and churn prediction.

3.3.2 Blockchain and distributed ledger technology (DLT)

Blockchain technology has the potential to disrupt the very foundation of financial services by enabling secure, transparent, and tamper-proof transactions without intermediaries. Distributed ledger technology (DLT) records each transaction on a decentralized network, increasing trust and reducing fraud. Example: RippleNet facilitates real-time international payments across multiple currencies at lower costs. It aids in improving transparency, reducing reconciliation time, and increasing security. Smart contracts are self-executing contracts with the terms coded directly into the blockchain. They automate and enforce agreements, reducing the need for manual intervention. Example: Trade finance, insurance claims, syndicated loans.

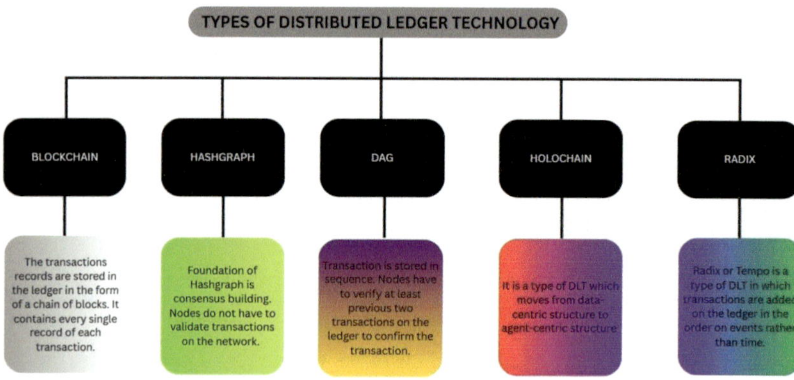

Figure 3.7 Types of DLT.

3.3.3 Cloud computing and Infrastructure as a Service (IaaS)

Cloud computing offers on-demand access to computing resources and storage, enabling financial institutions to scale operations and launch services faster. It supports innovation by eliminating the need for heavy infrastructure investment. Example: HSBC has moved many core banking functions to the cloud to increase resilience and scalability. It helps in achieving cost efficiency, business continuity, and faster time-to-market. Cloud platforms support APIs and integration with third-party services, essential for FinTech collaborations and open banking ecosystems.

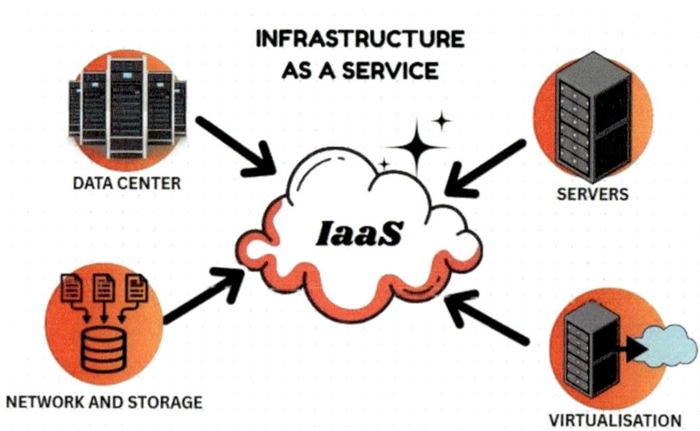

Figure 3.8 Infrastructure as a Service.

3.3.4 Robotic process automation (RPA)

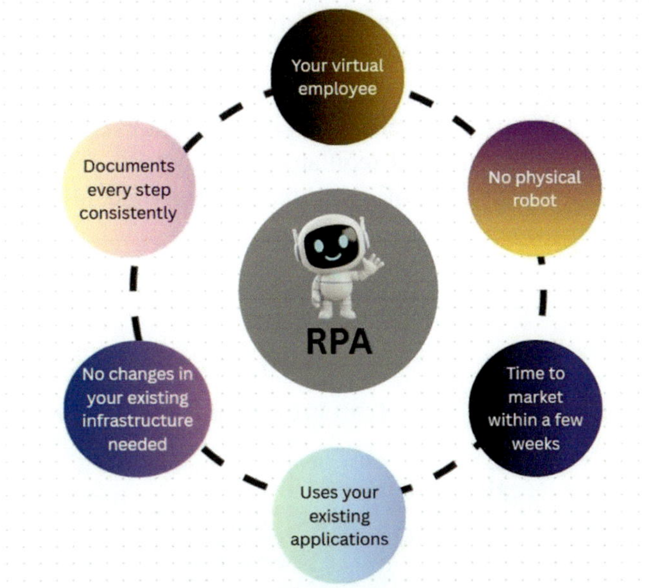

Figure 3.9 Robotic process automation.

RPA uses software bots to automate repetitive and rule-based tasks like data entry, compliance checks, and customer onboarding. This leads to reduced human error and operational costs. Example: Deutsche Bank uses RPA to streamline compliance reporting and KYC processes. It showed operational efficiency, quick regulatory compliance, and faster processing times. When integrated with AI, RPA can evolve into intelligent process automation (IPA), capable of handling complex tasks such as decision-making and exception management.

3.3.5 Big data and advanced analytics

Big data allows financial institutions to collect, store, and analyze massive datasets for actionable insights. Advanced analytics help in customer segmentation, fraud detection, credit risk analysis, and product development. Example: American Express leverages big data to predict consumer spending behavior and detect fraudulent activity. It improved strategic planning, customer targeting, and risk mitigation. Real-time analytics enhances customer engagement by providing instant insights and recommendations, improving customer retention and experience.

3.3.6 Cybersecurity technologies

As digital transactions grow, so do threats from cybercriminals. Financial institutions are investing in advanced cybersecurity measures such as biometric authentication, end-to-end encryption, behavior analytics, and intrusion detection systems. Example: Wells Fargo uses biometric voice recognition to authenticate users in their call centers. It reduced fraud, strengthened trust, and ensured regulatory compliance. AI is increasingly used to detect anomalies and mitigate threats in real time, offering proactive protection.

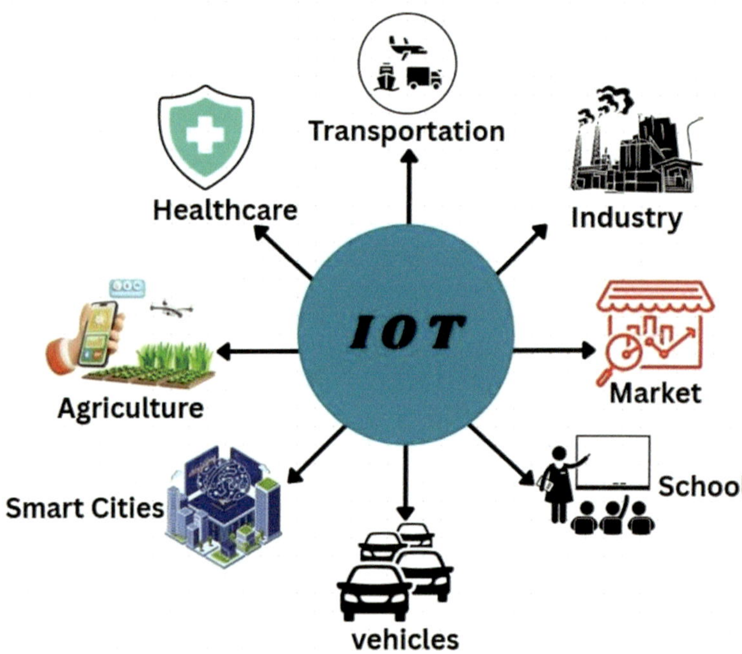

Figure 3.10 Internet of Things.

3.3.7 Internet of Things (IoT)

IoT enables the integration of physical devices with digital platforms, facilitating real-time monitoring and data sharing. Wearables, smart ATMs, and connected vehicles are examples of how IoT is shaping financial services.

Example: Insurance companies use telematics devices to track driving behavior and offer usage-based premiums. It aids in offering personalized services, risk-based pricing, and enhanced user experience.

3.3.8 Digital payments and mobile wallets

The surge in digital and mobile payments, driven by QR codes, NFC (near-field communication), and mobile wallets, is transforming retail and corporate banking. Platforms like PayPal, Apple Pay, and Google Pay have made digital payments ubiquitous. Example: Unified Payments Interface (UPI) in India processes billions of real-time, interoperable transactions each month. It increased financial inclusion, convenience, and transactional transparency. Central banks and financial institutions are adopting real-time gross settlement (RTGS) systems and instant payment networks to improve liquidity and transaction speed.

3.3.9 Chatbots and virtual assistants

AI-powered chatbots and virtual assistants are revolutionizing customer service in the financial sector. They handle queries, process transactions, and provide account insights round-the-clock. Example: Bank of America's virtual assistant "Erica" provides personalized financial advice and spending alerts. It reduced call center workload, improved customer engagement, and achieved operational cost savings. The crypto industry continues to evolve rapidly, influencing regulatory frameworks and investment strategies [19]. The global FinTech sector is projected to grow through collaboration, data-driven models, and cross-border scalability [20].

3.3.10 Quantum computing (emerging trend)

Quantum computing holds transformative potential for finance by solving complex optimization problems in milliseconds. While still in its infancy, it promises breakthroughs in risk modeling, fraud detection, and cryptography. Example: Institutions like Goldman Sachs and JPMorgan are investing in quantum research to future-proof their operations. It is expected to redefine algorithmic trading, portfolio optimization, and secure transactions.

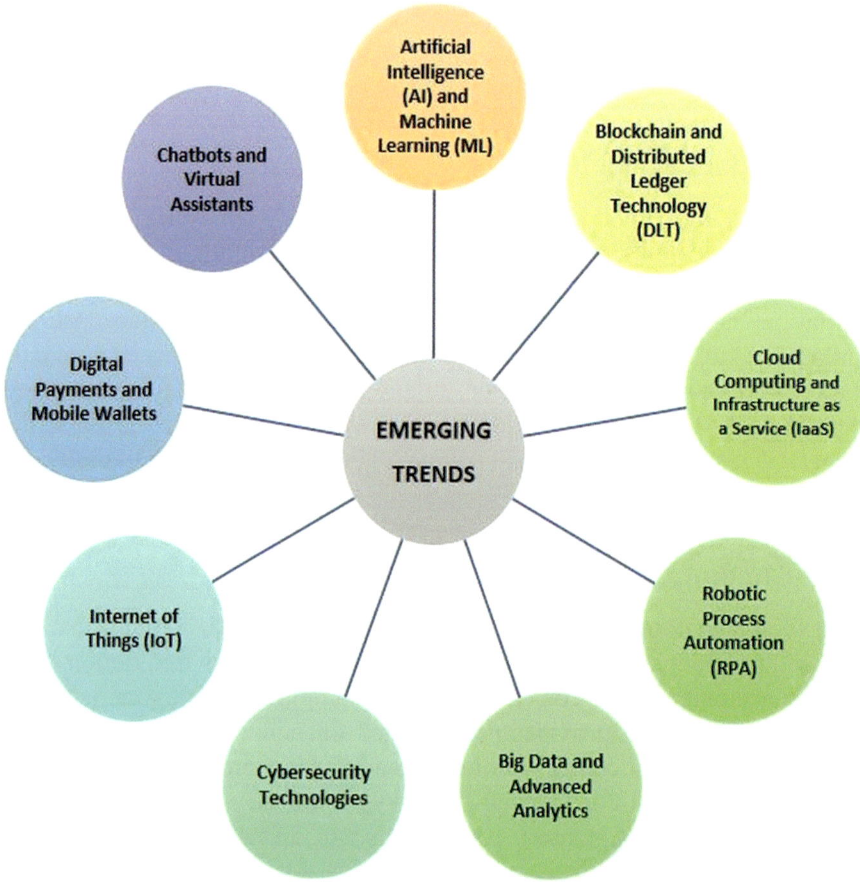

Figure 3.11 Emerging trends – financial sector.

Summary

The financial sector stands at the confluence of disruption and innovation, driven by powerful technological trends. From AI to blockchain, cloud computing to quantum algorithms, these technologies are not only transforming how financial services are delivered but also reshaping the competitive landscape. For institutions to remain relevant and resilient, embracing these technologies is not a choice but a strategic necessity. The key lies in aligning digital capabilities with customer-centric strategies, robust governance, and an innovation-first mindset. As the pace of technological change accelerates, the future of finance will be characterized by hyper-personalization, real-time decision-making, ecosystem collaboration, and unprecedented efficiency. Financial institutions that proactively adopt and integrate these trends will emerge as digital leaders in an increasingly data-driven world.

Case Study: DBS Bank: Leading Digital Transformation in Traditional Banking

DBS Bank, headquartered in Singapore, has emerged as a global exemplar of digital transformation within the traditional banking sector. Originally established as a conventional, paper-heavy financial institution, DBS recognized early on the disruptive potential of digital technologies and the pressing need for innovation in a rapidly evolving financial landscape. In response, the bank launched a bold and forward-looking strategy with the vision of transforming itself into a "technology company in banking." This shift was not merely cosmetic or operational; it was a fundamental overhaul of its organizational culture, technological infrastructure, and approach to customer engagement. To achieve this vision, DBS made substantial investments in emerging technologies such as cloud computing, artificial intelligence (AI), machine learning, and advanced data analytics. By leveraging these tools, the bank streamlined internal operations, enhanced real-time decision-making, and improved risk management capabilities. One of the standout features of its transformation journey has been the focus on reengineering customer journeys to be fully digital, intuitive, and personalized. From digital onboarding and paperless transactions to AI-powered chatbots and predictive financial insights, DBS sought to ensure that customer experience was at the heart of every innovation.

The bank's "digital to the core" strategy also emphasized the development of an agile, innovation-driven culture. It embraced startup-style experimentation, flattened hierarchies, and encouraged cross-functional collaboration. DBS established in-house innovation labs and partnered with FinTech firms to foster the co-creation of new financial solutions. The result was a significant reduction in time-to-market for new products and services and a more nimble response to changing consumer expectations. Moreover, DBS's transformation had a measurable business impact. The bank reported increased customer acquisition, improved operational efficiency, and a significant uptick in digital revenues. It also received international recognition for its digital leadership, being named "World's Best Digital Bank" multiple times by prestigious global financial publications.

By successfully bridging the gap between traditional banking and the digital age, DBS Bank has not only set new industry standards but also demonstrated that legacy institutions can adapt and thrive in the era of digital disruption. Its journey serves as a model for banks worldwide that are seeking to remain competitive and relevant in an increasingly digital financial ecosystem.

Discussion Questions

1. What strategic decisions enabled DBS Bank to successfully implement digital transformation?
2. How did DBS overcome the challenges of modernizing legacy systems?
3. In what ways did customer behavior influence DBS's digital strategy?
4. How can other traditional banks learn from DBS's transformation journey?
5. What role did leadership and organizational culture play in sustaining this transformation?

Keywords

- **Digital transformation:** Refers to the integration of digital technologies into all areas of a business, fundamentally changing how financial services operate and deliver value to customers.
- **Fintech:** Short for "financial technology," it refers to technology-driven innovations in financial services, including mobile payments, digital wallets, robo-advisors, and peer-to-peer lending.
- **Omnichannel strategy:** A business approach that provides a seamless customer experience across all digital and physical touchpoints, such as mobile apps, websites, and in-branch services.
- **Platform banking:** A model where banks offer digital platforms that integrate third-party financial services (via APIs), transforming from product providers into service ecosystems.

- **Customer-centricity:** A strategic focus on understanding and meeting the evolving needs and expectations of customers through personalized digital interactions.
- **Agile methodology:** A project management approach that promotes flexible planning, continuous improvement, and iterative development—especially useful in digital finance product launches.
- **Data-driven decision making:** The use of data analytics and business intelligence tools to guide strategic decisions in real-time, improving risk assessment, personalization, and efficiency.
- **Application Programming Interface (API):** A software intermediary that enables different applications or systems to communicate. In digital finance, APIs allow secure third-party service integration.
- **Digital-first strategy:** An approach where digital platforms are prioritized as the main channel for customer interaction, product delivery, and operations.
- **Cloud computing:** Use of remote servers and internet-based computing resources to store, manage, and process financial data, improving scalability and cost-efficiency.
- **Cybersecurity:** Protecting digital financial systems, transactions, and customer data from unauthorized access, fraud, or data breaches.
- **Blockchain:** A decentralized ledger technology offering secure, transparent, and tamper-proof transaction records, increasingly used in areas like payments, settlements, and identity management.
- **Robo-advisory:** Automated financial advisory services that use algorithms to manage and optimize client portfolios without human intervention.
- **Digital wallet:** An electronic device or software that allows individuals to make electronic transactions and store payment information securely.
- **Regulatory technology (RegTech):** Technology used to help financial institutions comply with regulatory requirements more efficiently and transparently.
- **Neobank:** A digital-only bank with no physical branches, offering streamlined banking services through mobile and online platforms.

- **Open banking:** A system that allows third-party financial service providers to access consumer banking data (with consent) through secure APIs, fostering competition and innovation.
- **Cost-to-income ratio:** A financial metric that measures operating efficiency by comparing costs to income—lower ratios indicate better efficiency, especially relevant in digital transformation.
- **Digital maturity:** The extent to which an organization has successfully adopted digital technologies and processes to create strategic value.
- **Innovation culture:** An organizational environment that encourages experimentation, agility, and continuous improvement to stay competitive in a digital landscape.

Discussion Questions

1. How does a digital-first strategy reshape the traditional business model of financial institutions?
2. What role does customer-centricity play in shaping digital finance strategies?
3. What are the risks and challenges of implementing a business strategy for digital finance in legacy banks?
4. In what ways has digital transformation affected the revenue streams of traditional banks?
5. How has digital transformation influenced the internal operations and workforce of banks?
6. Can traditional banks and FinTech companies collaborate effectively, or are they always competitors?
7. Which emerging technologies (e.g., AI, blockchain, cloud computing) are most critical to digital finance, and why?
8. What ethical concerns arise from the use of AI and data analytics in financial services?
9. How is the trend of open banking redefining competition and innovation in the financial sector?
10. Imagine you are the Chief Digital Officer of a mid-sized bank. What would be your 3-year roadmap for digital transformation?

References

[1] Ananda, S., Dalwai, T., & Singh, D. (Eds.). (2025). *Trends and challenges of electronic finance: Perspectives from emerging markets.* Palgrave Macmillan.

[2] Arner, D. W., Barberis, J. N., & Buckley, R. P. (2016). *The evolution of FinTech: A new post-crisis paradigm? Georgetown Journal of International Law, 47*(4), 1271–1319.

[3] Borri, N. (2025). *Corporate finance in the age of fintech: Scenarios and challenges.* arXiv.

[4] Chishti, S., & Barberis, J. (2016). *The FinTech Book: The Financial Technology Handbook for Investors, Entrepreneurs and Visionaries.* Wiley.

[5] Fund management needs to make digital shift. (2025, May 16). *Financial Times.*

[6] Rogers, D. L. (2023). *The digital transformation roadmap: Rebuild your organization for continuous change.* Columbia Business School Publishing.

[7] Omarini, A. (2017). *The digital transformation in banking and the role of FinTechs in the new financial intermediation scenario. International Journal of Finance, Economics and Trade, 1*(1), 1–6.

[8] Gomber, P., Kauffman, R. J., Parker, C., & Weber, B. W. (2018). *On the fintech revolution: Interpreting the forces of innovation, disruption, and transformation in financial services. Journal of Management Information Systems, 35*(1), 220–265. https://doi.org/10.1080/07421222.2018.1440766

[9] Bansal, N., & Taneja, S. (2025). *RegTech: The new regulatory technology.* In *Financial landscape transformation: Technological disruptions* (pp. 235–251). Emerald Publishing.

[10] Mer, A., & Virdi, A. S. (2025). *The influence of artificial intelligence on personal and corporate finance.* In *Financial landscape transformation: Technological disruptions* (pp. 253–268). Emerald Publishing.

[11] Mikula, J. (2024). *Banking as a service: Opportunities, challenges and risks of new banking business models.*

[12] Schmarzo, B. (2020). *The economics of data, analytics, and digital transformation.* Packt Publishing.

[13] Puschmann, T. (2017). *Fintech: A survey of developments, drivers, and challenges. Business & Information Systems Engineering, 59*(1), 69–76. https://doi.org/10.1007/s12599-017-0464-6

[14] Stefanelli, V., Manta, F., & Toma, P. (2022). *Digital financial services and open banking innovation: Are banks becoming invisible?* arXiv.

[15] Mehta, K., Sharma, R., & Yu, P. (2023). *Revolutionizing financial services and markets through fintech and blockchain.* IGI Global.

[16] Perez, C. (2003). *Technological revolutions and financial capital: The dynamics of bubbles and golden ages.* Edward Elgar Publishing.

[17] Schmarzo, B. (2020). *The economics of data, analytics, and digital transformation.* Packt Publishing.

[18] Key trends in rapidly changing crypto world. (2024, December). *The Australian.*

[19] The 6 disruptive tech trends CFOs need to know about. (2025). *The Australian* (Deloitte report).

[20] Where the fintech sector is headed next: QED–BCG Global Fintech Report 2025. (2025, June 2). *Economic Times* (India).

UNIT 2

FinTech Fundamentals and Ecosystem

4

Evolution and Typology of FinTech

Abstract

This chapter presents a comprehensive overview of the historical trajectory and classification of financial technology (FinTech), tracing its growth from foundational digital innovations to the current era of intelligent, data-driven financial solutions. By contextualizing the evolution of FinTech through clearly defined developmental phases – from FinTech 1.0 to FinTech 3.5 – the chapter captures the significant milestones that have redefined how financial services are created, delivered, and consumed.

The narrative begins with the early digitization of financial services (FinTech 1.0), progressing through the emergence of online banking and e-commerce (FinTech 2.0), the rise of mobile technologies and decentralized finance (FinTech 3.0), and the ongoing phase (FinTech 3.5), characterized by embedded finance, AI, blockchain, and hyper-personalized offerings. Each phase reflects broader shifts in technological capability, consumer behavior, and regulatory adaptation, painting a dynamic picture of FinTech's evolutionary journey. A critical component of the chapter is the typology of FinTech entities, providing a structured classification of players in the ecosystem. These include:

- **Infrastructure providers** (e.g., cloud computing, cybersecurity, payment gateways),
- **FinTech startups** (innovators developing customer-facing solutions in lending, payments, wealth tech, etc.), and
- **TechFins**, or large technology companies (like Google, Amazon, and Alibaba) that leverage their digital dominance to enter financial services.

The chapter also offers a focused analysis of FinTech growth in emerging economies, where mobile-first strategies, regulatory experimentation (such

DOI: 10.1201/9788743811244-6

as sandboxes), and high rates of digital adoption open up both immense opportunities and unique structural challenges. Financial inclusion limited traditional infrastructure, and supportive government initiatives often accelerate FinTech penetration in these markets, though obstacles like digital illiteracy, data privacy concerns, and capital access persist. Finally, the chapter explores how regional and global FinTech ecosystems are shaped by the interplay of innovation, regulation, and technology adoption. It emphasizes that FinTech growth is not uniform but rather influenced by cultural norms, infrastructure readiness, policy frameworks, and market maturity – necessitating localized strategies within a globally interconnected digital financial landscape. In essence, this chapter equips readers with a deep understanding of where FinTech has come from, how it is categorized, and what forces drive its proliferation across diverse economic and geographic environments.

Introduction

The rapid transformation of financial services through technology has given rise to the dynamic field of FinTech, which has evolved significantly over time. This chapter explores the historical progression of FinTech, tracing its development from early digitization efforts in FinTech 1.0 to the sophisticated, AI-driven innovations of FinTech 3.5. It also introduces a typology that categorizes FinTech into infrastructure enablers, agile startups, and TechFins, large technology firms entering the financial domain. By examining this evolution and classification, the chapter offers a structured understanding of how FinTech has reshaped financial ecosystems globally. Special focus is given to emerging economies, where FinTech presents both unprecedented opportunities for financial inclusion and considerable challenges related to infrastructure, regulation, and digital literacy.

4.1 FinTech 1.0 to 3.5: A timeline

Financial technology, commonly known as FinTech, refers to the innovative use of technology to deliver financial services and products. It encompasses a broad spectrum of applications ranging from mobile banking and digital payments to blockchain and robo-advisory platforms. The evolution of FinTech is not merely a technological journey but a transformation of the financial ecosystem itself, reshaping how individuals, businesses, and governments interact with money. The FinTech revolution represents a structural transformation in global finance, integrating technology with innovative business models [1]. Over the past decade, FinTech has evolved from peripheral disruption to a central driver of financial modernization [2]. FinTech's digital transformation has redefined traditional boundaries of the financial industry, reshaping market dynamics [3]. The sector's digital acceleration reflects the convergence of financial innovation and data-driven ecosystems [4].

The evolution of FinTech can be traced through distinct phases. FinTech 1.0 (1866–1967) laid the groundwork with foundational technologies like the telegraph and early banking infrastructure. FinTech 2.0 (1967–2008) marked the digitalization of traditional financial institutions, introducing electronic banking and global payment systems. The FinTech 3.0 era (2008–2014) saw the rise of startups that challenged conventional banking models, driven by the global financial crisis and the proliferation of smartphones. Today, in FinTech 3.5, we witness the integration of advanced technologies such as artificial intelligence, blockchain, and open banking, with Big Tech companies (TechFins) entering the financial domain.

Understanding the typology of FinTech is essential to grasp its diverse landscape. It includes:

- **Infrastructure providers**: Companies offering the technological backbone like APIs, cloud services, and cybersecurity.
- **FinTech startups**: Agile firms focused on specific financial services such as payments, lending, and investment.
- **TechFins**: Technology giants like Google and Alibaba that leverage their platforms to offer financial services at scale.

Table 4.1 Evolution of FinTech (Timeline).

Phase	Years	Key features
FinTech 1.0	1866–1967	Telegraph, transatlantic cables, first ATM (1967), early banking tech
FinTech 2.0	1967–2008	Mainframes, SWIFT, electronic, and online banking integration
FinTech 3.0	2008–2014	Post-crisis FinTech startups, mobile payments, and peer-to-peer lending
FinTech 3.5	2014–present	Big Tech enters finance (TechFins), blockchain, AI, open banking, and regulation

The BIS Innovation Hub identifies new typologies within FinTech, including RegTech, SupTech, and digital asset frameworks [5]. Digital financial services have played a vital role in expanding inclusion and reducing transaction costs in emerging economies [6]. FinTech has evolved through several distinct phases, each marked by technological advancements and shifts in financial service delivery. This section outlines the major milestones and characteristics of FinTech from its inception to the present day.

4.1.1 FinTech 1.0 (1866–1967): The foundation

- Introduction of telegraph and transatlantic cables.
- Emergence of early banking technologies, like the first ATM (1967).
- Focused on digitizing traditional banking infrastructure.

FinTech 1.0 marks the earliest phase of financial technology, characterized by the use of communication technologies like the telegraph and transatlantic cables to facilitate financial transactions across borders. The introduction of the first ATM in 1967 revolutionized banking by allowing customers to access cash without visiting a bank branch. This era laid the groundwork for digitizing traditional banking systems.

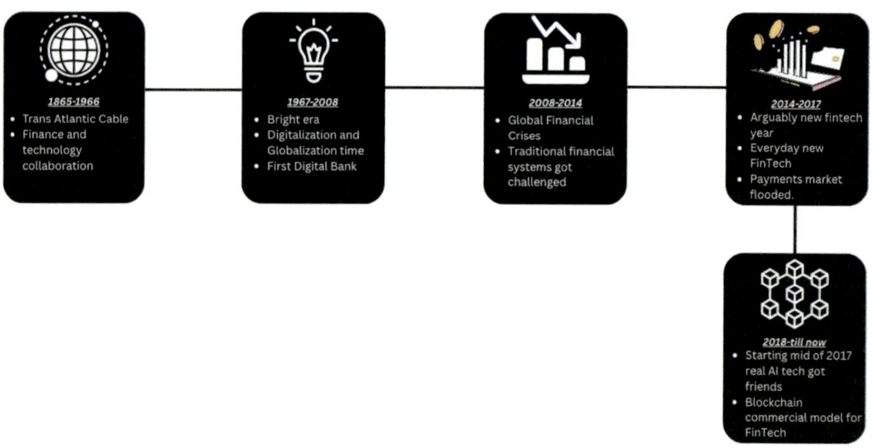

Figure 4.1 Timeline of FinTech 1.0 to 3.5

4.1.2 FinTech 2.0 (1967–2008): The digitalization era

- Rise of electronic banking and mainframe computers.
- Introduction of SWIFT (1973), online banking (1990s).
- Financial institutions began integrating IT systems.

During FinTech 2.0, financial institutions embraced digital technologies to streamline operations and improve customer service. Mainframe computers enabled large-scale data processing, while the SWIFT network standardized international financial communications. The 1990s saw the emergence of online banking, allowing users to manage their finances remotely. This era was pivotal in transitioning from analog to digital financial services.

4.1.3 FinTech 3.0 (2008–2014): The startup revolution

- Post-2008 financial crisis saw a surge in FinTech startups.
- Mobile payments, peer-to-peer lending, and robo-advisors emerged.
- Democratization of financial services.

The global financial crisis of 2008 catalyzed the rise of FinTech startups that aimed to disrupt traditional banking models. Innovations such as mobile payment platforms, peer-to-peer lending networks, and robo-advisors empowered consumers with more choices and control over their financial activities. FinTech 3.0 democratized access to financial services, making them more inclusive and user-friendly.

4.1.4 FinTech 3.5 (2014–present): Global expansion and integration

- Big Tech (TechFins) like Alibaba, Google, and Apple enter finance.
- Blockchain, AI, and open banking reshape the landscape.
- Regulatory frameworks like PSD2 and sandboxes emerge.

FinTech 3.5 represents the current phase of financial technology, characterized by the entry of technology giants into the financial sector. These TechFins leverage their massive user bases and data capabilities to offer financial services on a scale. Emerging technologies such as blockchain and artificial intelligence are transforming how financial services are delivered. Regulatory innovations like PSD2 and sandbox environments support experimentation and foster innovation while ensuring consumer protection. FinTech 3.5 marks the global reconfiguration of innovation ecosystems through cross-sector collaboration and AI integration [7]. Responsible FinTech emphasizes sustainability and ethical finance as core dimensions of future innovation [8]. Regulatory authorities across Europe highlight both opportunities and systemic risks arising from digital transformation [9]. Forces such as innovation, competition, and consumer empowerment underpin the ongoing FinTech revolution [10].

4.2 Typology: Infrastructure, Startups, TechFins

Typology in digital finance refers to the structured classification of various entities, business models, and enablers that collectively shape the evolving landscape of financial services in the digital age. It provides a clear analytical framework to distinguish between different actors based on their function, origin, technological intensity, and strategic approach. Understanding this typology is essential for academics, practitioners, and policymakers to navigate the complex digital finance ecosystem. Broadly, the typology includes three major categories: **Infrastructure providers**, **startups (FinTechs)**, and **TechFins**.

Infrastructure providers represent the foundational layer that supports the operation and delivery of all digital financial services. This includes core banking systems, payment gateways, digital identity platforms, data storage solutions, cloud computing, and cybersecurity frameworks. These elements ensure that transactions are processed securely, data is handled efficiently, and services can be scaled across geographies. Public infrastructure, such as UPI in India or the Aadhaar-enabled e-KYC system plays a significant role in fostering innovation and financial inclusion by enabling interoperability and regulatory compliance.

Startups, often referred to as FinTechs, are the innovation engines of digital finance. These technology-driven firms focus on specific verticals like mobile payments, digital lending, robo-advisory, insurance technology (InsurTech), and wealth management. They are agile, customer-focused, and often operate with lower overheads, enabling them to respond swiftly to changing market demands. Startups leverage cutting-edge technologies such as AI, blockchain, and big data to create efficient, accessible, and personalized financial services that challenge traditional banking norms.

TechFins, on the other hand, are large technology firms like Google, Apple, Amazon, Alibaba, and Tencent that expand into financial services by embedding them into their broader digital platforms. Unlike FinTechs, TechFins originate from the technology sector and integrate finance as a secondary but strategic component to enhance user engagement and ecosystem value. Their scale, data capabilities, and digital infrastructure gives them a powerful edge in delivering seamless, embedded financial services across payments, credit, insurance, and more.

Altogether, the typology of digital finance provides clarity in understanding the roles, innovations, and influence of different players within the financial ecosystem. It helps stakeholders analyze how infrastructure, startups, and TechFins interact, collaborate, and compete, thereby shaping the future of finance in an increasingly digital, data-driven world.

4.2.1 Infrastructure providers

In the context of digital finance, **infrastructure** refers to the foundational technological, institutional, and regulatory systems that enable the secure and efficient functioning of digital financial services. This infrastructure forms the backbone of a country's financial ecosystem, facilitating transactions, data flow, interoperability, risk management, and regulatory compliance. Without a robust digital financial infrastructure, even the most innovative financial products and services cannot function reliably or at scale.

The core components of digital financial infrastructure include **payment systems, digital identity frameworks, data networks, cloud computing environments, cybersecurity protocols, and regulatory technology (RegTech)**. Among these, **digital payment systems** such as Real-Time Gross Settlement (RTGS), Immediate Payment Service (IMPS), Unified Payments Interface (UPI), and card networks (Visa, Mastercard, RuPay) play a critical role by enabling instantaneous and secure transactions between individuals, businesses, and government entities. These systems must be interoperable to ensure that services from different providers can work together seamlessly.

Another crucial infrastructure layer is **digital identity**. Systems like Aadhaar in India have transformed access to financial services by providing biometric verification and enabling e-KYC (electronic Know Your Customer), which helps streamline customer onboarding, reduce fraud, and ensure compliance with anti-money laundering laws. Alongside digital ID, secure and open **data exchange networks** – often based on APIs – enable institutions to share customer data (with consent) for credit scoring, insurance underwriting, and fraud detection.

Cloud computing is another pillar of digital finance infrastructure. It provides scalable, cost-effective platforms for storing data, running applications, and deploying financial services across geographies without the need for heavy physical infrastructure. Cloud-based environments support innovation by enabling small firms and startups to enter the market with minimal capital investment.

Cybersecurity infrastructure ensures the protection of financial data and systems from breaches, identity theft, and cyber fraud. Firewalls, end-to-end encryption, biometric authentication, and multi-factor authentication are now standard components of financial cybersecurity frameworks. As financial activity increasingly moves online, robust cyber risk management is indispensable.

Governments and regulators also play a central role in building financial infrastructure by framing **regulatory and legal standards** that support innovation while ensuring consumer protection and financial stability. **RegTech** platforms help institutions stay compliant through automation and real-time regulatory reporting.

Public-private partnerships (PPPs) are often vital to expanding financial infrastructure. For example, in many countries, central banks, telecom operators, and commercial banks collaborate to develop inclusive payment platforms and agent networks, especially in rural or underserved areas. In sum, infrastructure is not a one-time investment but a dynamic, evolving layer that must adapt to emerging technologies, user behaviors, and regulatory needs. As digital finance grows more complex – with the rise of blockchain, AI, and cross-border transactions, financial infrastructure must evolve in tandem. A well-structured infrastructure ensures that the benefits of digital finance, such as speed, accessibility, transparency, and inclusion, are fully realized.

Key technologies

- **Cloud computing**: Enables scalable, secure, and cost-effective data storage and processing. It allows financial firms to manage vast amounts of data and deploy services globally with minimal physical infrastructure.

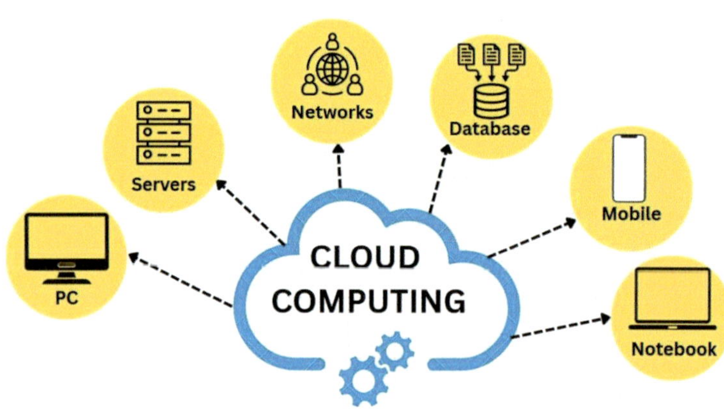

Figure 4.2 Cloud computing.

- **Application Programming Interfaces (APIs)**: Facilitate seamless integration between different financial systems and services. APIs allow developers to connect banking systems with third-party apps, enabling features like account aggregation, payments, and identity verification.

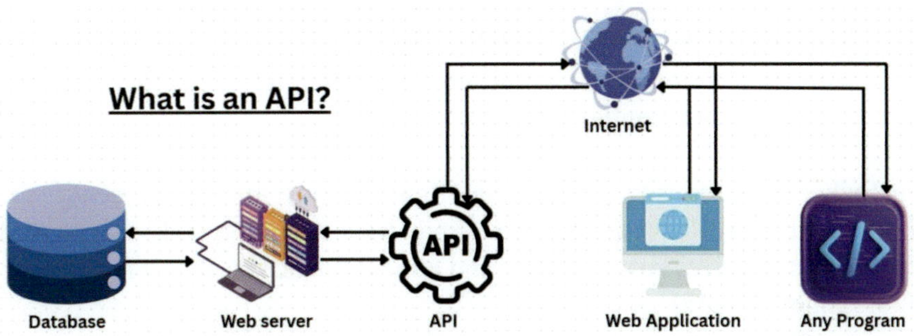

Figure 4.3 Application Programming Interface.

- **Cybersecurity**: Protects sensitive financial data from breaches and fraud. Infrastructure providers offer encryption, fraud detection, and compliance tools to ensure secure transactions and data integrity.

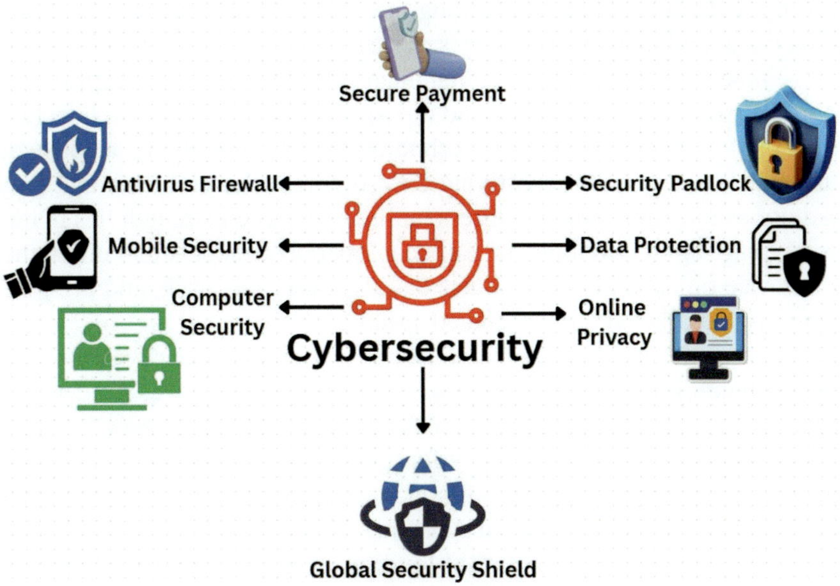

Figure 4.4 Cybersecurity (Global Security Shield).

Examples:

- **Plaid**: Offers APIs that connect consumer bank accounts to financial applications, enabling services like budgeting, payments, and lending.
- **Stripe**: Provides payment processing infrastructure for online businesses, supporting global transactions and fraud prevention.
- **Amazon Web Services (AWS)**: Delivers cloud computing solutions tailored for financial institutions, including data analytics, machine learning, and compliance support.

FinTech 3.5 marks the global reconfiguration of innovation ecosystems through cross-sector collaboration and AI integration [7]. Responsible FinTech emphasizes sustainability and ethical finance as core dimensions of future innovation [8].

FinTech startups

In the realm of digital finance, **startups** play a transformative and often disruptive role. These agile, technology-driven companies challenge traditional financial models by offering innovative, customer-centric solutions that leverage the latest digital technologies. Typically referred to as **FinTech startups**, these companies operate across various segments of the financial services industry, including payments, lending, insurance, wealth management, digital banking, and financial advisory services.

Unlike traditional banks, digital finance startups are **born-digital** – they build their services from the ground up using modern software architectures, cloud platforms, and data-driven technologies. They are highly adaptive and customer-focused, often identifying and solving niche problems that larger institutions may overlook or address inefficiently. Their strength lies in rapid prototyping, agile development, and lean operating models that allow them to innovate quickly, iterate products based on user feedback, and bring new solutions to market at unprecedented speeds.

One of the most prominent categories of digital finance startups is in the **payments sector**. Companies such as Razorpay, PhonePe, and Paytm in India, or Stripe and Square internationally, have revolutionized how businesses and individuals transfer money, pay for goods and services, or receive digital receipts. These startups leverage APIs and mobile platforms to deliver seamless, fast, and secure transactions, often bypassing the traditional card-based systems.

Another major area is **digital lending**, where startups use alternative data sources and AI-driven credit scoring models to evaluate borrower risk and disburse loans – often instantly. Companies like LendingClub, KreditBee, and Capital Float use digital channels to target underserved customers who may lack formal credit histories, including small business owners, gig workers, and first-time borrowers. By minimizing physical paperwork and branch-based interactions, they significantly reduce overheads and processing times.

InsurTech startups – those innovating in the insurance sector – leverage digital platforms to streamline policy distribution, claim management, and customer service. Startups such as Acko and Digit Insurance in India provide paperless insurance options with transparent pricing models and app-based claims processing. These companies often use behavioral and sensor data (from mobile phones or wearables) to offer personalized insurance products.

In the area of **wealth management and personal finance**, startups like Groww, Zerodha, and ETMoney empower retail investors with tools to manage investments, trade stocks, and plan for financial goals. Robo-advisors – automated digital platforms – help users build portfolios and rebalance investments based on risk appetite, offering low-cost alternatives to traditional financial advisors.

What sets these startups apart is their use of **emerging technologies** such as blockchain, artificial intelligence, machine learning, big data analytics, and natural language processing. These tools allow startups to offer real-time services, predictive analytics, chat-based interfaces, and personalized financial experiences. They also rely on **API-based architecture**, enabling them to plug into larger financial ecosystems or partner with traditional banks through Banking-as-a-Service (BaaS) models. However, digital finance startups face several challenges, including intense competition, regulatory uncertainty, funding constraints, and the need to build consumer trust. Many operate in a highly regulated industry where compliance with laws such as KYC, AML (Anti-Money Laundering), and data privacy is critical. Startups must balance innovation with compliance – a task often tackled through partnerships with RegTech providers or by hiring compliance specialists early in their growth journey. Economic liberalization and technological progress have jointly accelerated FinTech adoption worldwide [11]. The rise of digital banking introduces both operational efficiencies and complex cybersecurity challenges [12].

Startups also contribute to financial inclusion by reaching segments traditionally excluded from the formal financial system. Mobile-based micro-lending apps, peer-to-peer (P2P) lending platforms, and low-cost investment tools have brought financial services to millions of first-time users, especially in emerging markets. In conclusion, startups are an integral part of the digital finance typology. They serve as innovation engines, pushing the boundaries of what is possible and reshaping the financial services landscape through disruption, democratization, and digitization. As they continue to evolve, collaborate, and mature, digital finance startups are likely to play an even greater role in shaping the future of financial services.

Characteristics:

- Operate with lean teams and rapid development cycles.
- Prioritize user-friendly interfaces and mobile-first solutions.
- Often target underserved markets or offer more affordable alternatives.

Key categories:

- **Payments**: Companies like **PayPal** simplify digital transactions, enabling peer-to-peer payments and online purchases.
- **Lending**: Platforms such as **LendingClub** offer alternative lending models, including peer-to-peer loans and credit scoring innovations.
- **WealthTech**: Startups like **Robinhood** democratize investing by offering commission-free trading and easy-to-use mobile apps.

These startups often scale quickly and adapt to changing regulations and consumer demands, making them highly competitive in the financial space.

TechFins

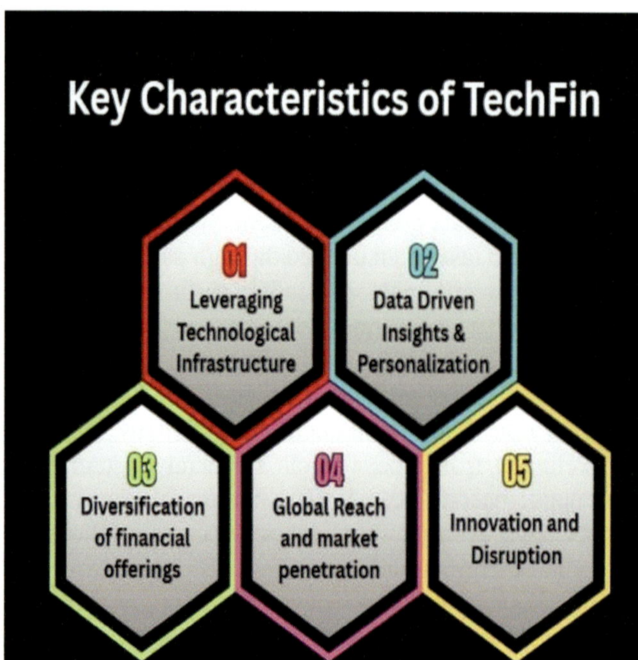

Figure 4.5 Key characteristics of TechFin

In the modern financial ecosystem, **TechFins** represent a distinct and rapidly growing typology within digital finance. The term "TechFin" was coined to distinguish large technology companies that enter the financial services space not as financial institutions first, but as technology-driven enterprises expanding into finance. Unlike FinTechs, which are startups leveraging technology to provide financial services, TechFins are typically established technology giants such as **Google, Amazon, Apple, Facebook, Alibaba, Tencent, and Baidu**, which use their massive digital platforms, customer bases, and data ecosystems to embed financial services into their existing offerings.

At their core, TechFins prioritize **technology-first solutions** and view financial services as a value-added component of a much broader digital ecosystem. These companies do not necessarily aim to replace banks but to complement or integrate financial offerings into their platforms, enhancing user engagement, retention, and monetization. For example, Alibaba launched **Ant Group**, a financial arm offering mobile payments (Alipay), wealth management, credit scoring, and insurance products – all deeply embedded within the Alibaba e-commerce environment. Similarly, Apple launched Apple Pay and Apple Card as part of its digital wallet and services expansion, integrating payments into the user experience of iPhones and iOS devices.

A key characteristic of TechFins is their ability to **leverage massive user data sets** to develop hyper-personalized financial services. Through insights derived from user activity, purchasing habits, search behavior, and digital footprints, TechFins can assess creditworthiness, personalize offers, and even automate financial decisions. For instance, Amazon offers small business loans and credit options to its merchants based on real-time sales performance, logistics, and inventory data, all of which are already part of its ecosystem. This gives TechFins an immense advantage in **risk management and customer targeting**, without relying on traditional financial indicators.

TechFins also benefit from **platform economics**, meaning their services scale easily across millions of users with low marginal cost. Their existing infrastructure, such as cloud services, data analytics platforms, and app ecosystems, allows for the rapid deployment of financial services. In contrast to banks that must build or buy new infrastructure for every service, TechFins can embed financial features such as "Buy Now, Pay Later" (BNPL), digital wallets, and savings options directly into platforms where users already spend time.

Another notable feature of TechFins is their role in **embedded finance**. Through APIs and partnerships, they allow non-financial companies to offer financial services as part of their customer journeys. For instance, ride-sharing apps like Uber and Ola offer in-app payments, driver loans, and insurance through integrated financial systems powered by TechFin platforms. This seamless integration of finance into day-to-day apps has revolutionized user convenience and broadened financial access.

Despite their innovations, TechFins face significant **regulatory scrutiny**, particularly concerning data privacy, anti-competitive practices, and systemic risk. Governments and regulators around the world are increasingly concerned about the dual role of TechFins as platform owners and financial service providers, which could lead to market dominance, reduced transparency, and data monopolization. China's suspension of Ant Group's IPO in 2020 and its subsequent regulatory tightening illustrate the challenges TechFins can face when they grow too large or influential in the financial domain.

TechFins are also reshaping the competitive dynamics of the financial industry. Traditional banks and even FinTech startups must now compete with these powerful digital ecosystems that have high brand loyalty, user engagement, and technological prowess. In response, many financial institutions are adopting **banking-as-a-platform** models or collaborating with TechFins to access their infrastructure and user bases.

In conclusion, TechFins represent a transformative force in digital finance. By embedding financial services into everyday digital experiences, leveraging big data, and deploying scalable platforms, they are redefining how financial products are delivered, consumed, and monetized. As regulators and market players adapt to this new paradigm, the role of TechFins will continue to expand, blurring the boundaries between technology and finance, and ultimately changing the future shape of the global financial landscape. FinTech in Asia demonstrates rapid scaling through advanced digital infrastructure and a young tech-savvy population [13]. The integration of blockchain within FinTech ecosystems enables transparency, automation, and cross-border efficiency [14].

Key features:

- **Platform integration**: Financial services are embedded into existing ecosystems (e.g., messaging apps, e-commerce platforms).
- **Data-driven personalization**: Use of big data and AI to tailor financial offerings to individual users.

- **Global reach**: Ability to scale rapidly due to established infrastructure and brand trust.

Examples:

- **Ant Financial**: A subsidiary of Alibaba, offering digital payments, credit scoring, and wealth management through platforms like Alipay.
- **Google Pay**: Integrates with Google's ecosystem to offer seamless mobile payments and financial services.
- **Apple Card**: A credit card service integrated with Apple Pay, offering unique features like real-time spending tracking and cashback rewards.

TechFins are reshaping the financial landscape by merging convenience, data intelligence, and global accessibility.

4.3 Opportunities in Emerging Economies

FinTech offers transformative opportunities in emerging economies by addressing long-standing gaps in financial inclusion, access, and efficiency. With widespread mobile phone penetration and increasing internet connectivity, FinTech platforms enable underserved populations to access banking, payment, credit, and insurance services, often for the first time. Digital wallets, peer-to-peer lending, and mobile banking have become tools for empowering small businesses, rural populations, and the unbanked. Additionally, FinTech fosters innovation by supporting startups and entrepreneurs, creating job opportunities, and driving economic growth. The agility of FinTech firms, especially in payments and microfinance, allows them to cater to local needs faster than traditional banks. Governments and central banks in several emerging nations are also adopting regulatory sandboxes and digital ID frameworks to promote innovation while safeguarding consumers. Global FinTech investment trends indicate sustained growth, with AI, payments, and lending dominating innovation pipelines [15]. India's digital payments revolution showcases how regulatory frameworks can foster inclusion while ensuring consumer protection [16]. The Indian FinTech ecosystem continues to evolve as a model of innovation, entrepreneurship, and adaptive regulation [17]. Across Africa, FinTech is driving financial access, entrepreneurship, and poverty reduction through mobile-led innovation [18].

4.3.1 Financial inclusion: Mobile money (e.g., M-Pesa) reaches unbanked populations

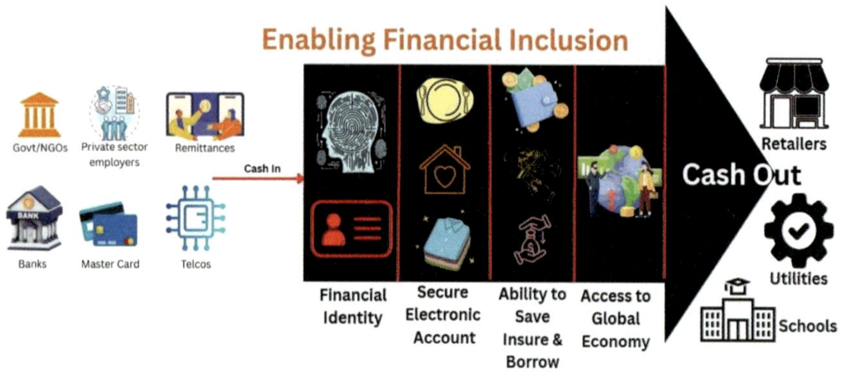

Figure 4.6 Financial inclusion: Mobile money (e.g., M-Pesa) reaches the unbanked population.

Financial inclusion is one of the most transformative impacts of FinTech in emerging economies. Mobile money platforms like M-Pesa in Kenya have enabled millions of people without access to traditional banking to perform financial transactions using basic mobile phones. These services allow users to deposit, withdraw, transfer money, and pay for goods and services, thereby integrating them into the formal financial system. This has led to increased economic participation, improved savings behavior, and enhanced financial resilience among underserved populations.

4.3.2 Leapfrogging: Bypassing legacy systems with mobile-first solutions

Emerging economies often lack the extensive legacy banking infrastructure found in developed countries. This absence allows them to leapfrog directly to modern, mobile-first financial solutions. For example, instead of building physical bank branches, countries can deploy mobile banking apps and digital wallets that provide instant access to financial services. This leapfrogging accelerates financial inclusion and innovation, enabling faster adoption of cutting-edge technologies like blockchain and AI.

4.3.3 Entrepreneurship: Local startups solving region-specific problems

FinTech fosters entrepreneurship by enabling local startups to address unique financial challenges in their regions. These startups often develop tailored solutions for issues such as micro-lending, agricultural finance, and remittance services. By leveraging local knowledge and digital tools, they create inclusive financial products that cater to underserved communities, stimulate job creation, and contribute to economic development.

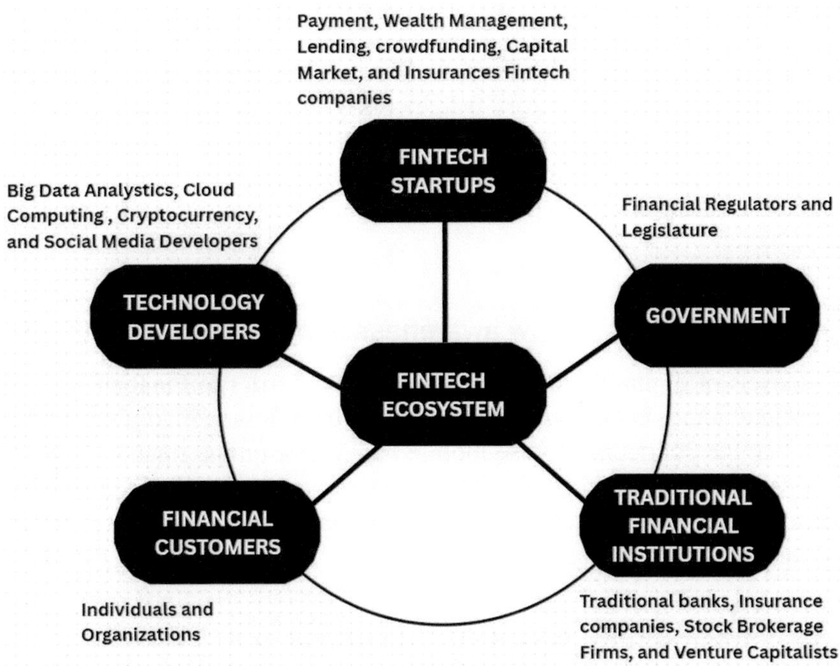

Figure 4.7 FinTech ecosystem in emerging economies.

4.4 Challenges in Emerging Economies

Despite its promise, FinTech adoption in emerging economies faces several challenges. Infrastructural limitations such as unreliable internet, limited smartphone access, and inconsistent digital literacy restrict widespread use. Regulatory uncertainty and fragmented policy environments also pose barriers to scaling FinTech innovations. Cybersecurity risks, data privacy concerns, and the digital divide between urban and rural users further complicate adoption. Moreover, many FinTech startups struggle with funding and sustainability due to underdeveloped venture capital ecosystems. While TechFins and infrastructure enablers have the potential to bridge these gaps, a coordinated approach involving governments, regulators, and private stakeholders is essential to harness FinTech's full potential responsibly and inclusively.

4.4.1 Regulatory uncertainty: Lack of clear frameworks

One of the major hurdles for FinTech in emerging markets is the absence of clear and consistent regulatory frameworks. Uncertainty around licensing, compliance, and consumer protection can deter investment and innovation. Moreover, rapidly evolving technologies often outpace regulatory development, creating a gap that can lead to legal ambiguities and operational risks.

4.4.2 Digital literacy: Low awareness and trust in digital finance

Low levels of digital literacy pose a significant barrier to FinTech adoption. Many individuals in emerging economies are unfamiliar with digital tools and may lack the confidence to use mobile banking or online financial services. This can result in mistrust, misuse, or underutilization of FinTech solutions. Educational initiatives and user-friendly interfaces are essential to bridge this gap and build trust in digital finance.

4.4.3 Infrastructure gaps: Limited internet and mobile penetration

Reliable internet connectivity and mobile network coverage are critical for the success of FinTech. However, many rural and remote areas in emerging economies suffer from poor infrastructure, limiting access to digital financial services. Addressing these gaps requires investment in telecommunications, electricity, and digital infrastructure to ensure equitable access to FinTech innovations.

In emerging economies, FinTech presents both opportunities and challenges. It fosters financial inclusion, enables leapfrogging over legacy systems, and stimulates local innovation. However, it also faces hurdles such as regulatory ambiguity, limited digital literacy, and infrastructural constraints. This chapter delves into the historical progression of FinTech, categorizes its key players, and examines its impact – particularly in developing regions. Through a case study on India, we explore how FinTech typology evolves in response to local needs and global trends, offering insights into the future of financial innovation. Example: United Kingdom: Regulatory Leadership and Open Banking. The UK has positioned itself as a global FinTech hub, especially after the 2008 financial crisis. The FinTech evolution accelerated with government-supported innovation and the introduction of Open Banking regulations under PSD2.

Typology

- **Startups: Revolut**, **Monzo**, and **Starling Bank** lead the neobanking revolution, offering multi-currency accounts, budgeting tools, and crypto access.
- **Infrastructure:** The **Open Banking Implementation Entity (OBIE)** and government-backed innovation hubs support API infrastructure and compliance.
- **TechFin:** While the UK lacks domestic TechFins, global players like Amazon and Google integrate their services with UK FinTech firms.

Outcome: **The UK FinTech ecosystem showcases** how proactive regulation and public-private partnerships can enable secure innovation. The regulatory sandbox model adopted by the FCA (Financial Conduct Authority) has since been **replicated worldwide.**

Summary

This chapter explains the evolution of modern payment systems and how technology has transformed financial transactions. It covers systems like RTGS and NEFT that enable secure bank-to-bank fund transfers, along with mobile payments and digital wallets that allow users to make quick transactions using smartphones. The chapter also discusses UPI as a real-time payment platform that has simplified peer-to-peer and merchant payments. In addition, it highlights the role of APIs in connecting banks with fintech platforms, enabling smooth data exchange and innovation in digital financial services. Overall, the chapter shows how digital payment technologies have improved speed, convenience, and financial inclusion.

Case Study: Ant Group and the Chinese Fintech Ecosystem: A Comprehensive Study of Fintech Evolution and Typology

China stands as one of the most vivid illustrations of how FinTech has evolved from rudimentary digital financial services to an integrated, AI-driven ecosystem deeply embedded into everyday life. This case study focuses on Ant Group, the financial arm of Alibaba, and explores how China's FinTech journey reflects the broader global evolution from FinTech 1.0 to 3.5. It also demonstrates the development and interconnection of the three primary FinTech typologies: infrastructure enablers, startups, and TechFins. China's case further highlights the opportunities and challenges that arise from the rapid expansion of FinTech applications in an emerging economy context. In its earliest phase, during FinTech 1.0 (pre-2000s), China's financial system was underdeveloped, relying heavily on cash transactions and lacking widespread banking infrastructure. With the advent of the internet and e-commerce in the early 2000s (FinTech 2.0), Alibaba launched Alipay in 2004 to support secure payments on its Taobao platform. This marked the beginning of China's digital payment revolution. As smartphones and mobile internet became widespread during FinTech 3.0 (2010–2015), mobile finance, microlending, and peer-to-peer (P2P) lending flourished. Ant Group's introduction of Yu'e Bao in 2013 enabled everyday users to invest idle funds from their Alipay wallets into money market accounts, democratizing investment for millions. In the current FinTech 3.5 phase (2015 onward), technologies such as artificial intelligence, blockchain, and machine learning have powered services like automated credit scoring, real-time fraud detection, and blockchain-enabled cross-border payments. Super apps like Alipay and WeChat Pay have seamlessly integrated financial products – including loans, insurance, and investment – into social and lifestyle platforms, redefining financial engagement.

Typologically, China's FinTech space is dominated by TechFins, with Ant Group serving as a prime example. By leveraging Alibaba's vast consumer data, Ant Group offers credit (Huabei, Jiebei), insurance (Xiang Hu Bao), and wealth management services through intelligent algorithms. Tencent's WeChat Pay, embedded within the WeChat app, is ubiquitous in Chinese daily life, used for everything from online purchases to local transactions. FinTech startups also surged during the 2010s, with platforms like Lufax, Dianrong, and Qudian using alternative data for credit assessments and SME financing. However, the absence of early regulatory oversight led to market saturation and eventual corrections. Complementing this ecosystem are infrastructure enablers such as UnionPay and JD Digits, which provide critical backend services including APIs, credit engines, cloud infrastructure, and identity verification systems – essential for scaling digital financial services securely.

Regulatory responses in China have evolved significantly over time. Initially characterized by non-interference, the regulatory stance shifted to active oversight in the mid-2010s. The proliferation of unregulated lending and systemic risks led authorities to establish frameworks such as regulatory sandboxes for testing innovation, data protection laws aligned with international norms, and strict controls over large FinTech entities. A defining moment came in 2020 when Ant Group's planned IPO was halted, followed by its restructuring into a financial holding company subject to banking regulations. In parallel, the People's Bank of China introduced the Digital Yuan (e-CNY), a sovereign digital currency directly competing with private digital wallets and signaling the state's intention to assert control over digital finance.

China's FinTech landscape offers both vast opportunities and notable challenges. On one hand, mobile-based platforms have expanded financial inclusion, reaching rural and previously unbanked populations. AI-driven credit scoring has enabled more accurate risk assessments for borrowers without formal credit histories. Digital tools have empowered SMEs with accessible financial products, and leading FinTech firms are now expanding into international markets, especially Southeast Asia and Africa, exporting a mobile-first financial model. On the other hand, rapid expansion has led to regulatory volatility, data privacy concerns, and the rise of monopolistic platforms. The ease of accessing microloans has contributed to growing personal debt, particularly among younger demographics, raising questions about consumer protection and digital literacy. The Chinese experience offers vital lessons for other emerging economies. It shows how TechFins can scale rapidly by leveraging existing digital ecosystems, but also underscores the need for robust regulation to ensure market stability and consumer protection. Strong infrastructure, including digital identity systems and cloud-based services, plays a pivotal role in scaling financial access. Regulatory foresight, such as the use of sandboxes, is essential to balancing innovation with systemic safety. Above all, a diverse ecosystem that includes startups, infrastructure providers, and large tech players ensures resilience and sustained innovation.

In conclusion, China's FinTech evolution – from basic payment facilitation to comprehensive AI-powered ecosystems – serves as a pioneering example of how financial services can be transformed through technology. Ant Group's trajectory illustrates the complex interplay between innovation, market dynamics, and regulation in shaping digital finance. While the model offers a blueprint for other nations, it also serves as a cautionary tale on the risks of unregulated growth. For policymakers, industry leaders, and researchers, China's case highlights the transformative potential of FinTech when guided by user-centric innovation and adaptive governance.

Case Discussion Questions

1. How did China's unique combination of market size, technological infrastructure, and regulatory flexibility contribute to the rapid evolution of FinTech from 1.0 to 3.5, and what implications does this have for other emerging economies?
2. In what ways do TechFins like Ant Group and Tencent differ from traditional financial institutions and FinTech startups in terms of business models, risk exposure, and regulatory challenges?
3. Considering the suspension of Ant Group's IPO and the introduction of the Digital Yuan, how should governments balance innovation and financial inclusion with the need for regulatory control and systemic stability in the digital finance ecosystem?

Keywords

- **Financial technology (FinTech):** The use of technology to deliver financial services in innovative, efficient, and accessible ways, transforming traditional banking, insurance, lending, and investment systems.
- **FinTech 1.0 – 3.5:** A historical timeline representing the evolution of FinTech, from early digitization of finance (1.0), the rise of online banking and e-commerce (2.0), to mobile apps, AI, and decentralized technologies in recent phases (3.0–3.5).
- **TechFin:** Large technology companies (like Google, Amazon, or Alibaba) are entering the financial services space by leveraging user data, cloud infrastructure, and digital platforms.

- **Startups (FinTech startups):** Small, agile, and innovation-driven companies that develop niche financial services, often disrupting traditional financial institutions.
- **Infrastructure providers:** Companies or platforms that offer the technological foundation for FinTech services, such as APIs, cloud computing, digital identity, and payment gateways.
- **Financial inclusion:** The process of ensuring access to appropriate financial products and services to all individuals – especially the underserved and unbanked – in a fair and affordable manner.
- **Digital wallet:** An application or software-based system that allows individuals to store, send, and receive money electronically using a smartphone or other device.
- **Regulatory sandbox:** A controlled environment where FinTech companies can test their innovations under a regulator's supervision without immediately being subject to full regulatory obligations.
- **Peer-to-peer (P2P) lending:** A form of direct lending between individuals or businesses through digital platforms, bypassing traditional financial intermediaries like banks.
- **Digital divide:** The gap between individuals who have access to modern information and communication technology (like the internet and smartphones) and those who do not.

Discussion Questions

1. Describe the key differences between FinTech 2.0 and FinTech 3.0.
2. What are the main categories in the typology of FinTech?
3. How do TechFins differ from traditional FinTech startups?
4. Discuss two major challenges FinTech faces in emerging economies.
5. Analyze the role of India Stack in transforming India's FinTech landscape.
6. Explain how blockchain technology is impacting the FinTech industry.
7. What are the regulatory challenges faced by FinTech companies worldwide?

8. Discuss the significance of open banking in FinTech development.
9. How is artificial intelligence transforming financial services within FinTech?
10. Identify the key factors driving FinTech growth in developing countries.

References

[1] Accenture. (2023). *The future of FinTech: Disruptive technologies and new business models.*

[2] Arner, D. W., Barberis, J. N., & Buckley, R. P. (2022). *The evolution of FinTech: A new post-crisis paradigm?* In D. Lee Kuo Chuen (Ed.), *Handbook of Blockchain, Digital Finance, and Inclusion* (pp. 491–507). Elsevier.

[3] Alt, R., Beck, R., & Smits, M. T. (2018). FinTech and the transformation of the financial industry. *Electronic Markets, 28*(3), 235–243. https://doi.org/10.1007/s12525-018-0310-9

[4] Baur, D. G., & Lucey, B. M. (2019). FinTech: The financial sector's digital transformation. *Financial Analysts Journal, 75*(3), 20–29.

[5] BIS Innovation Hub. (2024). *FinTech typologies and regulatory technology frameworks.* Bank for International Settlements. https://www.bis.org

[6] Chen, H., & Huang, Y. (2020). FinTech and financial inclusion: The role of digital financial services. *World Economic Review, 12*(2), 76–94.

[7] Deloitte. (2024). *FinTech 3.5: Global reconfiguration of financial innovation ecosystems.* https://www2.deloitte.com

[8] Dorfleitner, G., Utz, S., & Wimmer, M. (2017). Sustainable and responsible FinTech: A conceptual framework and exploration of two cases. *Journal of Business Ethics, 155*(2), 463–481.

[9] European Banking Authority (EBA). (2022). *The digital transformation of financial services: Opportunities and risks* [Report].

[10] Gomber, P., Kauffman, R. J., Parker, C., & Weber, B. W. (2018). On the FinTech revolution: Interpreting the forces of innovation, disruption, and transformation in financial services. *Journal of Management Information Systems, 35*(1), 220–265.

[11] Haddad, C., & Hornuf, L. (2019). The emergence of the global FinTech market: Economic and technological determinants. *Small Business Economics, 53*(1), 81–105. https://doi.org/10.1007/s11187-018-9991-x

[12] Klein, M., & Pearce, R. (2021). Digital banking and innovation in FinTech: Challenges and opportunities. *Banking & Finance Review, 13*(4), 89–101.

[13] McKinsey & Company. (2024). *FinTech in Asia: Scaling new heights.* https://www.mckinsey.com

[14] Mehta, K., Sharma, R., & Yu, P. (2023). *Revolutionizing financial services and markets through FinTech and blockchain.* IGI Global.

[15] QED Investors & BCG. (2023). *The future of FinTech: 2023 and beyond.* https://www.bcg.com/publications/2023/the-future-of-fintech

[16] Sahay, R., & Saha, S. (2022). FinTech and digital payments in India: A regulatory perspective. *Reserve Bank of India Bulletin.*

[17] Vardhan, H. (2023). *FinTech in India: A practitioner's guide to developments and regulatory frameworks.* Oxford University Press.

[18] World Bank Group. (2023). *FinTech and the future of finance in Africa.* https://documents.worldbank.org

5

Key Players in FinTech

Abstract

This chapter delves into the evolving landscape of key stakeholders shaping the FinTech ecosystem. It explores the dynamic roles played by FinTech startups and technology providers, who are at the forefront of introducing disruptive innovations that redefine customer experience, efficiency, and financial inclusion. The narrative highlights how traditional financial institutions – such as banks, insurance firms, and NBFCs – are undergoing strategic digital transformations to remain competitive, often through partnerships, acquisitions, or in-house innovation initiatives. A major focus of the chapter is the complex relationship between established financial incumbents and emerging FinTech players, where competition and collaboration coexist. While startups drive agility and customer-centric solutions, traditional institutions bring scale, trust, and regulatory experience to the ecosystem.

The chapter analyzes these synergies and tensions, offering case studies and examples of collaborative FinTech models such as Banking-as-a-Service (BaaS), co-lending platforms, and embedded finance. To cement learning, the chapter integrates practical exercises encouraging readers to map the FinTech stakeholder environment, examine real-world alliances, and reflect on evolving business models. Ultimately, this chapter provides a comprehensive understanding of the ecosystem's main actors and how their interplay continues to redefine the financial services industry in a digital-first world.

Introduction

The FinTech ecosystem, an abbreviation for "Financial Technology," has undergone a radical transformation over the past two decades, fueled by technological innovation, regulatory support, and evolving consumer preferences. At the heart of this transformation lies a complex interplay of key players

DOI: 10.1201/9788743811244-7

who together shape the direction and dynamism of the sector. These stakeholders range from traditional financial institutions to cutting-edge startups, from regulatory bodies to technology providers, each playing a critical role in redefining financial services for the digital era. The FinTech ecosystem today consists of both emerging startups and well-established financial institutions driving innovation [1]. Startups and technology providers act as the key disruptors by introducing AI, blockchain, and analytics in financial processes [2]. These firms, free from legacy systems, are creating niche solutions that enhance accessibility and improve customer experiences [3].

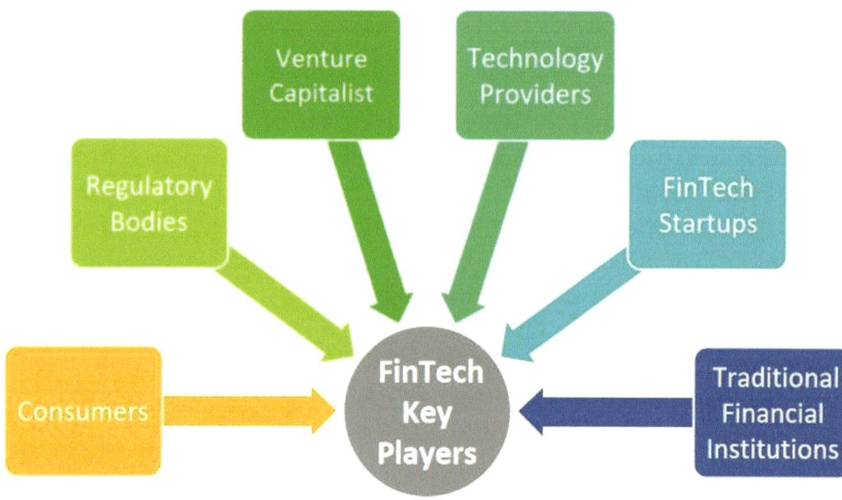

Figure 5.1 Key players in FinTech.

5.1 Startups and Technology Providers in the FinTech Ecosystem

The FinTech ecosystem is a complex and collaborative space where multiple stakeholders interact to shape the future of financial services. Major technology giants and payment firms like Mastercard are also entering the FinTech and crypto space, expanding competition [4]. The diagram titled "Key Players and Dynamics" visually represents six critical participants in the FinTech landscape and illustrates the multidirectional relationships and flow of influence between them. These six players are: (1) traditional financial institutions, (2) FinTech startups, (3) regulatory bodies, (4) technology providers, (5) consumers, and (6) venture capitalists and angel investors.

5.1.1 Traditional financial institutions

Traditional financial institutions like banks, insurance companies, and non-banking financial corporations (NBFCs) serve as the foundation of the financial system. In the FinTech ecosystem, these institutions are no longer isolated; they are deeply interconnected with newer digital players. Traditional institutions often collaborate with FinTech startups to modernize legacy systems, digitize services, and reach underserved markets. The diagram shows these institutions feeding into the ecosystem, indicating both their influence and their dependence on emerging technologies and partnerships for relevance and innovation.

5.1.2 FinTech startups

FinTech startups are agile, innovation-driven firms that develop digital solutions for banking, payments, insurance, lending, and wealth management. These startups are shown at the heart of the diagram's rightward flow, highlighting their role in driving technological change and challenging established norms. They benefit from capital and tech support while influencing customer expectations and financial models. The ecosystem encourages them to not only disrupt but also partner with traditional banks and integrate with regulatory and tech frameworks to scale their operations responsibly.

5.1.3 Regulatory bodies

Regulatory agencies ensure that all financial activities, whether by traditional banks or FinTech firms, adhere to legal, ethical, and security standards. They play a balancing role – enabling innovation while protecting consumers and the economy. In the diagram, their leftward arrow suggests that they exert a strong influence on how other players, especially FinTechs and technology providers, operate. At the same time, regulators must adapt to the evolving landscape by updating laws around digital identity, cryptocurrency, data privacy, and cross-border transactions.

5.1.4 Technology providers

Technology providers, such as cloud service firms, cybersecurity companies, and API developers, act as enablers of digital transformation. Their presence on the right side of the diagram reflects their role in powering the core infrastructure that FinTechs and traditional banks use. Whether through artificial intelligence (AI), blockchain, Internet of Things (IoT), or data analytics, tech providers create the tools and platforms that facilitate innovation. Their dynamic with FinTech startups is particularly strong, as most new-age financial solutions are built on tech-enabled services.

5.1.5 Consumers

Consumers, both individual and business users, are central to the FinTech revolution. Their expectations for faster, cheaper, and more user-friendly services fuel the demand for innovation. Represented by a leftward arrow, consumers impact the design and evolution of financial products. Their behavior, feedback, and adoption patterns drive FinTech startups to continuously improve offerings. Moreover, digital literacy and trust are crucial here; if consumers feel insecure or overwhelmed, adoption drops, making user experience and education a vital part of the ecosystem.

5.1.6 Venture capitalists and angel investors

Finally, the financial backing of the FinTech world largely comes from venture capitalists (VCs) and angel investors. Shown at the top of the diagram with a rightward arrow, they provide the funding required for startups to build, test, and scale their platforms. These investors assess not just profitability but also innovation potential and regulatory viability. Their support accelerates FinTech growth but also introduces performance expectations that can shape business models and timelines.

The diagram clearly illustrates that the FinTech ecosystem is not a linear supply chain but a **dynamic, multidirectional network** of players. Each stakeholder – be it a regulator or investor, a startup or a bank – contributes to and benefits from the others. Their interactions are shaped by technological advancements, regulatory shifts, market needs, and funding availability. Understanding these relationships is essential for anyone studying or entering the FinTech industry, as collaboration and adaptability are the key forces that define success in this space.

In a nutshell, the FinTech ecosystem is a multifaceted and collaborative network of players, each contributing to the sector's dynamism in unique ways. From nimble startups to robust incumbents, from tech behemoths to regulatory stewards, and from infrastructure enablers to strategic investors, the FinTech landscape thrives on synergy, competition, and innovation. As financial services continue to digitalize, the interactions and evolution of these players will determine the shape of global finance in the decades to come.

Fintech startups

FinTech startups are the trailblazers of innovation in the financial services sector. Born in the digital age, these agile, tech-driven firms aim to solve long-standing inefficiencies and gaps in traditional financial systems by leveraging disruptive technologies. Unlike legacy institutions, FinTech startups operate with lean structures, customer-centric models, and rapid innovation cycles, allowing them to adapt quickly to market demands and regulatory changes. These startups typically focus on niche areas within the financial services spectrum, such as digital payments, peer-to-peer lending, robo-advisory, blockchain solutions, regtech (regulatory technology), neobanking, and micro-insurance. For instance, Razorpay in India has revolutionized digital payments for SMEs, while Robinhood in the U.S. has democratized stock trading for retail investors through commission-free platforms. Their strength lies in their ability to offer personalized, accessible, and frictionless services, often through mobile-first platforms that cater to tech-savvy millennials and Gen Z customers.

Figure 5.2 Top 16 FinTech startups in USA. (2022)
Source:https://startuptalky.com/usa-fintech-startups/

Key characteristics:

- **Agile and innovative**: They adopt rapid development cycles, allowing them to launch and test new financial products quickly.
- **User-centric**: FinTech startups often prioritize user experience, offering simplified interfaces, seamless onboarding, and personalized services.
- **Digital-first**: Most operate entirely online or through mobile apps, minimizing the need for physical branches.

- **Specialized services**: Many focus on specific functions such as digital payments (e.g., Razorpay, Stripe), peer-to-peer lending (e.g., LendingClub), robo-advisory (e.g., Betterment), or cryptocurrency trading (e.g., CoinDCX, Coinbase).

Impact:

- Empower consumers with more choices and control over their finances.
- Increase competition and drive innovation in the financial sector.
- Help boost financial inclusion by reaching underbanked populations.

One of the standout features of FinTech startups is their use of alternative data and predictive analytics. For example, startups in the lending space may assess creditworthiness using behavioral data, mobile phone usage patterns, or e-commerce transaction histories, thereby enabling credit access for the underbanked or unbanked populations. In regions with limited access to formal banking, such as parts of Southeast Asia or Sub-Saharan Africa, these models provide financial inclusion at scale. FinTech startups also serve as incubators for new business models, such as the Buy Now, Pay Later (BNPL) trend, pioneered by firms like Klarna and Afterpay, or the rise of embedded finance, where financial services are seamlessly integrated into non-financial platforms (e.g., loans offered at the point-of-sale in e-commerce). However, these startups face challenges as well. Scaling operations, complying with complex and evolving regulatory environments, building consumer trust, and maintaining cybersecurity are all significant hurdles. Despite this, their role in pushing boundaries, accelerating digital transformation, and fostering financial democratization makes them indispensable actors in the FinTech ecosystem.

Technology providers

Technology providers form the digital backbone of the FinTech revolution. While FinTech startups focus on customer-facing innovation, technology providers enable and sustain the infrastructure on which these innovations are built. They are the architects of scalability, security, and speed in financial technology. At the core of this group are cloud service providers, such as Amazon Web Services (AWS), Google Cloud Platform (GCP), and Microsoft Azure. These platforms allow FinTech firms to deploy applications rapidly, handle massive datasets, ensure uptime, and scale globally without needing extensive physical infrastructure. Cloud-native architectures also enhance flexibility, cost-efficiency, and data-driven innovation, making them crucial to the success of both startups and established players.

Figure 5.3 Top trends for tech providers 2022.
Source: https://siliconangle.com/2022/05/08/top-trends-driving-technology-providers- 2022/

In addition to cloud platforms, cybersecurity firms play a vital role. As FinTech deals with sensitive financial and personal data, ensuring data privacy and protection against fraud, hacking, and breaches is non-negotiable. Companies like Palo Alto Networks, McAfee, and CrowdStrike provide next-generation firewalls, endpoint protection, and threat intelligence services to safeguard digital financial operations. API developers and integration platforms are also key enablers. FinTech thrives on open banking and interconnectivity, where different systems and services can communicate seamlessly. Companies like Plaid and MuleSoft provide APIs that allow FinTech apps to securely connect with banks, credit bureaus, and payment gateways. This interconnection is foundational to enabling services like real-time payments, automated personal finance tools, and multi-account management dashboards.

Key characteristics:

- **Cloud computing platforms**: Such as Amazon Web Services (AWS), Microsoft Azure, or Google Cloud, which host and scale FinTech applications.
- **Cybersecurity solutions**: Ensuring safe digital transactions, protecting data, and preventing fraud (e.g., Palo Alto Networks, FireEye).
- **Payment gateways and APIs**: Enabling digital payments, wallet integration, and banking-as-a-service (e.g., Visa, Mastercard, PayU).
- **AI and data analytics tools**: Helping with credit scoring, fraud detection, and personalized financial recommendations.
- **Core banking solutions**: Firms like Infosys Finacle, Temenos, and FIS offer core banking software for digital transformation.

Impact:

- Enable fast, secure, and scalable operations.

- Bridge the technological gap for traditional banks entering the digital space.
- Help startups reduce infrastructure costs and time-to-market.

Another subset of technology providers includes blockchain infrastructure firms, such as Consensys, Ripple, or Chainalysis, which facilitate decentralized finance (DeFi), smart contracts, and secure transaction validation. These players are essential in enabling trustless systems, reducing transaction costs, and improving transparency, especially in cross-border finance.

Artificial intelligence (AI) and machine learning (ML) solution providers are increasingly important as well. They offer tools for predictive modeling, fraud detection, chatbots, robo-advisors, and automated underwriting. AI-based decision engines are being used to assess risk, tailor financial advice, and deliver personalized customer experiences. Firms like DataRobot, H2O.ai, and various SaaS AI platforms help FinTechs build and deploy such models efficiently. Furthermore, payment infrastructure providers like Visa, Mastercard, Stripe, and Adyen offer foundational services for enabling online transactions, tokenization, merchant onboarding, and compliance with global payment standards (e.g., PCI DSS). These technology providers are integral to the functioning of e-commerce and digital wallets, and often act as the glue connecting merchants, banks, and customers. Collectively, technology providers may not always be visible to the end user, but they are the silent enablers of FinTech innovation. Their tools, platforms, and systems empower startups and institutions alike to deliver seamless, secure, and scalable financial solutions. By ensuring operational resilience, real-time capabilities, and continuous innovation, they help drive the evolution of digital finance in a sustainable and compliant manner.

In essence, startups and technology providers play complementary roles in the FinTech ecosystem. While startups innovate at the edge, delivering customer-centric products that challenge traditional norms, technology providers build and maintain the robust infrastructure that enables these innovations to scale, remain secure, and comply with regulatory demands. Together, they form the innovation core and operational spine of the digital finance revolution, transforming how individuals and businesses access, use, and manage financial services in the 21st century.

5.2 Traditional Financial Institutions in the FinTech Ecosystem

Traditional financial institutions such as commercial banks, cooperative banks, insurance companies, non-banking financial companies (NBFCs), and legacy investment firms – have long been the pillars of the global financial system. Historically characterized by centralized operations, manual processes, and hierarchical decision-making structures, these institutions are undergoing a profound transformation in the wake of the FinTech revolution. Far from becoming obsolete, they are evolving into hybrid players that blend conventional finance with cutting-edge technology, thereby emerging as formidable actors in the FinTech ecosystem. Initially, the rise of FinTech startups posed an existential threat to traditional institutions. Agile, customer-focused, and unburdened by legacy systems, these startups began attracting a growing share of tech-savvy consumers with intuitive interfaces, faster services, and lower costs. Recognizing the disruptive potential, traditional financial institutions gradually shifted from resistance to collaboration and adaptation. Today, many banks and insurance firms actively integrate digital innovations into their operations, either through internal digitization, strategic partnerships, or investments in FinTech ventures. Traditional financial institutions are increasingly investing in digital transformation and open banking to remain relevant [5]. Bureaucratic structures and legacy systems often hinder innovation within bank-led FinTech initiatives [6]. Despite these limitations, large banks are adopting new technologies and collaborations to sustain competitiveness [7]. The rise of generative AI in finance is further reshaping operations, risk management, and customer interaction in traditional banks [8].

Figure 5.4 Traditional banks vs FinTech.
Source: https://www.scnsoft.com/finance/fintech

5.2.1 Internal digital transformation

One of the most significant contributions of traditional institutions to the FinTech landscape is their own digital overhaul. Many banks have launched innovation labs, digital-only branches, and AI-driven platforms to enhance customer experience and reduce operational inefficiencies. For example, JPMorgan Chase developed Contract Intelligence (COiN), an AI platform that analyzes legal documents, while Wells Fargo launched an AI-powered chatbot within its mobile banking app. In India, ICICI Bank and HDFC Bank have heavily invested in digital banking platforms and mobile apps that rival those of FinTech startups.

These institutions now embrace cloud computing, , big data analytics, and cybersecurity solutions to optimize internal workflows and minimize human error. The adoption of digital Know Your Customer (KYC) processes, e-signatures, and paperless loan processing are just a few examples of how legacy institutions are aligning with FinTech best practices.

5.2.2 Collaborations with FinTech startups

Rather than competing outright, many traditional players have adopted a collaborative approach, forming alliances with FinTech startups to co-create value. These partnerships often involve white-labeled services, platform integrations, or joint ventures. For instance, Goldman Sachs partnered with Apple to launch the Apple Card, combining Goldman's banking infrastructure with Apple's tech ecosystem. In India, State Bank of India (SBI) has partnered with several startups to enhance digital payments, lending, and customer analytics.

Such collaborations allow banks to quickly integrate innovative services without undergoing complete structural overhauls, while startups gain access to large customer bases, compliance expertise, and funding support. This model of open innovation is increasingly facilitated by open banking regulations, which mandate that banks expose certain data and infrastructure to third-party developers via application programming interfaces (APIs). This fosters a collaborative ecosystem where traditional banks become platform enablers rather than isolated service providers.

5.2.3 Investments and acquisitions

Traditional institutions are also becoming active investors in FinTech startups. Through corporate venture arms and innovation funds, banks and insurance companies acquire equity in promising startups, ensuring early access to disruptive technologies. Examples include Citi Ventures, HSBC Ventures, and American Express Ventures, which routinely invest in FinTech companies operating in areas such as blockchain, cybersecurity, and payments. In some cases, traditional firms pursue full acquisitions to absorb FinTech capabilities directly into their business models. For instance, Goldman Sachs acquired personal finance startup Clarity Money to enhance its digital consumer banking offerings under the Marcus brand. These investments not only foster innovation but also accelerate the digital transformation of incumbent institutions.

5.2.4 Role in financial inclusion and trust building

Despite the rise of digital-native competitors, traditional financial institutions still hold a crucial advantage in terms of customer trust, regulatory compliance, and systemic stability. Their longstanding reputations, physical branch networks, and established risk management frameworks make them uniquely positioned to bridge the trust gap in emerging FinTech services – particularly in economies where informal financial practices dominate. Moreover, they are key enablers of financial inclusion when empowered with FinTech tools. For example, Indian banks have leveraged the Unified Payments Interface (UPI) and Jan Dhan-Aadhaar-Mobile (JAM) trinity to extend basic financial services to rural and unbanked populations. With government support, traditional institutions have deployed digital banking kiosks, biometric authentication systems, and microcredit products tailored to underserved segments, thus playing a pivotal role in inclusive growth.

5.2.5 Regulatory alignment and risk governance

Another area where traditional institutions add substantial value to the FinTech ecosystem is in regulatory alignment and risk management. Having operated under strict regulatory scrutiny for decades, these institutions possess deep expertise in areas such as anti-money laundering (AML), capital adequacy, data privacy, and consumer protection. As FinTech companies mature and expand, they often struggle with the compliance burden – a gap that traditional banks can help bridge through shared service models or advisory roles.

Additionally, traditional institutions are often the first point of call for regulators when formulating FinTech policies and sandboxes. Their insights and historical data play an essential role in designing frameworks that balance innovation with systemic stability. In many regions, regulators are encouraging "TechFin" – where technology is embedded into financial services offered by regulated entities – as a safer path to digital transformation.

In sum, traditional financial institutions have reinvented themselves as active and strategic players in the FinTech ecosystem. No longer bound by legacy thinking, these institutions are embracing digital innovation through internal transformation, partnerships with startups, venture investments, and new service models. They bring to the table a powerful combination of scale, compliance strength, customer trust, and capital resources, enabling them to serve as both stabilizers and accelerators in the digital finance revolution. Rather than being eclipsed by FinTech startups, traditional institutions are now co-architects of the future of finance, blending the credibility and governance of legacy banking with the agility and innovation of modern technology. As the FinTech ecosystem matures, their role will continue to evolve from service providers to platform curators, ecosystem enablers, and digital transformation leaders, making them indispensable in shaping the next frontier of global financial services.

5.3 Collaboration and Competition: The Dual Dynamics in the FinTech Ecosystem

In the evolving FinTech ecosystem, collaboration and competition are not mutually exclusive but rather coexisting forces that drive innovation, shape market dynamics, and redefine traditional financial relationships. These dual dynamics – sometimes termed as "coopetition" – underscore the nuanced and strategic interactions among various FinTech stakeholders, including startups, traditional financial institutions, BigTech firms, technology providers, and regulators. Together, these interactions influence the pace and direction of financial innovation across the globe. Collaboration between FinTech startups and banks combines agility with financial strength and consumer trust [9]. These partnerships are redefining the industry by creating hybrid models that merge innovation with regulation [10]. Digital lending, AI-based scoring, and blockchain-based payments are key examples of FinTech–bank collaborations [11]. The global shift toward blockchain-enabled financial ecosystems illustrates how partnerships enhance efficiency [12]. In India, FinTech collaborations have expanded financial inclusion and digital access at an unprecedented rate. Traditional banks are also responding to FinTech competition through innovations like deferred payment solutions [13].

5.3.1 Collaboration: Building synergistic alliances

Collaboration in the FinTech landscape is increasingly seen as a strategic imperative rather than a mere option. The complexity of digital transformation, evolving customer expectations, and stringent regulatory requirements compel diverse players to **join forces and leverage each other's strengths**.

5.3.2 Startups and traditional financial institutions

One of the most common forms of collaboration is between **FinTech startups and incumbent banks**. While startups bring agility, innovation, and cutting-edge technology, traditional banks offer trust, scale, regulatory expertise, and access to vast customer bases. These collaborations are often structured as:

White-label partnerships: where banks offer FinTech-developed solutions under their brand (e.g., robo-advisory, mobile wallets).

API integrations: enabling startups to plug into banks' core systems for real-time data exchange (e.g., account aggregation, payments).

Joint ventures: forming new digital platforms that combine the best of both worlds.

For instance, Axis Bank's partnership with FinTech startup FreeCharge allowed the bank to tap into the growing youth market through digital wallets and payments. Globally, BBVA's acquisition of Simple (a neobank) reflected a trend of traditional players embedding digital DNA through FinTech partnerships.

5.3.3 FinTech and BigTech collaborations

BigTech firms such as Google, Amazon, Facebook, and Apple increasingly collaborate with FinTechs to extend financial services to their user bases. Through embedded finance, these platforms integrate FinTech solutions like lending, insurance, or payments directly into their apps. For example:

Apple Card (Apple + Goldman Sachs)

Google Pay partners with various Indian banks for digital lending

Amazon Lending collaborates with FinTech underwriters and banks

These collaborations allow FinTechs to scale rapidly, while BigTech platforms deepen customer engagement and expand into financial services.

5.3.4 Cross-sector collaborations

FinTech also fosters cross-industry collaboration, such as between telecommunications companies, insurance providers, and financial institutions. In Africa, M-Pesa – a mobile money service – grew through partnerships between Safaricom (a telecom operator) and financial institutions, revolutionizing payments and financial inclusion.

Regulator–FinTech collaboration

Regulators are no longer mere overseers but **enablers of innovation**. Through **regulatory sandboxes**, open banking mandates, and innovation hubs, they collaborate with FinTechs to test new models in a controlled environment. This fosters mutual learning, ensures customer protection, and allows agile policy adaptation.

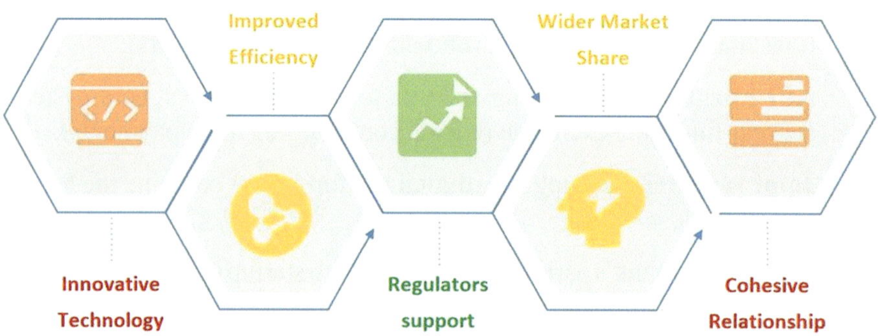

Figure 5.5 Advantages of FinTech collaboration.

Competition: Driving innovation and market realignment

While collaboration fosters growth, competition fuels transformation. FinTech startups often enter markets with the goal of disrupting traditional models – offering better user experience, faster services, and cost efficiency. This disruption forces incumbents to reassess their strategies and adopt digital-first approaches.

Startups vs traditional institutions

Many FinTech startups position themselves as **challengers to banks**, particularly in areas such as:

Digital lending (e.g., LendingClub, Kabbage)

Payments (e.g., Paytm, PhonePe)

Personal finance management (e.g., Mint, YNAB)

WealthTech and robo-advisory (e.g., Wealthfront, Zerodha)

These firms compete by leveraging data analytics, automation, and intuitive design, which often outperform traditional players on speed and personalization.

Neobanks vs legacy banks

Neobanks – fully digital banks with no physical branches – pose a direct challenge to traditional banking models. They provide seamless user experiences, zero-fee banking, and app-based interfaces. In markets like the UK and India, players like Monzo, Revolut, and Jupiter have rapidly gained traction, particularly among younger demographics.

BigTech as financial competitors

BigTech firms, with their vast ecosystems, data access, and technological prowess, are fast becoming competitors in financial services. For example:

Amazon Pay competes in the payments domain.

Google's digital banking partnerships threaten traditional deposit models.

Facebook's Novi project aimed at digital currency-based transactions.

These firms often bypass traditional channels, embedding financial services into user journeys in e-commerce, social media, or communication platforms, thus blurring the boundaries between sectors.

Tech providers entering financial services

Technology firms that once served financial institutions are now entering the market as direct competitors. For example, Stripe, initially a payments infrastructure provider, now offers loans and business banking features. This vertical integration allows tech firms to move up the value chain and capture larger revenue shares.

Coopetition: The emerging norm

The FinTech ecosystem is now defined by "coopetition" – a blend of cooperation and competition. Institutions may compete in one domain while collaborating in another. For example, two banks might partner to build a shared blockchain infrastructure for settlements while competing fiercely in retail lending. This hybrid model reflects the modular nature of FinTech, where value chains are unbundled and rebundled through APIs, platforms, and alliances. It allows:

Shared risk and innovation through consortia (e.g., R3 blockchain alliance)

Cost efficiencies through pooled infrastructure (e.g., shared KYC utilities)

Faster go-to-market strategies through ecosystem partnerships

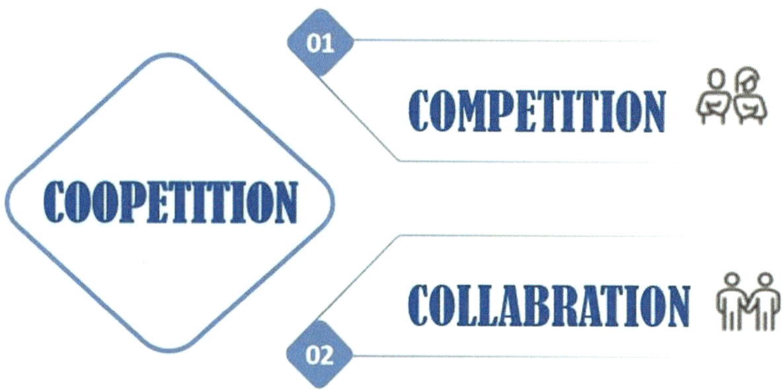

Figure 5.6 Coopetition.

In a nutshell, collaboration and competition are not opposing forces, but complementary mechanisms that shape the FinTech ecosystem's evolution. Collaboration enables access to capabilities, compliance, and customers, while competition drives differentiation, efficiency, and innovation. The most successful FinTech players – whether startups, banks, or BigTechs – are those that navigate this duality strategically, forming alliances where beneficial and competing when necessary. As FinTech matures, this dual dynamic will deepen, resulting in a convergent ecosystem where players co-create, co-exist, and co-compete to redefine the future of finance. Recognizing and embracing this complexity is essential for policymakers, entrepreneurs, and investors aiming to thrive in the digital financial era.

5.3.5 Overview of strategic FinTech collaborations: Apple, Google, and Amazon

In the rapidly evolving financial services industry, BigTech firms such as Apple, Google, and Amazon have ventured into financial services not by becoming banks themselves, but through strategic collaborations with traditional financial institutions and FinTech providers. These partnerships exemplify how digital platforms are reshaping the delivery of financial products by embedding them within technology-driven ecosystems. Each initiative, like Apple Card, Google Pay Lending, and Amazon Lending, illustrates a unique approach to bridging technology and finance.

Summary

Chapter 5 explores the major stakeholders that are shaping the FinTech revolution. It begins by highlighting the role of startups and technology providers, which are at the forefront of innovation. These agile players leverage advanced technologies such as AI, blockchain, and mobile platforms to disrupt traditional financial services and deliver more efficient, personalized solutions. In Section 5.2, the chapter examines how traditional financial institutions are responding to this disruption. While these incumbents have the advantage of scale, customer trust, and regulatory experience, they face challenges such as legacy systems and slow innovation cycles. Many are now investing in digital transformation to modernize their operations and compete effectively in a digital economy. Finally, the next section discusses the complex landscape of collaborations and competition between FinTech startups and traditional institutions. The concept of "coopetition" has emerged, where partnerships and strategic alliances are formed alongside market rivalry. Initiatives like open banking, API integration, and regulatory sandboxes are enabling these collaborations, driving innovation while managing risk. Overall, this chapter emphasizes that the future of finance is being shaped by a dynamic ecosystem where diverse players must work together, adapt continuously, and innovate responsibly to meet evolving customer needs and technological possibilities.

Caselet 1: Apple Card – A Strategic Collaboration Between Apple and Goldman Sachs

Overview:
Launched in August 2019, the Apple Card represents a pioneering collaboration between Apple Inc., a global BigTech leader, and Goldman Sachs, a major Wall Street investment bank. This partnership marks Apple's entry into financial services and Goldman Sachs' foray into consumer banking at scale.

Key features:

- A digital-first credit card built directly into the Apple Wallet on iPhones.
- Offers real-time transaction alerts, AI-powered financial insights, and Daily Cash rewards.
- Emphasizes data privacy – Apple does not know where the user shopped or what they bought.
- Goldman Sachs handles underwriting, customer support, and transaction processing.

Apple leverages its massive iOS user base and design ecosystem, while Goldman Sachs brings banking infrastructure, regulatory compliance, and risk expertise. The Apple Card stands out for its lack of fees, intuitive budgeting tools, and seamless user experience, made possible by the tight integration of finance and technology. Apple rapidly gained a share of the U.S. credit card market, particularly among millennials and digital natives. Goldman Sachs acquired millions of new retail customers, reinforcing its brand in consumer banking via the Marcus by Goldman Sachs initiative.

Caselet 2: Google Pay – Partnerships with Indian Banks for Digital Lending

Overview:
In India's booming digital payments ecosystem, Google Pay has emerged as a leading player. Moving beyond payments, it has partnered with Indian financial institutions to offer digital lending services through its app, leveraging UPI infrastructure, data analytics, and user trust. Main partners were HDFC Bank, ICICI Bank, Kotak Mahindra Bank, and Federal Bank, among others. In this partnership, Google Pay acts as a technology interface, facilitating pre-approved instant loans via bank partners. The process is paperless and entirely digital, with loan offers pushed through Google Pay based on customer profile and transaction history. Banks remain the lenders of record, managing credit risk, disbursement, and recovery.

Banks tap into Google's massive distribution channel, especially among India's growing digital-savvy population. Google enhances customer engagement by offering value-added financial services, without taking on credit risk. The model supports financial inclusion, offering easy access to microloans and short-term credit. Banks benefit from lower acquisition costs and real-time creditworthiness insights based on behavioral and transactional data.

Caselet 3: Amazon Lending – FinTech-Enabled Working Capital for Sellers

Overview:
Launched in 2011, Amazon Lending is a B2B initiative aimed at providing working capital loans to small and medium-sized businesses (SMBs) that sell on the Amazon marketplace. Rather than acting as a full-fledged bank, Amazon partners with banks and FinTech underwriters to deliver financing.

Key features:

- Loans are typically short-term, ranging from $1,000 to $750,000.
- Sellers are pre-qualified based on sales data, inventory levels, and platform behavior.
- Loan repayment is automated, deducted from future sales on Amazon.

Goldman Sachs: Partnered with Amazon to offer loans via the Marcus platform to selected merchants. Lendistry and other FinTech firms have worked with Amazon to offer microloans to underrepresented business owners. In India, Amazon has worked with Capital Float and IDFC First Bank to facilitate seller financing. Amazon utilizes its data analytics to assess creditworthiness without traditional credit scores. Financial partners manage loan disbursement, compliance, and underwriting. The offering strengthens seller loyalty and boosts sales on the platform by reducing liquidity constraints. Thousands of SMBs across the U.S., UK, India, and Japan have accessed credit through Amazon. The model reduces friction in supply chains, particularly for e-commerce sellers who need quick inventory restocking.

Table 5.1 Cross-case insights.

Aspect	Apple Card	Google Pay Lending	Amazon Lending
Primary player	Apple	Google	Amazon
Financial partner(s)	Goldman Sachs	ICICI, HDFC, Kotak, Federal Bank	Goldman Sachs, Capital Float, IDFC, etc.
Target audience	Retail iPhone users	Indian digital payment users	Amazon marketplace sellers
Product type	Credit card	Personal digital loans	Working capital loans
Delivery mode	iPhone Wallet + physical card	Google Pay app	Amazon Seller Central + APIs
Risk management	Bank handles underwriting	Bank handles risk and disbursement	FinTechs/banks handle underwriting
Innovation edge	Seamless UI, privacy, rewards	UPI integration, data-driven loan offers	Sales-data-based credit evaluation

These caselets show how BigTech companies are redefining finance through embedded partnerships, combining scale, data intelligence, and customer engagement with banking and regulatory expertise. This fusion of strengths illustrates the coopetition model that now defines the global FinTech landscape.

Case Study: Mobile Payments In Retail – Apple Pay, Google Pay, and Paytm

Sarah, a small business owner running a boutique retail shop in a bustling urban marketplace in India, caters primarily to tech-savvy millennials and urban professionals. With the increasing demand for digital and contactless payment options, she decided to upgrade her existing point-of-sale (POS) system to accommodate mobile payments. Her objective was to enhance customer experience, reduce checkout times, and increase overall sales conversions, particularly during peak hours. After initial research, Sarah narrowed her choices to three widely adopted mobile payment platforms: Apple Pay, Google Pay, and Paytm. Her decision required balancing customer preferences, infrastructure costs, transaction speed, and security. Apple Pay and Google Pay utilize Near Field Communication (NFC) technology, allowing customers to make payments by tapping their smartphones against an NFC-enabled POS terminal. This system provides a fast and seamless transaction process where customers authenticate the payment through biometric verification, such as facial recognition or fingerprint scanning. These platforms offer several advantages. First, they ensure rapid and convenient checkouts without the need to enter PINs or sign receipts. Second, they provide advanced security through tokenization, which substitutes sensitive card information with a secure token, thereby reducing fraud risk. Third, both platforms are globally recognized, offering seamless compatibility with international cards, which is beneficial for tourists and global customers. Lastly, the contactless nature of NFC transactions promotes hygiene and speed – attributes highly valued in the post-COVID retail environment.

Despite their advantages, NFC-based systems also pose certain challenges. Device compatibility remains a major barrier, as Apple Pay and Google Pay require smartphones with NFC capabilities, potentially excluding customers with older or budget phones. Additionally, implementing NFC-enabled terminals may incur significant costs for small merchants, particularly those operating with limited capital or in regions where digital infrastructure is still evolving.

In contrast, Paytm offers a QR code-based payment system that allows customers to scan the merchant's QR code using the Paytm mobile app and instantly complete the transaction. This approach has gained immense popularity in India due to its simplicity and accessibility. One of the major advantages of Paytm is its low setup cost – merchants only need a smartphone and a printed or digital QR code to begin accepting payments. Furthermore, its intuitive interface makes it user-friendly for both merchants and customers, especially in semi-urban and rural markets where NFC-enabled devices are not widespread. Moreover, Paytm's role in enhancing financial inclusion in India has been significant, enabling small vendors and rural merchants to adopt digital payments without investing in expensive POS infrastructure.

However, Paytm also presents its own set of limitations. The platform requires both the merchant and the customer to have the specific Paytm app, which restricts flexibility when compared to more universally accepted NFC-based systems. Additionally, QR code transactions depend heavily on stable internet connectivity, which may be unreliable in remote or densely populated areas.

After weighing the pros and cons of each system, Sarah determined that using a combination of payment methods would best suit her customer base. In her urban setting, where many customers own modern smartphones and demand speed, Apple Pay and Google Pay provide a high-quality digital experience. For local walk-in customers, especially those from surrounding areas who are more familiar with Paytm, a QR code system ensures inclusivity and ease of access. By integrating both NFC and QR-based options, Sarah can offer flexibility and convenience, thereby optimizing sales and customer satisfaction.

This case emphasizes the importance of choosing the right digital payment system in retail based on the demographic and technological readiness of the target audience. It also underlines how FinTech can play a transformative role in improving the retail payment experience, even for small business owners.

Challenges faced:

- Device compatibility: NFC-based systems require smartphones with specific hardware, potentially excluding customers with older or non-smart devices.
- Infrastructure cost: Upgrading to NFC-enabled POS systems can be expensive for small businesses.
- Limited app dependency: QR-based systems like Paytm require specific apps, which may limit customer flexibility.
- Internet dependency: QR code systems are sensitive to internet availability, which can cause transaction delays in areas with poor connectivity.

Case Discussion Questions:

1. What are the main differences in infrastructure and user requirements between NFC-based systems and QR code-based payment systems?
2. How do mobile payment solutions like Apple Pay, Google Pay, and Paytm influence customer purchasing behavior in urban retail environments?
3. In what ways can small businesses benefit from adopting multiple digital payment options instead of relying on a single method?
4. How does tokenization in NFC payments enhance transaction security for both merchants and customers?
5. What are the broader implications of mobile payment adoption on financial inclusion in emerging markets like India?

Keywords

- **FinTech startups:** New and agile companies using technology to disrupt traditional financial services by offering faster, cheaper, or more innovative solutions.
- **Technology enablers:** Companies that supply critical technological infrastructure (cloud services, AI tools, cybersecurity platforms) to support FinTech operations.
- **Digital-only banks (Neobanks):** Banks that operate entirely online without physical branches, offering simplified and low-cost banking solutions.
- **Payment gateways:** Technology platforms that facilitate online transactions between customers and merchants, often integrated with FinTech apps.
- **Peer-to-peer (P2P) lending platforms:** Online platforms that connect borrowers directly with individual lenders, bypassing traditional banks.
- **InsurTech:** A subset of FinTech startups focusing on innovating the insurance industry through technology like AI-driven underwriting and usage-based pricing.
- **Legacy banks:** Well-established banks with long histories, extensive branch networks, and traditional operating models.
- **Financial intermediaries:** Institutions (like banks, insurance firms, and brokers) that act as middlemen between savers and borrowers or buyers and sellers.
- **Digital transformation units:** Internal departments within traditional banks focused on modernizing technology, improving customer experience, and fostering innovation.
- **Core banking systems:** Back-end systems used by banks to process daily transactions and manage accounts. Many legacy institutions are modernizing these for better agility.
- **Incumbents:** Established financial firms that face disruption from newer, more agile FinTech entrants.

- **Coopetition:** A strategic blend of cooperation and competition where FinTechs and traditional banks partner for mutual gain while still competing in certain areas.
- **Open banking:** A regulatory framework and practice that allows third-party developers to access banking data through APIs, promoting innovation and customer choice.
- **Strategic alliances:** Formal partnerships between FinTechs and financial institutions to co-develop new services, share technology, or expand market reach.
- **Acquihire:** A strategy where larger firms acquire FinTech startups primarily to gain access to their talent and technical expertise rather than their products.
- **Embedded finance:** Integration of financial services into non-financial platforms (e.g., payments in e-commerce apps), enabled through collaboration between FinTechs and various businesses.
- **Regulatory sandboxes:** Controlled environments created by regulators where FinTech firms can test new products or services under relaxed regulatory conditions.
- **API economy:** An ecosystem where APIs enable seamless collaboration between banks and FinTechs, allowing real-time service integration and innovation.

Discussion Questions

1. How are FinTech startups redefining customer expectations in the financial services industry?
2. What advantages do technology providers bring to the FinTech ecosystem, and how do they shape innovation?
3. Why are neobanks gaining popularity among younger users, and what risks do they face in scaling up?
4. What barriers do traditional banks face in keeping pace with FinTech innovation?
5. How are traditional financial institutions using digital transformation to stay competitive in a FinTech-driven market?

6. In what ways can traditional banks leverage their strengths (e.g., customer base, trust, compliance experience) to compete with FinTechs?
7. Do collaborations between FinTechs and banks lead to genuine innovation or are they just survival tactics?
8. What are the key factors that determine whether a FinTech-bank collaboration will be successful?
9. How is the concept of "coopetition" reshaping the competitive dynamics of the financial sector?
10. What role do regulatory sandboxes play in encouraging responsible innovation and collaboration in FinTech?

References

[1] Gomber, P., Kauffman, R. J., Parker, C., & Weber, B. W. (2018). *On the FinTech revolution: Interpreting the forces of innovation, disruption, and transformation in financial services. Journal of Management Information Systems, 35*(1), 220–265. https://doi.org/10.1080/07421222.2018.1440766

[2] Mehta, K., Sharma, R., & Yu, P. (2023). *Revolutionizing Financial Services and Markets through FinTech and Blockchain.* IGI Global.

[3] Chishti, S., & Barberis, J. (2016). *The FinTech Book: The Financial Technology Handbook for Investors, Entrepreneurs and Visionaries.* Wiley.

[4] Business Insider. (2025, March). *How Mastercard is building the Venmo of crypto.* Business Insider.

[5] Stefanelli, V., Manta, F., & Toma, P. (2022). *Digital financial services and open banking innovation: Are banks becoming invisible?* arXiv.

[6] Financial Times. (2025, February). *Why bank-backed fintechs get stuck in corporate quicksand. FT.com.*

[7] PwC. (2022). *Financial services technology 2020 and beyond: Embracing disruption.* Retrieved from https://www.pwc.com

[8] Saha, B., Rani, N., & Shukla, S. K. (2025). *Generative AI in financial institutions: A global survey of opportunities, threats, and regulation.* arXiv.

[9] Arner, D. W., Barberis, J., & Buckley, R. P. (2016). *The evolution of FinTech: A new post-crisis paradigm. Georgetown Journal of International Law, 47*(4), 1271–1319.

[10] Arner, D. W., Barberis, J., & Buckley, R. P. (2022). *The evolution of FinTech: A new post-crisis paradigm?* In D. L. Chuen (Ed.), *Handbook of Blockchain, Digital Finance, and Inclusion* (pp. 491–507). Elsevier.

[11] Lee, L. (2024). *Enhancing financial inclusion and regulatory challenges: A critical analysis of digital banks and alternative lenders through digital platforms and ML integration.*

[12] World Economic Forum. (2021). *The Future of Financial Infrastructure: An Ambitious Look at How Blockchain Can Reshape Financial Services.* Retrieved from https://www.weforum.org

[13] Financial Times. (2025, April). *Big banks play catch-up with fintech start-ups in deferred payments. FT.com.*

6

Funding and Growth

Abstract

This chapter offers a comprehensive exploration of the financial lifelines that fuel innovation and expansion in the FinTech sector. It begins by outlining the diverse funding avenues accessible to FinTech enterprises, ranging from traditional sources such as venture capital, private equity, and angel investors to more strategic options like partnerships with incumbent financial institutions. The chapter emphasizes the critical role that early and growth-stage investments play in shaping a startup's trajectory, from product development to market entry and scale. Expanding on modern financing alternatives, the chapter delves into emerging models such as crowdfunding and peer-to-peer (P2P) lending. These democratized funding platforms not only empower startups to access capital outside conventional channels but also enable retail investors and communities to participate in FinTech innovation. The risks and regulatory implications of these models are also critically examined.

A major theme of the chapter is scaling – both the opportunities it presents and the inherent challenges it poses. Readers gain insight into common obstacles FinTech firms face while expanding, such as maintaining regulatory compliance across jurisdictions, managing complex technology infrastructure, and acquiring and retaining a growing customer base in a crowded market. The chapter underscores the importance of building sustainable growth models that balance innovation with sound governance, risk management, and strong investor relations. Ultimately, this chapter equips readers with the knowledge to navigate the financial and operational strategies essential for nurturing and expanding a successful FinTech venture in an increasingly competitive and regulated environment.

DOI: 10.1201/9788743811244-8

Introduction

This chapter explores the financial backbone that supports the development and expansion of FinTech startups. It begins by examining various FinTech funding channels, including venture capital, angel investors, corporate partnerships, and emerging models like initial coin offerings (ICOs) and government grants. The chapter then highlights the role of crowdfunding as a democratic and accessible way for startups to raise capital directly from the public, often leveraging online platforms to pitch innovative ideas. It also discusses peer-to-peer (P2P) lending, which enables individuals to borrow and lend money without traditional financial intermediaries, offering both funding solutions and alternative investment opportunities. Finally, the chapter delves into the strategies for scaling up a FinTech startup, emphasizing the importance of building customer trust, achieving regulatory compliance, managing growth risks, and forming strategic alliances. Altogether, the chapter provides a comprehensive overview of how FinTech firms secure capital and scale sustainably in a competitive market.

6.1 FinTech Funding Channels

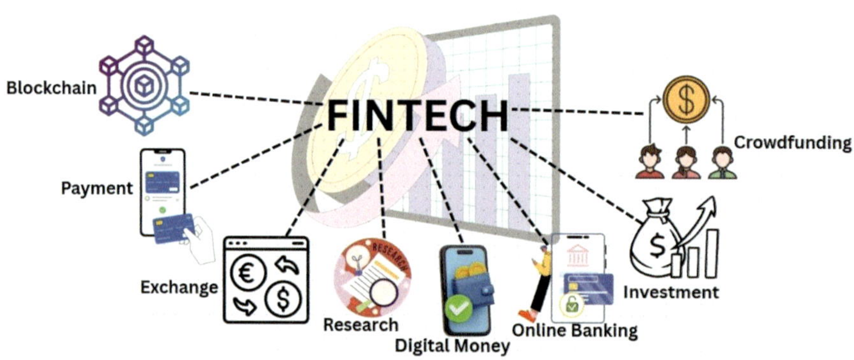

Figure 6.1 Fintech funding channels.

FinTech funding channels refer to the various sources through which financial technology startups and firms secure capital to develop, scale, and innovate their products and services. These channels range from traditional methods like venture capital (VC) and private equity to more modern approaches such as crowdfunding, initial coin offerings (ICOs), and corporate investments from established financial institutions. Angel investors also play a key role in providing early-stage funding, while government grants and incubator programs support innovation in regions promoting digital finance. In recent years, strategic partnerships with banks and tech giants have emerged as hybrid funding avenues, offering not just capital but also market access and technological expertise.FinTech firms today rely on hybrid funding sources, including venture capital, private equity, and corporate investment partnerships [1]. The integration of digital ecosystems has transformed traditional financing into scalable, data-driven growth strategies [2]. Scaling FinTech companies demand balancing innovation speed with operational efficiency and compliance [3]. Firms like Stripe illustrate how funding innovation drives global financial expansion and digital infrastructure growth [4]. Institutional investors and regulators increasingly shape FinTech's funding landscape through policy and stability frameworks [5]. The continuous inflow of capital from mergers, acquisitions, and global investors sustains market momentum [6].

Table 6.1 FinTech funding channels.

Funding type	Purpose	Examples
Seed funding	Early idea development	Angel investors, incubators
Venture capital (VC)	Scaling product and operations	Series A, B+, corporate VC arms
Private equity and growth funding	Expansion, acquisitions	PE firms, growth equity funds
Strategic partnerships	Innovation via collaboration	Tech giants (e.g., Apple, Google)
Crowdfunding	Community-driven capital	SeedInvest, Kickstarter
IEOs and STOs	Blockchain-based fundraising	Token sales via crypto platforms
Debt financing	Non-equity capital with repayment	Venture debt, convertible notes
Government/public funding	Innovation and inclusion Grants	EU grants, SBIR programs

The choice of funding channel often depends on the FinTech firm's stage of growth, business model, regulatory environment, and long-term vision. These diverse funding options have contributed significantly to the rapid expansion of the FinTech sector globally.

6.1.1 Seed funding

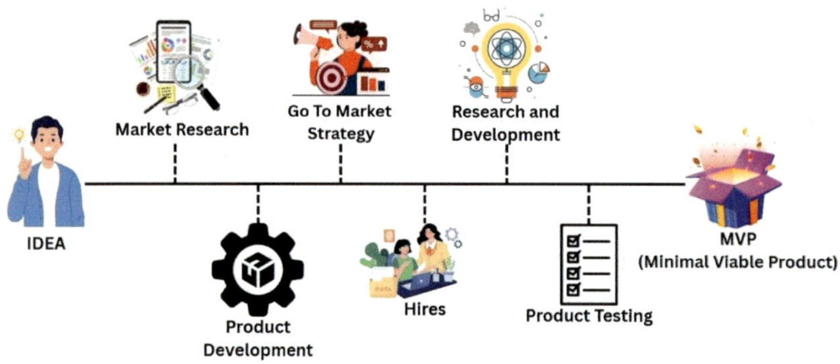

Figure 6.2 Process of seed funding.

Initial capital to develop an idea or product, often from personal savings, friends, or angel investors.

Sources:

- **Angel investors**: High-net-worth individuals providing early-stage capital.
- **Friends and family**: Personal networks supporting the startup.
- **Accelerators/incubators**: Programs offering initial funding, mentorship, and resources (e.g., Y Combinator, Techstars).
- **Seed funds**: Venture funds focusing on early-stage investments.

6.1.2 Venture capital (VC) funding

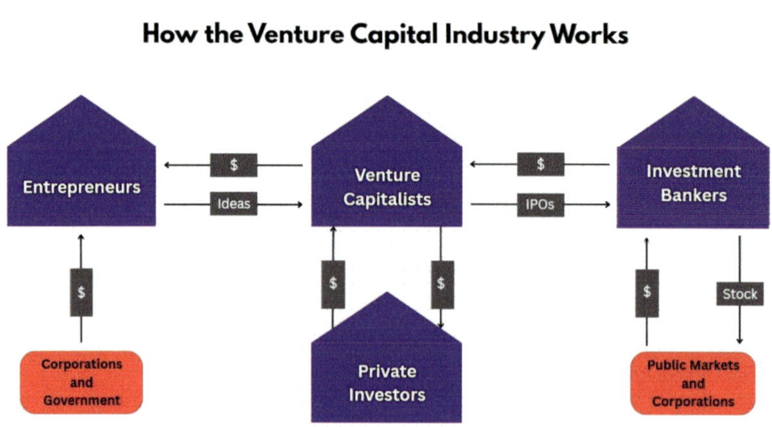

Figure 6.3 Working of venture capital industry.

Stages:

Series A: Funding to optimize product, grow user base, and scale operations.

Series B and beyond: Larger investments to expand market reach, develop new products, or acquire competitors.

Sources:

- **Venture capital firms**: Specialized funds investing in high-potential startups.
- **Corporate venture arms**: Corporations investing strategically in FinTech innovations (e.g., Goldman Sachs, Citi).
- **Institutional investors**: Large entities like pension funds or endowments seeking high-growth opportunities.

6.1.3 Private equity and growth funding

Later-stage funding for established FinTech companies aiming for expansion, mergers, or acquisitions.

Sources:

- **Private equity firms:** Focused on raising funds from institutional investors such as pension funds, insurance companies, sovereign wealth funds, and high-net-worth individuals.
- **Growth equity funds**: Focused on scaling proven business models.

6.1.4 Strategic partnerships and corporate investments

Investments by big FinTech or financial institutions seeking strategic synergies.

Examples:

- Banks investing in FinTech startups.
- Technology giants (e.g., Google, Apple) investing or partnering for innovation.

6.1.5 Crowdfunding and community funding

- **Equity crowdfunding**: Raising capital from a large group of investors via online platforms (e.g., Seed Invest, Crowd cube).
- **Rewards and donation-based**: Less common for FinTech but may be used for niche projects.

6.1.6 Initial exchange offerings (IEOs) and security token offerings (STOs)

- **Description**: Token-based fundraising leveraging blockchain technology.
- **Applications:** Fintech projects, especially in crypto, looking to raise capital directly from the community without traditional intermediaries.

6.1.7 Debt financing

- **Venture debt**: Loans extended to startups, typically after initial funding rounds.
- **Convertible notes**: Debt that converts into equity at a later stage.
- **Bank loans and credit facilities**: For more mature FinTech firms with proven revenue streams.

6.1.8 Government and public funding

- **Grants and subsidies**: Provided by government agencies for innovation and tech development.
- **Public funding programs**: e.g., European Union grants, US Small Business Innovation Research (SBIR) program.

6.2 Crowdfunding

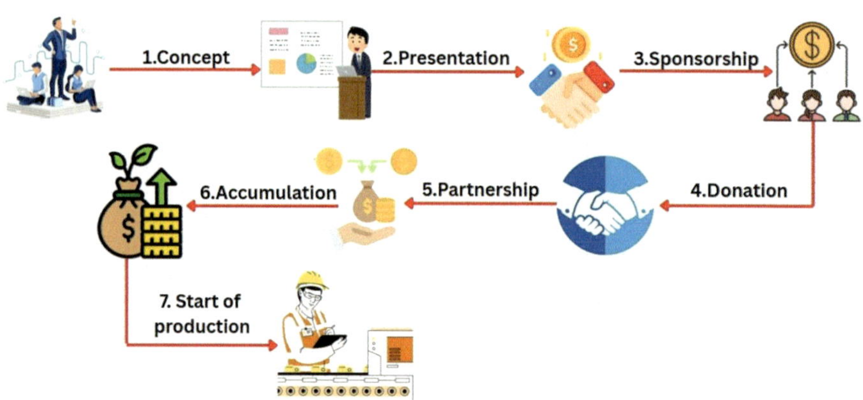

Figure 6.4 Process of crowdfunding.

Crowdfunding is a method of raising capital from a large number of individuals, typically via online platforms, where each contributor invests small amounts toward a project, startup, or venture. In other words, **Crowdfunding** is a modern fundraising model that allows startups, creative projects, social initiatives, and even FinTech ventures to raise small amounts of money from a large number of people, typically via online platforms. Unlike traditional funding methods that rely on institutional investors or banks, crowdfunding democratizes finance by giving everyday individuals the opportunity to contribute to causes or businesses they believe in. There are several types of crowdfunding, including **donation-based**, **reward-based**, **equity- based**, and **debt-based** models. For example, in equity crowdfunding, contributors receive ownership shares in the business, while in reward-based crowdfunding, they may receive early access to a product or exclusive perks. Platforms like Kickstarter, Indiegogo, and Crowdcube have gained popularity by offering streamlined, tech- enabled processes to connect fundraisers with global contributors. Crowdfunding not only provides capital but also validates business ideas by gauging public interest before launch. However, it also comes with challenges such as platform fees, regulatory restrictions, intellectual property risks, and the need for robust digital marketing to attract backers. Crowdfunding platforms democratize finance by connecting investors and entrepreneurs through digital channels [7]. Artificial intelligence enhances platform transparency, project evaluation, and investor protection in crowdfunding ecosystems [8]. Regulatory policies play a pivotal role in managing risks and maintaining credibility within crowdfunding markets [9]. Sustainable innovation in crowdfunding promotes inclusive growth and environmentally responsible investments [10].

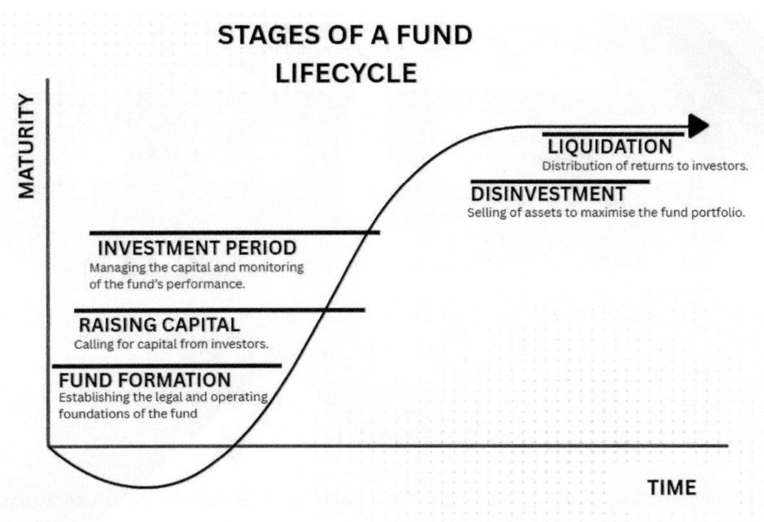

Figure 6.5 FinTech funding lifecycle.

6.2.1 Types of crowdfunding

Reward-based crowdfunding

- Contributors receive non-monetary rewards such as products, services, or experiences.
- Example platforms: Kickstarter, Indiegogo.
- Common in innovative tech and consumer product sectors, including FinTech prototypes.

Equity crowdfunding

- Investors receive equity shares or a stake in the company.
- Suitable for startups seeking early-stage investment.
- Regulatory environment is more complex; platforms include Seed Invest, Crowd cube.

Debt-based crowdfunding (peer-to-peer lending)

- Investors lend money to businesses or individuals and earn interest.
- Runs as a marketplace connecting lenders and borrowers directly.

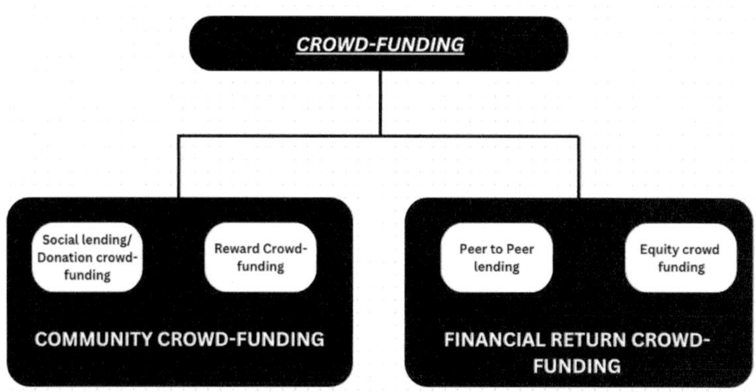

Figure 6.6 Crowdfunding models infographic.

6.3 Peer-To-Peer Lending (P2P Lending)

P2P lending, also known as **crowdlending**, is a form of debt crowdfunding where individuals lend money directly to borrowers via online platforms, passing through traditional financial institutions. **Peer-to-peer (P2P) lending**, on the other hand, is a type of alternative finance that connects individual borrowers and lenders through online platforms, eliminating traditional financial intermediaries like banks. In this model, investors can earn interest on their funds by lending directly to individuals or businesses, while borrowers often gain access to more competitive interest rates and faster approval times. Platforms like LendingClub, Prosper, and Funding Circle facilitate credit risk assessment, loan disbursement, and repayment management, often using proprietary algorithms and credit scoring technologies. P2P lending is particularly useful for individuals with limited access to conventional credit or small and medium-sized enterprises (SMEs) seeking quick funding. While the model offers flexibility and efficiency, it also carries significant risks such as borrower default, regulatory uncertainty, and platform solvency. To mitigate such risks, many platforms now offer diversified investment options, insurance-like protections, or tie-ups with institutional partners. Peer-to-peer lending transforms credit delivery by linking lenders and borrowers directly through online marketplaces [11]. FinTech credit channels bridge financial gaps while fostering inclusion and competition in credit markets [12]. Digital lending models expand accessibility and affordability for underserved populations in emerging economies [13]. New frameworks in digital finance and open regulation support sustainable growth of P2P platforms [14]. FinTech regulation ensures balance between innovation, consumer protection, and systemic stability [15]. The evolution of FinTech governance outlines future-oriented strategies for digital financial ecosystems [16]. Innovation and adaptability will define the next phase of FinTech-based lending transformation [17].

Overall, P2P lending represents a disruptive shift in how credit is accessed and distributed, emphasizing transparency, decentralization, and technology-driven decision-making.

6.3.1 Steps in P2P Lending Process

Registration on P2P platform

Both borrowers and lenders create accounts on a P2P lending platform (e.g., LendingClub, Funding Circle) and submit basic details.

Borrower application

Borrowers submit a loan request with the desired amount, purpose of the loan, and repayment term.

Credit assessment and risk profiling

The platform evaluates the borrower's creditworthiness using credit scores, income verification, and risk algorithms to assign an interest rate.

Loan listing for lenders

Approved loan applications are listed on the platform, where lenders can view details like borrower profile, loan purpose, and risk grade.

Lender investment

Lenders browse available loans and choose to fund them fully or partially. Multiple lenders can contribute to one loan (fractional lending).

Loan disbursement

Once the funding target is reached, the platform disburses the loan amount to the borrower's account after deducting any processing fees.

Repayment schedule

Borrowers repay the loan in monthly installments (including interest) as per the agreed schedule.

Return to lenders

The platform collects repayments and distributes the principal and interest to the lenders periodically.

Monitoring and recovery

The platform monitors repayments, handles delays or defaults, and may initiate recovery proceedings if necessary.

Features:

Interest rates: Generally attract higher returns for lenders compared to traditional savings accounts.

Loan terms: Typically 3–5 years.

Risk-reward: Investors face credit risk if borrowers default.

Popular platforms: Lending Club, Prosper (US), Funding Circle (UK), Mintos, Peer Berry (Europe)

Several prominent platforms have played a crucial role in shaping the global peer-to- peer (P2P) lending ecosystem by offering streamlined, tech-driven alternatives to traditional banking systems. In the United States, LendingClub and Prosper are among the earliest and most popular P2P lending platforms. LendingClub primarily connects individual investors with borrowers seeking personal loans, leveraging advanced credit risk models to match them efficiently. Prosper, another U.S.-based platform, focuses on unsecured personal loans and allows fractional investments, enabling lenders to diversify their portfolios across multiple borrowers to reduce risk.

In the United Kingdom, Funding Circle has emerged as a key P2P platform specializing in small and medium enterprise (SME) lending. It enables individual and institutional investors to lend directly to vetted businesses, supporting entrepreneurship and economic growth while offering competitive returns. Meanwhile, Europe hosts a range of dynamic P2P platforms such as Mintos and PeerBerry, which operate as loan marketplaces rather than direct lenders. These platforms aggregate loans from various originators across multiple countries, giving investors access to a wide array of consumer, car, and business loans. Their cross-border model, combined with buyback guarantees and risk ratings, has made them particularly attractive to retail investors seeking diversification and higher yields.

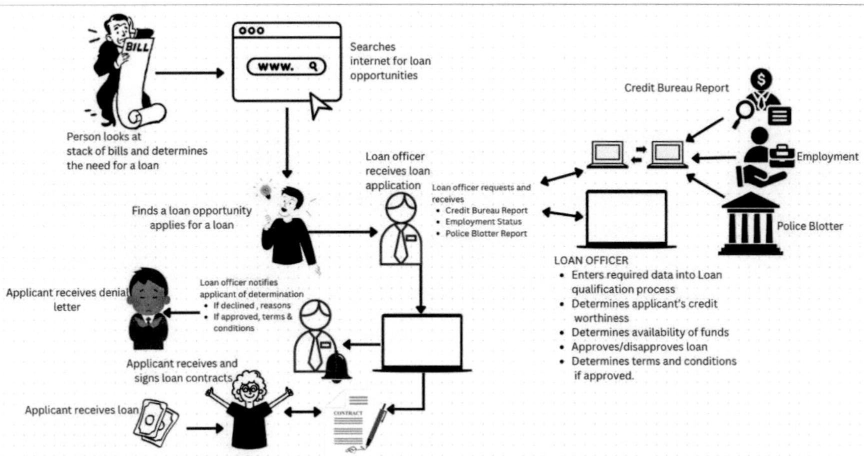

Figure 6.7 P2P lending workflow diagram.

Target borrowers:

Consumers (personal loans, credit card debt consolidation)

Small businesses seeking growth capital

Real estate projects

Advantages:

For lenders: Attractive returns, short investment cycles.

For borrowers: Faster approval, less stringent collateral requirements.

Democratizes access to credit and investment.

Risks:

Borrower default

Platform failure or insolvency

Regulatory changes impacting operation

Regulatory environment varies significantly across jurisdictions, typically regulated as financial service providers. Transparency and investor protection are key regulatory concerns. Both crowdfunding and P2P lending leverage technology to extend financial services. They enable inclusion by reaching underserved populations. Data analytics help in credit scoring and risk assessment.

6.3.2 Scaling up a FinTech startup – detailed notes

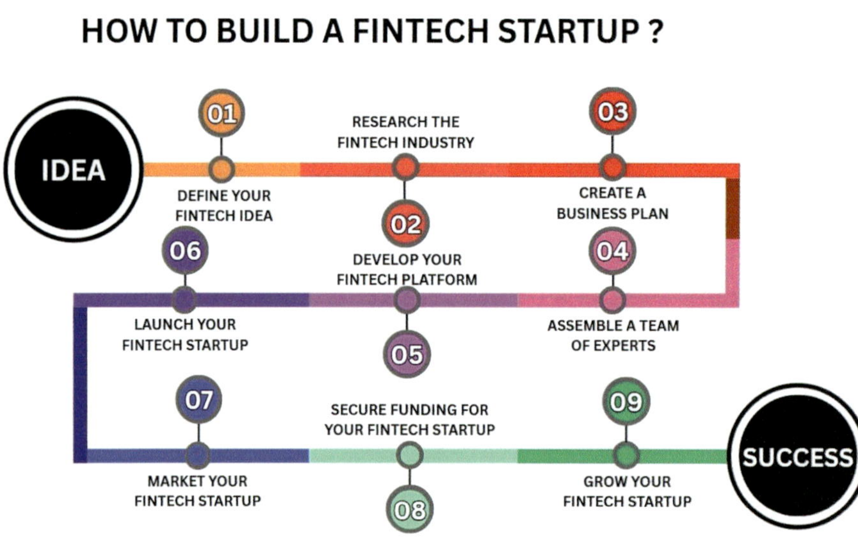

Figure 6.8 Process of building a FinTech startup.

Scaling up a FinTech startup refers to the process of expanding operations, customer base, revenue streams, and technological capabilities to transition from a small, early-stage venture to a robust, sustainable enterprise. Unlike traditional businesses, FinTech startups operate at the intersection of technology and finance, requiring them to balance rapid innovation with regulatory compliance, cybersecurity, and trust-building among users. The first step in scaling involves refining a scalable and compliant business model. FinTech startups must ensure their core technology infrastructure – such as payment gateways, lending algorithms, or robo-advisory tools – is reliable, secure, and adaptable to increasing volumes of transactions and user data. A strong backend infrastructure helps prevent system crashes, fraud, and data breaches as the business grows.

Funding is critical at this stage. Most FinTech startups seek Series A or B venture capital investments to fuel hiring, product enhancement, and marketing. Capital is also used to enter new geographies or develop adjacent services. For example, a startup offering digital wallets may expand into credit lending or investment management. However, scaling too quickly without a clear customer acquisition strategy or regulatory understanding can result in unsustainable growth and reputational risks. Regulatory compliance becomes more complex as a startup grows across borders or adds financial products. Startups must comply with financial laws, data protection standards (like GDPR), anti-money laundering (AML) rules, and know-your-customer (KYC) norms. Building legal and compliance teams or partnering with RegTech firms can mitigate these challenges.

Customer acquisition and retention are equally vital. Scaling requires not only increasing user numbers but also improving customer experience to ensure loyalty and reduce churn. FinTechs often leverage digital marketing, referral programs, and partnerships with banks or retailers to expand their reach. Finally, talent acquisition and organizational culture must evolve. As the team grows, leaders must implement structures that promote agility, innovation, and accountability. Strategic hires in technology, finance, compliance, and data science help the startup remain competitive and responsive to market demands. In essence, scaling up a FinTech startup is a multifaceted challenge that involves managing growth sustainably while maintaining trust, security, and regulatory alignment. Successful scaling transforms a promising startup into a market leader capable of reshaping financial ecosystems and delivering value at scale.

6.3.3 Key strategies for scaling a FinTech startup

Strengthen core infrastructure

Scaling requires a transition from MVPs or pilot systems to highly secure, scalable, and robust platforms. FinTech startups must invest in cloud computing for flexibility, automate operations like onboarding and compliance (KYC/AML), and integrate APIs for smoother partnerships and service delivery. Cybersecurity becomes non-negotiable to protect customer data and meet regulatory standards.

Ensure regulatory compliance and licensing

As startups grow into new markets, understanding local financial regulations becomes crucial. Securing licenses, implementing strong AML and KYC protocols, and maintaining data privacy in line with global standards (e.g., GDPR) is essential. Dedicated legal and compliance teams or partnerships with RegTech firms help in navigating this complexity.

Expand markets and customer segments

Geographic expansion should be data-driven, considering local financial infrastructure, culture, and regulatory conditions. FinTechs should also diversify their customer base – targeting individuals, SMEs, and enterprises – with customized solutions and localized marketing campaigns to deepen user engagement.

Diversify product offerings and innovate

Scaling is not just about doing more of the same. FinTechs must innovate by integrating emerging technologies like AI, blockchain, or machine learning. Feedback loops should guide product refinement, and customer-centric design should be prioritized to enhance satisfaction and retention.

Build strategic partnerships and secure funding

Collaborations with banks, payment processors, cloud providers, and retail players can open distribution channels and unlock new markets. Simultaneously, securing Series B/C funding is essential to support growth while ensuring strong financial management, profitability planning, and the hiring of top-tier talent across operations, compliance, and tech.

Challenges and risks during scaling

- **Regulatory and legal risks:** Navigating international compliance requirements and managing license acquisitions and legal reviews.
- **Operational risks:** Ensuring system reliability and security, and maintaining customer service quality during rapid growth.
- **Market risks:** Competitive responses and market saturation, and changing customer preferences.
- **Technological risks:** Data breaches, cyber-attacks, Platform downtime, and scalability issues.
- **Financial risks:** Overexpansion without sufficient revenue and dilution of ownership and control with new funding rounds.

Scaling a FinTech startup requires strategic planning, agility, stakeholder collaboration, and adherence to regulatory standards. It is a balance of harnessing innovation, expanding responsibly, and managing risks.

Summary

Chapter 6: Funding and Growth explores the financial backbone that supports the development and expansion of FinTech startups. It begins by examining various FinTech funding channels, including venture capital, angel investors, corporate partnerships, and emerging models like initial coin offerings (ICOs) and government grants. The chapter then highlights the role of crowdfunding as a democratic and accessible way for startups to raise capital directly from the public, often leveraging online platforms to pitch innovative ideas. It also discusses peer-to-peer (P2P) lending, which enables individuals to borrow and lend money without traditional financial intermediaries, offering both funding solutions and alternative investment opportunities. Finally, the chapter delves into the strategies for scaling up a FinTech startup, emphasizing the importance of building customer trust, achieving regulatory compliance, managing growth risks, and forming strategic alliances. Altogether, the chapter provides a comprehensive overview of how FinTech firms secure capital and scale sustainably in a competitive market.

Case Study: Stripe – A Global Blueprint For FinTech Funding and Growth

Stripe, founded in 2010 by Irish entrepreneurs Patrick and John Collison, has emerged as one of the most prominent FinTech companies in the world. Specializing in online payment processing for internet-based businesses, Stripe's evolution from a fledgling startup to a global financial infrastructure powerhouse exemplifies the strategic interplay between funding acquisition, technological innovation, and aggressive market expansion. Its growth narrative not only underscores the importance of timely capital infusion but also highlights how product innovation and ecosystem thinking can drive long-term success in FinTech.

The company's funding journey began with an impressive seed round between 2010 and 2012, in which it raised approximately $2 million from influential backers such as Y Combinator, Founders

Fund, and Sequoia Capital. This early capital allowed Stripe to refine its core offering – an intuitive and developer-friendly API that enabled seamless online payment integration. By 2014, Stripe had completed its Series B round, raising $70 million at a valuation of $1.4 billion. This phase focused on expanding the engineering team, improving fraud prevention systems, and launching initial efforts toward international market entry. The subsequent Series C round in 2015 added $80 million to its capital pool, with a sharper focus on scaling infrastructure and deepening its market reach.

In 2018, Stripe achieved a landmark with a Series D funding round worth $250 million, elevating its valuation to $35 billion. This capital surge supported Stripe's aggressive global expansion, including new product lines such as Stripe Capital (for small business lending), Stripe Issuing (to manage virtual and physical cards), and Stripe Treasury (banking-as-a-service offerings). One of the company's major milestones came in 2020 when it opted for a direct listing on the New York Stock Exchange, achieving a staggering valuation of approximately $95 billion, later crossing the $100 billion mark – making it one of the most valuable privately held tech companies globally.

Stripe's growth strategy was built on four key pillars. First, its commitment to global expansion was evident as it quickly extended its footprint from the U.S. into Europe, Asia, and Latin America, adapting to local currencies, compliance mandates, and payment preferences. Second, Stripe pursued product diversification, evolving from a single-purpose payment gateway into a comprehensive financial infrastructure platform offering merchant services, credit issuance, treasury management, and capital lending. Third, it prioritized robust, developer-centric technology by building customizable APIs and streamlined user experiences, which greatly enhanced its adoption rate across small startups and tech giants alike. Fourth, Stripe cultivated an open, innovation-driven ecosystem by partnering with major platforms like Shopify, Amazon, and Apple while also acquiring firms to enhance its capabilities in fraud detection, compliance, and global transaction processing.

As a result of these deliberate strategies, Stripe today processes billions of dollars in daily transactions and serves millions of companies across multiple continents. Its consistent success in securing large-scale funding rounds validated its reputation as a reliable and scalable FinTech innovator. Stripe's transformation from a niche U.S. startup to a global FinTech giant illustrates several key lessons: the impact of visionary leadership, the strategic deployment of capital, the importance of customer-centric innovation, and the value of early internationalization. Stripe's case continues to serve as a benchmark for FinTech startups seeking sustainable growth through technology, capital, and global thinking.

Case Discussion Questions

1. How did Stripe's developer-centric approach to product design contribute to its rapid adoption and funding success across different stages of its growth journey?
2. In what ways did Stripe strategically use its funding rounds to support diversification and international expansion, and what lessons can other FinTech startups learn from this sequencing of growth initiatives?
3. Considering Stripe's evolution into a global FinTech infrastructure provider, what are the potential risks and regulatory challenges it may face as it continues to scale, especially in non-U.S. markets?

Keywords

- **FinTech funding channels:** Various sources of capital – including venture capital, angel investment, and bank loans – used by FinTech startups to finance their growth and operations.
- **Crowdfunding:** A fundraising approach where small contributions from a large number of individuals are pooled, typically via online platforms, to support startups or projects.
- **Peer-to-peer (P2P) lending:** A form of debt financing that enables individuals to lend and borrow money directly without traditional financial intermediaries like banks.
- **Angel investor:** A high-net-worth individual who provides capital to early-stage startups in exchange for ownership equity or convertible debt.
- **Venture capital (VC):** A form of private equity financing provided by investors to startups and small businesses with long-term growth potential.

- **Initial coin offering (ICO):** A fundraising method used by blockchain-based companies where digital tokens are issued to investors in exchange for capital.
- **Scalability:** The ability of a startup or business model to grow in capacity and capability without proportionately increasing costs.
- **Burn rate:** The rate at which a startup spends its capital before generating positive cash flow or breaking even.
- **Exit strategy:** A planned approach by which investors or founders intend to liquidate their stake in a startup, typically through acquisition, IPO, or merger.
- **Regulatory compliance:** The process by which FinTech firms adhere to legal and financial regulations required by governing bodies, especially important as firms scale.

Discussion Questions

1. What are the primary factors driving the growth of FinTech companies today?
2. How does funding influence the development and scaling of FinTech startups?
3. What are the key challenges faced by FinTech firms during growth phases?
4. What are the common sources of funding for early-stage and growth-stage FinTech startups?
5. How do venture capital and private equity differ in their approach to FinTech funding?
6. What role do government grants and public money play in FinTech development?
7. How does crowdfunding differ from traditional financing methods?
8. What are the main risks and benefits associated with P2P lending for investors and borrowers?
9. How are regulatory frameworks shaping the development of crowdfunding and P2P lending?
10. What are the critical steps involved in scaling a FinTech business?

References

[1] Accenture. (2020). *Scaling Fintech: Strategies for Growth.*

[2] Lee, I., & Shin, Y. J. (2018). *Fintech: Ecosystem, business models, techniques and challenges. Business Horizons, 61*(1), 35–46.

[3] Renaud, G. (2018). *Scaling Fintech Companies: Challenges and Opportunities. Journal of Banking & Finance.*

[4] Stripe official resources. (2023). *Stripe's Funding Journey and Growth Strategy.*

[5] Allen, F., Carletti, E., & Claessens, S. (Eds.). (2021). *FinTech and Big Tech Finance: Implications for Financial Stability and Regulation.* CEPR Press.

[6] KPMG. (2022). *Pulse of Fintech H2 2022.*

[7] Montagne, F., & Bounaba, F. (2020). *Crowdfunding and Peer-to-Peer Lending: A Systematic Review. Journal of Business Venturing Insights.*

[8] Chishti, S., & Puschmann, T. (2023). *The AI Book: The Artificial Intelligence Handbook for Investors, Entrepreneurs and FinTech Visionaries.* Wiley.

[9] OECD. (2020). *Crowdfunding and the Regulatory Environment.* [OECD Report].

[10] Nassiry, D., & Pickering, J. (2023). *Innovating for Sustainability in FinTech: Pathways to Inclusive Growth.* Edward Elgar Publishing.

[11] Claessens, S., Frost, J., Turner, G., & Zamil, R. (2022). *FinTech Credit: Market Structure, Business Models and Financial Stability Implications.* International Monetary Fund Publications.

[12] Arner, D. W., Barberis, J., & Buckley, R. P. (2016). *The evolution of FinTech: A new post-crisis paradigm.* In D. L. Chuen (Ed.), *Handbook of Blockchain, Digital Finance, and Inclusion, Volume 1* (pp. 491–507). Academic Press.

[13] World Bank. (2021). *Fintech and Financial Inclusion.*

[14] Gomber, P., Klaus, T., & Siering, M. (Eds.). (2022). *Digital Finance and FinTech: Business Models and Regulation.* Palgrave Macmillan.

[15] Zetzsche, D. A., Buckley, R. P., Arner, D. W., & Barberis, J. N. (2020). *FinTech: Finance, Technology and Regulation.* Cambridge University Press.

[16] Puschmann, T. (Ed.). (2022). *FinTech and the Future of Finance.* Springer.

[17] Leong, C., & Sung, C. Y. (2023). *FinTech Innovation and the Future of the Financial Services Industry.* Routledge.

UNIT 3

Financial Institutions and Infrastructure

7

Banking and Non-Banking Systems

Abstract

This chapter delves into the dynamic transformation of the financial services landscape through the emergence of digital banking and the expanding role of non-banking financial companies (NBFCs). It begins by tracing the evolution of digital banking models, highlighting how technology is revolutionizing traditional financial institutions through increased efficiency, automation, and customer-centric innovation. The chapter explores new-age banking formats such as neobanks, virtual banks, and cloud-native platforms, which operate without physical branches but offer robust, app-based financial ecosystems tailored to modern consumer needs. A critical focus is placed on NBFCs, detailing their regulatory frameworks and financial functions within the broader economic system. These institutions play a pivotal role in promoting financial inclusion by serving credit-deficient and high-risk sectors such as microenterprises, rural populations, and low-income groups that often remain underbanked by traditional banks. Through their innovative lending models and risk tolerance, NBFCs contribute significantly to credit dispersion and economic democratization.

Furthermore, the chapter investigates the rapid rise and impact of mobile and online banking technologies. It analyzes how the integration of smartphones, APIs, and cloud infrastructure has enabled seamless, secure, and accessible banking experiences across user demographics. Special emphasis is placed on the evolving paradigms of cybersecurity, user authentication, and digital literacy that underpin trust in mobile and internet banking platforms. By interlinking advancements in both banking and non-banking systems, the chapter paints a comprehensive picture of a financial ecosystem in transition – shifting from legacy models to agile, technology-led frameworks. It invites readers to critically assess how regulatory clarity, customer trust, and technological innovation collectively shape the future of inclusive and resilient financial services.

DOI: 10.1201/9788743811244-10

Introduction

Chapter 7 focuses on the evolving landscape of banking and non-banking financial institutions (NBFCs) in the digital era. It begins with an exploration of digital banking models, which highlight how traditional banks are transforming through technology adoption, including fully digital banks, branchless banking, and hybrid models. The chapter then discusses the role of NBFCs, which have emerged as critical players complementing banks by offering flexible financial products and reaching underserved segments. Finally, it examines online and mobile banking, the primary channels driving customer convenience, financial inclusion, and real-time service delivery. This chapter provides a comprehensive understanding of the structural dynamics, innovations, and challenges shaping modern banking and NBFC sectors. The financial ecosystem today is evolving through technology-driven reforms that reshape both banking and non-banking structures [1].

7.1 Banking and Non-Banking System

The financial system of any country plays a crucial role in facilitating economic activities by enabling savings, investments, and credit flows. Traditionally, this system has been categorized into two primary components: **Banking financial institutions (BFIs)** and **non-banking financial institutions (NBFIs)**. In recent years, Financial Technology (FinTech) has emerged as a transformative force, reshaping the operations, outreach, and efficiency of both sectors. This chapter explores the structural features of banking and non-banking systems and analyzes the revolutionary role of FinTech in each. Banking financial institutions, commonly referred to as banks, are licensed entities authorized to accept public deposits and extend credit facilities. These institutions are regulated by a central monetary authority (such as the Reserve Bank of India or the Federal Reserve in the United States) and are essential for maintaining monetary stability and supporting financial intermediation. The banking system comprises institutions like commercial banks, cooperative banks, development banks, and central banks, which are regulated by a central authority (e.g., RBI in India, Federal Reserve in the US). They accept deposits, provide loans, and offer a range of financial services. The traditional banking system continues to be the cornerstone of financial intermediation and economic development [2]. Non-banking systems complement banks by offering alternative credit and financial services, often serving niche and underserved markets [3]. The Reserve Bank of India plays a pivotal role in regulating both banking and non-banking entities to maintain systemic stability [4]. The integration of FinTech innovation has bridged gaps between conventional banks and emerging financial intermediaries [5].

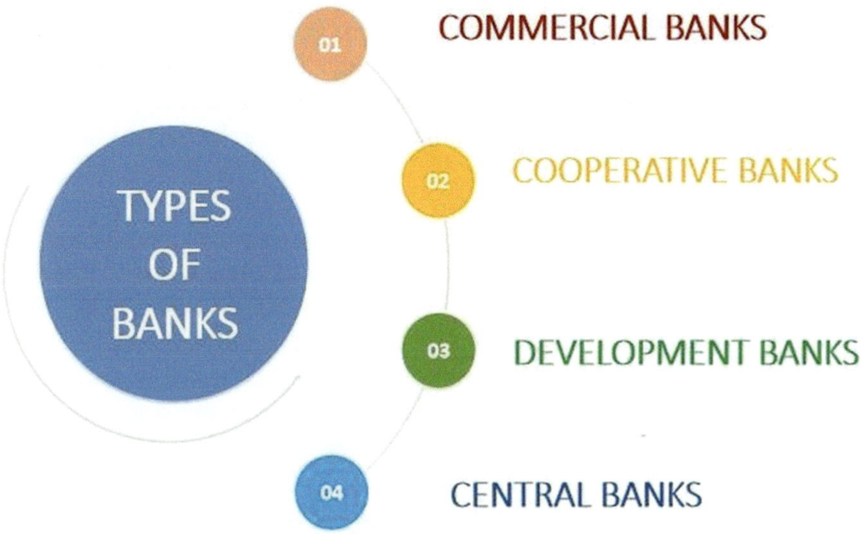

Figure 7.1 Types of banks.

7.1.1 Types of banks

Commercial banks

Commercial banks are financial institutions that offer a wide range of banking services to individuals, businesses, and the government. Their primary functions include accepting deposits, providing loans, issuing credit cards, and offering savings and checking accounts. They aim to earn profits through interest on loans and fees. Examples include State Bank of India (SBI), Bank of America, and HDFC Bank inIndia. These banks are regulated by the central bank of the country and operate under strict guidelines to ensure financial stability.

Development banks

Development banks are specialized financial institutions that provide long-term capital to support large-scale development projects. Their goal is not immediate profit but to promote economic development in sectors such as infrastructure, industry, and agriculture. They offer financial assistance in the form of loans, equity participation, or guarantees. Examples include NABARD (for agriculture and rural development) and SIDBI (for small industries in India). These banks play a crucial role in national growth and planning.

Cooperative banks

Cooperative banks are community-based financial institutions owned and operated by their members. These banks function on the principle of cooperation and mutual help. They primarily serve rural areas, farmers, small-scale industries, and low-income groups. Profits are usually reinvested into the community or shared among members. They are regulated by both the Reserve Bank of India (RBI) and state cooperative bodies. An example is a local agricultural cooperative bank that offers affordable loans to farmers.

Central bank

The central bank is the apex monetary authority of a country, responsible for managing the nation's currency, money supply, and interest rates. In India, the Reserve Bank of India (RBI) serves this role. The central bank regulates and supervises other banks, ensures financial stability, issues currency, manages foreign reserves, and formulates monetary policy. It does not deal directly with the public but acts as a banker to the government and commercial banks. For example: RBI, ECB, Federal Reserve.

7.1.2 Core functions of a bank

- Accepting savings, current, and fixed deposits
- Providing personal, commercial, and industrial loans
- Facilitating domestic and international payments
- Issuing debit and credit cards
- Offering wealth management and financial advisory services

7.1.3 Role of FinTech in banking

FinTech is revolutionizing the banking system through the integration of technology in financial services. Key innovations include:

- **Digital banking platforms**: Banks offer complete financial services through mobile apps and online portals.
- **Neobanks**: FinTech firms like Niyo and Jupiter provide digital-only banking services with streamlined onboarding.
- **Artificial intelligence (AI)**: Used for fraud detection, chatbots, risk assessment, and personalized services.
- **Open banking and APIs**: Allows third-party developers to build innovative services on top of banks' infrastructure.
- **Blockchain technology**: Improves transparency, speeds up cross-border transactions, and reduces settlement risk.

Non-banking financial companies (NBFCs)

Non-banking financial companies (NBFCs) refer to entities that offer financial services similar to those of banks but **do not hold a full banking license**. They are **not permitted to accept demand deposits**, yet play a vital role in credit distribution, especially in sectors underserved by traditional banks.

Key types of NBFCs

Types of NBFCs

Microfinance institutions (MFIs)

These NBFCs provide small loans (microloans) to low-income individuals or groups, especially in rural or semi-urban areas. They focus on financial inclusion for people who may not have access to traditional banking services.

Asset finance companies (AFCs)

AFCs specialize in financing physical assets such as vehicles, machinery, or equipment. They help individuals or businesses purchase capital goods by offering loans or lease financing.

Investment companies

These NBFCs primarily deal with acquiring and managing securities and investments such as shares, bonds, and other financial instruments. They earn income from interest, dividends, or capital gains.

Infrastructure finance companies (IFCs)

IFCs provide long-term financial support for large-scale infrastructure projects like roads, bridges, power plants, and airports. These companies are crucial for national economic development.

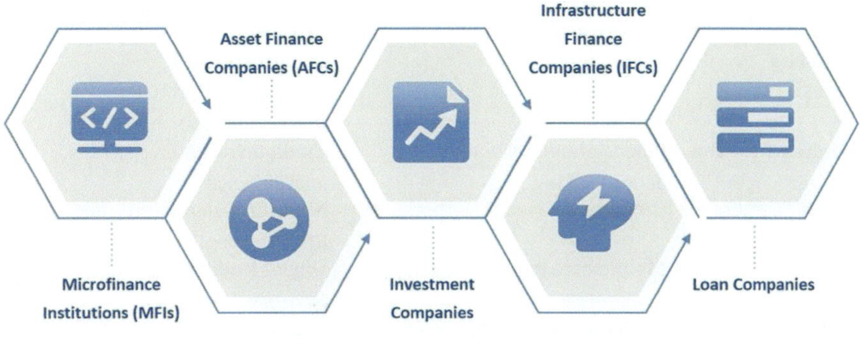

Figure 7.2 Types of NBFCs.

Loan companies

These are general-purpose NBFCs that offer loans and advances to individuals or businesses for various purposes, without accepting demand deposits like banks.

Traditional functions of an NBFC:

- Lending to individuals, SMEs, and corporates
- Financing consumer durables, vehicles, and housing
- Providing leasing and hire-purchase services
- Disbursing microloans and emergency credit
- Offering insurance and investment advisory services

FinTech innovations in NBFC:

FinTech has empowered the non-banking system in ways such as:

- **Digital lending**: NBFCs and FinTechs use alternative data (mobile usage, social profiles, utility bills) to assess credit risk and provide instant loans.
- **P2P lending platforms**: FinTechs like **Faircent** (India) directly connect borrowers with investors.
- **InsurTech**: Firms like **PolicyBazaar** provide comparison-based policy selection and digital claims processing.
- **Digital microfinance**: Apps like **Kiva** and **CreditMantri** reach underserved populations via mobile-first credit offerings.
- **WealthTech**: Robo-advisory platforms like **Groww** and **Zerodha** automate investment strategies and enable small-ticket investing.

Table 7.1 Banking and non-banking system.

Parameter	Banking institutions	Non-banking institutions
Regulatory authority	Central Bank (e.g., RBI)	RBI, SEBI, IRDAI (sector- specific)
Deposit taking	Permitted (demand and time deposits)	Mostly not allowed (except payment banks)
Primary function	Financial intermediation, deposit-taking	Credit delivery, investments, microfinance
Target segments	Broad-based (retail, corporate)	Niche or underserved (rural, MSMEs, youth)
FinTech integration	Mobile banking, chatbots, BaaS	Digital lending, P2P, robo-advisory, InsurTech
Flexibility and innovation	Moderate (high compliance)	High (light-touch regulations)

FinTech as the bridge between banking and NBFC

FinTechs increasingly act as a **bridge between banking and non-banking systems** by:

- Enabling **co-lending partnerships** between banks and NBFCs (e.g., digital loan disbursement through shared risk models)
- Creating **financial inclusion** by serving remote or low-income populations via smartphones
- Unbundling services (payments, credit, insurance) and delivering them through a modular, API-based architecture

Figure 7.3 FinTech as a bridge between bank and NBFC

The convergence of FinTech with banking and non-banking systems is transforming the financial ecosystem from a bank-centric model to a platform-centric model. In this new paradigm, Banks are evolving into Banking-as-a-Service (BaaS) providers, NBFCs, and FinTechs are leading innovation in customer acquisition, credit scoring, and last-mile delivery. Consumers benefit from faster, more personalized, and inclusive financial solutions. The distinction between traditional banking and non-banking systems is becoming increasingly blurred due to the FinTech revolution. While banks focus on compliance, stability, and full-spectrum services, non-banking entities – often supported by FinTech innovations – are driving inclusion, agility, and product innovation. Together with the integration of FinTech, these systems are building a more resilient, inclusive, and technologically advanced financial ecosystem.

Example of banking services: HDFC Bank's SmartHub: A Digital Suite for Small Business Banking, Payments, and Analytics

HDFC Bank's SmartHub is a digital platform designed to cater to the banking needs of small and medium-sized enterprises (SMEs), retailers, and entrepreneurs. It provides a comprehensive set of banking services, payment solutions, and analytics tools, aiming to simplify financial management for businesses.

Key features of SmartHub:

- **Payment solutions**: SmartHub enables businesses to accept payments through various channels, including QR codes, point-of-sale (POS) terminals, UPI, and online payment gateways. This flexibility allows businesses to serve customers through physical and digital mediums seamlessly.
- **Digital banking**: Businesses can manage their current accounts, access working capital loans, and make bulk payments through the platform. It also supports automated payroll processing.
- **Business analytics**: SmartHub provides SMEs with detailed financial analytics, offering insights into transaction patterns, cash flow management, and customer behavior. These insights help businesses optimize their operations and make data-driven decisions.
- **Invoicing and billing**: The platform enables business owners to generate invoices, track payments, and manage receivables easily. It also integrates with GST-compliant tools for tax filing and compliance.
- **Lending:** Small businesses can apply for loans through the platform, with instant approval based on their transaction history and credit score. The platform uses machine learning algorithms to assess creditworthiness quickly.

For HDFC Bank: SmartHub helps HDFC Bank cater to the growing SME market by offering a tailored, digital-first solution. It also promotes cross-selling of HDFC's financial products like business loans and insurance.

For SMEs: The platform makes it easy for businesses to accept payments, manage finances, and access credit, all through a single interface, reducing reliance on multiple vendors and streamlining operations.

For customers: It allows for faster, more secure transactions, enhancing the customer experience at retail businesses.

SmartHub is an example of how banks can empower SMEs by providing integrated digital tools that go beyond basic payment processing. By combining payment acceptance, analytics, and financial services in one platform, HDFC Bank is positioning itself as a one-stop financial partner for small businesses.

7.2 Digital Banking Models in the Modern Financial Landscape

Digital banking represents a paradigm shift from traditional brick-and-mortar banking to a digital-first approach. It leverages technology to provide seamless, secure, and efficient banking services, enhancing both the customer experience and operational efficiency. The rise of FinTech innovations has spurred a transformation in how banking services are delivered, leading to the development of different digital banking models. This chapter explores these models in detail, categorizing them based on their operational characteristics, customer interactions, and technological integration. Digital-only banks are redefining consumer expectations with personalized, seamless, and real-time financial services [6]. FinTech advancements have introduced innovative business models such as neobanks and open banking ecosystems [7]. The evolution of digital finance has compelled banks to redesign customer experience, operational frameworks, and data strategies [8]. Digital banking initiatives support financial inclusion, particularly in emerging economies like India [9]. Digital banking models are fundamentally changing how banks operate and how consumers interact with financial services. These models can be broadly classified into four primary categories based on their structure and the degree of digital integration:

- **Traditional banks with digital transformation**
- **Neobanks**
- **Challenger banks**
- Banking-as-a-Service (BaaS) **Providers**

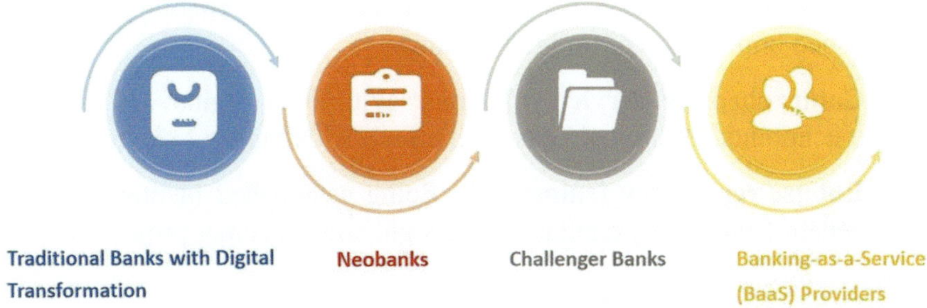

Figure 7.4 Digital banking models

Each model has unique characteristics and serves different market segments based on customer needs and technological innovations.

7.2.1 Traditional banks with digital transformation

Traditional banks, such as **HSBC**, **Citibank**, and **State Bank of India (SBI)**, have long histories and established customer bases. In the digital age, these institutions have **digitized their existing services** to offer customers online and mobile banking options. These banks still maintain physical branches but have significantly invested in **digital banking platforms**, mobile apps, and cloud infrastructure to enhance their service delivery and operational capabilities.

Characteristics

- **Hybrid model**: While they maintain traditional banking services (physical branches, customer service), they have integrated digital tools like mobile banking apps, online portals, and digital payment platforms to provide seamless services.
- **Customer-centric approach**: Focus on digitally transforming customer touchpoints by offering services like online account opening, 24/7 mobile banking, and AI-driven customer support (chatbots).
- **Innovation in legacy systems**: Banks enhance legacy systems by integrating modern technologies such as blockchain for secure transactions, big data analytics for better customer insights, and cloud computing for scalability.
- **Omnichannel experience**: A combination of physical branches and digital services to cater to diverse customer needs, providing flexibility and convenience.

Advantages

- **Trust and reputation**: Customers benefit from the reliability and established brand value of traditional banks.
- **Comprehensive service offerings**: With both digital and physical touchpoints, traditional banks can offer a wide range of services.
- **Robust regulatory framework**: Being established institutions, they benefit from strong regulatory oversight and consumer protection.

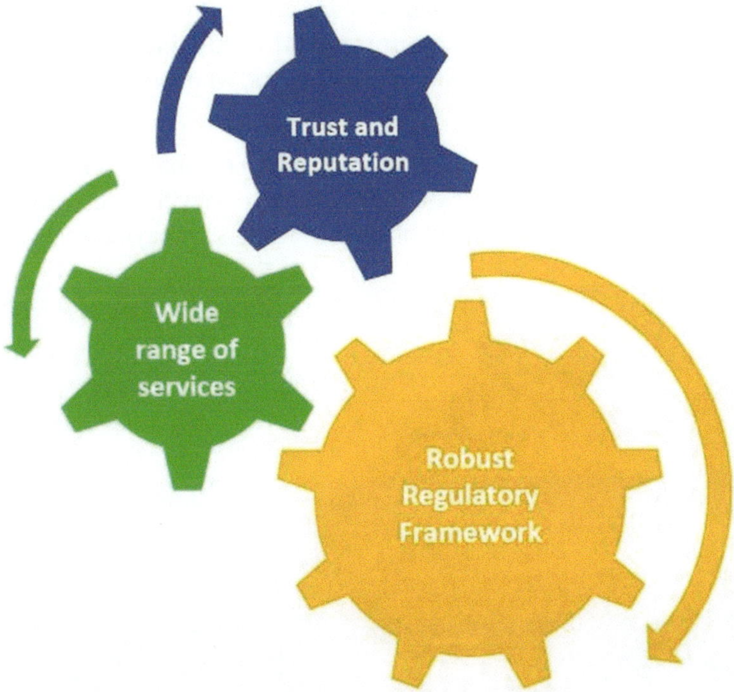

Figure 7.5 Traditional bank with digital transformation.

7.2.2 Neobanks

Neobanks are **digital-only financial institutions** that operate without any physical branches. They focus on offering **online-only banking services**, leveraging technology to provide better customer experiences at lower costs. Neobanks are typically startups or FinTech companies with a strong digital-first ethos.

Characteristics

- **Fully digital**: They have no physical branches and operate exclusively through mobile apps and web platforms.
- **Lower fees and higher accessibility**: Neobanks tend to have lower operational costs due to their digital nature, which translates to lower fees for customers. They are also more accessible to underserved and niche market segments.

- **Targeted services**: Neobanks often focus on specific banking services, such as **savings accounts**, **debit cards**, **loans**, and **budgeting tools**, catering to **tech-savvy customers** who prefer simplicity and convenience.
- **Open banking**: Many neobanks embrace **open banking** principles, which allow customers to **integrate** their financial data with third-party financial services, such as investment platforms, lenders, or payment systems.

Figure 7.6 N26 Image.
Source: https://n26.com/en-de/sim

Examples

- **N26**: A German neobank offering a full suite of banking services entirely through its mobile app. N26 has expanded to various European markets and the United States.
- **Revolut**: A UK-based neobank that offers banking services, cryptocurrency trading, and currency exchange through its app.
- **Chime**: A US-based neobank known for offering no-fee checking accounts and a user-friendly mobile app.

Advantages

- **Lower operating costs**: Without physical branches, neobanks operate at significantly lower costs.

- **User experience**: These banks are optimized for the **digital-first generation**, providing intuitive interfaces and seamless user journeys.
- **Innovation**: Neobanks are highly agile, often implementing cutting-edge technologies like **AI**, **blockchain**, and **big data analytics** to enhance their offerings.

7.2.3 Challenger banks

Challenger banks are **small, specialized digital banks** that compete with traditional financial institutions by offering innovative and **consumer-friendly banking products**. While they may have some physical presence, they primarily focus on **digital platforms** to challenge the status quo of traditional banking.

Characteristics

- **Regulated banks**: Unlike neobanks, challenger banks are fully regulated financial institutions and often have banking licenses (e.g., Monzo in the UK or Atom Bank).
- **Focus on innovation**: These banks innovate in customer experience, offering simple and transparent banking services such as fee-free accounts, real-time payments, and instant access to funds.
- **Tech-driven platforms:** They often use AI, machine learning, and big data to offer personalized services and enhance decision-making, such as instant loan approval and predictive budgeting.

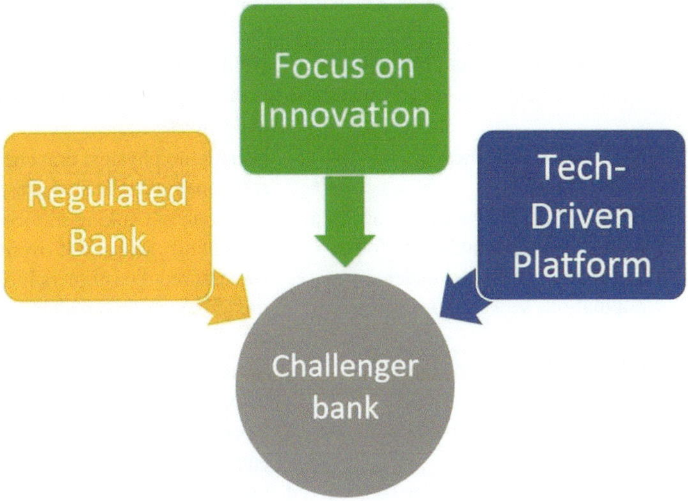

Figure 7.7 Challenger bank.

Examples

- **Monzo**: A UK-based challenger bank known for its transparent pricing model and innovative budgeting tools that allow users to set aside funds for different goals.
- **Atom bank**: A UK challenger bank that offers mortgages, savings accounts, and personal loans via a completely mobile app.
- **Starling bank:** Another UK-based bank that provides current accounts, savings, and small business banking with an emphasis on user-friendliness and low fees.

Advantages

- **Customization**: Challenger banks are highly focused on tailoring services to customer needs, offering highly personalized products.
- **Innovation and flexibility**: They can quickly introduce new features and services without the constraints of legacy infrastructure, making them highly agile.
- **Transparency:** Challenger banks are often more transparent than traditional banks regarding fees, loan terms, and product offerings.

Table 7.2 Neobank vs challenger bank.

Aspect	Neobank	Challenger bank
Definition	A digital-only financial service provider that operates without a banking license.	A fully licensed digital bank that competes with traditional banks.
Regulatory status	Typically operates in partnership with a licensed bank; not directly regulated.	Holds a full banking license and is directly regulated by financial authorities.
Physical presence	No physical branches; entirely online or app-based.	Usually no physical branches, but some may have limited presence.
Core services	Basic banking services like payments, money transfers, budgeting tools.	Full suite of banking services, including savings, loans, and overdrafts.
Target market	Tech-savvy users and underserved populations seeking convenience.	General retail customers looking for modern, tech-driven alternatives to big banks.
Examples	Chime (USA), Open (India), YONO Lite (India)	Monzo (UK), Starling Bank (UK), N26 (Europe)
Business model	Depends on partner banks for core banking operations.	Operates independently as a licensed bank.
Risk and compliance	Lower compliance burden (outsourced to partner bank).	Full responsibility for compliance and risk management.

7.2.4 Banking-as-a-Service (BaaS) providers

Banking-as-a-service (BaaS) is a model where traditional banks or other financial institutions provide their banking infrastructure to non-bank entities (such as **FinTechs**, **retailers**, and **third-party developers**) via Application Programming Interfaces (APIs). This allows non-banking entities to integrate banking services into their products or platforms.

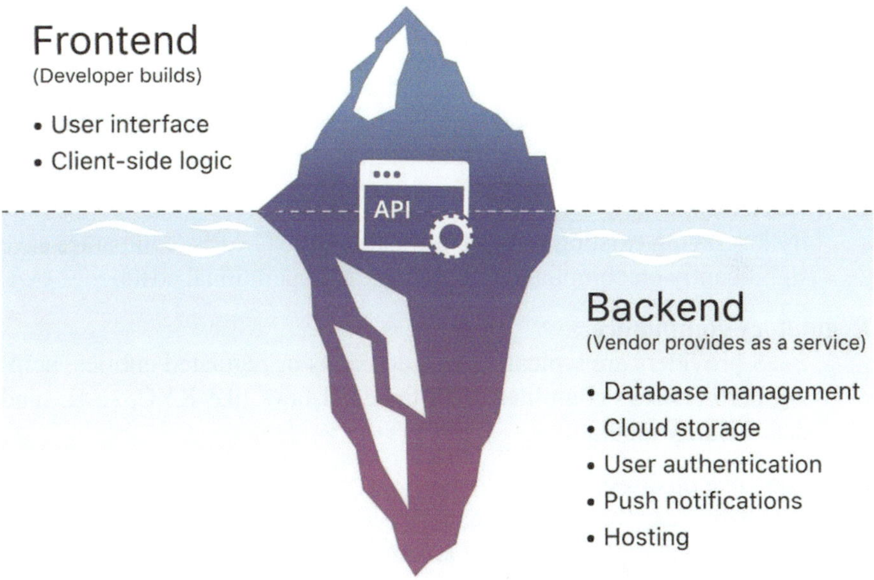

Figure 7.8 BaaS – frontend and backenCd.
Source: https://www.cloudflare.com/en-gb/learning/serverless/glossary/backend-as-a-service-baas/

Characteristics

- **API integration**: BaaS providers offer a suite of **APIs** that allow third-party developers to access banking functions such as **payments**, **lending**, **account opening**, and **transactions**.
- **White-label solutions**: Many BaaS providers offer **white-label solutions**, allowing non-banking companies to **brand** and market the services as their own.
- **Flexible partnerships**: BaaS is increasingly popular among **FinTechs**, **e-commerce platforms**, and **other digital businesses** looking to integrate financial products into their offerings without building the infrastructure themselves.

Examples

- **Solarisbank**: A German BaaS provider that offers digital banking services to businesses, including payment services, digital banking, and identity verification.
- **Finix**: A BaaS provider offering payment processing solutions for companies to manage their payment infrastructures.

Advantages

Faster time to market
BaaS allows FinTechs, startups, and even non-financial companies to quickly launch banking services like payments, lending, or digital wallets without building a bank from scratch.

Cost efficiency
By leveraging existing banking infrastructure via APIs, companies save significantly on compliance, licensing, and operational costs.

Regulatory compliance
BaaS providers are typically licensed banks or regulated entities, helping partners stay compliant with financial laws like KYC, AML, and data security regulations.

Focus on core business
Companies can focus on user experience, innovation, and branding while leaving the complex backend banking operations to BaaS providers.

Scalability
BaaS platforms are cloud-native and API-driven, making it easier to scale services across regions and customer segments without major infrastructure investments.

Easy integration
Modern BaaS platforms use plug-and-play APIs, enabling smooth integration into apps, websites, and platforms with minimal technical overhead.

The emergence of digital banking models marks a significant shift in the financial services landscape. Traditional banks with digital transformation, neobanks, challenger banks, and BaaS providers are all leveraging technology to offer more convenient, cost-effective, and customer-centric banking services. As technology continues to advance, these models will continue to evolve, offering more innovative financial products, improved customer experiences, and greater financial inclusion. This comprehensive exploration of digital banking models should serve as a valuable resource in understanding the dynamic landscape of modern banking, including the role of technology and FinTech in shaping the future of financial services.

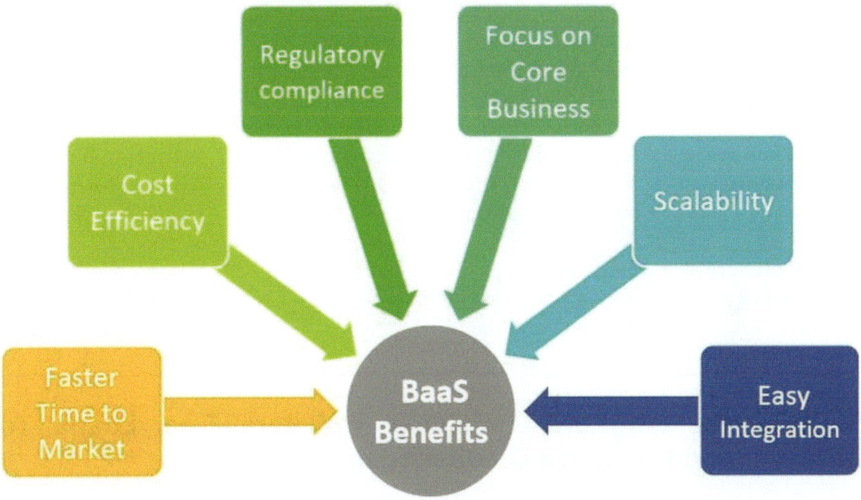

Figure 7.9 BaaS benefits.

Technology has rapidly evolved to support scalable, efficient, and on-demand services through cloud-based models like **IaaS (Infrastructure as a Service), PaaS (Platform as a Service), SaaS (Software as a Service), and BaaS (Banking as a Service)**. These models represent different layers of digital transformation. IaaS provides the foundational infrastructure – such as virtual servers and storage – enabling businesses to avoid the cost and complexity of physical data centers. PaaS builds on this by offering platforms that support application development and deployment, allowing developers to focus on coding without managing backend systems. SaaS delivers complete software solutions via the cloud, making it easy for users to access and use tools like email, CRM, or collaboration apps. In the financial world, BaaS has emerged as a specialized model where licensed banks provide core banking infrastructure via APIs, enabling non-banking companies to embed financial services like payments, lending, or digital wallets into their own platforms. Together, these technologies showcase how continuous upgradation is driving flexibility, innovation, and accessibility across industries.

Table 7.3 BaaS, IaaS, PaaS, SaaS.

Type	Full form	What it provides	Users	Examples
BaaS	**Banking as a Service**	Ready-made digital banking infrastructure (accounts, payments, compliance) via APIs	FinTechs, non-bank companies wanting to offer financial services	Solarisbank, Treasury Prime, BBVA Open Platform
IaaS	**Infrastructure as a Service**	Virtualized computing resources: servers, storage, networking	IT admins, system engineers	Amazon Web Services (EC2), Microsoft Azure, Google Compute Engine
PaaS	**Platform as a Service**	A platform with tools and frameworks for building, testing, and deploying apps	Developers	Google App Engine, Heroku, Microsoft Azure App Service
SaaS	**Software as a Service**	Fully functional software applications delivered over the internet	End-users	Google Workspace, Dropbox, Salesforce, Zoom

Example: LendingKart: Providing Collateral-Free Loans To MSMEs Using Predictive Credit Models

LENDINGKA₹T

Simplifying MSME Finance

LendingKart is a prominent **FinTech company** that offers **collateral-free loans** to **micro, small, and medium enterprises (MSMEs)**, helping businesses overcome the challenge of securing traditional bank loans that typically require physical assets as collateral.

Key features of LendingKart:

- **Data-driven credit assessment**: LendingKart uses **predictive credit models** and **big data analytics** to assess the creditworthiness of borrowers. The platform analyzes over **200 variables**, including **banking transactions**, **business performance data**, **social media activity**, and other digital footprints to predict the risk profile of MSMEs. This is in contrast to traditional lending models, which often rely on **physical collateral** and **historical financial statements**.

- **Speed and accessibility**: By leveraging digital technology and data analytics, LendingKart offers **instant loan approvals**. The application process is fully online, requiring minimal paperwork, which significantly reduces the time it takes to process loans. This makes **financing accessible to businesses** that may not have the necessary physical collateral or a long credit history.

- **Loan amount and terms**: LendingKart provides MSMEs with loans ranging from **INR 50,000 to INR 2 crore** (approximately USD 550 to USD 220,000). The repayment terms are also flexible, and businesses can access funds for **working capital** or **business expansion** purposes.
- **Alternative credit scoring**: LendingKart's use of **alternative data sources** (like GST returns, tax filings, and business cash flows) enables it to offer loans to businesses that may not have access to traditional forms of credit.

Impact and value proposition:

- **For MSMEs**: It opens up access to capital for **small businesses** that might otherwise be unable to secure loans from traditional financial institutions. This helps them **expand their operations**, improve cash flow, and invest in growth without the need for collateral.
- **For the economy**: By empowering **MSMEs**, LendingKart plays a crucial role in supporting **economic growth** and **job creation** in emerging markets like India. MSMEs contribute significantly to national economies but often face barriers when accessing credit, which LendingKart helps overcome.
- **For the FinTech sector**: LendingKart sets a powerful example of how **technology** (especially **AI**, **machine learning**, and **big data**) can be used to **innovate** financial services and cater to **underserved markets**.

Example: Zerodha (Rainmatter)

ZERODHA

A WealthTech Platform Revolutionizing Online Stock Trading with Low Fees and Simplified Interfaces. Zerodha is India's largest online stock trading platform, offering services such as discount brokerage, equity trading, commodities trading, derivatives trading, and mutual fund investments. Zerodha's mission is to make stock trading accessible to everyone, especially retail investors, by offering low-cost, efficient, and transparent trading services. Rainmatter is Zerodha's FinTech incubator, which fosters innovation by supporting startups and projects that are aligned with Zerodha's vision of democratizing finance and improving the accessibility of wealth-building tools for Indians.

Key features of Zerodha:

- **Low brokerage fees**: Zerodha introduced a discount brokerage model where traders pay a flat fee (or no fee) per trade, as opposed to traditional brokers who charge a percentage-based fee on each transaction. This has led to massive cost savings for individual traders and investors.
- **Simplified user interface**: Zerodha offers a highly intuitive and user-friendly platform with tools like Kite (its trading app), Coin (for mutual funds), and Varsity (for learning resources). The design prioritizes a clean interface, real-time data, and speed, making it easier for both beginners and seasoned traders to navigate the platform.
- **Zero maintenance fee**: Unlike many competitors, Zerodha charges no maintenance fee for holding shares, making it a more affordable option for retail investors.
- **Innovative products**: Zerodha provides a range of advanced trading products for active traders, such as futures and options, margin trading, and access to global markets. The platform is also working on offering blockchain-based services for enhanced transparency and security.

Rainmatter incubates projects and businesses that align with Zerodha's goal of making financial markets more accessible. For instance, Rainmatter has supported small startups working on AI in finance, low-cost mutual fund platforms, and financial literacy tools. It has also contributed to the financial literacy movement by providing resources, hosting events, and working on open-source financial technology to empower individuals with the knowledge to manage their wealth effectively.

Impact and value proposition:

- **For retail investors**: Zerodha has **revolutionized online stock trading** by offering **low-cost, easy-to-use platforms** for retail investors. It provides access to financial markets without the high fees and complicated interfaces of traditional brokerage firms.

- **For the FinTech sector**: Zerodha and Rainmatter are significant players in the **WealthTech** space, driving the **digitization of financial services** and opening up the financial markets to a broader, tech-savvy audience. It encourages **financial inclusivity** and supports **entrepreneurial ventures** in the **FinTech ecosystem**.
- **For the Indian economy**: Zerodha has contributed to a rise in **stock market participation** in India, especially among **younger investors**, promoting a culture of **savings** and **investments** among the middle class.

These **FinTech examples – LendingKart**, and **Zerodha** – illustrate the growing role of technology in reshaping traditional financial services. LendingKart leverages predictive models to empower MSMEs with collateral-free loans and Zerodha lowers the cost of stock trading and enhances investment accessibility through its low-fee model and user-friendly platform. Together, these companies demonstrate how technology and data are breaking down barriers in the financial services industry, creating more inclusive, efficient, and customer-focused solutions.

Collabration examples:

JPMorgan Chase (USA) × Onyx by JPM & Collaborations with FinTechs

FinTech collaborations:

- Partnership with Plaid **(USA):**

  JPMorgan collaborated with Plaid, a leading open banking platform, to improve customer data access and enable third-party financial app integrations with user consent.

- Acquisition of WePay (2017):

  JPMorgan acquired WePay, a FinTech that specializes in integrated payment solutions for small businesses. This allowed the bank to offer advanced digital payment infrastructure to clients in direct competition with Stripe and Square.

- Blockchain via Onyx:

  Through its digital arm **Onyx by JPMorgan**, the bank has launched:

- **JPM Coin** (a blockchain-based digital currency for institutional transfers)

- **Liink** (a blockchain-based network for secure interbank data exchange, developed in collaboration with over 75 global banks and FinTechs)

As a result, there is improved digital onboarding and API infrastructure, strengthened JPMorgan's position in B2B payments and blockchain innovation, and enhanced customer-centric FinTech integrations via Plaid and WePay.

HSBC (UK) × Google Cloud, Tradeshift & Nova Credit

FinTech collaborations:

- Google Cloud partnership:

  HSBC partnered with Google Cloud to modernize its data and analytics infrastructure, enabling better risk modeling, real-time fraud detection, and personalized services using machine learning and big data tools.

- Tradeshift (supply chain FinTech):

  HSBC collaborated with **Tradeshift**, a cloud-based supply chain financing platform, to offer real-time invoice financing and improve working capital access for corporate clients. This helps businesses unlock liquidity directly through digital invoice networks.

- Nova Credit (Cross-border Credit Scoring):

  HSBC partnered with **Nova Credit**, a FinTech that helps immigrants bring their international credit history to new countries. This helps HSBC expand its customer base among expatriates and migrants, a major segment in the UK and globally. As a result, accelerated transition to cloud-native, AI-powered banking operations, enhanced cross-border credit inclusion, and SME supply chain finance offerings and positioned HSBC as a digitally progressive, partner-driven bank.

These collaborations demonstrate that even the largest global banks are leveraging the agility and innovation of FinTech giants to stay competitive, modernize their offerings, and cater to the evolving needs of digital-first customers. These partnerships signal a shift from competition to collaboration in the global financial ecosystem.

7.3 The Role of Non-Banking Financial Companies (NBFCs) in the FinTech Era

Non-banking financial companies (NBFCs) have long been an integral part of the financial services ecosystem, offering services that complement traditional banking, especially in markets where access to formal banking is limited. With the rise of **FinTech**, the role of NBFCs has evolved significantly. They have adapted by leveraging technology to offer **innovative**, **accessible**, and **customer-centric financial solutions**. This chapter explores the growing influence of NBFCs in the **FinTech era**, outlining their role, key contributions, and how they are transforming the financial landscape. Non-banking financial companies (NBFCs) have become critical players in credit delivery and financial deepening across developing economies [10]. They enhance competition and accessibility, filling gaps left by traditional banks in SME and consumer lending [11]. The rise of FinTech credit markets has further expanded NBFC operations by integrating technology into lending practices [12].

Non-banking financial companies (NBFCs) are financial institutions that provide a wide range of services similar to traditional banks but do not hold a banking license. These services may include **lending**, **asset management**, **leasing**, **investment**, **insurance**, and **microfinance**. NBFCs typically serve **unbanked or underbanked** populations and are pivotal in **financial inclusion**.

NBFCs differ from banks in the following key ways:

- They cannot offer **demand deposits** (checking accounts).
- They are not authorized to operate as **clearing houses** or **settling payments**.
- They can provide **loans**, **leasing**, and other financial services, but cannot accept **public deposits** in the same manner as banks.

However, despite these limitations, NBFCs play a crucial role in extending credit and offering other financial services in both **urban** and **rural areas**, particularly in emerging economies.

7.3.1 The Impact of FinTech on NBFCs

Embracing digital transformation

With the advent of **FinTech innovations**, NBFCs have increasingly **embraced digital tools** to enhance service delivery and broaden their reach. The rise of **digital lending platforms**, **peer-to-peer lending**, **artificial intelligence (AI)**, and **blockchain** has significantly influenced the way NBFCs operate. By adopting these technologies, NBFCs can:

- **Automate** loan processing, approval, and disbursement.
- Use **big data** and **machine learning algorithms** to better assess credit risk and offer more personalized products.

- Simplify **loan application procedures**, reducing the time and documentation involved in traditional lending.

This digital transformation has enabled NBFCs to **scale up** and **reach previously underserved markets**, including **small and medium-sized enterprises (SMEs)** and **individual borrowers** who may not have access to traditional banking services.

New business models

The **FinTech revolution** has spurred the development of innovative business models among NBFCs. For example:

- **Online lending platforms**: Many NBFCs have launched **digital-only lending services** that allow customers to apply for personal, business, or micro loans through mobile apps or websites. These platforms use **data-driven models** to assess creditworthiness and determine loan eligibility without the need for traditional paperwork or physical collateral.

- **Peer-to-peer (P2P) lending**: Some NBFCs have entered the **P2P lending space**, acting as intermediaries between investors and borrowers. This model allows individuals to lend money directly to other individuals or businesses, bypassing traditional financial intermediaries.

- **Buy Now, Pay Later (BNPL)**: NBFCs have increasingly become key players in the **BNPL** segment, offering consumers the ability to make purchases and pay for them in installments. By leveraging FinTech, NBFCs can assess risk and approve loans in real-time, making this model efficient and appealing for both consumers and merchants.

Financial inclusion

NBFCs, with their digital-first approach, play a crucial role in enhancing financial inclusion, a key objective of the FinTech ecosystem. They provide financial services to unbanked and underbanked populations, especially in rural areas and smaller towns, where traditional banks may not have a significant presence. Their use of technology, including mobile apps, digital wallets, and online lending platforms, enables them to offer services to a wider audience.

- **Microfinance**: Many NBFCs specialize in microloans and small-value loans, helping individuals and small businesses access credit that they otherwise could not obtain from traditional banks.

- **Data-driven credit scoring:** By leveraging alternative data sources, such as utility payments, social media activity, and mobile phone usage, NBFCs can assess credit risk for individuals without formal credit histories. This opens up lending opportunities to a larger demographic, particularly in emerging markets.

7.3.2 Key roles of NBFCs in the FinTech ecosystem

Digital lending and credit accessibility

Digital lending is one of the most significant contributions of NBFCs in the FinTech space. Using advanced data analytics and artificial intelligence (AI), NBFCs can process loan applications much faster and more efficiently than traditional banks. By providing quick access to credit for individuals, businesses, and SMEs, NBFCs play a critical role in driving financial inclusion. For example, loan origination platforms that use AI to assess risk based on real-time data, such as bank transactions, to offer collateral-free loans. SME lending platforms: NBFCs are often the preferred choice for SMEs due to their ability to provide quick loans without requiring extensive documentation or collateral. This helps businesses access working capital and grow without the barriers imposed by traditional banks.

Innovations in payment solutions

Many NBFCs have partnered with FinTech startups or created their own digital wallets and payment solutions to improve financial services. By integrating payment technologies, they can streamline transactions, facilitate cross-border payments, and provide more secure and efficient payment systems. Payment Gateways and Wallets: Some NBFCs offer their own payment gateways and wallet services, providing easy access to money transfers, bill payments, and e-commerce payments.

Facilitating wealth management and investments

NBFCs are also increasingly involved in WealthTech by leveraging technology to offer investment products and wealth management services. They are providing customers with access to mutual funds, stocks, and bonds through digital platforms with low fees and greater transparency. For example, some NBFCs have adopted robo-advisory services, which use algorithms to suggest optimal investment portfolios based on individual risk preferences and financial goals.

Insurance and risk management

As part of the InsurTech ecosystem, NBFCs have ventured into the insurance sector, often partnering with traditional insurers or InsurTech startups to offer customers digital insurance products. These may include microinsurance: Affordable insurance policies for low-income individuals or small businesses, and on-demand insurance: Pay-per-use models where customers pay only for the coverage they need at a specific time, enabled through mobile apps and digital platforms.

7.3.3 Challenges and opportunities for NBFCs in the FinTech era

Challenges

Despite their growth, NBFCs face several challenges in the FinTech space:

Regulatory constraints: NBFCs are often subject to stricter regulations than traditional banks, especially concerning capital requirements and lending limits. This can limit their ability to scale quickly.

Technology adoption: While many NBFCs have embraced digital platforms, others still rely on legacy systems, making the transition to digital models challenging.

Cybersecurity risks: As NBFCs handle sensitive financial data, they are vulnerable to **cyber threats**, requiring constant upgrades to their **security infrastructure**.

Opportunities

On the other hand, NBFCs also have tremendous opportunities, such as by collaborating with FinTech startups, NBFCs can expand their product offerings, reach new customer segments, and leverage cutting-edge technology without building everything from scratch. With their flexibility and ability to offer microloans and financing solutions, NBFCs are well-positioned to target underserved markets, such as rural populations and SMEs.

In the FinTech era, NBFCs have emerged as key players in the digital transformation of financial services. Through digital lending, payment innovations, and wealth management solutions, NBFCs are making financial services more accessible, affordable, and inclusive. By embracing technology and data analytics, they can overcome traditional barriers and drive the future of financial inclusion. As the FinTech landscape continues to evolve, NBFCs are poised to play an even more significant role in reshaping the financial ecosystem globally.

7.4 Online and Mobile Banking in the FinTech Ecosystem

In the digital age, online banking and mobile banking have become crucial components of the FinTech ecosystem, playing a pivotal role in transforming the way individuals and businesses access and manage their financial services. These innovations not only increase the efficiency of banking operations but also promote financial inclusion, particularly for underserved populations, and reduce the reliance on traditional brick-and-mortar banking infrastructure. Online banking refers to the use of the internet to conduct financial transactions and access banking services through a computer or other internet-enabled devices. The introduction of online banking has significantly disrupted traditional banking by providing customers with 24/7 access to their accounts and financial services from anywhere in the world. Online and mobile banking innovations are reshaping customer engagement through ease of access and transaction efficiency [13]. Technological convergence and AI-based personalization have improved service quality and reduced operational costs in mobile banking [14]. Modern banking systems are evolving into hybrid ecosystems, balancing digital and physical touchpoints [15]. The Indian financial system reflects a dynamic shift toward integrated, digital-first service delivery models [16].

7.4.1 The role of online and mobile banking in the FinTech ecosystem

Online and mobile banking play a central role in the FinTech ecosystem by serving as the primary channels through which users access digital financial services. These platforms have transformed traditional banking by offering convenient, 24/7 access to core services such as account management, fund transfers, bill payments, and loan applications. Powered by advanced technologies like biometric authentication, AI-based chatbots, and real-time notifications, online and mobile banking enhances user experience while reducing operational costs for financial institutions. They also act as key enablers of financial inclusion, bringing banking access to underserved populations through smartphones and internet connectivity. As consumer expectations evolve, these digital channels continue to drive innovation, customer engagement, and the seamless integration of FinTech solutions into everyday financial life.

Enabling digital transformation in banking

Online and mobile banking represent the forefront of digital transformation in the banking sector. These platforms enable banks to rethink traditional banking models by providing digital-first services that are faster, more cost-effective, and customer-centric. The shift to digital banking allows institutions to better cater to the needs of tech-savvy customers who demand convenience, speed, and accessibility.

Financial inclusion and accessibility

One of the major advantages of online and mobile banking is the boost to financial inclusion. In emerging markets, many people lacked access to traditional banking services due to factors such as geographical isolation, lack of physical infrastructure, or high service fees. Online and mobile banking platforms provide a solution by offering users access to banking services directly through their phones or computers, effectively bringing banking services to the unbanked or underbanked populations. For example, in countries like India, Africa, and Southeast Asia, mobile money platforms such as M-Pesa have revolutionized access to financial services by allowing individuals to make payments, transfer money, and access savings and loans via their mobile phones, even in remote areas without banking branches.

Collaboration with FinTech startups

The rise of FinTech startups in the digital banking space has led to increased collaborations between traditional banks and FinTechs to create more innovative solutions. These partnerships allow for the integration of third-party services and enhanced features in online and mobile banking platforms, creating a more dynamic user experience. For example, neobanks (digital-only banks) have emerged as challengers to traditional banks, offering services like real-time payments, budgeting tools, and investment management via mobile apps with no need for physical branches. FinTechs have provided the technological infrastructure for these banks to succeed, which often includes cloud-based core banking systems, AI-powered customer service, and machine learning-based fraud detection.

Enhanced customer experience and personalization

Online and mobile banking have shifted the focus toward offering more personalized services. Banks now use data analytics and artificial intelligence (AI) to analyze customer behavior and offer tailored products and services. Personal Finance Management (PFM) features in mobile banking apps use transaction data to offer users personalized insights into their spending habits, provide budgeting tips, and suggest savings plans. AI-powered chatbots can also provide personalized customer support, assisting users with inquiries about account balances, transaction history, and product offerings.

Security and fraud prevention

With the increasing use of online and mobile banking, the need for robust security has never been more critical. FinTech companies and traditional banks are investing heavily in advanced security features to protect customer data and transactions. Some of the key security features include protecting sensitive data during transmission, using fingerprints, facial recognition, or voice authentication to verify the identity of users and enhancing account security by requiring an additional layer of verification beyond just passwords.

7.4.2 Online banking

Online banking has played a transformative role in the FinTech ecosystem by digitizing traditional banking services and making them more accessible and efficient. Through secure web-based platforms, users can manage accounts, transfer funds, pay bills, and access loan or investment services without visiting a physical branch. FinTech has enhanced online banking with features such as AI-driven chatbots, automated financial planning tools, and real-time fraud detection. This integration not only streamlines financial operations for institutions but also allows consumers to enjoy faster, safer, and more personalized services. As digital adoption continues to grow, online banking remains a vital interface between consumers and the expanding universe of FinTech innovations.

Key features of online banking:

- **Account access**: Customers can check their account balances, view transaction history, and manage their accounts without the need to visit a physical branch.
- **Fund transfers**: Customers can easily transfer funds between accounts or to third-party recipients (national or international) through secure platforms.
- **Bill payments**: Online banking platforms allow users to pay **utility bills**, **loan installments**, **credit card bills**, and **tax payments** directly from their accounts.
- **Loan management**: Borrowers can apply for personal loans, mortgage loans, or business loans online. The application process is simplified, and users can track their loan status digitally.
- **Investment services**: Many banks provide online tools for customers to invest in **stocks**, **bonds**, **mutual funds**, and other financial products directly through their online platforms.

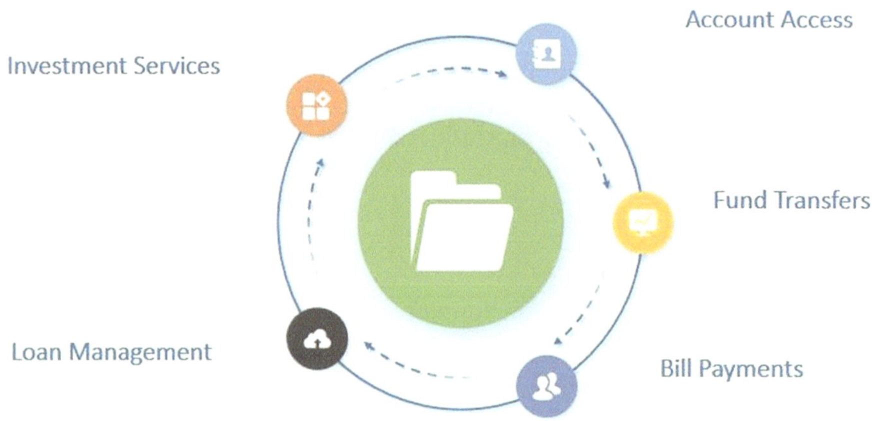

Figure 7.10 Features of online banking

Benefits of online banking:

- **Convenience**: Customers can manage their finances from the comfort of their homes or offices, eliminating the need for physical visits to a bank.
- **Cost reduction**: Banks reduce operational costs by offering services through online platforms, allowing them to cut down on infrastructure and branch network expenses.
- **Efficiency**: Online banking speeds up processes like fund transfers, loan applications, and bill payments, reducing the time it takes to complete banking tasks.
- **Financial inclusion:** Online banking has enabled customers from rural and remote areas to access banking services without the need to travel long distances to physical branches.

Mobile banking

Mobile banking, a key advancement within FinTech, brings banking services directly into the hands of users through smartphone applications. It allows customers to perform everyday financial tasks – like checking balances, transferring money, depositing checks, and receiving instant transaction alerts – anytime and anywhere.

FinTech has revolutionized mobile banking by embedding features such as biometric authentication, voice-enabled transactions, and AI-based budgeting tools. In many regions, especially developing countries, mobile banking has significantly boosted financial inclusion by reaching unbanked populations that lack access to traditional banking infrastructure. As smartphones become more powerful and widespread, mobile banking continues to lead FinTech's mission of making finance more inclusive, real-time, and user-centric.

Key features of mobile banking:

- **Mobile payments**: Mobile banking apps allow users to make payments via QR codes, NFC technology, and mobile wallets such as Google Pay, Apple Pay, and Samsung Pay.
- **Real-time notifications**: Customers receive real-time alerts on transactions, account activity, bill reminders, and loan due dates, helping them stay on top of their financial obligations.
- **Mobile wallets**: Many mobile banking apps feature integrated mobile wallet services, allowing users to store and manage their credit/debit cards, loyalty cards, and other digital currencies directly on their phones.
- **Peer-to-peer (P2P) transfers**: Mobile banking platforms enable instant money transfers between users, even without requiring the recipient's bank account number, using services like Paytm or Venmo.
- **Personal finance management (PFM):** Mobile banking apps often include budgeting tools, expense tracking, and financial goal setting features, helping users manage their finances more effectively.

Benefits of mobile banking:

- **Accessibility and portability**: Mobile banking provides customers with access to their accounts at any time and from any place, as long as they have a mobile device and an internet connection. This accessibility is particularly important for customers in remote or underserved areas.
- **Instant transactions**: Mobile banking enables real-time processing of transactions, making fund transfers, bill payments, and payments for goods and services quicker and more efficient.
- **Secure transactions**: Many mobile banking platforms use biometric authentication (such as fingerprint scans or face recognition) and two-factor authentication (2FA) to enhance the security of financial transactions.
- **Convenience for on-the-go users**: Mobile banking is ideal for individuals who are always on the go, allowing them to access banking services without being tied to a desktop computer or visiting a branch.

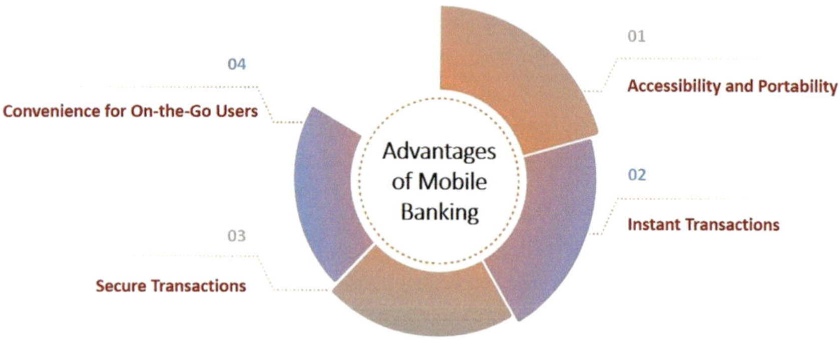

Figure 7.11 Advantages of Mobile banking.

7.4.3 Challenges of online and mobile banking

Cybersecurity threats

While digital banking offers convenience, it also exposes users to an increased risk of cybersecurity breaches. Hackers target mobile banking apps and online platforms to gain access to personal information, financial data, and accounts. Ensuring the security of online and mobile banking services remains a top challenge for financial institutions and FinTechs alike.

Regulatory compliance

The rise of online and mobile banking services is closely monitored by financial regulatory bodies to ensure consumer protection and data privacy. Banks and FinTechs need to comply with various regulations, such as KYC (Know Your Customer), AML (Anti-Money Laundering), and GDPR (General Data Protection Regulation) in certain regions.

Digital divide and accessibility

While online and mobile banking have expanded access to financial services for many, there is still a significant portion of the global population that remains excluded due to factors such as lack of internet access, technological literacy, or lack of smartphones. Overcoming this digital divide is a key challenge for the broader FinTech ecosystem. Online and mobile banking are at the heart of the FinTech ecosystem, revolutionizing how consumers access, manage, and optimize their financial lives. By offering convenience, accessibility, and cost efficiency, these platforms have enhanced the user experience, especially in terms of financial inclusion and real-time transactions. Despite challenges such as cybersecurity threats and regulatory compliance, online and mobile banking continue to drive the digital transformation of the financial services industry, paving the way for a more connected, inclusive, and innovative future for financial services globally.

Summary

This chapter examines the changing face of banking systems amid rapid digitization. It introduces various digital banking models, including traditional banks adopting digital channels, neobanks operating exclusively online, and hybrid models blending physical and digital services. These models emphasize customer-centricity, automation, and seamless experiences. The chapter also highlights the increasing importance of NBFCs in providing credit, leasing, and other financial services, particularly to SMEs and retail customers who may be underserved by traditional banks. Finally, the chapter explores the rise of online and mobile banking, detailing their role in expanding access to financial services, enhancing transaction speed, and promoting financial literacy. Overall, the chapter underscores the synergy and competition between banks and NBFCs in delivering modern financial services.

Case Study: ING Bank (Netherlands) – Leading Digital Transformation Through FinTech Integration

ING Bank N.V., headquartered in **Amsterdam, Netherlands**, is one of Europe's largest and most influential commercial banks. The bank was officially formed in **1991** through a merger between Nationale-Nederlanden (an insurance company) and NMB Postbank Group (a bank). Today, ING operates in more than 40 countries, serving over 38 million customers across retail, commercial, and investment banking segments. In its early decades, ING followed a traditional banking model, relying on physical branches, paper-based processes, and conventional financial products. However, by the late 2000s and early 2010s, the global financial landscape began to shift dramatically Customer expectations changed, with users demanding faster, mobile-accessible, and personalized financial services. FinTech startups began disrupting core banking functions like payments, lending, personal finance, and wealth management. Regulatory reforms such as the European Union's Revised Payment Services Directive (PSD2) encouraged open banking and data-sharing through APIs.

Recognizing these tectonic shifts, ING made a bold strategic pivot toward digital transformation. Instead of viewing FinTech as a threat, ING chose to embrace FinTech as a partner and accelerator of innovation. Its leadership adopted a vision of "banking without a bank" – aiming to deliver seamless financial services embedded within customers' digital lifestyles. Founded in 1991 and headquartered in Amsterdam, ING Bank is one of Europe's major commercial banking institutions. Serving over 38 million customers globally, ING has gained recognition not only for its robust financial services but also for its forward-thinking digital transformation strategy. By the early 2010s, ING faced increasing competition from digital-only banks and FinTech startups offering personalized, low-cost, and mobile-first services.

Customers expected faster service, digital onboarding, and predictive financial tools – challenging ING's traditional branch-based model. To respond to these shifts, ING undertook a comprehensive digital transformation powered by FinTech tools and partnerships, centered on three pillars:

- **Customer-centric digital platforms: ING's mobile banking App** was enhanced with AI-driven features such as real-time spending insights, budgeting tools, and voice-activated commands. **One App Strategy** consolidated various services (loans, investments, daily banking) into a seamless digital experience.
- **FinTech collaborations and investments:** ING launched ING Ventures, a €300 million fund to invest in promising FinTech startups. It invested in companies like Yolt (UK): An open banking app for personal finance management, WeLab (Asia): A digital lending platform and Cobase (Netherlands): A multi-banking platform for corporate clients. ING also partnered with Scalable Capital, a robo-advisory platform for wealth management.
- **Open banking and API strategy:** ING actively embraced **PSD2** regulations by offering **o**pen APIs for third-party developers. Through ING's Developer Portal, FinTechs and SMEs could build tools connected to ING's infrastructure, fostering an ecosystem of innovation.

96% of customer interactions now take place digitally. Significant drop in operational costs due to automation. Yolt reached over 1.5 million users before being spun off. Recognized by Forrester and Deloitte as one of Europe's top digital banks. Improved customer satisfaction and retention, especially among younger demographics. Digital transformation in banking requires not just technology, but a cultural shift toward agile, customer-first thinking. Strategic FinTech partnerships accelerate innovation faster than internal development alone. Banks must invest in open platforms and APIs to stay relevant in a collaborative digital ecosystem. ING Bank's journey illustrates how a traditional European commercial bank can thrive by integrating FinTech at the core of its operations. Through investments, partnerships, and internal innovation, ING has transitioned into a digital banking leader, setting a benchmark for commercial banks across Europe.

Discussion Questions: ING Bank and FinTech integration

1. What were the key factors that motivated ING Bank to adopt FinTech solutions and undergo digital transformation?
2. How have ING's partnerships with FinTech startups (like Yolt and Scalable Capital) contributed to its competitive advantage?
3. In what ways has ING leveraged emerging technologies like AI, blockchain, and APIs to improve customer experience and operations?
4. What are the major risks and regulatory challenges associated with ING's FinTech-driven digital strategy?
5. How can traditional banks like ING balance innovation with trust and customer security in a rapidly evolving digital ecosystem?

Keywords

- **Digital banking models:** Frameworks defining how banks deliver services using digital channels, including fully digital banks, branchless banks, and hybrid models combining physical and digital.
- **Neobank:** A type of digital-only bank that operates without physical branches, offering services primarily through mobile apps and web platforms.
- **Branchless banking:** Banking services delivered without traditional branches, often using agents, kiosks, or digital channels to reach customers.
- **Non-banking financial companies (NBFCs):** Financial institutions providing banking-like services such as loans and credit facilities, but do not hold a banking license.
- **Microfinance institutions (MFIs):** NBFCs or other entities providing small loans and financial services to low-income individuals or groups, often focusing on financial inclusion.

- **Online banking:** Access to banking services and transactions via the internet, typically through secure web portals.
- **Mobile banking:** Banking services accessed via mobile devices such as smartphones, often through dedicated apps or mobile-optimized websites.
- **Financial inclusion:** The process of making financial products and services accessible and affordable to all individuals and businesses, especially underserved populations.
- **Real-time payments:** Instantaneous transfer of funds between accounts, enabling faster transaction settlements.
- **Digital wallets:** Electronic applications that store payment information, allowing users to make digital transactions securely.

Discussion Questions

1. What are the main differences between traditional banks, neobanks, and branchless banking models?
2. How have digital banking models improved customer experience and financial inclusion?
3. In what ways do NBFCs complement traditional banking systems?
4. What challenges do NBFCs face in competing with banks in the digital era?
5. How has mobile banking transformed the way customers interact with financial institutions?
6. What security concerns arise from increased reliance on online and mobile banking?
7. How do real-time payment systems impact the efficiency of banking operations?
8. What role do digital wallets play in modern banking ecosystems?
9. How can banks and NBFCs collaborate to serve underserved populations more effectively?
10. What regulatory considerations are important in overseeing digital banking and NBFC operations?

References

[1] EY. (2021). *Global banking outlook: Reinventing financial services for a digital age.*

[2] Ghosh, S. (2017). *Banking Principles and Operations.* S. Chand Publishing.

[3] Sundararajan, V., & Balasubramanian, R. (2019). *Indian Financial System.* Pearson Education.

[4] Reserve Bank of India. (2021). *Report on trend and progress of banking in India.* Retrieved from https://www.rbi.org.in

[5] Arner, D. W., Barberis, J., & Buckley, R. P. (2016). In D. L. Chuen (Ed.), *Handbook of Blockchain, Digital Finance, and Inclusion* (Vol. 1). Academic Press.

[6] Accenture. (2022). *The rise of digital-only banks: Are consumers ready?* Retrieved from https://www.accenture.com/us-en/insights/banking/digital-only-banks

[7] Chishti, S., & Barberis, J. (2016). *The FinTech Book: The Financial Technology Handbook for Investors, Entrepreneurs and Visionaries.* Wiley.

[8] Gomber, P., Klaus, T., & Siering, M. (Eds.). (2022). *Digital Finance and FinTech: Business Models and Regulation.* Palgrave Macmillan.

[9] Ghosh, S. (2021). *Digital Banking and Financial Inclusion: Strategies and Challenges.* Routledge.

[10] Sengupta, R., & Vardhan, H. (2017). *Non-banking financial companies: Role and risks. Economic and Political Weekly, 52*(11), 47–54.

[11] World Bank. (2020). *Non-bank financial institutions: Assessment of development and risks.* Retrieved from https://www.worldbank.org/en/publication/gfdr

[12] Claessens, S., Frost, J., Turner, G., & Zhu, F. (2018). *Fintech credit markets around the world: Size, drivers and policy issues. BIS Quarterly Review,* September.

[13] Deloitte. (2023). *The future of mobile banking: Innovation and adoption trends.* Retrieved from https://www2.deloitte.com/global/en/pages/financial-services/articles/mobile-banking-trends.html

[14] Puschmann, T. (Ed.). (2022). *FinTech and the Future of Finance.* Springer.

[15] Singh, B., & Upadhyay, A. (2021). *Banking and Financial Systems.* Kalyani Publishers.

[16] Khan, M. Y. (2014). *Indian Financial System* (9th ed.). McGraw Hill Education.

8

Payment Technologies

Abstract

The rapid digital transformation of financial services has brought payment systems to the forefront of modern economic activity. This chapter explores the mechanisms, workflows, and comparative efficiency of traditional and contemporary fund transfer systems such as Real-Time Gross Settlement (RTGS) and National Electronic Funds Transfer (NEFT). It further examines the growing prominence of mobile payments and digital wallets, which have revolutionized the way individuals and businesses engage in financial transactions by providing greater convenience, accessibility, and speed. Special attention is devoted to the Unified Payments Interface (UPI) and Application Programming Interface (API) infrastructure, which serve as foundational elements in creating seamless, interoperable, and scalable payment ecosystems. By analyzing their architecture and significance, the chapter highlights how these innovations have enhanced integration across banking and non-banking financial platforms. Additionally, it evaluates the benefits and challenges associated with these technologies, including issues of security, regulatory compliance, customer adoption, and inclusivity. Overall, the discussion provides a comprehensive understanding of how payment technologies have evolved, their role in shaping the digital economy, and the critical considerations necessary for sustaining trust, efficiency, and innovation in the financial system.

Introduction

In this chapter, we explore the transformative landscape of payment technologies, focusing on traditional fund transfer systems, mobile payments, digital wallets, and the innovative infrastructure that powers digital transactions. The adoption of payment technologies is reshaping industries, enabling faster, more secure, and cost-effective transactions.

DOI: 10.1201/9788743811244-11

We delve into the various payment technologies that have evolved to meet the demands of today's fast-paced financial landscape. From traditional systems like RTGS and NEFT to cutting-edge mobile wallets, these technologies not only streamline the transfer of funds but also play a critical role in fostering financial inclusion and innovation. As the global financial ecosystem continues to evolve, so do the payment technologies that support it. By examining established systems such as RTGS, NEFT, and newer innovations like mobile payments and UPI, we can better understand the impact these technologies have on our daily transactions and broader economic systems. The evolution of FinTech has introduced innovative frameworks that enhance banking efficiency, including real-time fund transfer systems [1]. Technological disruption is reshaping financial services, enabling faster and more secure interbank settlement systems such as RTGS and NEFT [2]. FinTech integrates financial operations with digital technologies to improve transparency and operational effectiveness in fund transfers [3].

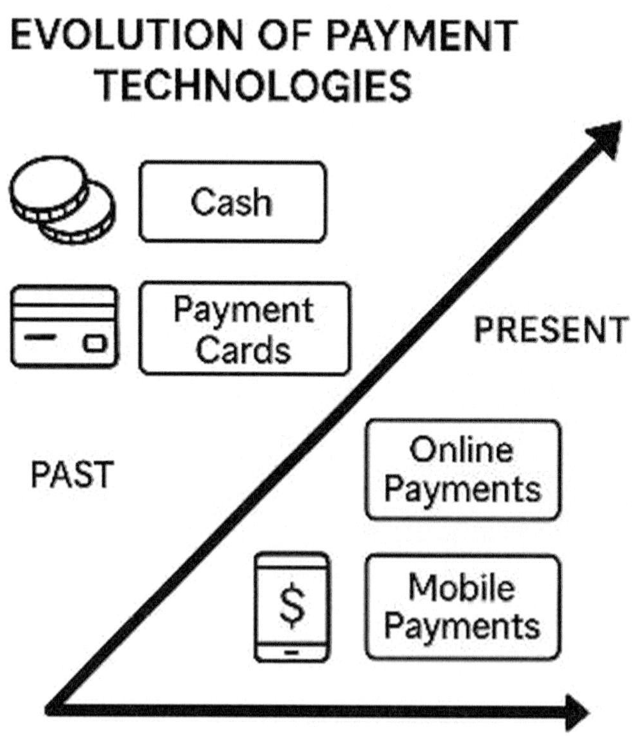

Figure 8.1 Evolution of payment technologies.

8.1 RTGS, NEFT, Fund Transfer Systems

Real-Time Gross Settlement (RTGS) and **National Electronic Fund Transfer (NEFT)** are two foundational systems for electronic fund transfers that have enabled individuals and businesses to make fast, secure, and reliable transactions between banks. **RTGS**: RTGS allows for real-time settlement of funds on a gross basis. In this system, transactions are settled immediately, one at a time, without netting. RTGS is primarily used for large-value transactions, typically exceeding ₹2 lakh in India. It is considered highly secure due to its real-time settlement and the absence of intermediaries. Global payment systems continue to evolve, ensuring secure, resilient, and interoperable settlements across institutions [4]. Beyond traditional banking, digital innovations allow financial institutions to provide 24 × 7 real-time transfers, reducing settlement delays [5].

8.1.1 Real-Time Gross Settlement (RTGS)

How It Works: RTGS is a system that settles payments on a **gross basis** and in **real time**. This means that every payment is processed individually and immediately. The system eliminates the need for batching or waiting periods, offering the fastest settlement option for large transactions. A bank sends the payment request to the RTGS system, which processes the transaction immediately. After validation, the payment is completed in real time, and the amount is deducted from the sender's account and credited to the receiver's account.

Advantages: RTGS guarantees immediate finality, meaning once the payment is made, it cannot be undone. This makes it highly secure and reliable, particularly for large-value transactions.

- **Immediate settlement**: As funds are transferred immediately, RTGS is ideal for urgent, high-value transactions such as business-to-business payments or interbank transfers.

- **Security**: The use of encrypted data and the direct involvement of central banks ensure high security in RTGS transactions.

- **Example**: A corporation making a payment of ₹f,00,000 to a vendor for a large supply order would likely use RTGS to ensure the payment clears immediately and with finality.

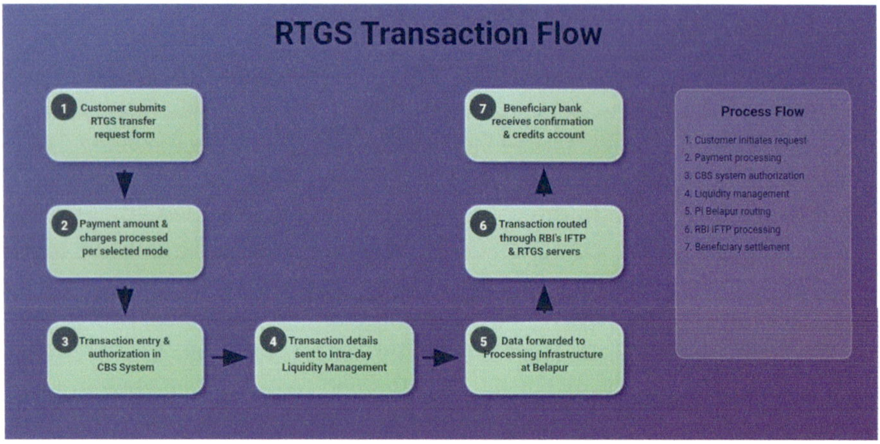

Figure 8.2 RTGS transaction flow.

8.1.2 NEFT

Unlike RTGS, NEFT operates on a batch processing basis. Transactions are processed in intervals throughout the day. NEFT is used for smaller-value transactions, and there is no upper limit on the amount that can be transferred. Payments are processed in batches at specified intervals, meaning that the transaction is not instantaneous. While it is not as fast as RTGS, it remains a popular and widely used system for fund transfers.

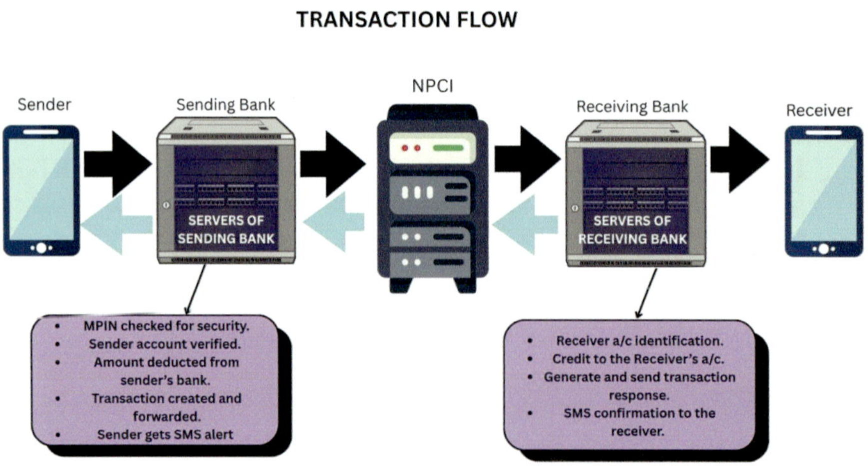

Figure 8.3 Transaction flow in NEFT.

- **How it works**: NEFT processes payments in **batches**, typically at hourly intervals, rather than in real-time. The system works well for smaller-value transactions and is widely used for personal and business transactions. NEFT provides **settlement on a net basis**, meaning payments are consolidated and processed at specific intervals.

- **Transaction process**: The sender initiates the transaction, and it is queued for processing in the next available batch. While this system is not as fast as RTGS, it is extremely reliable for smaller transactions that don't require immediate settlement.

Advantages: NEFT is an affordable and efficient method for transferring smaller amounts, and it is widely available to the public. It supports transfers up to ₹o lakh or more.

- **Affordability**: NEFT is generally cheaper than RTGS, making it more suitable for everyday payments.

- **Accessibility**: The system operates 24 × 7, though transactions are settled only during the bank's working hours, and it supports payments to any bank in India.

- **Example**: An individual transferring ₹50,000 to a relative in another city would likely use NEFT, as it is affordable and efficient for transactions of this size.

The primary difference between RTGS and NEFT lies in the settlement speed and the transaction volume. RTGS is for high-value transactions, settled in real-time, while NEFT is for smaller transactions and settled in batches.

Example: If a corporate entity wants to make a large payment to a supplier, RTGS would be the preferred choice due to its real-time settlement and high-value transfer capabilities. On the other hand, for smaller retail transactions, NEFT remains an ideal option for individuals transferring money across bank accounts.

Table 8.1 Difference between RTGS and NEFT.

Feature	RTGS	NEFT
Speed	Real-time, immediate settlement	Batch-wise settlement (not instant)
Transaction size	High value (₹2 lakh and above)	Low to moderate value
Transaction cost	Higher cost, especially for corporate payments	Lower cost, suitable for personal transactions

8.2 Mobile Payments and Digital Wallets

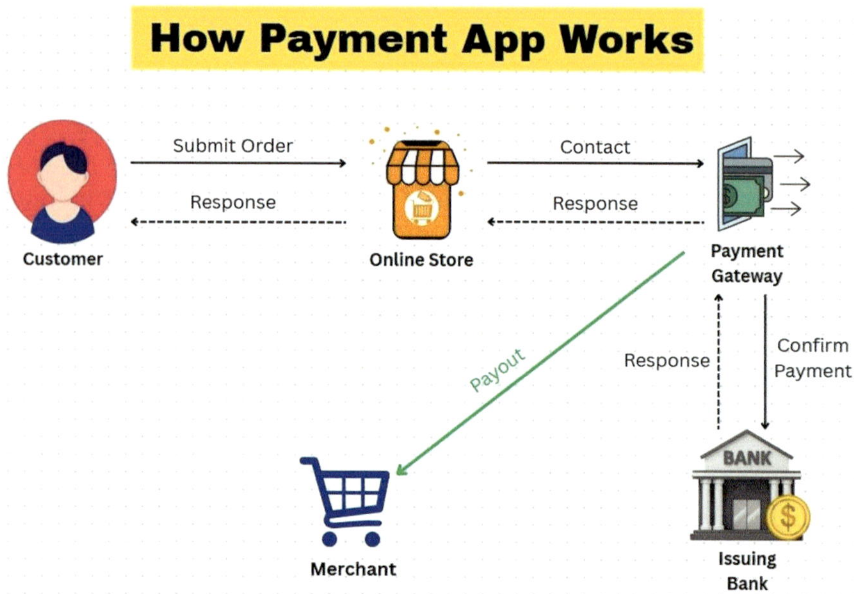

Figure 8.4 Working of payment app.

In recent years, **mobile payments** and **digital wallets** have significantly changed how consumers interact with money. By combining convenience with security, these technologies have facilitated a rapid shift from traditional methods of payment to digital-first transactions. They have revolutionized how consumers interact with financial services. These technologies provide a convenient, secure, and often seamless way to make payments using smartphones and digital platforms.

Mobile payments have become a dominant force in how consumers make everyday transactions. Technologies like near field communication (NFC), QR codes, and dedicated digital wallets are transforming how payments are made, both online and offline. Mobile payments allow users to conduct transactions directly from their smartphones. Whether it's tapping a phone at a POS terminal, scanning a QR code, or sending money via apps, mobile payments have become the cornerstone of modern transactions. NFC allows users to make payments by simply tapping their smartphones against a point-of-sale terminal. The transaction is completed using wireless communication, and no physical card is required. This technology is based on radio-frequency identification (RFID) and works over very short distances (usually within 4 cm). **Example**: In stores that accept Apple Pay or Google Pay, customers can simply tap their phones against a terminal to complete a purchase. This method is popular for its speed and ease of use. QR codes offer another simple method for conducting payments. Users can scan a merchant's or recipient's QR code to transfer funds. QR codes are increasingly used for peer-to-peer (P2P) transactions and merchant payments. A consumer can scan a merchant's QR code to make a payment, or the merchant can scan the consumer's code to collect payment. **Example**: In India, **Paytm** and **PhonePe** allow users to scan merchant QR codes for direct payments, making them ideal for small businesses and vendors. Alternative finance platforms, including mobile payments, have expanded financial access and inclusion, particularly in underbanked regions [6].

8.2.1 Benefits of mobile payments

Figure 8.5 Advantages of online payment system.

- **Convenience**: Users no longer need to carry physical cards or cash, and payments can be made with a tap or scan. Payments can be made anytime, anywhere, without the need to carry cash or cards.
- **Speed**: Transactions are processed almost instantly, providing a seamless experience for consumers and merchants. Mobile payment solutions aim to streamline the transaction process to make purchases faster and more efficient.
- **Security**: With features like two-factor authentication and tokenization, mobile payments are considered highly secure.

8.2.2 Digital wallets

Digital wallets, also known as e-wallets, are applications that securely store payment information, such as credit card or bank account details. They allow users to make online purchases and in-store transactions. Examples include PayPal, Venmo, Apple Wallet, and Google Wallet. A digital wallet stores payment information, such as credit/debit card details, and allows users to make secure transactions online or in-store. Digital wallets are typically tied to an app that can be linked to the user's bank account. Most digital wallets use tokenization, which replaces sensitive card details with a unique identifier, reducing the risk of fraud. Instead of storing credit card numbers, digital wallets store a token, which is a unique identifier that cannot be traced back to the original account information, thus enhancing security. In addition, digital wallets incorporate biometric authentication, such as fingerprint or facial recognition, to enhance security. India's digital payment infrastructure, including mobile wallets, has significantly reduced reliance on cash transactions [7]. Innovative payment services enhance convenience and accessibility for both consumers and small businesses [8]. Mobile payment technologies help bridge gaps in financial inclusion, connecting unbanked populations to formal banking systems [9].

Examples:

- **PayPal**: A globally accepted digital wallet that allows users to store funds, make purchases, and send money.
- **Apple wallet**: A wallet that allows users to store boarding passes, tickets, and payment methods on their Apple devices.
- **Google wallet**: An app that lets users store credit cards, debit cards, and loyalty cards, and make payments directly from their smartphones.
- **Venmo**: Primarily used in the United States, Venmo allows for P2P (peer-to-peer) money transfers via a linked bank account or debit card.

Types of digital wallets:

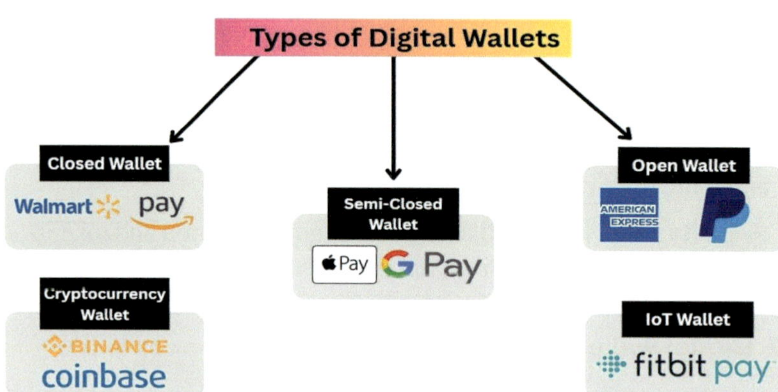

Figure 8.6 Types of digital wallets.

- **Closed wallets**: Used exclusively for transactions within the platform. For example, Paytm's wallet can only be used to make payments to merchants that accept Paytm.
- **Semi-closed wallets**: Allow users to make payments at multiple merchants, but there may be some restrictions. An example of this is the Amazon Pay Wallet.
- **Open wallets**: These wallets are generally linked to a bank account and can be used for a broad range of payments, including ATM withdrawals, making them the most versatile.

Advantages:

- **Centralization**: Multiple forms of payment (credit, debit, loyalty) can be managed within a single wallet.
- **Integration**: Digital wallets can integrate with other services, such as insurance or shopping apps, providing users with a unified experience.

Table 8.2 Difference between mobile payments and digital wallets.

Aspect	Mobile payments	Digital wallets
Definition	The act of making a payment using a mobile device (e.g., smartphone, tablet)	A software-based system that securely stores users' payment information and passwords
Function	Focuses on the transaction process – sending money or paying for goods/services	Focuses on storing and managing various types of digital financial instruments (cards, vouchers, crypto, etc.)
Examples	Apple Pay at a POS terminal, QR code payments via Paytm	PayPal, Google Wallet, Apple Wallet
Technology used	NFC (Near Field Communication), QR codes, SMS-based payments	Cloud-based storage, tokenization, encryption
Scope	Primarily used for making payments	Broader functionality – includes loyalty cards, tickets, and IDs, along with payments
Device dependence	Usually requires a mobile device	Can be used on mobile, desktop, or even wearables, depending on the platform

8.3 UPI and API Infrastructure

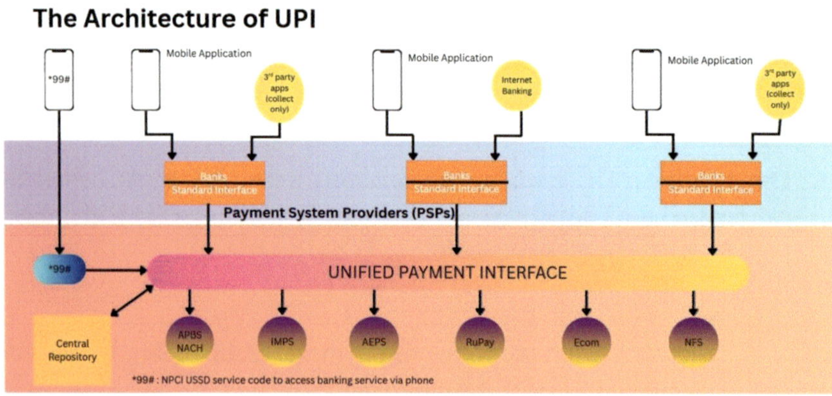

Figure 8.7 UPI architecture.

Unified Payments Interface (UPI) was officially launched on April 11, 2016, by the National Payments Corporation of India (NPCI), with the support of the Reserve Bank of India (RBI) and the Indian Banks' Association (IBA). UPI is one of the most innovative developments in payment technologies. It allows users to transfer money between bank accounts instantly using their smartphones. **API** stands for **Application programming interface**. It is a set of rules, protocols, and tools that allows different software applications to communicate with each other. An API is a software intermediary that enables interaction between different systems, programs, or components by exposing a set of functions, commands, or endpoints. UPI allows users to link multiple bank accounts to a single mobile application and make seamless, real-time transactions. It supports features like bill payments, peer-to-peer transfers, and merchant payments, all from a single platform. The introduction of **BHIM UPI** app helped accelerate the adoption of UPI in India. The success of UPI is powered by a robust **API infrastructure**. APIs allow third-party developers to create applications that interface directly with the UPI platform, enabling a wide range of financial services to be offered to consumers. The ease of integration with banking systems has made UPI a preferred platform for many businesses and FinTech startups. The development of open API infrastructure and UPI has transformed India's digital payment ecosystem, enabling seamless interbank transactions [10]. FinTech-driven marketplace lending and API-based integrations facilitate faster, secure, and interoperable financial services [11]. RBI reports indicate substantial growth in digital payments driven by API-enabled systems and consumer adoption [12].

Unified Payments Interface (UPI) is one of India's most innovative payment solutions, allowing for seamless and instant money transfers. UPI has become a global benchmark for real-time, interoperable digital payments across multiple banks and FinTech platforms [13]. Surveys show that small businesses increasingly adopt mobile and UPI-based solutions, improving digital participation [14]. The market is shifting from wallet-based to UPI-integrated systems, reflecting user preference for unified payment platforms [15].

- **How it works**: UPI allows users to link multiple bank accounts to a single mobile application and conduct seamless transactions. The system is powered by real-time settlement, and users can transfer money, pay bills, and even make merchant payments through UPI.

  Key features:

- **Interoperability**: UPI is bank-agnostic, meaning it allows users to send money between different banks using a single application, like Google Pay or PhonePe.
- **Request to pay**: UPI also facilitates "Request to Pay" features, where users can request payments from others directly.
- **Security**: UPI uses **two-factor authentication (2FA)** for security, and all transactions are encrypted.
- **Example**: A user can transfer money to a friend or pay for groceries by scanning a QR code or entering the recipient's UPI ID (e.g., example@upi).

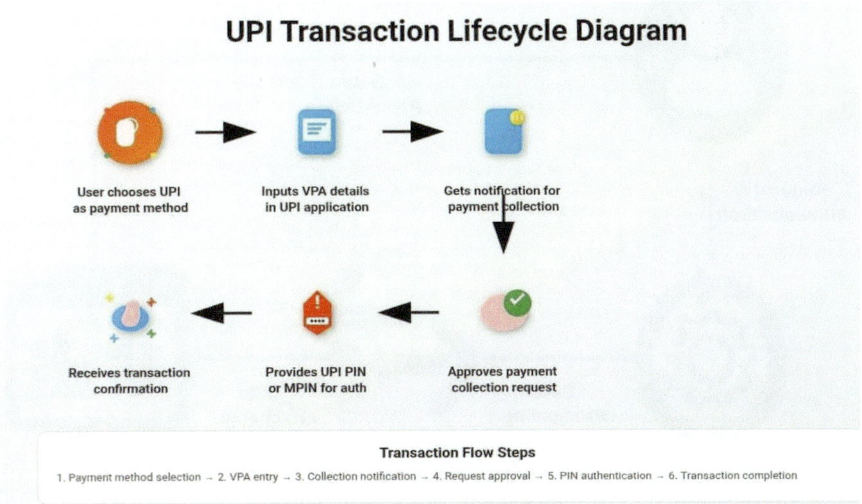

Figure 8.8 UPI transaction lifecycle.

API infrastructure:

- **How APIs power UPI**: UPI is built on an API-based architecture that allows third-party apps to easily integrate UPI functionality into their platforms. This API infrastructure will enable developers to create payment solutions that work seamlessly with the UPI ecosystem.
- **Benefits of API infrastructure**: APIs make it possible for businesses to quickly add payment features to their services, allowing for faster innovation in the payment space.
- **Example**: **PhonePe** and **Google Pay** are built on UPI APIs, offering users seamless payment experiences across various services, from paying bills to making investments.

The **Unified Payments Interface (UPI)** is a groundbreaking technology that has reshaped India's payments ecosystem, offering a seamless, interbank payment system that enables real-time transfers. UPI's **API-driven architecture** plays a significant role in making it accessible to millions of users through third-party apps and financial services. Online and mobile banking channels have become central to India's digital finance transformation, enabling secure, real-time financial management for consumers and businesses [16].

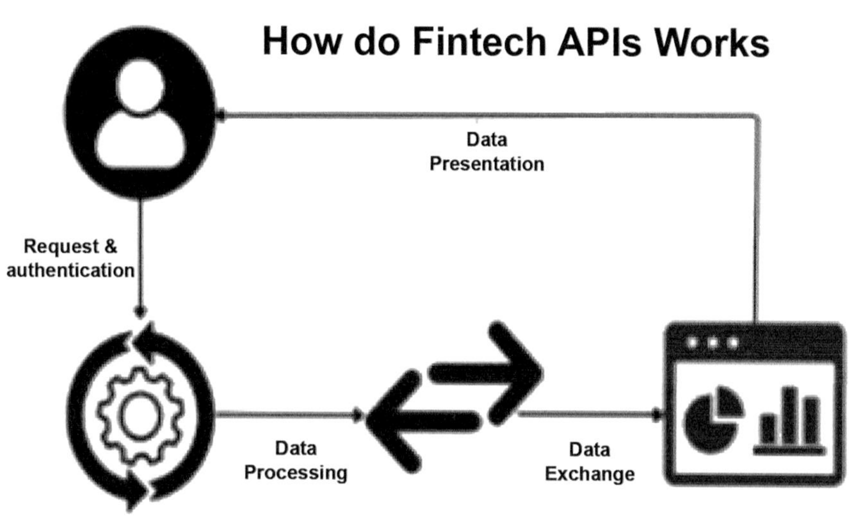

Figure 8.9 Working of API.

Summary

This chapter focuses on the various mechanisms and technologies that enable modern digital payments. It begins by explaining the workflows and operations of traditional fund transfer systems like Real-Time Gross Settlement (RTGS) and National Electronic Funds Transfer (NEFT). It then highlights the growing importance of mobile payments and digital wallets, which have revolutionized how consumers and businesses conduct transactions. The discussion extends to the architecture of Unified Payments Interface (UPI) and API-based infrastructure, which are central to enabling real-time, seamless, and interoperable digital payments. Finally, it evaluates both the benefits – such as speed, convenience, and financial inclusion – and the challenges – like cybersecurity risks and system scalability – associated with different payment technologies.

Case Study: RTGS vs. NEFT in Corporate Payments – A Strategic Decision by XYZ Corp

XYZ Corp., a global conglomerate with operations in India, recently received a critical shipment of raw materials from its key supplier, ABC Ltd. The invoice for the shipment amounted to ₹1 crore, and per the agreement, the payment needed to be made promptly to maintain business continuity and preserve goodwill. The finance team at XYZ Corp. was tasked with choosing the most appropriate electronic funds transfer method to remit the amount from its corporate account to ABC Ltd.'s bank account. The options under India's electronic payment infrastructure included Real-Time Gross Settlement (RTGS) and National Electronic Funds Transfer (NEFT). The team needed to weigh various factors, including transaction urgency, operational ease, cost, and compliance.

RTGS is designed for high-value transactions and enables real-time fund transfers. It processes payments on a gross basis, meaning each transaction is settled individually and immediately, making it highly suitable for large, time-sensitive payments. In this case, the funds would be debited from XYZ Corp's account and credited to ABC Ltd's account within minutes. The primary advantages of RTGS are its speed, security, and suitability for high-value transactions above ₹2 lakh. It also minimizes the risk of fraud and avoids delays, which is vital when business continuity is at stake. NEFT, on the other hand, operates in half-hourly batches, resulting in a delay between initiation and settlement. While it is more cost-effective and available throughout the day, it may not be ideal for urgent or large-sum transactions.

After evaluating both options, XYZ Corp. opted for RTGS due to the urgency and the large value of the transaction. Although NEFT was a less expensive option, it did not guarantee immediate settlement, which was critical in this case. The company likely used secure corporate banking platforms integrated with the Reserve Bank of India's infrastructure, ensuring real-time tracking, authorization, and regulatory compliance. The outcome was a successful, fast, and secure transaction that upheld business operations, built trust with the supplier, and demonstrated the company's financial responsiveness. Moreover, RTGS helped XYZ Corp. avoid potential disruptions in its production process that could have occurred due to payment delays.

However, the case was not without challenges. The finance team had to carefully balance transaction costs against the need for speed. RTGS transactions are typically limited to banking hours, and missing a cut-off could lead to delays. High-value transactions also require multiple levels of approval and precise documentation, which can sometimes introduce internal delays. Trust in the digital infrastructure and ensuring error-free processing were also important considerations.

This case highlights the strategic importance of selecting the right payment mechanism for corporate finance. RTGS is best suited for urgent, high-value payments, whereas NEFT is more appropriate for routine, low-value transfers that are not time-critical. The ability to make such decisions efficiently requires financial awareness, operational preparedness, and robust digital banking infrastructure.

Case Discussion Questions:

1. What key operational and financial factors influenced XYZ Corp.'s decision to choose RTGS over NEFT?
2. In what types of business scenarios would NEFT be a more appropriate choice than RTGS?
3. How do real-time settlement systems like RTGS contribute to business efficiency and risk mitigation?

4. What role do digital infrastructure and banking technology play in facilitating corporate payments?
5. How can companies develop payment policies to optimize cost without compromising on urgency or security?

Keywords

- **Real-Time Gross Settlement (RTGS):** A payment system where the transfer of money happens in real-time and on a gross basis. Each transaction is settled individually without netting, making it ideal for large, urgent transactions.
- **National Electronic Funds Transfer (NEFT):** A system for transferring funds between banks in India. NEFT works on a batch processing model, meaning transactions are grouped and processed at specified intervals throughout the day.
- **Mobile payments:** A method of paying for goods or services through a mobile device, typically via an app or mobile wallet. Examples include Google Pay, Apple Pay, and Paytm.
- **Digital wallets:** Electronic systems that allow users to store and manage payment information, such as credit card details, bank accounts, and other digital payment methods. Examples include PayPal, Apple Wallet, and Google Pay.
- **Unified Payments Interface (UPI):** A real-time payment system developed in India that allows users to send and receive money instantly using mobile devices. It integrates multiple bank accounts into one mobile app and facilitates both peer-to-peer and business payments.
- **Application Programming Interface (API):** A set of tools and protocols that allow one software application to interact with another. In payments, APIs enable third-party applications to process payments, access banking information, and integrate payment systems.
- **Near Field Communication (NFC):** A short-range wireless technology that enables devices, such as smartphones or cards, to communicate with one another by bringing them close together. It is commonly used in contactless payment systems like Apple Pay and Google Pay.

- **Tokenization:** The process of replacing sensitive data, such as credit card numbers, with a unique token that is useless if intercepted. Tokenization enhances payment security by protecting sensitive information during transactions.
- **QR code payments:** A type of payment where customers scan a QR code displayed by the merchant to complete a transaction. This is popular in mobile wallets and is an affordable alternative to NFC-based systems.
- **Contactless payments:** A type of payment where a user can make transactions by waving or tapping their card or mobile phone near a point-of-sale terminal, without having to physically insert or swipe the card.
- **Payment systems:** Broadly refers to the infrastructure that enables money transfers, including technologies like card networks, mobile payment platforms, and bank transfer systems.
- **Banking infrastructure:** Refers to the entire set of technologies, services, and networks that banks use to process and facilitate payments, including ATMs, payment gateways, clearinghouses, and settlement systems.
- **Fraud prevention:** The set of technologies, techniques, and protocols used to detect and prevent unauthorized transactions or fraudulent activities in payment systems. This can include encryption, multi-factor authentication, and machine learning algorithms.
- **Transaction speed:** Refers to the time it takes for a transaction to be completed in a payment system. Systems like RTGS offer instant transfers, while systems like NEFT may have a delay due to batch processing.
- **Payment gateway:** A technology that securely processes payment transactions by transmitting the payment information from the merchant to the bank or payment processor. Examples include Stripe, PayPal, and Square.
- **Banking regulations:** The rules and laws governing the operation of financial institutions, including how payments and funds are handled, ensure security, transparency, and consumer protection.
- **Secure payment technologies:** Technologies designed to ensure that payment transactions are conducted safely. These include encryption, tokenization, multi-factor authentication, and secure protocols like HTTPS.
- **Fund transfer systems:** Systems used to transfer money from one account to another. This can include both real-time systems (like RTGS) and batch processing systems (like NEFT).

- **Peer-to-peer payments:** A type of payment that allows individuals to send money to each other without going through traditional financial intermediaries like banks. Examples include Venmo, Zelle, and Paytm.
- **Cross-border payments:** Payments that are made between parties in different countries. These transactions often involve currency exchange and need to adhere to international regulations and security standards.

Discussion Questions

1. Explain the key differences between RTGS and NEFT in terms of transaction speed, cost, and transaction size.
2. In what situations would a business prefer to use RTGS over NEFT? Provide an example scenario.
3. Discuss the security features that make mobile payments secure, such as tokenization and encryption.
4. Why are these features crucial in protecting users from fraud, and how do they compare to traditional payment methods like credit cards?
5. Explain how UPI has improved financial inclusion in rural and underserved areas.
6. What challenges still exist in adopting UPI in rural areas, and how can they be overcome?
7. List the advantages and disadvantages of using a digital wallet over a physical wallet.
8. How can digital wallets contribute to reducing cash dependency in the economy?
9. Describe how an API infrastructure enables third-party apps to use UPI for payments.
10. What are the key benefits of using APIs in payment systems for both users and businesses?

References

[1] Arner, D. W., Barberis, J., & Buckley, R. P. (2015). The evolution of FinTech: A new post-crisis paradigm? *Georgetown Journal of International Law, 47*(4), 1271–1319.

[2] Gomber, P., Kauffman, R. J., Parker, C., & Weber, B. W. (2018). On the FinTech revolution: Interpreting the forces of innovation, disruption, and transformation in financial services. *Journal of Management Information Systems, 35*(1), 220–265. https://doi.org/10.1080/07421222.2018.1440766

[3] Schueffel, P. (2016). Taming the beast: A scientific definition of FinTech. *Journal of Innovation Management, 4*(4), 32–54.

[4] Bank for International Settlements (BIS). (2020). *Payments – Status, challenges, and outlook*. https://www.bis.org

[5] McWaters, J., Galaski, R., & World Economic Forum. (2017). *Beyond FinTech: A pragmatic assessment of disruptive potential in financial services*. World Economic Forum. https://www.weforum.org

[6] Ziegler, T., Shneor, R., Garvey, K., Wenzlaff, K., & Yerolemou, N. (2021). *The global alternative finance market benchmarking report*. Cambridge Centre for Alternative Finance.

[7] Agarwal, A., & Goel, M. (2023). *Digital payments & payment systems in India: Economics, operations, challenges*. Routledge.

[8] Rajeshwari, R. K., & Balasubramanian, G. (2022). *Payment systems and services: Trends and innovations*. Sage Publications.

[9] Pathak, B. (2021). *Financial inclusion through payment technologies*. Springer.

[10] Pusukas, I. (2022). *Modern banking infrastructure & FinTech systems*. Palgrave Macmillan.

[11] Litan, R. E., & Singer, A. (2020). *Marketplace lending and emerging financial technology*. Brookings Institution Press.

[12] Reserve Bank of India (RBI). (2024). *Report on trends and progress of digital payments in India 2023–24*. Reserve Bank of India.

[13] National Payments Corporation of India (NPCI). (2024). *UPI annual review 2023–2024*. https://www.npci.org.in

[14] PayNearby. (2025). *MSME digital index survey report: Digital payments adoption in small businesses*. PayNearby.

[15] PwC India. (2024). *Digital wallets vs UPI: Market shift and future outlook*. PricewaterhouseCoopers India.

[16] International Monetary Fund (IMF). (2025). *Growing retail digital payments: Value of interoperability – India case study* (IMF Working Paper).

9

Market Provisioning and Investment Management

Abstract

The evolution of financial services in the digital era has redefined the structure, delivery, and consumption of banking and related services. This chapter provides an overview of emerging digital banking models and evaluates their transformative impact on traditional banking systems, reshaping how financial institutions operate and compete. It examines the critical role of non-banking financial companies (NBFCs) in bridging credit gaps and supporting financial inclusion, particularly in underserved markets. The chapter also explores the rapid rise of online and mobile banking platforms, highlighting their convenience, accessibility, and growing importance in customer engagement. In addition, it introduces consumer-focused financial technologies that are reshaping the user experience in finance, including innovations in personalization, automation, and real-time services. Special focus is given to the concept of embedded finance, which integrates financial services into non-financial platforms, thereby creating seamless and contextual customer experiences. Furthermore, the chapter discusses the features and benefits of personal financial management (PFM) applications, which empower users to make informed financial decisions through budgeting, tracking, and analytics tools. Collectively, these innovations are portrayed as powerful enablers of consumer empowerment, offering greater financial control, accessibility, and inclusion while setting new benchmarks for efficiency and customer-centricity in the financial ecosystem.

Introduction

This chapter explores the transformative impact of technology on market provisioning and investment management. It focuses primarily on the emergence of robo-advisors and AI-based investing tools that automate investment

DOI: 10.1201/9788743811244-12

decision-making and portfolio optimization, making sophisticated strategies accessible to a wider range of investors. The chapter also examines portfolio management platforms that integrate data analytics, real-time monitoring, and personalized services to enhance investment outcomes. Through these innovations, investment management is becoming more efficient, transparent, and customer-centric, fundamentally reshaping how individuals and institutions approach wealth creation and asset allocation. The digital revolution has not only transformed the backend operations of financial institutions but has also redefined the way consumers interact with financial products and services. This chapter further explores how technology is reshaping consumer experiences through innovations that are highly integrated, intuitive, and personalized. The focus lies on embedded finance and personal financial management (PFM) Apps, two powerful developments that are making financial services more accessible, contextual, and customer-friendly. As traditional banking gives way to more seamless and invisible financial interactions, consumer-centric technologies are emerging as a core driver of financial inclusion, engagement, and empowerment. FinTech innovations have created new business models in investment management, including the proliferation of robo-advisors that automate portfolio allocation and client advisory services [1]. The post-crisis evolution of FinTech has accelerated the integration of digital platforms in investment processes, reshaping traditional advisory models [2]. This chapter provides insights into the mechanisms, benefits, and implications of these technologies for both users and financial service providers.

9.1 Robo-Advisors

The landscape of investment management has undergone a profound transformation in recent years, driven largely by advances in technology. Two key innovations at the forefront of this evolution are robo-advisors and AI-based investing. These technologies leverage automation, big data, and artificial intelligence (AI) to democratize access to investment advisory services, optimize portfolio management, and enhance decision-making precision. This detailed explanation explores the concepts, mechanisms, benefits, challenges, and future outlook of robo-advisors and AI-based investing within the broader context of financial technology (FinTech). Digital footprints and alternative credit scoring techniques used by FinTechs highlight the ability of technology to enhance investment decision-making and risk assessment [3]. Adaptive market theory suggests that financial markets evolve rapidly under technological innovations, providing fertile ground for automated investment systems [4].

Figure 9.1 Robo-advisor.

Robo-advisors are digital platforms that provide automated, algorithm-driven financial planning and investment management services with minimal human intervention. Robo-advisors have the potential to optimize asset allocation and reduce costs while providing scalable solutions for individual and institutional investors [5]. Platforms such as Betterment, Wealthfront, and Indian equivalents have seen exponential growth in assets under management, reflecting growing investor trust in automated advisory services [6]. Unlike traditional financial advisors who offer personalized advice through face-to-face meetings or calls, robo-advisors use software algorithms to gather client information, assess risk tolerance, financial goals, and time horizon, then recommend and manage an appropriate investment portfolio. The typical robo-advisor process involves:

- **Client profiling:** Users answer questions about their financial situation, investment goals, risk appetite, and time horizon.
- **Algorithmic portfolio construction:** Based on client inputs, the robo-advisor's algorithm selects a diversified portfolio of assets-often exchange-traded funds (ETFs) -optimized to meet the client's objectives.
- **Automated portfolio management:** Robo-advisors continuously monitor the portfolio and automatically rebalance assets to maintain target allocations in response to market fluctuations.
- **Tax optimization:** Some platforms incorporate tax-loss harvesting, which strategically sells securities at a loss to offset capital gains and reduce tax liability.
- **Low-cost model:** By automating these functions, robo-advisors offer services at a fraction of the cost of traditional financial advisors.

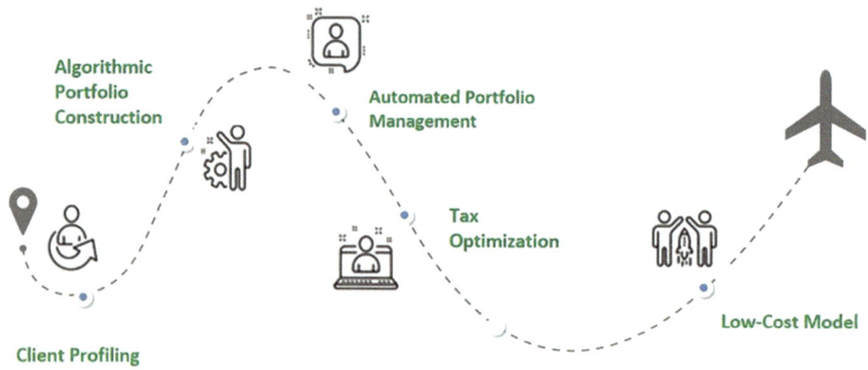

Figure 9.2 Robo-advisor process.

9.1.1 Robo-advisor examples

Betterment (USA): Betterment, launched in 2008, is one of the earliest and most successful robo-advisors globally. Based in the United States, it provides automated investment management services designed for individuals seeking low-cost, hands-off investing. The users can create separate portfolios for goals like retirement, emergency funds, or travel. It includes features like tax-loss harvesting and asset location optimization. It is based on Modern Portfolio Theory (MPT), and it automatically diversifies investments across global ETFs. It also offers hybrid plans with access to certified financial planners. Betterment popularized robo-advising as a trusted alternative to traditional wealth management. Its intuitive user interface, transparent fee structure, and strong regulatory compliance (SEC and FINRA in the U.S.) made it a model for emerging robo platforms worldwide.

Nutmeg (UK): Founded in 2011 and based in London, Nutmeg is the UK's largest robo-advisor and one of Europe's most recognized digital wealth managers. It offers a mix of automated investment portfolios and personalized financial services. The users choose risk levels, and Nutmeg allocates funds accordingly using ETFs. It offers ESG (environmental, social, governance) and socially responsible investment options. It is powered by J.P. Morgan Asset Management for active, AI-enhanced strategies. It has a flat fee structure with real-time tracking and no hidden costs. Nutmeg has been instrumental in bringing robo-advisory to mainstream British investors. Its acquisition by J.P. Morgan in 2021 signals the global financial industry's endorsement of automated platforms as part of the future of investment management.

9.2 AI-Based Investing

While robo-advisors primarily focus on portfolio construction and management based on client profiling, AI-based investing encompasses a broader spectrum of investment strategies powered by artificial intelligence and machine learning. AI-based investing applies advanced algorithms to analyze massive datasets, recognize patterns, forecast market trends, and make predictive decisions, often in real-time. Artificial intelligence (AI) is transforming investment management by enabling predictive analytics, risk modeling, and personalized strategies at unprecedented speed [7]. The digital transformation of the financial sector leverages AI to enhance efficiency, automate trading, and improve decision-making in portfolio management [8].

9.2.1 Key AI techniques used

- **Machine learning (ML):** ML models learn from historical market data to identify correlations and predict asset price movements.
- **Natural language processing (NLP):** NLP analyzes news, social media sentiment, earnings calls, and other textual data to gauge market sentiment.
- **Deep learning:** A subset of ML using neural networks to detect complex patterns in financial data.
- **Reinforcement learning:** AI agents learn optimal trading strategies through trial and error in simulated environments.

9.2.2 Applications of AI in investing

Artificial intelligence has significantly advanced various aspects of modern finance, particularly in investment and credit-related functions. In algorithmic trading, AI enables the automated execution of trades based on pre-defined rules and real-time data, increasing speed and efficiency in financial markets. Sentiment analysis tools leverage news articles and social media activity to gauge public mood and inform strategic buy or sell decisions. AI is also widely used in risk assessment, where models analyze market conditions and portfolio compositions to predict potential exposures and recommend appropriate mitigation strategies. AI-powered investment tools help investors navigate complex markets, reducing human bias while increasing precision in asset selection [9]. AI-enabled systems are increasingly integrated into robo-advisory platforms, combining automation with data-driven insights for improved investment outcomes [10]. Furthermore, AI improves accuracy in credit scoring and asset valuation by evaluating vast amounts of financial data, thereby enhancing decision-making in lending and investment processes.

- **Algorithmic trading:** Automated execution of trades based on pre-set AI-driven rules.
- **Sentiment analysis:** Using social media and news sentiment to inform buy/sell decisions.
- **Risk assessment:** AI models predict portfolio risk exposures and suggest mitigations.
- **Credit scoring and asset valuation:** AI enhances accuracy in evaluating financial instruments and borrowers.

Figure 9.3 Applications of AI in investing.

9.2.3 Benefits of robo-advisors and AI-based investing

Robo-advisors lower the entry barrier to professional investment management by offering low-cost, automated services accessible to retail investors who may not meet the minimum asset requirements or afford traditional advisors. Other advantages are listed below:

- **Cost efficiency:** Automation reduces the need for human labor, cutting operational costs. Fees for robo-advisors typically range from 0.2% to 0.5% of assets under management (AUM), significantly less than traditional advisors who may charge 1% or more.

- **Consistency and discipline:** Algorithms enforce disciplined investment strategies, minimizing emotional biases that can impair human decision-making. Automated rebalancing ensures portfolios remain aligned with risk profiles.
- **Personalization at scale:** AI and robo-advisor platforms can tailor portfolios and advice to individual client goals using data-driven insights, making personalized investing feasible for a large customer base.
- **Enhanced data processing:** AI's ability to analyze vast volumes of structured and unstructured data enables more informed and timely investment decisions, uncovering opportunities that humans might miss.
- **Real-time monitoring and adaptation:** AI systems can monitor market conditions 24/7 and adjust strategies dynamically, improving responsiveness to volatile markets.

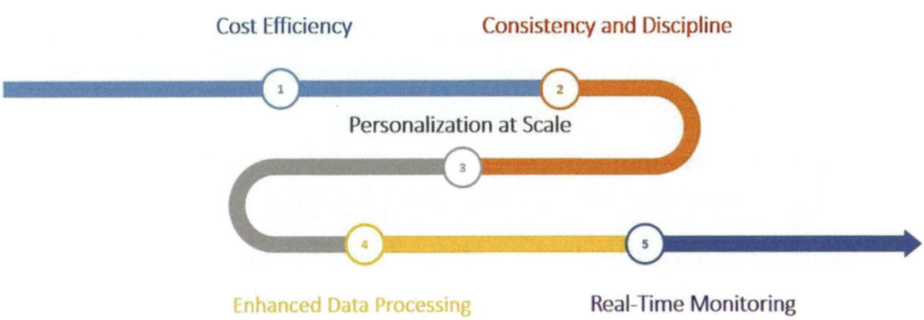

Figure 9.4 Advantages of using robo-advisor.

Challenges and limitations

- **Model risks and over-reliance on algorithms:** Algorithms rely on historical data and programmed rules, which may not always predict future market behavior accurately, especially during unprecedented events or market shocks.
- **Lack of human judgment:** While automation excels at routine tasks and pattern recognition, it may lack the nuanced judgment required for complex financial situations, behavioral coaching, or crisis management.
- **Data quality and bias:** AI models are only as good as the data they are trained on. Poor data quality or biased datasets can lead to inaccurate predictions and flawed investment advice.

- **Regulatory and compliance issues:** The evolving regulatory landscape poses challenges for AI-driven investment platforms, including ensuring transparency, protecting investor interests, and addressing cybersecurity risks.
- **Client trust and adoption barriers:** Some investors remain skeptical of fully automated advisory services due to concerns about control, security, and the impersonal nature of digital platforms.

The future of robo-advisors and AI-based investing is promising, with ongoing developments expected to enhance their capabilities:

- **Hybrid models:** Combining AI automation with human advisors to offer personalized, nuanced advice alongside efficient portfolio management.
- **Explainable AI:** Increasing demand for transparency in AI decision-making processes to build trust and meet regulatory standards.
- **Integration of alternative data:** Utilizing unconventional data sources such as satellite imagery, IoT data, and Environmental, Social, Governance (ESG) metrics for richer insights.
- **Advanced personalization:** Deeper customization of investment strategies incorporating behavioral finance principles.
- **Global expansion:** Robo-advisors and AI investing tools will continue to grow in emerging markets, driving financial inclusion.

Robo-advisors and AI-based investing represent a paradigm shift in the investment management industry, driven by technology's ability to provide accessible, efficient, and data-driven services. While challenges remain in terms of accuracy, regulation, and client trust, the benefits of automation and artificial intelligence in enhancing investment decision-making are significant. As these technologies mature, they are poised to redefine how investors of all sizes manage wealth, making investment management more inclusive, adaptive, and intelligent.

9.3 Portfolio Management Platforms

Portfolio management has traditionally been a complex, resource-intensive task, often requiring the expertise of professional fund managers and financial advisors. However, the advent of digital technologies has revolutionized this landscape through the development of **portfolio management platforms** – digital tools that facilitate the construction, monitoring, analysis, and optimization of investment portfolios. These platforms leverage advanced analytics, real-time data, automation, and increasingly, artificial intelligence (AI), to improve investment outcomes, enhance transparency, and streamline the investor experience. This comprehensive explanation explores the concept, features, types, benefits, challenges, and future trends associated with portfolio management platforms in the contemporary investment ecosystem. Portfolio management platforms are digital systems designed to assist investors, asset managers, financial advisors, and institutions in managing investment portfolios more efficiently and effectively. *These platforms provide a centralized environment to:*

- Construct diversified portfolios aligned with client goals and risk tolerance.
- Track portfolio performance and asset allocations in real time.
- Analyze risks, returns, and correlations among portfolio components.
- Automate routine tasks such as rebalancing and reporting.
- Facilitate compliance and regulatory oversight.

Figure 9.5 Platform management services shown in devices.
Source: https://www.advisoryhq.com/articles/5-great-portfolio-management-software-ranking-and-reviews/

By consolidating these functions, portfolio management platforms empower users to make data-driven investment decisions while reducing manual workload and operational costs.

9.3.1 Types of portfolio management platforms

Portfolio management platforms vary widely depending on the target users and functionalities offered. The primary categories include:

Retail investor platforms

These platforms cater to individual investors seeking to manage their personal portfolios with minimal technical expertise. They often integrate with online brokerages and provide user-friendly dashboards, goal-based investing tools, and educational resources. **Examples:** Personal Capital, SigFig, Wealthfront (portfolio management features).

Robo-advisory platforms

Robo-advisors are a subset of portfolio management platforms that combine automated portfolio construction and management with minimal human intervention. They emphasize algorithm-driven asset allocation and automated rebalancing. **Examples:** Betterment, Wealthfront, Schwab Intelligent Portfolios.

Institutional portfolio management systems

These sophisticated platforms serve asset management firms, hedge funds, pension funds, and other institutional investors. They offer advanced analytics, multi-asset class support, scenario analysis, and compliance tools. **Examples:** BlackRock Aladdin, Bloomberg AIM, FactSet Portfolio Analytics.

Advisor-focused platforms

Designed for financial advisors and wealth managers, these platforms facilitate managing multiple client portfolios, client reporting, billing, and regulatory compliance, often integrating CRM (Customer Relationship Management) features. **Examples:** Orion Advisor Services, Envestnet, Tamarac.

Features of portfolio management platforms

A modern portfolio management platform typically offers a suite of integrated features that cover the end-to-end investment management lifecycle:

Figure 9.6 Types of portfolio management platforms.

Portfolio construction and optimization

Platforms use quantitative models to build portfolios aligned with investor objectives and risk profiles. They employ optimization techniques like mean-variance optimization to balance expected returns against risk.

Real-time performance monitoring

Users can monitor portfolio returns, asset allocation, and benchmark comparisons in real time through intuitive dashboards and visualizations.

Risk management tools

Risk metrics such as Value at Risk (VaR), beta, standard deviation, and stress testing help assess potential downside scenarios and volatility.

Automated rebalancing

To maintain desired asset allocations, platforms automatically execute portfolio rebalancing by buying or selling securities as market values fluctuate. Also, Platforms often integrate with custodians, brokerages, market data providers, and CRM systems to consolidate information and provide a unified view.

Tax optimization

Features like tax-loss harvesting help reduce tax liabilities by strategically realizing losses to offset gains.

Reporting and compliance

Platforms generate customized performance reports for clients and facilitate regulatory compliance by tracking transaction histories, disclosures, and audit trails.

How portfolio management platforms work

The functioning of portfolio management platforms involves several interconnected processes:

- **Data aggregation:** Collecting portfolio data, market prices, benchmark indices, client information, and transaction histories from multiple sources.
- **Analysis and modeling:** Applying financial models and algorithms to evaluate portfolio performance, risks, and expected returns.
- **Decision support:** Generating actionable insights and recommendations for portfolio adjustments based on predefined rules or AI-driven predictions.
- **Execution and automation:** Enabling automated trade execution for rebalancing, tax strategies, or strategic shifts.
- **Client communication:** Delivering performance summaries, risk disclosures, and investment advice through portals or reports.

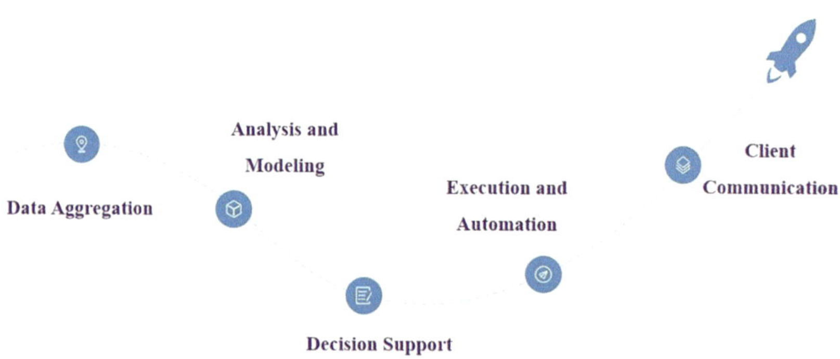

Figure 9.7 Process of portfolio management platforms.

Benefits of portfolio management platforms

- **Improved efficiency:** Automating routine tasks like performance tracking, rebalancing, and reporting frees up time for portfolio managers and advisors to focus on strategic decision-making.

- **Data-driven decision-making:** Platforms provide sophisticated analytics and visualization tools that enhance understanding of portfolio risks, returns, and correlations, leading to more informed investment choices.
- **Enhanced transparency:** Real-time access to portfolio information increases transparency for investors, building trust and enabling better communication between clients and advisors.
- **Scalability:** Advisors and institutions can manage larger numbers of portfolios or clients without a proportional increase in resources due to automation and centralized management.
- **Customization and personalization:** Platforms allow tailoring portfolios to individual goals, risk appetites, and constraints, supporting personalized investment experiences.
- **Cost savings:** By reducing manual processes and errors, portfolio management platforms lower operational costs, potentially translating into lower fees for investors.

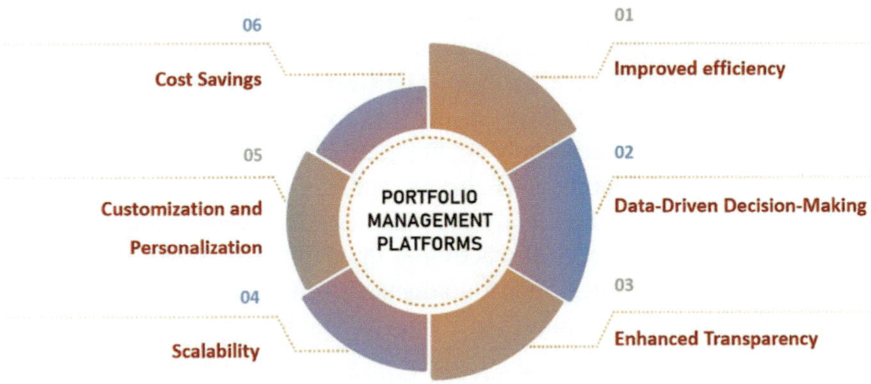

Figure 9.8 Advantages of using portfolio management platforms.

Challenges and limitations

Despite their advantages, portfolio management platforms face several challenges:

- **Complexity and usability:** Some platforms may have steep learning curves, especially for retail investors unfamiliar with investment terminology or analytics.

- **Data security and privacy:** Handling sensitive financial data requires robust cybersecurity measures and compliance with data protection regulations.
- **Integration issues:** Seamless integration with various data sources and brokerage platforms can be technically complex and costly.
- **Algorithmic lmitations:** Automated models depend on historical data and may fail to anticipate black swan events or sudden market disruptions.
- **Regulatory compliance:** Navigating complex regulatory environments across jurisdictions requires continuous updates to platform features and disclosures.

9.3.2 Role of AI and machine learning in portfolio management platforms

Artificial intelligence is playing a transformative role in financial services by enhancing decision-making and operational efficiency. Predictive analytics uses AI models to forecast asset price movements and market trends by analyzing both historical and alternative datasets. Natural language processing (NLP) enables sentiment analysis by scanning news articles and social media to assess market mood and adjust portfolios accordingly. Additionally, machine learning offers behavioral insights by identifying client behavior patterns, allowing for personalized financial advice and nudges that can improve individual outcomes. AI also strengthens security by enabling real-time fraud detection and anomaly identification, as algorithms quickly flag unusual transactions or portfolio activities that may indicate errors or fraudulent behavior. Increasingly, portfolio management platforms incorporate AI and machine learning techniques to enhance capabilities:

- **Predictive analytics:** AI models forecast asset price movements and market trends based on historical data and alternative datasets.
- **Sentiment analysis:** NLP processes news and social media feeds to gauge market sentiment and adjust portfolios accordingly.
- **Behavioral insights:** Machine learning can identify client behavior patterns, enabling personalized advice and nudges to improve financial outcomes.
- **Fraud detection and anomaly identification:** AI algorithms flag unusual transactions or portfolio activities that could indicate errors or fraud.

These advancements contribute to more proactive, adaptive, and intelligent portfolio management.

Examples of portfolio management platforms

- **BlackRock Aladdin:** An institutional platform that combines risk analytics, portfolio management, and trading operations, widely used by asset managers and pension funds.
- **Orion Advisor Services:** Provides comprehensive tools for financial advisors including portfolio accounting, rebalancing, and client reporting.
- **Personal Capital:** A hybrid platform serving retail investors with aggregated financial data, investment tracking, and advisory services.
- **Tamarac:** Offers an integrated suite for advisors combining portfolio management, trading, and client communication.

Figure 9.9 Examples of portfolio management platforms.

The evolution of portfolio management platforms is expected to continue along several trajectories:

Greater AI integration

Advanced AI capabilities will enable platforms to offer deeper insights, hyper- personalization, and dynamic portfolio adjustments in real time.

Blockchain and smart contracts

Blockchain technology may facilitate transparent, tamper-proof transaction records and automate compliance via smart contracts.

Open architecture and API ecosystems

Platforms will increasingly adopt open APIs to enable third-party integrations, fostering innovation and interoperability.

Focus on ESG investing

Integration of environmental, social, and governance (ESG) criteria will become standard, allowing investors to align portfolios with sustainability goals.

Enhanced user experience

Improved interfaces, mobile accessibility, and educational resources will broaden adoption among retail investors.

Portfolio management platforms represent a significant advancement in how investments are managed and optimized. By leveraging technology, these platforms provide efficiency, transparency, and personalization previously unattainable at scale. While challenges such as data security, integration, and regulatory compliance persist, the ongoing infusion of AI and emerging technologies promises to make portfolio management more intelligent, responsive, and accessible. As these platforms continue to evolve, they will play an increasingly central role in shaping the future of wealth management for individuals and institutions alike.

9.4 Embedded Finance: Transforming the Financial Ecosystem from the Inside Out

Embedded finance is one of the most transformative concepts in the modern financial technology landscape. It represents the integration of financial services – such as payments, lending, insurance, and investment – into non-financial platforms. Rather than being standalone offerings accessible only through banks or financial institutions, financial products are now seamlessly woven into the platforms that consumers and businesses already use daily, such as e-commerce websites, ride-hailing apps, social media, and enterprise software. This fusion has dramatically altered the way individuals and businesses access financial services. It breaks the traditional model where customers go to a bank or financial institution to initiate a transaction. Instead, finance comes to them contextually and conveniently exactly when and where it is needed.

Embedded finance enables financial services to be integrated directly into non-financial platforms, creating seamless investment and payment experiences [11]. The future of embedded finance includes

Banking-as-a-Service (BaaS) models, allowing FinTech firms to provide investment tools without being traditional banks [12]. This chapter aims to explore the architecture, drivers, use cases, benefits, and challenges of embedded finance in detail.

Embedded finance refers to the incorporation of financial services into the digital interfaces of non-financial companies. It enables users to complete financial transactions such as making a payment, getting credit, or purchasing insurance within the platform they are already using, without being redirected to a separate financial institution. For example, when a customer buys a product on an e-commerce website and opts for "Buy Now, Pay Later" at checkout, they are using embedded lending. The customer remains on the platform but accesses a loan service in real time. BaaS platforms offer both opportunities and challenges, facilitating access to investment products while requiring careful regulatory compliance [13]. Embedded finance is creating a $7 trillion opportunity by integrating investment and banking functionalities into everyday apps and services [14].

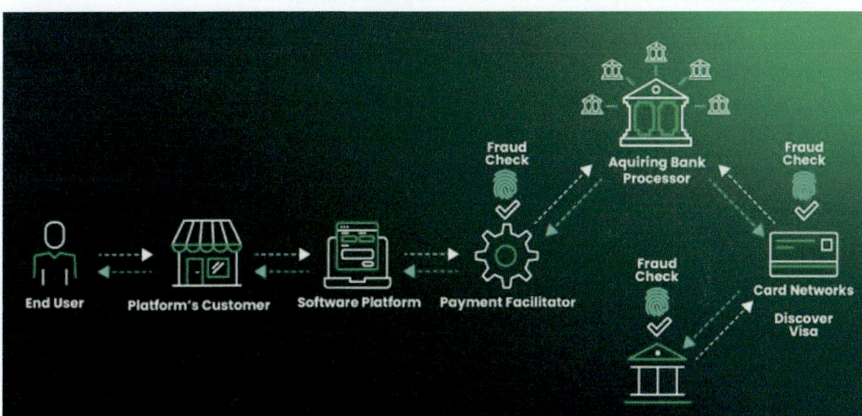

Figure 9.10 Process of embedded finance.
Source: https://forbytes.com/blog/embedded-finance/

Key components

Embedded finance typically involves collaboration between three types of players:

- **Non-financial platforms**: Businesses that offer core services like e-commerce, ride-sharing, or healthcare.
- **Financial service providers**: Banks, NBFCs, and FinTechs that provide the actual financial infrastructure.

- **Technology enablers**: Companies that offer APIs (Application Programming Interfaces) to integrate financial services seamlessly into the platform.

Evolution and growth drivers

Historically, financial services have been siloed – offered only through physical branches or proprietary digital portals. The unbundling of banking services began with FinTechs offering digital wallets, peer-to-peer lending, and robo-advisory platforms. The next evolution has been the re-bundling of finance within digital ecosystems through embedded models. Several technological developments have fueled the rise of embedded finance:

- **APIs and open banking**: APIs enable secure, real-time data exchange between systems, allowing for integration without compromising security.
- **Cloud computing**: Scalability and real-time processing support vast data handling required in embedded transactions.
- **Artificial intelligence (AI)**: AI enhances credit scoring, fraud detection, and personalized financial recommendations.
- **Mobile-first ecosystems**: Smartphones have made it easier to offer financial services within consumer-facing apps.

Types of embedded finance

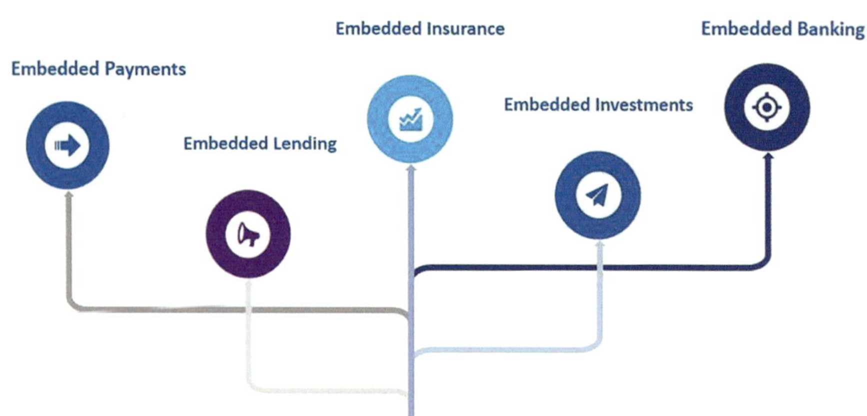

Figure 9.11 Particles of embedded finance.

Embedded payments

This is the most common form. It allows users to make payments without leaving the platform. Examples include **Amazon Pay**, integrated within the Amazon app and **Uber**, where users pay for rides without needing a separate wallet.

Embedded lending

Platforms offer users credit at the point of purchase. This includes **Buy Now, Pay Later (BNPL)** solutions (e.g., Affirm, Klarna). Also, In-app working capital loans for small businesses using platforms like Shopify.

Embedded insurance

This allows consumers to buy insurance within the purchase flow of a non-insurance platform. Examples: Travel insurance during flight bookings on airline websites. Mobile phone insurance is offered during smartphone purchases.

Embedded investments

Users can invest in stocks, mutual funds, or cryptocurrencies directly through non- financial platforms. For instance, **Cash App** or **Robinhood** integrating stock and crypto trading within personal finance apps.

Embedded banking (Banking-as-a-Service)

Non-banking platforms offer bank-like services such as account creation or issuing debit cards. Example: **Chime**, offering banking services without being a traditional bank.

Benefits of embedded finance

For consumers

- **Convenience**: Users can access financial services without switching apps or platforms.
- **Personalization**: Services are tailored based on user behavior and context.
- **Accessibility**: It increases financial inclusion by reaching users where they already are.

For businesses (non-financial platforms)

- **New revenue streams**: Monetization through financial product offerings (e.g., commission on loans or insurance).

- **Improved user experience**: Reducing friction improves customer loyalty and engagement.
- **Customer retention**: Offering embedded finance increases platform stickiness.

For financial institutions

- **Wider reach**: Partnering with consumer platforms gives banks access to untapped markets.
- **Operational efficiency**: Through API-based services, banks can reduce the cost of acquisition and servicing.

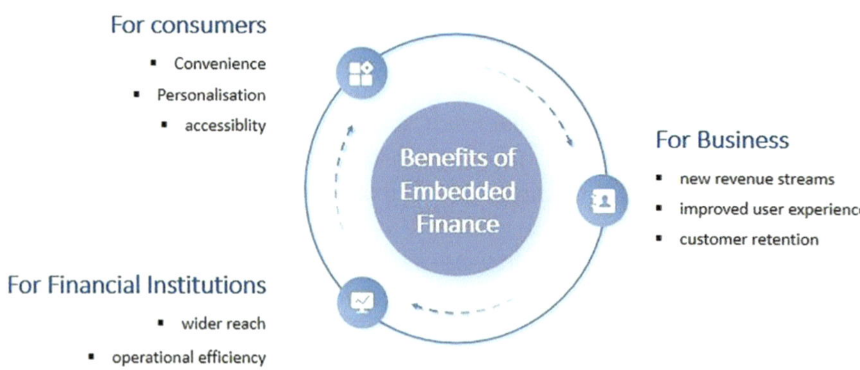

Figure 9.12 Benefits of embedded finance.

Table 9.1 Use cases across industries.

Industry	Examples
E-Commerce	BNPL at checkout, instant refunds, loyalty wallets
Healthcare	Insurance embedded during appointments or medical procedures
Transportation	Auto insurance and digital wallets in ride-sharing apps
SaaS Platforms	Payroll services, corporate credit cards for small businesses
Hospitality	Travel insurance or installment-based hotel bookings
Education	Student loans or EMI options on EdTech platforms

Embedded finance vs traditional finance

Embedded Finance represents a paradigm shift from the conventional structures of Traditional Finance by integrating financial services directly into non-financial platforms and customer journeys. Unlike traditional finance, where consumers must interact with standalone banks or financial institutions to access services like payments, loans, or insurance, Embedded finance allows these services to be seamlessly offered within apps or platforms they already use – such as e-commerce sites, ride-hailing apps, or digital wallets. This integration enhances convenience, personalization, and real-time financial decision-making, whereas Traditional finance often involves more rigid procedures, longer approval cycles, and siloed service delivery. As a result, embedded finance offers a more customer-centric, accessible, and agile financial experience, positioning itself as a key driver in the future of financial inclusion and innovation.

Table 9.2 Traditional finance vs embedded finance.

Aspect	Traditional finance	Embedded finance
Access point	Bank branches, bank apps	Within non-financial apps
Customer journey	Starts with the bank	Starts with the consumer's core activity
Experience	Often fragmented	Seamless and integrated
Reach	Limited to bank customers	Broader, including underserved populations
Customization	One-size-fits-all	Contextual and personalized

Regulatory and security considerations

Embedded finance brings with it a complex web of regulatory obligations. These include:

- **KYC/AML compliance**: Platforms must ensure customer verification and monitor for financial crime.
- **Data privacy**: Managing and sharing sensitive financial data must comply with regulations like GDPR or India's DPDP Act.
- **Licensing requirements**: Depending on the jurisdiction, platforms may need a banking license or partner with licensed entities.
- **Consumer protection**: Transparency around fees, loan terms, and dispute resolution is essential.

Challenges in embedded finance implementation

- **Technical integration:** While APIs simplify connectivity, ensuring reliability, scalability, and security across systems remains a challenge.

- **Trust and brand perception:** Non-financial brands offering financial services must work harder to gain trust, especially in high-stakes areas like lending and insurance.
- **Liability and risk sharing:** Defining responsibility between the platform, the financial service provider, and the technology enabler is critical to avoid legal disputes.
- **Fragmented regulation:** Different geographies have varied rules for financial services, making it hard for platforms to scale internationally without heavy compliance burdens.

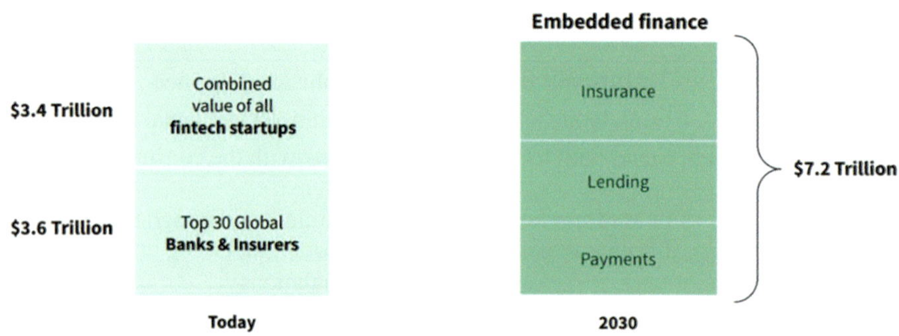

Figure 9.13 Embedded finance.
Source: Deal Room and ABN Amro, https://www.forbes.com/sites/ronshevlin/2022/04/25/the-7-trillion-embedded-finance- and-baas-gold-rush/

The embedded finance industry is projected to reach $7 trillion globally by 2030, according to various FinTech market research reports. Key future trends include:

- **Expansion into B2B**: Embedded credit lines and accounts payable automation for businesses.
- **Crypto integration**: Platforms enabling users to pay or invest in cryptocurrencies directly.
- **Smart contracts**: Use of blockchain to automate transactions and enforce financial agreements.
- **Greater personalization**: AI-driven, hyper-personalized financial services embedded in user workflows.
- **FinTech-as-a-feature**: Financial services becoming just another feature of software products, similar to how messaging or GPS became ubiquitous.

Embedded Finance is revolutionizing how people and businesses engage with financial services. By integrating these services into non-financial platforms, it not only offers unmatched convenience and efficiency but also expands financial inclusion by reaching previously underserved demographics. As technology matures and regulations adapt, embedded finance is set to become a defining characteristic of the financial services industry in the digital era. Rather than seeing finance as a separate domain, we are now witnessing a world where "every company can be a FinTech company." This shift holds tremendous potential for democratizing access to credit, savings, insurance, and investments – empowering consumers and businesses alike.

9.5 Personal Financial Management (PFM) Apps: Revolutionizing Individual Financial Well-Being

Personal finance management has undergone a dramatic transformation in recent years, driven by rapid advances in mobile technology, artificial intelligence (AI), and financial data integration. What was once a tedious process of manual budgeting and record-keeping has now evolved into a seamless digital experience through the use of personal financial management (PFM) Apps. These applications empower users to take control of their financial lives by providing real-time visibility, intelligent insights, and actionable recommendations related to income, expenses, budgeting, savings, investments, and credit. This chapter provides a detailed exploration of PFM apps from their core functionalities and evolution to the technology that powers them and their implications for consumers, financial institutions, and the broader digital economy. Personal financial management (PFM) apps are reshaping retail investment by providing tools for budgeting, portfolio tracking, and goal-oriented savings [15]. Economic forces, such as financial literacy and digital adoption, are driving the PFM revolution, enhancing investor engagement and wellness [16]. The rise of PFM tools reflects a broader trend toward financial wellness, emphasizing personalized investment strategies and automated portfolio monitoring [17].

Personal financial management (PFM) apps are software applications – typically mobile or web-based – that help individuals manage their personal finances. These tools allow users to track their spending, set budgets, monitor savings goals, manage debt, plan investments, and receive personalized financial advice. Most PFM apps offer dashboards and analytics to help users make informed decisions based on real- time financial data. Example: YNAB – You Need A Budget. Uses the "zero-based budgeting" technique and encourages users to assign every rupee a job. It promotes saving and debt elimination through financial discipline.

9.5.1 Objectives of PFM apps

- Provide visibility into personal financial activities.
- Promote financial discipline through automated tracking and reminders.
- Offer insights and advice using analytics and AI.
- Encourage goal-based planning and long-term wealth creation.

9.5.2 Historical evolution of PFM tools

PFM apps have evolved through several key stages:

- **Pre-digital era**: Financial planning was manual, relying on ledgers, spreadsheets, or financial advisors.
- **Early 2000s**: Desktop-based software like Microsoft Money and Quicken provided basic budgeting and financial tracking.
- **2010–2020**: The rise of mobile banking apps and third-party FinTechs like Mint, YNAB (You Need A Budget), and PocketGuard offered advanced user interfaces and financial integrations.
- **2020s onwards**: Integration with AI, open banking APIs, and embedded financial services marked the era of intelligent, real-time, and highly personalized financial management.

9.5.3 Key features and functionalities of PFM apps

- **Expense tracking**
  PFM apps categorize spending across different verticals such as groceries, dining, travel, and utilities. Some apps automate this through bank integration, while others allow manual entry.
- **Budgeting tools**
  Users can create monthly or category-specific budgets. Apps notify users when they exceed limits or identify overspending habits.
- **Goal setting and savings management**
  Users can set financial goals such as building an emergency fund, saving for a vacation, or paying off loans. The app suggests savings plans and monitors progress.

- **Bill reminders and alerts**
  PFM apps provide timely alerts for upcoming bill payments, credit card due dates, or subscription renewals, helping users avoid penalties.
- **Net worth and portfolio tracking**
  Advanced apps offer dashboards to calculate users' total assets and liabilities, offering a dynamic view of net worth. Integration with investment accounts allows tracking of mutual funds, stocks, and retirement plans.
- **Credit score monitoring**
  Some PFM apps integrate with credit bureaus to provide regular updates on credit scores and tips to improve them.
- **Personalized financial advice**
  Using machine learning and AI, apps provide tailored suggestions on how to reduce expenses, increase savings, or invest wisely.

Technological infrastructure behind PFM apps

Open banking APIs

Open banking frameworks allow third-party apps to securely access financial data from banks, enabling real-time updates of transaction history, balances, and financial behavior patterns.

Artificial intelligence and machine learning

AI/ML algorithms help categorize expenses automatically, detect anomalies or fraudulent activities, predict future spending, and provide personalized recommendations.

Data encryption and security

Given the sensitive nature of financial data, PFM apps employ end-to-end encryption, multi-factor authentication (MFA), and compliance with regulations like GDPR and India's DPDP Act.

Cloud computing

Cloud infrastructure enables scalability, data storage, and processing power for real- time analytics and sync across multiple devices.

Table 9.3 Types of PFM app.

Type	Description
Bank-Integrated PFM apps	Offered by banks as value-added services within mobile banking apps.
Third-party FinTech apps	Independent apps like Mint, Walnut, or Goodbudget focused solely on PFM.
Niche PFM apps	Focused on specific needs – debt reduction (Tally), investment (Groww), etc.
B2B2C White-label solutions	FinTech infrastructure providers like Tink and Plaid that allow banks to build PFM tools.

Figure 9.14 Types of personal financial management apps.

Benefits of PFM Apps For Consumers

- **Financial awareness**: Track all accounts in one place for holistic financial visibility.
- **Behavioral change**: Encourages users to control spending and prioritize savings.
- **Goal realization**: Helps users plan and achieve short- and long-term financial goals.
- **Reduced debt**: Monitors credit usage, avoids penalties, and aids debt repayment.
- **Convenience**: 24/7 access to financial information through smartphones.

For financial institutions

- **Customer engagement**: Increases app usage and stickiness.

- **Cross-selling opportunities**: Insights allow targeted product offerings like loans or insurance.
- **Data enrichment**: Improves segmentation and personalization using behavioral analytics.

For society

- **Financial inclusion**: Reaches underbanked and young users with simplified interfaces.
- **Improved financial literacy**: Teaches money management in real time through app usage.

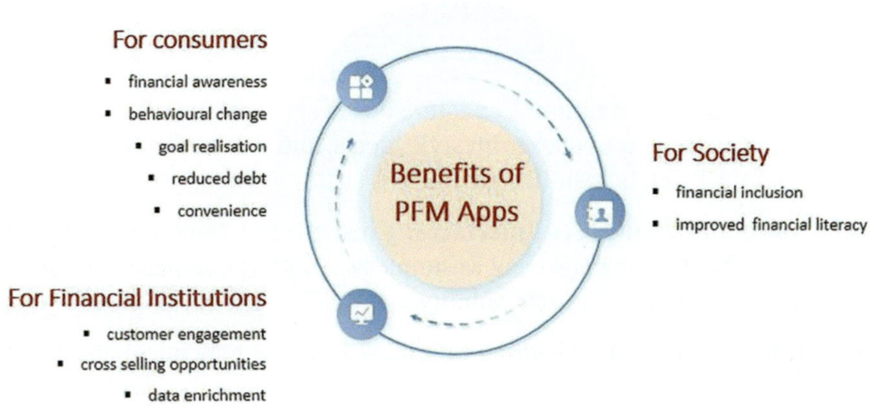

Figure 9.15 Benefits of PFM apps.

Challenges and limitations

- **Data privacy concerns:** Many users are skeptical about sharing sensitive financial information with third-party apps, especially in light of increasing cyber threats.
- **Integration with banks:** Not all banks offer open APIs, which makes real-time syncing difficult in some countries or smaller regions.
- **Low user engagement:** Some users install PFM apps but abandon them due to complexity or lack of perceived value.
- **Financial illiteracy:** Despite technological advancement, many users struggle to understand charts, insights, or financial terminology, limiting the impact of PFM apps.

Figure 9.16 Challenges – PFM apps.

Future of PFM apps

- **Hyper-personalization:** The future lies in apps that understand not just financial behavior but user lifestyle, goals, and risk preferences. AI will offer nuanced, human-like advice.
- **Voice and chat-based interfaces:** Chatbots and voice assistants will make financial management as simple as speaking commands or asking questions, improving accessibility.
- **Integration with embedded finance:** PFM apps may integrate embedded financial products such as instant loans, insurance, or BNPL options for contextual recommendations.
- **Gamification:** Gamifying saving goals, credit score improvement, or budgeting challenges can improve user engagement and financial behavior.
- **Financial ecosystems:** PFM apps could evolve into full-service financial platforms, integrating investments, credit, taxes, and insurance under one umbrella.

Personal financial management apps are playing a transformative role in helping individuals take control of their financial lives. By leveraging real-time data, intuitive design, and intelligent analytics, these apps make complex financial decisions simpler and more accessible. They are fostering a generation of financially aware, goal- oriented individuals who can save more, invest wisely, and reduce unnecessary financial stress. As the digital finance ecosystem continues to grow, PFM apps are poised to become an essential companion in every individual's financial journey democratizing access to financial literacy, discipline, and wellness. With increased adoption, better security, and enhanced AI capabilities, PFM tools will become not just reactive trackers, but proactive financial coaches embedded into daily life.

Summary

This chapter analyzes key innovations in investment management driven by technology. It begins with the rise of robo-advisors, automated platforms that use algorithms and AI to offer personalized investment advice and portfolio rebalancing with minimal human intervention. The chapter also covers AI-based investing, which employs machine learning to analyze market data, identify trends, and predict asset performance for smarter investment decisions. Next, it discusses portfolio management platforms, which combine analytics, risk management, and client reporting functionalities to streamline investment oversight for advisors and investors alike. Overall, the chapter highlights how digital transformation enhances market provisioning by making investment processes more data-driven, efficient, and scalable. This chapter further delves into the evolution and impact of consumer- centric innovations in financial technology. It begins with Embedded Finance, a model that integrates financial services into non-financial platforms such as e- commerce sites, ride-hailing apps, or social media platforms. The chapter then moves to personal financial management (PFM) Apps, which are designed to help individuals track income, expenses, savings, debt, and investment goals through user- friendly interfaces. Together, these innovations emphasize a shift from institution- centered to customer-centered finance, highlighting the need for personalization, context-awareness, and real-time financial engagement. The chapter concludes by discussing the future implications of these technologies in driving financial empowerment and reshaping the customer journey.

Case Study: Nord Investments (Denmark) – Democratizing Portfolio Management Through Robo-Advisory

Nord Investments A/S, founded in 2015 and headquartered in Copenhagen, Denmark, is a fast-growing FinTech company specializing in automated portfolio management, commonly referred to as robo-advisory. Targeting everyday investors in Denmark and the broader Nordic region, Nord aims to simplify wealth management and make professional-grade investment strategies accessible to a wider audience – especially those without prior financial knowledge or access to private wealth services. The company was born out of a need to bridge the gap between traditional wealth advisors and retail investors who often faced high fees, complex products, or lack of access to expert advice. Nord Investments leveraged digital innovation to automate the entire portfolio construction, monitoring, and rebalancing process. Traditional portfolio management services in Denmark – offered by banks or private advisors – were often with high management fees and hidden commissions. It is primarily catering to high-net-worth individuals. It lacks user transparency and real- time reporting. Retail investors, particularly millennials and tech-savvy professionals, sought more cost-effective, transparent, and digital-first investment solutions. They wanted automated, long-term investing strategies that aligned with their risk profiles and life goals. Nord Investments introduced a fully digital robo-advisory platform that offers:

a. Automated portfolio construction: Users complete an online questionnaire assessing their risk appetite, time horizon, and goals. Nord's algorithm allocates funds into a globally diversified ETF portfolio based on modern portfolio theory principles.
b. Low-cost, passive investing: The platform uses low-fee ETFs (exchange-traded funds), reducing annual costs significantly compared to traditional asset management. No trading fees, performance fees, or hidden charges – just a transparent annual advisory fee (around 0.6%).
c. Real-time portfolio monitoring: Clients can access performance dashboards, allocation breakdowns, and risk metrics through Nord's intuitive web and mobile platforms. The platform automatically rebalances the portfolio as markets fluctuate or when client inputs change.
d. Tax optimization: Nord integrates Danish tax reporting, making it easier for users to comply with capital gains tax rules.
e. Sustainable investment options: Users can opt for ESG-compliant portfolios, aligning with Denmark's strong focus on sustainability and responsible investing.

Nord's platform is built on a modern FinTech stack combining:

- **AI and algorithmic decision engines**: Used for personalized investment strategy recommendations and continuous optimization.

- **Cloud infrastructure (e.g., AWS)**: Ensures scalability, data protection, and seamless client experience.
- **API integrations**: Connects with custodial banks and ETF providers to automate transactions and data flows.
- **Bank-grade security**: Incorporates multi-factor authentication (MFA), end-to- end encryption, and compliance with the **EU's MiFID II and GDPR**.

As of 2024, Nord manages over DKK 2.5 billion (~$350 million USD), showing rapid adoption in Denmark. Thousands of Danish investors, especially between 25 and 45 years old, have shifted from banks to Nord for investment management. Clients save 30–50% annually on investment costs compared to traditional advisors. High retention rates and consistent 4.5+ ratings on Trustpilot.Nord Investments was listed on Nasdaq First North Denmark in 2021, further increasing investor confidence.

A local focus on tax, compliance, and language adaptation helped Nord stand out in a crowded European robo-advisory market. It offers sustainable investing options helped align with Denmark's eco-conscious investors.Nord Investments exemplifies how FinTech can transform portfolio management in developed economies by offering affordable, accessible, and transparent investment solutions. By leveraging technology, Nord removed traditional entry barriers and empowered Danish retail investors to take control of their long-term financial futures. As the FinTech ecosystem in Denmark continues to mature, Nord stands as a leader in the digital wealth management revolution, with potential for expansion across the Nordics and broader European market.

Case Discussion Questions

1. What specific gaps in traditional wealth management did Nord Investments aim to address, and how did FinTech help fill those gaps?
2. How does Nord's robo-advisory model enhance transparency, efficiency, and affordability in portfolio management compared to conventional banks?
3. What are the key technological components that enable Nord's digital platform to deliver personalized and automated investment strategies?

4. In what ways does offering sustainable ESG investment portfolios align with customer expectations in Denmark's market?
5. What challenges might Nord face in scaling its operations beyond Denmark, and how can it maintain trust while expanding into new regions?

Keywords

- **Robo-advisors:** Automated platforms that use algorithms to provide investment advice and manage portfolios without direct human involvement.
- **Artificial intelligence (AI)-based investing:** The use of AI and machine learning techniques to analyze financial markets and inform investment decisions.
- **Algorithmic trading:** Trading strategies executed by computer algorithms based on pre-set criteria, aiming to optimize trade execution.
- **Portfolio management platform:** Digital tools that assist in constructing, monitoring, and managing investment portfolios through analytics and reporting features.
- **Asset allocation:** The process of dividing investments among various asset categories to balance risk and return.
- **Personalized investment advice:** Investment recommendations tailored to an individual's financial goals, risk tolerance, and preferences.
- **Portfolio rebalancing:** The practice of realigning portfolio assets periodically to maintain desired asset allocation.
- **Machine learning:** A subset of AI where systems improve automatically through experience and data analysis.
- **Risk management:** The identification, assessment, and mitigation of financial risks within investment portfolios.
- **Financial technology (FinTech):** Technology-driven innovations that improve or automate financial services, including investment management.
- **Embedded finance:** Integration of financial services such as payments, lending, or insurance into non-financial digital platforms.

- **Consumer-centric innovation:** Innovations focused on improving the experience, accessibility, and value for end-users or consumers.
- **PFM apps:** Personal Financial Management applications that help users manage budgets, expenses, and goals.
- **Application Programming Interface (API):** A set of tools and protocols enabling apps to interact and share data, especially in embedded finance.
- **Contextual finance:** Delivery of financial services at the moment of consumer need within a non-financial environment.
- **Financial empowerment:** The ability of individuals to make informed financial decisions using accessible tools and information.
- **AI-powered recommendations:** Personalized suggestions generated using artificial intelligence based on user behavior and data
- **Customer journey mapping:** The process of analyzing how consumers interact with a brand across different stages and touchpoints.

Discussion Questions

1. How do robo-advisors differ from traditional financial advisors in terms of service delivery and cost?
2. How does algorithmic trading influence market liquidity and volatility?
3. What challenges do investors face when relying on automated investment advice?
4. How can portfolio rebalancing strategies impact long-term investment performance?
5. What ethical considerations arise from the use of AI and algorithms in investment decision-making?
6. How might future technological advancements further disrupt traditional investment management?
7. What are the advantages and potential risks of integrating financial services into non-financial platforms?
8. In what ways do personal financial management apps empower users to make better financial decisions?

9. How can financial institutions leverage PFM tools to build stronger customer relationships?

10. What technological factors have enabled the rise of embedded finance and PFM apps?

11. Discuss the role of APIs in enabling embedded finance ecosystems.

12. How can PFM apps contribute to improving financial literacy among millennials and Gen Z?

13. What privacy and data security challenges arise from the use of consumer-centric financial apps?

14. Do you think embedded finance could replace traditional banking channels in the future? Why or why not?

References

[1] Puschmann, T. (2017). Fintech: Business model framework. In D. Gimpel, T. Alt, & R. Blohm (Eds.), *FinTech in Germany* (pp. 69–86). Springer.

[2] Arner, D. W., Barberis, J., & Buckley, R. P. (2016). The evolution of FinTech: A new post-crisis paradigm? *Georgetown Journal of International Law, 47*(4), 1271–1319.

[3] Berg, T., Burg, V., Gombović, A., & Puri, M. (2020). On the rise of fintechs – Credit scoring using digital footprints. *Review of Financial Studies, 33*(7), 2845–2897. https://doi.org/10.1093/rfs/hhz041

[4] Lo, A. W. (2017). *Adaptive markets: Financial evolution at the speed of thought*. Princeton University Press.

[5] Statista. (2024). Assets under management in robo-advisors worldwide from 2017 to 2024. https://www.statista.com/statistics/800426/worldwide-robo-advisors-aum/

[6] Morningstar. (2023). The rise of robo-advisors: What investors need to know. https://www.morningstar.com/articles

[7] Organisation for Economic Co-operation and Development (OECD). (2021). *The impact of AI on the financial sector: Risks and opportunities*. https://www.oecd.org/finance/the-impact-of-ai-on-the-financial-sector.htm

[8] World Economic Forum. (2020). *Digital transformation of the financial services industry*. https://www.weforum.org/reports/digital-transformation-of-the-financial-services

[9] Deloitte. (2021). AI and investment management: Navigating a new era. https://www2.deloitte.com

[10] Chishti, S., & Barberis, J. (2021). *The FinTech Book: The Financial Technology Handbook for Investors, Entrepreneurs and Visionaries*. Wiley.

[11] Arner, D. W., Barberis, J., & Buckley, R. P. (2020). The evolution of FinTech: A new post-crisis paradigm? *Georgetown Journal of International Law, 47*(4), 1271–1319.

[12] World Economic Forum. (2021). *The future of embedded finance*. https://www.weforum.org

[13] Accenture. (2022). *Banking-as-a-Service: Opportunity and threat in embedded finance*. https://www.accenture.com

[14] Deal Room and ABN Amro, https://www.forbes.com/sites/ronshevlin/2022/04/25/the-7-trillion-embedded-finance-and-baas-gold-rush/

[15] Langley, P., & Leyshon, A. (2021). Platform capitalism in the personal finance industry: The case of FinTech PFM apps. *Economic Geography, 97*(3), 213–233. https://doi.org/10.1080/00130095.2020.1831648

[16] Frost, J. (2020). The economic forces shaping the PFM revolution. *Bank for International Settlements – BIS Papers No. 113*.

[17] PwC. (2023). Financial wellness and the rise of PFM tools. https://www.pwc.com

Table 10.1 Types of blockchain.

Feature	Public	Private	Consortium	Hybrid
Access	Open to everyone	Restricted	Restricted to a group	The mix of public and private
Decentralization	Fully decentralized	Centralized	Partially decentralized	Balanced
Speed and scalability	Low	High	Moderate	High
Transparency	High	Low	Moderate	Controlled
Governance	Community-based	Single entity	Group of organizations	Flexible
Use case examples	Bitcoin, Ethereum	Hyperledger, Corda	IBM Food Trust, EWC	Dragonchain, XinFin

How blockchain works: A technical walkthrough

Blockchain operates through a defined sequence of actions aimed at maintaining transparency, security, and decentralization. It begins when a user initiates a transaction, which is broadcast to a peer-to-peer (P2P) network of connected nodes. These nodes validate the transaction using consensus protocols such as Proof of Work or Proof of Stake. Once validated, the transaction is grouped into a new block and linked to the existing chain. The distributed ledger is then updated and synchronized across all nodes, guaranteeing both accuracy and immutability. For example, in a Bitcoin transaction, if Alice transfers 0.5 BTC to Bob, she authorizes it through a digital signature. Miners validate it and add it to a block, and once the block is successfully appended to the chain, Bob receives the BTC after six confirmations – highlighting the secure and irreversible nature of blockchain transactions. Blockchain is a decentralized digital ledger that securely records transactions across a distributed network [1]. It eliminates the need for intermediaries and enhances transparency, trust, and immutability in digital interactions [2]. The system operates through block data structures containing transactions that are cryptographically linked to form a continuous chain [3]. Each block holds a unique hash value and connects with the previous block, creating a tamper-resistant ledger [4].

Advantages of blockchain

- Transparency: All transactions are publicly verifiable.
- Security: Uses advanced cryptographic methods.
- Decentralization: No central point of failure.

- Reduced costs: Fewer intermediaries.
- Traceability: Ideal for supply chains and audit trails.

Challenges and limitations

- Scalability: Public blockchains often suffer from low transaction throughput (e.g., Bitcoin processes 7 TPS).
- Energy consumption: PoW systems require substantial computational power, raising environmental concerns.
- Legal and regulatory issues: Governments struggle to adapt regulations to decentralized systems. Issues include taxation, KYC/AML compliance, and legal recognition of smart contracts.
- Interoperability: Lack of standards across blockchain limits communication between platforms.
- Data privacy: Public visibility of transactions may conflict with data protection laws like GDPR.

Blockchain vs. traditional databases

In the digital age, the decision of choosing between blockchain technology and traditional databases can significantly affect the efficiency, security, and scalability of various business processes. Both systems are designed to store and manage data, but they differ greatly in architecture, governance, and applications. Traditional databases are best suited for centralized, high-speed applications, whereas blockchain introduces a decentralized, immutable way to store data securely. This chapter explores the distinctions between these two technologies, offering a detailed comparison to help guide their appropriate use in different contexts.

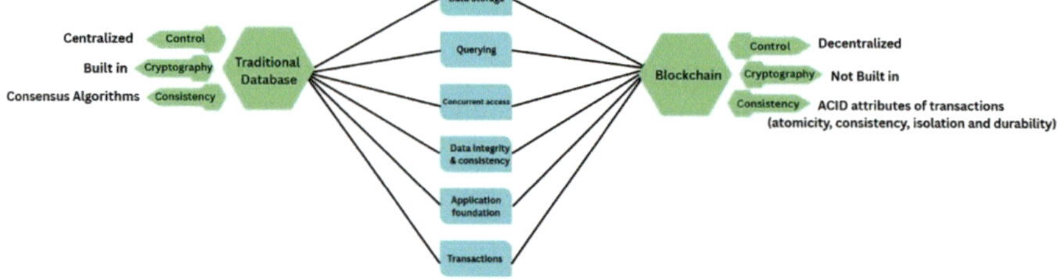

Figure 10.3 Blockchain vs traditional database.

Architecture overview

Traditional databases typically follow a client-server architecture, where a central database server holds and manages data. Clients interact with this server to query, modify, or update the data. This architecture relies on an administrator or organization to manage access control, security, and overall system operations.

- Centralized: A single entity or organization controls the database.
- Types: Relational (SQL) databases, NoSQL databases (e.g., MongoDB, Cassandra).
- Data management: Data is stored in tables or collections, with updates directly reflecting on the database.

Blockchain

In contrast to centralized systems, blockchain employs a distributed peer-to-peer (P2P) framework where each node holds its own copy of the ledger. This structure allows all participants to interact directly with the blockchain without relying on a single governing authority.

- Decentralization: The system operates without a central controller, with data maintained collectively across numerous nodes.
- Immutable ledger: Information is recorded in blocks that are securely linked in sequence, forming an unalterable chain – hence the term "blockchain."
- Consensus protocols: Network nodes authenticate transactions using various consensus methods, including Proof of Work (PoW) and Proof of Stake (PoS).

Data storage mechanism

Traditional database model

Traditional databases organize data using schemas that define the structure of tables, rows, and columns in relational databases. In relational databases, links between data entities are created through the use of primary and foreign keys. In contrast, NoSQL databases organize data in formats such as documents, key-value pairs, graphs, or wide-column stores, offering greater flexibility in storage and retrieval.

- Mutable data: Data is easy to update or delete as needed.
- CRUD operations: Standard operations include create, read, update, and delete for managing data records.

- Transactions: Conventional databases adhere to the ACID principles – atomicity, consistency, isolation, and durability which guarantee the preservation of data integrity throughout transaction processing.

Blockchain data model

Within a blockchain, information is organized into blocks that record multiple transactions. Each block typically includes:

- A timestamp
- Specific details of the transactions
- The cryptographic hash of the preceding block, which secures the chain's immutability

The blockchain's chain-like structure guarantees that once a block is recorded, it cannot be modified or removed. Additional blocks are added sequentially, and altering any block would necessitate changes to all subsequent blocks, a computationally impractical task.

- Immutability: Once recorded, data cannot be changed.
- Transparency: In public blockchains, anyone can view all data on the blockchain.
- Distributed ledger: Data is replicated across all nodes, ensuring redundancy and fault tolerance.

Trust and authority

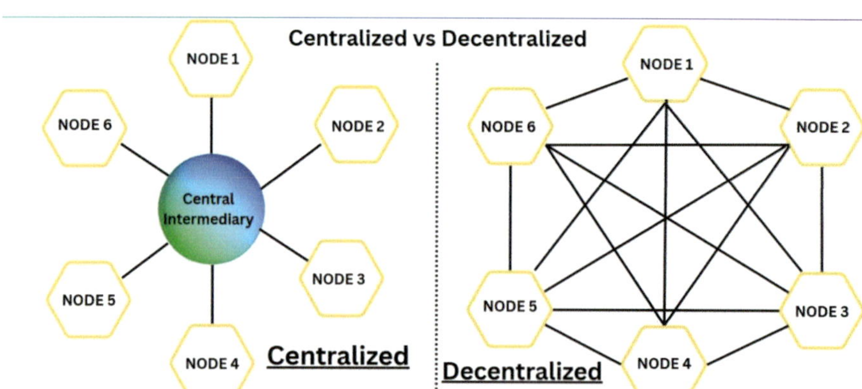

Figure 10.4 Centralized vs decentralized.

Table 10.2 Use case comparison blockchain vs. traditional database – unified comparison table.

Aspect/use case/ feature	Traditional database system	Blockchain
Financial transactions	High-speed, centralized	Transparency, audit trail
Supply chain management	Integrates well with ERP systems	Traceability, transparency
Voting systems	Vulnerable to fraud	Immutable, transparent
Healthcare data	Centralized, secure	User-controlled, immutable
Identity management	Centralized and easy to manage	Decentralized, secure
Control	Centralized	Decentralized
Data modifiability	Mutable	Immutable
Speed	High	Moderate to Low
Transparency	Limited	High (public)
Security	Authentication-based	Cryptography-based
Cost	Low (except for large-scale systems)	High (especially for public blockchains)
Scalability	High	Moderate
Speed and scalability (recommendation)	Recommended	Not preferred
Immutable audit trail (Recommendation)	Not preferred	Recommended
Multi-party trustless interactions	Not ideal	Recommended
Centralized control and management	Recommended	Not preferred
Distributed ledger for transparency	Not ideal	Recommended

Centralized trust model in databases

Traditional databases are managed by a central authority or a single organization. This central authority holds the power to update, modify, or delete data. Access control is typically based on permissions granted to users, which can range from full access to read-only access.

- Administrator control: The organization controls all aspects of the database, including maintenance, access, and security.
- Trusted third party: Users and applications must trust the authority managing the database.

Decentralized trust model in blockchain

In a blockchain network, trust is collectively shared among all participants. Instead of relying on a single central authority, consensus algorithms allow all nodes to agree on the legitimacy of transactions. This approach eliminates the role of intermediaries and establishes trust through cryptographic methods.

- No single point of control: Consensus protocols ensure that no single entity has complete control over the network.
- Trustless systems: Users do not need to trust any central party; trust is established through the decentralized network and cryptographic verification.

10.2 Blocks, Transactions, and Merkle Trees

"Understanding the components that make up a blockchain is essential to grasp the underlying mechanics of how decentralized systems ensure security, data integrity, and consensus. This chapter explores blocks, transactions, and Merkle trees – key elements that make blockchain technology powerful." In the realm of blockchain technology, the concepts of transactions, blocks, and Merkle trees are foundational to the operation and security of decentralized systems. Transactions represent the core unit of data on a blockchain, blocks act as containers for transactions, and Merkle trees ensure the efficient and secure storage of data within these blocks. This chapter delves deeply into these elements to understand how they interact within blockchain networks and contribute to the technology's key features – security, transparency, and immutability.

Understanding transactions

Within a blockchain, a transaction serves as the basic data unit, signifying the exchange of assets or information between participants in the network. Whether it is sending cryptocurrency, updating a smart contract, or changing a record in a decentralized application (dApp), every blockchain operation is structured as a transaction.

Structure of a transaction

A typical blockchain transaction involves several key components:

- Sender: The unique address associated with the participant who initiates the transaction.
- Receiver: The unique address corresponding to the participant who receives the transaction.

- Amount: The quantity or asset being transferred, such as cryptocurrency or data.
- Timestamp: The exact date and time at which the transaction is created or initiated.
- Transaction ID: A distinct identifier assigned to each transaction.
- Signature: A cryptographic code produced using the sender's private key to verify authenticity.
- Nonce: A number used to prevent replay attacks by ensuring each transaction is unique.
- Fee: The transaction fee paid to the validators or miners (in Proof of Work systems).

Transaction validation

After a transaction is initiated, it is transmitted across the network for verification. The validators or miners then confirm that the sender possesses adequate funds or the necessary rights to execute the transaction.

- The transaction is properly signed and conforms to the rules of the blockchain network.
- The transaction is legitimate (e.g., not a double-spending attempt).

Once validated, the transaction is included in a block and added to the blockchain.

Blocks in blockchain

In blockchain, a block serves as a container for storing multiple transactions and acts as a fundamental data unit of the system. These blocks are linked in sequence to form an unalterable chain. The addition of each block to the blockchain is governed by a consensus protocol, such as Proof of Work (PoW) or Proof of Stake (PoS). Transactions on the blockchain are verified through cryptographic algorithms and stored in distributed nodes, ensuring security and data integrity [5]. The Merkle tree structure enables efficient verification of large datasets by linking transaction hashes in a hierarchical format [6]. Consensus mechanisms like Proof of Work (PoW) and Proof of Stake (PoS) determine how nodes agree on the validity of transactions [7].

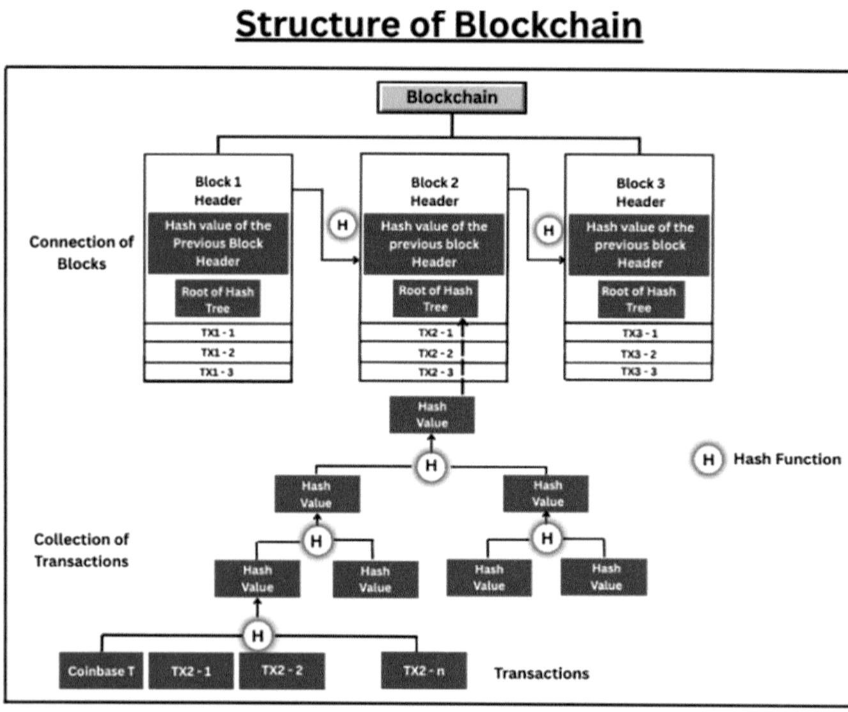

Figure 10.5 Structure of a Blockchain.

A typical blockchain block includes the following key components:

Block header:

- Previous block hash: A reference to the hash of the previous block, ensuring the immutability of the blockchain by making tampering with earlier blocks computationally infeasible.
- Timestamp: The time when the block was mined or created.
- Merkle root: A cryptographic hash representing all transactions within a block, acting as a unique fingerprint of the block's data.
- Block height: The position of the block within the blockchain.
- Nonce: A value used in Proof of Work systems to generate a hash below a certain target.
- Transaction data: This includes the actual transactions included in the block.

- Block hash: A unique identifier generated by hashing the block's contents, ensuring its integrity.

How blocks are linked in a blockchain

Each new block references the hash of the previous block, creating a chain of blocks. This structure provides blockchain with its core feature – immutability, which makes it tamper-resistant and secure. This connection guarantees that once information is stored in a block, altering it would require modifying all subsequent blocks and obtaining the approval of the majority of nodes in the network – an undertaking that is computationally impractical.

Merkle trees

A Merkle tree, also known as a binary hash tree, is a hierarchical structure used in blockchain to effectively summarize and confirm the integrity of extensive datasets, such as all transactions within a block. In this arrangement, each leaf node contains the hash of a specific transaction, whereas each non-leaf node holds a hash generated from its corresponding child nodes.

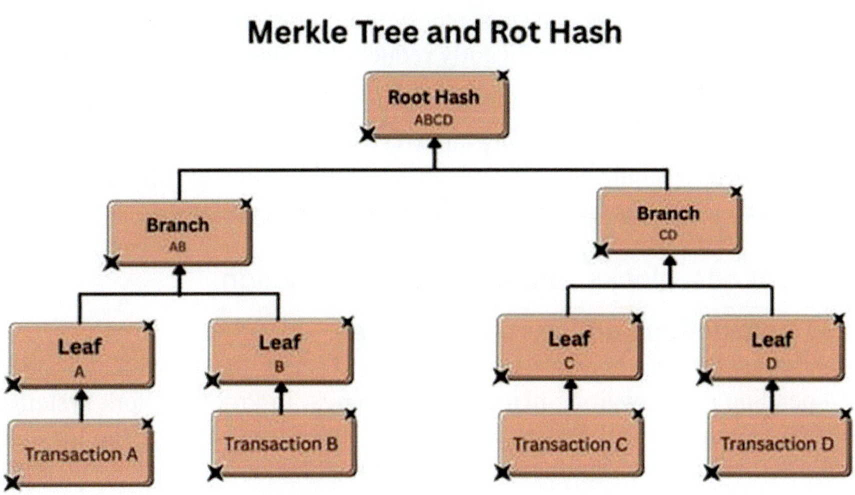

Figure 10.6 Merkle tree and rot hash.

Structure and function of Merkle trees

- Leaf nodes: At the base of the Merkle tree, each leaf node contains the cryptographic hash of a transaction.

- Non-leaf nodes: These nodes contain hashes of their child nodes. This process continues up the tree, where each parent node is the hash of its two child nodes.
- Merkle root: The single top node, also called the root, represents the entire set of transactions in the block. It is the cryptographic fingerprint of all transactions contained within the block.

The Merkle tree design allows for fast and secure verification of a transaction's inclusion within a block. By providing the Merkle root, a blockchain can offer proof of a specific transaction without needing to reveal the entire block's transaction history.

Role of Merkle trees in blockchain

Merkle trees play a crucial role in preserving the integrity of data within a blockchain.

- Efficient data verification: Instead of validating each transaction individually, a node only needs to verify the Merkle root. If the root matches, it confirms the integrity of all transactions in the block.
- Proof of inclusion: To verify that a specific transaction exists within a block, a participant can present a limited set of hashes, referred to as a Merkle proof. This significantly reduces the amount of data needed for validation.
- Scalability: By summarizing large datasets with a small fixed-size hash, Merkle trees enhance blockchain scalability, allowing the network to handle more transactions without compromising security.

Transactions, blocks, and Merkle trees in action

How transactions are stored in blocks

After a transaction is generated, it is distributed across the network and added to a pending pool, awaiting placement in a block. In Proof of Work systems, miners, and in Proof of Stake systems, node operators, validate the transaction's authenticity before it is accepted into the block.

The newly formed block includes:

- A collection of verified transactions.
- A Merkle root summarizing all transactions within the block.

- A hash reference to the preceding block, ensuring the blockchain remains a continuous and tamper-proof sequence of blocks.

The role of Merkle trees in transaction integrity

The Merkle tree ensures that the data integrity of transactions is maintained in a space-efficient manner. The Merkle root in the block header serves as a summary of the block's contents, enabling fast verification. If a malicious actor tries to modify a transaction within the block, the Merkle root would change, immediately signaling the tampering attempt.

10.3 Consensus Mechanisms: PoW and PoS

Consensus mechanisms are fundamental to blockchain functionality, allowing participants in a decentralized environment to collectively agree on transaction validity without depending on a central governing body. This section focuses on two of the most prominent consensus models – Proof of Work (PoW) and Proof of Stake (PoS) – exploring their frameworks, strengths, and drawbacks. The objective is to provide an in-depth perspective on how these protocols secure blockchain networks and build trust among participants. Blockchain is revolutionizing industries by enabling decentralized, transparent, and tamper-resistant data management. At its heart lies the concept of consensus, which ensures uniform agreement on the state of the ledger across all network nodes. Consensus mechanisms are the algorithms that make this agreement possible, preventing inconsistencies and fraudulent activities. This chapter examines the widely adopted PoW and PoS approaches to demonstrate how blockchain preserves integrity, decentralization, and security.

Consensus mechanisms

In distributed networks, consensus protocols allow all nodes to synchronize on the blockchain's current state without oversight from entities like banks or governments.

These mechanisms validate transactions, safeguard the network from malicious activity, and prevent double-spending. As a result, every node maintains an identical and verified copy of the ledger. By ensuring that only legitimate transactions are added, consensus mechanisms uphold the reliability of blockchain systems.

Significance in blockchain networks

Without consensus algorithms, blockchains would be highly susceptible to manipulation and cyberattacks. These mechanisms guarantee:

- Decentralization: No single entity controls the network.
- Security: Transactions are authenticated and securely recorded.
- Immutability: Once added, a block cannot be altered without the consent of the majority.
- Trust: Participants can rely on the authenticity of transactions in a distributed setup.

Proof of Work (PoW)

PoW, first implemented in Bitcoin, requires miners to compete in solving challenging cryptographic puzzles (hashes) to validate transactions and create new blocks. PoW, used in Bitcoin, requires solving complex puzzles to validate blocks, ensuring security but consuming high energy [8]. PoS, introduced in Ethereum, selects validators based on stake ownership, making it more sustainable [9]. These mechanisms safeguard the blockchain against fraud and double spending [10]. The EU Blockchain Observatory (2020) highlights blockchain's convergence with AI and IoT for smarter digital ecosystems [11]. The procedure involves:

- Mining: Collecting pending transactions into a candidate block.
- Puzzle Solving: Determining a nonce – a random value – that, when combined with block data and hashed, meets the network's difficulty target (e.g., a set number of leading zeros).
- Block Submission: Broadcasting the solved block to the network for verification by other nodes.
- Rewards: Successful miners receive newly minted cryptocurrency and transaction fees.

PoW in Bitcoin

Bitcoin, as the pioneering cryptocurrency, employs PoW to maintain its decentralized and secure network. Miners compete to solve hash puzzles, ensuring only valid transactions are recorded. This process not only strengthens the network against tampering but also reinforces its distributed nature.

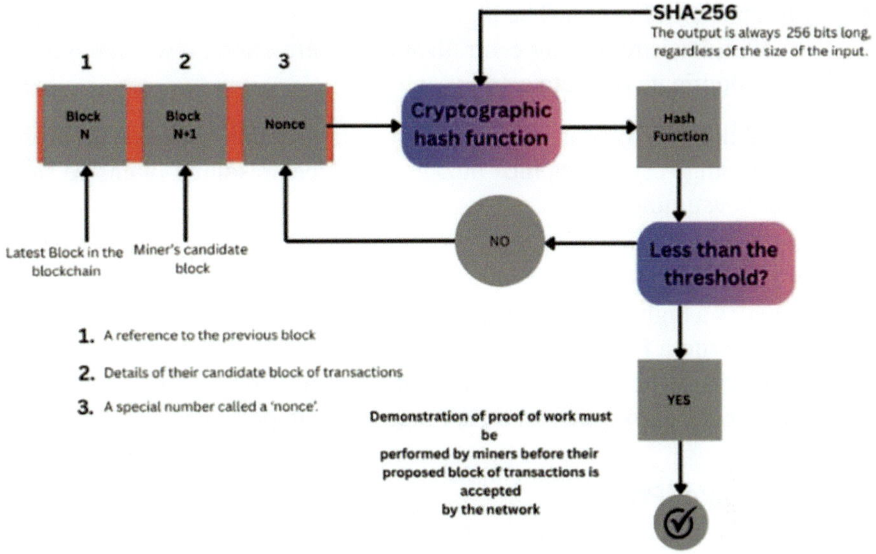

Figure 10.7 Proof of Work (PoW) flow.

- Block time: The time taken to solve a block is approximately 10 minutes.
- Difficulty adjustment: The difficulty of the puzzle adjusts every 2,016 blocks to ensure that block times remain consistent, despite the increase in mining power.

Advantages and disadvantages of PoW Advantages:

- Security: Proof of Work offers strong security because solving its cryptographic puzzles demands significant computational resources.
- Decentralization: No central authority controls the network. Anyone with computing power can participate in the mining process.
- Immutability: Once a block is appended to the chain, modifying it would require re-computing the Proof of Work for all following blocks, a computationally unfeasible task.

Disadvantages:

- Energy consumption: Proof of Work demands substantial computational resources, resulting in high energy usage. In fact, Bitcoin's electricity consumption is frequently likened to that of entire nations.

- Mining centralization: The high cost of mining equipment and electricity often leads to mining centralization, where only a few large mining pools dominate the network.
- Scalability: PoW can lead to slower transaction processing times, as solving cryptographic puzzles can be resource-intensive and time-consuming.

Security in PoW

PoW provides a high level of security by making it difficult to alter the blockchain. To rewrite a block, an attacker would need to outpace the entire network of miners, which would require more computational power than exists in the network, making such an attack practically impossible.

Proof of Stake (PoS)

Proof of Stake (PoS) serves as an alternative consensus mechanism to Proof of Work, developed to overcome its drawbacks – most notably excessive energy usage. In PoS, the role of block creation is assigned to validators instead of miners. These validators are chosen based on the amount of cryptocurrency they possess and are prepared to "stake" as a form of collateral. The process generally involves:

- Staking: Validators deposit a specified amount of cryptocurrency into a staking pool as collateral.
- Block Proposal: Validators are chosen – often randomly but weighted by the size of their stake and other factors such as stake age – to propose the next block.
- Validation: The proposed block is reviewed by other validators, and if a majority confirms its validity, it is appended to the blockchain.
- Reward: Validators contributing to the consensus process receive transaction fees and, in some cases, newly issued cryptocurrency.

PoS in Ethereum 2.0

Ethereum, the second-largest blockchain platform, is in the process of shifting from the Proof-of-Work (PoW) model to the Proof-of-Stake (PoS) framework as part of its Ethereum 2.0 upgrade. This transition aims to drastically reduce energy consumption, improve scalability, and speed up transaction throughput.

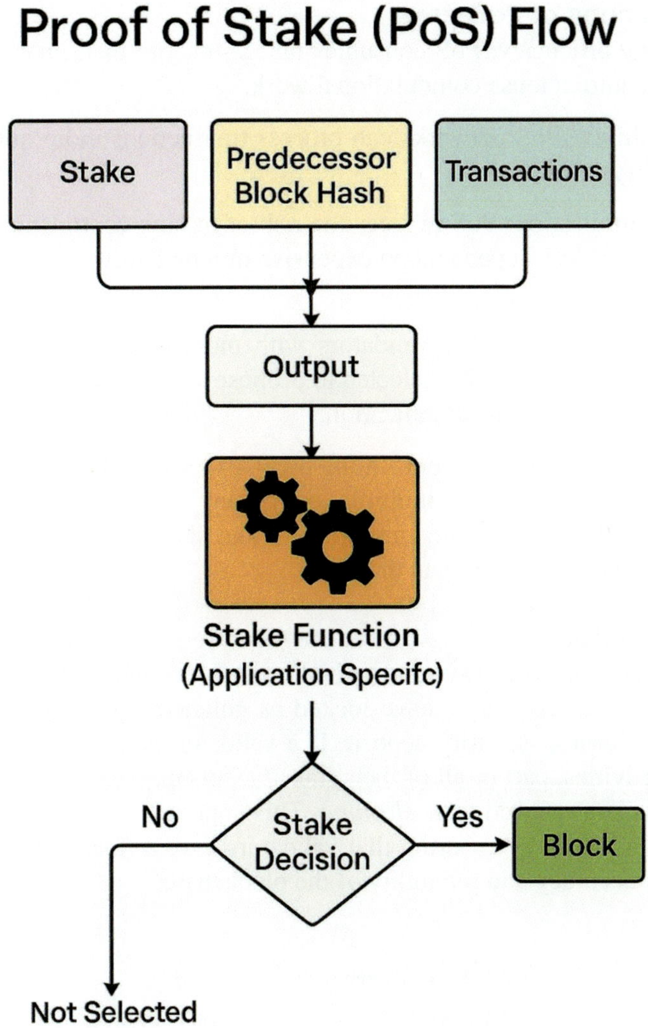

Figure 10.8 Proof of Stake (PoS) flow.

- Staking requirement: To operate as a validator in Ethereum 2.0, participants must stake a minimum of 32 ETH as collateral within the network.
- Validator incentives: Validators receive ETH rewards and transaction fees for validating transactions and proposing new blocks to the blockchain.

Pros and cons of PoS Pros:

- Energy efficiency: PoS consumes far less energy than PoW, as it does not require intense computational work.
- Scalability: PoS networks can process transactions more quickly than PoW systems.
- Decentralisation: PoS reduces the risk of mining centralization, as the process is less dependent on expensive mining hardware.

Cons:

- Wealth concentration: Validators with more cryptocurrencies have a higher chance of being selected to propose and validate blocks, leading to potential wealth centralization.
- Nothing-at-stake problem: In the early stages of PoS, validators could theoretically validate multiple conflicting chains, leading to double-spending. However, mechanisms like slashing (penalties for dishonest behavior) mitigate this issue.

Security in PoS

In a Proof-of-Stake (PoS) system, validators are motivated to act in good faith by the cryptocurrency they have locked as collateral. This staked amount serves as a form of security deposit. If a validator engages in dishonest or harmful activities, part or all of their staked assets may be forfeited – a penalty mechanism referred to as *slashing*. This approach strengthens the security of the network by ensuring that validators have a financial incentive to uphold the accuracy and reliability of the blockchain.

Table 10.3 Comparison of PoW and PoS.

Feature	Proof of Work (PoW)	Proof of Stake (PoS)
Energy consumption	High, due to computational mining work	Low, as it does not require energy-intensive mining
Security	High requires significant computational power to attack	High, but relies on stake and penalties for dishonest behavior
Scalability	Low, due to slow block	High, which allows for faster
Feature	Proof of Work (PoW) generation and high energy costs	Proof of Stake (PoS) transaction processing
Decentralization	Can be affected by mining pools	Can be affected wealth concentration among validators
Environmental impact	Significant carbon footprint	Low environmental impact
Transaction speed	Slow, 10 minutes per block in Bitcoin	Faster, as it does not require extensive computational work

Hybrid consensus mechanisms in blockchain

In blockchain networks, hybrid consensus mechanisms integrate two or more consensus algorithms to optimise the strengths of each while addressing the inherent limitations of individual methods. One of the most common combinations is Proof of Work (PoW) and Proof of Stake (PoS). By merging these mechanisms, hybrid systems strive to achieve a balance between security, decentralisation, scalability, and energy efficiency. This approach leverages the robustness of PoW in securing the network and the resource efficiency of PoS, thereby mitigating the drawbacks associated with using either mechanism in isolation.

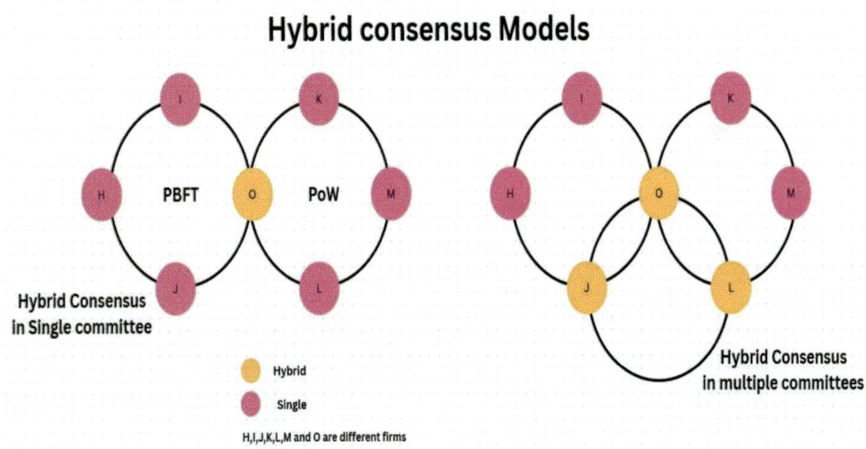

Figure 10.9 Hybrid consensus models.

The hybrid models are designed to leverage:

- PoW's proven security and ability to resist attacks by making it computationally expensive to alter the blockchain.
- PoS's energy efficiency and scalability by reducing the need for resource- intensive mining and offering faster block finality.

Hybrid consensus mechanisms can offer enhanced performance by using the strengths of multiple algorithms while attempting to address weaknesses like scalability issues, energy consumption, or centralization.

Consensus mechanisms are essential for safeguarding the integrity and security of blockchain networks. Proof of Work (PoW), in particular, has long been regarded as the foundational model for ensuring trust and preventing malicious activity within decentralized systems. While PoW is highly effective in maintaining security, it also presents notable drawbacks-most prominently, its intensive energy requirements and inherent scalability limitations. On the other hand, Proof of Stake (PoS) provides a more energy-efficient solution and improves scalability, but it is concerned about wealth centralization. Both mechanisms play a pivotal role in the operation of blockchain systems, and their differences influence the choice of blockchain platform depending on the use case and desired outcomes. According to the World Economic Forum [12] and IBM [13], blockchain fosters enterprise innovation in supply chain, finance, and governance. NIST [14] defines standardized frameworks ensuring interoperability and security. Policymakers emphasize regulatory alignment and fair competition to support blockchain adoption (OECD, 2022) [15]. The Cambridge Centre for Alternative Finance [16] notes its rapid integration into financial infrastructure. Recent trends show evolution toward hybrid and energy-efficient consensus models [17], while research focuses on architecture optimization [18]. Future directions include secure, sustainable blockchain applications in sectors such as healthcare and logistics [19].

Summary

Chapter 10 introduces the foundational concepts behind blockchain technology. It begins by explaining what a blockchain is decentralized, distributed ledger that securely records transactions across a network without relying on a central authority. The chapter then explores the structure of blocks, how transactions are added, and the role of Merkle Trees, which efficiently verify and summarize large volumes of data to ensure integrity. Finally, it covers consensus mechanisms, focusing on Proof of Work (PoW) and Proof of Stake (PoS), the two primary methods used to validate transactions and secure blockchain networks. Together, these concepts form the technical backbone of blockchain systems used in cryptocurrencies and beyond.

Case Study: Bitcoin and Ethereum – Evolution of Blockchain Applications

Bitcoin, launched in 2009 by the anonymous figure or group known as Satoshi Nakamoto, stands as the pioneering implementation of blockchain technology. As the first decentralized cryptocurrency, Bitcoin introduced the concept of a peer-to-peer digital cash system that eliminates the need for intermediaries such as banks or centralized financial institutions. Its core strength lies in the decentralization of control, where a network of distributed nodes, commonly referred to as miners, collectively validates and records transactions. This system ensures that no single entity can manipulate the ledger, thus promoting trust and transparency. The principle of immutability is also demonstrated strongly in Bitcoin; once transactions are recorded on the blockchain, they cannot be altered or erased, thereby reinforcing the integrity of the system. Furthermore, Bitcoin's consensus mechanism, known as Proof-of-Work (PoW), requires miners to solve complex cryptographic puzzles using SHA-256 hashing. This process not only validates transactions but also determines who gets to add the next block to the chain. Technically, new blocks are generated approximately every 10 minutes, and miners are incentivized through block rewards, which initially started at 50 BTC and halve every 210,000 blocks – roughly every four years.

The launch of Bitcoin marked a revolutionary shift in the way digital value could be stored and transferred without relying on centralized entities. It demonstrated that decentralized systems secured through cryptographic and economic incentives could function on a global scale. Bitcoin laid the groundwork for a multitude of other blockchain-based cryptocurrencies and applications, setting the stage for widespread innovation in decentralized systems. From a foundational perspective, Bitcoin validated several key blockchain principles: secure cryptographic operations, distributed consensus, economic incentivization, and the structural integrity of immutable ledgers. At the same time, it revealed limitations, particularly with respect to scalability and energy efficiency inherent in PoW systems.

Building on the principles laid by Bitcoin, Ethereum emerged in 2015 as a second- generation blockchain platform that significantly expanded the utility of blockchain technology beyond simple value transfer. Founded by Vitalik Buterin and a team of developers, Ethereum introduced the concept of smart contracts – self-executing code that runs when predefined conditions are met, without the need for intermediaries. This programmability was enabled through the Ethereum Virtual Machine (EVM), a decentralized computing environment in which developers could build decentralized applications (dApps). The platform supports trustless interactions across domains like finance, insurance, and supply chain management, facilitating more complex, conditional, and automated transactions. Ethereum also introduced the concept of "gas," a measure used to quantify computational effort and prevent misuse of the network by attaching costs to each operation.

One of Ethereum's most notable applications was the creation of the Decentralized Autonomous Organization (DAO), a venture capital fund managed entirely by smart contracts. Although the DAO was famously exploited due to a vulnerability in its code, it demonstrated both the power and risks associated with blockchain programmability. The Ethereum network has since become the foundation for major innovations such as Decentralized Finance (DeFi) and Non-Fungible Tokens (NFTs), reshaping digital ownership and financial systems. The impact of Ethereum extended into areas like digital identity, decentralized governance, and tokenized assets, thereby significantly broadening blockchain's real-world applications.

Case Discussion Questions:

1. How did Bitcoin validate the core principles of blockchain technology, and what limitations did it expose?
2. In what ways does Ethereum extend blockchain functionality beyond cryptocurrency?
3. What are the risks associated with programmability in Ethereum, and how can they be mitigated?
4. How do consensus mechanisms like Proof-of-Work affect the scalability and energy efficiency of blockchain systems?
5. Compare the roles of Bitcoin and Ethereum in the broader FinTech and digital innovation ecosystems. How do their use cases differ?

Keywords

- **Blockchain**: A distributed, decentralized digital ledger that records transactions across a network of computers. Once recorded, these transactions cannot be altered, ensuring transparency, security, and permanence.
- **Merkle tree**: A unique type of binary tree structure used to efficiently verify and validate that the data within a block has not been altered.
- **Block**: A data unit in a blockchain that acts as a container, holding a batch of verified transactions before being added to the chain.

- **Nonce**: A numeric value used during mining in Proof of Work (PoW) systems to help discover a valid hash and solve the computational challenge.
- **Merkle root**: The root hash in a Merkle tree, representing a condensed cryptographic summary of all the transactions within a block.
- **Mining**: The PoW-based process of validating transactions and appending new blocks to a blockchain.
- **Validator**: A participant in a Proof of Stake (PoS) system who is responsible for approving transactions and proposing new blocks.
- **Slashing**: A disciplinary action in PoS systems where dishonest or non-compliant validators lose part of their staked assets.
- **Staking**: The process of locking up cryptocurrency to participate in transaction validation and governance within a PoS network.
- **Distributed ledger technology (DLT)**: A shared record-keeping system distributed across multiple nodes in a network. Each participant maintains a synchronized copy of the ledger, eliminating the need for a central authority.
- **Hashing**: The cryptographic process of converting input data into a fixed-length string, called a hash. In blockchain, algorithms like SHA-256 ensure data integrity, as any data change produces a completely different hash output.
- **Proof of Work (PoW)**: A consensus process where miners solve complex mathematical problems to verify transactions and produce new blocks. While secure, it demands substantial computational power and energy.
- **Proof of Stake (PoS)**: A consensus protocol that selects validators to create blocks based on the amount of cryptocurrency they lock as collateral, offering greater energy efficiency than PoW.
- **Smart contract**: A self-executing program stored on the blockchain that automatically enforces the terms of an agreement when predefined rules are met, eliminating the need for intermediaries.
- **Public blockchain**: A permissionless blockchain open to all participants for transaction validation and consensus, characterized by full decentralization and transparency, e.g., Bitcoin and Ethereum.

- **Private blockchain**: A permissioned blockchain allowing only authorized entities to participate, typically managed by a single organization for secure internal operations.
- **Consortium blockchain**: A partially decentralized blockchain governed by multiple organizations, blending features of public and private networks for collaborative use cases like banking alliances or supply chains.
- **Immutability**: A blockchain property ensuring that once data is recorded and confirmed, it cannot be altered or removed without consensus and modification of subsequent blocks.
- **Consensus mechanism**: The protocol enabling distributed blockchain participants to agree on transaction validity and ledger state, examples include PoW, PoS, and PBFT.
- **Decentralization**: The distribution of control and decision-making across a network, enhancing transparency, resilience, and trust by eliminating central authority dependence.
- **Nonce** (duplicate term in PoW context): A one-time numeric value miners adjust to meet the required hash difficulty when generating a new block.
- **Cryptographic hash function**: An algorithm that transforms an input into a fixed-size hash value, which is deterministic, secure against collisions, and fundamental to blockchain security.
- **Byzantine Fault Tolerance (BFT)**: The ability of a distributed network to maintain correct functionality even if some participants act maliciously or fail, as implemented in consensus models like PBFT.
- **Transaction**: A discrete piece of data on the blockchain that records the exchange of assets or information.

Discussion Questions

1. Explain the evolution of blockchain technology from Bitcoin to Blockchain 3.0. Provide real-world examples.
2. Describe the structure of a blockchain block. What is the significance of hashing?

3. Compare and contrast PoW and PoS. Discuss their strengths and weaknesses.
4. What are the main challenges in implementing blockchain in government and financial sectors?
5. Identify three industries where blockchain is making a significant impact. Describe one use case for each.
6. Explain how a Merkle tree works and why it is important for blockchain systems.
7. How does the inclusion of a Merkle root in a block header help ensure blockchain integrity?
8. What is the relationship between transactions, blocks, and Merkle trees in a blockchain network?
9. Describe how Merkle proofs are used to verify individual transactions within a block.
10. Discuss the advantages and limitations of using Merkle trees in blockchain networks.
11. Explain the key differences between PoW and PoS and their respective advantages and disadvantages.
12. How does PoS address the scalability issues of PoW? Discuss the trade-offs.
13. What is the "Nothing-at-Stake" problem in PoS, and how is it mitigated?
14. Analyse the impact of centralization in PoW and PoS. Which mechanism offers better decentralization, and why?
15. What are some emerging consensus mechanisms, and how do they differ from PoW and PoS?

References

[1] Antonopoulos, A. M. (2017). *Mastering Bitcoin: Programming the open blockchain* (2nd ed.). O'Reilly Media.

[2] Mougayar, W. (2016). *The business blockchain: Promise, practice, and application of the next internet technology.* Wiley.

[3] Drescher, D. (2017). *Blockchain basics: A non-technical introduction in 25 steps.* Apress.

[4] Swan, M. (2015). *Blockchain: Blueprint for a new economy.* O'Reilly Media.

[5] Bashir, I. (2020). *Mastering blockchain: Unlocking the power of cryptocurrencies, smart contracts, and decentralized applications* (3rd ed.). Packt Publishing.

[6] Narayanan, A., Bonneau, J., Felten, E., Miller, A., & Goldfeder, S. (2016). *Bitcoin and cryptocurrency technologies: A comprehensive introduction.* Princeton University Press.

[7] Tapscott, D., & Tapscott, A. (2016). *Blockchain revolution: How the technology behind Bitcoin is changing money, business, and the world.* Penguin.

[8] Tiana, G., & Minetti, M. (2022). *Decoding blockchain: Essentials for building the decentralized web.* Springer.

[9] Buterin, V. (2022). *Proof of stake: The making of Ethereum and the philosophy of blockchain.* Seven Stories Press.

[10] Gaurav, V. (2021). *Blockchain for beginners: A guide to decentralized technologies.* Wiley India.

[11] European Union Blockchain Observatory and Forum. (2020). *Convergence of blockchain and artificial intelligence.* EU Blockchain Report.

[12] World Economic Forum. (2021). *Blockchain development toolkit.* World Economic Forum.

[13] IBM Institute for Business Value. (2020). *The practical guide to blockchain: Tech primer for enterprise.* IBM.

[14] National Institute of Standards and Technology (NIST). (2018). *Blockchain technology overview (NISTIR 8202).* U.S. Department of Commerce.

[15] Organisation for Economic Co-operation and Development (OECD). (2022). *Blockchain and competition policy.* OECD Publishing.

[16] Cambridge Centre for Alternative Finance. (2020). *Global blockchain benchmarking study.* University of Cambridge.

[17] Deloitte Insights. (2023). *Blockchain trends: Evolving consensus models and efficiency.* Deloitte.

[18] Accenture. (2021). *Blockchain: Realizing the potential – Architecture and principles.* Accenture Research.

[19] Ramachandran, M. (2025). *Blockchain engineering: Secure, sustainable frameworks for healthcare applications* (1st ed.). Springer Nature Singapore.

11

Blockchain in Finance

Abstract

The advent of blockchain technology has introduced transformative possibilities for the banking and financial sector by enabling decentralized, transparent, and secure transaction systems. This chapter identifies various blockchain banking models and examines their practical applications across payment processing, trade finance, cross-border remittances, and smart contracts. It critically analyzes how blockchain addresses systemic inefficiencies in traditional financial processes, including issues of high transaction costs, settlement delays, and risks associated with centralized data management. Real-world implementations, such as Ripple for cross-border payments and Ethereum for decentralized finance (DeFi) and programmable smart contracts, are evaluated to illustrate the scope, benefits, and limitations of blockchain solutions in financial ecosystems. The chapter further discusses the profound impact of blockchain on conventional finance infrastructure and practices, highlighting its potential to disrupt legacy systems, enhance transparency, and strengthen trust while also acknowledging regulatory, scalability, and interoperability challenges. Collectively, the chapter underscores blockchain's role as a foundational innovation in reshaping the future of banking and finance.

Introduction

The banking industry has long been reliant on centralized systems to manage and track financial transactions, maintain customer data, and execute a range of financial operations. However, with the advent of blockchain technology, traditional banking models are facing significant disruption. Blockchain's decentralized, secure, transparent, and immutable nature offers several advantages for the banking sector, including enhanced efficiency, reduced operational costs, and better security.

DOI: 10.1201/9788743811244-15

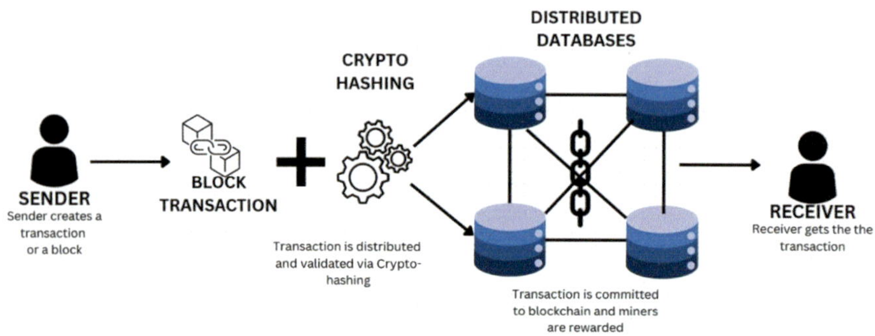

Figure 11.1 Process of blockchain.

Blockchain banking models are frameworks through which financial institutions can leverage blockchain to streamline operations, provide innovative financial services, and improve customer experience. These models vary depending on the scope of implementation, with some banks adopting blockchain to enhance existing services, while others explore the possibility of decentralizing entire banking operations. Blockchain technology has become a transformative force in the financial sector, offering transparency, security, and decentralization [1]. Modern blockchain banking models aim to replace traditional intermediaries with distributed ledgers that streamline operations [2]. By removing centralized control, blockchain enables faster settlements and reduces operational costs in financial institutions [3]. A research also empirically demonstrated that blockchain adoption enhances financial performance among Australian banks through improved efficiency [4]. This section will explore different blockchain banking models in detail, highlighting their benefits, challenges, and real-world examples.

11.1 Blockchain Banking Models

11.1.1 Traditional banking on blockchain (blockchain for existing banking systems)

In this model, traditional banks adopt blockchain technology to enhance existing services. Rather than entirely changing the structure of the bank, blockchain is integrated into existing operations like payment systems, clearing and settlement, and record-keeping to improve efficiency and reduce costs.

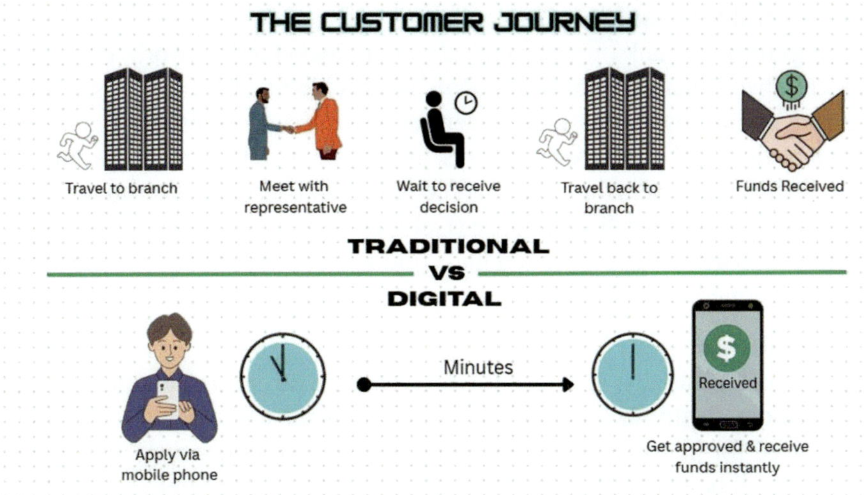

Figure 11.2 Traditional vs digital banking.

Key features:

- Payment systems: Blockchain can be used to streamline payment systems, reducing transaction times from days to minutes. It provides secure and near- instantaneous transfers, especially for cross-border payments, where intermediaries and lengthy processing times are common.
- Clearance and settlement: Blockchain's ability to provide real-time settlement of securities and financial transactions reduces delays and improves the efficiency of the clearing and settlement process.
- Record-keeping: Blockchain can be used to create an immutable record of all transactions, improving transparency and reducing the risk of fraud.

Example: JPMorgan and Quorum: JPMorgan Chase has developed a blockchain platform called Quorum, based on Ethereum, which is designed for the financial sector to enable faster and more secure transactions. It is used for various purposes, including payments and smart contract applications within the bank.

Benefits:

- Faster and cheaper cross-border transactions
- Reduced fraud and errors due to immutability and transparency
- Streamlined back-office operations through automation

Decentralized banks

A decentralized bank operates entirely on a blockchain network, leveraging decentralized finance (DeFi) protocols to provide financial services without relying on intermediaries such as central banks, payment processors, or traditional financial institutions. In this model, financial services are directly provided to customers through smart contracts and decentralized applications (dApps). The decentralized finance (DeFi) ecosystem builds upon these principles, offering peer-to-peer lending, trading, and insurance without traditional intermediaries [5].

Key features:

- Smart contracts: DeFi banks rely heavily on smart contracts, which automatically execute the terms of financial agreements without the need for intermediaries. For example, lending, borrowing, and staking can all be managed by smart contracts that are transparent and secure.
- P2P lther without relying on traditional lending institutions.
- Staking and yield farming: These platforms offer users the ability to earn returns by staking their digital assets or participating in yield farming.

Example:

- Compound: A decentralized finance platform that allows users to lend and borrow cryptocurrencies. Compound uses smart contracts to manage the lending and borrowing process, eliminating the need for a central authority to oversee transactions.
- Aave: Another decentralized finance platform that enables users to lend and borrow digital assets. Aave leverages blockchain technology and smart contracts to enable trustless financial transactions.

Benefits:

- Full decentralization removes the need for intermediaries, reducing costs and increasing transparency.
- Increased privacy and security due to blockchain's cryptographic nature.
- 24/7 availability, as decentralized banks are not bound by traditional business hours.

Challenges:

- Lack of regulatory oversight can lead to security concerns and vulnerability to exploits.

- Potential for scalability issues as decentralized systems handle growing transaction volumes.
- Limited adoption among non-crypto native individuals, who may find decentralized platforms difficult to navigate.

Blockchain-enabled digital banking platforms

Blockchain-enabled digital banks are a hybrid between traditional and decentralized banks. These platforms leverage blockchain for specific functions while still operating within a centralized structure. The focus is on providing digital banking services, such as digital wallets, payments, and loans, using blockchain to improve operational efficiency and customer experience.

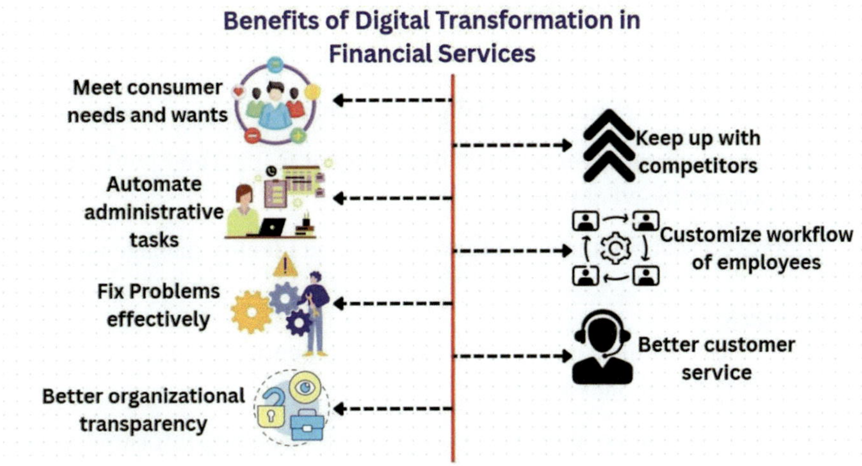

Figure 11.3 Benefits of digital transformation in financial services.

Key features:

- Blockchain-based payments: Blockchain technology is used to streamline digital payments, enabling instant, low-cost transactions, particularly for cross-border payments.
- Digital identity: Banks can use blockchain to manage customer identities in a secure and decentralized manner, reducing fraud and enhancing security. Digital identities can also streamline the Know Your Customer (KYC) process.

- Digital asset management: Blockchain allows customers to hold and manage digital assets (e.g., cryptocurrencies, tokenized assets) in a secure manner, providing a one-stop shop for traditional and digital asset management.

Example:

- Revolut: Revolut, a digital banking app, allows users to buy, sell, and hold cryptocurrencies. It uses blockchain for cryptocurrency transactions and settlements, while also providing traditional banking services such as debit cards, money transfers, and loans.
- Paxos: Paxos is a regulated blockchain platform offering digital asset custody and tokenization services for financial institutions. It bridges the gap between traditional finance and blockchain, enabling institutions to offer digital asset services securely.

Benefits:

- Access to both traditional and digital financial services on one platform.
- Enhanced customer experience using digital wallets and low-cost, fast blockchain-based payments.
- Improved security through blockchain-based identity management.

Challenges:

- Regulatory hurdles around integrating cryptocurrencies and blockchain with traditional banking systems.
- Integration complexities with existing legacy banking infrastructure.
- Customer adoption rates for blockchain-based services in traditional digital banking environments.

Blockchain-based custody and asset management services

This model focuses on the use of blockchain technology to provide secure custody solutions for digital assets and enhance asset management services. It allows banks and financial institutions to offer custody services for cryptocurrencies and tokenized assets, providing the same level of security and insurance as traditional asset management systems.

Key features:

- Digital asset custody: Banks use blockchain-based solutions to securely store and manage cryptocurrencies and other digital assets. This ensures that assets are protected against theft or loss.

- Tokenized assets: Blockchain allows for the tokenization of real-world assets like real estate, stocks, and commodities, making them easier to trade and manage.
- Fractional ownership: Tokenization allows for fractional ownership of high- value assets, making it easier for retail investors to access traditionally inaccessible investment opportunities.

Example:

- Fidelity digital assets: Fidelity offers blockchain-based custody services for cryptocurrencies, including Bitcoin and Ethereum. The firm provides a secure solution for institutional investors to store and manage their digital assets.
- Anchorage: Anchorage offers a regulated digital asset custody solution, enabling financial institutions to store and manage cryptocurrencies securely.

Benefits:

- Enhanced security and protection of digital assets.
- Easier access to tokenized real-world assets and fractional ownership.
- Increased efficiency in asset management and reduced fees through tokenization.

Challenges:

- Regulatory clarity around digital asset custody, especially in highly regulated markets.
- The complexity of integrating blockchain-based custody systems with traditional asset management practices.
- Need for higher levels of institutional adoption and trust.

Hybrid blockchain banking models

Hybrid blockchain banking models combine elements from both traditional centralized banks and decentralized finance platforms. These models offer a blend of flexibility, transparency, and security, allowing banks to provide innovative financial products while maintaining certain aspects of traditional banking services.

Key features:

- Blockchain integration with legacy systems: Hybrid models use blockchain to enhance specific banking functions (e.g., cross-border payments, KYC) while still relying on centralized systems for other functions.

- Regulatory compliance: These models work within existing regulatory frameworks to provide blockchain-based services while ensuring compliance with local financial regulations.
- Enhanced customer interaction: Banks use blockchain to offer new customer engagement features, such as crypto trading, digital wallets, and decentralized lending, alongside traditional services.

Example:

- Banco Bilbao Vizcaya Argentaria (BBVA): BBVA has implemented blockchain technology for trade finance, using it to streamline and automate the processing of transactions. They have also experimented with smart contracts for loan issuance and payments.
- Goldman Sachs: Goldman Sachs is exploring hybrid blockchain applications that offer the benefits of blockchain's transparency and security while adhering to the regulatory requirements of traditional banking systems.

Benefits:

- Best of both worlds combines the security and regulatory compliance of traditional banks with the innovation and transparency of blockchain.
- Increased operational efficiency by automating processes and eliminating intermediaries.
- Improved customer service through innovative offerings such as crypto trading and digital asset management.

Challenges:

- Balancing innovation with regulatory compliance.
- Potential conflicts between traditional banking practices and decentralized finance principles.
- Complexity in managing both centralized and decentralized elements within the same platform.

Blockchain banking models represent a significant shift in the financial services industry. From improving traditional banking systems with blockchain to fully decentralizing financial services, these models offer substantial benefits in terms of efficiency, transparency, and security. However, challenges such as regulatory compliance, integration with legacy systems, and scalability remain. Blockchain enhances transparency and trust, which are essential for combating fraud and ensuring accountability in finance [6]. Financial institutions are experimenting with hybrid blockchain models that balance decentralization with regulatory compliance [7]. The research highlights that blockchain's governance mechanisms redefine how financial systems manage risk and incentives [8]. FinTech Magazine [9] reports that banks integrating blockchain experience significant improvements in customer experience and data security. In Jordan, blockchain adoption reduced operational redundancies and improved efficiency in transaction management [10]. According to a research, the finance sector leads blockchain research due to its measurable economic and technological benefits [11].

The future of blockchain in banking will likely involve greater hybridization, where traditional banks integrate blockchain-based services into their operations while maintaining their existing infrastructure. As blockchain technology continues to mature and regulatory frameworks evolve, more innovative banking models will emerge, further disrupting and transforming the financial services landscape.

11.2 Solving Systemic Inefficiencies

Systemic inefficiencies in the traditional financial system have long plagued both institutional and retail users. These inefficiencies manifest in the form of high transaction costs, slow settlement times, lack of transparency, fraud vulnerabilities, over-reliance on intermediaries, and data silos. With increasing globalization, the demand for real-time, cost-effective, and secure financial services has grown rapidly, exposing the limitations of legacy infrastructure.

Blockchain technology, with its decentralized, immutable, and transparent architecture, presents an innovative solution to many of these challenges. This chapter explores how blockchain can solve systemic inefficiencies across key areas of financial operations and beyond.

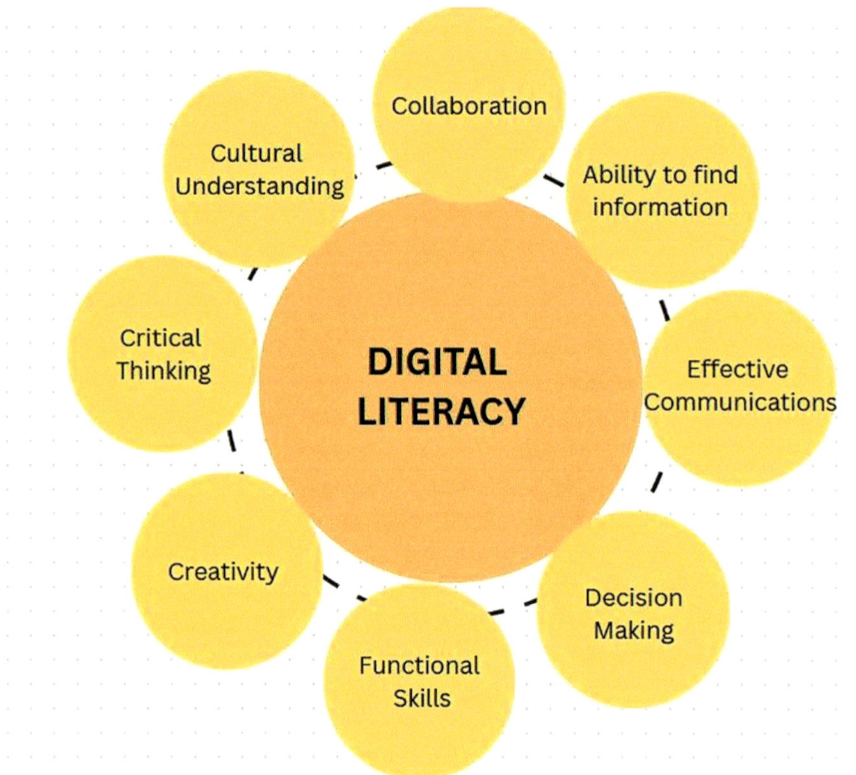

Figure 11.4 Digital literacy.

11.2.1 Understanding systemic inefficiencies in traditional finance

Systemic inefficiencies refer to structural issues within financial systems that prevent optimal performance. These inefficiencies include:

- **Settlement delays**: Traditional systems take days for the settlement and clearing of transactions due to intermediary involvement.
- **Intermediary dependence**: Banks, clearinghouses, and third-party service providers act as trusted intermediaries, adding friction, time, and costs.
- **Opaque record-keeping**: Centralized ledgers make audit trails difficult to access and increase the risk of fraud or manipulation.

- **High transaction fees**: Cross-border transactions, remittances, and financial services come with high costs due to layers of intermediaries.
- **Limited financial inclusion**: Many people globally remain unbanked due to geographic, bureaucratic, or economic barriers.
- **Data silos**: Financial institutions maintain separate databases, resulting in fragmented and redundant information.

11.2.2 Blockchain as a tool for transformation

Blockchain technology addresses these inefficiencies through the following mechanisms:

Decentralization

By removing the need for a central authority, blockchain allows peer-to-peer transactions. This reduces overhead and removes the reliance on costly intermediaries, such as banks or clearing houses.

Use case: In cross-border remittances, blockchain enables direct transfers without the need for SWIFT intermediaries, reducing transaction costs and time.

Immutability and transparency

All records on a blockchain are timestamped and immutable, meaning once data is entered, it cannot be altered without consensus. This provides an auditable trail for regulators and increases trust among participants.

Use case: In trade finance, documents like letters of credit can be recorded on a blockchain, reducing fraud and enabling real-time verification by all stakeholders.

Smart contracts

Smart contracts automate processes by executing pre-set rules encoded in code. This reduces paperwork, manual errors, and enforcement costs.

Use case: Insurance claims processing can be streamlined by smart contracts, where a contract automatically releases payments once conditions (e.g., flight delay or weather data) are verified.

Interoperability and data sharing

Blockchain can provide a shared ledger accessible to multiple institutions while maintaining confidentiality through encryption. This promotes synchronized data sharing and eliminates duplication.

Use case: KYC/AML procedures are often duplicated across institutions. Blockchain can streamline compliance by enabling shared identity verification.

Tokenization of assets

Physical assets like real estate, gold, or even art can be digitized (tokenized) and represented on a blockchain, allowing easier and fractional access.

Impact: Tokenization increases market liquidity and opens new avenues for investment, even in traditionally illiquid asset classes.

11.2.3 Sector-wise application of blockchain for efficiency payments and settlements

- **Inefficiency**: Time-consuming settlement cycles, especially in cross-border transactions.
- **Blockchain solution**: Instantaneous transactions with reduced fees and no need for intermediaries.
- **Example**: Ripple Net offers a blockchain-based system that settles cross-border payments in seconds.

Trade finance

- **Inefficiency**: Paper-heavy processes and manual verifications.
- **Blockchain solution**: Digitized documentation, real-time tracking, and smart contract automation.
- **Example**: Marco Polo Network and Trade Lens use blockchain to streamline trade documentation and logistics.

Securities clearing and settlement

- **Inefficiency**: Delays due to multiple intermediaries and reconciliations.
- **Blockchain solution**: Near real-time clearing and immutable records.
- **Example**: The Australian Securities Exchange (ASX) is replacing its CHESS system with a blockchain-based platform to reduce costs and settlement time.

Identity management

- **Inefficiency**: Repetitive KYC/AML checks across institutions.
- **Blockchain solution**: Shared digital identity records that are secure and verifiable.

- **Example**: Sovrin Network enables self-sovereign identities based on blockchain.

Supply chain finance

- **Inefficiency**: Opaque supply chains, fraud, and long payment cycles.
- **Blockchain solution**: Transparent tracking and faster invoice financing using verifiable on-chain data.
- **Example**: IBM Food Trust tracks product provenance from farm to store, ensuring authenticity and improving trust.

Benefits of solving inefficiencies with blockchain

- **Cost savings**: Reduced operational costs from eliminating intermediaries and manual processes.
- **Speed**: Real-time processing and settlements.
- **Security**: Cryptographic protection of data and reduced fraud.
- **Transparency**: Immutable and auditable records.
- **Accessibility**: Broader financial inclusion through decentralized platforms.
- **Automation**: Smart contracts remove human error and bias in enforcement.

Challenges and considerations

Despite its potential, blockchain implementation also presents challenges:

- **Scalability**: Some blockchain networks struggle with processing high volumes of transactions.
- **Regulatory uncertainty**: Jurisdictional ambiguity and compliance concerns can hinder adoption.
- **Integration with legacy systems**: Merging blockchain with traditional infrastructure is complex.
- **Privacy vs. transparency**: Balancing open ledgers with confidentiality requirements remains a challenge.

As blockchain matures and regulatory clarity improves, the adoption of blockchain to solve systemic inefficiencies will increase. Interoperable, scalable, and regulated blockchain ecosystems are expected to become integral to the digital transformation of finance.

Developments like Central Bank Digital Currencies (CBDCs), enterprise blockchain platforms (e.g., Hyperledger, R3 Corda), and decentralized financial protocols (DeFi) will collectively redefine efficiency benchmarks in global financial systems.

11.3 Industry Examples – Ripple and Ethereum

Blockchain technology has evolved beyond a theoretical innovation into a practical infrastructure for numerous industries, especially in finance. Two of the most influential blockchain platforms in the financial technology ecosystem are **Ripple** and **Ethereum**. Each addresses different systemic needs: Ripple focuses on revolutionizing cross-border payments, while Ethereum provides a decentralized platform for deploying smart contracts and decentralized applications (dApps). This chapter examines the architectures, features, use cases, and impacts of these platforms on the financial services industry. Bitcoin and Ethereum laid the foundation for decentralized financial systems through public blockchains [12]. Ripple, a blockchain-based payment protocol, focuses on real-time gross settlements and cross-border transfers [13]. Comparative studies reveal Ripple's network provides lower transaction costs and higher speed than SWIFT systems [14]. Ethereum's programmable smart contracts enable financial innovation by automating trust-based transactions [15].

Ripple: Blockchain for cross-border payments

Ripple is a real-time gross settlement system (RTGS), currency exchange, and remittance network created by Ripple Labs Inc. Unlike most public blockchains, Ripple does not rely on Proof of Work (PoW) or Proof of Stake (PoS). Instead, it uses a **unique consensus mechanism** known as the Ripple Protocol Consensus Algorithm (RPCA).

Architecture and components

- **Ripple net**: A network of banks and financial institutions that use Ripple's technology to process payments.
- **XRP ledger (XRPL)**: A decentralized, open source blockchain that supports the XRP token.
- **XRP token**: The native digital currency used as a bridge asset in currency exchange and liquidity provision.
- **Interledger protocol (ILP)**: Enables interoperability between different payment networks and ledgers.

Use cases

- **Cross-border remittances**
  Ripple enables banks to settle international transactions in real-time with end-to-end tracking. Traditional systems such as SWIFT can take several days to complete similar transactions.
- **Liquidity provision**
  XRP can be used as a bridge currency in markets where direct exchange pairs may not exist. This reduces the need for pre-funded nostro accounts.
- **Banking infrastructure**
  Ripple is used by over 300 financial institutions, including Santander, SBI Holdings, and PNC Bank, for fast and low-cost remittance and settlement.

Advantages

- **High speed**: Transactions settle in ~3-5 seconds.
- **Low cost**: Minimal transaction fees (fractions of a cent).
- **Energy efficient**: No mining; low computational requirement.
- **Scalability**: Can handle ~1,500 transactions per second (TPS).

Criticism and challenges

- **Centralization concerns**: Critics argue Ripple's node control is more centralized than other blockchain platforms.
- **Regulatory issues**: Ripple Labs has faced legal battles, most notably with the U.S. Securities and Exchange Commission (SEC) over the classification of XRP as a security.

Ethereum: Decentralized smart contract platform

Launched in 2015, Ethereum is a decentralized, open-source blockchain platform that enables the development and execution of smart contracts and decentralized applications. Created by Vitalik Buterin and others, Ethereum goes beyond simple currency transactions to support complex programmable logic on the blockchain.

Ethereum 1.0 vs. Ethereum 2.0

- **Ethereum 1.0**: Used Proof of Work (PoW) consensus, like Bitcoin.
- **Ethereum 2.0 (The Merge)**: Transitioned to Proof of Stake (PoS) in 2022, enhancing scalability, reducing energy consumption, and improving security.

Core features

- **Smart contracts**: Self-executing contracts with the terms of agreement written into code.
- **Ethereum virtual machine (EVM)**: A Turing-complete virtual machine that enables execution of smart contract code.
- **Ether (ETH)**: The native cryptocurrency used for transaction fees and contract execution.
- **Gas fees**: Charges paid in ETH to perform operations and prevent spam on the network.

Use cases

- **Decentralized finance (DeFi)**
  Ethereum powers platforms like Uniswap, Aave, and Compound that allow users to lend, borrow, trade, and earn interest on digital assets without intermediaries.
- **Tokenization**
  Ethereum's ERC-20 and ERC-721 standards enable the creation of fungible and non-fungible tokens (NFTs), respectively, revolutionizing asset ownership and management.
- **Decentralized applications (dApps)**
  Thousands of dApps are deployed on Ethereum for various purposes, including gaming, social networking, and finance.
- **Initial Coin Offerings (ICOs)**
  Ethereum has facilitated the launch of new cryptocurrencies and blockchain projects via token sales.

Advantages

- **Programmability**: Supports custom smart contracts and dApps.
- **Large developer community**: Leading blockchain in terms of development activity.
- **Network effect**: High adoption and integration in DeFi and NFT sectors.

Challenges

- **Scalability**: High network congestion and gas fees have been persistent issues.

- **Security risks**: Smart contract bugs can be exploited, as seen in the DAO hack.
- **Regulatory uncertainty**: As a leading DeFi platform, Ethereum faces scrutiny from global regulators.

Table 11.1 Comparative analysis: Ripple vs. Ethereum.

Feature	Ripple	Ethereum
Primary focus	Cross-border payments	Smart contracts and dApps
Consensus mechanism	Ripple Protocol Consensus Algorithm (RPCA)	Proof of Stake (Ethereum 2.0)
Speed	~3–5 seconds	~12 seconds (variable based on congestion)
Token	XRP	ETH
Energy usage	Low	Low (post-PoS)
Smart contract support	Limited	Extensive
Use in traditional finance	High	Moderate to high (especially in DeFi)
Adoption	Banks and payment providers	Developers, startups, and DeFi projects

Ripple and Ethereum exemplify how blockchain can address different financial challenges – Ripple focuses on optimizing cross-border settlements, while Ethereum enables programmable finance through smart contracts. Together, they highlight the adaptability and transformative power of blockchain technology in the modern financial world. Understanding their differences, applications, and limitations is crucial for professionals aiming to innovate or invest in blockchain-based financial solutions.

Summary

Chapter 11 introduces the foundational concepts of blockchain technology and highlights how it differs from traditional databases. It begins by comparing blockchain systems with conventional databases, emphasizing the decentralized, immutable, and transparent nature of blockchains, unlike the centralized control seen in traditional systems. The chapter then explains the structure of blockchain blocks, how transactions are recorded, and the role of Merkle Trees in ensuring data integrity and efficient verification. Finally, it explores consensus mechanisms – particularly Proof of Work (PoW) and Proof of Stake (PoS) – which are crucial for validating transactions and maintaining trust across decentralized networks. Together, these concepts lay the groundwork for understanding how blockchain ensures security, reliability, and decentralization in digital systems.

Case Study: RippleNet – A Model For Cross-Border FinTech Collaboration

RippleNet, developed by Ripple Labs Inc., a FinTech company headquartered in San Francisco, represents one of the most transformative initiatives in the realm of cross-border financial technology. Designed to modernize and streamline international money transfers, RippleNet has emerged as a global payments network connecting over 300 financial institutions – including banks, non-banking financial companies, and payment service providers – across more than 40 countries. This case illustrates how FinTech innovation, combined with strategic cross-border collaboration, can disrupt traditional financial models and create more inclusive and efficient global payment systems. Traditional cross-border payment mechanisms are often plagued by inefficiencies such as high fees, lengthy settlement times, and limited transparency. These issues are particularly burdensome for small and medium-sized enterprises (SMEs), migrant workers sending remittances, and institutions in developing markets. RippleNet addresses these challenges by utilizing blockchain technology to facilitate real-time gross settlement and employing its digital asset, XRP, as a bridge currency. This allows transactions to be executed in seconds rather than days, significantly reducing transaction costs and currency exchange complexities.

The strength of RippleNet lies in its collaborative model. By partnering with established financial institutions around the world, Ripple has created an interoperable and decentralized network that blends legacy infrastructure with cutting-edge FinTech solutions. Institutions such as Santander Bank (Spain), SBI Remit (Japan), Siam Commercial Bank (Thailand), and Standard Chartered (UK) are notable members of RippleNet. These partnerships allow banks to offer enhanced cross-border services without overhauling their existing core systems. The use of Ripple's APIs enables easy integration, making it a scalable solution for both large financial players and emerging FinTech firms.

RippleNet's role extends beyond technology; it plays an active part in fostering international regulatory cooperation. Ripple Labs works closely with regulators in different jurisdictions to ensure that its operations comply with local laws related to anti-money laundering (AML), know-your-customer (KYC), and data protection. This commitment to regulatory alignment has positioned RippleNet as a trusted partner for financial institutions navigating the complex landscape of cross-border compliance. Moreover, its efforts contribute to the creation of standardized frameworks that encourage innovation while maintaining financial stability. Another key element in RippleNet's success is its ability to support financial inclusion. By significantly reducing the costs and barriers associated with international transfers, RippleNet empowers SMEs to expand globally and allows migrant workers to send money home quickly and affordably. Its model promotes a more equitable financial ecosystem where access is not limited by geography or institutional size. Furthermore, the use of digital identity systems and secure data-sharing protocols ensures that cross-border interactions remain safe, efficient, and transparent.

In conclusion, RippleNet exemplifies how cross-border FinTech collaboration can reshape global finance. By merging innovative blockchain-based solutions with existing financial infrastructures and by fostering strong international partnerships, RippleNet has created a robust, inclusive, and efficient payments network. It showcases the power of collaborative ecosystems where public and private stakeholders, guided by forward-thinking regulation and technology, come together to build the future of financial connectivity.

Discussion Questions

1. Discuss the technological advantages in terms of speed, cost, and transparency, and compare them.
2. Analyze how Ripple's engagement with global regulators contributes to its scalability and trust, and explore the challenges posed by inconsistent international regulations.
3. Examine the social and economic impacts of low-cost, real-time international transfers, and discuss how smaller Fintech can benefit from such global networks.

Keywords

- **Blockchain**: A decentralized, distributed ledger technology that records transactions in a secure and immutable way across a network of computers.
- **Cryptocurrency**: A digital or virtual currency that uses cryptography for security, typically built on blockchain technology.
- **Central Bank Digital Currency (CBDC)**: A digital currency issued and regulated by a country's central bank, using blockchain technology to facilitate secure and efficient payments.
- **Smart contract**: A self-executing contract where the terms of the agreement are written directly on lines of code, automatically executing when predefined conditions are met.
- **Decentralized finance (DeFi)**: A financial ecosystem that operates without intermediaries, leveraging blockchain to provide services such as lending, borrowing, and trading.
- **Tokenization**: The process of converting assets or rights into digital tokens that can be traded on blockchain networks.
- **Peer-to-peer (P2P) lending**: A decentralized system where individuals lend and borrow money directly from each other, typically facilitated by a blockchain-based platform.
- **Systemic inefficiency**: Structural problems in financial systems cause delays, high costs, and errors.
- **Intermediaries**: Third-party entities that facilitate transactions in traditional systems.
- **Immutable ledger**: A blockchain ledger where data, once recorded, cannot be altered.
- **Smart contract:** A blockchain-based code that automatically executes financial agreements.
- **Tokenization**: Converting real-world assets into digital tokens on a blockchain.
- **Interoperability**: The ability of different systems or blockchains to share and use information.
- **Ripple**: A blockchain-based platform for fast, cost-effective cross-border payments.

- **XRP**: The native cryptocurrency of the Ripple network.
- **Ethereum**: A decentralized platform for smart contracts and decentralized applications.
- **Smart contract**: Code that automatically enforces the terms of an agreement on the blockchain.
- **DeFi**: Decentralized financial systems built on blockchain without intermediaries.
- **Gas fees**: Transaction fees paid in ETH to execute operations on the Ethereum network.
- **Proof of stake (PoS)**: A consensus mechanism where validators are chosen based on the amount of cryptocurrency they stake.

Discussion Questions

1. Explain the concept of blockchain and how it is different from traditional database systems.
2. Discuss the role of blockchain in revolutionizing the payment and cross-border transaction systems.
3. What are Central Bank Digital Currencies (CBDCs), and how do they differ from cryptocurrencies like Bitcoin and Ethereum?
4. Describe how blockchain technology can be used to improve the lending process in decentralized finance (DeFi) platforms.
5. In what ways does blockchain enhance transparency and reduce fraud in the insurance industry? Provide examples.
6. How does tokenization of assets on a blockchain improve liquidity and accessibility in financial markets?
7. Identify the potential challenges faced by financial institutions in integrating blockchain technology into their existing systems.
8. Discuss the importance of smart contracts in automating financial transactions. Provide an example of their use in real-world financial applications.
9. Explain how blockchain is transforming the securities trading and settlement processes. What are the benefits and challenges?
10. What is the future potential of blockchain technology in the finance industry, and what trends do you predict will emerge over the next five years?

11. Define systemic inefficiency and explain how it affects traditional financial systems.

References

[1] Tapscott, D., & Tapscott, A. (2016). *Blockchain revolution: How the technology behind bitcoin is changing money, business, and the world.* Penguin.

[2] Parkhi, S., Karande, K., & Palande, B. (2024). Blockchain and its use cases in banking, accounting and finance. In B. Alareeni & A. Hamdan (Eds.), *Navigating the Technological Tide: The Evolution and Challenges of Business Model Innovation* (pp. 63–71).

[3] Sakarneh, B., & Kilani, Y. M. (2024). The role of blockchain technology in managing efficiency and cost reduction in the banking sector in Jordan. *Journal of System Management Sciences, 14*(5), 251–267. https://doi.org/10.33168/JSMS.2024.0516

[4] Almadadha, R. (2025). Blockchain and financial performance: Empirical evidence from major Australian banks. *Frontiers in Blockchain, 8,* 1463633. https://doi.org/10.3389/fbloc.2025.1463633

[5] Amler, H., Eckey, L., Faust, S., Kaiser, M., Sandner, P., & Schlosser, B. (2021). DeFi-ning DeFi: Challenges & pathway. In *Proceedings of BRAINS 2021.* https://doi.org/10.48550/arXiv.2101.05589

[6] Seshadrinathan, S., & Chandra, S. (2025). Trusting the trustless blockchain for its adoption in accounting: The mediating role of the technology-organization-environment framework. *Financial Innovation, 11,* 44. https://doi.org/10.1186/s40854-024-00685-5

[7] Basdekidou, V., & Papapanagos, H. (2024). Blockchain technology adoption for disrupting FinTech functionalities: A systematic literature review for corporate management, supply chain, banking industry, and stock markets. *Digital, 4*(3), 762–803. https://doi.org/10.3390/digital4030039

[8] Böhme, R., Christin, N., Edelman, B., & Moore, T. (2015). Bitcoin: Economics, technology, and governance. *Journal of Economic Perspectives, 29*(2), 213–238.

[9] FinTech Magazine. (2024). Blockchain technology and modern banking systems. *FinTech Magazine.*

[10] Sakarneh, B., & Kilani, Y. M. (2024). The role of blockchain technology in managing efficiency and cost reduction in the banking sector in Jordan. *Journal of System Management Sciences, 14*(5), 251–267. https://doi.org/10.33168/JSMS.2024.0516

[11] Bulut Karadag, A., Zaim, A. H., & Akbulut, A. (2024). Blockchain in finance: A systematic literature review. *Journal of Business Economics and Finance, 13*(2), 113–129.

[12] Nakamoto, S. (2008). *Bitcoin: A peer-to-peer electronic cash system.* https://bitcoin.org/bitcoin.pdf

[13] Ahmadova, S., & Erek, M. (2022). A review on Ripple, a financial intermediary coin. *Journal of Academic Projection, 7*(2), 117–130.

[14] *Analysis of blockchain-based Ripple and SWIFT.* (2022). *Asian Journal of Electrical and Electronic Engineering, 2*(1), 1–8. https://doi.org/10.69955/ajoeee.2022.v2i1.26

[15] Li, W., Bu, J., Li, X., & Chen, X. (2022). Security analysis of DeFi: Vulnerabilities, attacks and advances.

12

Cryptocurrencies and Digital Assets

Abstract

This chapter delves into the evolving landscape of cryptocurrencies and digital assets, offering a comprehensive understanding of their foundations, functions, and financial implications. It begins by distinguishing between cryptocurrencies and stablecoins, unpacking their technological frameworks, value mechanisms, and economic roles within the broader digital finance ecosystem. As decentralized currencies gain mainstream traction, the chapter critically examines the legal and regulatory complexities that differ widely across jurisdictions – highlighting challenges such as investor protection, anti-money laundering (AML) compliance, and central bank policies. Furthermore, the chapter explores the behavioral economics of crypto investors, shedding light on psychological drivers like speculation, herd behavior, and risk perception. Various valuation models, including network value-to-transactions (NVT) and sentiment analysis, are discussed to understand how digital assets are priced in volatile and often opaque markets. Lastly, the chapter evaluates the risks and opportunities of investing in digital assets, balancing concerns over security breaches, market manipulation, and regulatory uncertainty with the potential for high returns, diversification, and financial democratization. Through this multidimensional lens, the chapter equips readers with the analytical tools and critical perspective necessary to navigate the dynamic world of digital finance.

Introduction

The advent of blockchain technology has introduced a revolutionary shift in the financial ecosystem, giving rise to cryptocurrencies and a broad category of digital assets. These innovations are redefining how value is stored, transferred, and managed in a decentralized, secure, and transparent manner. This

DOI: 10.1201/9788743811244-16

chapter explores the foundational concepts, classifications, mechanisms, benefits, and challenges associated with cryptocurrencies and digital assets, with a focus on their significance in the modern financial landscape.

12.1 Digital Assets

Digital assets encompass a broader category that includes any asset that is created and stored in a digital format, which has ownership and value. These may include:

- **Cryptocurrencies**
- **Utility tokens**
- **Security tokens**
- **Non-fungible tokens (NFTs)**
- **Central Bank Digital Currencies (CBDCs)**

Cryptocurrencies

Cryptocurrencies are **digital or virtual currencies** secured by cryptography and typically decentralized through blockchain technology. They serve as a medium of exchange, store of value, and unit of account without reliance on a central authority.

Table 12.1 Classification of digital assets.

Type	Description	Examples
Cryptocurrency	Used primarily as a currency or store of value.	Bitcoin, Litecoin
Utility token	Provides access to a product or service on a blockchain.	Ether (ETH), Binance Coin (BNB)
Security token	Represents a share in a real-world asset and is subject to regulation.	Securitize tokens
Stablecoin	Pegged to a stable asset (e.g., fiat) to reduce volatility.	USDT, USDC
NFT	The non-fungible token represents unique digital ownership.	Art NFTs, in-game assets
CBDC	Government-issued digital currencies backed by a central bank.	Digital Yuan, eNaira

Key characteristics

- **Decentralization:** Operate on distributed ledgers.
- **Transparency:** Transaction records are publicly verifiable.
- **Security:** Employ cryptographic techniques for protection.
- **Immutability:** Once confirmed, transactions cannot be altered.

Key cryptocurrencies

Figure 12.1 Key cryptocurrencies.

Bitcoin (BTC)

- **Launch:** In 2009 by pseudonymous creator Satoshi Nakamoto.
- **Use case:** Store of value, decentralized payment.
- **Consensus:** Proof of Work (PoW).
- **Limit:** 21 million coins.

Ethereum (ETH)

- **Launch:** In 2015 by Vitalik Buterin and team.
- **Use case:** Smart contracts and decentralized applications (dApps).
- **Consensus:** Transitioned from PoW to PoS (Ethereum 2.0).

Other notable cryptocurrencies

- **Ripple (XRP):** Cross-border payments.
- **Litecoin (LTC):** Faster alternative to Bitcoin.
- **Cardano (ADA):** Academic-driven PoS platform.
- **Solana (SOL):** High-speed, low-cost blockchain.

Role in the financial ecosystem

- **Payments and transfers**
  Cryptocurrencies allow fast, low-cost global payments without intermediaries, making them attractive for remittances and micropayments.
- **Investment and speculation**
  Digital assets are treated as investment vehicles due to their high return potential and volatility, attracting retail and institutional investors.
- **Financial inclusion**
  They enable unbanked populations to access financial services through a mobile device and an internet connection.
- **Asset tokenization**
  Real-world assets such as real estate, equities, and art can be tokenized, making them more liquid and tradable.

Advantages

- **Decentralization:** Eliminates intermediaries and censorship.
- **Transparency:** Open access to transaction histories.
- **Accessibility:** Available to anyone with internet access.
- **Programmability:** Smart contracts can automate and enforce agreements.

Table 12.2 Challenges and risks.

Challenge	Explanation
Volatility	Price fluctuations limit use as a stable currency.
Regulatory Uncertainty	Legal status varies across jurisdictions.
Security	Vulnerable to hacking and phishing scams.
Scalability	Networks may face congestion and high fees.
Environmental impact	Some cryptocurrencies (e.g., Bitcoin) require significant energy use.

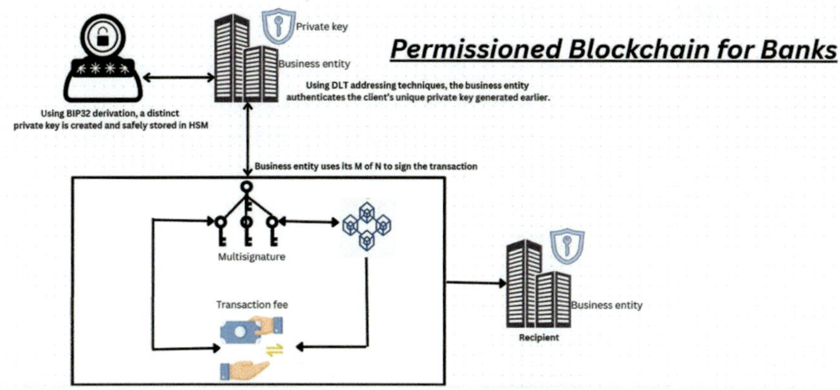

Figure 12.2 Permissioned blockchain for banks.

Emerging trends

- **Decentralized Finance (DeFi)**
  Uses blockchain to replicate traditional financial instruments without centralized control, offering lending, borrowing, and trading services.

- **Stablecoins and CBDCs**
  Aim to combine stability with blockchain features, gaining traction in payment systems and monetary policy implementation.

- **Institutional adoption**
  Large firms and investment funds are integrating cryptocurrencies into portfolios and balance sheets, signaling growing mainstream acceptance.

- **Tokenization of assets**
  Illiquid assets are being **digitized and fractionalized**, enabling broader participation and new investment opportunities.

Cryptocurrencies and digital assets represent a paradigm shift in how individuals and institutions perceive money, investment, and ownership. Their underlying technology – blockchain – offers unparalleled benefits in transparency, security, and efficiency. However, challenges such as regulatory compliance, volatility, and scalability must be addressed to realize their full potential. As the digital economy evolves, cryptocurrencies and digital assets will likely become integral components of global finance.

12.2 Cryptocurrency and Stablecoins

In the evolving world of FinTech, **cryptocurrencies** have emerged as a revolutionary force, disrupting traditional financial systems with the promise of decentralization, transparency, and financial inclusion. Beginning with Bitcoin in 2009, cryptocurrencies have rapidly expanded, forming a diverse ecosystem of digital assets with various use cases. Despite their potential, these digital currencies are often marked by volatility and regulatory uncertainty, prompting the development of a specialized subset: **stablecoins**. Stablecoins aim to combine the best of both worlds – the efficiency of cryptocurrencies with the price stability of fiat currencies.

Cryptocurrencies emerged as decentralized digital currencies operating on blockchain networks, redefining the concept of money [1]. Bitcoin introduced a peer-to-peer model, eliminating intermediaries through cryptographic proof and consensus algorithms [2]. Blockchain technology enables transparent, immutable ledgers that support various digital asset applications [3]. Stablecoins, unlike volatile cryptocurrencies, are pegged to fiat currencies to maintain value stability [4]. Tokenization of assets allows fractional ownership and liquidity in previously illiquid markets [5]. This chapter explores the origins, evolution, and mechanics of cryptocurrencies and stablecoins, examining their implications for the broader financial ecosystem.

12.2.1 Understanding cryptocurrencies

A **cryptocurrency** is a digital or virtual currency secured by cryptography, which makes it nearly impossible to counterfeit or double-spend. Unlike traditional fiat currencies, cryptocurrencies operate on decentralized networks based on blockchain technology – a distributed ledger enforced by a network of computers (nodes).

Key features of cryptocurrencies

- **Decentralization**: Operate without a central authority (e.g., banks or governments).
- **Cryptographic security**: Transactions and wallets are secured through complex encryption algorithms.
- **Transparency and immutability**: All transactions are recorded on a public ledger, ensuring traceability.
- **Limited supply**: Most cryptocurrencies have a fixed supply cap (e.g., Bitcoin's 21 million cap).

- **Peer-to-Peer transactions**: Facilitate direct transactions without intermediaries.

The first modern cryptocurrency, **Bitcoin**, was introduced by an anonymous entity known as *Satoshi Nakamoto* in 2008 through a white paper titled "Bitcoin: A Peer-to- Peer Electronic Cash System." This white paper proposed a new system for electronic transactions that did not rely on trust or centralized financial institutions.

Types of cryptocurrencies

Bitcoin (BTC)

The pioneer and most widely recognized cryptocurrency, primarily used as a **store of value** or **digital gold**.

Altcoins

"Alternative coins" to Bitcoin, with varied features and use cases:

- **Ethereum (ETH)** – Introduced smart contracts and decentralized applications (dApps).
- **Ripple (XRP)** – Focuses on real-time, cross-border payments.
- **Litecoin (LTC)** – Known for faster transaction confirmations than Bitcoin.

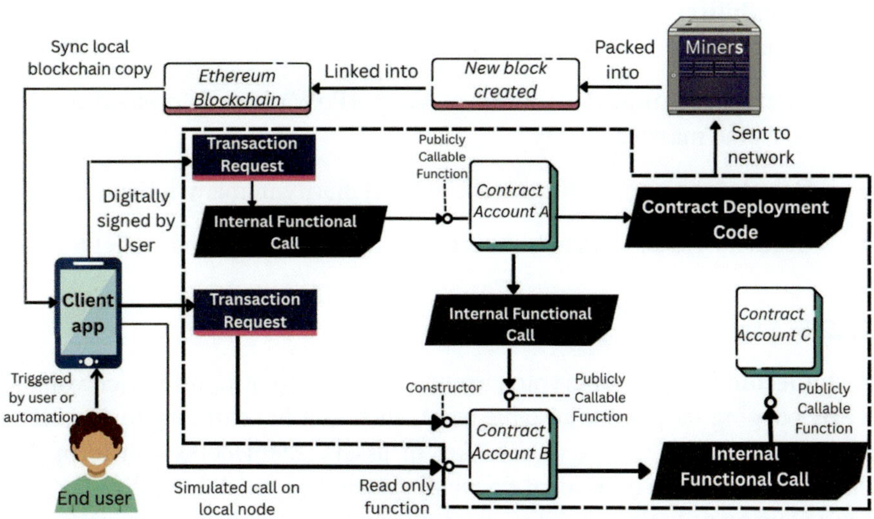

Figure 12.3 Ethereum: Smart contract in action.

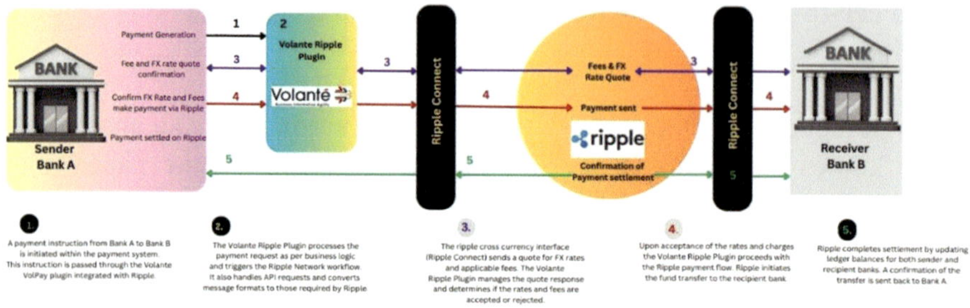

Figure 12.4 Ripple transaction flow.

- **Cardano (ADA), Polkadot (DOT)** – Emphasize scalability and interoperability.

12.2.2 Utility Tokens vs. Security Tokens

- **Utility tokens**: Provide access to a product or service (e.g., Filecoin).
- **Security tokens**: Represent ownership of assets, subject to securities regulation.

Challenges and limitations of cryptocurrencies

- **Price volatility**: Major swings in value hinder their use as a stable medium of exchange.
- **Scalability**: Networks like Bitcoin face limitations in transaction throughput.
- **Energy consumption**: Proof-of-Work (PoW) based cryptocurrencies consume massive energy.
- **Regulatory uncertainty**: Lack of legal clarity in many jurisdictions.
- **Security risks**: Vulnerabilities to hacking, phishing, and wallet theft.

12.2.3 Stablecoins

A **stablecoin** is a type of cryptocurrency designed to minimize price volatility by pegging its value to a stable asset, such as a fiat currency (e.g., USD), a commodity (e.g., gold), or a basket of assets. Stablecoins aim to bridge the gap between the traditional financial system and the decentralized crypto ecosystem by providing stability, liquidity, and efficiency in digital payments and DeFi (Decentralized Finance) applications.

Classification of stablecoins

Fiat-collateralized stablecoins

Backed 1:1 by fiat currencies held in reserve by custodians.

- **Examples**: Tether (USDT), USD Coin (USDC), TrueUSD (TUSD)
- **Pros**: High stability, simple model
- **Cons**: Requires trust in custodians and centralization

Crypto-collateralized stablecoins

Backed by overcollateralized crypto assets stored in smart contracts.

- **Examples**: DAI (by MakerDAO)
- **Pros**: Decentralized and transparent
- **Cons**: Subject to crypto market volatility, complex mechanisms

Algorithmic stablecoins

Maintain peg through algorithmic control of supply and demand rather than backing by reserves.

- **Examples**: TerraUSD (now defunct), Ampleforth
- **Pros**: Fully decentralized, no collateral needed
- **Cons**: High risk of de-pegging, market instability

Use cases of stablecoins

- **Remittances**: Lower cost and faster international money transfers
- **DeFi Ecosystem**: Used in lending, borrowing, and liquidity pools
- **Hedging Instrument**: Protection against crypto volatility
- **E-Commerce Payments**: Merchants can accept crypto without facing price swings
- **Central Bank Digital Currency (CBDC) Models**: Influence and inspire state-issued digital currencies

Regulatory considerations

Stablecoins have attracted significant attention from regulators due to their systemic importance:

- **U.S. SEC and FinCEN**: Increased scrutiny on whether stablecoins are securities or money transmitters

- **EU's MiCA (Markets in Crypto-Assets)**: Aims to provide legal clarity on stablecoins and crypto-assets
- **Global Organizations (e.g., BIS, IMF)**: Emphasize risk management and international coordination

Key regulatory concerns include:

- Lack of transparency in reserves
- Systemic risks to traditional finance
- Consumer protection and anti-money laundering (AML)

Risks and challenges of stablecoins

- **Centralization** (in fiat-backed models) contradicts the decentralized ethos of blockchain.
- **Reserve auditability**: Limited transparency on whether reserves back the stable coin.
- **De-pegging risk**: Failure to maintain the pegged value, especially in algorithmic models.
- **Regulatory crackdowns**: Governments may restrict or ban certain stablecoin operations.
- **Loss of trust**: Incidents like the collapse of TerraUSD (UST) show the fragility of some models.

Stablecoins are likely to play a central role in both retail and institutional adoption of crypto technology, serving as a gateway to decentralized finance and potentially transforming how value is stored and transferred globally. Cryptocurrencies have introduced a transformative way of conducting transactions without intermediaries, leveraging blockchain technology to foster decentralization and transparency. However, their inherent volatility limits their usability in everyday transactions, a gap that stablecoins aim to fill. By offering stability while retaining the core benefits of blockchain, stablecoins are poised to be a cornerstone of the digital financial future. Yet, their evolution must be balanced with appropriate regulatory oversight to safeguard users and maintain systemic stability.

12.3 Legal and Regulatory Implications

The rapid evolution of financial technologies, especially the proliferation of cryptocurrencies, stablecoins, and blockchain-based platforms, has

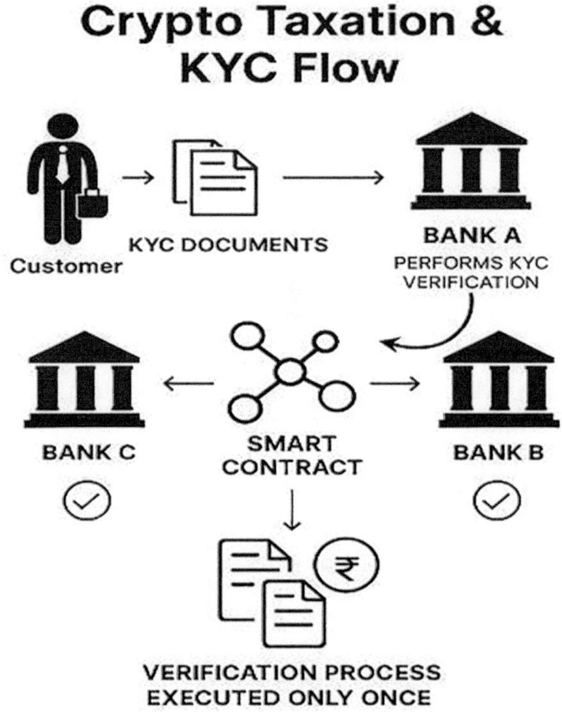

Figure 12.5 Crypto Taxation and KYC Flow

posed significant challenges to established legal and regulatory frameworks. FinTech innovations often transcend national borders and operate in decentralized environments, where traditional jurisdictional boundaries, compliance mechanisms, and supervisory models are difficult to apply. Regulatory authorities globally are framing standards to manage crypto-related financial stability risks [6]. The IMF emphasizes that rapid crypto adoption can threaten macro-financial stability if left unregulated [7]. The World Bank highlights the need for clear policies to balance innovation and investor protection in developing economies [8]. The European Central Bank warns that interconnectedness between crypto-assets and traditional finance poses systemic vulnerabilities [9]. OECD findings suggest that digital asset tokenization may blur legal boundaries between securities and commodities. Decentralized finance (DeFi) introduces regulatory challenges due to its borderless and code-driven governance structure [10]. Governance models must evolve to integrate blockchain accountability within corporate and legal frameworks [11]. This chapter explores the legal and regulatory implications of FinTech, focusing on cryptocurrencies, stablecoins, decentralized finance (DeFi), and associated technologies. It examines how different jurisdictions are responding, the key risks regulators seek to address, and the path toward harmonized oversight that balances innovation with consumer and investor protection, market integrity, and financial stability

12.3.1 Importance of regulation

Consumer and investor protection: Ensures transparency, fairness, and recourse against fraud or mismanagement.

Market integrity: Prevents manipulation, insider trading, and systemic risks.

Financial stability: Maintains trust in the financial system by mitigating volatility and contagion.

Anti-money laundering (AML) and counter-terrorism financing (CTF): Prevents misuse of financial systems for illicit activities.

Tax compliance and reporting: Ensures that digital assets are appropriately taxed and reported.

12.3.2 Regulatory challenges in FinTech

Anonymity and pseudonymity: Difficulties in tracking and identifying users on blockchain networks.

Decentralized systems: No clear legal entity to hold accountable.

Cross-border operations: Services accessible globally but subject to varying local laws.

Technology outpacing regulation: Legal systems struggle to keep up with rapid innovations.

12.3.3 Legal classification of digital assets

Cryptocurrencies

Regulators categorize cryptocurrencies differently:

Currency: Treated as legal tender in a few jurisdictions (e.g., El Salvador).

Commodity: Classified by the U.S. CFTC as commodities (e.g., Bitcoin).

Security: If it passes the **Howey Test**, it may be classified as a security (e.g., some ICO tokens).

Property: Treated as property for tax purposes in jurisdictions like the U.S. and UK.

Stablecoins

Stablecoins are more complex due to their fiat-pegged nature and reserve mechanisms:

Payment Instruments: Some jurisdictions treat stablecoins as instruments akin to electronic money.

Deposits: In some cases, stablecoin issuance may trigger banking regulations.

Securities: Where stablecoins offer returns, they may fall under securities law.

Global regulatory approaches

United States

SEC (Securities and Exchange Commission): Focuses on whether tokens are securities.

CFTC (Commodity Futures Trading Commission): Oversees commodity derivatives like crypto futures.

FinCEN: Enforces AML/CTF obligations for crypto exchanges and wallet providers.

State-level licensing: New York's Bit License regime imposes strict rules on crypto firms.

European Union (EU)

MiCA (Markets in Crypto-Assets Regulation):

Establishes a comprehensive framework for crypto-asset issuance and service providers.

Classifies stablecoins as either **asset-referenced tokens (ARTs)** or **e- money tokens (EMTs)**.

Emphasize transparency, governance, and capital requirements.

United Kingdom

FCA (Financial Conduct Authority):

Mandates registration for crypto firms under AML/CTF rules.

Bans certain crypto derivatives for retail investors due to high risk.

Plans to regulate stablecoins used for payments under the **Financial Services and Markets Act 2023**.

Asia-Pacific

China: China has banned cryptocurrency trading and mining while promoting a central bank digital currency (CBDC) – the Digital Yuan.

Singapore: Singapore uses a pro-innovation framework through the **Payment Services Act**, encouraging licensing and risk-based supervision.

Japan: Japan requires crypto exchanges to register and maintain capital and security standards.

India

Currently lacks a comprehensive framework; taxation rules impose a 30% tax on crypto gains.

Regulatory developments are in progress via the **Reserve Bank of India (RBI)** and **SEBI**.

12.3.4 Regulatory implications for FinTech stakeholders

For FinTech companies

Licensing and registration: Required to operate legally in many jurisdictions.

AML/KYC compliance: Firms must implement Know-Your-Customer (KYC) procedures and report suspicious activity.

Consumer protection: Need for clear disclosures, grievance mechanisms, and risk warnings.

Data privacy and cybersecurity: Compliance with data protection laws (e.g., GDPR in Europe).

For investors

Disclosure requirements: Investors need access to accurate and timely information.

Protection from fraud and scams: Regulation helps reduce the risk of rug pulls and Ponzi schemes.

Clear tax guidance: Clarity on how digital asset transactions are taxed.

Emerging regulatory trends

Regulatory sandboxes allow FinTech companies to test innovations in a controlled environment under regulator supervision (e.g., UK, Singapore, India). Central Bank Digital Currencies (CBDCs). As a response to stablecoins, many central banks are exploring or launching CBDCs. These are government-backed digital currencies aimed at providing a safe and regulated alternative to private digital currencies. Organizations such as the Financial Action Task Force (FATF), Bank for International Settlements (BIS), and International Organization of Securities Commissions (IOSCO) are working toward global standards for crypto regulation.

12.3.5 Risks of regulatory arbitrage and fragmentation

Regulatory Arbitrage: Companies may choose jurisdictions with lax rules, undermining investor protection.

Inconsistent Regulations: Lack of harmonization complicates compliance and inhibits innovation.

Overregulation: Excessively rigid rules may stifle innovation and limit financial inclusion.

Under regulation: Too little oversight can lead to fraud, instability, and loss of public trust.

12.3.6 The future of legal and regulatory frameworks

Principle-based regulation: Flexible and technology-neutral approaches are gaining traction.

Dynamic regulation: Real-time monitoring and algorithmic supervision (Sup Tech) may evolve.

Public-private collaboration: Cooperation between regulators, developers, and financial institutions is essential for creating effective rules.

Global standards: A unified international regulatory regime could facilitate cross-border innovation while managing systemic risks.

12.4 Behavior Analysis and Valuation

The intersection of human behavior and financial decision-making is at the core of the behavioral finance field that seeks to explain market anomalies, irrational investment patterns, and bubbles that traditional theories fail to capture. In FinTech, and particularly in crypto markets, behavioral factors are significantly more pronounced due to 24/7 trading, high volatility, lack of traditional valuation metrics, and rapid information dissemination via social media. The economic value of blockchain systems derives from their capacity to reduce transaction costs and enable trustless exchange [12]. Crypto valuation models emphasize user adoption, network effects, and technological scalability [13]. (Bank for International Settlements research notes that stablecoins and CBDCs could reshape monetary systems through programmable money features [4]. Market data shows that criminal misuse of cryptocurrencies remains a small but persistent risk factor [14]. World Economic Forum reports suggest that tokenized assets may redefine capital market infrastructure and investor participation [15]. Early studies reveal that crypto assets often exhibit speculative behavior rather than stable investment fundamentals [16]. Academic and institutional analyses agree that digital assets will continue to evolve as a major frontier in global finance [17].

In this chapter, we explore the psychological underpinnings of investor behavior, how emotions affect pricing, and methodologies for analysing and valuing digital assets in the FinTech ecosystem.

Table 12.3 Traditional vs. behavioral finance.

Aspect	Traditional finance	Behavioral finance
Investor assumption	Rational and utility- maximizing	Irrational with cognitive biases
Market behavior	Efficient (EMH)	Often inefficient
Decision-making	Based on full information	Influenced by psychology and emotion

12.4.1 Core concepts in behavioral finance

Herding behavior: Tendency to follow the crowd, especially during price surges or crashes.

Overconfidence: Belief in one's ability to predict market moves, often leading to excessive trading.

Anchoring: Relying heavily on the first piece of information (e.g., historical highs) when making decisions.

Loss aversion: Tendency to prefer avoiding losses rather than acquiring equivalent gains.

Mental accounting: Treating money differently depending on its source or intended use.

12.4.2 Behavior in crypto and FinTech markets

High volatility and emotional trading

Cryptocurrency markets are highly volatile due to low liquidity, speculative demand, and the absence of intrinsic valuation anchors. Investors often react impulsively to:
Sudden price spikes (FOMO – Fear of Missing Out)

Sharp declines (FUD – Fear, Uncertainty, Doubt)

News events or regulatory updates

Influencer or celebrity endorsements (e.g., Elon Musk tweets)

Role of social media and sentiment

Social media platforms like Twitter, Reddit (r/Crypto), Telegram, and Discord significantly influence investor behavior.

Sentiment analysis: Techniques that assess public opinion or mood from textual data to predict market movements.

Meme coins: Assets like Dogecoin or Shiba Inu often surge in value due to viral memes, despite lacking fundamental value.

Tools for behavioral analysis

Sentiment indicators

Fear and greed index: Measures investor sentiment on a scale from extreme fear to extreme greed.

Social volume: Measures frequency of crypto mentions across platforms.

Google trends: Tracks search interest over time to gauge retail investor curiosity.

On-chain analytics

HODL waves: Show the distribution of held assets over time, indicating long-term vs. short-term holding patterns.

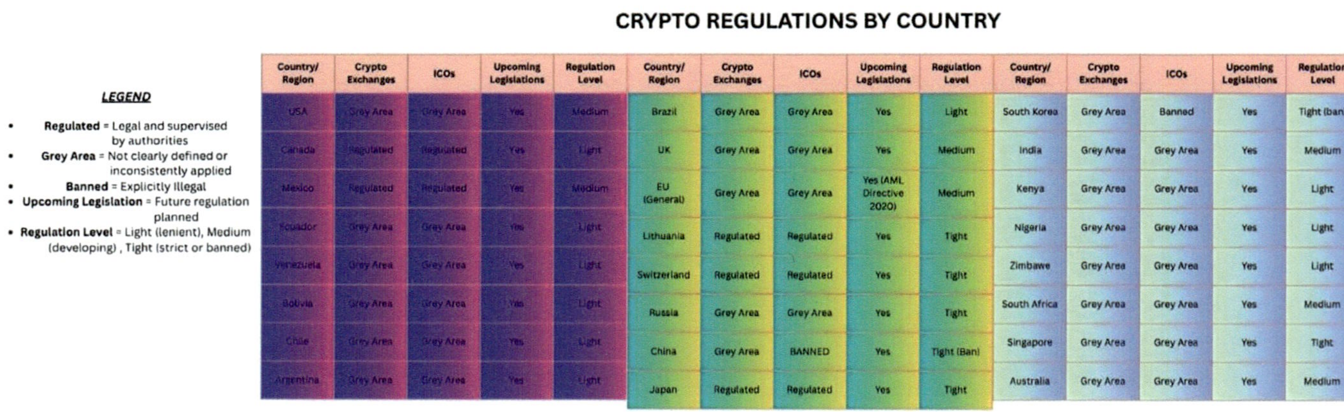

CRYPTO REGULATIONS BY COUNTRY

LEGEND

- **Regulated** = Legal and supervised by authorities
- **Grey Area** = Not clearly defined or inconsistently applied
- **Banned** = Explicitly Illegal
- **Upcoming Legislation** = Future regulation planned
- **Regulation Level** = Light (lenient), Medium (developing), Tight (strict or banned)

Country/ Region	Crypto Exchanges	ICOs	Upcoming Legislations	Regulation Level	Country/ Region	Crypto Exchanges	ICOs	Upcoming Legislations	Regulation Level	Country/ Region	Crypto Exchanges	ICOs	Upcoming Legislations	Regulation Level
USA	Grey Area	Grey Area	Yes	Medium	Brazil	Grey Area	Grey Area	Yes	Light	South Korea	Grey Area	Banned	Yes	Tight (ban)
Canada	Regulated	Regulated	Yes	Light	UK	Grey Area	Grey Area	Yes	Medium	India	Grey Area	Grey Area	Yes	Medium
Mexico	Regulated	Regulated	Yes	Medium	EU (General)	Grey Area	Grey Area	Yes (AML Directive 2020)	Medium	Kenya	Grey Area	Grey Area	Yes	Light
Ecuador	Grey Area	Grey Area	Yes	Light	Lithuania	Regulated	Regulated	Yes	Tight	Nigeria	Grey Area	Grey Area	Yes	Light
Venezuela	Grey Area	Grey Area	Yes	Light	Switzerland	Regulated	Regulated	Yes	Tight	Zimbawe	Grey Area	Grey Area	Yes	Light
Bolivia	Grey Area	Grey Area	Yes	Light	Russia	Grey Area	Grey Area	Yes	Tight	South Africa	Grey Area	Grey Area	Yes	Medium
Chile	Grey Area	Grey Area	Yes	Light	China	Grey Area	BANNED	Yes	Tight (Ban)	Singapore	Grey Area	Grey Area	Yes	Tight
Argentina	Grey Area	Grey Area	Yes	Light	Japan	Regulated	Regulated	Yes	Tight	Australia	Grey Area	Grey Area	Yes	Medium

Figure 12.6 Crypto regulations by country.

Wallet activity: Spike in new wallet addresses or whale movements can indicate potential behavioral shifts.

Network growth: Rapid network growth often reflects speculative activity.

Behavioral metrics in FinTech apps

FinTech platforms use behavioral analytics to:

Monitor **user engagement** (e.g., login frequency, trade patterns)

Personalize **notifications** based on user sentiment

Detect **behavioral anomalies** to prevent fraud

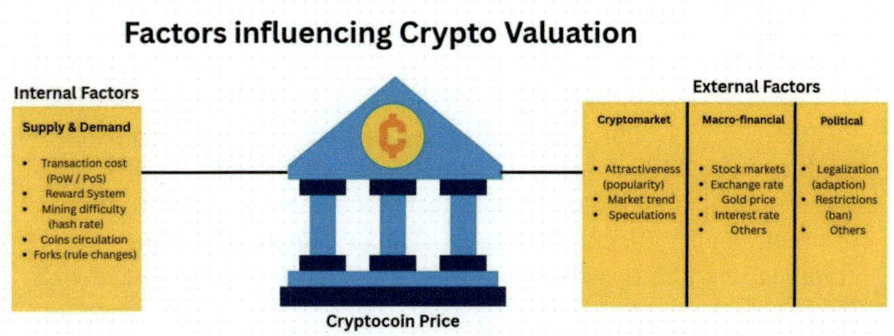

Figure 12.7 Factors influencing crypto valuation.

Summary

This chapter introduces cryptocurrency as a form of digital asset built on blockchain technology. It explains different types of crypto assets, including stable coins that aim to reduce price volatility by linking their value to traditional assets. The chapter also discusses the legal and regulatory challenges faced by governments in controlling and monitoring cryptocurrency markets. Since crypto operates across borders, issues like taxation, fraud, and investor protection become complex. Additionally, the chapter explores investor behavior in crypto markets, noting how speculation, social media influence, and risk-taking attitudes impact price movements and decision-making.

Case Study: Bhutan's Green Cryptocurrency Initiative

Bhutan, a small Himalayan kingdom renowned for its development philosophy based on *Gross National Happiness* rather than *Gross Domestic Product*, has emerged as a pioneering example of how sustainable energy resources can be leveraged for digital innovation. In recent years, Bhutan has sought to diversify its economy beyond traditional sectors like agriculture, tourism, and hydropower exports to India. The Covid-19 pandemic and increasing climate-related uncertainties exposed vulnerabilities in the country's economic structure, prompting an urgent need for diversification. Simultaneously, youth unemployment and a growing brain drain created pressure on policymakers to identify new avenues for income generation and skill-based employment. These circumstances laid the foundation for an ambitious national initiative focused on cryptocurrency mining powered entirely by renewable energy.

In 2023, it was revealed that Bhutan, through its state-owned investment arm Druk Holding and Investments (DHI), had been secretly mining Bitcoin since 2017 using surplus hydroelectric energy. The initiative gained global attention after court documents related to the bankruptcy of crypto lender BlockFi disclosed Bhutan's financial dealings in the cryptocurrency ecosystem. Soon after, Bhutan officially partnered with Bitdeer Technologies, a Nasdaq-listed digital asset mining company, to establish a $500 million fund aimed at building green mining infrastructure. The strategy involved placing data centers near hydroelectric plants to reduce transmission losses, while Bitdeer contributed mining hardware, technical expertise, and access to international capital. The project was designed not only to generate digital asset income but also to create tech-oriented employment, attract global FinTech attention, and maintain alignment with environmental, social, governance (ESG) principles.

Bhutan's initiative yielded substantial results. It became the first country to publicly support state-run cryptocurrency mining powered entirely by renewable energy. The project demonstrated that blockchain and sustainability can coexist, challenging common criticisms about the carbon footprint of crypto mining. It created new jobs in areas such as blockchain analytics, data center management, and renewable energy engineering, and further expanded Bhutan's interest in blockchain technology to areas such as national digital identity and tokenized assets. However, the country also encountered key challenges, including Bitcoin's price volatility, which complicates revenue forecasting, and regulatory uncertainty, given the evolving global landscape of digital asset compliance. Additionally, as digital infrastructure scales, cybersecurity threats become a major concern.

Challenges faced

- Market volatility: The fluctuating value of Bitcoin affects revenue stability and planning.
- Regulatory pressure: Bhutan may face international scrutiny and need to comply with emerging global cryptocurrency regulations.
- Cybersecurity risks: Expanding digital infrastructure introduces potential threats from hacking and cybercrime.
- Public transparency: Delayed disclosure of the project raised concerns about governmental openness and regulatory oversight.

Case Discussion Questions

1. How did Bhutan align its national development strategy with digital asset innovation?
2. In what ways does Bhutan's initiative challenge traditional criticisms of cryptocurrency mining?
3. What are the potential risks and rewards of relying on Bitcoin mining as a national revenue stream?
4. How can Bhutan scale its crypto operations while ensuring compliance with evolving global regulations?
5. What can other small nations learn from Bhutan's model of combining sustainability with blockchain technology?

Keywords

- **Cryptocurrency**: A digital currency that uses cryptography and runs on decentralized blockchain networks like Bitcoin or Ethereum.
- **Stablecoin**: A cryptocurrency with a stable value, usually tied to assets like fiat money or gold.

- **Fiat-collateralized**: Stablecoins backed by actual money held in reserve, like USDC and Tether.
- **Algorithmic stablecoin**: A coin that uses software rules to keep its price stable without holding real-world assets.
- **Volatility**: How much and how quickly an asset's price moves up or down.
- **Decentralization**: Power and control are spread across many users instead of a single authority.
- **Smart contracts**: Self-running digital agreements on blockchains that execute automatically when conditions are met.
- **Central Bank Digital Currency (CBDC)**: A government-issued digital currency that is backed and controlled by a central bank.
- **Decentralized Finance (DeFi)**: Financial services like lending or trading that run without banks, using blockchain and smart contracts.
- **Pegging**: The method of keeping a stablecoin's value tied to another asset, like 1 USD.
- **Behavioral finance**: The study of how emotions and psychology influence financial decisions.
- **Herding**: When people follow the crowd in financial markets, often ignoring their own judgment.
- **Fear of Missing Out (FOMO)**: Buying into an asset due to the fear of missing profit as others jump in.
- **Fear, Uncertainty, Doubt (FUD)**: Negative feelings or news that cause panic selling in markets.
- **Metcalfe's law**: A network's value grows as more users join it – used to value platforms like Bitcoin.
- **NVT ratio**: A metric comparing a crypto's market value to its usage; like a P/E ratio for crypto.
- **Stock-to-flow (S2F) model**: A scarcity-based model used to predict the long- term price of assets like Bitcoin.
- **Tokenomics**: The economic setup of a crypto token, including its supply, use, and incentives.

- **On-chain analytics**: Analysis of public blockchain data to study crypto trends and user behavior.
- **Sentiment analysis**: Using software to read public opinions and feelings in crypto markets.
- **Behavioral biases**: Mental shortcuts or emotions that cause people to make irrational financial decisions.
- **Anti-money laundering (AML)**: Rules to prevent criminals from using financial systems to hide illegal money.
- **Know your customer (KYC)**: A process where financial firms verify the identity of their clients.
- **Markets in Crypto-Assets Regulation (MiCA)**: EU rules to standardize and regulate crypto assets and platforms.
- **Financial Action Task Force (FATF)**: A global body that sets rules to fight financial crimes like money laundering.
- **Regulatory sandbox**: A testing space where FinTechs can try new ideas under light regulations.
- **Securities law**: Rules that govern the issue and trading of investment assets, including crypto tokens.
- **Licensing and compliance**: Legal approvals and rules that FinTechs must follow to operate safely and legally.
- **Regulatory arbitrage**: Moving operations to countries with easier rules to avoid strict regulation.
- **Financial stability**: A healthy financial system that can handle shocks without breaking down.

Discussion Questions

1. Define cryptocurrency and describe how it differs from digital fiat currencies.
2. List and explain the main types of stablecoins with examples.
3. Discuss the role of stablecoins in enabling decentralized finance (DeFi).
4. Evaluate the regulatory risks associated with stablecoins.

5. Compare and contrast Bitcoin and USDC in terms of volatility, use case, and structure.
6. Define and differentiate between cryptocurrencies and digital assets.
7. What are the primary use cases of Bitcoin and Ethereum?
8. How do stablecoins address the issue of volatility in the crypto market?
9. Explain how tokenization improves liquidity and market access.
10. Discuss the challenges faced by regulators in managing cryptocurrency markets.
11. What role do smart contracts play in the digital asset ecosystem?

References

[1] Vigna, P., & Casey, M. J. (2015). *The age of cryptocurrency: How Bitcoin and digital money are challenging the global economic order.* St. Martin's Press.

[2] Narayanan, A., Bonneau, J., Felten, E., Miller, A., & Goldfeder, S. (2016). *Bitcoin and cryptocurrency technologies: A comprehensive introduction.* Princeton University Press.

[3] Tapscott, D., & Tapscott, A. (2016). *Blockchain revolution: How the technology behind Bitcoin is changing money, business, and the world.* Penguin.

[4] Bank for International Settlements. (2022). CBDCs and stablecoins: Regulatory perspectives (BIS Papers No. 125). https://www.bis.org/publ/bppdf/bispap125.htm

[5] Organisation for Economic Co-operation and Development. (2020). *The tokenisation of assets and potential implications for financial markets.* https://www.oecd.org/finance/The-Tokenisation-of-Assets-and-Potential-Implications-for-Financial-Markets.htm

[6] Financial Stability Board. (2022). *Assessment of risks to financial stability from crypto-assets.* https://www.fsb.org/wp-content/uploads/P111122.pdf

[7] International Monetary Fund. (2021). *The crypto ecosystem and financial stability challenges* (Global Financial Stability Report, October 2021, Chapter 2). https://www.imf.org/en/Publications/GFSR

[8] World Bank Group. (2022). *Crypto-asset regulation and developing economies: Policy challenges and options.* https://www.worldbank.org

[9] European Central Bank. (2022). *Decrypting financial stability risks in crypto-asset markets* (Occasional Paper Series No. 276). https://www.ecb.europa.eu/pub/pdf/scpops/ecb.op276~8b9a4b9d18.en.pdf

[10] Schär, F. (2021). Decentralized finance: On blockchain- and smart contract-based financial markets. *Federal Reserve Bank of St. Louis Review, 103*(2), 153–174. https://doi.org/10.20955/r.103.153-74

[11] Yermack, D. (2017). Corporate governance and blockchains. In E. Brousseau, J. Glachant, & M. Janssen (Eds.), *The economics of blockchain* (pp. 127–145). Brookings Institution Press.

[12] Catalini, C., & Gans, J. S. (2016). *Some simple economics of the blockchain.* MIT Sloan Research Paper No. 5191-16.

[13] MIT Digital Currency Initiative. (2021). *Toward a comparatively stable ecosystem: Valuing crypto assets.* Massachusetts Institute of Technology. https://dci.mit.edu

[14] Chainalysis. (2023). *Crypto crime report 2023.* https://www.chainalysis.com/reports

[15] World Economic Forum. (2021). *Digital assets, distributed ledger technology, and the future of capital markets.* https://www.weforum.org/whitepapers

[16] Chuen, D. L. K. (Ed.). (2015). *Handbook of digital currency: Bitcoin, innovation, financial instruments, and big data.* Academic Press.

[17] Baur, D. G., & Lucey, B. M. (2019). Fintech: The financial sector's digital transformation. *Financial Analysts Journal, 75*(3), 20–29.

UNIT 5

Alternative and Specialized FinTech Domains

13

Digital and Alternative Finance

Abstract

This chapter provides a critical exploration of the digital and alternative finance landscape, emphasizing innovative financing mechanisms and their growing influence on the global financial ecosystem. It begins by unpacking the concepts of crowdfunding and initial coin offerings (ICOs), explaining how these models have emerged as viable alternatives to traditional capital-raising channels by leveraging decentralized technologies and online investor communities. The discussion then extends to marketplace lending platforms, offering insights into their operational dynamics, scalability, and the unique risks they pose, such as credit default, platform dependency, and regulatory ambiguity. A significant focus is placed on the emergence of Chinese TechFins, whose data-driven models and rapid market penetration are reshaping global FinTech dynamics. The chapter analyzes how players like Ant Group and Tencent are transforming financial inclusion and service delivery through AI, digital wallets, and super-app ecosystems, while also sparking geopolitical and regulatory scrutiny.

Finally, the chapter evaluates the regulatory and market challenges faced by digital finance platforms worldwide. Issues such as jurisdictional mismatches, consumer protection, cybersecurity, and compliance with evolving legal frameworks are critically examined. Through a multi-layered perspective, this chapter enables readers to understand both the promise and pitfalls of alternative finance, equipping them with the knowledge to assess its future direction and regulatory implications.

Introduction

The financial services sector is currently experiencing a profound transformation in its structure and operations. Digital and alternative finance

DOI: 10.1201/9788743811244-18

represent a category of new financial instruments and delivery mechanisms made possible by internet-based platforms, digital technologies, and decentralized architectures. These innovations challenge the traditional banking model by increasing access to capital, reducing intermediation, and enabling personalized and real-time financial services. While digital finance focuses on the use of technology to deliver conventional financial services more efficiently, alternative finance encompasses new funding models outside the traditional banking sector. The landscape of digital and alternative finance has evolved rapidly, integrating technology with financial intermediation to expand access and efficiency [1]. Together, they form the backbone of the FinTech revolution. Post-crisis developments have accelerated fintech-driven disruption, reshaping financial regulation and inclusion worldwide [2]. The rise of digital finance reflects a paradigm shift where innovation drives value creation across both retail and institutional segments [3].

13.1 Digital Finance

Digital finance encompasses the provision of financial services via electronic platforms, including mobile devices, online networks, and technologies like distributed ledgers. It includes:

- Mobile banking
- Online lending platforms
- Digital wallets
- Robo-advisors
- Open banking

13.1.1 Components of digital finance

- **Digital infrastructure**: APIs, cloud computing, and 5G connectivity.
- **Digital identity**: e-KYC (electronic Know Your Customer), biometric verification.
- **Real-time payments**: UPI in India, Faster Payments in the UK, and SEPA in the EU.

Data Analytics and AI Digital finance encompasses the provision of financial services via electronic platforms, including mobile devices, online networks, and technologies like distributed ledgers.

Benefits

- Lower transaction costs
- Enhanced financial inclusion
- Greater transparency
- Faster service delivery
- Data-driven decision-making

Alternative finance: Overview

Alternative finance involves financial tools and platforms that operate beyond conventional banking and capital market frameworks. These include:

- Peer-to-peer (P2P) lending
- Equity crowdfunding
- Invoice trading
- Initial Coin Offerings (ICOs)
- Buy Now Pay Later (BNPL)

Table 13.1 Comparison: Traditional vs. alternative finance.

Feature	Traditional finance	Alternative finance
Intermediaries	Banks, brokers	Platforms, marketplaces
Access to credit	Strict eligibility	Flexible and inclusive
Regulation	Heavily regulated	Lightly or variably regulated
Speed	Slower processes	Rapid, real-time approvals
Technology use	Moderate	High and disruptive

Models of alternative finance

- **Mechanism**: It enables borrowers to access funds directly from individual lenders through digital platforms
- **Examples**: Lending Club, Funding Circle, Faircent.
- **Advantages**: Lower interest rates, reduced credit barriers, and wider access to loans.
- **Risks**: Credit default risk, platform risk, and lack of insurance.

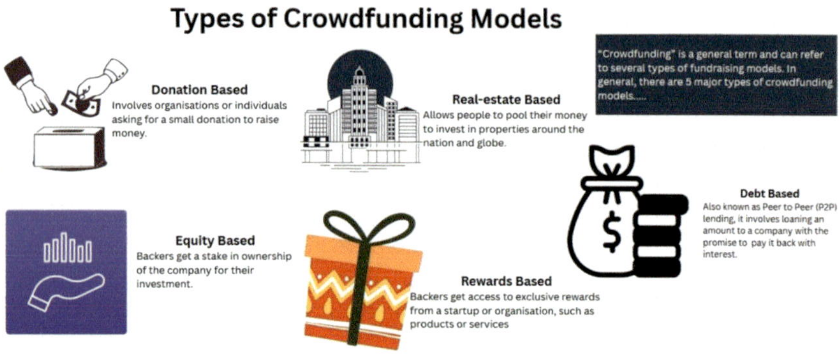

Figure 13.1 Types of crowdfunding models.

Equity crowdfunding

- **Mechanism**: Startups raise capital from many small investors in exchange for equity.
- **Examples**: SeedInvest, Crowdcube, Republic.
- **Advantages**: Democratized investing, startup visibility.
- **Risks**: Illiquidity, high startup failure rates, valuation ambiguity.

Invoice and supply chain finance

- **Mechanism**: Businesses sell unpaid invoices to raise quick liquidity.
- **Platforms**: MarketInvoice, KredX.
- **Use cases**: Helps small businesses manage cash flow and working capital.

Embedded finance

- **Definition**: Embedding financial services within platforms that primarily serve non-financial purposes. (e.g., loans via e-commerce apps).
- **Examples**: Amazon Pay Later, Shopify Capital.
- **Technologies**: APIs, AI, cloud platforms.

Buy now, pay later (BNPL)

- **Mechanism**: Enables consumers to split payments into interest-free instalments.
- **Popular providers**: Klarna, after pay, Affirm.

- **Concerns**: Over-indebtedness and lack of transparency.

Token-based financing (ICOs, STOs, IDOs)

- **Mechanism**: Fundraising through blockchain-issued tokens.
- **Advantages**: Borderless, fast capital access, smart contract automation.
- **Regulatory issues**: Fraud risk, lack of investor protection, KYC/AML concerns.

Technologies powering digital and alternative finance

Digital and alternative finance rely on several key technologies to deliver innovative financial services. Blockchain enables decentralized finance (DeFi), smart contracts, and trustless peer-to-peer transactions without intermediaries. Artificial intelligence (AI) is widely used in robo-advising, credit risk assessment, and fraud detection. Application programming interfaces (APIs) support open banking by allowing third- party services to securely access financial data. Cloud computing provides the scalability and flexibility needed for deploying financial platforms efficiently. Data analytics helps generate real-time insights and enables the creation of tailored financial products.

Regulatory landscape

Different countries are adopting varied regulatory approaches to support innovation while ensuring stability. In the European Union, regulations like PSD2 and MiFID II promote open banking and consumer protection. In the United States, lending platforms are regulated at the state level, and the SEC monitors token offerings. India's RBI oversees non-banking financial companies (NBFCs) and digital lenders under specific norms. Meanwhile, Singapore's MAS encourages innovation by offering regulatory sandboxes where FinTech startups can test their products in a controlled environment.

Risks and challenges

Despite rapid growth, digital and alternative finance face several challenges. Cybersecurity threats remain a major concern due to increasing online transactions. The lack of standardized regulations across jurisdictions leads to compliance confusion. Platform reliability and the risk of insolvency pose operational risks for users. Consumer protection and proper disclosure are often inadequate, especially for novice investors. Finally, regulatory arbitrage, where companies exploit gaps in laws by operating in loosely regulated regions, undermines global financial integrity.

Case studies in innovation

Several platforms illustrate the power of digital finance in action. Ant Group (China) offers an integrated ecosystem combining payments, credit scoring, and micro- lending through a super-app. M-Pesa (Kenya) transformed financial inclusion in Africa by providing mobile-based money transfer and microfinance services to millions. Funding Circle (UK) is a peer-to-peer lending platform that connects small businesses with both individual and institutional lenders, supporting SME growth outside traditional bank systems.

The future of digital finance is poised for deeper integration and smarter services. Embedded finance will grow, with banking features built directly into B2B and B2C platforms. AI and predictive analytics will enable more personalized and proactive financial experiences for users. DeFi and traditional finance may converge, creating hybrid models that are both decentralized and regulated. As these innovations progress, increased regulation is expected to maintain consumer trust and systemic safety without stifling growth and creativity. Digital and alternative finance represent the most dynamic shift in financial services in the 21st century. Through technological innovation, new business models, and more inclusive access to capital, these systems have created opportunities and challenges for regulators, users, and financial institutions. The key to sustainable growth lies in balancing innovation with transparency, ethics, and robust risk management.

13.2 Crowdfunding and ICOs

Alternative finance has become a vital enabler of innovation and financial inclusion. Among its most transformative methods are **crowdfunding** and **Initial Coin Offerings (ICOs)**. Both mechanisms offer novel ways for startups, small businesses, and decentralized projects to raise capital without depending on conventional venture capital sources or banking systems. While crowdfunding leverages community backing through digital platforms, ICOs utilize blockchain technology to issue cryptographic tokens in exchange for investment. These models signify the convergence of finance, technology, and democratized access to capital. Crowdfunding has emerged as a participatory funding model enabling individuals to finance innovation and entrepreneurship online [4]. ICOs, built on blockchain technology, have democratized capital raising but also raised complex regulatory concerns [5]. Early ICO markets highlighted both investor enthusiasm and regulatory gaps that later shaped global policy responses [6]. Blockchain infrastructure has underpinned the evolution of decentralized fundraising, redefining how trust and verification are managed [7]. Digital currencies and tokenized assets are expanding financial participation in emerging economies [8].

13.2.1 Crowdfunding

It involves collecting modest contributions from a large number of individuals, usually through online platforms, to support a project or business initiative. It is used across sectors, including business, arts, healthcare, and social causes.

Table 13.2 Types of crowdfunding.

Model	Description
Donation-based	Contributors donate without expecting returns (e.g., charity projects).
Reward-based	Funders receive non-financial rewards like products or merchandise.
Equity-based	Investors receive shares in the company (ownership stake).
Debt-based (P2P Lending)	Investors lend money in exchange for interest repayments.

Platforms

Popular crowdfunding platforms include:

- **Kickstarter** – Reward-based funding for creative projects.
- **Indiegogo** – Flexible fundraising options for startups.
- **GoFundMe** – Donation-based platform for personal causes.
- **SeedInvest/Crowdcube** – Equity-based platforms for startups.

Advantages and disadvantages of crowdfunding

Advantages

- **Access to capital**: Enables startups to raise funds without giving up control to VCs.
- **Market validation**: Positive crowdfunding outcomes indicate product-market fit.
- **Community engagement**: Builds loyal communities around the brand.
- **Marketing exposure**: Public campaigns increase visibility and outreach.

Disadvantages

- **Uncertain funding**: Campaigns may fail to reach their goals.
- **Reputation risk**: Public failure may damage brand perception.

- **Intellectual property theft**: Ideas can be copied during public campaigns.
- **High competition**: Platforms are saturated with campaigns seeking attention.

Initial coin offerings (ICOs): Overview

An initial coin offering (ICO) is a fundraising approach built on blockchain technology, where emerging ventures distribute digital tokens in return for cryptocurrencies such as Bitcoin or Ethereum. These tokens can function as utility assets within the project's platform or act as speculative investment instruments.

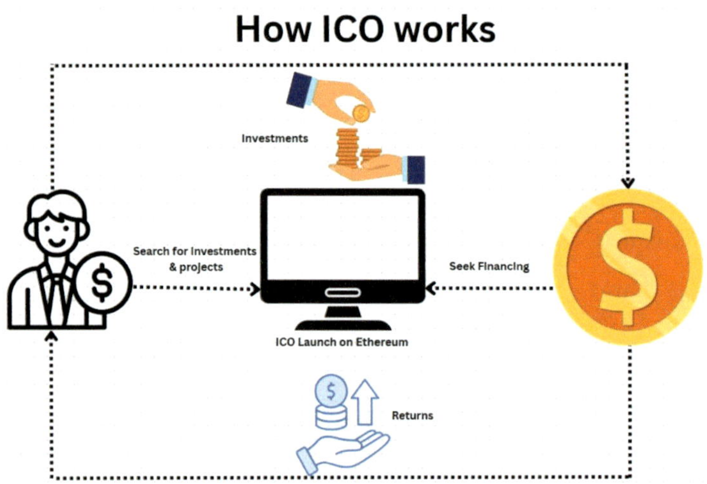

Figure 13.2 Working of an ICO.

How ICOs work

- **Whitepaper release** – The project publishes a document outlining its objectives, tokenomics, and roadmap.
- **Token creation** – Tokens are issued via smart contracts on a blockchain (often Ethereum).
- **Fundraising phase** – Investors purchase tokens using crypto assets.
- **Token listing** – Tokens may be traded on crypto exchanges post-ICO.

Token types

- **Security tokens**: Represent ownership or profit-sharing, akin to traditional securities.
- Utility tokens grant users the right to use a specific product or service within a platform.
- **Governance tokens**: Allow holders to vote on protocol changes in decentralized projects.

Table 13.3 ICO vs crowdfunding.

Feature	Crowdfunding	ICO
Legal Framework	More regulated (esp. equity crowdfunding)	Often unregulated or evolving
Investor Type	General public	Crypto-savvy individuals and institutions
Currency	Fiat (e.g., USD, EUR)	Cryptocurrency (e.g., ETH, BTC)
Returns	Product/rewards/equity	Tokens (utility/security)
Platforms	Kickstarter, SeedInvest	Ethereum, Binance Smart Chain

Regulatory landscape

Global regulations

- **USA**: SEC treats many ICOs as securities; crowdfunding is regulated under JOBS Act.
- **EU**: Crowdfunding is regulated by the European Crowdfunding Service Providers Regulation (ECSPR).
- **India**: Crowdfunding is lightly regulated; ICOs are not legally recognized.
- **Singapore**: ICOs are permitted under certain conditions; regulated by the MAS.

Key concerns

- Investor protection
- Anti-money laundering (AML) and know your customer (KYC) compliance
- Transparency and disclosure

- Fraud and scam prevention
- Cross-border jurisdiction challenges

Table 13.4 Risks and challenges.

Risk type	Description
Fraud risk	Many ICOs and crowdfunding campaigns have been exposed as scams.
Lack of liquidity	Tokens or shares may be illiquid or delisted from platforms.
Regulatory uncertainty	Varying regulations create compliance risk.
Overvaluation	Projects may be overhyped and fail to deliver on promises.
Cybersecurity	Platforms and smart contracts can be hacked.

13.3 Marketplace Lending

Marketplace lending — often referred to as peer-to-peer (P2P) or platform-based lending — is an innovative FinTech model that facilitates direct connections between borrowers and investors through online platforms, effectively eliminating the need for conventional financial intermediaries such as banks. By leveraging data analytics, automation, and digital onboarding, marketplace lending offers faster credit access and attractive returns for lenders. Originally launched to democratize lending, this model has evolved into a mature financial ecosystem involving retail investors, institutions, and alternative data tools. Its rise aligns with the broader digital transformation of finance.

Marketplace lending is the practice of matching borrowers and lenders via an online platform. The platform facilitates loan origination, risk assessment, fund transfer, and repayment, but it does not typically take loans onto its balance sheet.

Table 13.5 Comparison with traditional lending.

Aspect	Traditional bank lending	Marketplace lending
Intermediary	Bank	Online platform
Loan origination	Internal underwriting	Platform-driven matching
Capital source	Bank deposits	Individual and institutional investors
Speed	Days to weeks	Often within 24–48 hours
Credit evaluation	Conservative, FICO-based	Alternative data-driven
Interest rates	Based on risk and bank policies	Risk-based pricing via algorithms

13.3.1 Evolution and growth

2005: Launch of Zopa in the UK – the first true P2P platform.

2006: Prosper and LendingClub start in the U.S.

2010s: Rise of hybrid models involving institutional investors.

2020s: Integration with AI, Open Banking, and embedded finance solutions.

"As reported by the Cambridge Centre for Alternative Finance, marketplace lending has evolved into a global industry worth billions of dollars, with significant traction in countries like China, the United States, the United Kingdom, and India."

Business models

Peer-to-peer lending

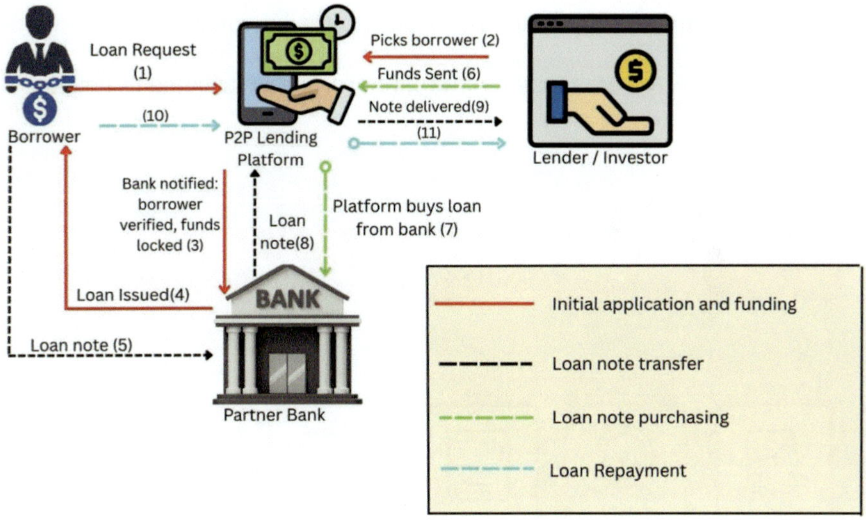

Figure 13.3 Peer-to-peer lending.

Direct match between individual borrowers and lenders. Returns vary based on risk class.

Peer-to-business lending

SMEs raise working capital or expansion funding from a pool of lenders.

Institutional marketplace lending

Platforms partner with hedge funds, banks, and asset managers for bulk funding.

Balance sheet lending (Hybrid)

Some platforms partially underwrite or fund loans from their own balance sheet.

Platform operation workflow

Borrower application – Digital KYC, income verification, and credit profiling.

Risk assessment – Credit scoring using traditional and alternative data.

Loan listing – Loan published on a platform with rate and terms.

Lender investment – Investors select and fund listed loans.

Loan disbursement – Funds are transferred to the borrower.

Repayment – Borrowers repay monthly; returns are distributed to lenders.

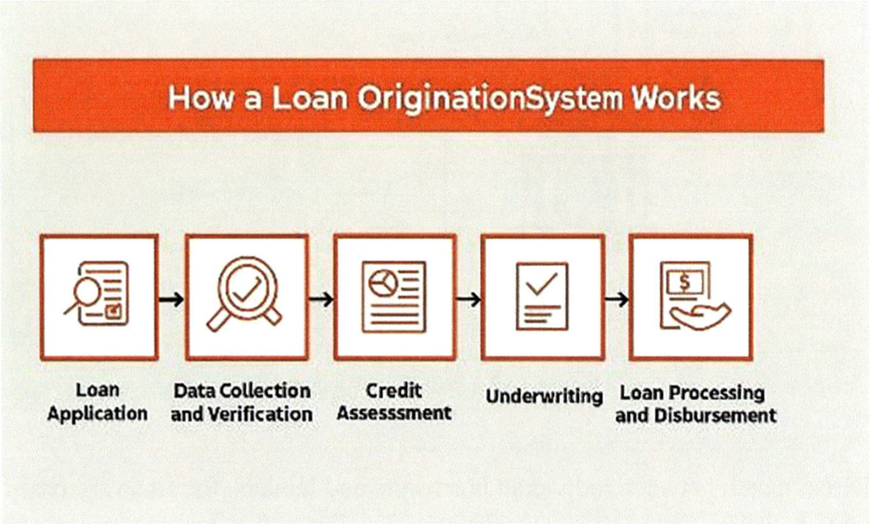

Figure 13.4 Working of the loan origination system.

Technology in marketplace lending credit

Scoring algorithms

Use of machine learning to assess non-traditional metrics such as social media behavior, utility payments, mobile phone usage, and psychometric data.

Automation and APIs

Fully automated onboarding, loan servicing, and data sharing through APIs and integrated platforms.

Blockchain and smart contracts (Emerging)

Ensures transparency, immutability, and automated loan agreements using smart contracts.

Table 13.6 Benefits and opportunities.

Stakeholder	Benefits
Borrowers	Faster access to credit, competitive rates, and fewer collateral requirements
Lenders	Diversified investment portfolio, higher yields
Platforms	Scalable business model with low operational costs
Economy	Financial inclusion, SME growth, and competition in lending

Table 13.7 Risks and challenges.

Risk type	Description
Credit risk	Borrower defaults can lead to investor losses.
Liquidity risk	Loans are illiquid; resale options are limited.
Platform risk	Platform failure or exit can disrupt loan servicing.
Regulatory risk	Regulatory uncertainty and jurisdictional differences can hinder growth.
Data security risk	Cyberattacks may compromise borrower and lender information.

Regulatory Framework

United States

SEC and CFPB regulate depending on the platform structure. Lending Club registered as a public company in 2014.

United Kingdom

Regulated by the Financial Conduct Authority (FCA) with detailed rules on risk disclosure and investor categorization.

India

RBI classifies P2P lenders as non-banking financial companies (NBFC-P2P). Platforms must adhere to capital requirements, risk disclosure norms, and KYC obligations.

China

After initial rapid growth, regulatory crackdowns in 2018–2020 led to the closure of most platforms due to fraud and loan bubbles.

The future of marketplace lending

Embedded lending: Integration with e-commerce and SaaS platforms for contextual lending.

AI and predictive analytics: It enhances loan approval and fraud detection.

ESG integration: Platforms may offer green loans or social impact lending.

Tokenization: Potential to issue debt tokens for trading and transparency.

Global collaboration: Cross-border P2P lending through regulatory harmonization.

Marketplace lending has emerged as a disruptive alternative to traditional credit systems, providing efficient, transparent, and scalable financial solutions. Driven by technology and data, it facilitates capital flow from savers to borrowers through platforms, reshaping how credit is accessed and offered. While it holds promises for financial inclusion and SME support, success depends on robust risk management, regulatory clarity, and technological resilience. Peer-to-peer lending platforms have transformed traditional credit markets by connecting borrowers and lenders directly [9]. Fintech credit markets have become significant alternative channels, particularly in regions underserved by conventional banks [10]. Global alternative finance models are increasingly diversifying, with Asia and Europe leading in platform-based lending [11]. Fintech start-ups' entry into lending has pressured incumbent banks to adopt new digital strategies [12]. The World Bank notes that digital financial services are critical to broadening access and resilience in developing economies [13].

13.4 Rise of Chinese TechFins

In the last decade, China has become a global leader in digital finance, largely driven by the emergence of **TechFin** firms – technology companies entering and reshaping the financial services landscape. Unlike traditional FinTech startups that enhance financial services through innovation, TechFins are primarily technology giants that expand into finance, leveraging their massive user bases, data ecosystems, and digital infrastructure. China's rapid fintech expansion showcases how regulatory frameworks influence innovation outcomes [14]. TechFins like Alibaba and Tencent illustrate a model where technology firms, not banks, dominate financial ecosystems [15]. Cross-border data integration and payments innovation have positioned Chinese firms as global leaders in alternative finance [16]. The fintech revolution in China highlights a dynamic fusion of policy, consumer demand, and digital infrastructure [17]. Digital platforms capitalize data to reshape financial intermediation [18]. The Global Findex Database underscores the role of digital finance in promoting financial inclusion across emerging markets [19]. Research highlights that economic and technological forces jointly determine fintech adoption, explaining China's rapid TechFin dominance [20]. The **rise of Chinese TechFins** reflects the intersection of mobile-first consumer behaviour, regulatory flexibility (initially), and the absence of entrenched financial institutions in key domains. Giants like **Ant Group (Alibaba)**, **Tencent (WeChat)**, and **JD.com** have disrupted banking, payments, credit, asset management, and insurance at an unprecedented scale.

Table 13.8 Defining TechFin vs. FinTech.

Feature	FinTech	TechFin
Core business	Financial services, enhanced by tech	Technology, expanding into finance
Examples	Stripe, SoFi, Robinhood	Ant Group, Tencent, JD Digits
Strategy	Build better financial products	Embed financial services in tech ecosystems
Risk profile	More aligned with the banking sector	Less regulated (initially), platform- driven

The term **TechFin** was popularized by **Jack Ma**, the founder of Alibaba, to describe technology companies using their platforms to offer financial services without becoming banks.

13.4.1 Drivers of TechFin growth in China

Digital and mobile penetration

China leapfrogged traditional internet infrastructure with mobile-first adoption. By 2023, China had over 1 billion internet users, most accessing services via smartphones. This created fertile ground for mobile payments, lending, and digital wealth management.

Regulatory flexibility (2005–2019)

Initially, Chinese regulators allowed tech platforms to experiment with financial services. This sandbox-like environment enabled rapid scaling without the constraints traditional banks face.

Financial inclusion gaps

Large parts of China's rural and urban lower-middle-income populations were underserved by traditional banks. TechFins offered accessible, low-cost, and data- driven alternatives.

Platform ecosystems

Chinese TechFins were born within **super-apps** – integrated platforms where users could shop, chat, pay bills, invest, borrow, and book services, all in one interface.

Key Chinese TechFin companies

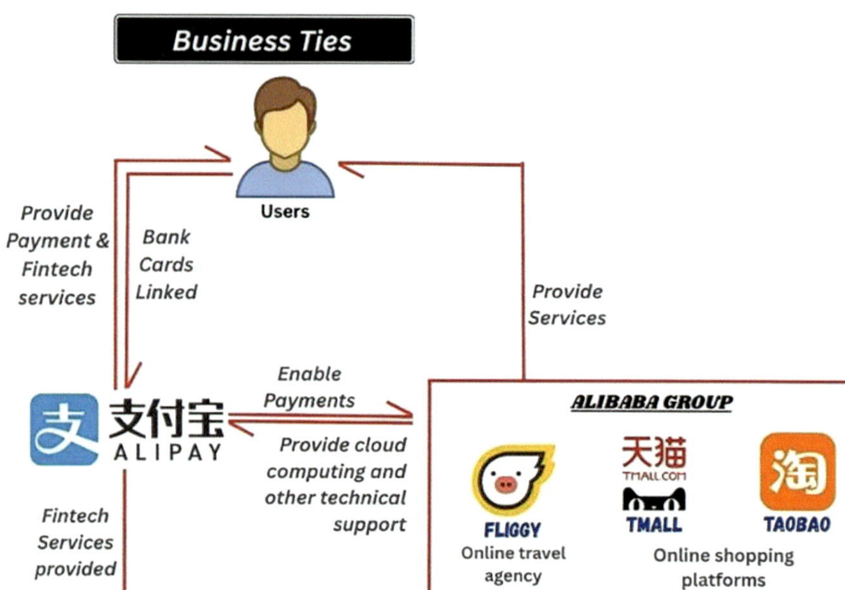

Figure 13.5 Ant Group and Alibaba business data.

Ant Group (Alibaba)

Core services: Alipay (payments), Huabei (credit), Jiebei (consumer loans), Yu'e Bao (wealth management), AntChain (blockchain), MYbank (online-only bank)

Key innovations: QR code payments, money market funds for retail, AI-based credit scoring

Business model: Platform-centric, monetizing through commissions, interest spreads, and technology licensing

Scale: Over 1 billion users, managing trillions of RMB in payment volume annually

Tencent (WeChat Pay)

Core services: WeChat Pay, WeBank (digital bank), Licaitong (investment services), insurance distribution

Integration: Financial services embedded into the WeChat social messaging and lifestyle app

Strategy: Monetization through embedded financial products, data-driven insights, and partnerships

JD Digits (JD Technology)

Services: Supply chain finance, SME lending, consumer credit, AI-based risk control, digital wallets

Advantage: Deep integration with JD.com's e-commerce and logistics platforms

TechFin business models

Payments as a Gateway

Mobile payments (Alipay and WeChat Pay) served as entry points to the financial ecosystem. Once users transacted digitally, platforms upsold loans, investment products, and insurance.

Lending and credit services

Using alternative data from shopping behavior, social interactions, and mobile usage, TechFins developed credit scoring models (e.g., Sesame Credit) to offer unsecured loans instantly.

Wealth and asset management

Ant's Yu'e Bao, launched in partnership with Tianhong Asset Management, allowed users to invest idle wallet balances into money market funds with high liquidity and returns.

InsurTech

Platforms enabled micro-insurance, usage-based coverage, and AI-based underwriting. Mutual aid programs and gamified health insurance became mainstream.

Regulatory response and transformation

Initial phase: Light-touch regulation

From 2005 to 2018, regulators took a hands-off approach, allowing rapid innovation. This led to massive growth but also rising risks in shadow banking and consumer over-indebtedness.

Crackdown phase (2020–2022)

Ant IPO Halt (2020): Regulators stopped Ant's $35B IPO, citing systemic risk concerns and poor governance.

Reclassification: TechFins were reclassified as financial holding companies subject to bank-like capital and compliance requirements.

Tightening credit rules: Lending practices were scrutinized. Platforms had to contribute to loan provisioning and comply with interest rate ceilings.

Data security and anti-monopoly: New laws demanded data localization, user consent for data use, and restrictions on monopolistic practices.

Global impact and expansion

Southeast Asia: Ant Financial and Tencent have invested in e-wallets and digital banks in Indonesia, the Philippines, and Malaysia.

Africa: Alipay's technology stack has been licensed to mobile money providers.

Partnership model: TechFins now operates more as an infrastructure provider and enabler, rather than a direct financial service provider abroad.

Table 13.9 Challenges ahead.

Challenge	Description
Regulatory uncertainty	Shifting policies affect business models and investor confidence
Data privacy	New rules on data storage, usage, and consent impact operations
Geopolitical tensions	Trade restrictions and data concerns hinder global partnerships
Sustainability	Need for risk control, transparent governance, and compliance-oriented growth

Future outlook

Bank-tech partnerships: Collaboration between TechFins and traditional financial institutions to combine reach with compliance.

Cross-border infrastructure: Export of FinTech platforms and APIs to developing markets.

AI and blockchain integration: Continued innovation in credit, compliance, and smart contract execution.

The integration of China's central bank digital currency (CBDC), the Digital Yuan, is expected to significantly transform the way TechFin firms deliver payment and lending services.

The rise of Chinese TechFins represents one of the most transformative developments in global finance. By embedding financial services into daily digital life, companies like Ant Group and Tencent redefined consumer finance, payments, and credit scoring. However, the regulatory clampdown highlights the balance between innovation and stability. As Chinese TechFins recalibrate for a more regulated future, their global footprint and technological prowess continue to influence the evolution of FinTech worldwide.

Summary

Chapter 13 delves into the rapidly growing domain of digital and alternative finance, highlighting how technology is reshaping access to capital and financial intermediation. It begins with a discussion on crowdfunding and ICOs, which provide innovative ways for startups to raise funds outside traditional capital markets. The chapter then explores marketplace lending (P2P), where digital platforms match borrowers directly with individual or institutional lenders. It also examines the rise of Chinese TechFins, showcasing how major technology firms like Alibaba and Tencent are leading a new model of financial service delivery through integrated digital ecosystems. These developments reflect the broader shift toward decentralized, accessible, and data-driven financial services.

Case Study: Filecoin ICO – Pioneering Decentralized Storage Through Blockchain-Based Fundraising

In 2017, Protocol Labs introduced Filecoin, a decentralized blockchain-based file storage network designed to transform the cloud storage industry. The platform enables users to rent out unused digital storage space and earn compensation in the form of FIL tokens, the native cryptocurrency of the Filecoin network. This initiative aimed to address persistent challenges associated with traditional centralized storage systems provided by firms like Amazon Web Services (AWS), Google Cloud, and Dropbox – including issues of monopolistic control, vulnerability to outages, and lack of transparency. To fund the development of the platform, Protocol Labs conducted an Initial Coin Offering (ICO) through the CoinList platform in August 2017. The ICO was structured in two phases: a private token sale targeting early-stage venture capital investors like Sequoia Capital and Andreessen Horowitz, followed by a public sale restricted to accredited investors, in compliance with U.S. SEC Regulation D. The ICO successfully raised over $257 million, positioning it as one of the largest token sales of its time. The funds were designated for network development, research, and long-term sustainability.

Filecoin operates using novel consensus mechanisms – Proof-of-Replication (PoRep) and Proof-of-Spacetime (PoSt) – which allow the system to verify that data is uniquely stored and maintained over a specified period. These mechanisms ensure the reliability of storage providers in a decentralized context. FIL tokens serve multiple purposes, acting as a medium of exchange, incentive layer, and governance token within the ecosystem. Governance was initially centralized under Protocol Labs, with future plans to decentralize decision-making as the protocol matured.

Despite delays in launching the mainnet, which finally went live in October 2020, Filecoin achieved significant adoption milestones. By 2024, the network was offering more than 1 EiB (exbibyte) of decentralized storage capacity globally. The FIL token achieved a peak market capitalization of over $10 billion in 2021, demonstrating the platform's traction and the credibility of its business model. Filecoin emerged as a reference point for legally compliant ICOs and an early example of infrastructure- based blockchain innovation.

The challenges faced:

- Launch delays: The Filecoin mainnet launch was postponed multiple times due to technical complexity and testing requirements, which created uncertainty among stakeholders.
- Legal restrictions on participation: By limiting the public ICO to accredited investors, global retail participation was restricted, potentially affecting decentralization in early token distribution.

- High development expectations: Given the size of the ICO and the high-profile investors involved, public and institutional expectations placed significant pressure on timely and scalable delivery.
- Market volatility: FIL token price fluctuations following the launch added volatility and speculative behavior, complicating long-term utility goals.
- Technical sophistication: The PoRep and PoSt mechanisms, while innovative, required rigorous testing and infrastructure, posing scalability and usability challenges in early adoption.

Case Discussion Questions

1. What core issues in centralized cloud storage systems did Filecoin aim to resolve through decentralization?
2. How did regulatory compliance affect investor trust and the structure of Filecoin's ICO?
3. What are the advantages and trade-offs of limiting token sales to accredited investors only?
4. In what ways did Filecoin's novel consensus mechanisms contribute to its storage reliability?
5. How can blockchain-based infrastructure projects manage stakeholder expectations during prolonged development cycles?

Keywords

- **Crowdfunding:** A method of raising small amounts of money from a large number of people, typically via online platforms, to fund a project, startup, or cause.
- **Initial coin offering (ICO):** A blockchain-based fundraising method where new cryptocurrencies or tokens are sold to investors in exchange for existing crypto like Bitcoin or Ethereum.
- **Marketplace lending:** Also known as peer-to-peer (P2P) lending, it connects borrowers and investors directly through digital platforms without traditional banks.
- **TechFin:** Financial services offered by technology companies (like Alibaba or Tencent), often embedded into large digital ecosystems rather than being stand-alone financial products.

- **Alternative finance:** Non-traditional financial services and instruments, including crowdfunding, P2P lending, and ICOs, that operate outside the conventional banking system.
- **Tokenization:** The process of converting real-world assets (like real estate or equity) into digital tokens that can be traded on blockchain networks.
- **Risk assessment in P2P lending:** The evaluation of borrower creditworthiness by algorithms or platform-defined criteria in marketplace lending, often without full banking oversight.
- **Chinese FinTech giants:** Refers to large tech-driven financial service providers in China (e.g., Ant Group, WeBank), who lead in digital payments, lending, and wealth management through integrated platforms.

Discussion Questions

1. Differentiate between digital finance and alternative finance with real-world examples.
2. Explain how P2P lending platforms manage risk and facilitate credit assessment.
3. Analyse the pros and cons of BNPL schemes from the perspective of both consumers and merchants.
4. Describe the regulatory concerns associated with ICOs and suggest mitigation measures.
5. Discuss how embedded finance is transforming the e-commerce landscape.

References

[1] Allen, F., Gu, X., & Jagtiani, J. (2022). A survey of fintech research and policy discussion. In A. N. Berger, P. Molyneux, & J. O. S. Wilson (Eds.), *Oxford Handbook of Banking* (3rd ed., pp. 896–918). Oxford University Press.

[2] Arner, D. W., Buckley, R. P., Zetzsche, D. A., & Barberis, J. N. (2020). The evolution of FinTech: A new post-crisis paradigm? In R. P. Buckley, D. W. Arner, & J. N. Barberis (Eds.), *The RegTech Book* (pp. 91–100). Wiley.

[3] Chen, M. A., Wu, Q., & Yang, B. (2019). How valuable is FinTech innovation? *The Review of Financial Studies, 32*(5), 2062–2106. https://doi.org/10.1093/rfs/hhz002

[4] De Buysere, K., Gajda, O., Kleverlaan, R., & Marom, D. (2012). A framework for European crowdfunding. European Crowdfunding Network. https://eurocrowd.org

[5] IOSCO. (2017). Initial Coin Offerings (ICOs): Consultation report. International Organization of Securities Commissions. https://www.iosco.org/library/pubdocs/pdf/IOSCOPD609.pdf

[6] Zetzsche, D. A., Buckley, R. P., Arner, D. W., & Barberis, J. N. (2019). Initial Coin Offerings: A critical review of regulatory approaches. In R. P. Buckley, D. W. Arner, & J. N. Barberis (Eds.), *FinTech and RegTech in a Nutshell* (pp. 55–89). Elgar Publishing.

[7] Tapscott, D., & Tapscott, A. (2016). *Blockchain revolution: How the technology behind Bitcoin is changing money, business, and the world.* Penguin.

[8] Chuen, D. L. K. (Ed.). (2015). *Handbook of digital currency: Bitcoin, innovation, financial instruments, and big data.* Academic Press.

[9] Milne, A., & Parboteeah, P. (2016). The business models and economics of peer-to-peer lending. European Credit Research Institute (ECRI) Research Report No. 17. https://www.ceps.eu/ceps-publications/business-models-and-economics-peer-peer-lending/

[10] Claessens, S., Frost, J., Turner, G., & Zhu, F. (2018). Fintech credit markets around the world: Size, drivers and policy issues. *BIS Quarterly Review.* https://www.bis.org/publ/qtrpdf/r_qt1809e.htm

[11] Ziegler, T., Shneor, R., Wenzlaff, K., Johanson, D., Lopez, A., Hao, R., & Zhang, B. (2021). *The Global Alternative Finance Market Benchmarking Report 2020.* Cambridge Centre for Alternative Finance. https://www.jbs.cam.ac.uk/faculty-research/centres/alternative-finance/publications/

[12] Li, Y., Spigt, R., & Swinkels, L. (2017). The impact of FinTech start-ups on incumbent retail banks' share prices. *Financial Innovation, 3*(26), 1–16. https://doi.org/10.1186/s40854-017-0076-7

[13] World Bank. (2020). *Digital financial services.* https://www.worldbank.org/en/topic/financialinclusion/brief/digital-financial-services

[14] Huang, Y. (2020). Fintech in China: The impact of regulation on innovation. In E. G. Carayannis et al. (Eds.), *The Palgrave Handbook of FinTech and Blockchain* (pp. 211–226). Palgrave Macmillan.

[15] Gai, K., Qiu, M., & Sun, X. (2018). A survey on FinTech. *Journal of Network and Computer Applications, 103*, 262–273. https://doi.org/10.1016/j.jnca.2017.10.011

[16] Frost, J. (2020). The economic forces driving fintech adoption across countries. *Bank for International Settlements Working Paper No. 838.* https://www.bis.org/publ/work838.pdf

[17] Gomber, P., Kauffman, R. J., Parker, C., & Weber, B. W. (2018). On the fintech revolution: Interpreting the forces of innovation, disruption, and transformation in financial services. *Journal of Management Information Systems, 35*(1), 220–265. https://doi.org/10.1080/07421222.2018.1440766

[18] Langley, P., & Leyshon, A. (2021). Platform capitalism: The intermediation and capitalisation of digital finance. In P. Mader, D. Mertens, & N. van der Zwan (Eds.), *The Routledge International Handbook of Financialization* (pp. 293–302). Routledge.

[19] Demirgüç-Kunt, A., Klapper, L., Singer, D., Ansar, S., & Hess, J. (2018). *The Global Findex Database 2017.* World Bank Publications.

[20] Haddad, C., & Hornuf, L. (2019). The emergence of the global fintech market: Economic and technological determinants. *Small Business Economics, 53*(1), 81–105. https://doi.org/10.1007/s11187-018-9991-x

14

Specialized FinTech Domains

Abstract

This chapter offers an in-depth exploration of specialized FinTech domains, focusing on how technological innovations are reshaping distinct sectors within the financial ecosystem. It begins by identifying key verticals such as InsurTech, PropTech, and TechFin, each representing the application of financial technology in insurance, real estate, and technology-led financial services, respectively. The chapter discusses how these domains leverage advanced tools – such as AI, big data, IoT, and blockchain – to solve industry-specific challenges, including claims automation in insurance, digital property transactions, and financial service delivery by non-traditional players like tech giants.

In addition, the chapter analyzes emerging market trends and innovative business models within these sectors, ranging from peer-to-peer insurance and tokenized real estate to platform-based financial ecosystems. It highlights how specialized FinTech solutions promote efficiency, transparency, and customer-centricity, while also disrupting legacy processes and value chains.

A critical evaluation is presented on how these innovations are influencing traditional financial institutions, compelling them to adopt agile technologies, reconfigure value propositions, and reshape customer engagement strategies. The chapter also examines shifts in consumer behavior, driven by hyper-personalized offerings, digital convenience, and increased expectations for trust and control. By synthesizing technological, market, and behavioral dimensions, this chapter enables a comprehensive understanding of the evolving FinTech landscape across specialized domains.

DOI: 10.1201/9788743811244-19

Introduction

The progression of FinTech has not only reshaped conventional banking and payment infrastructures but has also led to the emergence of specialized segments within the financial services landscape. Areas such as InsurTech, RegTech, and WealthTech are leveraging advanced technologies, including artificial intelligence (AI), blockchain, big data, and cloud computing, to redefine traditional practices. As the industry evolves, FinTech is transitioning from a disruptive force to an integrative component of financial systems, enabling targeted innovations across specific domains. These specialized FinTech sectors offer customized solutions that enhance operational performance, improve customer engagement, mitigate risk, and support broader financial inclusion. Specialized FinTech domains such as InsurTech, PropTech, and TechFin reflect the widening scope of digital transformation in financial services [1]. These domains move FinTech from generic financial innovation toward sector-specific technological advancements [2].

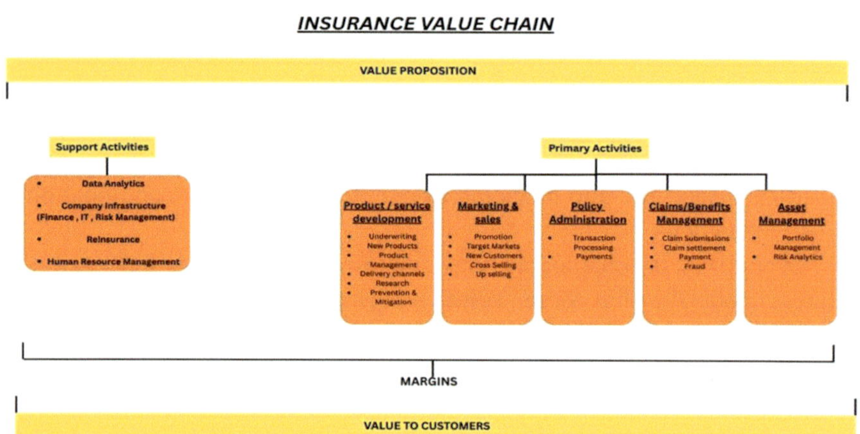

Figure 14.1 Insurance value chain.

14.1 Insurance Technology (InsurTech)

InsurTech is the segment of FinTech dedicated to transforming the insurance industry through technology. Traditional insurance models often involve complex paperwork, lengthy underwriting processes, and opaque claim procedures. InsurTech addresses these inefficiencies with automation, data analytics, and digital platforms. InsurTech has redesigned insurance value chains using automation, AI-driven underwriting, and digital claims processing.

Digital insurance ecosystems now incorporate cloud computing, data analytics, and IoT solutions to improve customer outcomes [3]. The rapid growth of InsurTech is supported by increased collaboration between insurers and digital startups [4].Technological Drivers

- **AI and machine learning**: Enable predictive underwriting and fraud detection.
- **IoT devices**: Smart sensors in cars and homes provide real-time risk data.
- **Blockchain**: Ensures transparency and trust in claims processing and policy validation.
- **Mobile applications**: Streamline customer onboarding, policy management, and claims.

14.1.1 Business models

- **Peer-to-peer insurance**: Pooling premiums among members, e.g., Friendsurance.
- **Usage-based insurance**: Insurance premiums based on real-time behavior, e.g., Metromile.
- **On-demand insurance**: Instant coverage for temporary needs, e.g., Trov.

Lemonade (USA): A disruptor in renters and homeowners' insurance, Lemonade uses AI-powered chatbots to handle claims in seconds. It donates unclaimed premiums to social causes, enhancing trust and customer loyalty.

14.1.2 Regulatory Technology (RegTech)

RegTech originated as a response to the heightened regulatory demands that followed the 2008 global financial crisis. It supports financial institutions in adhering to changing compliance requirements, minimizing the risk of penalties, and promoting greater transparency in operations.

Core applications

- **AML and CFT**: Automated monitoring of transactions to flag suspicious activity.
- **KYC**: Digital onboarding and identity verification using biometrics and AI.

- **Risk and compliance management**: Real-time dashboards for compliance officers.
- **Regulatory reporting**: Automating reporting formats for central banks and regulators.

Technological enablers

- Natural language processing for parsing regulatory texts
- Big data analytics for transaction monitoring
- Secure cloud environments for audit trails

Onfido (UK): Offers digital identity verification using facial recognition and document verification. It is widely used for onboarding in banks, crypto exchanges, and e-commerce platforms.

14.1.3 Wealth Management Technology (WealthTech)

WealthTech democratizes wealth management by offering digital investment advice and portfolio management tools. Traditionally accessible only to high-net-worth individuals (HNWIs), modern platforms offer services to retail investors.

Features

- **Robo-advisors**: Algorithms provide personalized investment strategies.
- **Goal-based planning**: Investment aligned with life goals.
- **Micro-investing**: Round-up models that invest spare change.
- **Portfolio rebalancing**: Automated risk and allocation adjustments.

Innovations

- Gamification of investing (e.g., Acorns)
- Real-time data dashboards
- ESG investment filters

14.1.4 LendingTech and robo-advisory – Redefining digital investment and credit access

The financial technology landscape has evolved rapidly to accommodate changing consumer behavior and technological advancement. Among the most transformative developments are **robo-advisory services** and **LendingTech platforms**, which are disrupting traditional financial advisory and lending models by introducing automation, algorithmic decision-making, and alternative data usage.

Two key areas are explored:

Betterment (USA) as a pioneering robo-advisor delivering goal-based investment services. **LendingTech models**, which include peer-to-peer lending, Buy Now Pay Later (BNPL), and AI-driven credit scoring, with global examples such as **Kiva** and **LendingClub**. These technologies address critical challenges in financial accessibility, especially in underbanked and emerging economies.

Traditional investment and lending systems present several barriers:

- **High advisory fees** and **minimum investment thresholds** exclude low- income users from accessing wealth management tools.
- **Credit systems** heavily reliant on formal income and credit history data exclude individuals with informal employment or thin credit files.
- **Financial exclusion** remains high in emerging economies where access to banks is limited, but smartphone and mobile wallet usage is widespread.

Betterment (Robo-Advisory – USA)

Betterment is a US-based robo-advisory platform that leverages **algorithms and artificial intelligence** to provide low-cost, automated investment services. Key features include:

- **Goal-based portfolio allocation**, customized based on user preferences and timelines.
- **Tax-loss harvesting**: Automatically sells underperforming assets to offset gains and reduce tax liabilities.
- **Automatic rebalancing**: AI ensures portfolios remain aligned with target asset allocations.

Betterment democratized wealth management by lowering entry barriers and eliminating manual advisory dependence.

LendingTech Innovations

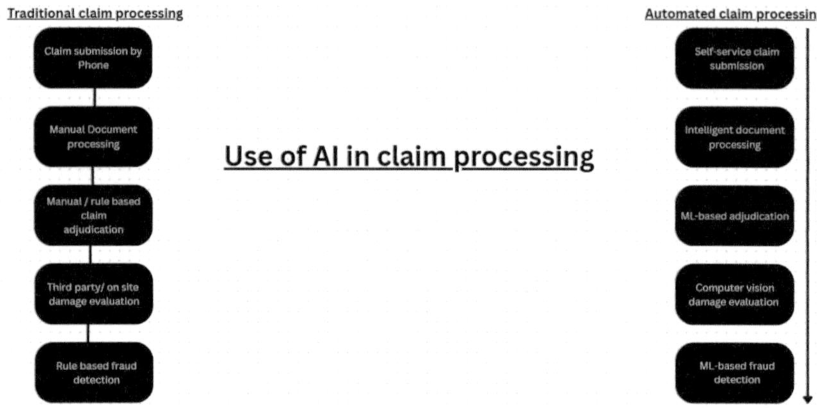

Figure 14.2 Use of AI in claim processing.

Lending tech platforms utilize digital infrastructure and alternative data to extend credit in new ways:

P2P Lending (e.g., LendingClub – USA)

- Connects individual borrowers and lenders through a digital marketplace.
- Reduces overhead and offers competitive rates outside traditional bank channels.

Buy Now, Pay Later (BNPL – e.g., Klarna, Afterpay)

- Offers short-term credit at the point of sale with interest-free installments.
- Integrated into e-commerce platforms, improving customer purchasing flexibility.

AI-driven credit scoring

- Uses **non-traditional data** sources such as social media behavior, mobile phone usage, utility bill payments, and e-commerce history.
- Facilitates access to credit for individuals without formal credit histories.

Kiva (global microcredit platform)

Kiva is a **non-profit microlending platform** operating in over 80 countries. It:

- Facilitates crowdfunding of small loans to entrepreneurs in underserved communities.

- Uses a peer-to-peer funding model that emphasizes **social impact over profit**.
- Enables capital access for women, farmers, and artisans in regions without formal banking infrastructure.

Betterment

- Serves over **800,000 clients** and manages billions in assets.
- Reduced advisory fees significantly (as low as 0.25% per annum).
- Proven that **digital investment platforms** can offer personalized services at scale.

Lending tech platforms

- **Lending Club** has facilitated over **$60 billion** in loans since its inception.
- **BNPL** usage has skyrocketed globally, especially among Gen Z and millennials.
- AI-driven underwriting has improved loan approval rates and reduced default risks in data-rich but credit-thin populations.

Kiva

- Over **$1.8 billion** in loans disbursed to more than **4.5 million borrowers**.
- Maintains a high repayment rate (~96%), indicating the **effectiveness of social lending** even in high-risk regions.

Table 14.1 Learnings/Implications.

Key insights	Description
Automation enables inclusion	Robo-advisory tools like Betterment allow small investors to access advanced financial planning with minimal cost.
Alternative data enhances lending access	LendingTech models broaden credit access for users without traditional documentation.
Digital models build resilience	Kiva's decentralized, crowdfunded lending system is resilient in fragile economies and during crises.
Regulatory adaptation is crucial	As LendingTech and BNPL expand, governments must update consumer protection laws and data governance policies.

The convergence of AI, alternative data, and digital platforms has redefined how financial services are delivered and accessed. Betterment showcases the potential of robo-advisory tools in democratizing investment, while LendingTech platforms like LendingClub, Klarna, and Kiva demonstrate how digital lending can close credit gaps globally. Together, these innovations signify a shift from institutional dependence to data-driven, customer-centric finance, especially in reaching underserved markets.

14.1.5 Property and real estate technology (PropTech)

PropTech applies financial technology concepts to improve the real estate industry's transparency, operational efficiency, and security.

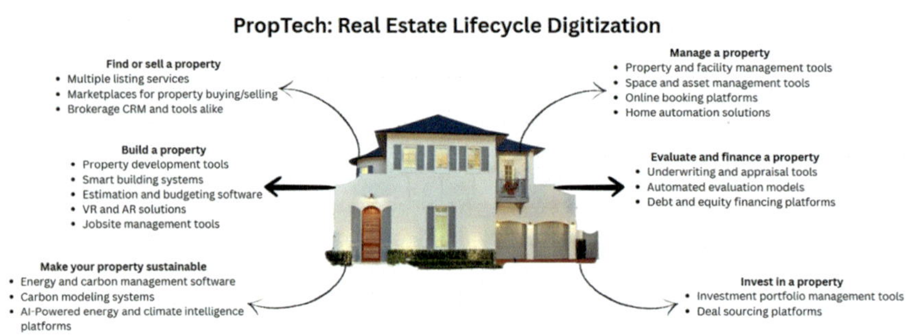

Figure 14.3 PropTech: Real estate lifecycle digitization.

Major applications

- **Digital mortgages**: Paperless, fast loan approvals.
- **Real estate tokenization**: Fractional ownership of property using blockchain.
- **Smart contracts**: Automating purchase/sale agreements.

Example

Propy is a real estate platform powered by blockchain technology that facilitates complete online property transactions, including title transfers and the execution of legal agreements.

Green FinTech (Sustainable Finance)

As climate change becomes a critical issue, Green FinTech applies financial technology to support environmentally sustainable practices and green investments.

Core services

- **ESG analytics**: Evaluate companies based on environmental, social, and governance performance.
- **Carbon accounting tools**: Help individuals and companies track their carbon footprint.
- **Green bonds via blockchain**: Transparent and traceable sustainable investments.

Global example:

Doconomy (Sweden): A banking app that shows users the carbon impact of their purchases and offers CO_2 offsetting options.

14.1.6 EduFinTech

EduFinTech aims to bridge the financial gap in education through student-focused financial solutions.

Offerings

- **Student loan platforms**: Non-traditional lenders offering better terms.
- **Tuition management systems**: For institutions and parents.

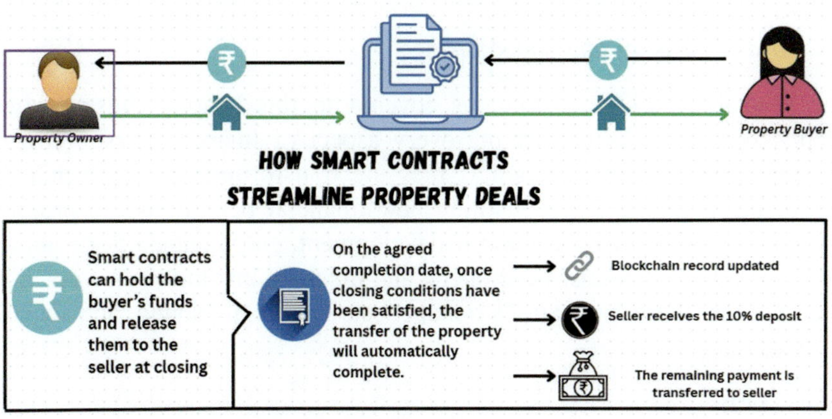

Figure 14.4 PropTech use case: Smart contracts in property deals.

- **Education crowdfunding**: Platforms like GoFundMe for student aid.

- **Prodigy finance**: Provides postgraduate education loans to international students based on future earning potential rather than credit history.

14.1.7 AgriFinTech

AgriFinTech focuses on financial inclusion for rural and farming communities, offering credit, insurance, and savings tools via mobile technologies.

Innovations

- **Weather-indexed insurance**: Automatically triggers payouts based on satellite data.
- **Digital supply chain financing**: Reduces cash flow gaps in agricultural production.
- **Mobile microloans**: Disbursed via USSD or SMS platforms.
- **FarmDrive (Kenya)**: Uses machine learning and mobile data to assess farmers' creditworthiness and facilitate loans.

14.1.8 Emerging Trends Across Specialized Domains

Convergence and Collaboration

- Cross-domain integration: e.g., Green WealthTech, Islamic RegTech
- Partnerships between FinTech startups and traditional institutions
- Use of APIs for embedded finance

The specialized FinTech domains covered in this chapter illustrate how deeply technology is penetrating every aspect of finance. These verticals are not just enhancing efficiency; they are transforming business models, improving inclusivity, and enabling new financial paradigms. To promote sustainable and inclusive economic development, coordinated efforts among policymakers, technology developers, and financial institutions are essential to ensure that these innovations remain secure, ethically sound, and socially responsible.

InsurTech

InsurTech, short for insurance technology, involves the application of advanced technologies to transform and enhance the insurance sector. It includes digital solutions that streamline and automate various components of the insurance value chain, such as underwriting, pricing, policy administration, and claims handling. With consumers expecting faster, personalized, and more transparent insurance services, InsurTech plays a pivotal role in modernizing this centuries-old sector.

Key technologies

- **Artificial intelligence (AI)**: AI algorithms enable predictive risk modeling, customer segmentation, and personalized policy recommendations.
- **Blockchain**: Facilitates secure, tamper-proof contracts (smart contracts), transparent claims history, and fraud prevention.
- **Internet of Things (IoT) devices** – such as smart home sensors and wearable fitness trackers – enable the collection of real-time data, which supports dynamic pricing models and more accurate risk evaluation in the insurance industry.
- **Big data and analytics**: Insurance firms use large datasets to analyse behavior, price premiums, and manage risk.
- **Telematics**: Especially used in auto insurance for pay-as-you-drive or behavior-based pricing models.

Core applications

- **Digital onboarding**: Mobile-based, paperless customer registration and KYC.
- **Peer-to-peer (P2P) insurance**: Groups individuals with similar needs to pool resources (e.g., Lemonade).
- **Usage-based insurance (UBI)** determines premiums according to individual customer behavior, such as driving patterns and habits.
- **Claim automation**: AI-driven bots and optical character recognition (OCR) tools accelerate claims approval.

14.2 PropTech

PropTech, or Property Technology, signifies the modernization of the real estate sector through the integration of FinTech solutions and emerging digital technologies. It includes platforms and tools that improve the way people buy, sell, rent, finance, and manage properties. With urbanization and smart city development on the rise, PropTech is addressing inefficiencies in the property market. PropTech represents real-estate innovation driven by digital platforms, smart-property solutions, and data integration. Market maps show rapid growth in PropTech sub-sectors, such as digital brokerage, real-estate analytics, and construction technology [5]. PropTech advancements align with global FinTech innovation trends, emphasizing platformization and data-driven decision making [6]. Digital real-estate ecosystems are expanding due to increased investment and technological scalability in property markets [7].

Key technologies

- **Blockchain**: Enables fractional ownership, digital land registries, and immutable transaction records.
- **AI and machine learning**: Predicts property values, demand trends, and buyer preferences.
- **AR/VR**: Virtual tours enhance remote property exploration and decision-making.
- **Big data analytics**: Provides insights on pricing, location trends, and consumer behavior.
- **IoT**: Enhances smart building management with automation in lighting, energy use, and security.

Major PropTech applications

- **Real estate marketplaces**: Platforms like Zillow, Magic Bricks, and 99acres digitize property listings.
- **Digital mortgages**: FinTech integration enables faster loan processing and e- signatures.
- **Real estate crowdfunding**: Allows small investors to invest in commercial and residential properties.
- **Smart contracts**: Used for lease agreements, property sales, and escrow services.

14.2.1 Propy – Blockchain innovation in real estate transactions

Propy is a US-based PropTech company that leverages blockchain technology to facilitate end-to-end digital property transactions. Targeting the inefficiencies in traditional real estate systems, Propy allows buyers and sellers – especially in cross- border contexts – to complete the full property transaction cycle online, including payment, document verification, and title transfer, without relying on intermediaries. At its core, Propy uses smart contracts to automate and secure real estate deals. The platform aims to streamline property purchases globally, reducing fraud, increasing speed, and enhancing transparency. Traditional real estate transactions are often complex, paper-intensive, and highly reliant on intermediaries such as brokers, notaries, and escrow services. Common challenges include:

- **Time-consuming cross-border transactions** with legal and procedural delays
- **Lack of transparency**, leading to increased risk of fraud or miscommunication
- **High transaction costs** due to multiple layers of intermediaries
- **Limited access** to property investment for individuals in different jurisdictions

Propy addresses these challenges by creating a **digitally native, blockchain-based platform** for real estate transactions.

Implementation:

Blockchain-enabled platform

- Propy uses blockchain technology to ensure that transaction records are immutable, timestamped, and securely stored.
- Every property deal is recorded on a distributed ledger, providing transparency and auditability.

Smart contract automation

- Legal agreements, escrow conditions, and title transfers are automated using **smart contracts**, reducing the need for human mediation.
- Once predefined conditions are met (e.g., payment received), ownership is automatically transferred.

Global marketplace

- Buyers from any part of the world can view, initiate, and complete property purchases online.
- The platform supports digital identity verification and multi-currency payments, including cryptocurrencies.

Results:

- **Faster transactions**: Real estate deals that traditionally took weeks are completed in days, thanks to automation.
- **Reduced costs**: Propy eliminates multiple intermediaries, significantly lowering transaction fees.
- **Increased trust**: Immutable blockchain records and automated smart contracts enhance security and trust between parties.
- **Cross-border accessibility**: Investors worldwide can purchase properties in different jurisdictions with reduced legal complexity.

Opportunities and barriers

Opportunities

- Democratized real estate access

  Blockchain facilitates **fractional ownership**, allowing a broader demographic to invest in property.
- Transparency and security

  Immutable digital records prevent data manipulation and reduce fraud in property registration.
- Operational efficiency

  Automated workflows streamline documentation, compliance checks, and title transfers.

Barriers

- Legal and regulatory challenges

  Many jurisdictions do not yet recognize blockchain-based title deeds or smart contracts as legally binding.
- Digital literacy

  Users in certain markets may lack the technical knowledge to navigate blockchain-based platforms.
- Integration with legacy systems

  Real estate registries and public records offices often rely on traditional, paper-based systems, complicating digital integration.

Table 14.2 Learnings and implications.

Key insight	Description
Blockchain can streamline complex sectors	Propy demonstrates how blockchain enhances efficiency and trust in property transactions.
Legal frameworks must evolve	For blockchain-based PropTech to scale globally, governments must adapt property laws and recognition of digital deeds.
Education and adoption go hand in hand	User training and public awareness campaigns are essential to bridge the digital literacy gap.
Partnerships are critical	Collaboration with real estate authorities and registries is necessary to integrate with existing infrastructure.

Propy exemplifies the transformative potential of blockchain and smart contracts in the real estate sector. By digitizing the entire transaction process, Propy enhances efficiency, transparency, and accessibility in property buying and selling. However, its long-term success will depend on the evolution of legal frameworks, improved digital literacy, and integration with legacy systems. The case of Propy serves as a foundational model for how PropTech platforms can reshape the future of global real estate.

14.3 TechFin

TechFin is a term coined by Jack Ma (Alibaba) to explain the emergence of technology-driven firms offering financial services, traditionally provided by banks and other financial institutions. Unlike FinTechs that are startups emerging from the financial industry using technology, TechFins are technology giants entering finance with existing massive user bases and robust technological infrastructure. TechFin, unlike FinTech, describes financial services driven by technology firms rather than traditional financial institutions. Large technology platforms such as Alibaba and Tencent integrate payments, lending, and wealth services within digital ecosystems [8]. TechFin firms gain a competitive advantage by leveraging massive user data, algorithmic precision, and platform reach (OECD, 2020) [9]. The rise of TechFin signifies a paradigm shift from product-based finance to embedded, ecosystem-based financial services [10]. These specialized domains contribute to global financial transformation by expanding the diversity of digital business models [11]. Regulatory agencies are adopting supervisory frameworks to address risks emerging from TechFin and other digital models [12].

Key difference:

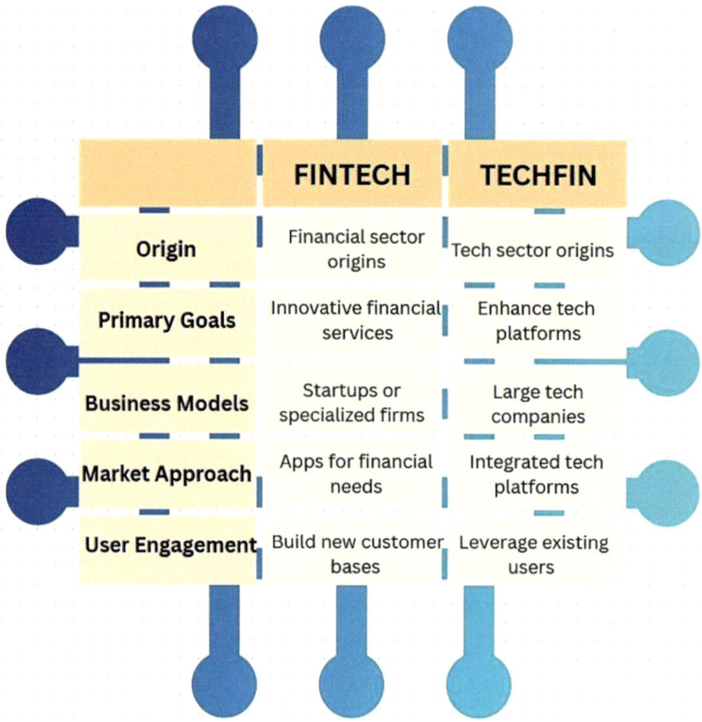

Figure 14.5 TechFin vs FinTech comparison.

FinTech = Financial company using tech

TechFin = Tech company offering financial services

Characteristics of TechFin

Platform-driven: Built on existing platforms like social media, e-commerce, or messaging apps.

Ecosystem-centric: Provides financial services as part of a broader digital ecosystem.

Data-rich: Leverages behavioral, transactional, and social data for better customer insights.

Key TechFin players

Alibaba (Ant Financial): Offers payments, lending, wealth management, and insurance via Alipay.

Amazon: Provides small business loans, digital wallets, and financial APIs.

Google Pay and Apple Pay: Offer payments, P2P transfers, and credit cards.

Facebook/Meta: Experimented with stablecoins and integrated P2P transfers in Messenger.

Advantages of TechFin

Massive scale: Billions of users can be instantly reached.

Deep data: Behavioural data aids in personalized financial product offerings.

Frictionless experience: Seamless integration of finance into digital daily life (e.g., one-click loans on e-commerce).

Regulatory concerns

Market dominance: Risk of monopolization due to market size.

Privacy issues: Combining financial and personal data raises ethical concerns.

Shadow banking risks: Operating outside traditional banking regulations.

Table 14.3 Tech Fin vs. FinTech: A comparative table.

Feature	FinTech	Tech Fin
Origin	Financial sector	Technology sector
Example companies	PayPal, Stripe, Lending Club	Amazon, Alibaba, Google
User base	Built from scratch	Pre-existing large ecosystem
Core focus	Financial innovation	Ecosystem enhancement
Data source	Financial data	Behavioral, e-commerce data

The rise of specialized FinTech domains like InsurTech, PropTech, and TechFin is reshaping the traditional boundaries between industries. Each domain responds to sector-specific challenges with innovative digital solutions, offering better efficiency, inclusivity, and customer experience. As these domains mature, regulatory frameworks and collaborative ecosystems will play crucial roles in shaping sustainable growth. International reports highlight sustained investment momentum in InsurTech, PropTech, and platform-based finance [13]. Blockchain, AI, and API-driven connectivity further accelerate innovation across these specialized FinTech verticals [14]. Collectively, these domains illustrate how FinTech is evolving into a multi-layered, platform-driven ecosystem shaping the future of financial services [15].

Figure 14.6 Area of interest for FinTech regulation.

Summary

Chapter 14 explores the evolving landscape of specialized FinTech sectors that are transforming traditional industries through technology-driven innovation. It begins with InsurTech, which enhances insurance services using data analytics, AI, and digital platforms to improve underwriting, claims processing, and customer experience. The chapter then covers PropTech, where real estate is being revolutionized by technologies like virtual property tours, blockchain-based land registries, and smart property management systems. Lastly, it introduces TechFin, a model where technology companies – rather than traditional financial firms – offer financial services by leveraging vast user data and digital ecosystems. Together, these domains highlight how FinTech is expanding beyond banking to redefine value delivery across multiple sectors.

Case Study: InsurTech – Ping A Good Doctor and the Smart Insurance Ecosystem

Ping An Insurance, one of China's largest financial conglomerates, launched Ping A Good Doctor as part of its broader digital transformation strategy aimed at modernizing insurance through health technology. This platform represents an innovative integration of telemedicine, insurance services, and artificial intelligence, offering users a one-stop digital health ecosystem. The development was driven by the need to overcome the inefficiencies of traditional insurance and healthcare models, which often involved delays, excessive paperwork, and limited personalization.

Ping A Good Doctor provides instant medical consultation through an AI-powered diagnostic system, enabling users to receive treatment recommendations in real time. This system reduces dependence on physical hospital visits for preliminary assessments, allowing doctors to focus on more complex cases. Moreover, the platform links directly with electronic health records, enabling faster claims processing and reducing administrative burdens. One of the unique features of the ecosystem is its integration with wearables and Internet of Things (IoT) devices. These tools collect health data such as blood pressure, heart rate, and physical activity in real time, which is then used to inform insurance underwriting decisions and support dynamic policy pricing based on lifestyle and risk.

The results of implementing this technology-driven model were significant. Ping An Good Doctor reached over 400 million registered users, making it one of the largest digital health platforms globally. Its use of automation and AI led to a reduction in insurance claims processing time by more than 80%, improving customer satisfaction and enabling Ping An to operate at a much lower cost structure. The integration of health data and predictive analytics has helped transition the company's insurance offering from a reactive to a preventive model, where early intervention and personalized monitoring can help avoid costly medical conditions.

While the platform has been a major success in terms of scale and innovation, it also faces some challenges. Managing sensitive health data requires robust cybersecurity measures to maintain user trust and regulatory compliance. Moreover, expanding the platform beyond China presents difficulties, including navigating different health regulations and adapting to varying levels of digital literacy. Nonetheless, Ping An Good Doctor remains a leading example of how insurance and healthcare can be reimagined through technology.

Case Discussion Questions

1. How does integrating healthcare services with insurance improve customer outcomes and operational efficiency?
2. What are the ethical considerations in using AI and wearables for underwriting insurance policies?
3. In what ways can data from wearables contribute to preventive healthcare and dynamic pricing models?
4. What challenges might Ping An face in replicating the Ping An Good Doctor model in international markets?

Case Study: PropTech – Smart Cities and Real Estate Digitization by Ping An

Ping An Group extended its digital transformation strategy into the property technology (PropTech) sector by leveraging its technological capabilities and strategic partnerships. Working through subsidiaries such as Lufax Holding and in collaboration with municipal governments, the company positioned itself at the forefront of smart city development and real estate digitization across China. Recognizing the inefficiencies and vulnerabilities in traditional real estate systems – such as property fraud, bureaucratic delays, and lack of transparency – Ping An aimed to reimagine urban development through integrated technological solutions.

The company's smart city platforms incorporate artificial intelligence and Internet of Things (IoT) sensors to manage essential urban functions. These systems enable real-time monitoring of traffic, pollution levels, energy consumption, and utility management, allowing cities to optimize their operations and improve residents' quality of life. One of the most transformative implementations was the introduction of a blockchain-based land registry system. This technology ensures that property ownership records are tamper-proof, reducing opportunities for fraud and enabling faster, more secure property transfers.

Furthermore, Ping A developed comprehensive online real estate platforms that facilitate property search, digital valuation, and mortgage processing. These services are powered by AI algorithms that provide personalized property recommendations to users, streamlining the home-buying journey. By integrating various services into a single digital platform, Ping A significantly reduced transaction times and improved access to real estate services, even in rapidly urbanizing areas.

The scale of Ping An's involvement in smart infrastructure is considerable, with operations extending to over 150 cities in China. The deployment of digital tools and secure registries has led to greater market transparency and improved liquidity in

property transactions. Although implementation at this scale presents logistical and regulatory challenges, Ping An's PropTech efforts represent a leading example of how financial and technological integration can reshape urban development.

Case Discussion Questions

1. How does Ping A use technology to improve real estate services?
2. What role does blockchain play in reducing property fraud?
3. Why is AI important in smart city platforms?
4. What challenges might Ping A face in expanding smart cities?
5. How do online real estate platforms benefit customers and cities?
6. Can Ping An's model work in other countries? Why or why not?
7. What risks come with using AI for property valuation?
8. How does PropTech support digital governance in China?

Keywords

- **InsurTech:** Refers to the application of emerging technologies – such as artificial intelligence, machine learning, big data analytics, and automation – to modernize and enhance various aspects of the insurance industry.
- **PropTech:** Short for "Property Technology," it refers to digital innovations in the real estate industry, such as virtual tours, automated valuations, and smart buildings.
- **TechFin:** Financial services offered by technology firms (e.g., Google, Amazon, Alibaba), in contrast to FinTech, which involves tech-led innovations by financial institutions.
- **Peer-to-peer (P2P) insurance:** Peer-to-peer insurance is an alternative risk-sharing model in which individuals form groups to collectively pool their premiums, thereby insuring one another.
- **Usage-based insurance (UBI):** A model where insurance premiums are calculated based on individual behavior, such as driving habits or health metrics, collected through IoT devices.
- **Claims automation:** The use of AI and digital tools to process insurance claims more efficiently, reducing human error and speeding up settlements.
- **Smart contracts:** Smart contracts are digitally encoded agreements deployed on blockchain platforms that autonomously execute and enforce the terms of a contract once specified conditions are fulfilled.

- **Real estate tokenization:** The division of real estate assets into digital tokens on a blockchain, enabling fractional ownership and easier asset transfer.
- **Virtual property tours:** Digital or VR-based walkthroughs of real estate properties that allow potential buyers or renters to explore remotely.
- **Blockchain in real estate:** The use of blockchain to securely record property transactions, ownership, and leasing agreements with transparency and tamper-proof records.
- **Real estate crowdfunding:** A model where multiple investors contribute smaller amounts of capital via online platforms to fund property development or purchase.
- **Embedded finance:** Embedded finance refers to the seamless incorporation of financial services – such as payments, credit, insurance, or investment— into non-financial digital platforms, including e-commerce applications, ride- sharing services, and social media.
- **Super apps:** multi-functional mobile applications (such as Alipay or WeChat) that combine messaging, shopping, and a wide range of financial services.
- **AI-driven credit scoring:** AI-driven credit scoring utilizes machine learning algorithms and non-traditional data sources – such as social media activity, mobile phone usage, e-commerce behavior, and utility payments – to evaluate the creditworthiness of individuals or enterprises.

Discussion Questions

1. Define InsurTech and explain its role in streamlining insurance processes.
2. What are the major technologies used in RegTech, and how do they support compliance?
3. Describe the role of robo-advisors in WealthTech.
4. How does LendingTech improve credit access for underserved populations?
5. Explain the application of blockchain in PropTech with an example.
6. What differentiates Islamic FinTech from conventional FinTech services?

7. Discuss how Green FinTech contributes to climate-conscious consumer behavior.
8. What are the main technologies powering InsurTech innovations?
9. How is blockchain used in PropTech, and what benefits does it offer?
10. Differentiate between FinTech and TechFin with examples.
11. Explain how TechFins like Alibaba or Amazon pose challenges to traditional banks.
12. What is the role of AR/VR in PropTech?

References

[1] Arner, D. W., Barberis, J. N., & Buckley, R. P. (2016). The evolution of FinTech: A new post-crisis paradigm. In D. W. Arner, J. N. Barberis, & R. P. Buckley (Eds.), *The FinTech Book* (pp. 36–42). Wiley.

[2] Nicoletti, B. (2017). *The future of FinTech: Integrating finance and technology in financial services.* Palgrave Macmillan.

[3] Deloitte. (2021). Digital transformation in insurance: InsurTech and beyond. Deloitte Insights. https://www2.deloitte.com/insights/us/en/industry/financial-services/digital-transformation-in-insurance.html

[4] Ankenbrand, T., Dietrich, A., & Bieri, D. (2022). *Fintech Study 2022: From Hype to Relevance.* Lucerne University of Applied Sciences and Arts. https://doi.org/10.13140/RG.2.2.20500.04482

[5] CB Insights. (2023). *PropTech market map: 2023.* https://www.cbinsights.com/research/report/proptech-startups-market-map/

[6] Gomber, P., Kauffman, R. J., Parker, C., & Weber, B. W. (2018). On the FinTech revolution: Interpreting the forces of innovation, disruption, and transformation in financial services. *Journal of Management Information Systems, 35*(1), 220–265. https://doi.org/10.1080/07421222.2018.1440766

[7] Ziegler, T., Shneor, R., Garvey, K., Wenzlaff, K., Hao, R., & Zhang, B. (2020). *The Global FinTech Ecosystem Report.* Cambridge Centre for Alternative Finance.

[8] Zetzsche, D. A., Buckley, R. P., Arner, D. W., & Barberis, J. N. (2017). From FinTech to TechFin. *NYU Journal of Law and Business, 14*(2), 393–446.

[9] OECD. (2020). *The impact of digital transformation on competition in financial markets.* OECD Competition Committee.

[10] Arner, D. W., Barberis, J. N., & Buckley, R. P. (2016). The evolution of FinTech.

[11] Lee, I., & Shin, Y. J. (2018). Fintech: Ecosystem, business models, investment decisions, and challenges. *Business Horizons, 61*(1), 35–46. https://doi.org/10.1016/j.bushor.2017.09.003

[12] FCA. (2020). *Regulatory technology: Artificial Intelligence in financial services.* Financial Conduct Authority.

[13] KPMG. (2022). *Pulse of Fintech H2 2022.* KPMG International.

[14] World Economic Forum. (2015). *The future of financial infrastructure: How blockchain can reshape financial services.*

[15] Chishti, S., & Barberis, J. (2016). *The FinTech Book: The financial technology handbook for investors, entrepreneurs and visionaries.* Wiley.

15

FinTech in Audit, Compliance, and Capital Market

Abstract

This chapter examines the transformative influence of financial technology (FinTech) on audit, compliance, and capital markets – three pillars that sustain trust, transparency, and efficiency in the global financial system. Rapid advances in automation, artificial intelligence (AI), blockchain, and predictive analytics are reshaping how institutions manage risk, monitor transactions, conduct audits, and maintain regulatory adherence. FinTech applications are enabling real-time oversight, reducing manual errors, accelerating reporting cycles, and enhancing fraud detection capabilities through intelligent, data-driven systems. Simultaneously, capital markets are undergoing significant digital modernization, with algorithmic trading, tokenization, distributed ledger technologies (DLT), and digital asset platforms redefining how securities are issued, traded, and settled. By analyzing both operational advancements and emerging challenges, this chapter provides a comprehensive understanding of how FinTech is modernizing conventional financial processes while preparing institutions for a more automated, transparent, and resilient market environment.

Introduction

The integration of FinTech within audit, compliance, and capital markets represents one of the most impactful shifts in the evolution of traditional finance. Historically, these functions relied heavily on manual procedures, lengthy documentation, and fragmented information systems. Today, technologies such as robotic process automation (RPA), machine learning (ML), big data analytics, and blockchain are enabling organizations to monitor

DOI: 10.1201/9788743811244-20

risks continuously, verify transactions instantly, and ensure regulatory compliance with unprecedented accuracy. In the realm of audit and compliance, intelligent automation is streamlining data extraction, anomaly detection, and regulatory reporting, making these processes more agile, scalable, and resilient. Capital markets, meanwhile, are witnessing a digital transformation through innovations like high-frequency trading algorithms, crypto exchanges, tokenized assets, and real-time settlement mechanisms powered by DLT. As financial services become increasingly digitized and interconnected, this chapter aims to explore how FinTech is reshaping these critical sectors, the benefits it introduces, and the challenges it poses in ensuring stability, governance, and ethical technology adoption. FinTech-enabled RegTech solutions now automate compliance monitoring and streamline risk reporting in financial institutions [1]. The evolution of FinTech has introduced new regulatory expectations that influence how audit and compliance functions operate [2].

15.1 Audit and Compliance Automation

The integration of FinTech into the financial services sector has significantly transformed traditional audit and compliance functions through automation, making these processes faster, more accurate, and more transparent. Historically, auditing and compliance involved manual procedures, periodic reviews, and retrospective analysis, which were time-consuming and prone to human error. With the emergence of FinTech, technologies such as artificial intelligence (AI), machine learning (ML), robotic process automation (RPA), and blockchain have enabled real-time, continuous auditing and proactive compliance management. FinTech has introduced the concept of **continuous auditing**, where financial transactions and controls are monitored on an ongoing basis, allowing organizations to detect anomalies, fraud, and regulatory breaches as they occur. This represents a shift from the traditional end-of- period audits to a more dynamic and predictive approach. For instance, AI algorithms can analyze patterns across large datasets to flag unusual activities that could indicate money laundering or internal fraud. Similarly, ML models learn from historical compliance data to predict potential regulatory risks, enabling organizations to take preemptive action. The Basel committee on banking supervision emphasizes that FinTech innovations require banks to upgrade internal controls and compliance frameworks [3]. A prominent area where FinTech has driven automation is regulatory compliance, giving rise to what is known as **RegTech (Regulatory Technology)**. RegTech solutions automate critical compliance functions such as know your customer (KYC), anti-money laundering (AML), and transaction monitoring. Platforms like Trulioo and ComplyAdvantage exemplify this shift. Trulioo offers real-time digital identity verification across global databases, helping banks comply with KYC norms while ensuring smooth customer onboarding. ComplyAdvantage uses AI and natural language processing (NLP) to screen clients and transactions against sanctions lists, politically exposed persons (PEPs), and adverse media, enabling institutions to detect and prevent financial crimes more efficiently. These tools not only reduce manual workload but also ensure that compliance frameworks are updated automatically in response to regulatory changes. Another landmark development is the use of Blockchain technology in audit automation, particularly for tracking and verifying digital assets. PwC's "Halo for Blockchain" tool, for example, enables auditors to independently verify cryptocurrency balances and transactions directly from blockchain networks, bringing transparency and assurance to crypto audits. In addition, cloud-based platforms like KPMG Clara represent the new frontier in automated auditing. Blockchain and automation tools are transforming traditional audit procedures by enabling transparent and reliable data trails [4]. This platform combines data analytics, AI, and real-time collaboration tools to support end-to-end digital audits. It allows auditors to work interactively with clients, access real-time data feeds, and apply analytics to highlight key risk areas, thereby improving audit quality and efficiency. Overall, the automation of audit and compliance through FinTech offers multiple benefits: enhanced accuracy, reduced human error, improved regulatory adherence, cost savings, and faster audit cycles. However, it also presents new challenges such as data privacy risks, cybersecurity threats, and the need for ongoing updates in response to changing regulatory landscapes. Despite these concerns, the trajectory of audit and compliance automation driven by FinTech is clearly upward, offering a paradigm shift in how financial integrity and regulatory assurance are maintained in the digital age. As financial ecosystems grow more complex and digitized, FinTech's role in automating these core governance functions will become increasingly indispensable. Advanced analytics and intelligent automation are reshaping audit methodologies and enhancing audit quality [5]. Digital technologies are redefining financial oversight structures and strengthening risk controls across institutions [6]. FinTech-driven automation improves the efficiency of compliance functions by reducing human error and manual processing [7]. AI and data-driven tools support auditors in detecting anomalies faster and enhancing fraud monitoring processes [8].

15.1.1 Use cases of audit and compliance automation

Audit and compliance functions have traditionally been manual, labor-intensive, and retrospective processes in financial services. However, the rise of financial technology (FinTech) has significantly transformed these areas by introducing automation, real-time monitoring, and data-driven decision-making tools. Audit automation involves the use of software tools and algorithms to automatically review, analyze, and report on financial records and transactions. Compliance automation refers to the use of technology to monitor adherence to laws, regulations, and internal policies in real time or near real time. FinTech tools integrate artificial intelligence (AI), machine learning (ML), robotic process automation (RPA), and blockchain to bring speed, accuracy, and transparency to audit and compliance operations. These technologies are reshaping how financial institutions detect fraud, report financials, and maintain regulatory integrity.

Real-time transaction monitoring

- Continuously monitor financial transactions for anomalies or suspicious patterns.
- Automate alerts for potential fraud or AML violations.
- Used in banks, payment gateways, and digital wallets.

Automated KYC/AML screening

- Digitally verify customer identity using national databases and document scanning.
- Screen customers against sanctions lists, PEPs, and negative media.
- Common in onboarding for banks, NBFCs, and FinTech platforms.

Regulatory reporting automation

- Automatically generate and submit compliance reports (e.g., tax, capital adequacy).
- Ensure timely submission to regulators like RBI, SEBI, or global agencies (FATF, SEC).
- Reduces human error and increases accountability.

Smart audit trails

- Maintain immutable digital logs (often using blockchain) of financial and operational activities.
- Enhances traceability for both internal and external audits.

- Useful in accounting firms, crypto exchanges, and ERP systems.

Policy and risk compliance monitoring
- Track adherence to internal policies and industry regulations (GDPR, PCI-DSS, etc.).
- Identify and flag non-compliant behavior proactively.
- Employed in compliance-heavy sectors like insurance and wealth management.

Expense and reimbursement auditing
- Use RPA to match expense claims with receipts and company policy.
- Prevents fraud and speeds up approval workflows.
- Popular in corporate finance and HR audit functions.

Third-party and vendor risk management
- Automate due diligence and compliance checks on suppliers or partners.
- Monitor third-party behavior for ongoing compliance.
- Important in procurement, FinTech lending, and outsourcing firms.

Cybersecurity and data privacy compliance
- Automate risk scanning and privacy regulation compliance checks.
- Ensure continuous alignment with data protection laws like GDPR, CCPA, or India's DPDP Act.
- Crucial for digital banks, SaaS firms, and online brokers.

Tax compliance and reconciliation
- Automatically validate invoices, GST records, and TDS deductions.
- Reconcile tax filings with financial ledgers.
- Used by e-commerce platforms, SMEs, and accounting firms.

Cryptocurrency auditing
- Real-time audit of blockchain-based transactions and crypto wallets.
- Used to ensure asset ownership, prevent illicit activities, and meet digital asset regulations.
- Deployed by firms using tools like PwC's Halo for Blockchain.

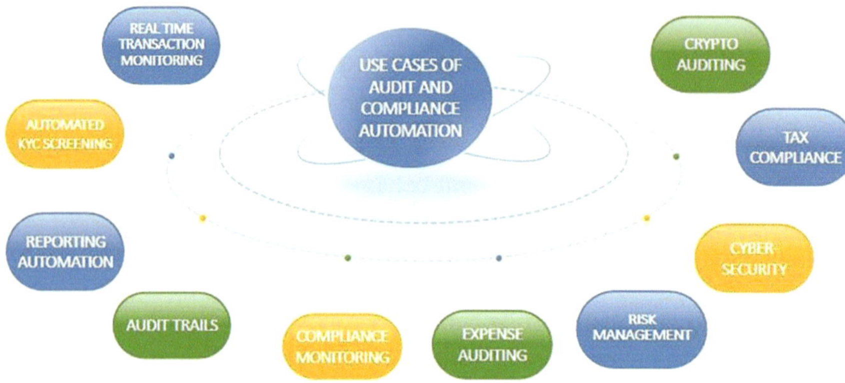

Figure 15.1 Use cases of audit and compliance automation.

KPMG Clara: KPMG Clara is a next-generation digital audit platform developed by KPMG International. It is part of the firm's efforts to transform traditional audit methodologies by embedding data analytics, cloud computing, and AI-driven risk assessment tools into the audit process.
Type: Audit platform **Function**: Cloud-based automation of financial auditing using data analytics, AI, and real-time collaboration.
Key features: • **Continuous auditing**: Allows real-time access to client financial data, enabling auditors to spot trends, anomalies, or risks throughout the year – not just at the end of a reporting period. • **Data analytics integration**: Leverages big data tools to analyze vast datasets for risk indicators, transaction anomalies, and financial inconsistencies. • **AI-powered insights**: Clara uses AI to guide auditors toward areas of highest risk, improving **audit quality and efficiency**. • **Collaboration portal**: Auditors and clients can interact within a single secure platform, streamlining communication and documentation.
The major advantages of using this platform are reducing audit cycle time, improving regulatory compliance, and increasing transparency and accountability.

PwC's Halo for Blockchain: PwC Halo for Blockchain is a suite of tools developed by PricewaterhouseCoopers (PwC) to support audits of companies dealing with cryptocurrencies and blockchain-based assets.
Type: Blockchain audit tool **Function**: Real-time auditing and verification of digital assets and blockchain transactions.

Key features:

- **Validates ownership and transaction history** of digital currencies like Bitcoin and Ethereum.
- **Connects directly to blockchain nodes**, allowing auditors to confirm balances and transactions independently.
- **Reconciles blockchain activity** with financial statements to ensure accuracy and integrity.

It is used in auditing crypto exchanges, digital asset firms, and blockchain startups. It also ensures clients are not involved in fraudulent or non-compliant crypto activities. It brings trust and transparency to blockchain environments, helps auditors meet assurance standards in a rapidly evolving digital asset space, and also sets new benchmarks in digital-era financial auditing.

15.1.2 Challenges faced by the audit and compliance department in the FinTech era

In the FinTech ecosystem, the audit department plays an essential role in maintaining financial integrity, ensuring compliance, and managing risks. With the increasing reliance on technology, auditors must evolve their practices to address the challenges posed by digital systems, cybersecurity risks, and regulatory compliance. By effectively leveraging data analytics, AI, and machine learning, auditors in FinTech companies can provide more proactive and insightful assessments of the financial and operational risks, ensuring that FinTech firms operate securely, transparently, and in line with legal requirements.

- **Rapid technological changes:** The fast pace of innovation in FinTech, with the introduction of blockchain, AI, big data, and cloud computing, creates challenges for auditors in understanding and auditing these complex systems. They must stay up to date with technological advances to effectively assess the risks and controls associated with new technologies.
- **Cybersecurity and fraud prevention:** With the increasing frequency and sophistication of cyberattacks, cybersecurity remains a significant concern for FinTech auditors. Ensuring that data is secure and financial transactions are protected is a key responsibility, requiring auditors to constantly assess and adapt to evolving cyber threats.
- **Data privacy and compliance:** As FinTech companies deal with vast amounts of sensitive data, auditors must ensure compliance with

stringent data privacy laws (e.g., GDPR). They also need to ensure that the company's systems are equipped to handle sensitive financial information securely.

- **Regulatory complexity**: FinTech companies often operate across multiple regions, each with different regulatory requirements. The audit department must navigate these regulatory complexities to ensure compliance with local, national, and international laws. The constantly changing nature of financial regulations also means auditors need to stay up to date with the latest requirements.

Figure 15.2 Challenges faced by audit department.

Case Study: Trulioo – Powering Global Identity Verification for Compliance in FinTech

Introduction

Founded in 2011 in Vancouver, Canada, Trulioo has emerged as a leading Regulatory Technology (RegTech) firm that enables companies to meet complex compliance, audit, and KYC/AML requirements across international jurisdictions. At its core, Trulioo provides electronic identity and business verification through its flagship product, GlobalGateway, allowing financial institutions, online marketplaces, and digital platforms to onboard customers securely, verify identities in real-time, and remain compliant with local and global regulations. Trulioo operates as a B2B SaaS platform, offering cloud-based API services that connect companies to over 400 trusted data sources across 100+ countries. It supports both individual and business verification through a unified platform that ensures speed, scalability, and regulatory compliance.

Key service areas include:

- **Identity verification (IDV)**: Real-time verification of personal identity using official data such as government ID records, voter lists, utility records, and mobile data.
- **Business verification (KYB)**: Automated know your business checks using global business registries to verify legal entities, ownership structure, and ultimate beneficial owners (UBOs).
- **Document verification**: OCR and AI-based document capture and validation for passports, driver's licenses, etc.
- **AML watchlist screening**: Checks against global sanctions, politically exposed persons (PEP) lists, and criminal databases.
- **Compliance automation**: Streamlines onboarding flows, record keeping, and audit trails to reduce human error and regulatory risk.

Use case in audit and compliance FinTech

Trulioo plays a critical role in enabling FinTechs, banks, cryptocurrency exchanges, and lenders to adhere to increasingly complex and evolving audit and compliance demands. It helps Trulioo's real-time screening and verification help organizations satisfy regulatory frameworks such as **FATF**, **FinCEN**, **GDPR**, and **eIDAS**. All verification and screening activities are automatically logged, timestamped, and stored in compliance-ready formats for auditing purposes. Early-stage identity checks prevent account fraud, money laundering, and synthetic identity creation. What once took days can now be done in minutes, significantly enhancing customer experience without compromising regulatory rigor. Trulioo leverages AI, machine learning, OCR, API integration, and blockchain-friendly identity standards to offer scalable, intelligent verification. Its cloud-native infrastructure ensures global reach with GDPR-compliant data handling and encryption.

Trulioo offers several key technical advantages that strengthen its position as a global leader in digital identity verification. Its GlobalGateway API enables seamless integration with financial platforms and apps through a single plug-in, simplifying compliance processes across jurisdictions. The use of AI and machine learning enhances fraud detection by identifying unusual patterns and generating anomaly alerts, while real-time notifications help internal audit teams respond swiftly to potential compliance risks or discrepancies. In terms of recent developments, Trulioo achieved unicorn status in 2021 after raising $394 million in Series D funding, pushing its valuation beyond $1.75 billion. The company has since expanded its offerings to include advanced biometric verification tools, anti-money laundering (AML) monitoring dashboards, and know-your-business (KYB) solutions tailored for small enterprises. Looking ahead, Trulioo plans to implement AI-powered risk scoring models and explore interoperability with blockchain-based digital identity systems, aiming to enhance both scalability and trust in global compliance ecosystems.

Trulioo stands as a cornerstone in the RegTech and compliance FinTech space, enabling businesses to build trust, efficiency, and auditability into their customer onboarding and regulatory reporting processes. It proves how digital identity verification and compliance automation can mitigate risks, reduce fraud, and ensure adherence to financial laws – all while enhancing the customer experience. As financial ecosystems grow more complex and global, Trulioo's case illustrates the rising importance of intelligent compliance technology in maintaining ethical, legal, and operational integrity.

Case Discussion Questions

1. How does Trulioo's global identity verification platform help FinTech companies address compliance challenges in multiple jurisdictions, and what trade-offs might arise between regulatory adherence, user experience, and cost?
2. In what ways could Trulioo's reliance on diverse data sources raise concerns about data privacy, ethical use, and algorithmic fairness, and how should the company balance accuracy with protection of individual rights?
3. What potential risks or limitations exist when FinTechs outsource identity verification to third-party providers like Trulioo, and how can firms mitigate issues related to vendor dependency and system resilience?

15.2 Securities Trading and Capital Markets in the FinTech Ecosystem

The **securities trading** and **capital markets** industry is undergoing a profound transformation, largely driven by the rise of financial technology

(FinTech). With the rapid digitization of trading platforms, automation, and the advent of innovative technologies, FinTech is reshaping how securities are traded, how capital is raised, and how market participants interact with financial markets. These changes are resulting in more efficient, transparent, and accessible financial markets, providing both retail and institutional investors with new tools to navigate the complex world of securities trading and capital markets. Capital markets increasingly rely on algorithmic trading and digital platforms to optimize transaction speed and liquidity [9]. FinTech ecosystems provide new business models that influence audit, compliance, and trading operations [10]. Integrated finance-technology systems are enabling more transparent and efficient compliance environments in traditional sectors [11]. Digital transformation in capital markets is enhancing operational resilience and data transparency [12].

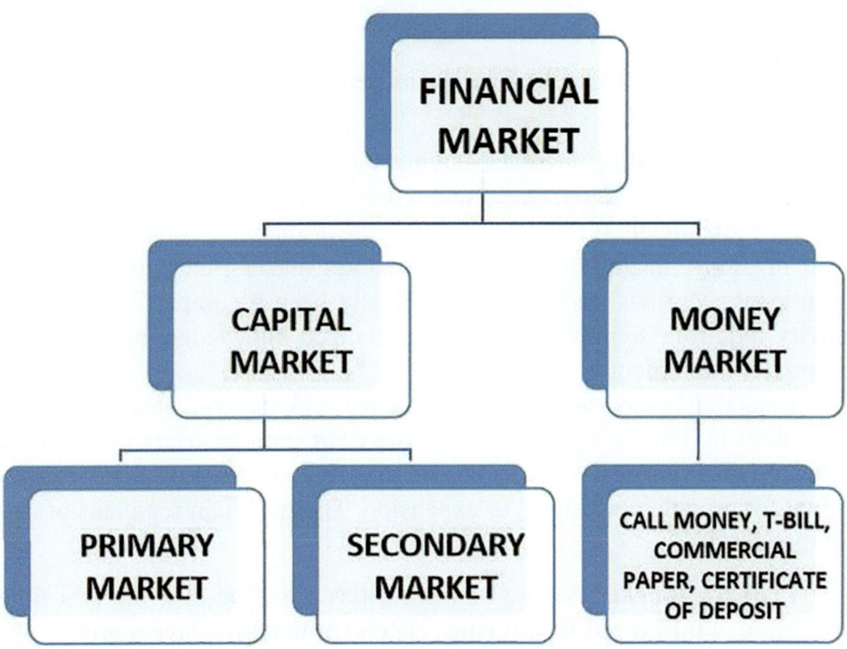

Figure 15.3 Types of financial market.

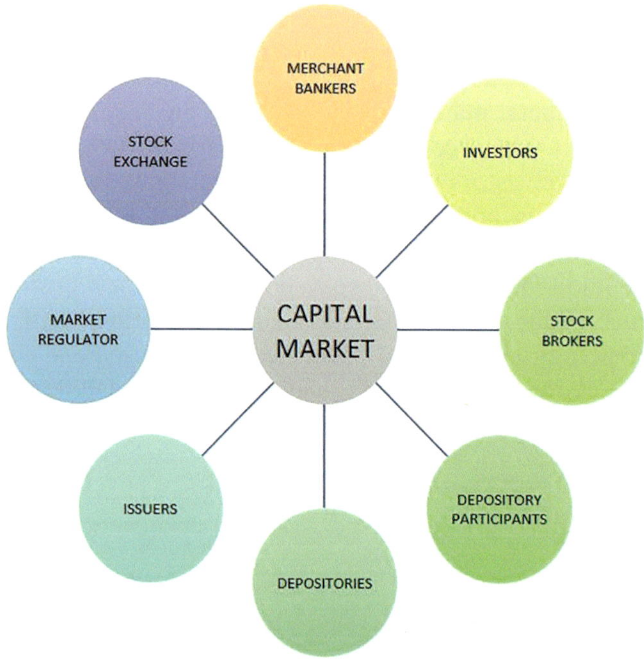

Figure 15.4 Capital market components.

Securities trading involves buying and selling financial instruments like stocks, bonds, derivatives, and commodities on various exchanges or over-the-counter (OTC) markets. The primary participants include retail investors, institutional investors, market makers, and broker-dealers. Traditional securities trading has historically been a complex, high-barrier activity requiring significant capital, specialized knowledge, and access to expensive infrastructure.

Capital markets are where companies and governments raise long-term funds by issuing **equity** (stocks) and **debt** (bonds). They facilitate the exchange of securities between buyers and sellers, enabling firms to raise capital for growth, operations, or expansion. The two main segments of capital markets are:

- **Primary market**: Where new securities are issued for the first time, often in **initial public offerings (IPOs)** or **private placements**.
- **Secondary market**: Where previously issued securities are bought and sold by investors.

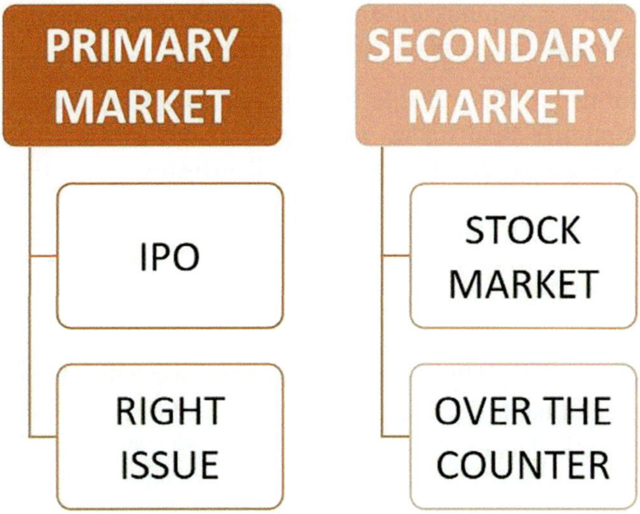

Figure 15.5 Primary and secondary market.

15.3 Impact of FinTech on Securities Trading

FinTech has introduced **digitalization**, **automation**, and **artificial intelligence (AI)** to the securities trading landscape, significantly altering how markets function. Here are several key ways in which FinTech is influencing the trading and investment ecosystem:

15.3.1 Digital trading platforms

One of the most significant innovations in FinTech has been the development of **digital trading platforms** that allow individuals and institutions to buy and sell securities without the need for traditional brokerage firms. These platforms are typically **cloud-based** and accessible via mobile apps and websites, enabling users to trade **stocks**, **options**, **cryptocurrencies**, and other financial instruments with greater ease. Some of the most notable digital trading platforms include:

- **Robinhood**: A popular app for commission-free stock trading, attracting millions of retail investors.
- **eToro**: A social trading platform that allows users to trade stocks, ETFs, and cryptocurrencies while copying the strategies of successful traders.

- **Freetrade**: A commission-free trading platform focused on equities and exchange-traded funds (ETFs) in the UK.

These platforms use **algorithmic trading** and **machine learning (ML)** to help users optimize their trades, and they have lowered the entry barriers to **securities trading**, enabling more **retail investors** to participate in the markets.

15.3.2 Robo-advisors

Robo-advisors are AI-driven platforms that provide automated, algorithm-based financial planning and investment advice. These platforms analyze a user's financial goals, risk tolerance, and time horizon, then automatically create and manage a diversified portfolio of securities. Examples of robo-advisors include Betterment, Wealthfront, and Nutmeg. These platforms democratize investment management by providing low-cost and customized portfolios that were previously available only to high-net-worth individuals. Robo-advisors help investors access capital markets with minimal effort and lower fees, as they do not require human intermediaries, such as financial advisors.

15.3.3 High-frequency trading (HFT)

High-frequency trading (HFT) refers to the use of advanced algorithms and high- speed data networks to execute a large number of orders at extremely high speeds. In the past, HFT was limited to institutional investors with access to costly infrastructure. However, with the development of cloud computing and access to sophisticated software, HFT has become more accessible.FinTech firms specializing in algorithmic trading and quantitative finance use HFT strategies to take advantage of minute price fluctuations in securities markets. Firms such as Two Sigma and Citadel are known for utilizing cutting-edge trading algorithms. HFT is widely used in capital markets to improve liquidity, reduce transaction costs, and enhance price discovery. It also increases the complexity of market dynamics and raises concerns about the potential risks of market manipulation or flash crashes.

15.3.4 Blockchain and tokenized securities

One of the most promising FinTech innovations in securities trading is blockchain technology. Blockchain enables decentralized and immutable transaction records, which enhances transparency, reduces fraud, and cuts down on the time and cost associated with traditional securities trading.

Security token offerings (STOs): Blockchain has made the tokenization of securities possible, enabling the issuance of digital representations of traditional securities like stocks and bonds. Security tokens can be traded on blockchain- based platforms, providing increased liquidity and reducing intermediaries like brokers and custodians.

Decentralized exchanges (DEXs): DEXs like Uniswap and SushiSwap allow the trading of digital assets and tokenized securities without a centralized authority, enhancing liquidity and enabling more efficient market functioning.

By providing a decentralized and transparent ledger, blockchain can fundamentally change the way capital markets function, enabling faster, more secure, and cost- effective securities trading.

15.3.5 Impact of FinTech on capital markets

FinTech is also transforming the broader capital markets, particularly in terms of **capital raising**, **market access**, and **investor participation**.

Crowdfunding and peer-to-peer (P2P) lending

Crowdfunding platforms, such as **Kickstarter**, **Indiegogo**, and **GoFundMe**, allow entrepreneurs and startups to raise capital directly from individuals. Similarly, **P2P lending platforms** such as **LendingClub** and **Prosper** enable individuals to lend money directly to borrowers, bypassing traditional banks and financial institutions.

Equity crowdfunding: FinTech platforms like **Crowdcube** and **Seedrs** allow small businesses to raise funds by offering equity to the public. This gives investors the opportunity to participate in early-stage ventures and access **private equity** markets.

Peer-to-peer lending: P2P platforms match borrowers and lenders directly, offering alternative funding sources outside traditional banking channels. This has revolutionized the **debt capital markets**, enabling faster and more efficient **capital allocation**.

Digital assets and cryptocurrencies

The rise of **cryptocurrencies** such as **Bitcoin**, **Ethereum**, and **Ripple** has disrupted traditional capital markets. These digital currencies provide an alternative to traditional **fiat currency** and offer new opportunities for investment, trading, and capital raising.

Initial coin offerings (ICOs): ICOs are fundraising mechanisms in which new cryptocurrency or token-based projects issue digital tokens to investors in exchange for capital. Similar to IPOs, ICOs have allowed startups to access funding outside traditional equity markets.

Security token offerings (STOs): As mentioned earlier, STOs allow companies to issue tokenized representations of traditional securities, opening new avenues for raising capital while maintaining compliance with securities regulations.

15.3.6 Robo-trading and artificial intelligence

Artificial intelligence (AI) and machine learning (ML) are increasingly being used to optimize trading strategies in capital markets. FinTech companies are developing AI-driven systems that can analyze vast amounts of data, identify market trends, and execute trades automatically with minimal human intervention.

Quantitative hedge funds: Hedge funds like Renaissance Technologies use advanced AI algorithms and quantitative strategies to manage vast amounts of data and generate consistent returns in the capital markets.

AI and ML improve efficiency by helping institutional investors and traders make faster, more informed decisions while reducing human error.

FinTech has radically transformed the securities trading and capital markets landscape by introducing digital platforms, automation, blockchain, and AI. These innovations have democratized access to capital markets, reduced transaction costs, increased market liquidity, and allowed for faster and more efficient trading. As a result, retail investors now have more opportunities to participate in financial markets, while institutional investors are leveraging advanced technologies to enhance their trading strategies.

Moving forward, FinTech will continue to push the boundaries of capital market innovation, facilitating smarter trading, more secure transactions, and greater market transparency. However, the increased use of technology also raises challenges related to regulation, security, and market volatility, which will need to be addressed as the ecosystem evolves.

Robinhood: Revolutionizing commission-free trading

Robinhood is a financial technology company that offers a commission-free trading platform primarily focused on stocks, options, cryptocurrencies, and exchange-traded funds (ETFs). It was founded in 2013 by Vlad Tenev and

Baiju Bhatt with the mission of democratizing finance and making it accessible to everyone. The app is particularly popular among millennials and retail investors due to its user-friendly interface, no-fee structure, and easy access to financial markets.

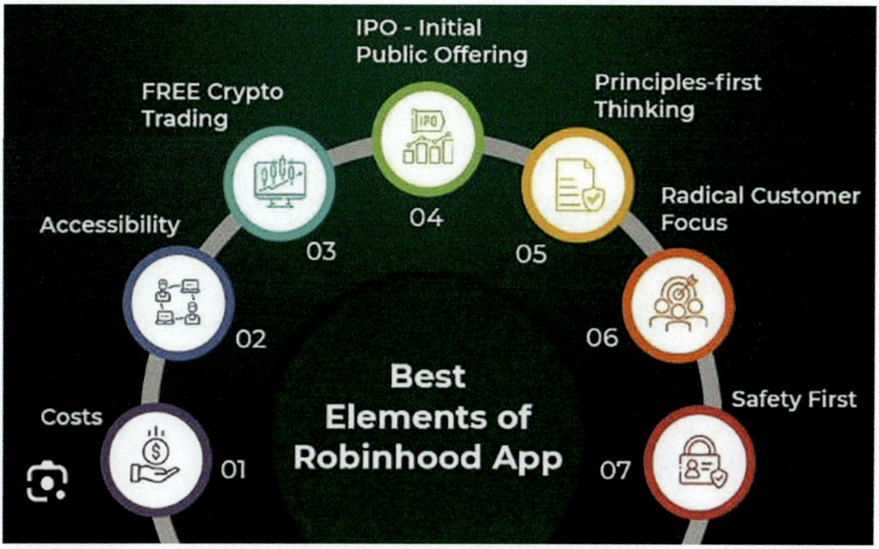

Figure 15.6 Robinhood app.

Key features of Robinhood

- **Zero commission fees**: Robinhood disrupted the traditional brokerage model by eliminating commissions on stock and ETF trades, which are typically charged by established brokerage firms like Charles Schwab or TD Ameritrade. This **zero-commission** approach allowed retail investors to trade without incurring the same level of fees that traditionally made investing expensive, particularly for small investors.
- **Fractional shares**: Robinhood allows users to buy fractional shares of stocks, meaning investors can purchase partial ownership of a stock rather than needing to buy a whole share. This makes high-priced stocks like Amazon and Tesla more accessible to small investors who might not have the capital to buy full shares.
- **Cryptocurrency trading**: In addition to traditional securities, Robinhood also offers commission-free trading for cryptocurrencies such as Bitcoin, Ethereum, and Dogecoin. This is a major draw for cryptocurrency enthusiasts, especially since many cryptocurrency exchanges charge substantial fees for trading.

- **Mobile app and user experience**: Robinhood's platform is primarily mobile-based, allowing users to trade from their smartphones with ease. The app is designed with simplicity in mind, offering a streamlined, intuitive user interface that appeals to both beginner and experienced investors.
- **Robinhood Gold**: For users looking to access additional features, Robinhood offers a **premium subscription** service called Robinhood Gold. This includes benefits like margin trading, extended hours trading, and access to research reports.

Business model and revenue generation

While Robinhood offers free trades, it still generates revenue through several alternative methods:

- **Payment for order flow (PFOF)**: Robinhood makes money by routing trades through market makers and receiving compensation for this order flow. While this practice has been controversial, as critics argue it could lead to conflicts of interest, it allows Robinhood to offer free trades without charging commissions.
- **Interest on cash balances**: Robinhood earns interest on uninvested cash sitting in users' accounts.
- **Margin trading fees**: Robinhood charges interest on margin loans provided to users who subscribe to **Robinhood Gold**.

Robinhood has played a crucial role in popularizing commission-free trading, forcing traditional brokerage firms to adapt and reduce their own trading fees. It has also made investing more accessible to a broader audience, particularly younger generations who may not have previously considered investing due to high fees. However, Robinhood has faced criticism, particularly over issues related to gamification, user protection, and the GameStop saga in early 2021, where the platform restricted trades on GameStop and other stocks during a massive short squeeze. Despite these controversies, Robinhood remains a prominent player in the retail investing space.

eToro: Social trading and investment platform

eToro is a social trading platform that allows users to trade various financial instruments, including stocks, ETFs, cryptocurrencies, commodities, and currencies. Founded in 2007 in Israel by Yoni Assia, Ronnen Ben-Cohen, and David Ring, eToro has grown to become one of the largest and most well-known social trading platforms globally. The company aims to democratize trading by combining traditional investing with social interaction.

Key features of eToro:

- **Social trading (CopyTrading)**: eToro is best known for its **social trading** features, particularly its **CopyTrading** functionality. This allows users to **copy the trades of successful investors** in real-time, essentially automating the process of investing by mimicking the strategies of top traders. Users can view the performance, risk profile, and portfolio details of professional traders before deciding to copy their strategies.
- **Wide range of assets**: eToro provides access to a wide variety of **assets**, including stocks, **ETFs**, **cryptocurrencies** (such as Bitcoin, Ethereum, and Litecoin), **commodities**, and **currencies**. This variety makes eToro a one-stop platform for investors seeking diverse investment opportunities.
- **Commission-free trading**: Similar to Robinhood, eToro offers **commission-free trading** for stocks and ETFs. However, it does charge spreads (the difference between the buying and selling price) on certain assets, such as cryptocurrencies and commodities.
- **Cryptocurrency trading**: eToro has established itself as one of the largest platforms for **cryptocurrency trading**, offering a broad range of digital assets. eToro allows users to trade and invest in cryptocurrencies with ease, making it particularly popular among beginners looking to enter the crypto market.
- **Mobile app and social feed**: eToro's mobile app includes a **social feed** that allows users to share updates, strategies, and market insights with others. This creates a community-driven environment where investors can collaborate, learn, and interact with one another.

Business model and revenue generation

eToro makes money primarily through:

- **Spreads**: eToro generates income from the **spread** (the difference between the buy and sell price) when users execute trades, particularly in **cryptocurrencies** and **commodities**.
- **Fees for withdrawals and inactivity**: eToro charges a **fee for withdrawals** from the platform and a **monthly inactivity fee** if an account is dormant for a certain period.

- **Interest on leverage**: eToro also charges interest on **leverage**, which allows users to trade with borrowed funds.

eToro's social trading model has redefined how people approach investing. It appeals to both beginners and experienced investors, enabling them to leverage the expertise of professional traders. By making investing a social activity, eToro has helped democratize financial markets and has made trading more transparent. Additionally, its integration of cryptocurrency trading has positioned it as a major player in the rapidly growing crypto space. Market modernization driven by FinTech adoption impacts competitiveness and regulatory alignment [13]. The rapid expansion of FinTech applications is reshaping audit planning and execution procedures across industries [14]. Disruptive digital technologies are altering financial market structures and influencing regulatory strategies globally [15].

Summary

In summary, FinTech has become a powerful catalyst in transforming audit operations, compliance functions, and capital market infrastructures. The adoption of automation and AI has made audits more efficient, data-driven, and predictive, while RegTech solutions are helping institutions navigate complex and evolving regulatory landscapes with ease. Technologies such as blockchain and advanced analytics are improving the integrity of records, reducing fraud, and supporting real-time monitoring and reporting. In capital markets, FinTech innovations from algorithmic trading to tokenized securities have enhanced liquidity, broadened investor participation, and accelerated settlement cycles, contributing to more open, efficient, and transparent markets. Clear definitions of FinTech help auditors and regulators better categorize technological risks and compliance needs [16]. Big data analytics enhances the auditor's ability to process complex datasets and identify risk patterns [17]. FinTech innovations introduce new competitive dynamics that affect capital market operations and compliance expectations [18]. Regulatory challenges continue to intensify as financial institutions adopt advanced technologies in trading and audit environments [19]. Despite the numerous advantages, challenges remain, including cybersecurity risks, integration issues with legacy systems, and regulatory uncertainties. Overall, the chapter emphasizes that FinTech's impact on traditional financial functions is profound and ongoing, highlighting the need for continuous innovation and strategic adaptation to harness its full potential.

Case Study: Freetrade: Commission-Free Equity and ETF Trading in the UK

Freetrade is a commission-free trading platform that provides users with the ability to trade stocks and exchange-traded funds (ETFs) without paying any fees. Founded in 2016 in London, Freetrade aims to democratize investing by making it easier and more affordable for UK investors to access the stock market. It is one of the prominent FinTech startups that have emerged in the UK, disrupting traditional brokerage models by focusing on simplicity and transparency.

Key features of Freetrade:

- **Commission-free trading**: Freetrade offers commission-free trading on a wide range of stocks and ETFs listed in the UK and US markets. This makes it attractive to retail investors who want to avoid the high commissions charged by traditional brokers. However, users who require access to advanced features may opt for a premium subscription.
- **Fractional shares**: Freetrade also allows users to invest in fractional shares, similar to Robinhood. This means users can buy a fraction of a share of high- priced stocks like Amazon or Tesla, making it more accessible to people with limited capital.
- **Easy-to-use mobile app**: Freetrade's platform is designed to be simple and user-friendly, with a mobile-first approach. Its clean interface makes it easy for beginners to get started with investing, while still offering the functionality needed by more experienced investors.
- **Freetrade Plus**: For users who want access to additional features such as market research, advanced tools, and the ability to trade more stocks and ETFs, Freetrade offers a premium subscription plan called Freetrade Plus. This plan also gives users access to ISA (Individual Savings Account) trading and the ability to invest in foreign stocks.
- **Safety and security**: Freetrade is regulated by the Financial Conduct Authority (FCA) and is a member of the Financial Services Compensation Scheme (FSCS), ensuring that users' funds are protected up to a certain limit in case of insolvency.

Freetrade generates revenue through the premium subscription service, which is a significant revenue stream, offering additional features and services to subscribers. Also, when trading international stocks, users may incur currency conversion fees, and like many trading platforms, Freetrade can generate income from holding uninvested cash in users' accounts. Freetrade has gained significant traction in the UK due to its low-cost structure and focus on transparency. As one of the first platforms to offer commission-free trading in the UK, it has pushed other traditional brokerage firms to re-evaluate their pricing structures, making investing more affordable for the average consumer. Freetrade's approach has also been influential in the growing trend of retail investing in the UK. All three platforms Robinhood, eToro, and Freetrade are redefining the landscape of securities trading by making it more accessible, affordable, and user-friendly. They have empowered millions of retail investors, especially young and tech-savvy individuals, to participate in financial markets that were once dominated by institutional investors. Each of these platforms leverages unique business models, such as commission-free trading, social trading, and fractional share investments, to attract new users and foster a culture of democratized finance. By focusing on innovation, transparency, and low costs, these platforms are driving the FinTech revolution in the securities trading and investment space.

Case Discussion Questions

1. How does Freetrade's commission-free model challenge traditional brokerage firms, and what long-term implications might this have for the broader financial services industry in the UK?
2. While Freetrade promotes affordability and accessibility, what ethical and financial risks could arise from encouraging inexperienced users to engage in active stock trading without fees?
3. What regulatory and technological safeguards should platforms like Freetrade implement to ensure user education, transparency, and responsible investing in a digital-first environment?

Keywords

- **Non-banking financial companies (NBFCs):** Financial institutions that provide banking services without holding a banking license, often focusing on loans and asset financing.

- **Digital lending platforms:** Online systems that enable quick loan application, approval, and disbursal using automated credit scoring and data analytics.
- **Robotic process automation (RPA):** Technology that automates repetitive and rule-based tasks such as audit checks and compliance reporting.
- **Compliance automation:** Use of software tools to ensure financial institutions adhere to regulatory requirements efficiently and accurately.
- **Algorithmic trading:** Automated trading using computer algorithms to execute orders at high speed and volume based on preset criteria.
- **Blockchain in capital markets:** Distributed ledger technology used to improve transparency, security, and settlement speed of trades and transactions.
- **Digital exchanges:** Online platforms that facilitate the buying and selling of securities electronically, enhancing market access and reducing costs.
- **Credit risk analytics:** Analytical techniques that assess the likelihood of borrower default using big data and machine learning.
- **Regulatory Technology (RegTech):** Technologies designed to help organizations comply with regulations more effectively.

Discussion Questions

1. What are the key benefits and challenges of implementing audit and compliance automation in financial institutions?
2. In what ways has algorithmic trading transformed securities markets, and what risks does it pose?
3. How can blockchain technology improve transparency and efficiency in capital markets?
4. What role does RegTech play in helping traditional sectors manage complex regulatory environments?
5. How do digital lending platforms affect financial inclusion, especially for underserved populations?
6. What are the implications of increased automation on jobs in audit and compliance departments?

7. How do digital exchanges differ from traditional stock exchanges in terms of operations and investor experience?

8. What measures should be taken to mitigate cybersecurity risks associated with digital transformation in traditional sectors?

9. How can traditional financial institutions balance innovation with regulatory compliance in adopting FinTech solutions?

References

[1] Accenture. (2020). *Driving compliance and risk transformation with RegTech*. Accenture Financial Services. https://www.accenture.com

[2] Arner, D. W., Barberis, J. N., & Buckley, R. P. (2016). The evolution of FinTech: A new post-crisis paradigm. In S. Chishti & J. Barberis (Eds.), *The FinTech Book* (pp. 36–42). Wiley.

[3] Basel Committee on Banking Supervision. (2018). *Sound practices: Implications of fintech developments for banks and bank supervisors*. Bank for International Settlements. https://www.bis.org

[4] Chishti, S., & Barberis, J. (Eds.). (2016). *The FinTech Book: The financial technology handbook for investors, entrepreneurs and visionaries*. Wiley.

[5] Deloitte. (2021). *The future of audit: Transforming audit through technology*. Deloitte Insights. https://www2.deloitte.com

[6] Dorfleitner, G., Hornuf, L., Schmitt, M., & Weber, M. (2017). *FinTech in Germany*. Springer.

[7] Ghosh, S. (2020). Fintech and the transformation of the financial industry. In D. A. Zetzsche et al. (Eds.), *The Palgrave Handbook of Technological Finance* (pp. 27–44). Palgrave Macmillan.

[8] Gomber, P., Kauffman, R. J., Parker, C., & Weber, B. W. (2018). On the fintech revolution: Interpreting the forces of innovation, disruption, and transformation in financial services. *Journal of Management Information Systems, 35*(1), 220–265. https://doi.org/10.1080/07421222.2018.1440766

[9] Gomber, P., Sagade, S., & Weber, M. C. (2020). Digital finance and capital markets – The future of trading. *Journal of Applied Corporate Finance, 32*(4), 36–48. https://doi.org/10.1111/jacf.12371

[10] Lee, I., & Shin, Y. J. (2018). FinTech: Ecosystem, business models, investment decisions, and challenges. *Business Horizons, 61*(1), 35–46. https://doi.org/10.1016/j.bushor.2017.09.003

[11] Nicoletti, B. (2017). *The future of FinTech: Integrating finance and technology in financial services*. Palgrave Macmillan.
[12] OECD. (2021). *The digital transformation of banking and capital markets*. Organisation for Economic Co-operation and Development. https://www.oecd.org
[13] Philippon, T. (2019). *The great reversal: How America gave up on free markets*. Harvard University Press.
[14] Puschmann, T. (2017). Fintech and financial services: Initial results of a structured literature review. *Journal of Financial Services Research, 51*(1), 95–116. https://doi.org/10.1007/s10693-017-0278-0
[15] PwC. (2022). *Financial services technology 2022 and beyond: Embracing disruption*. PricewaterhouseCoopers. https://www.pwc.com
[16] Schueffel, P. (2016). Taming the beast: A scientific definition of fintech. *Journal of Innovation Management, 4*(4), 32–54.
[17] Vasarhelyi, M. A., Kogan, A., & Tuttle, B. (2015). Big data in accounting: An overview. *Accounting Horizons, 29*(2), 381–396. https://doi.org/10.2308/acch-51071
[18] World Economic Forum. (2017). *Beyond Fintech: A pragmatic assessment of disruptive potential in financial services*. https://www.weforum.org
[19] Zetzsche, D. A., Buckley, R. P., Arner, D. W., & Barberis, J. N. (2017). From FinTech to TechFin: The regulatory challenges. *Journal of Financial Regulation, 3*(1), 75–105. https://doi.org/10.1093/jfr/fjx002

UNIT 6

Regulation, Supervision, and Governance

16

Regulation in FinTech

Abstract

This chapter provides a comprehensive overview of the regulatory landscape governing the FinTech ecosystem, with a focus on both Indian and global frameworks. It begins by identifying key regulatory bodies such as the Reserve Bank of India (RBI), Securities and Exchange Board of India (SEBI), Financial Conduct Authority (FCA), European Central Bank (ECB), and the U.S. Securities and Exchange Commission (SEC), among others, outlining their respective roles in monitoring, guiding, and shaping the FinTech environment.

The chapter critically examines regulatory initiatives that influence FinTech innovation and operational compliance, including data protection laws, anti-money laundering (AML) directives, payment regulations, and consumer protection norms. Special attention is given to the concept of regulatory sandboxes, which serve as controlled environments for FinTech experimentation. The benefits, such as fostering innovation, minimizing risk exposure, and improving regulatory understanding, are discussed alongside limitations like scalability concerns and jurisdictional constraints.

A core focus is placed on the rise of smart regulation, where technology is leveraged to improve regulatory oversight through tools like real-time data analytics, AI-based fraud detection, and automated reporting systems. This naturally leads into a deep dive into the Regulatory Technology (RegTech) ecosystem, where the interplay between regulators, financial institutions, technology providers, and compliance officers is unpacked. The chapter emphasizes how RegTech enables more agile, transparent, and effective compliance through innovation.

To ground these concepts in practice, the chapter presents case studies of successful RegTech implementations, highlighting how specific firms and regulators have adopted technologies to streamline compliance and enhance

DOI: 10.1201/9788743811244-22

regulatory collaboration. Overall, this chapter equips readers with a strategic and practical understanding of FinTech regulation, balancing the imperative for innovation with the necessity of robust oversight in an increasingly digital and data-driven financial world.

Introduction

As FinTech reshapes the landscape of traditional financial services, regulators globally are confronted with the dual challenge of promoting technological innovation while safeguarding consumer interests, preserving market integrity, and maintaining overall financial system stability. FinTech regulation encompasses the legal frameworks, policy guidelines, and oversight mechanisms designed to govern the operations of financial technology firms and ensure responsible innovation. This chapter explores the regulatory landscape of FinTech, its global approaches, challenges, and future directions. It emphasizes the need for balance between innovation and risk mitigation. In today's dynamic financial landscape, adhering to regulatory mandates has become more intricate and resource-intensive. The rapid expansion of FinTech has further amplified the demand for flexible, technology- enabled compliance mechanisms. Regulatory technology (RegTech) has consequently emerged as a pivotal innovation, offering financial institutions advanced tools to streamline risk management, ensure legal compliance, and facilitate more efficient interactions with regulatory authorities. This chapter explores the evolution, significance, and future trajectory of RegTech, tracing its development from manual regulatory processes to real-time, automated, and intelligent compliance frameworks.

16.1 Global Regulatory Bodies in FinTech

Global regulatory bodies play a crucial role in overseeing the safe and ethical growth of the FinTech industry by setting international standards and guidelines. Organizations such as the Financial Action Task Force (FATF) develop rules to combat money laundering and terrorist financing, while the International Organization of Securities Commissions (IOSCO) focuses on protecting investors and ensuring fair markets. The Basel Committee on Banking Supervision (BCBS) provides guidelines for capital adequacy and risk management, especially relevant for digital banks and lenders. In the European Union, regulations like Markets in Crypto-Assets (MiCA) and Revised Payment Services Directive (PSD2) aim to foster innovation while ensuring consumer protection. These global efforts help harmonize regulations, reduce systemic risks, and create a safer environment for FinTech innovation and cross-border financial services. Regulation in FinTech has evolved as digital finance expands rapidly, demanding new frameworks to ensure stability and innovation [1]. Global regulatory bodies increasingly focus on harmonizing standards to oversee cross-border digital finance activities [2]. International coordination is essential, as FinTech innovations often outpace traditional regulatory mechanisms [3]. Regulatory bodies such as the FCA, EU Commission, and FSB play critical roles in shaping modern FinTech oversight [4].

These regulatory institutions establish standards, guidelines, and frameworks to promote responsible innovation while protecting consumers, preventing financial crime, and maintaining financial stability. Below are some of the key global regulatory bodies and their roles in the FinTech ecosystem:

16.1.1 Financial Action Task Force (FATF)

The **FATF** is an intergovernmental organization that sets global standards to combat money laundering, terrorist financing, and other financial crimes. In the context of FinTech, the FATF has issued guidance on regulating virtual assets (VAs) and virtual asset service providers (VASPs), requiring them to implement know your customer (KYC) and anti-money laundering (AML) measures. One of its key policies is the travel rule, which mandates that crypto exchanges share information about the sender and receiver during digital asset transfers.

16.1.2 Basel Committee on Banking Supervision (BCBS)

The **Basel Committee**, part of the Bank for International Settlements (BIS), develops global banking standards like Basel III, which aims to strengthen bank capital and manage risk. As FinTech firms increasingly enter lending, payments, and banking services, these standards help ensure that digital banks and non-bank financial institutions maintain financial soundness and resilience.

16.1.3 International Organization of Securities Commissions (IOSCO)

IOSCO oversees the regulation of securities markets globally and provides principles for fair, efficient, and transparent markets. It has issued guidance on the use of technologies in securities issuance and trading, particularly focusing on initial coin offerings (ICOs), security tokens, and digital exchanges, ensuring investor protection and market integrity in FinTech-related activities.

16.1.4 International Monetary Fund (IMF) and World Bank

The **IMF** and **World Bank** support FinTech adoption globally by helping countries develop financial inclusion strategies and build regulatory capacity. They provide research, funding, and policy advice on areas like digital payments, central bank digital currencies (CBDCs), and inclusive financial technologies, especially in emerging markets.

16.1.5 European Union (EU) – MiCA and PSD2

Within the EU, regulatory initiatives such as Markets in Crypto-Assets Regulation (MiCA) and Revised Payment Services Directive (PSD2) aim to create a unified framework for FinTech. MiCA regulates crypto-assets, stablecoins, and service providers, ensuring transparency, risk control, and consumer protection. PSD2 promotes open banking by requiring banks to share customer data securely with third- party providers (with user consent), encouraging competition and innovation in financial services.

16.1.6 Financial Stability Board (FSB)

The **FSB** monitors and makes recommendations about the global financial system to avoid systemic risks. It closely examines the potential threats posed by FinTech innovations such as **stablecoins**, **DeFi**, and **BigTechs** entering finance. The FSB helps coordinate policies among countries to ensure financial innovation does not lead to instability or regulatory blind spots.

Global regulatory bodies ensure that FinTech innovations align with principles of security, fairness, and market stability. By creating consistent international standards, these institutions help prevent **regulatory arbitrage** (where companies exploit gaps in different jurisdictions), protect consumers, and promote cross-border cooperation. As FinTech grows in complexity and scale, these global regulators will continue to play a vital role in shaping a secure and inclusive financial future.

16.1.7 Collaboration and standardization

Cross-border collaboration

Global FinTech requires harmonized regulation. Organizations like **G20**, **FATF**, and **IOSCO** promote shared principles on:

- Cross-border payments
- Cybersecurity

- Crypto-asset taxation
- Anti-money laundering

Public-private partnerships

Collaborative FinTech frameworks are being developed where regulators work with startups to ensure compliance by design.

Challenges for regulators

- Rapid technological evolution
- Regulatory arbitrage (operating in loosely regulated jurisdictions)
- Cross-border data flow restrictions
- Cybersecurity threats
- Balancing innovation and risk management

Regulatory bodies – both in India and globally – are instrumental in shaping the FinTech landscape. While they must ensure safety and fairness, they are also increasingly fostering innovation through sandbox programs, collaborative frameworks, and RegTech tools. As FinTech matures, global cooperation and adaptive regulation will be critical to its sustainable growth.

16.2 Key Regulatory Initiatives in FinTech

Key regulatory initiatives in FinTech have been introduced globally to ensure innovation is balanced with safety, transparency, and consumer protection. One of the most significant is the European Union's Revised Payment Services Directive (PSD2), which mandates open banking by requiring banks to provide secure access to customer data through APIs, thereby encouraging competition and enabling new financial services. Similarly, the EU's Markets in Crypto-Assets (MiCA) regulation establishes a unified legal framework for cryptocurrencies and digital assets, aiming to protect investors and support innovation across member states. In the United States, the Securities and Exchange Commission (SEC) regulates digital asset offerings and trading platforms, ensuring compliance with securities laws, while the Commodity Futures Trading Commission (CFTC) supervises crypto derivatives and commodities. The Financial Action Task Force (FATF) has introduced global standards for anti-money laundering (AML) and counter-terrorism financing (CTF), including the "Travel Rule" for virtual asset service providers, which requires the sharing of customer data during transactions. Countries like Singapore have pioneered regulatory sandboxes, allowing FinTech firms to test innovative products under controlled conditions. Additionally, the Basel III framework guides digital banks on capital adequacy and risk management, reinforcing financial stability. Initiatives like the General Data Protection Regulation (GDPR) in the EU have also shaped how FinTechs handle personal data, emphasizing user privacy, consent, and data security. Collectively, these regulatory efforts aim to create a secure and inclusive digital financial ecosystem while addressing risks such as fraud, cyber threats, and systemic vulnerabilities. The EU's Digital Finance Strategy represents a comprehensive approach to governing digital financial services across member states [5]. Many jurisdictions now emphasize technology-neutral regulations to support innovation while maintaining consumer protection [6]. Key global initiatives include risk-based supervision, open banking rules, and cybersecurity mandates [7].

As FinTech evolves, regulators are proactively introducing policies, frameworks, and initiatives to balance innovation with risk management, consumer protection, and financial stability. These initiatives are designed to provide regulatory clarity, support innovation, and ensure compliance with global standards. This chapter outlines major regulatory initiatives at both the Indian and global levels that shape the FinTech landscape. It includes frameworks for digital lending, cybersecurity, cryptocurrency, digital identity, and sandbox environments. Example: Indian Regulatory Initiatives: The Reserve Bank of India (RBI) issued comprehensive guidelines to regulate digital lending platforms and apps.

Figure 16.1 Roles and functions of RBI.

Key features:

- **Loan disbursal** and **repayment** must occur directly between the borrower and regulated entities (REs), not intermediaries.
- **Transparency mandate**: Lenders must disclose **annual percentage rate (APR)**, terms and conditions, and charges.
- **Consent-based data collection**: Personal data collection must be explicit and limited.
- **Grievance redressal** mechanisms are mandatory.
- Introduction of the **cooling-off period** and a **key fact statement (KFS)** for borrowers.

Impact:

- Reduced predatory lending
- Improved consumer trust in digital loan apps
- Better integration of NBFCs and FinTech startups into formal regulatory channels

Account aggregator (AA) framework

Launched by the **Financial Stability and Development Council (FSDC)**, and regulated by **RBI**, the **AA framework** enables individuals to share their financial data securely across institutions.

Key features:

- Consent-based data sharing enables the secure exchange of financial information between financial information providers (FIPs) and financial information users (FIUs), contingent upon the explicit approval of the data owner. This model promotes data privacy, transparency, and user control within digital financial ecosystems.
- Promotes open banking and data empowerment
- Reduces reliance on physical documents

Impact:

- Facilitates **credit access for MSMEs**
- Enables real-time risk assessment for lenders

- Boosts innovation in **wealth management** and **personal finance tools**

Global regulatory initiatives

- **PSD2 (Revised Payment Services Directive – EU)**
  The Revised Payment Services Directive (PSD2) is a European Union regulation aimed at fostering open banking by requiring banks to provide secure access to customer account information through application programming interfaces (APIs) for authorized third-party providers (TPPs), thereby encouraging innovation and competition in the financial sector.

Key features:

- **Strong customer authentication (SCA)**
- Mandatory use of **APIs** by banks
- **Consent-driven** data access by FinTech's
- Separation of **data ownership** from banks

Impact:

- Catalysed open banking in Europe
- Improved competition in financial services
- Led to global inspiration (e.g., India's Account Aggregator)

FATF's travel rule for crypto

The financial action task force (FATF) implemented the travel rule to strengthen oversight in the virtual asset sector. Under this guideline, virtual asset service providers (VASPs) are obligated to collect, verify, and transmit information regarding both the originator and the beneficiary of digital asset transactions. This requirement aligns with broader efforts to enforce anti-money laundering (AML) and counter- terrorism financing (CTF) standards across jurisdictions.

Impact:

- Reduced anonymity in crypto transactions
- Enabled compliant crypto infrastructure

- Improved cross-border traceability

Financial Stability Board (FSB) global guidelines

The **FSB** released guidance for **global stablecoins** and **crypto assets**, addressing:

- Financial stability risks
- Operational resilience
- Governance structures
- Regulatory cooperation among countries

SEC and CFTC initiatives (USA)

- **SEC** oversees **initial coin offerings (ICOs)**, DeFi platforms, and securities tokens
- **CFTC** regulates **crypto futures and derivatives**

Both agencies are increasingly:

- Enforcing disclosure requirements
- Conducting audits of digital asset companies
- Issuing **no-action letters** for specific FinTech cases

Monetary Authority of Singapore (MAS) initiatives

Singapore's MAS has launched:

- **FinTech Regulatory Sandbox Plus**
- **Project Ubin** (blockchain-based interbank payments)
- **Project Orchid** (retail CBDC exploration)

MAS fosters innovation through **clear regulations**, **regulatory clarity**, and **international cooperation.**

Key regulatory initiatives are instrumental in shaping a robust, secure, and inclusive FinTech ecosystem. India, alongside global bodies, is actively creating **progressive policies**, **data-sharing frameworks**, and **risk control mechanisms** to support responsible innovation. Continued collaboration between governments, regulators, and private players will be essential for FinTech's sustainable future.

16.3 Regulatory Sandboxes in FinTech

The accelerated pace of innovation in financial technologies has often outstripped the ability of traditional regulatory systems to adapt. In response, the Regulatory Sandbox model has emerged as a practical solution to close the gap between regulation and innovation. These sandboxes provide a controlled and supervised space where FinTech companies can pilot novel financial products, services, or business models without immediately being subjected to the full spectrum of regulatory requirements. Regulatory sandboxes allow firms to test innovative products under controlled environments, reducing market-entry barriers [8]. Sandboxes have expanded globally as a tool to balance experimentation with investor protection [9]. Studies highlight that sandboxes foster responsible innovation and align regulators with technological change [10].

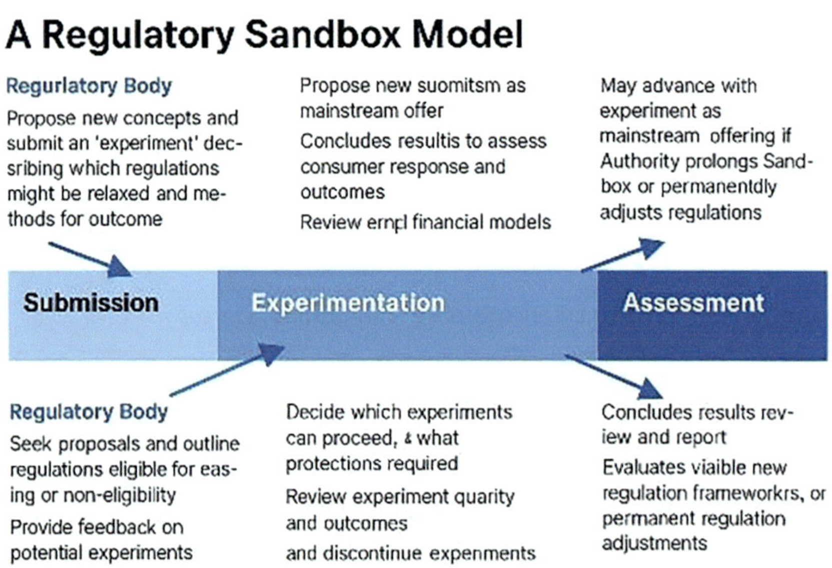

Figure 16.2 A regulatory sandbox model.

Globally adopted by financial authorities, Regulatory Sandboxes are designed to foster innovation while upholding critical policy goals such as consumer protection, financial system stability, and regulatory compliance.

A regulatory sandbox is a structured framework established by a financial regulatory authority that permits FinTech startups and other technology-driven innovators to test their solutions in real-world conditions, under regulatory oversight but with temporary relaxations or exemptions from standard rules. This approach allows for live experimentation while enabling regulators to monitor emerging risks and gather insights into the implications of new technologies on the financial ecosystem.

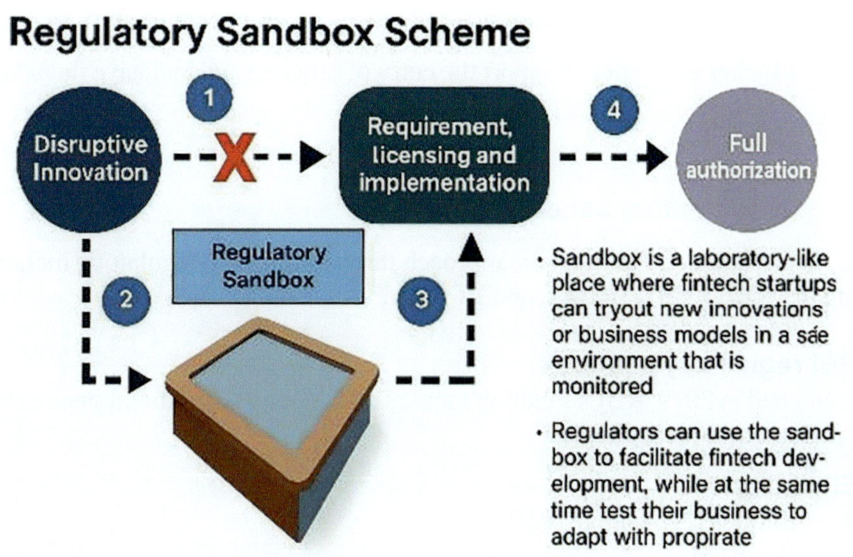

Figure 16.3 Regulatory sandbox scheme.

Key characteristics:

- **Limited timeframe**: Testing is allowed for a fixed period.
- **Controlled environment**: Experiments are limited in scale and participants.
- **Regulatory relaxation**: Some regulatory requirements are temporarily relaxed.
- **Close monitoring**: Regulators observe performance and risks in real-time.

16.3.1 Objectives of regulatory sandboxes

- **Encourage innovation**: Allow experimentation with new technologies, products, and delivery mechanisms.
- **Consumer protection**: Ensure safety mechanisms are in place while products are being tested.
- **Policy development**: Help regulators better understand new business models.
- **Risk mitigation**: Contain potential financial and operational risks.
- **Market efficiency**: Support the entry of efficient and inclusive financial services.

16.3.2 Regulatory sandboxes in India

India has adopted the sandbox approach through multiple regulators, including the **RBI, SEBI, IRDAI**, and **PFRDA**.

RBI regulatory sandbox

Launched in 2019, RBI's sandbox focuses on **innovative financial products, services, and technologies**.

Eligibility:

- Entities regulated by RBI
- Startups, banks, NBFCs, and tech firms
- Product must demonstrate **genuine innovation** and **public interest**

Notable themes:

- **Retail payments**
- **Cross-border payments**
- **Digital KYC**
- **Blockchain in finance**
- **Fraud prevention systems**

Procedure:

- **Application phase**
- **Selection and evaluation**

- **Testing in sandbox**
- **Exit and feedback reporting**

Outcome:
- Promoted UPI innovation and e-mandate features
- Enabled testing of API-based lending and biometric KYC models

SEBI innovation sandbox

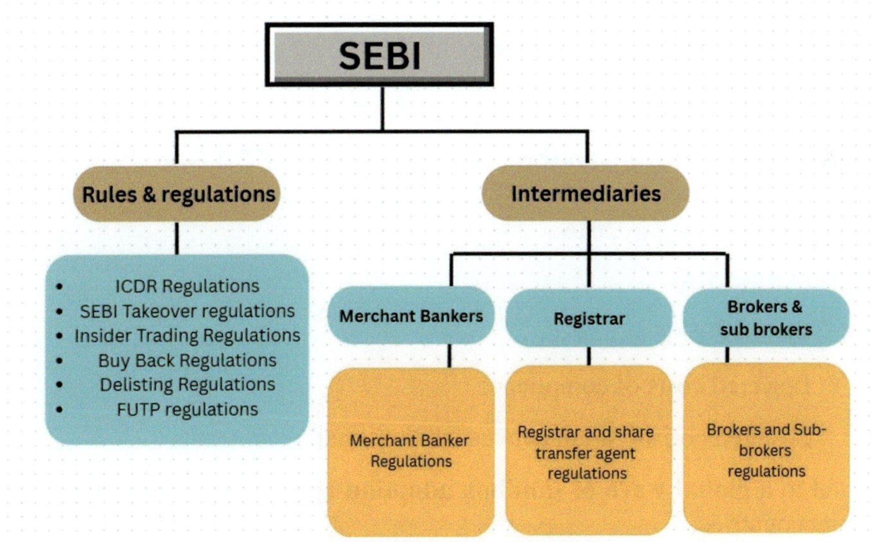

Figure 16.4 SEBI roles and regulation.

SEBI's sandbox, launched in 2020, provides market participants with **access to securities market data** for:
- Developing **algorithms**
- Testing **investment advisory tools**
- Building **trading and compliance systems**

Focus areas:
- Robo-advisory
- Algo-trading

- Regulatory reporting tools

IRDAI regulatory sandbox

IRDAI's sandbox, initiated in 2019, encourages **InsurTech experimentation** in:

- **Usage-based insurance**
- **On-demand policies**
- **Telematics and wearable-based underwriting**
- **AI chatbots for claims processing**

IRDAI allows **regulatory flexibility** for 6 to 12 months with monitored customer groups.

Global Regulatory Sandbox Initiatives: UK's FCA Sandbox

The **UK's Financial Conduct Authority (FCA)** introduced the world's first regulatory sandbox in **2016**.

Achievements:

- Reduced time to market
- Lowered costs of compliance
- Fostered collaboration between startups and incumbents

It led to a **global wave of sandbox adoption** and served as a blueprint for many countries.

Monetary Authority of Singapore (MAS)

MAS's sandbox framework is **industry-friendly and flexible**, aimed at:

- Digital payments
- Cross-border remittances
- Tokenized securities
- Digital identity solutions

Sandbox Express allows **fast-track approvals** for certain low-risk FinTech products.

Global Financial Innovation Network (GFIN)

Formed by over **60 regulators worldwide**, GFIN enables:

- Cross-border sandbox testing
- **Regulatory cooperation**
- Knowledge-sharing on FinTech regulation

This supports **interoperable FinTech regulation** across countries.

Table 16.1 Benefits of regulatory sandboxes.

Benefit	Description
Innovation enablement	Encourages experimentation in emerging areas like AI, blockchain, and IoT in finance.
Consumer safety	Limit exposure to untested risks through regulatory oversight.
Policy learning	Helps regulators frame informed and dynamic policies.
Faster time to market	Helps startups launch products without long delays from regulatory red tape.
Cost reduction	Reduces initial compliance burden on early-stage firms.

Challenges and criticisms

- **Limited scalability**: Testing environments do not always simulate real-world complexity.
- **Regulatory arbitrage**: Firms may exploit relaxed regulations.
- **Data privacy risks**: User data used during sandbox testing must be protected.
- **Entry barriers**: Application and selection processes can be complex.
- **Uncertain outcomes**: Products may fail after exiting the sandbox due to market or regulatory constraints.

Regulatory sandboxes represent a powerful tool for shaping the future of financial services. They not only support responsible innovation but also enable regulators to proactively adapt to new technologies. For FinTech entrepreneurs, sandboxes serve as an essential stepping stone to market readiness, while ensuring consumer interests are safeguarded. Marketplace insights show FinTech firms benefiting from sandbox participation through faster licensing and reduced compliance uncertainties [11].

Table 16.2 The rise and regulation of Revolut in the UK and EU.

Revolut, a UK-based digital bank founded in 2015, began as a simple currency exchange app and evolved into a fully-fledged FinTech "super app." As it grew, Revolut faced increasing regulatory scrutiny from multiple jurisdictions.

Regulatory challenges

- **Licensing:** Initially operated under an e-money license from the UK's FCA; later applied for a full banking license in the UK and EU.
- **AML/KYC compliance**: The organization encountered regulatory scrutiny due to deficiencies in its anti-money laundering (AML) and know your customer (KYC) protocols, particularly during periods of rapid expansion.
- **Data privacy regulations**: The company was mandated to adhere to the European Union's General Data Protection Regulation (GDPR), necessitating stringent controls over the collection, processing, and storage of user data.
- **Cross-border compliance:** Operating in multiple jurisdictions raised challenges in complying with varying financial and tax regulations.

Regulatory milestones

- **2018:** Obtained a European banking license from the Bank of Lithuania, allowing Revolut to passport banking services across the EU.
- **2021:** Applied for a UK banking license post-Brexit.
- **2022–2023:** Engaged with the Financial Conduct Authority (FCA) and Prudential Regulation Authority (PRA) over internal audit weaknesses.

Impact and outcome

- Significantly strengthened compliance and internal controls.
- Adopted **RegTech tools** for real-time monitoring and fraud detection.
- Adjusted organizational structure to satisfy cross-border banking rules.

BASIS	**GDPR**	**PDPA**
Territorial Scope	Applies to European Union(EU) and EEA countries and to any Organisation that process data of EU Citizens.	Applies to Singapore and any Organisation outside Singapore that process data of Singapore Citizens.
Definition of personal data	Broad definition that includes any information related to an identified or identifiable person.	Narrower definition that includes only data about individuals.
Data Protection Officer Requirement	Required for certain businesses.	Optional for businesses
Rights of Data Subjects	Individuals have rights to be informed about how their data is being processed and also have right to data portability which means they can request a copy of their data.	PDPA does not inform individuals how their data is being processed and also doesn't have right to data portability.

Figure 16.5 GDPR vs PDP Bill (India) comparison.

16.4 RegTech

Regulatory Technology (RegTech) involves the application of advanced digital technologies to optimize, automate, and modernize regulatory compliance processes within the financial industry. By leveraging tools such as data analytics, artificial intelligence, machine learning, blockchain, and cloud computing, RegTech enables institutions to effectively manage regulatory reporting, monitor risks, and ensure adherence to evolving legal requirements. RegTech has emerged as a parallel field that enhances regulatory compliance through automation and analytics [12]. Advances in AI help financial institutions detect anomalies and reduce compliance burdens significantly [13]. RegTech solutions increasingly rely on machine learning, NLP, and big data to streamline reporting and monitoring [14]. Industry reports show that RegTech adoption accelerates in response to rising regulatory complexity worldwide [15].

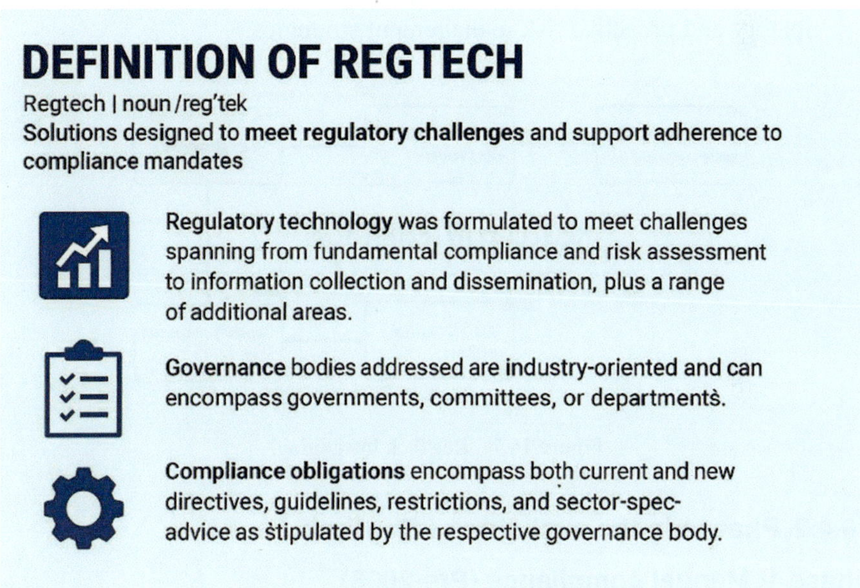

Figure 16.6 Definition of RegTech.

16.4.1 Drivers behind the emergence of RegTech Post-2008 Financial Crisis

Regulations

- Introduction of Dodd-Frank Act, MiFID II, Basel III, etc.
- Increased compliance requirements and monitoring.

Data explosion

- There is a growing necessity to handle large-scale, real-time processing of both structured and unstructured financial data to support timely decision-making and regulatory compliance.

Complexity and cost of compliance

- Rising costs in maintaining compliance departments and legal resources.

Technological advancements

- Availability of cloud infrastructure, APIs, real-time data feeds, and AI/ML capabilities.

Pressure from regulators

- Demand for **transparency**, **real-time reporting**, and facilitating anticipatory and proactive risk management strategies.

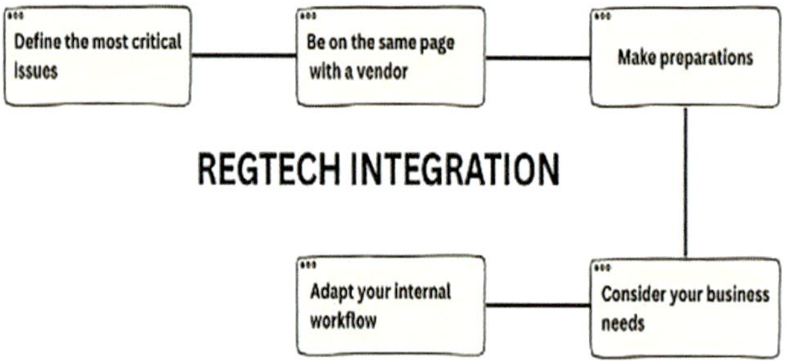

Figure 16.7 RegTech Integration.

16.4.2 Phases in the evolution of RegTech

Phase 1: Manual compliance (Pre-2008)

- Paper-based filings, spreadsheets, and static databases.
- Reliance on human compliance officers.
- Reactive and post-facto risk management.

Phase 2: Digital transformation (2008–2015)

- Introduction of **digitized compliance software**.
- Regulatory Information Management (RIM) tools.

- Automated document processing, archiving, and audit trails.

Phase 3: Emergence of RegTech (2015–2020)

- Coined formally in 2015 by the UK's FCA.
- Startups began offering **cloud-based, scalable, and real-time compliance tools**.
- Regulatory bodies began **digitizing rulebooks** and adopting API-based submissions.

Phase 4: Intelligent RegTech (2020–present)

- Integration of **AI, NLP, blockchain, and big data** into RegTech platforms.
- Shift from static compliance to **predictive and real-time monitoring**.
- Use of chatbots, robotic process automation (RPA), and fraud detection engines.

Phase 5: RegTech 5.0 (Emerging)

- **Hyper-automation**, self-regulating smart contracts, and **continuous compliance**.
- Integration with supervisory technology **(SupTech)**.
- Regulatory sandboxes fostering RegTech pilots.

Table 16.3 Core components and functions of RegTech.

Function	Technology used	Examples
Regulatory reporting	APIs, cloud systems	AxiomSL, Vizor, BearingPoint
Identity verification	Biometrics, KYC-AML Algorithms	Trulioo, Onfido, Jumio
Risk and compliance analytics	AI/ML, predictive analytics	Ayasdi, Quantifind
Transaction monitoring	Pattern recognition, RPA	Actimize, FICO, ComplyAdvantage
Regulatory change management	NLP, real-time notifications	Ascent RegTech, ClauseMatch
Document and data management	OCR, blockchain, Data Lakes	Chainalysis, Elliptic

16.4.3 Impact of RegTech on the financial industry

Benefits

- **Efficiency**: Reduces time, effort, and cost in compliance management.
- **Accuracy**: Minimizes human error in regulatory filings.
- **Speed**: Enables real-time reporting and fraud detection.
- **Transparency**: Enhances auditability and regulator trust.
- **Agility**: Adapts quickly to changes in regulations and compliance standards.

Challenges

- Integration with legacy systems
- Regulatory uncertainty and fragmentation
- Data privacy and security concerns
- High initial implementation cost
- Talent shortage in RegTech expertise

Global adoption and regulatory support

United Kingdom

- FCA actively promotes RegTech innovation.
- Launch of **TechSprint** initiatives to solve complex compliance issues.

United States

- RegTech is used in monitoring financial crimes, AML, and SEC filings.
- FinCEN and FDIC are exploring AI-powered compliance solutions.

Singapore

- MAS supports RegTech pilots through the **Financial Sector Technology and Innovation (FSTI)** scheme.

India

- RBI, SEBI, and IRDAI encourage RegTech for risk-based supervision, fraud detection, and e-KYC.

Table 16.4 Comparing insights – Comply Advantage, Signzy, and Ayasdi

Aspect	ComplyAdvantage (UK)	Signzy (India)	Ayasdi (USA)
Primary focus	AML/KYC risk data	Digital onboarding/KYC	AI-powered risk analytics
Technology core	NLP, machine learning	AI, biometrics, blockchain	TDA, unsupervised ML
Region focus	Global (EU/UK)	India, emerging markets	US and multinational banks
Key impact	False positives reduction	Financial inclusion	Detection of non-obvious risks
Regulatory support	FCA-aligned	RBI, UIDAI, IRDAI	FinCEN, federal reserve

The future of Regulatory Technology (RegTech) is poised for greater innovation and integration. One major trend is its convergence with Supervisory Technology (SupTech), enabling regulators to perform real-time supervision of financial activities. Continuous compliance systems are being developed to operate with minimal human input, ensuring regulations are met automatically and efficiently. As FinTech operates across borders, the push for global RegTech standards will help streamline compliance for international firms. The reconceptualization of financial regulation stresses data-driven oversight and dynamic supervision models [16]. Academic research suggests that FinTech–RegTech integration will redefine global regulatory architectures in the coming decade [17]. Ultimately, effective FinTech regulation must balance innovation, stability, consumer rights, and systemic resilience [18]. Additionally, AI-powered policy interpretation engines are emerging to help institutions understand and apply complex regulations accurately. Finally, smart contracts are expected to play a larger role in automated compliance, executing regulatory actions instantly when predefined conditions are met, thereby reducing delays and errors. The advancement of Regulatory Technology (RegTech) marks a fundamental transformation in the approach to regulatory compliance within the financial sector. As international regulatory frameworks grow increasingly complex and fragmented, the integration of technology has become essential for achieving dynamic, scalable, and real-time compliance capabilities. Beyond minimizing compliance costs and burdens, RegTech facilitates more secure, transparent, and operationally efficient financial processes, positioning it as a strategic asset in modern financial governance.

Summary

Chapter 16 explores the evolving regulatory landscape that governs the FinTech ecosystem, emphasizing the balance between innovation and compliance. It begins by examining the roles of global regulatory bodies such as the FATF, BIS, and IOSCO, which set international standards to ensure financial stability, data protection, and anti-money laundering compliance across jurisdictions. The chapter then outlines key regulatory initiatives like PSD2, MiCA, and GDPR, which promote transparency, open banking, and consumer protection. It also introduces regulatory sandboxes, which allow startups to test innovative financial products under relaxed regulations in a controlled environment. Additionally, the chapter delves into RegTech, a fast- growing sector that uses advanced technologies like AI, blockchain, and automation to simplify compliance and supervision processes. Together, these elements illustrate how regulation in FinTech is becoming more adaptive, data-driven, and collaborative to support safe and inclusive financial innovation.

Case Study: Regulatory Sandboxes in the United Kingdom – A Catalyst for FinTech Innovation

In recent years, as FinTech began disrupting traditional financial ecosystems with unprecedented speed, regulators faced a dual challenge: encouraging technological innovation while ensuring consumer protection and financial system stability. In response to this, the Financial Conduct Authority (FCA) of the United Kingdom introduced the concept of a **regulatory sandbox** in 2016. This initiative provided a supervised space where FinTech companies could test their innovations in real-market conditions with regulatory guidance but without immediately being subject to the full suite of financial regulations.

One notable participant in the FCA's sandbox was **SafeBank**, a startup offering AI- based micro-investment services targeted at underbanked users. Its business model focused on analyzing users' spending behavior to automatically invest spare change into low-risk portfolios. However, this raised various regulatory concerns related to data privacy (under the General Data Protection Regulation), investment advice compliance (under MiFID II), and the ethical use of artificial intelligence. Instead of facing these complexities alone, SafeBank was able to test its solution under the FCA sandbox. The company received temporary authorization to conduct trials with real users while receiving ongoing feedback and support from regulatory officers.

Through its participation in the sandbox, SafeBank adjusted its algorithms to enhance fairness and explainability, strengthened data protection protocols, and improved its risk assessment processes. After a successful six-month pilot, it secured full regulatory approval and launched its product to the broader UK market. This experience not only validated its model but also enhanced user trust and regulatory confidence in AI-based financial tools. The success of the UK's sandbox model inspired similar initiatives in other countries, including Singapore, Australia, and India.

The regulatory sandbox initiative has helped reduce the time-to-market for innovative financial solutions and created a more collaborative relationship between regulators and FinTech firms. However, challenges remain. Regulatory arbitrage is a risk where companies might seek out jurisdictions with lenient sandbox environments. Additionally, not all innovations fit neatly within a sandbox, especially those with global operations that encounter fragmented regulatory regimes. Despite these hurdles, the sandbox model represents a progressive shift in how financial regulation can be adaptive, forward-thinking, and innovation-friendly.

Case Discussion Questions

1. What benefits do regulatory sandboxes offer to both FinTech companies and regulators?
2. How can AI-driven financial services like SafeBank ensure ethical and transparent operations?
3. In what ways does regulatory collaboration during the sandbox phase differ from traditional oversight?
4. What are the limitations of sandbox environments in regulating global FinTech firms?
5. Should regulatory sandboxes expand to cover emerging areas like DeFi and tokenized assets?

Keywords

- **RegTech (Regulatory Technology):** Advanced technologies are leveraged to assist organizations in meeting regulatory obligations with greater efficiency and reduced operational costs.

- **Artificial intelligence (AI):** Algorithms that learn from data to identify compliance issues like fraud, suspicious transactions, and regulatory violations.
- **Topological data analysis (TDA):** A mathematical technique for discovering shape and structure in large data sets; used by Ayasdi to detect hidden relationships in financial data.
- **Compliance-as-a-Service (CaaS):** Outsourcing compliance functions to third-party RegTech providers via cloud platforms, reducing internal burden.
- **Behavioral analytics:** Techniques that analyse user Behavior to detect unusual activities, commonly used in fraud detection.
- **Real-time monitoring:** Continuous surveillance of transactions and communications to ensure immediate detection of potential regulatory breaches.
- **Regulatory reporting automation:** Automatically generating and submitting regulatory reports using structured data and APIs, reducing human error and cost.
- **Supervisory Technology (SupTech):** Tech used by regulators themselves to supervise, analyse, and audit financial institutions using RegTech principles.
- **False positives:** Incorrectly flagged compliance issues. AI-powered RegTech reduces these, improving efficiency in compliance systems.
- **Explainable AI (XAI):** Governance frameworks and operational procedures designed to maintain data integrity, ensure information security, and uphold compliance with regulations such as the GDPR and HIPAA.
- **Data governance regulatory change management:** Systems that track, interpret, and implement changes in laws and regulations in real-time.
- **Digital identity verification:** Use of biometrics, OCR, and blockchain to confirm customer identities remotely and securely.
- **Anti-money laundering (AML):** AML refers to a set of legal and regulatory measures designed to prevent the misuse of financial institutions for concealing the origins of illicit funds. RegTech solutions enhance AML compliance by employing artificial intelligence and automation to monitor transactions, detect suspicious patterns, and streamline reporting processes.

- **Know your customer (KYC):** KYC regulations mandate financial institutions to authenticate and evaluate the identities of their clients to mitigate financial crimes such as fraud, money laundering, and terrorism financing.

Discussion Questions

1. What are the core regulatory challenges faced by FinTech startups like Revolut?
2. How do sandbox initiatives help FinTech companies test new products legally?
3. What role does RegTech play in modern compliance management?
4. How can regulatory compliance be turned into a competitive advantage?
5. What are the implications of GDPR for FinTech firms operating in Europe?
6. How do licensing requirements differ between traditional banks and FinTech firms?
7. What is the importance of consumer data protection in the FinTech ecosystem?
8. What is the difference between RegTech and SupTech?
9. How does RegTech improve AML and KYC processes?
10. Why is explainability important in AI-driven RegTech systems?
11. What are the main challenges in adopting RegTech in legacy financial institutions?
12. How can RegTech assist in managing regulatory changes across jurisdictions?

References

[1] Arner, D. W., Barberis, J. N., & Buckley, R. P. (2017). FinTech and RegTech: Impact on Regulators and Banks. *Journal of Banking Regulation*, 19(1), 1–14. https://doi.org/10.1057/s41261-017-0031-6

[2] Financial Stability Board (FSB). (2017). Financial stability implications from FinTech: Supervisory and regulatory issues that merit authorities' attention. https://www.fsb.org/wp-content/uploads/R270617.pdf

[3] International Monetary Fund (IMF). (2019). The rise of RegTech: Promise and challenges. *IMF FinTech Notes No. 4.* https://www.imf.org/en/Publications/Fintech-Notes/Issues/2019/06/27/The-Rise-of-RegTech-Promise-and-Challenges-46944
[4] Financial Conduct Authority. (2021). FCA's Approach to FinTech and Innovation.https://www.fca.org.uk/publication/corporate/our-approach-fintech.pdf
[5] European Commission. (2020). Digital Finance Strategy for the EU. https://ec.europa.eu/info/publications/200924-digital-finance-proposals_en
[6] World Bank Group. (2020). Regulating fintech: Tools for developing countries. https://www.worldbank.org/en/topic/fintech
[7] KPMG. (2022). Smart regulation: Balancing innovation and compliance in financial services. https://home.kpmg
[8] Reserve Bank of India. (2020). Enabling framework for regulatory sandbox. https://rbi.org.in/Scripts/PublicationReportDetails.aspx?UrlPage=&ID=939
[9] Securities and Exchange Board of India (SEBI). (2023). Regulatory sandbox framework. https://www.sebi.gov.in
[10] Zetzsche, D. A., Buckley, R. P., Arner, D. W., & Barberis, J. N. (2020). Regulating a Revolution: From Regulatory Sandboxes to Smart Regulation. *Fordham Journal of Corporate & Financial Law*, 23(1), 31–103.
[11] Revolut Ltd. (2023). Annual Report and Regulatory Updates. https://www.revolut.com/legal/
[12] Deloitte. (2019). AI and Compliance: The Rise of RegTech in Financial Services. https://www2.deloitte.com
[13] Ayasdi. (2020). AI-Powered Compliance Solutions. https://www.ayasdi.com/
[14] KPMG. (2021). Evolving Role of RegTech in Financial Services. https://home.kpmg/xx/en/home/insights.html
[15] Deloitte. (2021). RegTech Universe 2021. https://www2.deloitte.com
[16] Arner, D. W., Barberis, J. N., & Buckley, R. P. (2017). FinTech, RegTech and the Reconceptualization of Financial Regulation. *Northwestern Journal of International Law & Business*, 37(3), 371–413.
[17] Zetzsche, D. A., Buckley, R. P., Arner, D. W., & Barberis, J. N. (2017). From FinTech to TechFin: The regulatory challenges. *Journal of Financial Regulation*, 3(1), 75–105. https://doi.org/10.1093/jfr/fjx002
[18] Chishti, S., & Barberis, J. (Eds.). (2016). *The FinTech Book: The financial technology handbook for investors, entrepreneurs and visionaries.* Wiley.

17

Supervisory Technologies (SupTech)

Abstract

This chapter delves into the rapidly evolving domain of Supervisory Technologies (SupTech), which represents the application of advanced technologies – particularly automation and artificial intelligence – to enhance the effectiveness and efficiency of financial supervision and regulatory compliance. It opens with an exploration of how automation is revolutionizing traditional regulatory processes, enabling real-time monitoring, predictive analytics, and early warning systems for regulatory breaches.

A significant portion of the chapter is devoted to the integration of AI-powered tools in supervisory frameworks, including machine learning models for anomaly detection, natural language processing for regulatory reporting, and algorithmic surveillance for complex market transactions. These tools not only increase oversight precision but also reduce the burden of manual compliance tasks on both regulators and financial institutions. The discussion then shifts to the necessary infrastructure redesign to support the deployment of SupTech solutions. This includes modernizing data collection systems, improving digital interoperability among institutions, and ensuring cybersecurity standards to safeguard supervisory data integrity. Attention is also given to the importance of data standardization and cross-border regulatory collaboration to fully harness the capabilities of SupTech.

Finally, the chapter provides a critical assessment of the challenges and benefits associated with implementing SupTech. While benefits include greater transparency, early risk identification, and cost efficiency, challenges such as regulatory capacity constraints, data privacy concerns, algorithmic accountability, and institutional resistance to change are also highlighted. By presenting both theoretical foundations and practical implications, the chapter equips readers with a well-rounded understanding of how SupTech is

DOI: 10.1201/9788743811244-23

reshaping financial regulation, positioning it as a cornerstone of future-ready governance in the FinTech era.

Introduction

Amid the continuous transformation of the financial ecosystem, the digital transformation of financial institutions has posed challenges for regulators and supervisors in terms of data volume, complexity, and real-time oversight. Supervisory Technology, or SupTech, has emerged as a powerful response, empowering regulators with advanced tools to enhance their supervisory capabilities. SupTech is the counterpart to RegTech. While RegTech helps financial institutions comply with regulations, SupTech enables regulatory bodies to enhance the precision, operational efficiency, and overall effectiveness of regulatory oversight.

Figure 17.1 Overview of SupTech.

17.1 SupTech

Supervisory Technology (SupTech) refers to the use of innovative technologies by regulatory and supervisory authorities to digitise, automate, and strengthen financial oversight. It aims to improve risk identification, market surveillance, and compliance monitoring through data-driven, intelligent systems. Supervisory Technologies (SupTech) represent the digital transformation of regulatory oversight functions in modern financial systems [1]. SupTech emerged as a response to increasing data complexity and the need for real-time supervisory insights [2].

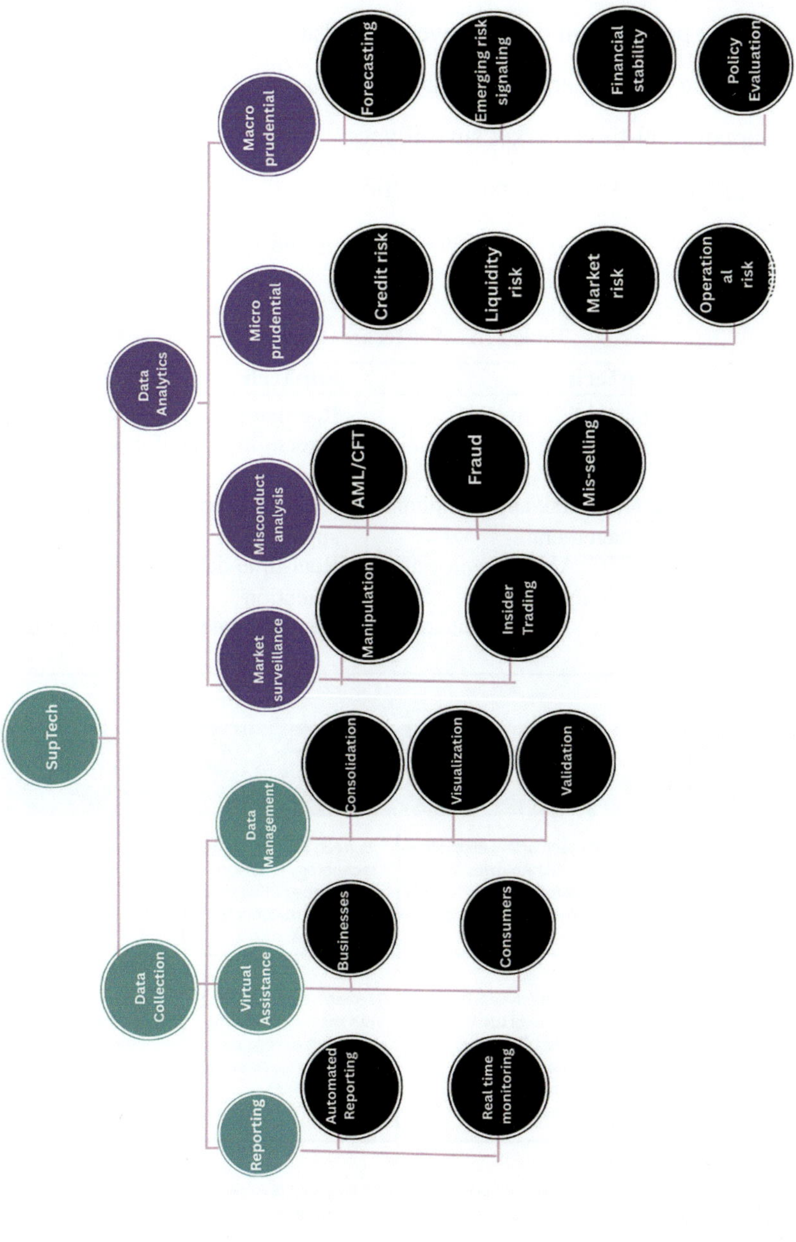

Figure 17.2 SupTech automation flowchart.

17.1.1 Objectives of SupTech

- Automate and streamline supervisory processes
- Enable proactive and predictive supervision
- Enhance data collection, validation, and analysis
- Support real-time market surveillance
- Improve fraud and anomaly detection
- Facilitate faster policy responses and regulatory decisions

Table 17.1 SupTech vs. RegTech.

Aspect	RegTech	SupTech
User	Financial institutions	Regulators and supervisory bodies
Goal	Compliance with regulations	Oversight and enforcement of regulations
Focus	Internal risk and compliance management	External monitoring and supervision
Example technologies	e-KYC, AML monitoring, risk analytics	Real-time data ingestion, anomaly detection
Key stakeholders	Banks, FinTechs, insurance firms	Central banks, financial regulators

Criteria	FinTech	RegTech	SupTech
Distinctive Advantage	Fintech offers innovative technologies for transforming the delivery & usage of financial services.	Regtech aims at using technology to ensure compliance of financial service providers to regulations.	Suptech works as a Regtech for supervisors in the financial services landscape.
Reason for Implementation	Fintech improves traditional banking and financial services with personalization , convenience and accessesibility.	Regtech helps in dealing with the overwhelming challenges of regulatory compliance for financial services.	Suptech helps provide supervisory agencies with effective tools to monitor risks and compliance breaches.
Target Audience	Financial service providers and users	Financial service providers	Supervisory authorities in the financial services landscape.

Figure 17.3 SupTech, RegTech, and FinTech comparison map.

17.1.2 Evolution of SupTech

Phase 1: Manual supervision

- Paper-based reporting and audits
- High latency in data collection and risk assessment
- Reactive supervision based on periodic reports

Phase 2: Digitization of supervision

- Excel and PDF-based digital submissions
- Limited analytics; still largely human-driven analysis

Phase 3: Advanced Sup Tech (current phase)

- Real-time digital submissions using APIs
- Machine Learning and AI for fraud detection
- Use of Natural Language Processing (NLP) to analyse regulatory filings
- Dashboards and visualisation tools for early warning systems

Phase 4: Predictive SupTech (Emerging)

- Predictive modelling for systemic risk
- Continuous monitoring and algorithmic supervision
- Use of decentralised data oracles and smart contracts

Table 17.2 Core Technologies in SupTech.

Technology	Function in SupTech
APIs and data portals	Real-time submission and ingestion of regulatory data
Artificial intelligence	Fraud detection, sentiment analysis, and predictive modelling
Big data analytics	Processing high-frequency market and transaction data
Natural language processing (NLP)	Parsing and analysing unstructured filings and financial news
Machine learning	Pattern recognition and anomaly detection
Blockchain	Ensuring the integrity and immutability of records
Cloud computing	Scalable data storage and compute infrastructure for regulators
Dashboards and visualisation tools	Risk monitoring, reporting, and decision-making

17.1.3 Applications of SupTech

Real-time transaction surveillance

- Detect unusual market behaviour and insider trading
- Monitor algorithmic trading platforms

Early warning systems

- Predict systemic risk and bank failures using AI models
- Generate alerts based on capital adequacy, liquidity, etc.

Regulatory reporting automation

- API-based digital regulatory filing from FIs
- Improved data validation and error checking

Onsite inspection optimization

- Use analytics to prioritize inspections based on risk profiles
- Remote supervision of branches and ATMs

Cyber risk monitoring

- Supervising cybersecurity frameworks of banks and FinTechs
- Aggregating real-time incident reports from institutions

17.1.4 Global examples of SupTech initiatives

Monetary Authority of Singapore (MAS)

- Launched **Project NOVA** to automate supervisory risk assessments
- Uses AI to analyse financial statements and detect misreporting

Bank of England (BoE)

- Developed a SupTech tool for **real-time liquidity monitoring**
- Partnered with RegTech startups to trial data visualization platforms

U.S. Federal Reserve and FDIC

- Use SupTech tools for stress testing and scenario analysis

- Leverage cloud-based platforms for consumer complaint analysis

Reserve Bank of India (RBI)

- Implements **SupTech dashboards** to monitor NBFCs and cooperative banks
- Working on AI models to assess the financial health of rural credit institutions

European Central Bank (ECB)

- Initiated **digital supervisory reporting** under the DPM (Data Point Model)
- Using SupTech for consistency checks across eurozone member banks

17.1.5 Benefits of SupTech

- Faster and more accurate risk detection
- Reduced supervisory lag
- Lower operational costs for regulators
- Data-driven decision-making
- Improved transparency and accountability
- Enhanced collaboration between regulators and institutions

Table 17.3 Challenges in Sup Tech adoption.

Challenge	Description
Data standardization	Variability in formats across institutions
Legacy systems	Difficulty integrating modern Sup Tech with old IT infrastructure
Cybersecurity risks	Protection of sensitive financial and regulatory data
Regulatory fragmentation	Differing approaches across jurisdictions
Skill gaps	Shortage of data scientists and AI experts in the public sector
Privacy and ethical concerns	Surveillance vs. rights of institutions and individuals

17.1.6 The future of SupTech

- **Continuous supervision**: Systems that monitor and flag anomalies 24/7
- **Digital twins for simulation**: Supervisors can simulate potential crises
- **Cross-border Sup Tech frameworks**: Harmonization of supervision globally
- **AI-driven policy feedback loops**: Real-time insight into the effectiveness of regulations
- **Collaborative Sup Tech ecosystems**: Regulatory sandboxes including supervisors and innovators

SupTech is revolutionizing how regulators operate by equipping them with data, analytics, and intelligent tools to supervise an increasingly digital financial system. It ensures that oversight keeps pace with innovation, while reducing risks and enhancing the resilience of financial markets. As financial systems become more complex and interlinked, Sup Tech will play a critical role in ensuring trust, stability, and regulatory effectiveness.

17.2 Automation in Regulatory Compliance

In the digital era, financial institutions face increasingly complex and dynamic regulatory landscapes. Compliance requirements span anti-money laundering (AML), data privacy, know your customer (KYC), taxation, risk management, and more. Traditionally, regulatory compliance involved manual processes, paperwork, and human interpretation of rules, leading to inefficiencies, high costs, and regulatory lapses. To overcome these challenges, the financial industry is increasingly embracing automation in regulatory compliance through technologies such as artificial intelligence (AI), machine learning (ML), robotic process automation (RPA), and application programming interfaces (APIs). This transformation is enabling real-time, accurate, and scalable compliance processes. It enhances regulatory efficiency by digitizing manual supervisory processes traditionally dependent on paper-based workflows [3]. Advances in cloud computing, analytics, and APIs have accelerated the global adoption of SupTech solutions [4].

17.2.1 Regulatory compliance automation

Regulatory compliance automation involves leveraging advanced technological solutions to digitize, streamline, and enhance compliance operations, ensuring alignment with evolving legal and regulatory requirements.

Key objectives:

- Reduce manual intervention and human error
- Ensure timely and accurate regulatory reporting
- Monitor compliance continuously in real time
- Improve risk management and decision-making
- Lower compliance costs and increase agility

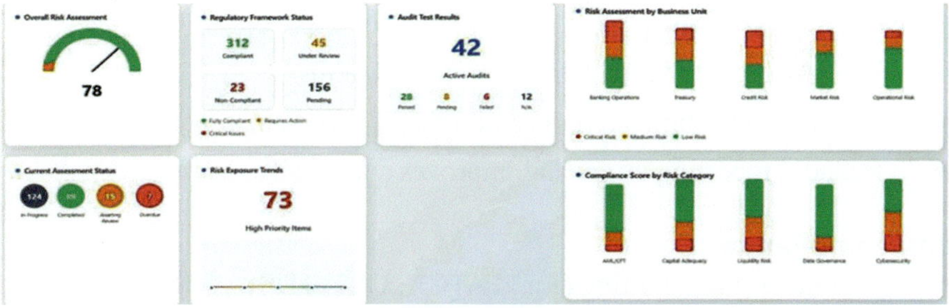

Figure 17.4 Central Bank compliance dashboard example.

Table 17.4 Key technologies powering automation.

Technology	Application in compliance
Artificial intelligence (AI)	Automates rule interpretation, alerts, and policy enforcement
Machine learning (ML)	Detects suspicious activity and adapts to new risk patterns
Robotic process automation (RPA)	Automates repetitive tasks like report generation or data extraction
Natural language processing (NLP)	Analyses legal texts and regulatory guidelines
APIs	Automates data exchange between internal systems and regulators
Blockchain	Enhances transparency and traceability of regulatory actions
Cloud computing	Enables scalable, secure compliance systems accessible across units

17.2.2 Core areas of compliance

Automation know your customer (KYC)

- Automates customer verification using digital identity solutions
- Integrates with government databases and AML watchlists
- Uses facial recognition and document scanning technologies

Anti-money laundering (AML)

- Real-time monitoring of transactions for red flags
- Machine learning algorithms to detect unusual behaviour
- Automated Suspicious Activity Report (SAR) filing

Regulatory reporting

- Uses APIs to gather data from internal systems
- Formats and submits reports automatically to regulators
- Reduces reporting errors and improves audit trails

Tax compliance

- Automates tax reporting (e.g., FATCA, GST, TDS)
- Ensures real-time tracking of taxable events
- Minimizes risks of tax penalties or audit discrepancies

Data privacy and protection

- Automates enforcement of data retention and deletion policies
- Tracks consent and access control under GDPR or PDPA
- Logs data movement across borders for audit readiness

Table 17.5 Benefits of automation in compliance.

Benefit	Explanation
Efficiency	Reduces time and resources spent on manual compliance tasks
Accuracy	Minimizes human errors in data entry and analysis
Real-time monitoring	Enables proactive detection of compliance issues
Cost reduction	Lowers operational and staffing costs
Audit readiness	Maintains consistent and transparent logs of compliance actions
Scalability	Handles regulatory updates or higher data volumes with ease

Table 17.6 Challenges in automating compliance.

Challenge	Description
Changing regulatory landscapes	Frequent changes in rules require agile and adaptive systems
Integration with legacy systems	Older systems may resist automation or pose compatibility issues
Data quality and standardization	Poor-quality data undermines AI/ML model effectiveness
Cybersecurity risks	Compliance systems must protect sensitive data from breaches
Ethical considerations	Biased AI models may trigger unfair compliance decisions
Cost of implementation	Initial automation costs can be high for small and medium-sized firms

17.2.3 Regulatory expectations and global trends

- **Regulators encourage automation** to ensure timely, high-quality submissions
- **Basel Committee**, **FATF**, and **IOSCO** support digital compliance initiatives
- **EU's digital finance strategy** emphasizes RegTech and automation in financial regulation
- **India's RBI and SEBI** are pushing for API-based regulatory filings and SupTech integrations

17.2.4 Automated AML compliance transformation

HSBC, one of the world's largest banking institutions, faced significant reputational damage and regulatory scrutiny following its involvement in multiple high-profile money laundering cases during the early 2010s. The bank was fined approximately $1.9 billion by U.S. authorities in 2012 for failing to implement adequate anti-money laundering (AML) controls, especially concerning its operations in Mexico and other high-risk regions. This regulatory failure highlighted critical weaknesses in HSBC's compliance infrastructure, particularly in its ability to monitor cross-border transactions, detect suspicious activity, and respond to compliance alerts in a timely and consistent manner. In response to these deficiencies and to restore public and regulatory trust, HSBC embarked on a comprehensive digital transformation of its compliance function. The initiative focused on the automation of AML processes using advanced technologies such as artificial intelligence (AI), robotic process automation (RPA), and API-based integration systems. Regulators now use SupTech tools for automated data collection, reducing reporting burdens on financial institutions [5]. SupTech strengthens oversight by increasing data accuracy through machine-readable and machine-executable regulatory reporting formats [6]. Platforms like APIX support regulators in testing digital regulatory tools within controlled environments [7]. Automation in regulatory compliance minimizes human error and accelerates the detection of compliance breaches [8].

Actions and technologies implemented

To rebuild its compliance framework and prevent future lapses, HSBC adopted several strategic measures:

- **AI-based transaction monitoring:** Machine learning algorithms were deployed to analyse millions of transactions in real-time, identifying suspicious patterns that might indicate money laundering.
- **Robotic process automation (RPA):** Automated bots were used to handle routine compliance tasks such as reviewing flagged transactions, escalating cases to compliance officers, and updating internal systems.
- **API integration for regulatory submissions:** HSBC established secure APIs for real-time, machine-readable regulatory reporting to bodies such as the Financial Conduct Authority (FCA) and Financial Crimes Enforcement Network (FinCEN).

Outcomes and impact

The automation initiatives led to measurable improvements in HSBC's AML compliance performance:

- **60% reduction in false positives,** improving investigative efficiency
- Enhanced **risk categorization**, enabling faster and more accurate prioritization of high-risk cases
- **Significantly improved regulatory alignment**, reducing the risk of further sanctions and fines
- HSBC also reported **better internal audit outcomes** and increased confidence from global regulators in its AML compliance capabilities

Best practices for compliance automation

From HSBC's transformation journey, several best practices have emerged that can guide other financial institutions in adopting compliance automation:

- **Map regulatory obligations** directly to automated workflows and processes.
- Use a **modular system architecture** that allows flexible updates as regulations evolve.
- **Collaborate with compliance officers** during the system design phase to ensure operational relevance.
- Prioritize **auditability and explainability** in AI models to maintain trust and regulatory compliance.
- Provide **continuous training for staff** to interpret and act on AI-generated insights.
- Conduct **regular testing and validation** under simulated real-world regulatory scenarios.

HSBC's digital transformation following its AML compliance failures demonstrates how large financial institutions can use RegTech to rebuild regulatory credibility. The integration of AI, RPA, and real-time APIs not only improved operational efficiency but also positioned HSBC as a forward-looking leader in automated compliance. This case highlights the strategic value of adopting intelligent compliance systems in the modern regulatory environment. Automation in regulatory compliance marks a significant step forward in ensuring robust, agile, and cost-effective adherence to financial regulations. As the regulatory environment grows more complex, automation not only helps institutions keep pace but also proactively mitigates risks, enhances transparency, and fosters innovation. While implementation comes with challenges – especially around data, ethics, and integration – the long-term gains in efficiency, accuracy, and accountability are undeniable.

17.3 AI-Powered Supervision

In an increasingly digitized financial ecosystem, supervisory authorities face a rapidly expanding volume of complex and high-frequency data. Traditional regulatory oversight mechanisms – often reliant on manual audits, retrospective reporting, andperiodic assessments are no longer sufficient to detect emerging risks or prevent systemic failures in real time. To address this challenge, financial regulators around the world are turning to artificial intelligence (AI) to enhance supervision, improve regulatory agility, and ensure market stability. This shift is giving rise to what is now known as AI-powered supervision or Supervisory Technology (SupTech), driven by AI. Regulated entities also benefit as automated compliance systems reduce operational costs and improve reporting timeliness [9]. SupTech systems enable supervisors to monitor systemic risks by rapidly analyzing large volumes of structured and unstructured data [10]. AI-powered SupTech tools help authorities identify anomalies, fraud patterns, and emerging risks more accurately [11].

AI-powered supervision involves incorporating artificial intelligence tools – such as machine learning algorithms, natural language processing (NLP), and predictive analytics – into the oversight functions of financial regulators to enhance the effectiveness, speed, and accuracy of regulatory processes.

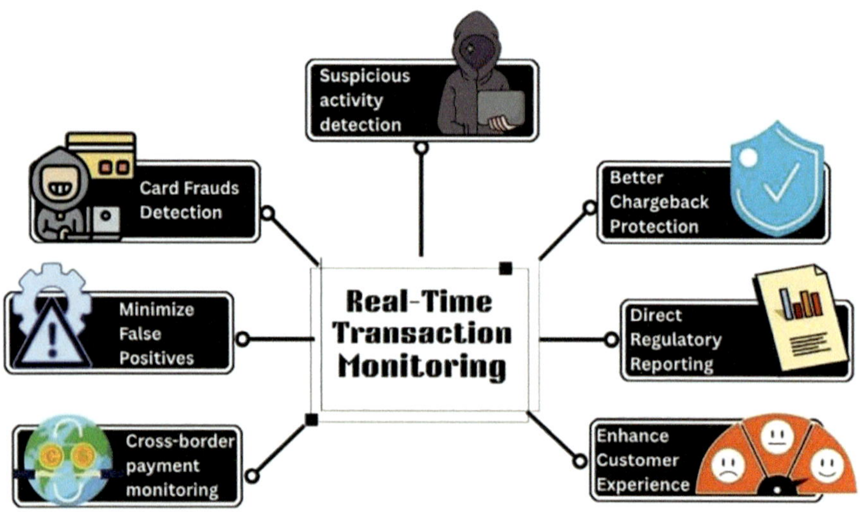

Figure 17.5 AI for real-time transaction monitoring.

It enables regulators to move from **reactive** to **proactive** and even **predictive** models of oversight.

17.3.1 Objectives of AI in supervision

- Real-time monitoring of financial activities
- Early detection of systemic risks

- Fraud and anomaly detection
- Automated regulatory reporting
- Streamlined decision-making
- Data-driven policy formulation

17.3.2 Applications of AI-powered supervision

Automated risk assessment

- Classifies institutions based on real-time risk profiles
- Continuously recalibrates risk models using machine learning

Table 17.7 Core AI technologies in supervision.

Technology	Function in supervision
Machine learning (ML)	Learns from historical patterns to predict future risks
Natural language processing (NLP)	Analyses unstructured data like legal texts or filings
Deep learning	Enables complex pattern recognition in large datasets
Predictive analytics	Forecasts potential non-compliance or financial distress
Computer vision	Analyses visual documents (e.g., scanned contracts, KYC IDs)
Reinforcement learning	Helps optimize supervisory actions based on feedback loops

Real-time transaction surveillance

- Monitors payment networks, trading platforms, and lending operations
- **Detects anomalies like insider trading or market manipulation**

Predictive compliance monitoring

- Flags institutions likely to violate regulations before breaches occur
- **Triggers pre-emptive supervisory actions or requests for clarification**

Document intelligence

- Uses NLP to analyse and extract data from annual reports, contracts, and disclosures

- Identifies compliance gaps, inconsistencies, or missing statements

AI chatbots for regulatory support

- Assists institutions in understanding compliance requirements
- Reduces the burden on supervisory staff for routine queries

Figure 17.6 NLP use in regulatory reporting.

Table 17.8 Benefits of AI in supervision.

Benefit	Explanation
Proactive oversight	Enables early identification of irregularities and system vulnerabilities
Operational efficiency	Reduces manual audits and paperwork
Scalable supervision	Handles high data volumes across institutions and geographies
Timely regulatory intervention	Supports faster decision-making to avert crises
Enhanced transparency	Improves audit trails and policy justification
Data-driven policy making	Empowers regulators to revise rules based on observed data trends

Table 17.9 Challenges and risks.

Challenge	Implication
Data quality issues	Poor data can distort AI outputs and lead to incorrect decisions
Model bias and fairness	Algorithms may reflect historical discrimination
Explainability of AI decisions	Lack of transparency may undermine trust in supervisory decisions
Cybersecurity risks	AI systems can be targeted for manipulation or sabotage
Skill gaps in regulatory bodies	Requires upskilling of supervisors and new hiring strategies
Legal and ethical compliance	Must ensure AI adheres to privacy, transparency, and fairness laws

Examples

Monetary Authority of Singapore (MAS)

- Launched **Project Veritas**, which explores the ethical use of AI in finance
- **Uses AI for AML, risk scoring, and predictive supervision**

European Central Bank (ECB)

- Uses ML for stress testing and macroprudential supervision
- **Applies NLP to extract insights from supervisory reports**

Financial Conduct Authority (UK)

- Deployed AI in **Digital Regulatory Reporting** pilots
- Studies AI transparency and explainability as part of RegTech collaboration

Reserve Bank of India (RBI)

- Invests in **data-driven SupTech platforms**
- Explores AI for real-time reporting and fraud surveillance

Artificial intelligence in SEC market surveillance (United States)

The U.S. financial markets are among the most active and complex in the world, processing millions of transactions every trading day across equities, derivatives, and other instruments. The Securities and Exchange Commission (SEC), as the primary regulator of these markets, is responsible for maintaining market integrity, ensuring fair trading practices, and protecting investors. Traditionally, the SEC relied on manual audits, tip-based investigations, and rule-based surveillance systems to detect market misconduct such as insider trading, market manipulation, and front-running.

However, the rapid growth of high-frequency trading (HFT), algorithmic trading, and the increasing volume of real-time digital transactions began to outpace the SEC's legacy systems. Detecting illicit activity manually or through rigid rule-based systems became inefficient and ineffective, particularly when perpetrators used subtle, hidden patterns spread across multiple transactions, timeframes, or platforms.

Additionally, market misconduct has grown more sophisticated – often involving encrypted communication, unstructured data sources, and cross-border transactions – making traditional tools obsolete. To remain effective in this fast-evolving landscape, the SEC recognized the need to augment its surveillance framework with advanced data analytics and AI technologies that could process vast datasets, identify hidden patterns, and detect anomalies in real time.

The turning point came in the late 2010s, when the SEC began investing heavily in supervisory technology (SupTech). Collaborating with data scientists, AI researchers, and regulatory technologists, the SEC piloted AI-based models for detecting irregular trading behavior. These models were trained using historical enforcement data, enabling the system to "learn" what types of behavior had previously led to enforcement actions.

In parallel, the SEC began applying natural language processing (NLP) to analyze press releases, earnings reports, regulatory disclosures, and news articles to establish whether trading activity correlated suspiciously with material public information or insider knowledge. By integrating structured data (e.g., trade logs) with unstructured data (e.g., news feeds), the SEC was able to achieve a multidimensional view of trading behavior – one that could not be obtained through traditional surveillance techniques. This AI-powered transformation not only enhanced the SEC's detection accuracy and efficiency but also significantly reduced the number of false positives, which had previously clogged investigative pipelines and strained regulatory resources.

Infrastructure redesign for regulation

The swift digital transformation of financial services, driven by FinTech advancements, has significantly reshaped the regulatory environment. Conventional regulatory frameworks rooted in manual workflows, paper-centric documentation, and fragmented data silos have proven inadequate in addressing the increased scale, complexity, and velocity of today's financial systems. As a result, regulators worldwide are undergoing a strategic infrastructure redesign to modernize their tools, systems, and frameworks. This chapter explores how regulatory bodies are reengineering their technological and organizational infrastructure to ensure real-time supervision, data-driven policy-making, and collaborative oversight in a digital economy. Machine-learning-based early warning systems allow regulators to act proactively rather than reactively to market vulnerabilities [12]. Countries like Singapore have pioneered AI-driven supervisory frameworks to enhance fintech ecosystem stability [13]. The Covid-19 pandemic accelerated SupTech adoption as digital oversight became essential for operational continuity [14].

Infrastructure redesign for regulation refers to the transformation of the tools, technologies, processes, and institutional frameworks used by regulatory authorities to supervise and enforce financial regulations in a digitally native and scalable manner. This redesign involves:

- Digital transformation of legacy systems
- Integration of emerging technologies (AI, cloud, APIs)
- Streamlining of regulatory reporting channels
- Collaboration with FinTech and RegTech ecosystems

Table 17.10 Drivers for infrastructure redesign.

Driver	Explanation
Data explosion	Huge volumes of structured and unstructured financial data
Real-time compliance needs	Demand for continuous and instantaneous monitoring
Rise of decentralized finance	New financial products bypass traditional infrastructures
Cross-border transactions	Need for interoperability among international regulators
Cybersecurity concerns	Higher risks due to data centralization and digital vulnerabilities
Innovation in financial products	Complex, fast-evolving financial services need agile supervision

Components of regulatory infrastructure redesign

Digital data hubs

Regulators are shifting from periodic data submissions to centralized **digital data platforms** where financial institutions stream structured data in real time.

- Benefits: Instant access, better data quality, efficient analytics
- Example: Bank of England's Digital Regulatory Reporting (DRR) initiative

API-based regulatory interfaces

Financial entities can integrate with regulators via **application programming interfaces (APIs)** to submit data, receive alerts, and stay updated on compliance requirements.

- APIs promote real-time, standardized communication.
- Example: Monetary Authority of Singapore's regulatory API architecture

Cloud-native supervision systems

Cloud-based systems offer scalability, resilience, and storage for high-volume datasets. Regulators can perform complex analytics and simulations without local infrastructure limitations.

- Enables rapid data processing and deployment of AI tools
- Enhances disaster recovery and cybersecurity

Advanced analytics and AI engines

Modern supervisory systems are embedded with **AI and machine learning models** for risk detection, fraud monitoring, and trend analysis.

- AI helps flag outliers and predict systemic risks
- NLP engines process legal texts and disclosures automatically

Regulatory sandboxes and innovation hubs

To support FinTech innovation, regulators redesign infrastructure to allow **controlled experimentation environments** (sandboxes) and **collaborative innovation hubs**.

- Encourages testing without compromising stability
- Feedback from innovators enhances regulatory frameworks

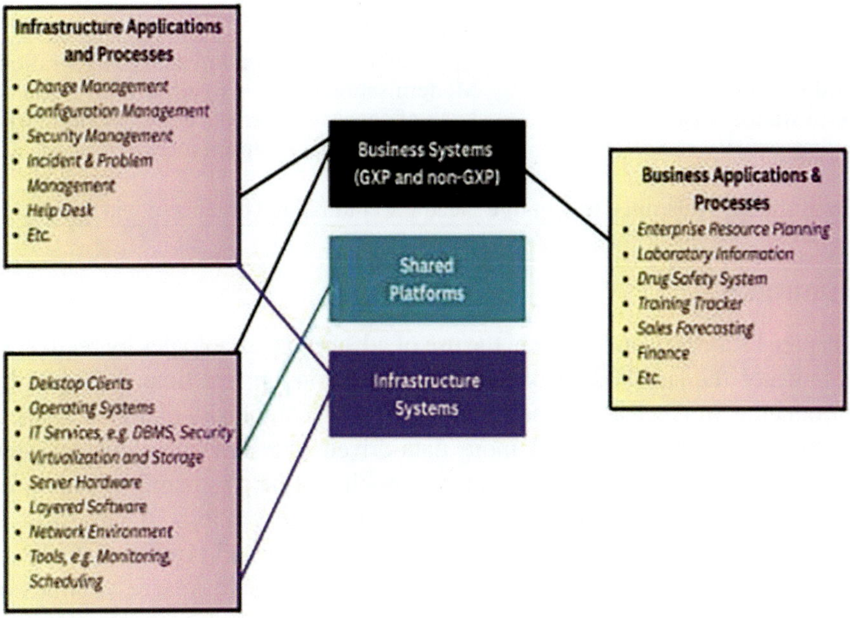

Figure 17.7 Modern regulatory IT infrastructure.

Interoperability and cross-border integration

Modern regulatory infrastructure includes **international data-sharing standards**, secure messaging protocols, and aligned frameworks for **global financial supervision**.

- Helps track cross-jurisdictional risks

- Examples: BIS Innovation Hub, GFIN (Global Financial Innovation Network)

Table 17.11 Key benefits of infrastructure redesign.

Benefit	Impact
Increased efficiency	Faster processing, fewer manual tasks
Improved transparency	Standardized data and audit trails
Enhanced decision-making	Data-driven insights and predictive capabilities
Adaptive regulation	Flexible architecture supports evolving FinTech landscape
Risk mitigation	Early detection of systemic and compliance risks

Table 17.12 Challenges in implementation.

Challenge	Explanation
Legacy systems	Outdated infrastructure resistant to integration
Budget constraints	Modernisation requires significant investment
Data standardisation issues	Lack of consistent formats across institutions
Cybersecurity risks	Expanded digital footprint increases attack surface
Institutional resistance to Change	Need for cultural and organizational shift

Summary

Chapter 17 focuses on SupTech, the use of advanced technologies by regulators to enhance the supervision of financial institutions in real time. It begins by introducing SupTech as a response to the growing complexity of digital finance, enabling smarter, faster, and more data-driven oversight. The chapter then explores how automation in regulatory compliance helps streamline processes like risk reporting, anomaly detection, and regulatory filings. A key focus is on AI-powered supervision, where machine learning and predictive analytics enable early identification of risks and irregularities across large volumes of financial data. Lastly, the chapter highlights the importance of infrastructure redesign, emphasizing the need for digital platforms, standardized data formats, and integrated systems to support continuous monitoring and efficient regulatory operations. Together, these advancements represent a shift from traditional supervision to proactive, technology-enabled oversight in the FinTech era.

Case Study: United Kingdom – Digital Regulatory Reporting (DRR)

In an effort to modernize the way financial institutions report data to regulators, the Financial Conduct Authority (FCA), in partnership with the Bank of England, initiated the Digital Regulatory Reporting (DRR) project. The DRR initiative emerged as a response to the rising complexity and volume of regulatory requirements imposed on firms, especially after the 2008 financial crisis. Traditionally, compliance processes relied heavily on manual interpretation of legal text, which had to be translated into technical reporting frameworks across various systems. This approach led to inconsistencies, increased operational costs, and frequent errors in regulatory submissions.

Financial firms in the UK faced considerable challenges in keeping up with evolving regulations. Due to fragmented systems and manual workflows, compliance teams often struggled to accurately and efficiently produce required reports, resulting in penalties, delays, and a strained relationship with supervisory authorities. The DRR project aimed to resolve these inefficiencies by transforming regulatory rules into machine-readable code. Rather than viewing regulation as static legal documents, DRR reimagines it as programmable logic that financial systems can interpret and apply automatically.

Pilot programs were developed using synthetic data and sandbox environments where financial firms and regulators could jointly experiment with this new model. Application programming interfaces (APIs) were introduced to streamline data transmission and ensure standardized reporting formats across institutions. This collaborative effort helped reduce duplicative work and clarified regulatory expectations.

As a result of the DRR initiative, compliance processes became more consistent and cost-effective. The transition toward "regulation-as-code" fostered a culture of collaboration between regulators and financial institutions, enabling both sides to adapt more quickly to regulatory changes. This case represents a forward-looking approach to financial regulation, offering a scalable blueprint for other countries aiming to integrate technology with governance.

Case Discussion Questions

1. What issues in the traditional regulatory reporting process led to the development of the DRR initiative in the UK?
2. How does "regulation-as-code" improve consistency in compliance across financial institutions?
3. In what ways did DRR reduce compliance costs and increase efficiency?
4. What role did collaboration between regulators and financial firms play in the DRR pilot projects?
5. Can DRR serve as a model for global regulatory reform in FinTech? Why or why not?

Keywords

- **Real-time data monitoring:** Use of live data streams to observe financial institutions' activities, enabling immediate action.
- **Regulatory reporting automation:** Auto-generating regulatory submissions using APIs and standard data formats, reducing errors and compliance costs.
- **Natural language processing (NLP):** A form of AI that allows regulators to analyse large volumes of text-based regulatory reports and contracts.
- **Predictive supervision:** AI-based systems that forecast risks and compliance breaches before they occur.
- **Machine learning algorithms:** Self-improving systems used by regulators to identify patterns in transactions and flag suspicious activity.
- **APIX (API Exchange):** A digital platform initiated by MAS and ADB for regulators to prototype and test SupTech solutions.
- **Infrastructure redesign:** Overhauling regulatory systems (data storage, cloud architecture, security) to support scalable and agile supervision.
- **Digital regulatory reporting (DRR):** A model where financial firms report data digitally and directly into regulators' systems in structured formats.

- **Data lakes:** Centralized repositories for storing raw regulatory and financial data, used for advanced analytics.
- **Explainable AI (XAI):** Facilitates the interpretability and auditability of AI- driven regulatory decisions, ensuring that outcomes are transparent and comprehensible to human supervisors.
- **Supervisory dashboards:**Real-time visual interfaces showing compliance status, risk scores, and performance metrics of institutions.
- **Anomaly detection:** Identification of outlier behaviour in transactions or reports using AI – useful in fraud or risk detection.
- **Digital twin for regulation:** Simulated models of financial systems are used by regulators to test policy impacts before real-world implementation.
- **Cloud-native supervision:** Regulatory tools and systems built for scalability, security, and flexibility on cloud infrastructure.
- **Supervisory Technology (SupTech):** Technology is adopted by regulators to enhance supervision, enforcement, and compliance oversight.

Discussion Questions

1. What is SupTech, and how does it differ from RegTech?
2. How has the Monetary Authority of Singapore applied SupTech in real-world regulatory processes?
3. What role does AI play in enhancing supervisory effectiveness?
4. Why is infrastructure redesign important for future-proof regulation?
5. How do supervisory dashboards contribute to better oversight?
6. What are the risks and limitations of adopting SupTech tools?
7. How can SupTech help prevent financial crises or systemic risks?
8. In what ways can natural language processing improve regulatory compliance?
9. How do digital twins support policy testing and regulatory forecasting?
10. What are the global implications of adopting SupTech in developing economies?

References

[1] Arner, D. W., Barberis, J. N., & Buckley, R. P. (2021). FinTech, RegTech and SupTech: Innovation in Financial Services Supervision. *Asian Journal of Comparative Law, 16*(1), 1–28. https://doi.org/10.1017/asjcl.2021.6

[2] Bank for International Settlements (BIS). (2019). *Innovative technology in financial supervision (SupTech) – The experience of early users.* https://www.bis.org/publ/bppdf/bispap108.htm

[3] World Bank Group. (2020). *The Role of SupTech in Modern Financial Supervision.* https://documents.worldbank.org

[4] Gai, K., Qiu, M., & Sun, X. (2018). A survey on FinTech. *Journal of Network and Computer Applications, 103*, 262–273. https://doi.org/10.1016/j.jnca.2017.10.011

[5] Financial Stability Board (FSB). (2020). *The use of supervisory and regulatory technology by authorities and regulated institutions.* https://www.fsb.org/2020/10

[6] Deloitte. (2022). *SupTech: Reshaping regulatory oversight in the digital age.* Deloitte Insights. https://www2.deloitte.com

[7] ADB & APIX. (2022). *APIX Platform and Regulator Adoption.* https://www.apixplatform.com

[8] Zetzsche, D. A., Buckley, R. P., & Arner, D. W. (2020). RegTech for regulators: Re-engineering compliance. *Journal of Banking Regulation, 21*(4), 273–282. https://doi.org/10.1057/s41261-020-00118-9

[9] Arner, D. W., Barberis, J. N., & Buckley, R. P. (2017). Fintech, Regtech, and the reconceptualization of financial regulation. *Northwestern Journal of International Law & Business, 37*(3), 371–413.

[10] Financial Stability Board (FSB). (2021). *Supervisory and Regulatory Technology (SupTech and RegTech) Developments.* https://www.fsb.org

[11] International Monetary Fund (IMF). (2021). *Supervisory technology (SupTech) for AML/CFT.* IMF Fintech Note No. 2021/001. https://www.imf.org/en/Publications/Fintech-Notes

[12] KPMG. (2021). *The next frontier in supervision: How SupTech is revolutionizing regulatory monitoring.* https://home.kpmg

[13] MAS (Monetary Authority of Singapore). (2021). *Harnessing Technology for a Smart Financial Centre.* https://www.mas.gov.sg

[14] Cambridge Centre for Alternative Finance (CCAF). (2021). *Global COVID-19 FinTech Market Rapid Assessment Study.* https://www.jbs.cam.ac.uk

18

Data-Driven Financial Services

Abstract

This chapter explores the transformative impact of artificial intelligence (AI) and data analytics in reshaping modern financial services, emphasizing the growing shift toward data-driven decision-making in the digital financial ecosystem. Beginning with a foundational understanding of machine learning paradigms – supervised, unsupervised, and reinforcement learning – the chapter outlines how each approach contributes uniquely to the processing and interpretation of financial data for real-time applications. A major focus is placed on the role of AI in governance and regulatory compliance, where intelligent systems aid in automating complex reporting, detecting anomalies, and ensuring adherence to dynamic regulatory frameworks. The chapter then transitions into an evaluation of AI applications in risk management, including credit risk modeling, fraud detection, and predictive analytics, as well as in personalized financial services, such as robo-advisors, customer segmentation, and behavior-based product recommendations.

However, the integration of AI into finance also presents critical challenges. The chapter delves into concerns surrounding algorithmic bias, black-box decision- making, and lack of accountability, which can undermine fairness and erode public trust. To mitigate these concerns, the chapter introduces key concepts such as differential privacy, data minimization, and ethical data governance, which are crucial in protecting users against data breaches and misuse.

The discussion also addresses broader ethical and privacy dilemmas – including questions of data ownership, the adequacy of informed

DOI: 10.1201/9788743811244-24

consent, and the need for transparency in AI-driven financial decisions. Through case studies and empirical insights, the chapter illustrates how data-driven insights can enhance customer- centricity, improve operational efficiency, and foster innovation, while simultaneously underscoring the importance of robust data ethics and responsible AI deployment. Ultimately, this chapter equips readers with a critical understanding of how financial institutions must balance innovation with integrity in leveraging data to build resilient, inclusive, and accountable financial services for the future.

Introduction

In today's digital landscape, data has emerged as a critical asset, fundamentally reshaping the financial services industry. From product innovation to risk evaluation, data is influencing every facet of financial operations. Institutions are increasingly harnessing large-scale structured and unstructured data to offer more intelligent, agile, and tailored financial solutions. This transformation reflects a broader shift from conventional financial models to ecosystems driven by data, where decisions are guided by insights generated through analytics, machine learning, and artificial intelligence.

This chapter explores the core principles, enabling technologies, real-world applications, advantages, challenges, and future prospects of data-centric financial services. Artificial intelligence (AI) has become a disruptive innovation within the financial services sector. Through data-driven learning and the simulation of human cognitive functions, AI technologies can execute tasks such as predictive analysis, decision-making, pattern detection, and interpretation of natural language. The integration of AI into finance, often referred to as AI in FinTech, has revolutionized operations across banking, insurance, asset management, and capital markets. From chatbots and robo-advisors to credit scoring and fraud detection, AI is reshaping the traditional financial landscape by improving efficiency, accuracy, and customer experience, while also raising important considerations about ethics, fairness, and regulatory compliance. Data-driven financial services leverage big data, AI, and advanced analytics to transform traditional banking operations into intelligent, adaptive systems [1]. By analyzing massive datasets, financial institutions can detect patterns, optimize decisions, and personalize customer experiences [2]. Metadata plays a critical role in organizing, categorizing, and deriving actionable insights from structured and unstructured financial data [3].

18.1 Data-Driven Financial Services

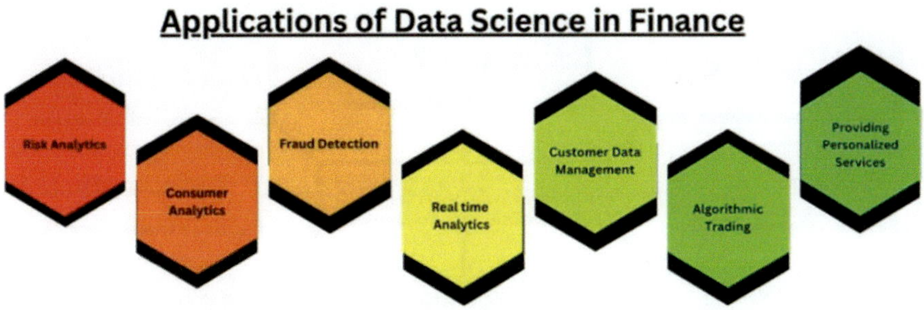

Figure 18.1 Application of data science in finance.

Data-driven financial services involve leveraging data analytics and advanced digital technologies to optimize the design, delivery, and administration of financial products and services. These services are distinguished by:

- Customer-centric design
- Real-time decision-making
- Predictive risk modelling
- Automated compliance and fraud detection
- Personalized product offerings

Such services depend extensively on technologies like Big Data, artificial intelligence, cloud infrastructure, and application programming interfaces (APIs) to collect, analyse, and utilize both financial and behavioral data.

Table 18.1 Types of data in financial services.

Type of data	Examples
Transactional data	Credit card purchases, bank transfers, and mobile payments
Behavioral data	Online browsing patterns, mobile app interactions
Financial data	Credit scores, loan repayment history, and account balances
Alternative data	User behavior on social media platforms, payment histories for utility services, geographic location tracking, and patterns in mobile top-up transactions.
Third-party data	Data from credit bureaus, financial partners, and open banking APIs

Technologies powering data-driven finance

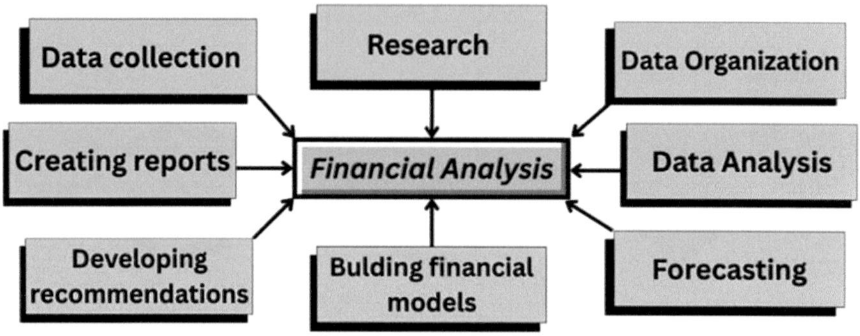

Figure 18.2 Financial data analytics flow.

- Big data analytics
  Analyses large and diverse data sets to identify patterns, detect trends, and generate actionable insights that support real-time decision-making.
- Artificial intelligence and machine learning
  Used for risk modelling, personalized recommendations, fraud detection, and dynamic pricing.
- Cloud computing
  Provides scalable infrastructure for data storage and computational capabilities, facilitating advanced analytics and the delivery of digital financial services.
- Application programming interfaces (APIs)
  Facilitate data exchange across financial institutions, third-party developers, and customers.
- Data lakes and warehouses
  Centralized storage platforms for structured and unstructured data, critical for analytical processing.

18.1.1 Key applications in financial services

- **Credit scoring and underwriting**
  Data-driven models assess creditworthiness using both traditional and alternative data, improving access to credit for underserved populations. **Example**: FinTech lenders like Tala and Upstart use behavioral and smartphone data to assess loan risk.

Structured Data	Unstructured Data
Can be displayed in rows, columns and relational databases	Cannot be displayed in rows, columns and relational databases
Numbers, dates and strings	Images, audio, video, word processing files, e-mails, spreadsheets
Estimated 20% of enterprise data (Gartner)	Estimated 80% of enterprise data (Gartner)
Requires less storage	Requires more storage
Easier to manage and protect with legacy solutions	More difficult to manage and protect with legacy solutions

Figure 18.3 Structured vs unstructured data in FinTech.

- **Personalized banking**
  Banks and FinTech's analyse customer spending, savings habits, and goals to recommend tailored financial products. **Example**: AI-powered chatbots offering savings advice based on spending history.
- **Fraud detection and AML**
  Machine learning-powered real-time anomaly detection systems identify irregular activities promptly, thereby enhancing the prevention of fraud and money laundering. **Example**: Transaction monitoring systems that learn from past fraud patterns.
- **Robo-advisory and wealth management**
  Algorithms analyse market data and customer profiles to offer personalized investment portfolios. **Example**: Wealth front, betterment, and other robo-advisors offering AI-based investment strategies.
- **Insurance pricing and claims management**
  Insurtech firms use data from devices (e.g., telematics in cars) to personalize premiums and automate claims.
- **SME and microfinance lending**
  Alternative data, such as transaction records or utility bills, help lenders assess the credit risk of unbanked or underbanked businesses.

Figure 18.4 Data-driven decision-making.

Table 18.2 Benefits of data-driven financial services.

Benefit	Description
Enhanced customer experience	Personalized, responsive services based on customer behavior
Better risk management	Predictive analytics improves risk modelling and early warning systems
Operational efficiency	Automation and data integration reduce manual processes and costs
Financial inclusion	Alternative data helps reach underbanked or thin-file customers
Faster decision-making	Real-time data allows for instant credit decisions or fraud alerts

Table 18.3 Challenges in implementation.

Challenge	Explanation
Data privacy and security	Sensitive financial data must be protected against breaches and misuse
Bias in AI models	Machine learning models can replicate social or economic biases
Data quality issues	Inaccurate or incomplete data can lead to wrong decisions
Regulatory compliance	Must comply with data protection laws like GDPR or India's DPDP Act
Integration complexity	Legacy systems may not be compatible with modern data technologies

18.2 Data Analytics and Metadata in FinTech

In today's digital financial ecosystem, data is not just an asset – it is the foundation of innovation, efficiency, and competitiveness. **Data analytics** and **metadata** are two pillars supporting the intelligent use of information in financial technologies (FinTech). From customer behavior predictions to real-time fraud detection and algorithmic trading, data-driven strategies define modern financial services. This chapter explores the significance, technologies, and applications of data analytics and metadata in the FinTech ecosystem, emphasizing how these elements drive informed decision-making, regulatory compliance, and personalized financial services.

Data analytics involves analysing, converting, and modelling data to uncover meaningful insights. Within the FinTech sector, it plays a crucial role in turning raw transaction data into strategic business intelligence.

Table 18.4 Types of data analytics.

Type	Purpose	Example in FinTech
Descriptive analytics	Understand historical data trends	Monthly customer spending summary
Diagnostic analytics	Understand why something happened	Analysing the causes of increased loan defaults
Predictive analytics	Forecast future events based on trends and patterns	Predicting customer churn or credit risk
Prescriptive analytics	Recommend actions based on predictions	Portfolio rebalancing advice from robo-advisors

18.2.1 Tools and technologies

- **Data warehouses** (e.g., Snowflake, Google Big Query)
- **BI Tools** (e.g., Tableau, Power BI)
- **Machine learning frameworks** (e.g., TensorFlow, Scikit-learn)
- **Real-time analytics** (e.g., Apache Kafka, Spark Streaming)

18.2.2 Applications in financial services

- Credit risk scoring
- Fraud detection and prevention
- Customer segmentation
- Real-time trading algorithms
- Personalized financial planning

18.2.3 Role of metadata in financial systems

Metadata is "data about data." It provides contextual information about data assets, making it easier to locate, interpret, and manage them within a system.

Table 18.5 Types of Metadata.

Type	Description	Example
Descriptive metadata	Provides information about the content	"Customer: John Doe, Transaction: ₹5,000, Date: 2025-05-01"
Structural metadata	Describes how data is organized and formatted	Table schema for a bank's transaction database
Administrative metadata	Offers information on data governance	Data owner: Risk department; Access: Read-only
Provenance metadata	Shows origin and changes to the data	Created by: ATM network; Processed by: Anti-fraud engine

Functions of metadata

- Enhances data discoverability and management
- Supports regulatory reporting and audits
- Enables data lineage and traceability
- Facilitates integration across platforms

Metadata and data governance

Metadata plays a vital role in effective data governance by helping maintain the accuracy, consistency, security, and regulatory compliance of data.

Key elements include:

- **Data stewardship**
- **Data quality management**
- **Access control**
- **Audit trails**

Regulatory importance

Financial institutions must maintain metadata for:

- Anti-money laundering (AML) compliance
- Know your customer (KYC) verification

- GDPR, CCPA, and RBI guidelines
- Basel III and MiFID II reporting

Integration of data analytics and metadata

Metadata enhances the effectiveness of data analytics by providing meaning and structure. For instance, metadata in a credit scoring model ensures that inputs are correctly labelled and interpreted, thus ensuring accurate risk assessments.

Metadata-driven analytics pipeline

- **Data ingestion** → Metadata captures source details
- **Data cleaning** → Metadata ensures correct format and usage
- **Model training** → Metadata labels, variables, and parameters
- **Interpretation** → Metadata explains outputs for decision-makers

Example: Fraud detection system

- **Analytics**: Real-time pattern recognition
- **Metadata**: Tracks transaction source, timestamp, location, device fingerprint

Challenges and future trends

Challenges

- **Data silos** limit visibility
- **Poor metadata quality** leads to misinterpretation
- **Privacy concerns** around metadata exposure
- **Integration complexity** across legacy systems

18.2.4 Personalized credit scoring for the underbanked

In many developing regions, a significant portion of the population remains underbanked or financially excluded due to the absence of formal credit histories or access to traditional banking institutions. This lack of financial documentation often disqualifies individuals from obtaining loans or other financial services through conventional credit evaluation methods. In response to this issue, a FinTech startup has introduced an innovative, data-driven solution aimed at redefining how creditworthiness is assessed.

Rather than relying on standard financial records such as income statements or prior loan histories, the startup utilizes alternative digital footprints generated through daily mobile and online activities. These include mobile phone recharge patterns, geographic movement tracked via geolocation data, and interactions on social media platforms. Such behavioral data provides nuanced insights into a user's financial habits, lifestyle stability, and reliability, offering a more holistic and inclusive picture of credit risk. The strategy is particularly effective in targeting populations that are digitally active but financially undocumented, such as informal sector workers, young adults without banking experience, or individuals in rural or semi-urban areas. By tapping into data already available through smartphones and apps, the startup is able to design a personalized credit scoring mechanism that adapts to real-time behavioral changes, ensuring continuous evaluation rather than a one-time snapshot.

This model not only broadens access to credit but also empowers financial institutions to make more informed and dynamic lending decisions. It bridges the gap between digital presence and financial identity, paving the way for a more inclusive financial ecosystem.

Technological approach

The platform employs advanced data analytics techniques to evaluate non-traditional data sources such as mobile recharge behavior, user geolocation patterns, and social media engagement. These behavioral indicators provide valuable insights into financial habits and risk profiles. By analyzing these diverse data points, the system can build a comprehensive understanding of an individual's creditworthiness, even in the absence of historical banking data.

Role of metadata

Metadata plays a foundational role in this credit scoring model. It helps classify and organize data from various sources, timestamps the collection process, and supports the enforcement of data governance policies. This ensures that all data handling practices remain transparent, traceable, and compliant with privacy and regulatory standards.

Outcome

The implementation of this model has enabled the startup to deliver real-time and dynamic credit scoring with enhanced accuracy. By incorporating alternative data, the system has broadened financial inclusion, allowing underserved individuals to access credit facilities that were previously unavailable through traditional evaluation methods.

Behavioral analytics combined with strong metadata governance can significantly improve the reach and fairness of credit scoring systems. This approach offers a scalable solution for financial inclusion in regions with limited access to formal financial institutions.

The synergy between **data analytics** and **metadata** forms the backbone of intelligent financial ecosystems. By contextualizing data through metadata and analysing it with advanced techniques, FinTech firms can unlock deeper insights, enhance customer experiences, and remain compliant in a dynamic regulatory landscape. As FinTech evolves, the mastery of data and metadata will continue to be a competitive and strategic imperative.

18.3 Differential Privacy and Data Breach Risks in FinTech

With the growing reliance on data within financial services, concerns surrounding privacy and security have become increasingly significant. FinTech firms manage large volumes of sensitive financial and personal information, positioning them as key targets for data breaches and cyber threats. While data analytics empowers innovation, it also raises significant concerns about user privacy. **Differential privacy** has emerged as a modern technique for preserving individual privacy while enabling data analysis. Simultaneously, understanding and mitigating **data breach risks** have become an essential part of digital finance governance.

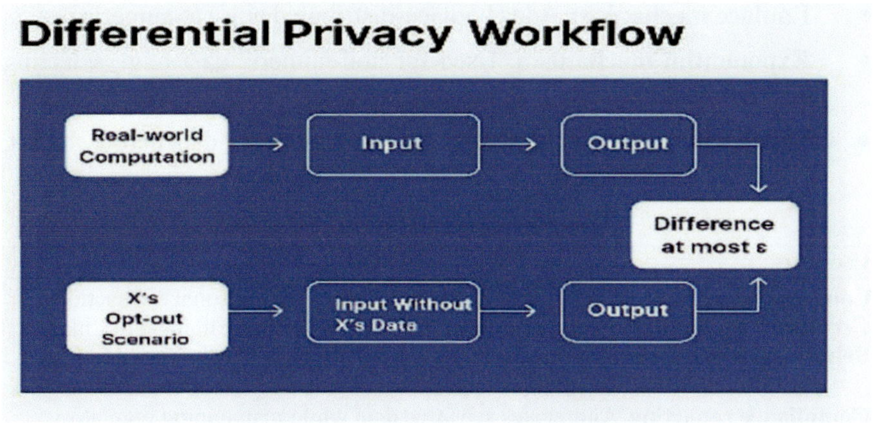

Figure 18.5 Differential privacy workflow.

This chapter explores the principles of differential privacy, the nature of data breach risks, and the intersection of these domains in FinTech systems.

Differential privacy is a **mathematical framework** that allows organizations to **analyse and share aggregate data** without revealing information about any individual within a dataset. It ensures that the output of any analysis is **statistically similar** regardless of whether an individual's data is included. The presence or absence of a single record should not significantly affect the outcome of data analysis. Differential privacy ensures individual data confidentiality while enabling analytics, helping prevent data breaches in financial systems [4]; [5]. Data breaches, as in the Capital One incident, highlight the importance of secure architecture and continuous monitoring for sensitive financial information [6]; [7]. Supervised learning techniques enable predictive modeling, such as credit scoring and fraud detection, using labeled historical datasets [8].

18.3.1 How it works

Differential privacy works by introducing random noise into datasets or query outputs, thereby masking specific individual data entries and enhancing privacy protection. The **privacy budget** (denoted by ε, or *epsilon*) quantifies the amount of privacy loss tolerated:

- **Lower** $\varepsilon \rightarrow$ More privacy, less accuracy
- **Higher** $\varepsilon \rightarrow$ Less privacy, more accuracy

18.3.2 Techniques used

- **Laplace mechanism**: Adds Laplace-distributed noise to numeric results
- **Exponential mechanism**: Used for non-numeric data (e.g., selecting best outputs)
- **Local differential privacy**: Each user perturbs their data before sharing

Table 18.6 Applications in FinTech.

Use case	Differential privacy benefit
Consumer analytics	Analyses trends without exposing personal transactions
Credit risk modelling	Protects individual credit histories while training risk models
Behavioral biometrics	Preserves user identity while analysing behavior for fraud detection
Compliance reporting	Aggregates sensitive data while maintaining regulatory standards

18.3.3 Data breach risks in FinTech

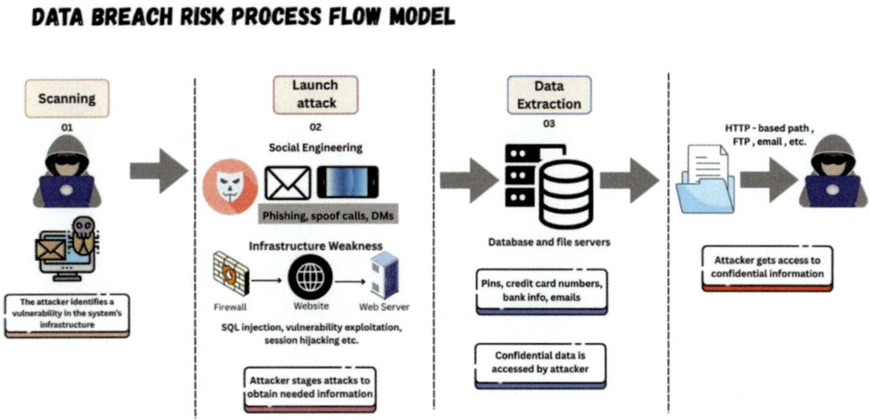

Figure 18.6 FinTech data breach risk management model.

A **data breach** is an unauthorized access or disclosure of confidential data. In FinTech, this typically involves personal identifiable information (PII), financial records, transaction histories, or login credentials.

Table 18.7 Common causes.

Cause	Description
Phishing and social engineering	Trick users or staff into revealing credentials
Weak authentication mechanisms	Poor password practices, lack of multi-factor authentication
Software vulnerabilities	Bugs or flaws in code that allow unauthorized access
Insider threats	Malicious or negligent actions by employees
Cloud misconfigurations	Incorrect settings in cloud environments expose data

Impact of data breaches

- **Financial losses**
- **Reputation damage**
- **Regulatory penalties**
- **Loss of consumer trust**

Table 18.8 Differential privacy vs traditional privacy techniques.

Feature	Traditional techniques	Differential privacy
Data anonymization	Removes PII	Adds noise to preserve group-level statistics
Data masking	Replaces sensitive values	Does not modify the original data but affects the results
Privacy guarantees	Often re-identifiable	Mathematically provable protection
Use in analytics	Limited due to loss of information	High utility with privacy trade-off
Re-identification risk	High with external datasets	Very low due to randomized noise injection

Regulatory and legal landscape

Regulatory mandates

- **GDPR (EU)**: Requires data minimization, privacy by design, and breach reporting
- **RBI (India)**: Mandates encryption, secure authentication, and incident reporting
- **CCPA (California)**: Enforces rights to access, delete, and restrict data usage

Differential privacy in policy

Some regulators and institutions now **recommend or require** differential privacy for:

- Public data releases (e.g., U.S. Census Bureau)
- FinTech open banking APIs
- Federated learning in mobile finance apps

Mitigating data breach risks with privacy engineering

Best practices

- Encrypt data at rest and in transit
- Implement multi-factor authentication
- Adopt zero-trust architecture
- Train employees on phishing and security
- Conduct regular penetration testing

Integrating differential privacy

- **In data analytics**: For internal reporting and customer insights
- **In federated learning**: Shared AI models without centralized data
- **In compliance**: Demonstrating privacy adherence during audits

As data becomes the foundation of FinTech innovation, ensuring privacy and security is not optional – it is essential. Differential privacy offers a mathematically robust solution for preserving individual anonymity while unlocking insights from big data. When integrated into modern FinTech architectures alongside strong cybersecurity protocols, it forms a powerful defence against both **data breaches** and **regulatory non-compliance**. To remain competitive and compliant, FinTech firms must adopt **privacy-first design principles**, guided by the principles of **differential privacy** and supported by continuous monitoring of **data breach risks**.

Differential privacy and data breach risks in FinTech

In the modern FinTech landscape, data serves as the fuel that powers digital financial innovation. From personalized financial products to fraud detection systems, data analytics enables institutions to better serve customers and enhance operational efficiency. Nonetheless, the extensive accumulation, storage, and analysis of personal and financial information heighten the vulnerability of both users and organizations to serious privacy and cybersecurity threats. As cyber threats grow more sophisticated and data breaches more prevalent, FinTech firms are under pressure to balance innovation with responsibility.

Differential privacy has emerged as a robust mathematical framework to ensure individual privacy in large-scale data analysis. Meanwhile, data breach risks are becoming central to FinTech risk management strategies. This chapter explores both concepts in depth, highlighting their implications, technologies, and best practices for secure and privacy-preserving financial ecosystems. Differential privacy is a mathematical framework designed to ensure the accuracy of statistical database queries while significantly reducing the risk of exposing individual data entries. The core idea is that whether a person's data is included in the dataset, the result of any analysis should not be significantly affected. A mechanism is said to provide ε- differential privacy if the probability of any output does not change by more than a factor of e^ε when a single data point is added or removed from the dataset.

Purpose in FinTech

- Ensures **user confidentiality** in financial data analytics
- Supports **privacy-by-design** in data infrastructure
- Enables **regulatory compliance** with frameworks like GDPR and CCPA
- Builds **trust** with privacy-conscious consumers

How differential privacy works

Differential privacy introduces **statistical noise** into queries and algorithms. The **amount and distribution of this noise** depend on a parameter called the **privacy budget** (ε):

- A **low ε value** means stronger privacy but lower accuracy.
- A **high ε value** provides more accurate results with weaker privacy guarantees.

Common mechanisms

- **Laplace mechanism**: Adds Laplace-distributed noise to numerical results.
- **Exponential mechanism**: Useful for categorical data.
- **Local differential privacy**: Each user perturbs their data before sharing.

Applications of differential privacy

FinTech personalized banking

Banks and FinTech firms can analyse spending behavior and usage patterns **without accessing exact transaction data**, enabling secure and personalized financial services.

Credit scoring and risk models

Differential privacy enables the training of AI models on customer financial data **without compromising individual identities**, making it suitable for underbanked and privacy-sensitive users.

Fraud detection

Real-time fraud detection systems can be built on differentially private datasets to **avoid profiling individuals**, especially in compliance with anti-discrimination laws.

Open banking APIs

Differential privacy ensures that **third-party developers** accessing financial data through open banking frameworks cannot reverse-engineer user identities.

Understanding data breach risks

A data breach is an event in which confidential, sensitive, or protected information is accessed, shared, or utilized without proper authorization. In FinTech, this includes personal identifiable information (PII), account credentials, credit histories, transaction records, and more.

Table 18.9 Common causes of data breaches.

Cause	Description
Phishing attacks	Deceptive emails or messages to steal user credentials
Weak access controls	Poor authentication methods or improper permission settings
Malware and ransomware	Malicious software that infiltrates systems and steals data
Insider threats	Employees or contractors misusing access privileges
Unsecured APIs	Improperly protected financial APIs are exposing data
Cloud misconfigurations	Incorrect cloud storage settings are making data publicly accessible

Impact of data breaches on FinTech

- **Financial losses**: Due to theft, lawsuits, and regulatory fines.
- **Reputational damage**: Loss of trust and brand value.
- **Customer attrition**: Users may abandon services post-breach.
- **Regulatory penalties**: Under laws like GDPR, CCPA, and RBI guidelines.
- **Operational disruption:** Systems may be taken offline or quarantined.

Linking differential privacy and data breach mitigation risk minimization

By using differential privacy, organizations can share and analyse data **without ever storing the exact sensitive values**, thereby reducing the **impact of a potential breach**.

Legal compliance

Differential privacy helps meet **data minimization and protection requirements** under global regulations likc:

- **General Data Protection Regulation (GDPR)**
- **California Consumer Privacy Act (CCPA)**

- **Reserve Bank of India (RBI) Guidelines**

Example: A FinTech app providing personalized financial advice uses differentially private algorithms to analyse user data for trends and suggestions. Even if the system is breached, the exposed data lacks **identifiable patterns**, rendering it **useless to attackers**.

Best practices for data privacy and breach prevention

Incorporate privacy by design

- Embed **differential privacy** in the development of data systems.
- Ensure **data minimization**: Only collect what is essential.

Strengthen security infrastructure

- Implement **multi-factor authentication (MFA)**
- **Conduct penetration testing**
- Apply encryption at rest and in transit

Staff training and awareness

- **Conduct regular cybersecurity training for employees.**
- Use simulation-based phishing exercises.

Incident response planning

- Have a **breach response team** in place.
- Develop **user notification protocols**.
- Maintain **audit trails and logs** for investigations.

As the FinTech sector grows in complexity and scale, so do its responsibilities in protecting user data. **Differential privacy** provides a mathematically sound approach to ensure privacy in analytics and innovation. At the same time, understanding and mitigating **data breach risks** is fundamental to business continuity and user trust. The future of FinTech lies in the ability to innovate responsibly, harnessing data without compromising privacy. By embedding privacy-first technologies like differential privacy and following robust security protocols, FinTech organizations can deliver secure, compliant, and consumer-centric financial services.

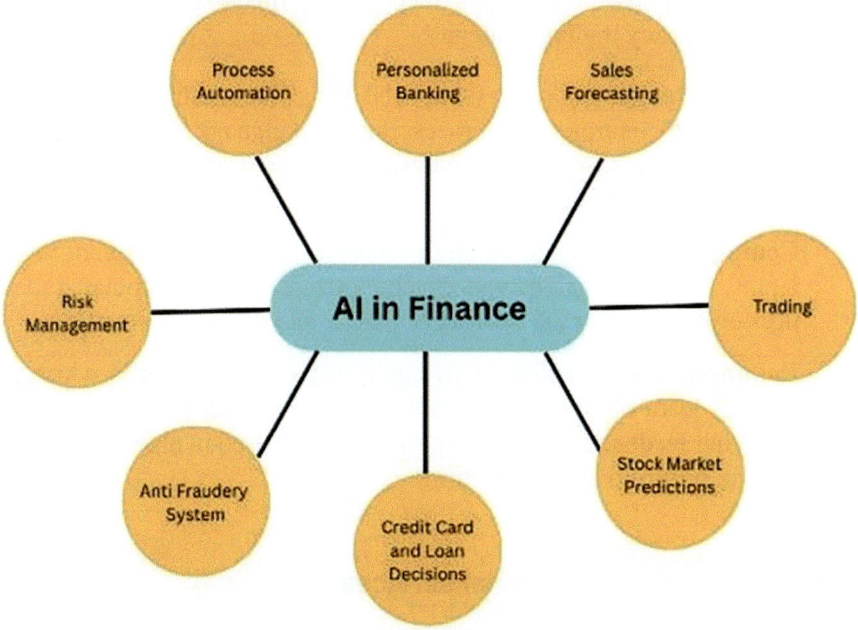

Figure 18.7 AI in financial services.

Foundations of artificial intelligence

Artificial Intelligence (AI) involves the development of machines capable of emulating human intelligence to perform functions such as reasoning, learning, perception, and natural language understanding. In the financial sector, AI facilitates the automation and enhancement of tasks that traditionally required human cognitive effort, thereby improving operational efficiency, decision-making, and customer service.

Key AI technologies in finance

- **Machine learning (ML):** A foundational component of AI, ML encompasses algorithms that analyse historical data to identify patterns and generate predictive insights, widely used in fraud detection, credit scoring, and market forecasting.

- **Deep learning:** A specialized branch of ML that utilizes artificial neural networks to model complex patterns. Deep learning is particularly effective in tasks like voice recognition, image classification, and high-frequency trading strategies.

- **Natural language processing (NLP):** This technology enables machines to interpret and process human language. In finance, NLP powers chatbots, sentiment analysis in market trends, and automated document processing.
- **Computer vision:** Focused on the analysis and interpretation of visual inputs, computer vision supports applications such as automated identity verification (e.g., KYC), surveillance, and document scanning.
- **Reinforcement learning:** A dynamic learning paradigm in which AI systems learn optimal strategies by interacting with environments and receiving feedback. This is increasingly being used in algorithmic trading and portfolio optimization.

Applications of AI in financial services

AI in banking

- **Chatbots and virtual assistants**: Automate customer service using NLP (e.g., HDFC's EVA, SBI's SIA).
- **Credit scoring**: ML models assess borrower risk using alternative data sources.
- **Fraud detection**: AI systems identify suspicious patterns and flag potentially fraudulent transactions.
- **Process automation**: Robotic Process Automation (RPA) for back-office functions like KYC, compliance checks, and account onboarding.

AI in wealth and asset management

- **Robo-advisors**: Algorithm-based financial advisors that recommend portfolios based on client preferences.
- **Portfolio optimization**: AI models analyse historical and real-time data for asset allocation.
- **Sentiment analysis**: NLP-based tools monitor social media and news to assess market sentiment.

AI in insurance (Insurtech)

- **Claims processing**: Automation of claim assessment through image recognition and NLP.
- **Risk assessment**: Predictive analytics to assess individual risk profiles.
- **Underwriting**: Real-time underwriting using data from IoT devices and AI- based evaluation.

AI in capital markets

- **Algorithmic trading**: High-frequency trading based on real-time data and predictive models.
- **Market surveillance**: Monitoring trading activities for manipulations or unusual behaviors.
- **Forecasting**: Predictive models forecast asset prices, volatility, and liquidity patterns.

Table 18.10 Benefits of AI in Finance.

Benefit	Description
Efficiency gains	Automates routine tasks and reduces processing time.
Enhanced accuracy	Reduces human errors in data analysis and decision-making.
Real-time insights	Enables instant processing and reaction to market changes.
Personalization	Offers tailored services to customers based on behavior and preferences.
Cost reduction	Minimizes manpower costs through automation.

Challenges and risks

- **Data quality and bias**
  AI models depend on high-quality data. Biased or incomplete data can lead to discriminatory outcomes, especially in credit scoring and insurance underwriting.
- **Model explainability**
  A significant concern with many AI models, especially those based on deep learning, is their "black box" nature – wherein the internal decision-making processes are not easily interpretable. This opacity creates challenges for regulatory compliance and undermines customer trust in AI-driven systems.

- **Regulatory compliance**
  AI-driven systems are required to adhere to data protection frameworks such as the General Data Protection Regulation (GDPR) and the Personal Data Protection Bill (PDPB), as well as comply with sector-specific financial regulations. Regulators demand explainability and fairness in AI-driven decisions.
- **Cybersecurity**
  AI systems themselves can be targeted by adversarial attacks, where manipulated inputs produce incorrect results.

AI governance and ethical considerations

- **Fairness and non-discrimination**
  AI should ensure fair access to financial services without reinforcing existing biases.
- **Transparency**
  Financial institutions must provide explanations for AI decisions, particularly in loan approvals or risk assessments.
- **Accountability**
  Clear ownership and human oversight are essential to prevent unregulated decision- making.
- **Data privacy**
  AI must process personal data within the boundaries of consent and privacy regulations.

Regulatory perspectives

Global level

- The **Basel Committee** is exploring the implications of AI in banking supervision.
- The European Union's AI Act seeks to establish a regulatory framework for high-risk AI systems, with particular attention to sectors, such as finance where algorithmic decisions can significantly impact individuals and institutions.

India:

- The **RBI** encourages responsible AI use in banking while emphasizing data security and customer protection.
- The **IRDAI** and **SEBI** are evaluating AI use in insurance and capital markets, respectively.

Future trends

- **AI-Powered Compliance (RegTech)**: Real-time compliance monitoring using ML.
- **Conversational AI**: Multilingual financial assistants powered by generative AI.
- **Explainable AI (XAI)**: Making model predictions more transparent and interpretable.
- **Federated learning**: Collaborative model training without centralized data sharing.

AI is redefining the future of finance by enabling smarter decision-making, automation, and superior customer experiences. However, its adoption must be approached with care, balancing innovation with ethics, compliance, and risk management. The successful deployment of AI in finance hinges on robust governance frameworks, high-quality data, and continuous monitoring of model behavior.

18.4 Supervised, Unsupervised, and Reinforcement Learning

Artificial intelligence (AI) comprises a broad spectrum of computational methods, among which machine learning (ML) stands out as a foundational subset. ML enables systems to learn patterns and make data-driven decisions without the need for explicit programming. In the context of financial services, ML is primarily applied through three core learning paradigms, each suited to different analytical and operational needs.

18.4.1 Supervised learning

Supervised learning involves training algorithms on labeled datasets, where each input is paired with a corresponding output. The model learns to recognize patterns and establish mappings between inputs and their correct outputs, enabling accurate predictions on new, unseen data.

Examples in finance

- **Credit scoring**: Predicting loan default based on historical borrower data.
- **Fraud detection**: Identifying fraudulent transactions by learning from past examples.

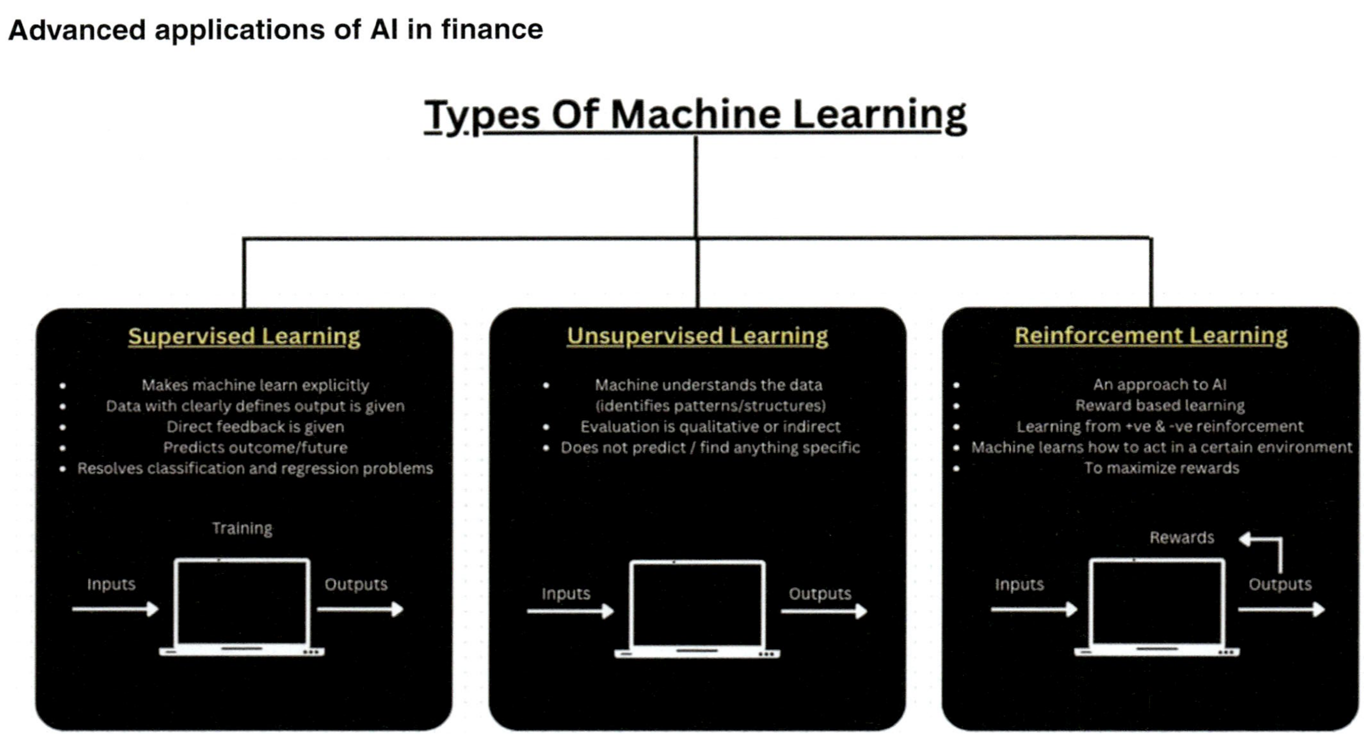

Figure 18.8 Supervised vs unsupervised vs reinforcement learning.

- **Stock price prediction**: Training models with past prices and market indicators.

Popular algorithms:

- Linear regression
- Decision trees
- Support vector machines (SVM)
- Neural networks

18.4.2 Unsupervised learning

Unsupervised learning operates on datasets that lack predefined labels, aiming to uncover underlying structures, patterns, or groupings within the data without prior knowledge of the outcomes. Unsupervised learning helps identify hidden patterns and anomalies, which can improve anti-money laundering and risk management strategies [9].

Examples in finance:

- **Customer segmentation**: Grouping customers by spending behavior.
- **Anomaly detection**: Identifying unusual transactions or outliers.
- **Portfolio clustering**: Creating diverse investment baskets based on asset similarities.

Popular algorithms:

- K-Means clustering
- Principal component analysis (PCA)
- Hierarchical clustering

18.4.3 Reinforcement learning

Reinforcement learning (RL) is a learning paradigm in which an autonomous agent interacts with its environment, gradually improving its performance through trial and error by receiving feedback in the form of rewards or penalties based on its actions. Reinforcement learning allows financial systems to adaptively optimize trading strategies and dynamic resource allocation over time [10].

Examples in finance:

- **Algorithmic trading**: RL agents learn to maximize returns by exploring strategies.
- **Dynamic pricing**: Adapting loan or insurance prices based on market response.
- **Portfolio optimization:** Continuously adjusting asset allocation based on market movements.

Key concepts:

- **Agent**: Learner or decision-maker.
- **Environment**: Financial market or system.
- **Reward function:** Guides learning by assigning positive/negative outcomes.

AI in governance and compliance

With increased regulatory scrutiny, AI is now central to ensuring financial institutions meet legal and ethical standards. It aids in automating regulatory compliance and improving governance frameworks. AI enhances governance and compliance by automating regulatory reporting and monitoring adherence to evolving financial regulations [11]; [12].

Regulatory technology (RegTech)

AI helps build intelligent RegTech systems capable of monitoring regulatory changes, automating compliance tasks, and ensuring timely filings.

Applications:

- **Automated reporting**: AI prepares and submits regulatory reports.
- **Transaction monitoring**: Identifies suspicious or illegal financial activities.
- **Policy mapping:** AI tools map internal policies to applicable regulations.

Governance frameworks

Artificial Intelligence strengthens corporate governance by facilitating real-time risk identification, promoting transparency in organizational processes, and enabling automated monitoring and compliance oversight. Ethical AI frameworks are increasingly adopted to ensure fairness, transparency, and accountability in automated financial decisions ([13]; [14]).

AI tools for governance

- **Audit bots**: Detect anomalies and inconsistencies in financial reports.
- **Behavioral analytics**: Monitor employee activities for fraud or unethical behavior.
- **Digital identity verification**: AI-based KYC tools ensure proper client due diligence.

Table 18.11 Challenges in AI-driven compliance.

Challenge	Description
Data privacy	Ensuring AI tools comply with GDPR, PDPB, and other regulations.
Model explainability	Regulators require that AI decisions be interpretable.
False positives in alerts	Over-alerting can waste compliance resources.
Regulatory maturity	Regulation often lags technological innovation.

AI in risk management and personalization

Risk and customer experience are two major areas transformed by AI. By analysing vast data, AI provides real-time, predictive insights that can mitigate risks and tailor services.

Risk management

AI offers predictive models that help financial institutions pre-emptively manage financial, credit, operational, and cyber risks.

Applications

- **Credit risk scoring**: Predicting a customer's likelihood of default.
- **Operational risk**: Detecting errors or fraud in business processes.
- **Market risk**: Simulating market stress scenarios using AI.
- **Cyber risk**: AI-based security systems detect intrusions and anomalies.

Tools used

- Predictive analytics

- Risk heat maps
- Automated risk assessment engines

Personalization of financial services

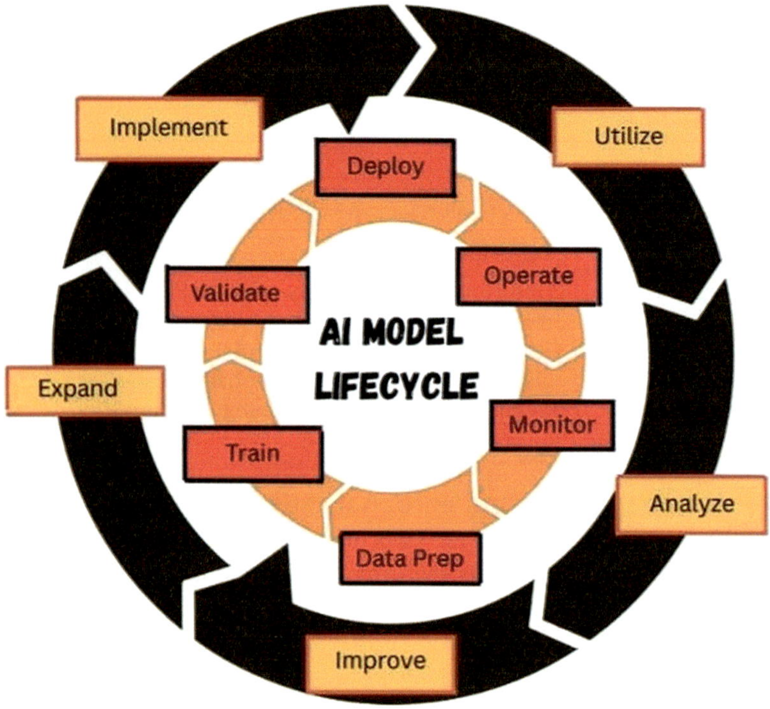

Figure 18.9 AI model lifecycle in finance.

AI-driven personalization enhances customer engagement by delivering targeted, relevant, and timely financial services.

Examples:

- **Customized investment portfolios**
  AI-driven advisory systems create tailored investment strategies by analysing individual user preferences, financial goals, and

risk tolerance levels, thereby enhancing portfolio suitability and engagement.

- **Intelligent chatbots and virtual assistants**
  AI-powered conversational agents offer round-the-clock customer service, responding to user queries in real time with context-aware and personalized assistance.
- **Spending analysis and budget optimization**
  Machine learning models evaluate a user's financial behavior, identifying spending trends and providing actionable recommendations to improve budgeting and promote savings.
- **Real-time loan pricing**
  Advanced AI algorithms dynamically adjust loan interest rates and terms by continuously analysing borrower behavior, creditworthiness, and prevailing market conditions.

AI is not merely a tool for efficiency – it is a critical enabler of strategic transformation in finance. From intelligent automation in governance to sophisticated modelling in risk management and hyper-personalized financial services, AI is driving a new wave of innovation and competitive advantage in FinTech. In risk management, AI models predict market, credit, and operational risks more accurately, helping institutions mitigate potential losses [15]. Personalized financial services, such as tailored loans and investment advice, are powered by AI-driven recommendation systems [16]. However, its adoption must be accompanied by strong governance, ethical considerations, and compliance mechanisms to mitigate associated risks.

18.5 AI in Governance and Compliance

In an era of growing regulatory complexity, artificial intelligence (AI) has emerged as a transformative tool in financial governance and compliance. Traditional compliance methods are often labor-intensive, reactive, and error-prone. AI, by contrast, enables proactive, scalable, and data-driven compliance frameworks that enhance transparency, reduce costs, and mitigate risk.

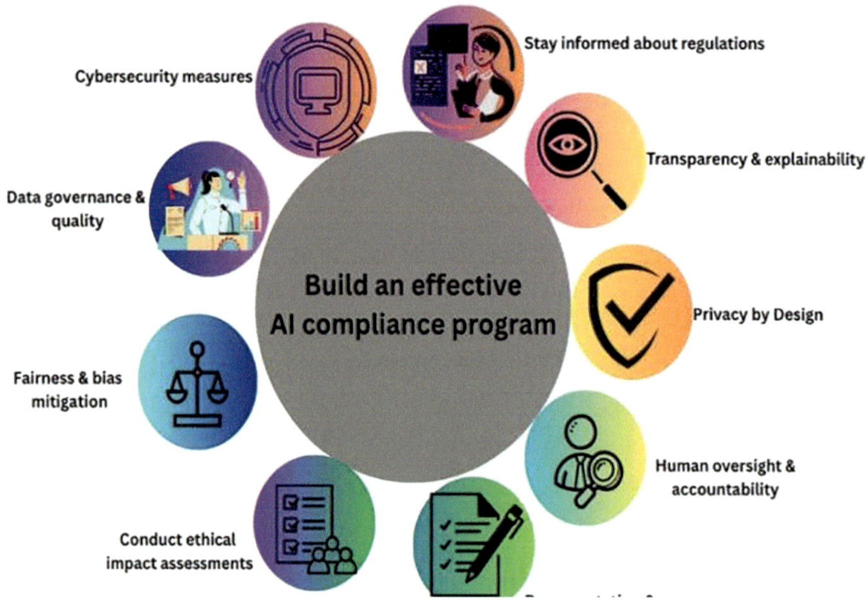

Figure 18.10 AI-powered regulatory compliance.

This chapter explores how AI is redefining compliance operations, regulatory reporting, ethical governance, and internal control systems in financial services.

18.5.1 Understanding governance and compliance in finance

- Governance refers to the frameworks, controls, and oversight mechanisms ensuring ethical behavior, strategic alignment, and risk mitigation in financial institutions.
- Compliance refers to the process of ensuring conformity with applicable external regulations, statutory requirements, and internal organizational policies that govern financial activities.

AI supports both by automating decision-making, reducing human bias, detecting anomalies, and enabling real-time monitoring.

Role of AI in governance

AI enhances **corporate governance** by providing tools to monitor internal behavior, identify conflicts of interest, and ensure organizational alignment with laws and standards.

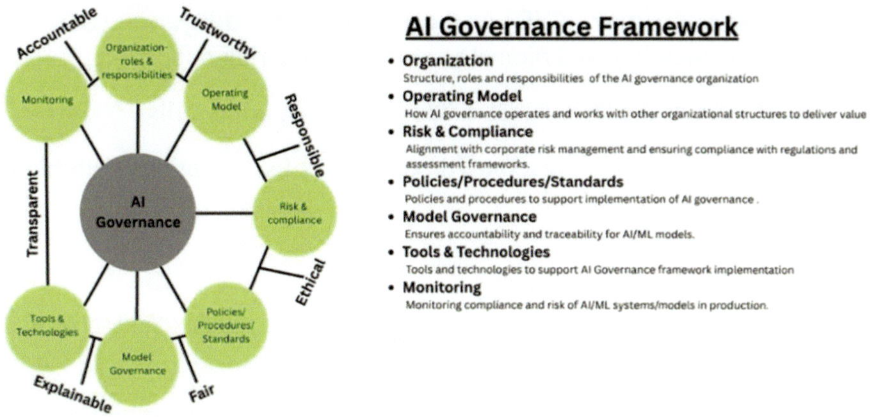

Figure 18.11 Explainable AI in governance.

Key areas

Internal audit automation

- AI audits financial statements, internal controls, and operational logs.
- Machine learning identifies inconsistencies or irregularities.

Behavior analytics

- AI monitors employee behavior, flagging suspicious actions like insider trading or data leaks.
- Useful in detecting **whistleblower cases**, unethical conduct, and breaches of fiduciary duty.

AI-driven ethics monitoring

- Natural language processing (NLP) scans communications (emails, chats) for regulatory red flags.
- AI models assess compliance with ethical standards and codes of conduct.

AI in regulatory compliance

Regulatory compliance involves processes such as reporting, surveillance, client onboarding (KYC), anti-money laundering (AML), and fraud detection. AI streamlines these functions with accuracy and scalability.

Know your customer (KYC) and customer due diligence (CDD)

- Facial recognition and biometric verification during onboarding.
- NLP extracts data from documents (ID proofs, utility bills).
- AI identifies politically exposed persons (PEPs) or entities with high-risk profiles.

Anti-money laundering (AML)

- AI analyses transaction patterns to detect anomalies and potential money laundering activities.
- Machine learning models evolve to new tactics used by criminals.

Transaction monitoring and alerting

- Real-time analysis of high-volume transactions.
- AI classifies and prioritizes alerts, reducing false positives.

Automated regulatory reporting

- AI auto-generates reports for regulatory submissions using structured and unstructured data.
- Ensures consistency, timeliness, and data integrity.

Table 18.12 Benefits of AI in governance and compliance.

Benefit	Description
Speed and efficiency	Real-time data processing and faster decision-making.
Accuracy and consistency	Reduction of human error and subjective judgment.
Scalability	Handles large volumes of transactions, entities, and compliance rules.
Predictive compliance	Anticipates risks and ensures proactive responses.
Cost reduction	Less manual labor and fewer compliance breaches lead to lower costs.

Table 18.13 Challenges and risks.

Challenge	Explanation
Bias and fairness	AI models trained on biased data may make discriminatory decisions.
Lack of explainability	Regulators demand transparency, which black-box models may not offer.
Regulatory uncertainty	Varying laws across jurisdictions make AI implementation complex.
Data privacy concerns	GDPR and similar laws restrict how data is collected and used by AI.
Over-reliance on technology	Automation may reduce human oversight and critical judgment.

18.5.2 Future trends in AI governance and compliance

- **Explainable AI (XAI):** More transparent and interpretable models for compliance decisions.
- **Real-time RegTech integration:** AI seamlessly integrated with live data sources and regulatory databases.
- **Self-regulatory compliance systems:** AI systems that auto-adjust compliance protocols based on regulatory changes.
- **Cross-border compliance engines:** Handling multi-jurisdictional regulatory requirements with AI logic layers.

AI is revolutionizing governance and compliance in financial services by making these processes faster, smarter, and more robust. As financial institutions continue to navigate an evolving regulatory landscape, AI tools can provide a significant competitive edge by enabling real-time oversight, reducing compliance costs, and proactively managing risk. However, responsible AI deployment requires attention to data ethics, model transparency, and cross-jurisdictional collaboration between regulators and FinTech innovators.

18.6 AI in Risk Management and Personalization

In modern financial ecosystems, managing risk and delivering personalized experiences are critical for both regulatory compliance and customer satisfaction. Traditional methods often fall short in handling massive, real-time datasets and predicting complex behaviors. Artificial Intelligence (AI), particularly machine learning and deep analytics, offers robust tools to address these challenges. Metadata-driven analytics also facilitate regulatory compliance and report efficiency in complex financial ecosystems. Differential privacy and secure multi-party computation reduce the risk of re-identification in shared financial datasets [17]; [18].

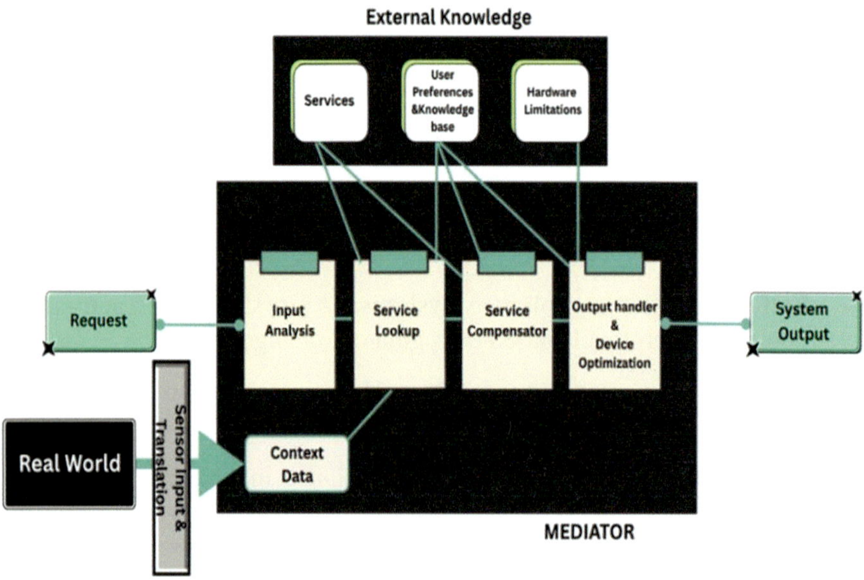

Figure 18.12 AI for financial risk prediction.

This chapter explores how AI enables proactive **risk management** and **hyper- personalization** of financial services, thereby improving operational efficiency, regulatory conformity, and customer loyalty.

18.6.1 AI in risk management

Financial risk can be broadly classified into:

- **Credit risk** – The possibility of a borrower defaulting.
- **Market risk** – Risk arising from fluctuations in asset prices or interest rates.

- **Operational risk** – Failures in internal processes or systems.
- **Liquidity risk** – Inability to meet short-term financial obligations.
- **Cyber risk** – Vulnerability to data breaches or cyberattacks.

AI helps in identifying, assessing, and mitigating these risks using advanced data analytics and predictive modelling.

Key applications of AI in risk management

Credit risk scoring

- AI analyses large datasets including credit history, income, social behavior, and transaction data.
- Machine learning models like logistic regression, XGBoost, and neural networks predict loan default probabilities.
- Provides real-time credit scoring for faster loan approvals.

Fraud detection

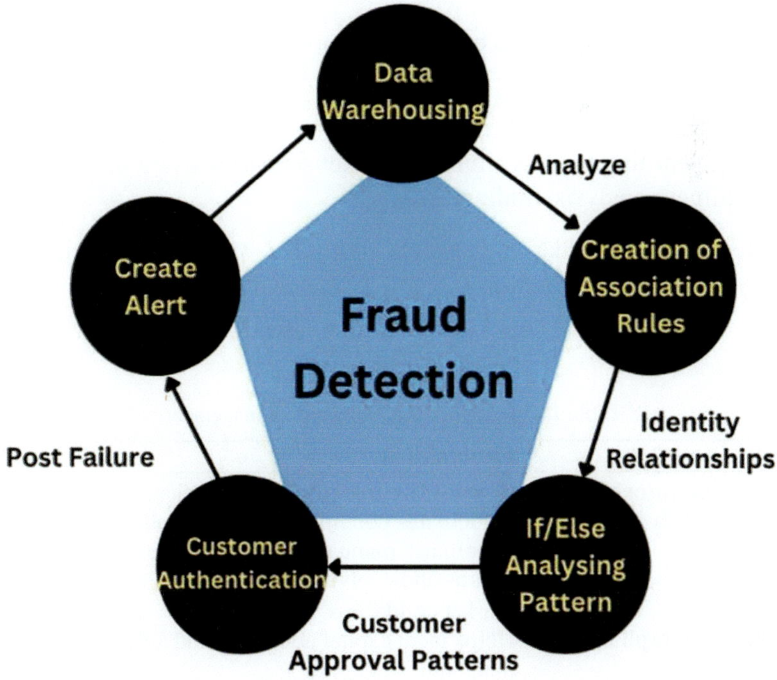

Figure 18.13 Key applications of AI in risk management with AI Use cases in risk management.

- AI uses anomaly detection to flag unusual behavior in real time.
- NLP analyses unstructured data (emails, documents) to detect fraud schemes.
- Behavioral biometrics, such as typing patterns and navigation habits, enhance identity verification.

Cybersecurity risk

- AI systems detect network anomalies, phishing attacks, and unauthorized access.
- Machine learning improves over time with exposure to new threats (adaptive defence).
- Real-time alerts and auto-response systems improve threat mitigation.

Operational risk monitoring

- AI models track internal processes to detect errors, inefficiencies, or compliance failures.
- Predicts system failures based on historical data and user patterns.

Market and liquidity risk modeling

- Deep learning models simulate market scenarios using big data (news, sentiment analysis, trading activity).
- Reinforcement learning agents optimize trading strategies under dynamic market conditions.

Table 18.14 Benefits of AI in risk management.

Benefit	Explanation
Real-time monitoring	Enables live tracking of risk indicators.
Predictive analysis	Anticipates potential defaults, fraud, or breaches.
Efficiency	Automates manual, repetitive risk evaluation tasks.
Adaptability	Learns and evolves with new types of risks and market conditions.
Regulatory compliance	Helps meet capital adequacy and anti-fraud mandates efficiently.

18.6.2 AI in personalization of financial services

Personalization refers to tailoring financial products, services, and communication to meet individual customer preferences and needs. AI makes this possible by analysing behavioral, transactional, and contextual data. Real-time analytics combined with AI enables faster detection of fraud and abnormal transactions, enhancing customer trust. Financial institutions integrating AI and big data achieve both operational efficiency and strategic innovation. Overall, data-driven financial services represent a paradigm shift toward intelligent, secure, and personalized financial ecosystems, balancing innovation with privacy and regulatory compliance.

Key personalization applications

Personalized investment advisory (robo-advisors)

- Dynamic rebalancing of portfolios using real-time market insights.
- AI-powered platforms generate personalized investment recommendations by analyzing factors such as an individual's financial objectives, risk appetite, age, and income profile.

Dynamic loan pricing and credit products

- AI assesses borrower data and market conditions to offer **customized loan terms**.
- Interest rates and repayment terms are adjusted based on predicted creditworthiness and customer behavior.

Intelligent chatbots and virtual assistants

- AI bots provide 24/7 customer support, answering queries, processing requests, and offering advice.
- NLP enables natural conversations with human-like understanding.

Transaction categorization and financial planning

- AI analyses spending patterns and suggests budgeting plans.
- Alerts users about upcoming bills, suspicious transactions, or saving opportunities.

Behavior-based marketing

- AI predicts product preferences and sends targeted offers and recommendations.

- Enhances engagement through personalized notifications and cross-sell opportunities.

Table 18.15 Used for personalization.

Technique	Application
Collaborative filtering	Recommends products based on similar users' behavior.
Content-based filtering	Recommendations are based on the user's past activity and preferences.
Reinforcement learning	Continuously improves personalization strategies through feedback.
Sentiment analysis	Understands customer emotions and opinions from feedback, social media, etc.

Table 18.16 Challenges and limitations.

Challenge	Explanation
Data privacy concerns	Collecting personal and behavioral data must comply with GDPR, PDPB, etc.
Bias in algorithms	Discriminatory outcomes may arise if the training data is not representative.
Model interpretability	Regulators require explainable decisions in lending and risk models.
Over-reliance on automation	Reduced human oversight can lead to missed judgment calls.
Integration with legacy systems	Older financial systems may not support AI deployment easily.

Summary

This chapter focuses on how financial institutions use data to improve decision-making and service delivery. It explains the importance of data analytics and metadata in understanding customer behavior and predicting financial risks. The chapter also addresses concerns such as data breaches and the need for strong cybersecurity systems to protect sensitive information. It introduces supervised and unsupervised learning techniques used in credit scoring, fraud detection, and customer segmentation. Finally, it discusses the role of artificial intelligence in governance, showing how AI helps regulators and institutions ensure transparency, compliance, and better risk management in modern financial systems.

Case Study: Mastercard Decision Intelligence – Real-Time Risk Assessment

As the volume of digital and card-based transactions surged globally, financial institutions encountered increasing difficulty distinguishing between fraudulent and legitimate activity. Conventional fraud detection systems – relying on preset rules like high transaction amounts or foreign activity – often failed to adapt to sophisticated and evolving fraud tactics. These outdated systems not only missed advanced fraud attempts but also led to a significant number of false positives, where legitimate transactions were wrongly declined. This not only eroded consumer trust but also caused revenue losses and reputational damage. Mastercard recognized the need for an adaptive, intelligent solution and responded by launching **Decision Intelligence** – an AI-powered fraud detection engine capable of analyzing every transaction in real time using a contextual, risk-based approach.

The platform leverages machine learning algorithms trained on a vast array of transactional data, analysing variables such as transaction location, amount, cardholder behavior, device information, and purchase timing. Unlike rule-based systems, Mastercard's AI continually evolves, learning from new data and refining its fraud detection models to adapt to emerging threats. As a result, the solution significantly reduced false positives while maintaining robust fraud prevention. Banks using Decision Intelligence reported improved authorization rates, better customer experiences, and fewer service disruptions. Mastercard's innovation shows how AI can shift fraud detection from a reactive defence to a proactive, user-centric strategy that safeguards security while enhancing trust and satisfaction in digital payment ecosystems.

Case Discussion Questions

1. How does Mastercard's Decision Intelligence differ from traditional fraud detection methods?
2. In what ways does real-time AI-based risk assessment enhance both security and customer experience?
3. What are the ethical or regulatory considerations in using AI for transaction monitoring?

Keywords

- **Supervised learning:** Machine learning, where models are trained on labelled data to predict known outcomes (e.g., fraud detection).
- **Unsupervised learning:** Identifies patterns or clusters in unlabelled data (e.g., customer segmentation or anomaly detection).
- **Reinforcement learning:** AI learns optimal decisions through trial and error, often used in algorithmic trading and dynamic portfolio optimization.
- **Natural language processing (NLP):** AI technique to interpret and analyse human language used in contract review, sentiment analysis, and chatbot services.
- **Model explainability (XAI):** Ensures that AI decision-making processes can be understood by regulators, stakeholders, and users.
- **Risk scoring models:** AI models that assign risk levels to loans, investments, or transactions based on financial Behavior and external data.
- **KYC/AML compliance:** AI automates the detection of fraudulent identity or suspicious transactions under anti-money laundering regulations.
- **AI governance:** Framework for managing ethical use, transparency, accountability, and lifecycle control of AI systems.
- **Bias mitigation:** Techniques that prevent AI from making unfair decisions, especially in lending and credit scoring.
- **Anomaly detection:** Identifying unusual or rare patterns in data, used in fraud detection or cyber risk monitoring.
- **Personalized financial advice:** AI tailors advice based on a client's profile, behavior, and financial goals.
- **Sentiment analysis:** Analyses news or social media to determine market mood used in robo-advisory and risk management.
- **Robo-advisors:** AI-driven platforms offering automated, algorithm-based financial planning services.
- **Dynamic portfolio management:** Using AI to rebalance investment portfolios in real time based on market changes and investor Behavior.
- **Compliance automation:** Leveraging AI to ensure institutions follow financial regulations without manual intervention.

Discussion Questions

1. What are the main differences between supervised, unsupervised, and reinforcement learning in finance?
2. How has JPMorgan Chase used AI to automate legal and compliance processes?
3. What are the benefits and risks of AI in financial governance?
4. What are the benefits and limitations of predictive analytics in banking?
5. Explain the concept of differential privacy and its application in financial services.
6. What security lessons can be learned from the Capital One data breach?
7. How does zero-trust architecture differ from traditional security models?
8. What are the challenges of using reinforcement learning in real-time trading systems?
9. How does AI help financial institutions comply with evolving regulatory requirements?

References

[1] Accenture. (2021). *AI in financial services: From personalization to risk management*. https://www.accenture.com

[2] Kshetri, N. (2021). Data-driven FinTech: Opportunities and risks. *Journal of Business Research, 134*, 167–175. https://doi.org/10.1016/j.jbusres.2021.04.029

[3] Varian, H. R. (2014). Big data: New tricks for econometrics. *Journal of Economic Perspectives, 28*(2), 3–28. https://doi.org/10.1257/jep.28.2.3

[4] Dwork, C., & Roth, A. (2014). The algorithmic foundations of differential privacy. *Foundations and Trends in Theoretical Computer Science, 9*(3–4), 211–407. https://doi.org/10.1561/0400000042

[5] Microsoft Azure. (2022). *Differential privacy in financial services*. https://azure.microsoft.com/en-us/resources/

[6] Capital One. (2020). *Post-breach security architecture: A case study*. https://www.capitalone.com

[7] U.S. Senate. (2020). *Examination of the Capital One cyber incident*. https://www.hsgac.senate.gov

[8] Russell, S., & Norvig, P. (2020). *Artificial intelligence: A modern approach* (4th ed.). Pearson.

[9] European Banking Authority. (2021). *Discussion paper on machine learning in credit risk*. https://www.eba.europa.eu

[10] Brynjolfsson, E., & McAfee, A. (2017). *Machine, platform, crowd: Harnessing our digital future*. W. W. Norton & Company.

[11] Arner, D. W., Zetzsche, D. A., & Buckley, R. P. (2022). FinTech, RegTech, and the reconceptualization of financial regulation. *Northwestern Journal of International Law & Business, 42*(1), 89–124.

[12] JPMorgan Chase. (2020). *COiN: Automating contract review with AI*. https://www.jpmorganchase.com

[13] Ghosh, S. (2020). Responsible AI and financial services: From risk management to ethical governance. In D. Zetzsche et al. (Eds.), *The Palgrave handbook of technological finance* (pp. 367–386). Palgrave Macmillan.

[14] Morley, J., Floridi, L., Kinsey, L., & Elhalal, A. (2021). From what to how: An initial review of publicly available AI ethics tools, methods and research to translate principles into practices. *Science and Engineering Ethics, 27*(4), 1–31. https://doi.org/10.1007/s11948-021-00300-4

[15] Bank for International Settlements (BIS). (2021). *The use of big data analytics and AI in supervisory technology*. https://www.bis.org/publ/bppdf/bispap117.pdf

[16] World Economic Forum. (2018). *The new physics of financial services: Understanding how AI is transforming the financial ecosystem*. https://www.weforum.org/reports

[17] Cavoukian, A. (2010). *Privacy by design: The 7 foundational principles*. Information and Privacy Commissioner of Ontario. https://www.ipc.on.ca

[18] Narayanan, A., & Shmatikov, V. (2008). Robust de-anonymization of large sparse datasets. *Proceedings of IEEE Symposium on Security and Privacy*. https://doi.org/10.1109/SP.2008.33

UNIT 7

Technology, Ethics and the Future

19

Emerging Technologies and Ethics In FinTech

Abstract

This chapter examines how emerging technologies – Internet of Things (IoT), Augmented and virtual reality (AR/VR), and advanced cybersecurity – are reshaping FinTech by enabling smarter, more secure, and customer-focused services. IoT supports real-time data collection for personalized banking, usage-based lending, and smart payment systems. AR/VR introduces immersive experiences such as virtual bank branches, 3D investment tools, and interactive financial advisory, enhancing engagement and accessibility. Alongside these innovations, the chapter addresses escalating cybersecurity threats and highlights solutions like biometric authentication, AI-driven threat detection, and encryption to build digital trust. It also critically evaluates the ethical and governance challenges in FinTech, including algorithmic bias, data privacy, and the risks of digital exclusion. The discussion emphasizes fair finance principles, responsible AI deployment, and the complexities of decentralized finance (DeFi) governance. Ultimately, the chapter advocates for integrating innovation with ethical safeguards to create inclusive, transparent, and resilient financial systems.

Introduction

The financial technology (FinTech) sector is experiencing a period of unprecedented innovation, driven by the rapid development and adoption of emerging technologies. These technological advancements are fundamentally transforming the traditional financial services landscape, creating new opportunities for efficiency, security, transparency, and inclusivity. As industry evolves, understanding these emerging technologies is essential for stakeholders, including

DOI: 10.1201/9788743811244-26

startups, established financial institutions, regulators, and consumers, to navigate the changing environment and leverage the benefits these innovations offer. The rapid rise of Financial Technology (FinTech) has dramatically reshaped the financial landscape. Traditional banking systems have given way to agile platforms that offer seamless mobile payments, peer- to-peer lending, AI-driven credit scoring, robo-advisory, blockchain-based assets, and decentralized finance (DeFi) ecosystems. With the ability to democratize access to financial tools, empower the underbanked, and boost economic participation, FinTech holds transformative power. However, this innovation also introduces profound ethical concerns – ranging from data misuse and algorithmic bias to financial exclusion and regulatory evasion. As FinTech becomes embedded in the global financial infrastructure, it is vital to examine the ethical framework that governs its deployment. The integration of emerging technologies is reshaping FinTech by expanding capabilities and raising new ethical considerations [1]. IoT plays a transformative role by enabling real-time data collection and seamless financial decision-making [2]. Smart IoT devices support personalized insurance pricing and risk assessment in financial services [3]. IoT-driven payment ecosystems reduce transactional friction and enhance customer experience [4].

19.1 IoT in Financial Services

The Internet of Things (IoT) refers to the network of interconnected devices capable of collecting, exchanging, and acting on data. In the financial services sector, IoT technologies are transforming traditional operations, enhancing customer experiences, improving risk management, and creating new revenue streams. The Internet of Things (IoT) also refers to a network of interconnected physical devices that collect, exchange, and process data through the internet. IoT services involve enabling seamless communication between devices such as sensors, smart meters, wearable gadgets, and connected systems. These services support real-time data monitoring, predictive analytics, automation, and remote management, which can significantly improve operational efficiency across industries. In financial services, IoT plays a crucial role in enabling personalized customer experiences, risk management, and smarter asset tracking.

19.1.1 Key applications of IoT in financial services

In the financial sector, IoT offers transformative applications ranging from insurance to banking operations. One key application is usage-based insurance, where IoT devices like vehicle trackers help insurers price premiums based on actual driving behavior. In banking, smart ATMs and IoT-enabled branches improve service delivery through real-time data and automation. IoT also aids in fraud detection by monitoring unusual activity patterns and enabling geo-fencing for secure transactions. Additionally, asset and supply chain tracking facilitated by IoT helps banks manage collateral and loans more effectively, especially in trade finance.

Fraud prevention and security

- IoT devices help monitor physical and digital transactions for suspicious activity.
- Smart sensors and biometric authentication (such as fingerprint, facial recognition) add layers of security.
- Real-time alerts and device authentication reduce identity theft and fraud.

Customer engagement and personalization

- Wearables and connected devices (smart watches, fitness trackers) provide data that help banks personalize services.
- Location-based services enable targeted offers and instant customer support.
- IoT-enabled ATMs and branches improve customer experience with smart interfaces and real-time diagnostics.

Asset and equipment management

- Financial institutions managing physical assets (like vaults, ATMs, and branches) use IoT sensors for real-time monitoring.
- Predictive maintenance reduces downtime and operational costs.
- Asset tracking and management improve security and efficiency.

Risk management

- IoT sensors provide real-time environmental data (e.g., in insuring properties or assets), enabling dynamic risk assessment.
- Insurers use IoT data (such as vehicle telematics or home sensors) to calculate premiums accurately and promote safe behavior.

Payment and transaction efficiency

- IoT facilitates contactless payments via connected devices like smartwatches or embedded chips in wearables.

- IoT enhances peer-to-peer (P2P) payments and enables smart contracts, which automatically execute transactions based on sensor data.

Insurtech

- IoT devices collect data for real-time monitoring of insured assets (vehicles, homes, health).
- Usage-based insurance models (UBI), driven by telematics or health devices, tailor premiums based on actual usage and behavior.

Figure 19.1 IoT applications in finance.

Benefits of IoT in financial services

- **Enhanced security:** Improved authentication and fraud detection.
- **Operational efficiency:** Automation and real-time data reduce costs.

- **Customer satisfaction:** Personalized experiences and faster services.
- **New revenue opportunities:** Innovative products like usage-based insurance and real-time risk assessment.

Challenges and risks

- **Data privacy and security:** IoT devices generate vast data, raising concerns about data breaches.
- **Interoperability:** Compatibility issues among diverse IoT devices.
- **High implementation cost:** Infrastructure investment may be significant.
- **Regulatory compliance:** Ensuring adherence to data protection laws (such as GDPR).

19.2 AR/VR Applications in Finance

Augmented reality (AR) and virtual reality (VR) are immersive technologies transforming how financial institutions interact with customers, analyze data, and operate internally. These technologies enhance engagement, improve decision-making, and streamline processes in the finance sector. Augmented reality (AR) and virtual reality (VR) services also create immersive and interactive experiences by overlaying digital information onto the real world (AR) or simulating entire environments (VR). These technologies are increasingly being adopted across sectors for training, customer engagement, and data visualization. In financial services, AR/VR services are used to enhance user interfaces, create virtual branches, and facilitate remote financial advisory. They enable new ways of interacting with data and services, improving customer understanding and decision-making.

19.2.1 Key applications of AR/VR in finance

AR and VR are redefining the way financial institutions engage with customers and data. One application is virtual banking environments, where customers can interact with a 3D virtual assistant or advisor for services like portfolio management and financial planning. AR enables dynamic data visualization, allowing users to see real-time financial trends or market data overlaid on physical environments, enhancing analysis and insights. AR/VR technologies are reshaping customer engagement by offering immersive financial advisory tools [5]. Virtual financial branches powered by VR enable remote onboarding and interactive service delivery [6]. AR interfaces are improving user comprehension of complex investment data and financial visualization [7]. These technologies are also used for staff training, simulating customer service scenarios or complex operations in risk-free virtual settings, improving readiness and efficiency.

Enhanced customer experience

- **Virtual branches:** Customers can explore virtual bank branches from anywhere, interacting with digital tellers and advisors in real-time.
- **AR-based product visualization:** Customers use AR to visualize financial products like insurance policies, investment portfolios, or loan options in a real- world context.
- **Interactive financial education:** VR environments simulate financial concepts or investment scenarios for training clients or staff.

Financial data visualization

- **3D data dashboards:** Traders and analysts view complex data sets and financial markets in immersive 3D environments, improving understanding and rapid decision-making.
- **Real-time market simulation:** VR platforms simulate live market conditions for training or strategic planning.

Risk management and fraud detection

- **Simulated scenarios:** VR simulations help staff practice responses to security threats or fraud attempts.
- **Visual analytics:** AR overlays provide real-time insights and alerts during operations, helping identify anomalies.

Training and employee development

- **Immersive training:** VR provides realistic, risk-free environments for training employees in complex tasks like trading, compliance, or customer handling.
- **Remote collaboration:** AR/VR facilitates remote teamwork for location-independent financial advisory or planning sessions.

Real estate and property investment

- **Virtual property tours:** Investors can view and evaluate real estate holdings via VR, making informed investment decisions without physical visits.

Insurance industry applications

- **Damage assessment:** AR tools assist insurance adjusters in assessing property damage remotely.
- **Customer education:** VR scenarios demonstrate insurance benefits or risk scenarios to clients.

19.2.2 Benefits of AR/VR in finance

- **Improved customer engagement:** Immersive experiences foster trust and satisfaction.
- **Better decision-making:** Enhanced data visualization aids analysts and traders.
- **Cost savings:** Virtual training reduces the need for physical infrastructure and travel.
- **Competitive advantage:** Early adoption positions financial firms as innovative leaders.

19.2.3 Challenges

- **High development cost:** Creating AR/VR applications requires significant investment.
- **Technological limitations:** Hardware accessibility and user adoption can be barriers.
- **Data security and privacy:** Ensuring secure handling of sensitive financial data in immersive environments.
- **Regulatory compliance:** Meeting regulations related to digital interactions and data protection.

19.2.4 Cybersecurity threats

Cybersecurity threats are evolving rapidly, driven by the rise of sophisticated technologies and increasingly complex digital infrastructures. One of the most alarming developments is the emergence of AI-driven attacks, where generative AI is used to craft highly personalized phishing emails and messages, dramatically increasing their success rate. Techniques like voice phishing (vishing) and business email compromise (BEC) are becoming more common, making traditional security measures less effective. Meanwhile, ransomware attacks continue to surge, especially with the growth of Ransomware-as-a-Service (RaaS) models, which allow even less technically skilled attackers to launch advanced attacks by exploiting zero-day vulnerabilities. Another growing concern lies in third-party and API risks, particularly in FinTech, where the heavy reliance on third-party services and external APIs creates new entry points for cybercriminals – especially when APIs are poorly secured. Cybersecurity remains a critical challenge as digital adoption increases the vulnerability surface of FinTech platforms [8]. The rise of sophisticated cyberattacks demands stronger encryption and multi-factor authentication systems [9]. Regulatory guidelines emphasize the need for robust cybersecurity frameworks to safeguard digital financial operations [10].

The increasing adoption of cloud infrastructure brings its own set of challenges, particularly cloud misconfigurations such as unsecured buckets and flawed CI/CD pipelines, which can expose sensitive financial and customer data. Even with cutting-edge systems in place, attackers still exploit legacy vulnerabilities, targeting outdated and unpatched software, which underscores the continued importance of robust patch management strategies. To counter these threats, institutions are investing in strategic cybersecurity solutions such as AI/ML-based fraud detection, where behavioral analytics and predictive machine learning models can identify anomalies in real-time and reduce false positives. Data protection techniques like end-to-end encryption, tokenization of sensitive data, and the implementation of Zero Trust Architecture are also gaining ground in minimizing access-related risks. Organizations are also adopting regulatory compliance automation tools that streamline risk assessments and ensure ongoing compliance with frameworks such as GDPR, PCI DSS, and ISO/IEC 27001.

Effective identity and access management (IAM) systems now incorporate adaptive and multi-factor authentication, along with role-based access controls to restrict unauthorized data access. Security information and event management (SIEM) systems, combined with global threat intelligence feeds, allow for real-time log analysis and proactive threat detection. Looking ahead, several emerging trends are set to shape the cybersecurity landscape. Generative AI is expected to automate up to 40% of cybersecurity tasks currently performed by humans by 2026, significantly altering workforce dynamics. Blockchain-based identity verification is gaining traction as a secure alternative to traditional credentials, while cyber resilience – the ability to recover and adapt quickly after cyberattacks – is becoming a boardroom- level concern, integrated into long-term business continuity planning rather than treated as a purely technical issue. Blockchain-based governance frameworks reduce the need for intermediaries while increasing transparency [11]. DeFi platforms challenge conventional regulatory structures by operating on decentralized protocols [12]. The decentralized paradigm introduces both opportunities for autonomy and risks of insufficient oversight [13]. FinTech evolution has broadened regulatory responsibilities, requiring adaptive governance mechanisms [14].

19.3 Cyber Security in FinTech

The practice of protecting systems, networks, and data from cyber attacks, unauthorized access, damage, or theft. FinTech is a prime target for cyber criminals because of sensitive financial data handled, large volumes of transactions, and increasing digital adoption.

	High Impact	Low Impact
High likelihood	Severe and likely risks; eg, ransomware attacks targeting critical infrastructure	Frequent but minimal impact risks; eg., regular but non-damaging malware infections.
Low likelihood	Severe but unlikely risks; eg, a sophisticated state-sponsored cyber attack	Minor and unlikely risks; eg,.a low level phishing attempt

Figure 19.2 Cybersecurity threats and solution matrix.

19.3.1 Importance of cybersecurity in FinTech

- Protection of **financial assets** and **customer data**.
- Maintaining **trust** and **reputation**.
- Compliance with **regulations** (e.g., GDPR, PCI-DSS, PSD2).
- Prevention of financial loss due to fraud or cybercrime.
- Ensures **business continuity** and operational resilience.

Table 19.1 Key cyber security measures in FinTech.

Security measure	Key practices
Data encryption	• Encrypt sensitive data in transit (using TLS/SSL) and at rest • Maintains confidentiality even if intercepted
Multi-factor authentication (MFA)	• Requires two or more factors (e.g., password + OTP) • Reduces unauthorized access risks
Secure software development (DevSecOps)	• Integrate security throughout development • Perform regular code reviews, penetration testing, and vulnerability scans
API security	• Use token-based authentication (e.g., OAuth) • Regular API monitoring • Apply rate limiting and throttling
Identity and access management (IAM)	• Assign roles/permissions on a need-to-know basis • Monitor access logs continuously
Fraud detection systems	• Leverage AI/ML to analyze transactions • Real-time alerts to block fraud
Network security	• Implement firewalls, IDS, and IPS • Use network segmentation to limit breach impact
Incident response planning	• Define clear incident response protocols • Conduct regular drills • Perform post-incident reviews
Employee training and awareness	• Regular training on phishing and social engineering • Foster a culture of cybersecurity awareness

19.3.2 Common cyber threats to FinTech

- **Phishing attacks:** Deceptive emails or messages to steal credentials.
- **Malware and ransomware:** Malicious software that can steal data or block access until a ransom is paid.
- **Man-in-the-Middle (MitM) attacks:** Intercepting communication between parties to steal information.
- **Distributed Denial of Service (DDoS) attacks:** Overwhelming server resources to disrupt services.
- **Insider threats:** Disgruntled employees or careless staff leaking information or creating vulnerabilities.

- **API vulnerabilities:** Exploiting weaknesses in application programming interfaces used by FinTech apps.
- **Social engineering:** Manipulating individuals to gain unauthorized access.
- **Credential stuffing:** Using leaked usernames and passwords to access accounts.

19.3.3 Regulatory and compliance considerations

- **General Data Protection Regulation (GDPR):** Protects customer privacy and data rights.
- **Payment Card Industry Data Security Standard (PCI-DSS):** Standards to protect credit card information.
- **Payment Services Directive 2 (PSD2):** Requires strong customer authentication in payments.
- **Local regulations:** Depending on geography, specific cyber and financial regulations apply.

19.3.4 Challenges in FinTech cybersecurity

- Rapid pace of innovation vs. security maturity.
- Legacy infrastructure integration challenges.
- Balancing usability and security.
- High-value targets attracting persistent attackers.
- Third-party risks from partnerships and cloud providers.

19.4 The Societal Impact of FinTech

FinTech promises to drive social inclusion by bringing financial services to underserved communities. Mobile banking, microfinancing, and digital wallets have enabled individuals in remote areas to participate in the financial ecosystem without needing access to traditional brick-and-mortar institutions. For example, platforms like M-Pesa in Kenya have revolutionized mobile money and brought millions into the financial fold. Yet, the same technology that fosters inclusion can also deepen inequalities if not handled ethically. Consider AI-powered credit scoring systems: while they provide quick access to loans, they often rely on alternative data sources (social media behavior, mobile phone usage, etc.) that may inadvertently discriminate against certain groups. If such systems are not transparent and accountable, they may entrench social biases, affecting marginalized populations disproportionately. Moreover, FinTech platforms are increasingly used by youth and individuals with limited financial literacy. Gamification elements in investing apps (like Robinhood) may encourage risky behavior without adequate understanding. Ethical FinTech design must include guardrails that protect users from harm and empower them with informed choices. Societal impacts of FinTech include expanded financial inclusion and access to digital financial services [15]. FinTech innovations continue to alter traditional structures of financial intermediation and customer behavior [16]. Ethical AI is crucial to ensuring transparent, explainable, and unbiased decision-making in financial algorithms [17].

19.4.1 Financial inclusion and accessibility

One of the most significant contributions of FinTech is its ability to bridge the financial gap for the unbanked and underbanked populations. With platforms like M-Pesa in Kenya, Paytm in India, and numerous micro-lending and neobanking apps, individuals without access to traditional banking can now perform essential financial tasks through a smartphone and internet connection. These innovations eliminate the need for physical branches and complex paperwork, empowering even informal workers and small entrepreneurs to participate in the formal economy. Peer-to-peer lending and invoice financing are also helping small businesses secure funding without the rigid collateral demands of conventional banks. However, the promise of inclusion comes with its own set of challenges. The digital divide remains a major barrier – many people in rural or economically weaker regions lack access to smartphones or internet connectivity. Additionally, language barriers and poor user interface design can exclude users who are not tech-savvy or fluent in English, limiting the reach of otherwise inclusive tools.

19.4.2 Personalization vs. privacy

FinTech's ability to tailor financial products to individual users has been revolutionary. Through AI and data analytics, platforms now offer personalized investment suggestions, risk-adjusted loan options, and even savings nudges to help users develop better financial habits. These data-driven insights make financial planning more efficient and accessible, especially for first-time investors or young users. However, personalization often comes at the cost of privacy. These customized services are built on deep and sometimes intrusive data collection – tracking users' spending, browsing habits, location data, and more. Many consumers remain unaware of how their data is harvested, used, or shared with third parties, raising ethical questions about transparency and consent in FinTech environments.

19.4.3 Democratization of investing and wealth management

FinTech has dramatically lowered the barriers to investing and wealth creation. Platforms such as Robinhood, Groww, and Zerodha allow retail investors to trade stocks with minimal capital and zero commissions. Robo-advisors have also emerged as affordable, automated portfolio managers that were once only available to high-net- worth individuals. Yet this democratization brings its own set of concerns. The gamification of investing – through flashy interfaces and reward-like feedback – can lead to overconfidence and impulsive decisions. Without adequate financial education, users may misinterpret trends, chase volatile assets, or fall prey to scams and misinformation.

19.4.4 Empowerment vs. exploitation

FinTech also empowers previously "credit-invisible" individuals by using alternative data, such as mobile phone usage and utility payments, for credit scoring. Micro- insurance products have further enhanced financial protection for low-income groups, offering coverage for health emergencies, crop failures, or accidents at minimal premiums. However, some FinTech lending apps engage in exploitative practices, offering high-interest loans with hidden fees and short repayment periods. These predatory models often lead to cycles of debt. Additionally, there is growing concern that algorithms used in credit decisions may carry hidden biases, perpetuating systemic inequalities when trained on flawed or discriminatory datasets.

19.4.5 Impact on employment and traditional banking

The rise of FinTech is reshaping the employment landscape. It has led to the creation of new jobs in technology, cybersecurity, data science, and customer experience design. At the same time, many traditional banks are now partnering with FinTech startups to modernize their systems and provide better services. Conversely, this digital transformation also results in job displacement. Automation reduces the need for roles like bank tellers and clerical staff, while increased reliance on digital platforms may lead to the closure of physical branches – potentially marginalizing rural populations and older adults who depend on face-to-face services.

19.4.6 Societal trust and behavioral shifts

FinTech is not only transforming financial systems but also reshaping user behavior. Digital transactions via UPI, QR codes, and online wallets have become normalized in many societies, replacing cash-based interactions. Blockchain-based platforms are promoting transparency by offering immutable records and traceable transaction histories, which help build trust in digital financial systems.

Nonetheless, the sector faces significant trust-related challenges. Incidents of fraud, phishing, fake investment platforms, and data leaks threaten user confidence. Moreover, an over-dependence on AI and automated systems in financial decision- making may reduce human oversight, leading to errors or biases that are difficult to detect and correct.

19.4.7 Regulatory and ethical dilemmas

The rapid pace of FinTech innovation often outpaces regulation. Many startups operate in a grey area where consumer protections are weak or nonexistent. Some even exploit regulatory arbitrage – choosing to operate in jurisdictions with less stringent rules to avoid compliance burdens. This creates uneven playing fields and increases risks for consumers. On a global scale, balancing cross-border functionality with local compliance remains a key challenge. Regulatory frameworks must evolve to ensure that innovation does not come at the cost of security, fairness, or consumer rights.

19.5 Ethical AI and Fair Finance

Artificial intelligence (AI) and machine learning (ML) lie at the core of many FinTech applications – from fraud detection to insurance pricing and loan approvals. However, these systems often operate as "black boxes," where decision-making logic is obscured from end-users. This raises three pressing ethical concerns:

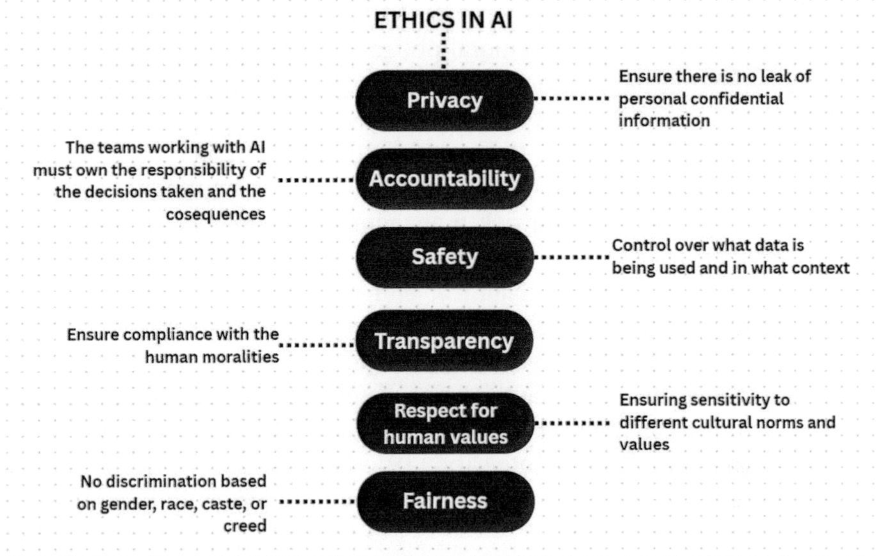

Figure 19.3 AI ethics in FinTech – bias vs fairness.

19.5.1 Bias and discrimination

AI systems can inherit biases from historical data. If past data reflect social inequities (e.g., racial, gender, or income disparities), AI algorithms may perpetuate or even amplify these issues. For instance, if women or certain ethnic groups were underrepresented in historical loan approvals, AI models trained on such data may continue to deny them credit.

To combat this, ethical FinTech should prioritize *algorithmic fairness*, incorporating techniques such as re-weighting data, auditing models for disparate impact, and involving diverse teams in model development.

Transparency and explainability

Users and regulators must be able to understand how decisions are made. An opaque system that declines a loan without explanation erodes trust. Ethical standards should require FinTech companies to provide explainable AI (XAI) solutions that justify decisions in clear, user-friendly terms.

Consent and data ethics

FinTech platforms collect vast amounts of personal data – financial history, location, social interactions, and more. Ethical data practices demand explicit user consent, data minimization (collecting only what is necessary), and secure storage. There is a moral obligation to avoid "surveillance capitalism," where users' behavioral patterns are monetized without informed consent.

AI in FinTech refers to the use of artificial intelligence and machine learning (ML) in financial services for tasks like Loan approvals and credit scoring, Fraud detection and risk management, algorithmic trading, customer service via chatbots, and robo-advisory and wealth management. While AI enhances speed, accuracy, and personalization, it also raises ethical challenges in areas like fairness, transparency, accountability, and privacy. AI-driven FinTech systems must address fairness concerns to prevent discriminatory lending and pricing outcomes [18]. Machine learning models deployed in finance require continuous monitoring to maintain accountability and ethical integrity [19]. Governance in decentralized financial systems demands trustless architectures supported by smart contracts [20].

19.5.2 Major ethical concerns in AI-driven finance

Algorithmic bias and discrimination: When AI models learn patterns from historical or skewed data that reflect societal prejudices (e.g., race, gender, income), leading to unfair or unequal outcomes. **Examples in FinTech:** Denial of loans or credit limits to women or minorities despite equivalent or better financial backgrounds. Insurance premiums higher for certain ZIP codes due to racial or socio-economic profiling.

Transparency and explainability: Many AI systems, especially deep learning models, do not offer human-readable explanations for their decisions. Users may not understand why they were denied credit. Regulators cannot assess whether a system is operating fairly. **Explainable AI (XAI)** methods to clarify how decisions are made (e.g., SHAP, LIME). Clear user-facing communication (e.g., "Your loan was denied due to a high debt-to-income ratio") **Informed consent and data ethics:** AI models rely on large datasets–often including sensitive financial, behavioral, and biometric data.

Key ethical questions

- Was data collected with explicit, informed consent?
- Are users aware of how their data is used, stored, or shared?
- Is data being used beyond its original purpose?

19.5.3 Principles for ethical FinTech development

To build a trustworthy and inclusive financial ecosystem, FinTech innovators must adhere to the following guiding principles:

- **Transparency** – Ensure users understand how their data is used and how decisions are made.
- **Fairness** – Mitigate algorithmic bias and avoid discriminatory outcomes.
- **Privacy and consent** – Prioritize user data rights with clear opt-in mechanisms and robust data protection.
- **Inclusivity** – Design for diverse populations, especially the financially vulnerable or technologically marginalized.
- **Accountability** – Establish clear responsibility structures, even in decentralized systems.
- **Security and resilience** – Invest in secure infrastructure to protect against data breaches and fraud.
- **Human-centric design** – Avoid manipulative UX features; promote informed, responsible user behavior.

Ethical AI is not just a technical challenge – it is a moral imperative. In FinTech, where decisions can shape lives, the stakes are especially high. Developers, regulators, and financial institutions must collaborate to ensure that innovation in AI leads not only to smarter systems but fairer financial outcomes for all.

19.6 Governance in Decentralized Systems

Governance in decentralized systems refers to the mechanisms, rules, and processes used to make decisions and manage operations within decentralized networks, such as blockchain platforms and distributed applications. Unlike traditional centralized systems, where a single entity or governing body makes key decisions, decentralized systems rely on community-driven, transparent, and consensus-based governance models. The primary goal is to ensure that all participants in the network have a voice and that the system evolves fairly, securely, and efficiently.

Governance in such systems typically includes protocol upgrades, dispute resolution, resource allocation, and setting operational parameters like transaction fees or consensus rules. It can be on-chain, where decisions are made and enforced directly through smart contracts (e.g., token-based voting in DAOs – Decentralized Autonomous Organizations), or off-chain, where discussions and decisions happen through forums or developer communities and are later implemented on-chain. Effective governance in decentralized systems must strike a balance between flexibility and security, empowering stakeholders while preventing malicious actors from taking control. It also demands clarity in voting rights, proposal processes, and upgrade mechanisms. As decentralized platforms scale globally, governance becomes even more complex, often involving diverse communities with competing interests. Well-structured governance ensures sustainability, community alignment, and resilience against hard forks or centralization risks. Therefore, it is a foundational aspect of building trust, accountability, and long-term success in any decentralized ecosystem.

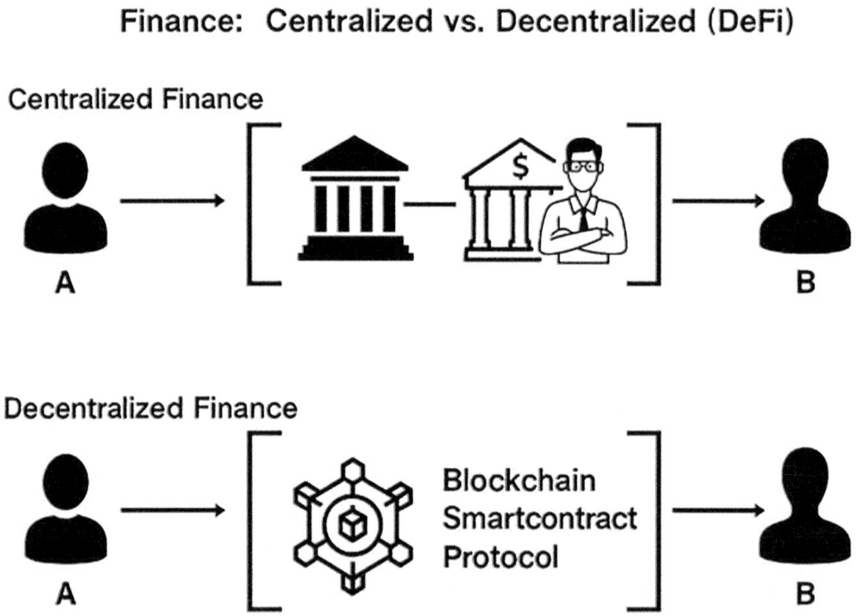

Figure 19.4 Governance in DeFi visual flow

19.6.1 Types of governance

- **On-chain governance**: Voting and decision-making happen directly on the blockchain via smart contracts (e.g., DAOs).

- **Off-chain governance**: Discussions and decisions occur off the blockchain (e.g., through community forums, GitHub) and are later implemented on-chain.

19.6.2 Common governance functions

- Protocol upgrades and bug fixes
- Managing treasury or community funds
- Adjusting system parameters (e.g., gas fees, inflation rates)
- Handling disputes and forks

19.6.3 Importance

- Ensures transparency, fairness, and adaptability in decentralized platforms.
- Builds trust among users and investors.
- Supports long-term sustainability and community alignment.

One of the most disruptive aspects of modern FinTech is the emergence of **decentralized finance**, which uses blockchain and smart contracts to bypass traditional financial intermediaries. While DeFi offers unparalleled transparency, efficiency, and global accessibility, it introduces unique ethical and governance challenges.

19.6.4 Lack of accountability

In decentralized systems, who is responsible when things go wrong? In the case of a smart contract bug or rug pull (fraudulent project exit), users often have no legal recourse. Traditional regulations do not map neatly onto these decentralized frameworks.

19.6.5 Regulatory arbitrage

DeFi platforms may operate across borders, selecting jurisdictions with lax regulations. This can lead to money laundering, terrorism financing, or tax evasion. Ethical FinTech must strive to operate above the minimum legal threshold and cooperate with global compliance frameworks like know your customer (KYC) and anti-money laundering (AML).

19.6.6 DAO ethics and tokenized governance

In Decentralized Autonomous Organizations (DAOs), decisions are often made by token holders voting on proposals. While this appears democratic, it can lead to plutocracy – where those with the most tokens (wealthiest users) dominate decision- making. An ethical DAO should implement checks and balances to prevent governance manipulation and ensure inclusivity.

Table 19.2 Governance examples.

Algorithmic bias in lending
In 2019, Apple's credit card, issued in partnership with Goldman Sachs, came under scrutiny when several users (including tech entrepreneur David Heinemeier Hansson) reported receiving significantly lower credit limits than their spouses – despite having better financial histories. This led to an investigation by New York regulators into potential gender discrimination. Although Goldman Sachs denied wrongdoing, the incident highlighted the urgent need for transparency and ethical oversight in algorithm-driven lending.
DeFi hacks and user protection
In 2021, Poly Network, a DeFi protocol, was hacked, resulting in a theft of over $600 million worth of cryptocurrency. Although the hacker eventually returned the funds, the incident exposed vulnerabilities in smart contracts and raised ethical questions about user protection in DeFi. Unlike traditional banks, there were no deposit protections or recovery mechanisms for affected users. This underscores the importance of secure coding, rigorous audits, and contingency planning in ethical DeFi development. FinTech is not merely a technological revolution; it is a social one. While it has the potential to unlock financial opportunities for billions, it also risks excluding or harming the very populations it seeks to uplift – unless guided by a robust ethical framework. Governments, regulators, developers, and users must work together to foster transparency, equity, and accountability in financial innovation. Ethics in FinTech is not just a matter of compliance – it is a commitment to building a fairer, more inclusive future. As we continue to navigate this exciting frontier, let innovation be tempered by integrity, and let every financial algorithm be underpinned by empathy.

19.6.7 Decentralized systems

In FinTech refer primarily to blockchain-based platforms that operate without centralized control. Examples include DeFi protocols (e.g., Uniswap, Aave), Decentralized Autonomous Organizations (DAOs) and smart contracts for peer-to-peer financial transactions. These systems are governed by code and consensus rather than centralized institutions like banks or regulatory bodies. While decentralization promotes autonomy, transparency, and resilience, it creates **complex** governance challenges and ethical concerns around accountability, fairness, and law enforcement.

19.6.8 Key ethical principles for decentralized governance

Key ethical principles for decentralized governance focus on ensuring fairness, transparency, inclusivity, and accountability within blockchain-based and decentralized systems. Since these systems operate without a central authority, ethical governance becomes crucial to maintain user trust and system integrity. Transparency is essential, as all decisions, proposals, and voting outcomes should be visible and verifiable on-chain. Inclusivity ensures that all stakeholders – regardless of their technical expertise or economic power – have meaningful opportunities to participate in decision-making. Fairness demands that no single group or entity dominates governance due to token wealth or technical control. Accountability is upheld through auditable smart contracts and clear community guidelines that define roles, responsibilities, and consequences for misconduct. Additionally, privacy rights, data protection, and resistance to censorship are important principles, especially in open financial networks. Ethical decentralized governance requires balancing collective autonomy with responsible oversight to ensure long-term sustainability and social impact. Emerging technologies demand a rethinking of financial regulation to ensure systemic stability and consumer protection [14]. Global ethical frameworks advocate responsible use of financial technologies to protect vulnerable populations [21]. AI adoption in finance must align with global ethical standards to maintain trust in digital ecosystems [22]. The rapid expansion of FinTech ecosystems highlights the need for secure, transparent, and ethically aligned innovation [23].

Table 19.3 Ethical principles for decentralized governance.

Principle	Application in DeFi
Transparency	All governance processes should be publicly visible
Inclusivity	Design mechanisms that empower all stakeholders, not just whales
Accountability	Create ways to trace and challenge harmful decisions
Resilience	Build in mechanisms for dispute resolution and error correction
Security-first design	Conduct regular audits and incentivize ethical hacking

Decentralized systems challenge traditional notions of governance, authority, and accountability. While they offer revolutionary financial freedom and disintermediation, they must evolve ethical frameworks that match their technical sophistication. Responsible governance in decentralized FinTech requires inclusive decision-making, transparent processes, fair token economics, and above all, a commitment to serving the public good over speculative gain. Without ethical governance, decentralization risks becoming a tool for unaccountable power rather than shared freedom.

Summary

This chapter examines how emerging technologies – Internet of Things (IoT), augmented and virtual reality (AR/VR), and cybersecurity – are reshaping financial services. IoT enables real-time data collection for improved efficiency, personalized banking, fraud detection, and asset tracking, supporting innovations like usage-based insurance and secure, data-driven banking. AR/VR enhances customer engagement and analysis through immersive experiences, enabling virtual advisory, 3D data visualization, and advanced digital interfaces. As these technologies expand, cybersecurity becomes critical, addressing threats such as AI-powered phishing, ransomware-as-a-service, insecure APIs, and cloud misconfigurations. Solutions include AI/ML fraud detection, encryption, secure development (DevSecOps), IAM, and blockchain-based identity verification, alongside employee awareness and regulatory compliance automation. The chapter also addresses ethical and governance challenges in FinTech. While FinTech fosters inclusion, transparency, and innovation, it risks digital exclusion, job loss, and privacy concerns. Ethical AI practices – ensuring fairness, explainability, and unbiased datasets – are vital to prevent discrimination. In decentralized finance (DeFi) and blockchain governance, DAOs, on-chain voting, and community consensus offer new models but face issues like voter manipulation, low participation, and unclear legal frameworks. The chapter concludes by emphasizing the need for ethics, accountability, inclusive design, and robust governance to ensure secure, equitable, and resilient FinTech systems.

Case Study: The Robinhood Controversy – Gamification, Ethics, and Investor Risk

Robinhood, a US-based FinTech company launched in 2013, revolutionized retail investing by offering commission-free stock and cryptocurrency trading through a mobile app designed to be intuitive and user-friendly. Its mission to "democratize finance for all" struck a chord with young, first-time investors, particularly during the Covid-19 pandemic when market activity surged, and more individuals sought digital access to investing. The platform's success was largely driven by its gamified interface, which included celebratory animations, real-time alerts, and a swipe-to- trade experience that resembled a game more than a traditional financial platform. By 2020, Robinhood had become a dominant force in the FinTech space. However, the same design features that made the platform accessible and engaging also sparked serious ethical and regulatory concerns, particularly after a tragic incident involving a young user.

In June 2020, a 20-year-old college student named Alex Kearns took his own life after seeing a negative balance of over $730,000 in his Robinhood account. He had attempted a complex options trade and misunderstood the temporary balance shown in the app, believing he was facing irreversible financial ruin. In reality, the loss was not yet finalized and was still pending settlement. In his suicide note, Alex questioned how a young person with no income or advanced financial knowledge could be given such massive financial leverage. His tragic death became a turning point in the public conversation around the ethical responsibilities of FinTech platforms, particularly those that market to inexperienced users. It also triggered widespread scrutiny of Robinhood's user interface, educational offerings, and customer support practices.

A central ethical concern in this case was Robinhood's use of gamification to encourage trading activity. The platform celebrated each trade with digital confetti and employed a vibrant, game-like design that critics argued resembled a casino environment. These behavioral nudges, though effective in engaging users, also incentivized frequent and sometimes reckless trading, especially among users with limited financial literacy. The ethical question arose: should a financial platform that deals with real monetary risks employ design elements that encourage impulsive behavior? The confetti, sound effects, and instant gratification mechanics arguably made trading feel like entertainment, downplaying the seriousness of financial risk. Another major issue was the lack of user education. While Robinhood offered powerful financial tools like options trading and margin accounts, it provided minimal guidance or training. Complex products were made easily accessible, often with no requirement to demonstrate knowledge or readiness. The app lacked adequate tutorials, simulations, or warnings that would prepare users for the risks involved. This created an environment where first-time investors could engage in high-risk activities without fully understanding the implications. The failure to educate or protect users raised concerns about informed consent and the ethical distribution of financial tools.

Robinhood's accessibility also led to questions about responsibility. The company's open-access model made investing simple, but it did little to ensure users were adequately screened before accessing high-risk features. Unlike traditional brokerage firms, Robinhood did not offer personal consultations or investment advice, and its user verification processes were basic. While ease of access was a major achievement, it blurred the line between empowering users and exposing them to harm. Critics questioned whether making finance easy should automatically equate to making it safe.

Perhaps the most alarming failure was in customer support. Following the incident involving Alex Kearns, it was revealed that he had reached out to Robinhood's support team via email but received no timely response. At the time, Robinhood lacked live customer support, a glaring oversight for a platform handling high-stakes financial transactions. This lack of real-time assistance during user crises pointed to a fundamental failure in the company's duty of care, further exacerbating the ethical lapse in user protection.

Regulatory authorities responded swiftly. The Financial Industry Regulatory Authority (FINRA), along with lawmakers and consumer advocacy groups, launched investigations into Robinhood's practices. In June 2021, FINRA fined the company $70 million – the largest penalty in its history – citing system outages, misleading communications, and harm to millions of users. As part of its settlement, Robinhood committed to strengthening its educational tools, adding risk disclosures, improving customer service, and introducing restrictions on complex trading features for new or inexperienced users. The Robinhood case remains a landmark example of how FinTech innovation must be balanced with ethical design, user education, and robust regulatory oversight to ensure technology serves, rather than exploits, its users.

Case Discussion Questions

1. What was Robinhood's original mission, and how did its app design support or contradict this mission?

2. Describe the event involving Alex Kearns and explain how Robinhood's platform may have contributed to the misunderstanding.
3. What regulatory actions were taken against Robinhood after the incident?

Keywords

- **Internet of Things (IoT):** A network of connected physical devices (like wearables or smart sensors) that collect and share data to automate and improve financial decision-making.
- **Augmented reality (AR):** Technology that overlays digital content (like charts or balances) onto the real-world view through devices like smartphones or AR glasses.
- **Virtual reality (VR):** A fully immersive digital environment that users can interact with, used in finance for training, investment simulations, and virtual banking.
- **Cybersecurity:** The protection of financial systems and customer data from unauthorized access, cyberattacks, and data theft.
- **Biometric authentication:** Security method that uses physical characteristics like fingerprints, face, or voice to verify a user's identity in financial apps.
- **Multi-factor authentication (MFA):** A security process that requires users to verify their identity through two or more different methods (e.g., password + OTP).
- **AI-powered fraud detection:** Using artificial intelligence and machine learning to identify suspicious transactions or behavior in real time.
- **Smart contracts:** Self-executing contracts with terms directly written into code, triggered automatically by predefined conditions (often used in insurance and lending).
- **Data encryption:** A method of converting data into unreadable code to prevent unauthorized access during storage or transmission.
- **Immersive finance:** The use of AR/VR to provide a more engaging and interactive financial service experience – such as virtual customer service or 3D financial planning.

- **FinTech ethics:** The application of moral principles in the design and delivery of financial technologies, ensuring fairness, transparency, accountability, and user well-being.
- **Algorithmic bias:** Systematic errors in AI or automated decision-making systems that lead to unfair treatment of certain groups, often due to biased data or flawed model design.
- **Ethical AI:** The development and use of artificial intelligence in ways that are fair, transparent, explainable, privacy-respecting, and free from discrimination or harm.
- **Data privacy:** The right of individuals to control how their personal financial data is collected, used, stored, and shared by FinTech companies or digital platforms.
- **Informed consent:** A process by which users are fully educated about what data is being collected and how it will be used, and they voluntarily agree to participate.
- **Decentralized finance (DeFi):** A blockchain-based financial ecosystem that operates without centralized institutions like banks, offering peer-to-peer services such as lending, borrowing, and trading.
- **Governance (in DeFi):** The mechanisms and decision-making processes – often involving token holders – that control how decentralized platforms are managed, upgraded, and regulated.
- **Regulatory arbitrage:** The practice of exploiting differences between regulatory systems in different jurisdictions to avoid strict rules, often used by FinTechs operating globally.
- **Transparency:** The principle of providing clear, accurate, and accessible information about how FinTech platforms function, especially regarding algorithms, data usage, and pricing.
- **Consumer protection:** Legal and ethical practices aimed at safeguarding FinTech users from fraud, unfair treatment, financial harm, or misuse of their personal data.

Discussion Questions

1. What are some of the major ethical concerns that arise with the rapid growth of FinTech?
2. Explain why ethical considerations are essential in FinTech, even if the technology complies with current regulations.
3. Describe two positive ways FinTech has contributed to financial inclusion in underserved populations.
4. What is the digital divide, and how does it impact the inclusivity of FinTech solutions?
5. What are algorithmic biases in FinTech, and how do they arise? Give a real-world example.
6. Explain the concept of "Explainable AI" (XAI). Why is it important in financial decision-making systems?
7. Define Decentralized Finance (DeFi) and explain how it differs from traditional finance in terms of governance.
8. What is regulatory arbitrage, and why is it a concern in the context of DeFi platforms?
9. List and briefly explain two emerging governance models designed to improve ethical accountability in decentralized systems.
10. If you were designing a FinTech app today, what ethical guidelines would you implement to balance innovation with user safety?
11. Should decentralized platforms be held to the same ethical and regulatory standards as centralized banks? Justify your answer.
12. How do emerging technologies impact customer experience in financial services?
13. How can IoT enhance customer personalization in FinTech?
14. What are the potential security risks associated with IoT in financial applications?

15. How are augmented reality (AR) and virtual reality (VR) technologies being used in finance?
16. Describe how AR can improve customer engagement for financial advisors.
17. What security measures can FinTech firms implement to protect user data?
18. Explain how multi-factor authentication (MFA) helps improve security in FinTech applications.

References

[1] Accenture. (2021). *Driving customer trust through secure emerging technologies*. https://www.accenture.com
[2] Madakam, S., Ramaswamy, R., & Tripathi, S. (2015). *Internet of Things (IoT): A Literature Review*. Journal of Computer and Communications, 3(5), 164–173.
[3] Zhou, T., & Piramuthu, S. (2015). *IoT and insurance: Exploring real-time data, smart contracts, and risk mitigation*. Decision Support Systems, 85, 50–60.
[4] Capgemini. (2023). *World FinTech Report*. https://www.capgemini.com/research/world-fintech-report-2023/
[5] Deloitte Insights. (2020). *Augmented reality and virtual reality in finance: A new frontier for customer engagement*.
[6] Shrier, D. L., Canale, M., & Pentland, A. (2016). *Frontiers of financial technology*.
[7] Gai, K., Qiu, M., & Sun, X. (2018). A survey on FinTech. *Journal of Network and Computer Applications, 103*, 262–273. https://doi.org/10.1016/j.jnca.2017.10.011
[8] Jain, A., & Bhaskar, S. (2021). *Cybersecurity Challenges in Indian FinTech Companies*. IJCSIS, 19(1), 90–97.
[9] Sinha, S. (2018). *FinTech Innovation and Cybersecurity Challenges in India*. Journal of Financial Services Marketing, 23, 194–206.
[10] Reserve Bank of India. (2020). *Guidelines on Cyber Security Framework in Banks*.
[11] Kshetri, N. (2017). Blockchain's roles in meeting key supply chain management objectives. *International Journal of Information Management*, 39, 80–89.

[12] Zetzsche, D. A., Buckley, R. P., Arner, D. W., & Barberis, J. N. (2020). *Decentralized finance (DeFi).* Journal of Financial Regulation, 6(2), 172–203

[13] O'Dwyer, R. (2015). *The revolution will (not) be decentralized: Blockchain-based financial technologies and the future of financial inclusion.*

[14] Arner, D. W., Barberis, J., & Buckley, R. P. (2016). *The Evolution of FinTech: A New Post-Crisis Paradigm?* Georgetown Journal of International Law, 47(4), 1271–1319.

[15] Lakshmi, R., & Kumaravel, A. (2021). *Paytm and Financial Inclusion in India.* International Journal of Management, 12(5), 123–129.

[16] Bank for International Settlements (BIS). (2022). *FinTech and the changing structure of financial intermediation.* https://www.bis.org

[17] Mittelstadt, B. D., Allo, P., Taddeo, M., Wachter, S., & Floridi, L. (2016). *The ethics of algorithms.* Big Data & Society, 3(2).

[18] OECD. (2021). *Ethics in AI in financial services.* https://www.oecd.org

[19] Kumar, N., & Singh, A. (2019). *Role of AI and Machine Learning in FinTech.* IJITEE, 8(9S), 268–272.

[20] Narula, N., & Catalini, C. (2019). *The need for trustless governance in blockchain-based financial systems.* HBR Digital Articles.

[21] United Nations Capital Development Fund (UNCDF). (2020). *Leaving no one behind in the digital era: Financial inclusion and digital ethics.*

[22] World Economic Forum (WEF). (2020). *Transforming paradigms: A global AI in financial services survey.*

[23] PwC. (2022). *Emerging technologies and their impact on financial services.* https://www.pwc.com

20

The Future of FinTech

Abstract

This chapter presents a forward-looking exploration of the evolving landscape of financial technology (FinTech), with a particular focus on emerging innovations, global collaboration, and the challenges that lie ahead. It begins by analyzing the transformative impact of big data, artificial intelligence (AI), and machine learning on financial services – driving automation, personalization, and predictive capabilities in areas such as lending, wealth management, and fraud detection. The chapter also addresses pressing ethical concerns surrounding data privacy, algorithmic transparency, and responsible AI deployment, which are vital to maintaining trust in digital finance. A key theme is the role of international cooperation and regulatory sandboxes in fostering FinTech innovation across borders. The chapter offers a strategic projection of the FinTech industry's evolution by 2030, highlighting expected advancements in digital infrastructure, financial inclusion, and regulatory harmonization. By comparing growth trajectories between developed and developing economies, it provides insight into infrastructure gaps and innovation potential in varied socio-economic contexts.

Through in-depth case studies from China, India, and the USA, the chapter illustrates how national policies, consumer behavior, and technological ecosystems shape the success of FinTech initiatives. It also identifies persistent barriers to global adoption, such as regulatory fragmentation, cybersecurity threats, and limited financial literacy. Ultimately, the chapter emphasizes the necessity for inclusive innovation, agile regulation, and cross-border collaboration. It advocates for the creation of localized, yet globally informed, policy frameworks that ensure FinTech's growth remains equitable, secure, and sustainable.

DOI: 10.1201/9788743811244-27

Introduction

The FinTech industry stands at the cusp of a new era, driven by unprecedented technological advances and an increasingly interconnected global financial ecosystem. As digital transformation in finance accelerates, the future of FinTech promises to be shaped by three key dimensions: data-driven innovation, cross-border collaborations, and a forward-looking vision that extends to 2030 and beyond. Data-Driven Innovation will be central to FinTech's next phase of growth. The ability to collect, analyze, and leverage massive amounts of financial and behavioral data enables companies to create highly personalized, efficient, and intelligent financial solutions. From AI-powered credit scoring to real-time fraud detection and robo-advisory services, data fuels greater customer insights and improved decision-making, making financial services more accessible and responsive. Simultaneously, cross-border FinTech Collaborations are set to redefine how financial services transcend geographical boundaries. Partnerships between startups, established financial institutions, technology providers, and regulators across countries will spur innovation and drive global financial inclusion. These collaborations can unlock new markets, streamline cross-border payments, and harmonize regulatory compliance, creating a truly global FinTech ecosystem. Looking ahead, Vision 2030 encapsulates the broad aspirations and transformative potential of FinTech over the next decade. It highlights not only the technological breakthroughs anticipated but also the evolving role of regulations, ethical considerations, and sustainability in shaping the industry's trajectory. The evolution of Financial Technology (FinTech) is not limited to any one geography – it is a global phenomenon. The future of FinTech is increasingly shaped by global digital transformation and proactive national innovation agendas [1]. Data-driven innovation now forms the backbone of FinTech competitiveness, enabling real-time insights and predictive capabilities [2]. Modern FinTech firms heavily rely on advanced analytics to enhance customer targeting and financial decision-making [3]. This chapter explores the dynamic FinTech landscape across different economic regions, comparing how developed and developing countries approach innovation, regulation, and adoption. While developed economies like the USA and the UK often lead in high-tech infrastructure and capital investment, developing nations like India and China have witnessed explosive FinTech growth driven by mobile penetration, digital public infrastructure, and financial inclusion efforts. By analyzing real-world case studies from China, India, and the United States, the chapter provides nuanced insights into the drivers and constraints of FinTech ecosystems across borders.

In addition, the section on challenges in global FinTech adoption sheds light on common hurdles, such as regulatory inconsistencies, data privacy issues, financial illiteracy, and cross-border technological compatibility. AI-enabled financial systems continue to expand, improving risk scoring, fraud detection, and algorithmic credit assessment [4]. BigTech-driven data ecosystems are reshaping global financial intermediation models at unprecedented scale [5]. Cross-border FinTech collaborations accelerate due to increasing global demand for seamless and low-cost transactions [6].

20.1 Data Driven Innovation

Data-driven innovation is poised to be a cornerstone of FinTech's evolution, transforming how financial services are designed, delivered, and consumed. By harnessing vast amounts of structured and unstructured data, FinTech companies can unveil deeper insights, create personalized products, optimize operations, and mitigate risks more effectively. This paradigm shift is fundamentally changing finance from intuition-based decision-making to evidence-driven strategies.

20.1.1 Key aspects of data-driven innovation in FinTech

Big data analytics

- The explosion of financial transactions, social media interactions, mobile usage, and IoT devices has led to enormous volumes of data.
- FinTech firms use big data analytics platforms to process and analyze this information in real time, uncovering patterns and trends that were previously invisible.
- Analytics enable predictive modeling, credit scoring, market forecasting, and dynamic risk assessments.

Artificial intelligence (AI) and machine learning (ML)

- AI and ML algorithms process historical and real-time data to automate decision- making.
- Applications include automated loan approvals by assessing creditworthiness beyond traditional credit reports, robo-advisors for wealth management, and fraud detection systems that identify unusual transaction patterns.

- Continuous learning models improve over time, enhancing accuracy and personalization.

Personalization and customer insights

- Data-driven approaches allow customization of financial products based on individual behaviors, preferences, and life stages.
- FinTech apps recommend payment plans, investment portfolios, or insurance products tailored to unique customer profiles.
- Personalized experiences improve customer engagement, satisfaction, and loyalty.

Real-time risk management and fraud prevention

- Through data analytics and machine learning, FinTech firms can monitor transactions and user behavior in real time.
- This enables faster detection and response to suspicious or fraudulent activities.
- Dynamic risk scoring helps in proactive blocking or flagging of high-risk transactions, reducing financial losses and increasing trust.

Enhanced regulatory compliance (RegTech)

- Data-driven automation assists FinTech companies in meeting complex regulatory requirements efficiently.
- Real-time monitoring, reporting, and auditing reduce manual errors and ensure transparency.
- RegTech solutions utilize data analytics to perform compliance checks, anti-money laundering (AML) screening, and know your customer (KYC) verification.

Integration with Internet of Things (IoT) and other emerging data sources

- IoT devices generate continuous streams of data related to user behavior, spending habits, and asset monitoring.
- Combining IoT data with financial datasets allows insurers and lenders to offer usage-based insurance (UBI) or dynamic credit risk assessments.
- This integration pushes the boundaries of traditional data analytics in FinTech.

20.1.2 Benefits of data-driven innovation in FinTech

- **Improved decision-making:** Data insights reduce reliance on gut-feeling, leading to more accurate financial decisions.
- **Cost efficiency:** Automation and predictive analytics streamline processes and reduce operational costs.
- **Financial inclusion:** Leveraging alternative data sources (e.g., mobile phone usage, social data) enables assessment of creditworthiness for unbanked or underserved populations.
- **Agility:** Real-time data processing allows FinTech firms to respond quickly to market changes and customer needs.
- **Customer trust:** Transparent and secure data handling builds deeper trust with users.

20.1.3 Challenges and considerations

- **Data privacy and security:** As data becomes central, protecting sensitive financial and personal information against breaches is critical.
- **Data quality and governance:** Ensuring accuracy, consistency, and ethical use of data requires strong governance frameworks.
- **Bias and fairness:** AI models trained on biased data can lead to unfair or discriminatory outcomes; FinTech firms must ensure equitable treatment.
- **Regulatory compliance:** Navigating evolving regulations around data collection, storage, and usage remains complex.

As the FinTech industry embraces data-driven innovation, future advancements – such as quantum computing and advanced AI – will further amplify capabilities. Collaborative ecosystems sharing data securely across institutions will enable holistic financial services that adapt fluidly to individual and market dynamics. Ultimately, data-driven innovation will be the engine powering FinTech's mission to create smarter, more inclusive, and resilient financial systems worldwide.

20.2 Cross-Border FinTech Collaborations

Cross-border collaborations in FinTech are becoming a defining trend in the industry's future growth, driven by globalization, regulatory harmonization, and interconnected digital ecosystems. FinTech companies, traditional financial institutions, regulators, and technology partners from different countries are increasingly joining forces to foster innovation, expand market reach, and enhance financial inclusion at a global scale. This collaborative approach allows FinTech firms to leverage complementary strengths, access new customer bases, and overcome regulatory and infrastructural challenges associated with international finance. Banks and FinTechs increasingly partner to deliver faster and more efficient cross-border payment solutions [7]. Innovative FinTech solutions are transforming small-business trade by reducing cross-border payment barriers [8]. Global FinTech adoption is driven by economic incentives, demographic changes, and digital readiness [9].

20.2.1 Key drivers of cross-border FinTech collaborations

Increasing global demand for seamless financial services

- Businesses and consumers operate in increasingly international environments, requiring efficient cross-border payments, currency exchanges, and credit facilities.
- Growing international trade, e-commerce, and migration create demand for accessible and affordable global financial solutions.

Expanding digital infrastructure and connectivity

- Advancements in smartphones, broadband, mobile money, and digital identification are lowering barriers to financial service adoption worldwide.
- Cloud computing and API-driven platforms enable scalable and interoperable FinTech solutions across national boundaries.

Regulatory evolution and harmonization

- Regulators are collaborating to create frameworks that accommodate cross-border FinTech services while managing risks.
- Initiatives such as the Financial Action Task Force (FATF) and Basel Committee cooperation help set global standards in AML/KYC and cybersecurity.
- Regional trade agreements and economic blocs (e.g., ASEAN, EU) promote integrated financial markets and cross-border FinTech projects.

20.2.2 Forms of cross-border FinTech collaborations

Partnerships between FinTech startups and traditional banks

- Banks seek partnerships with innovative FinTech startups from other countries to integrate new technologies like blockchain, AI, or open banking.
- Such alliances help banks expand international payment services, lending, and wealth management products.

Consortium and industry alliances

- Multiple FinTech firms and financial institutions form consortium to co-develop infrastructures, standards, and platforms that support cross-border transactions.
- Example: Global blockchain consortia working on cross-border payment solutions.

Regulatory sandboxes and innovation hubs

- Cross-border regulatory sandboxes allow FinTech firms to test products in new markets with temporary regulatory relaxations.
- Innovation hubs facilitate knowledge exchange and collaboration between international FinTech ecosystems.

Cross-border investment and M&A

- Increased investments across borders help scale FinTech innovations globally.
- Mergers and acquisitions enable consolidation, market entry, and access to talent and technology.

20.2.3 Benefits of cross-border collaborations in FinTech

- **Improved financial inclusion**
  Extending digital financial services across borders helps underserved populations, migrant workers, and small businesses access credit, payments, and insurance.
- **Enhanced innovation and product offering**
  Sharing diverse expertise fosters hybrid products combining strengths from different markets and faster adoption of international best practices.

- **Cost and time efficiency**
  Streamlining compliance, cross-border payments, and currency conversions through shared technology lowers transaction costs and settlement times.
- **Risk mitigation**
  Collaborative frameworks improve joint management of fraud, cyber threats, and compliance risks on a global scale.

20.2.4 Challenges and risks

- **Regulatory complexity and compliance**
  Differing regulations across jurisdictions around data privacy, anti-money laundering (AML), tax compliance, and consumer protection complicate operations.
- **Data privacy and security concerns**
  Protecting data shared across borders requires stringent security measures and clear policies, respecting both local and international laws.
- **Technological integration**
  Aligning different technology standards, protocols, and legacy systems can be complex and costly.
- **Cultural and language barriers**
  Differences in business practices, languages, and customer behaviors require adaptive strategies and localization.
- **Key examples of cross-border FinTech collaborations**
  Cross-border FinTech collaborations refer to strategic partnerships between financial technology companies, banks, governments, and regulatory bodies across different countries to develop and implement innovative financial solutions on a global scale. These collaborations aim to overcome challenges associated with international financial transactions, such as slow processing times, high costs, and inconsistent regulations. By working together, stakeholders can develop interoperable platforms, promote financial inclusion, enhance security, and accelerate digital transformation in global financial ecosystems.

Table 20.1 Cross-border FinTech collaborations examples.

1. PayPal and M-Pesa partnership – Digital wallet interoperability
In Africa, a groundbreaking collaboration between PayPal (a global digital payments platform) and M-Pesa (a Kenyan mobile money service operated by Safaricom) allows users in Kenya to transfer funds between their M-Pesa accounts and PayPal wallets. This cross-border integration enables freelancers, small businesses, and consumers in Kenya to engage in global e-commerce and receive international payments directly on their mobile phones. It demonstrates how digital wallet interoperability can empower emerging economies and promote financial inclusion.
2. TransferWise (Wise) – Borderless multi-currency accounts
Wise (formerly TransferWise) is a UK-based FinTech that partners with local banks and regulators in multiple countries to offer multi-currency borderless accounts and affordable cross-border transfers. By leveraging a local-to-local settlement model and regulatory approvals in various countries (e.g., the UK, EU, US, Australia, India), Wise enables users to send money internationally at real exchange rates with low fees. This collaboration model has transformed how individuals and businesses handle international payments.
3.Project Dunbar – Central Bank Digital Currency (CBDC) collaboration
Launched by the Bank for International Settlements (BIS) in partnership with the central banks of Australia, Singapore, Malaysia, and South Africa, Project Dunbar explores how multiple CBDCs can be used on a shared blockchain platform for efficient cross-border payments. The project demonstrates a new form of public- sector-led FinTech collaboration aiming to reduce the cost and time associated with traditional cross-border settlements and improve regulatory oversight.

The future of FinTech will be shaped by accelerating cross-border collaborations, driven by the widespread adoption of open banking APIs, decentralized finance (DeFi), and digital currencies, including central bank digital currencies (CBDCs). As international regulatory cooperation deepens, standardized compliance frameworks and innovation-friendly policies will support seamless global operations. Collaborative ecosystems involving both public and private sectors are expected to emerge, aiming to build inclusive and efficient global financial networks. In this landscape, digital identity systems and trusted data-sharing protocols will play a pivotal role in enabling secure and frictionless cross-border interactions. This collaborative model will empower smaller FinTech firms to scale globally at a faster pace, posing strong competition to traditional financial institutions. Inclusion-focused FinTech models are gaining traction, especially in underserved emerging markets [10]. Investment trends indicate continued global expansion of FinTech products, platforms, and technologies [11]. Asian FinTech ecosystems remain among the fastest growing, fueled by policy support and rapid digitization [12].

20.3 Challenges In Global FinTech Adoption

Despite the remarkable progress in FinTech across regions, several obstacles hinder its universal adoption and effectiveness. These challenges span technological, regulatory, social, and institutional dimensions. Despite growth, global FinTech faces challenges such as cybersecurity risks, data governance issues, and regulatory fragmentation [13]. Developing economies encounter barriers like low digital literacy, inconsistent infrastructure, and regulatory gaps (World Bank, 2022a) [14]. Vision 2030 economies, such as Saudi Arabia, are using FinTech to advance financial diversification and modernization [15]. Regulatory developments under national transformation agendas continue to shape long-term FinTech integrations [16].

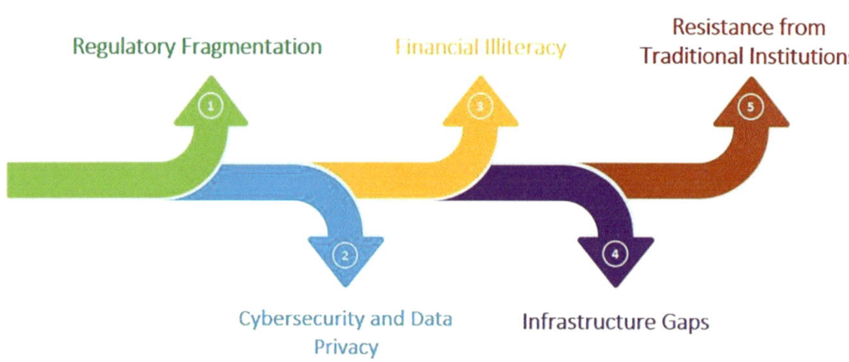

Figure 20.1 Challenges in Global FinTech adoption.

20.3.1 Regulatory fragmentation

One of the primary hurdles is the lack of standardized regulation across countries. Different legal definitions of digital currencies, data privacy laws, and financial products make it difficult for FinTech firms to operate across borders. For example, the General Data Protection Regulation (GDPR) in Europe imposes strict data management protocols that differ from Indian or U.S. standards.

20.3.2 Cybersecurity and data privacy

With increased digital transactions comes the risk of cyberattacks, fraud, and data breaches. Inconsistent enforcement of cybersecurity standards and weak data protection laws in developing nations make the situation more fragile.

20.3.3 Financial illiteracy

In many regions, especially in developing economies, the lack of basic financial and digital literacy inhibits the use of FinTech platforms. Consumers may be wary of digital payments or unable to understand complex products like digital insurance or crypto investments.

20.3.4 Infrastructure gaps

Internet connectivity, smartphone penetration, and digital identification systems are prerequisites for FinTech. However, many rural or economically disadvantaged areas still lack these essentials.

20.3.5 Resistance from traditional institutions

Traditional banks and financial institutions sometimes resist or delay FinTech partnerships due to concerns over disintermediation, technology costs, or regulatory compliance.

To overcome these challenges and realize the full potential of FinTech on a global scale, coordinated efforts among governments, regulators, and industry players are essential. Some actionable strategies include:

- **Cross-border regulatory cooperation**: Organizations like the Financial Stability Board (FSB) and G20 should foster uniform standards for data governance, digital ID, and payments interoperability.
- **Public-private partnerships (PPPs)**: Developing economies should invest in digital infrastructure with assistance from multilateral banks and private tech players.
- **Capacity building**: Financial literacy programs and digital skill development initiatives must accompany FinTech rollouts, especially in underserved regions.
- **Inclusive innovation**: Designing FinTech products with a human-centric approach ensures accessibility across age, literacy, and income groups.

- **Focus on ESG and sustainability**: FinTech can play a vital role in enabling green finance, carbon trading, and ethical investing in alignment with global sustainable development goals (SDGs).

The global FinTech scenario is one of both boundless opportunity and complex challenges. While countries like China and the USA lead in terms of innovation and capital, developing economies like India show the world how scalable infrastructure can democratize finance. The road ahead requires not just technological advancement but also policy harmonization, inclusive design, and shared vision. If executed well, FinTech holds the promise to create a more equitable, efficient, and transparent global financial system.

20.4 Vision 2030: What Lies Ahead in FinTech

As we look toward 2030, the FinTech industry is poised to undergo transformational changes fueled by rapid technological advances, evolving customer expectations, and a shifting regulatory landscape. The Vision 2030 for FinTech encompasses ambitious goals to create an inclusive, resilient, and highly efficient financial ecosystem that leverages emerging technologies while addressing challenges related to security, ethics, and sustainability. This section explores key trends, opportunities, and challenges that will define FinTech's path over the next decade.

20.4.1 Key drivers shaping FinTech by 2030

Advanced technology integration

- **Artificial intelligence (AI) and machine learning (ML):** Will become deeply embedded across financial services, powering advanced analytics, autonomous decision-making, and hyper-personalized customer experiences.
- **Quantum computing:** Expected to revolutionize encryption and computational capacities, enabling ultra-secure transactions and faster risk modeling.
- **Distributed ledger technology (DLT):** Blockchain and other DLTs will create decentralized, transparent financial networks that improve trust, reduce intermediaries, and enable smart contracts.
- **Internet of Things (IoT) and edge computing:** Real-time financial data from IoT devices will drive dynamic insurance policies, personalized lending, and seamless payment systems.

Widespread financial inclusion

- FinTech will further bridge gaps by providing affordable, accessible financial services to unbanked and underserved populations worldwide.
- Innovative credit scoring using alternative data will expand access to credit.
- Mobile-first solutions and digital identity systems will empower rural and marginalized communities.

Regulatory evolution and collaboration

- Regulators will continue evolving frameworks to balance innovation with consumer protection and systemic risk.
- International cooperation will be stronger, standardizing rules governing data privacy, cross-border flows, and digital assets.
- Regulatory sandboxes and innovation hubs will nurture experimentation while accelerating global market access.

Emergence of Central Bank Digital Currencies (CBDCs)

- Central banks globally will issue digital versions of their currencies, redefining monetary systems.
- CBDCs will promote faster payment settlements, reduce transaction costs, and enhance transparency.
- They will coexist with private digital currencies, requiring robust interoperability solutions.

Sustainable and ethical finance

- Environmental, social, and governance (ESG) factors will shape FinTech product offerings and investment flows.
- Green finance technologies will support climate change mitigation and sustainable development goals.
- Transparency and ethical AI use will become core to building trust.

Enhanced cybersecurity and privacy

- With growing digitization, cybersecurity will be paramount.

- Innovations like biometric authentication, decentralized identity, homomorphic encryption, and zero-trust frameworks will protect user data.
- Privacy-enhancing technologies (PETs) will enable compliant data sharing without compromising confidentiality.

Opportunities on the horizon

- **Hyper-personalization:** Financial products tailored in real time to individual needs, lifestyle, and risk appetite.
- **Embedded finance:** Integration of financial services directly within non- financial platforms (e.g., e-commerce, healthcare).
- **Decentralized finance (DeFi):** Expanded adoption of DeFi protocols enabling peer-to-peer finance without intermediaries.
- **Financial ecosystem platforms:** Open platforms allowing seamless service aggregation, switching, and innovation.
- **AI-powered advisory and automation:** Democratized wealth management and financial advice for all customer segments.

Challenges to address

- Ethical use of AI and algorithmic transparency to avoid bias and discrimination.
- Data sovereignty and cross-border data flow conflicts.
- Managing systemic risks from technological dependencies and emerging cyber threats.
- Ensuring digital literacy and bridging the skills gap for consumers and workforce alike.
- Balancing innovation speed with robust regulation and compliance.

Strategic imperatives for stakeholders

- **For FinTech firms:** Invest in scalable, secure, and interoperable technology infrastructures; foster cross-sector partnerships.
- **For regulators:** Promote principles-based regulation, support innovation sandboxes, and enhance international coordination.
- **For consumers:** Build awareness and trust through education and transparent communication.
- **For investors:** Focus on sustainable, scalable solutions with sound governance.

20.5 Global FinTech Scenario

The rapid evolution of financial technology, or FinTech, is reshaping how financial services are delivered and consumed worldwide. From mobile wallets to blockchain-based transactions, FinTech innovations have dramatically altered the landscape for both consumers and institutions. While the wave of digital disruption is global, the nature and pace of FinTech adoption vary significantly across different economies. Developed countries often lead in terms of technological sophistication and investment capital, whereas developing nations exhibit faster FinTech uptake due to a growing digital-savvy population and a need for financial inclusion. Understanding the global FinTech scenario requires examining these regional differences, identifying the key drivers of growth, and assessing the hurdles that stand in the way of seamless financial transformation. Regional financial development programs aim to create sustainable, innovation-ready digital ecosystems [17]. India's Vision Document highlights FinTech as a catalyst for inclusive and technology-driven financial growth [18]. Global assessments indicate that FinTech will continue expanding financial inclusion and digital payments worldwide [19]. This chapter explores the comparative FinTech landscape between developed and developing economies, offers case studies of leading nations like China, India, and the USA, and discusses the challenges impeding global FinTech harmonization.

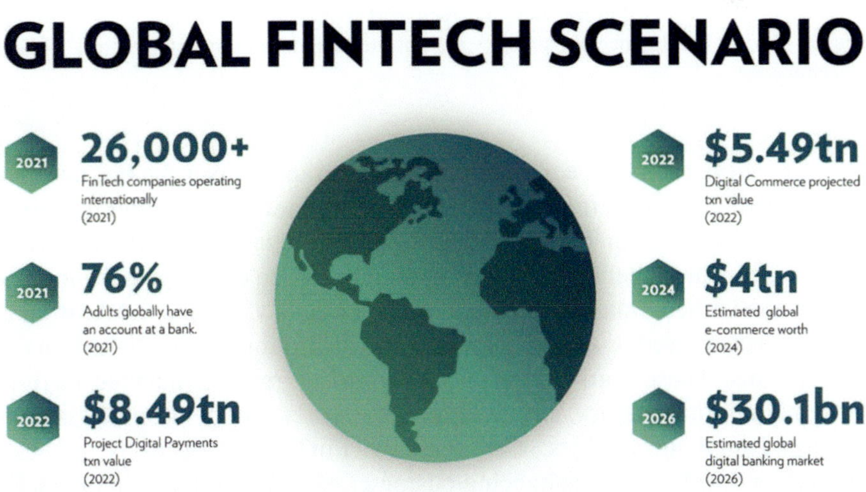

Figure 20.2 Global FinTech scenario.
Source: http://3.64.40.172/2022/11/29/digital-lending-and-fintech-impact-on-sme- lending/

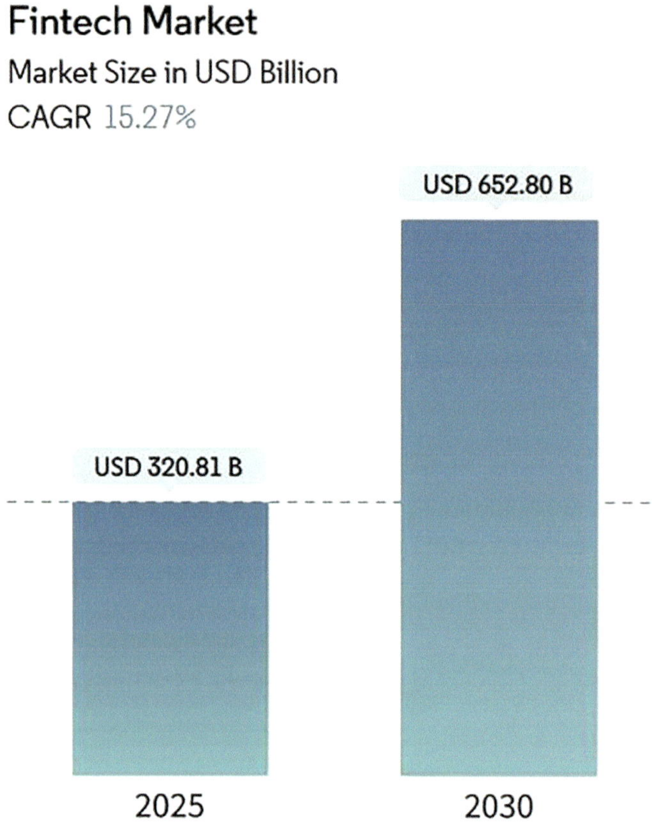

Figure 20.3 FinTech market projection.
Source: Mordor Intelligence https://www.mordorintelligence.com/industry-reports/global-fintech-market

The global FinTech ecosystem has grown rapidly over the last decade, but its manifestation differs significantly between developed and developing economies, driven by variations in infrastructure, regulation, market maturity, consumer behavior, and economic needs. In developed economies such as the United States, United Kingdom, Germany, Japan, and Australia, FinTech has evolved as an enhancement and disruption to established financial systems. These markets are characterized by mature financial institutions, high digital literacy, strong legal frameworks, and widespread access to formal banking services. Consequently, FinTech innovations in these regions tend to focus on enhancing customer experience, optimizing back-end efficiencies, and offering niche financial products like robo-advisory, algorithmic trading, buy-now-pay-later (BNPL), and decentralized finance (DeFi) applications. For instance, the U.S. hosts a robust FinTech ecosystem led by companies like Stripe, Robinhood, and Coinbase, while the UK is home to open banking pioneers such as Revolut and Monzo. These FinTechs compete or collaborate with incumbent banks, often focusing on personalization, speed, and cross-platform integration, capitalizing on high smartphone penetration, widespread broadband access, and digitally savvy consumers. Regulatory bodies in developed markets, such as the Financial Conduct Authority (FCA) in the UK or the Office of the Comptroller of the Currency (OCC) in the U.S., provide structured sandboxes and clear compliance protocols, enabling controlled innovation. Moreover, developed economies benefit from ample venture capital, established cybersecurity frameworks, and a more consistent enforcement of data privacy laws like GDPR or CCPA, which further boosts consumer trust in digital financial services.

In contrast, the FinTech boom in developing economies, such as India, Kenya, Brazil, Nigeria, Indonesia, and Vietnam, has been more transformational than evolutionary, often addressing fundamental gaps in financial inclusion and infrastructure. These regions are home to large unbanked or underbanked populations, limited access to traditional banking institutions, and cash-dominant economies. FinTech in these markets is not just an upgrade it is a lifeline. Mobile money platforms like M-Pesa in Kenya have revolutionized access to payments and basic banking services for millions without needing a bank account. Similarly, India's FinTech ecosystem, boosted by initiatives like Digital India, Aadhaar (biometric ID), UPI (Unified Payments Interface), and Jan Dhan Yojana (financial inclusion program), has allowed even rural populations to participate in real-time digital payments, microloans, and insurance. These innovations often leapfrog traditional systems, bypassing physical bank branches and credit bureaus. Instead, they rely on mobile-based KYC, AI-driven credit scoring, and agent banking models to reach the underserved. Additionally, platforms like Paytm, PhonePe, and Razorpay in India, and Nubank in Brazil, have emerged as household names by offering accessible, low-cost financial services. Government support plays a critical role in enabling FinTech growth in developing economies, where public-private partnerships, API-based digital infrastructures, and light-touch regulations encourage experimentation and inclusivity. Moreover, smartphone penetration and internet adoption, although lower in absolute terms than in developed nations, are growing rapidly, especially among the youth and informal workforce, creating a fertile market for FinTech innovations.

However, both developed and developing economies face their own sets of challenges in adopting FinTech. In developed markets, legacy infrastructure, customer inertia, and regulatory complexity can sometimes hinder agile innovation. Traditional banks may resist change due to high switching costs or vested interests in existing systems, and strict regulatory scrutiny can limit risk-taking by startups. Additionally, issues such as data monopolization, cybersecurity breaches, and ethical AI usage are growing concerns. Meanwhile, in developing countries, challenges include limited financial literacy, low credit penetration, patchy internet coverage, and trust deficits in digital platforms. Furthermore, FinTechs in these regions often struggle with access to funding, inadequate legal recourse, and unstable regulatory environments, which may lack clear definitions for emerging technologies like crypto or digital lending. Despite these hurdles, the impact per dollar invested in FinTech tends to be significantly higher in developing economies, as it directly contributes to financial empowerment, economic growth, and poverty alleviation.

Another key contrast lies in consumer behavior and expectations. In developed economies, consumers value customization, user experience, and multi-channel integration, often expecting seamless interactions between banking, shopping, and investing. In contrast, consumers in developing regions prioritize affordability, ease of use, and reliability, often via low-bandwidth mobile applications and USSD interfaces. Trust in institutions also varies, while banks in the West often enjoy established reputations, many FinTechs in developing countries have had to build trust from scratch, especially when serving populations that historically operated outside formal systems. This has led to unique innovations like agent-assisted digital banking, community-based lending, and gamified financial education platforms.

Despite these contrasts, a convergence is beginning to emerge. Global FinTech giants are expanding into developing markets through acquisitions, partnerships, and localized offerings, while successful models from the Global South are being adapted in advanced economies. For instance, India's UPI model is being studied by countries like France and Singapore, while African mobile money solutions are influencing Latin American FinTech rollouts. In both settings, embedded finance – the integration of financial services into non-financial apps is blurring traditional boundaries and unlocking new revenue streams. As such, while the trajectories may differ, the goal of creating accessible, efficient, and inclusive financial systems unites FinTech development across the world.

Figure 20.4 Fintech market overview.
Source: Mordor Intelligence https://www.mordorintelligence.com/industry-reports/global-fintech-market

In conclusion, the global FinTech scenario is characterized by contrast and complementarity between developed and developing economies. While the former are optimizing efficiency and personalizing financial services through advanced tech and data analytics, the latter are transforming lives by addressing deep-rooted access barriers using mobile-first, cost-effective innovations. FinTech in developed economies often complements existing institutions, whereas in developing economies, it replaces or leapfrogs them. The lessons from both sides of the spectrum are crucial: developed economies can learn agility, frugality, and inclusion from the Global South, while developing nations can gain from regulatory sophistication, investment ecosystems, and advanced cybersecurity from the Global North. Together, they form a global learning loop, in which FinTech continues to redefine the way the world transacts, saves, lends, and insures – one click at a time. The future of finance is marked by AI-enabled automation, embedded finance, and open-data ecosystems. Policy innovations such as regulatory sandboxes support safe FinTech experimentation and ecosystem growth [20]. Comparative evidence shows developed markets lead in innovation maturity, while developing economies lead in adoption speed and scale [21].

20.6 Developed vs. Developing Economies in FinTech

Developed economies

Developed economies such as the United States, the United Kingdom, Germany, and Japan benefit from high levels of financial literacy, robust digital infrastructure, and well-established regulatory systems. FinTech adoption in these regions often focuses on enhancing existing services, improving user convenience, and streamlining complex processes such as wealth management, insurance, and securities trading.

Key features include:

- Advanced technology stacks (cloud computing, AI, blockchain)
- Established capital markets and funding ecosystems
- Supportive regulatory bodies (e.g., Financial Conduct Authority in the UK)
- High smartphone and internet penetration
- Strong cybersecurity frameworks

FinTech in these economies primarily evolves around customer-centric innovations such as Robo-advisory services, RegTech (regulatory technology), InsurTech, and high-frequency trading platforms.

Developing economies

In contrast, developing economies such as India, Kenya, Brazil, and Indonesia see FinTech as a vehicle for **financial inclusion**. A significant portion of the population in these countries is underbanked or unbanked. Here, FinTech innovations are geared towards democratizing access to basic financial services through mobile technology and government-backed digital infrastructure.

Key features include:

- Mobile-first financial ecosystems
- Limited traditional banking infrastructure in rural areas
- Government-led initiatives for digital finance (e.g., UPI in India, M-Pesa in Kenya)
- Focus on microcredit, peer-to-peer lending, and low-cost remittances
- Challenges in regulatory enforcement and data protection

While developed economies innovate on top of mature systems, developing nations often leapfrog legacy systems entirely, adopting digital-first models that promote broad inclusion.

Table 20.2 Developed and developing nation economies in FinTech

Aspect	Developed nations	Developing nations
Technology infrastructure	Well-established internet, mobile, and digital banking infrastructure	Often limited or uneven access to internet and digital infrastructure
Primary drivers of adoption	Convenience, speed, personalization, and digital experience	Financial inclusion, mobile penetration, and lack of traditional banking
FinTech usage focus	Investment apps, robo-advisory, insurance tech, and digital payments	Mobile wallets, microloans, P2P lending, and remittances
Regulatory environment	Stable and mature regulations with active regulatory Sandboxes	Evolving frameworks, often less consistent across regions
Banking penetration	High traditional bank coverage	Large unbanked or underbanked population
Digital literacy	Generally high among consumers	Varies widely; often low in rural or underserved areas
FinTech–bank relationship	Competitive and collaborative (e.g., open banking, API ecosystems)	Often complementary to extend reach to the unbanked
Innovation focus	Advanced tech like AI, blockchain, and wealth tech	Mobile-first solutions and basic financial access tools
Challenges	Data privacy concerns, regulatory overreach, and tech saturation	Infrastructure gaps, trust issues, and a lack of digital education
Examples	USA, UK, Germany, Singapore	India, Kenya, Brazil, Nigeria

Table 20.3 Caselets: China, India, and the USA.

China: The mobile payment giant
China's FinTech landscape is arguably the most evolved in the world, with mobile payments becoming the dominant mode of transactions. Giants like **Ant Financial (Alipay)** and **Tencent (WeChat Pay)** have built ecosystems that combine social media, e-commerce, and financial services into one integrated experience. Key achievements include: • Over 90% mobile payment penetration in urban areas • Widespread use of QR code-based payments • Expansion of credit scoring systems like Sesame Credit • AI and blockchain integration for anti-fraud and identity verification The Chinese government has encouraged FinTech growth while keeping tight regulatory control, especially in areas like lending and data privacy. The recent crackdown on Ant Group's IPO is an example of balancing innovation with systemic risk control.
India: A FinTech lab for the world
India's FinTech success is driven by government-backed digital infrastructure such as the Aadhaar biometric ID, Unified Payments Interface (UPI), and Digital India movement. These initiatives have enabled rapid expansion of digital payments, peer- to-peer lending, and digital insurance products. Key developments include: • UPI processing over 10 billion monthly transactions (2025) • FinTech unicorns like Paytm, PhonePe, Zerodha, and Razorpay • Rise in financial literacy and smartphone penetration • Supportive policies through RBI's regulatory sandbox and NPCI governance India's model is globally recognized for its ability to combine public digital infrastructure with private innovation, especially in achieving financial inclusion.
USA: Capital-rich innovation hub
The United States remains a global hub for FinTech innovation due to its advanced capital markets, startup ecosystem, and technology leadership. The U.S. FinTech industry spans payments, lending, investing, and cryptocurrency, with strong players like **Stripe**, **Robinhood**, **Coinbase**, and **SoFi**. Key strengths: • Robust venture capital and IPO market for FinTech startups • Widespread use of digital banking and investment platforms • Leadership in blockchain and decentralized finance (DeFi) • Progressive regulators like the SEC and OCC (with limitations) However, the U.S. faces challenges due to fragmented regulatory oversight at the state and federal levels, sometimes slowing the adoption of newer models like central bank digital currencies (CBDCs).

Summary

This chapter delves into the global FinTech landscape by comparing the adoption patterns, regulatory frameworks, and innovation ecosystems of developed and developing economies. It begins with a comparative analysis between these two groups, highlighting differences in market maturity, customer behavior, and regulatory readiness. The chapter then presents detailed case studies from China, India, and the USA to illustrate the diversity of FinTech progress – China leading in mobile payments, India leveraging digital public infrastructure like UPI, and the USA focusing on investment tech and challenger banks. The chapter concludes by addressing the major challenges that hinder FinTech scalability and acceptance on a global level. These include regulatory fragmentation, cybersecurity threats, digital divide, and resistance from traditional financial institutions. Students are encouraged to think critically about how global cooperation, localized innovation, and inclusive policies can shape the future of global financial technology. By 2030, FinTech will not only transform financial services but also reshape the broader economic and social fabric by driving financial empowerment and inclusion globally. The vision is one of a smart, secure, and sustainable financial future accessible to all, underpinned by collaboration between technology innovators, regulators, and users. While the journey presents challenges, the opportunities to create resilient, equitable financial ecosystems are profound, paving the way for a digitized world where finance serves as an enabler for broader prosperity.

Case Study: Denmark's FinTech Journey with Danske Bank at the Forefront

Denmark, known for its high digital literacy and robust technological infrastructure, has emerged as a prominent FinTech hub in Europe. The country's FinTech ecosystem is characterized by strong government support, innovation-friendly regulation, and a highly connected population. A central player in this transformation is **Danske Bank**, Denmark's largest bank by assets, which has embraced digital transformation to compete with agile FinTech startups and changing customer demands.

Danske Bank's FinTech journey began with internal digitization but rapidly expanded into innovation through partnerships, startup accelerators, and AI-driven services. One of its most notable contributions to the FinTech landscape is MobilePay, a peer-to- peer (P2P) mobile payment app launched in 2013. Designed initially for Danske Bank customers, MobilePay was later made available across banks and is now one of the most widely used digital payment tools in Denmark, with over 4.5 million users in a country of just under 6 million people. MobilePay significantly reduced cash usage in Denmark and exemplifies how traditional banks can lead FinTech innovation.

Danske Bank has also been active in embracing open banking, complying early with the European Union's Revised Payment Services Directive (PSD2). It established API portals to allow third-party developers to build applications on its banking infrastructure, enhancing transparency and creating a collaborative ecosystem. This has fostered partnerships with various FinTech startups, especially in areas such as personal finance, cybersecurity, and investment advisory. The bank's internal innovation labs and partnerships with accelerators like Copenhagen FinTech – a major Danish FinTech hub – have helped it keep pace with the rapidly changing financial services environment. Danske Bank has invested in AI and machine learning to improve customer service through chatbots and intelligent advisory platforms. For example, the virtual assistant "June" offers investment guidance to customers based on individual risk profiles and market trends, making wealth management more accessible to the average customer.

Despite these advancements, the journey has not been without challenges. Danske Bank faced reputational setbacks in 2018 due to a high-profile money laundering scandal involving its Estonian branch. This incident highlighted the need for strong compliance mechanisms and ethical governance in the age of digital banking. In response, the bank has since invested heavily in regtech (regulatory technology), internal controls, and transparency, rebuilding public trust while continuing its innovation agenda. Moreover, Denmark's broader FinTech scene is thriving, with over 200 active FinTech startups operating in areas like blockchain, insurtech, and digital identity. The government and central bank have encouraged innovation through supportive policies and public-private collaborations. The use of NemID, Denmark's secure digital ID system, and the planned rollout of MitID have laid the groundwork for secure authentication in digital financial services.

In conclusion, Denmark's FinTech success is driven by a combination of technological readiness, consumer trust, collaborative innovation, and forward- thinking institutions like Danske Bank. While navigating regulatory challenges and reputational risks, Danske Bank's journey illustrates how traditional banks can transform themselves into digital leaders, shaping the future of finance not just in Denmark, but across the Nordic region and Europe.

Case Discussion Questions

1. How can traditional banks like Danske Bank balance innovation and risk management, especially after reputational challenges such as the money laundering scandal?
2. To what extent can internal innovation (like MobilePay) protect incumbent banks from FinTech disruption, compared to external partnerships or acquisitions?
3. What role should regulatory frameworks and public trust play in shaping the future of open banking initiatives led by large institutions like Danske Bank?

Keywords

- **Cross-border collaboration:** Cooperation between organizations or governments in different countries to offer or regulate financial services across national boundaries.
- **Open banking APIs:** Tools that allow third-party apps to securely access banking data and services to develop new financial products.
- **Decentralized finance (DeFi):** Financial services that run on blockchain technology without involving traditional banks or intermediaries, allowing peer- to-peer transactions.
- **Central Bank Digital Currency (CBDC):** A digital version of a country's official currency issued by its central bank for use in electronic payments.
- **Digital identity:** An electronic form of a person's identity used for verifying and accessing financial and digital services.
- **Data-driven innovation:** Creating new financial products and services based on insights drawn from large volumes of data using technologies like AI and analytics.
- **Blockchain technology:** A secure and transparent digital ledger system used to record financial transactions and other data without a central authority.

- **Financial inclusion:** Ensuring that individuals and businesses, especially in underserved regions, have access to useful and affordable financial services.
- **Regulatory sandboxes:** Controlled testing environments set up by regulators where FinTech startups can try new products with real users under relaxed regulations.
- **Interoperability:** The ability of different financial platforms and systems to work together and share information easily and securely.
- **Embedded finance:** The integration of financial services such as payments, loans, or insurance into non-financial platforms like online stores or apps.
- **Digital wallet:** A software-based system that securely stores users' payment information and enables them to make online or contactless transactions.
- **Real-time settlement:** Financial transactions that are completed instantly, reducing the delay between initiation and final confirmation of payment.
- **Global FinTech ecosystem:** The worldwide network of FinTech companies, banks, regulators, investors, and users working together to drive financial innovation
- **FinTech ecosystem:** The interconnected network of startups, regulators, banks, investors, and consumers involved in digital financial services.
- **Developed economies:** Economies with advanced technological infrastructure, high per capita income, and mature financial systems (e.g., USA, UK).
- **Developing economies:** Nations with lower income levels and emerging infrastructure but high FinTech growth potential (e.g., India, Kenya).
- **Financial inclusion:** The effort to make financial products and services accessible and affordable to all, especially underserved populations.
- **Regulatory sandboxes:** Controlled environments where FinTech startups test new products under regulatory supervision.
- **Digital public infrastructure:** Technology platforms like Aadhaar and UPI in India that support scalable digital services across the economy.

- **Mobile wallets:** Smartphone-based digital wallets used for payments, transfers, and sometimes credit or savings.
- **Neo-banks:** Digital-only banks that offer banking services without physical branches.
- **Cross-border payments:** Transactions where the payer and recipient are located in different countries, often involving regulatory and currency complexities.
- **Digital divide:** The gap between those with easy access to digital technology and those without.

Discussion Questions

1. Compare and contrast the FinTech ecosystems of developed and developing economies. What advantages and limitations do each face?
2. How has India's digital public infrastructure, such as Aadhaar and UPI, contributed to FinTech growth and financial inclusion?
3. What unique factors have driven China's dominance in mobile payments and digital lending?
4. Why are traditional banks in developing economies more resistant to FinTech adoption than in developed markets?
5. What are the top three challenges to global FinTech adoption, and how can they be mitigated through policy and innovation?
6. How do you envision the role of emerging technologies shaping the future financial ecosystem?
7. How can FinTech firms ensure ethical use of data and minimize bias in AI algorithms?
8. What role will real-time data analytics play in fraud detection and risk management in future FinTech solutions?
9. How might IoT data integration expand the scope and effectiveness of FinTech products?
10. What measures should be in place to protect data privacy and cybersecurity as FinTech services become more integrated and complex by 2030?

References

[1] Arner, D. W., Barberis, J. N., & Buckley, R. P. (2016). *The evolution of FinTech: A new post-crisis paradigm?* Georgetown Journal of International Law, 47(4), 1271–1319.

[2] Bayya, A. K. (2025). *Data-Driven Predictive Analytics and Decision-Making in FinTech Using MongoDB and High-Throughput Data Pipelines.* International Journal of Algorithms Design and Analysis Review, 3(1), 1–15.

[3] Shah, T. (2025). *Data-Driven Marketing in Fintech.* International Journal of Innovative Research in Science, Engineering and Technology, 14(3), 1915.

[4] OECD. (2021). *AI in finance: Challenges, opportunities, and the road ahead.*

[5] Frost, J., Gambacorta, L., Huang, Y., Shin, H. S., & Zbinden, P. (2019). *BigTech and the changing structure of financial intermediation.* BIS Working Papers No. 779.

[6] Edgar, Dunn & Company. (2025, June 1). *Fintech vs. Banks: The Future of B2B Cross-Border Payments.*

[7] PYMNTS.com. (2025, March 4). *Two-Thirds of Banks Team With FinTechs on Cross-Border Payments.*

[8] World Economic Forum. (2025, May 29). *How innovative fintech is helping small business in cross-border trade and payments.*

[9] Frost, J. (2020). *The economic forces driving FinTech adoption.* BIS Working Paper No. 838.

[10] Ghosh, S. (2022). *FinTech in emerging markets: Unlocking financial inclusion.* Palgrave Macmillan.

[11] KPMG. (2023). *Pulse of FinTech H2 2023.*

[12] McKinsey & Company. (2021). *FinTech in Asia: Accelerating financial inclusion and innovation.*

[13] PwC. (2020). *Global FinTech Report: Redrawing the lines.*

[14] World Bank. (2022). *FinTech and financial inclusion: Navigating risks and opportunities.*

[15] Alghofaili, A. S. (2025, June). *Fintech Adoption in Saudi Arabia… Vision 2030.*

[16] Almoammar, A. A., & Alonazi, A. H. (2025, April). *Integrating FinTech into Saudi Arabia's Financial Landscape… Vision 2030.*

[17] Saudi Arabia's Vision 2030. (2022). *Financial Sector Development Program Delivery Plan.*

[18] Reserve Bank of India. (2023). *FinTech in India – Vision document.*

[19] World Bank. (2022). *The future of finance: How FinTech is shaping the financial sector globally.*

[20] Zetzsche, D. A., Buckley, R. P., Arner, D. W., & Föhr, L. (2020). *Regulatory sandboxes and innovation hubs for FinTech.*

[21] Zhang, T., & Chen, H. (2021). *China's FinTech revolution: A critical analysis of policy and market drivers.* Journal of Financial Innovation, 7(2), 45–63.

Index

About the Authors

Dr. Neha Garg, Ph.D., UGC-NET, MBA (Finance), B.Com. (Hons.)
Assistant Professor, School of Business Administration, Bhagwan Parshuram Institute of Technology, New Delhi, India

Dr. Neha Garg graduated from Ramjas College, Delhi University, and is an ex-banker from Bank of Maharashtra. She did her MBA (Finance) from IBS, Hyderabad. She did her Ph.D. on Artificial Intelligence in Banking from a banker's perspective from Bharati Vidyapeeth Deemed to be University (Pune). Her present research interest areas are finance, banking, research analytics, business analytics, and FinTech. She has also co-authored a book on Business Analytics. She has published several research papers in UGC-Care, Scopus-indexed journals, and presented her research work at national and international conferences. She is also a reviewer for many journals of high repute. She has also received the Women leadership award for her valuable contribution in the field of financial literacy.

Dr Anoop Pandey, Ph.D., M.Com., B.Com.
HOD Commerce, Hemvati Nandan Bahuguna Garhwal University, (A Central University) Uttrakhand - 246001

Dr. Anoop Pandey is an excellent academician and researcher. He is presently working as a professor in the Department of Commerce in Dr. BGR Campus, Hemwati Nandan Bahuguna Garhwal University (A Central University), Uttarakhand. He has over 20 years of experience in the field of teaching and research. He has successfully completed seven research projects and published 120-plus quality research papers in reputed and indexed journals. Seven Ph.D. scholars have been awarded doctorate degrees under his guidance, and he has published three patents successfully. My major publication is in the field of SMEs and the entrepreneurship sectors. He has been called as a resource person in many research workshops, Seminars and conferences. Presently, he is working as a project director in ICSSR Sponsored research project titled "Strategic Technology Adoption and Acquisition: A Review of Policy Intervention and Performance of SMEs in India."

Ms. Nupur Tyagi, M. Tech, B.Tech.
Assistant Professor, Computer Science, Bhagwan Parshuram Institute of Technology, New Delhi, India

Nupur Tyagi, B.Tech in Information Technology, M.Tech (Cyber Security), Cybersecurity Specialist FinTech Professional Academician. Nupur Tyagi holds an M.Tech degree in Cyber Security from Swami Vivekanand University, Meerut, and a B.Tech degree from Subharti University, Uttar Pradesh. With a strong foundation in information technology and cybersecurity, she has built a multidisciplinary career at the intersection of technology, finance, and education. She has worked with various FinTech companies, gaining practical insights into digital finance, secure transaction systems, and the application of cybersecurity principles in financial technologies. With 4 years of corporate experience and three years of academic teaching, which bring a unique blend of industry expertise and academic depth. Her interests include network security, ethical hacking, cyber risk management, blockchain security, and the development of secure financial platforms. She is an active researcher in cybersecurity and FinTech innovation.

For Product Safety Concerns and Information please contact our
EU representative GPSR@taylorandfrancis.com Taylor & Francis
Verlag GmbH, Kaufingerstraße 24, 80331 München, Germany